PROMISE AND PERFORMANCE OF AMERICAN DEMOCRACY

PROMISE AND PERFORMANCE OF AMERICAN DEMOCRACY

Richard A. Watson

University of Missouri-Columbia

John Wiley & Sons, Inc.
New York · London · Sydney · Toronto

Cover Photograph, "A Fish-eye View of Convention Hall."
(*United Press International*)

To George A. Peek, Jr.
who first stimulated my interest in the basic course

And to my students
who have sustained it.

Preface

This textbook grows out of some twenty years of first-hand experience with the introductory course in American government, first as a Teaching Fellow at the University of Michigan where Professor George A. Peek, Jr. served as the Lecturer, and later as the Lecturer myself at the University of Missouri-Columbia. Over the years, my several thousand students have run the gamut from the eager freshman who badgered me about a future doctoral dissertation to the teary-eyed Home Economics major who pleaded that I pass her in this required course for graduation.

For future majors or one-time students alike, the introductory course in American government, as I view it, has three major purposes: first, conveying essential factual information; second, explaining basic concepts in political science to help students organize this information in order to comprehend how the American and other political systems operate; and third, stimulating students to think critically about our political system, to assess how democratic it is, and to evaluate how well it meets the major needs of our society.

These three major purposes of the introductory course are reflected in the kinds of texts that have been published over the years. Traditional books have done a good job of conveying a wealth of factual information to the student, but typically at the price of overwhelming and boring him in the process. They tell him more than he wants or needs to know, and leave him with a picture of the trees, but not the forest, of American government.

In the mid-1960s several texts began to provide students with various conceptual frameworks—systems analysis, theories of conflict and consensus, political culture—and the like. Although these are a healthy antidote to the excessive factualism of previous texts, they have their own problems: abstract jargon, a failure to capture the excitement of politics, and, all too often, a tendency to introduce a framework that is progressively ignored as the book proceeds.

More recently a spate of books that have appeared take a "point of view" (typically a highly critical one) toward the American political system.

These texts have served as a corrective for the sugar-coated treatment of the subject in many high schools, but most students who lack a good grounding in the fundamentals of American government are unable to evaluate them properly. I believe that provocative books of this nature are more appropriate for advanced students who can better judge their merits and place them in proper perspective.

In this text I have tried to maintain a balance of materials that serve all three purposes of the introductory course. Factual information is basic, yet I have omitted numerous detailed tables and charts that students seldom consult and rarely remember. I believe the book's over-all focus on democratic theory is more relevant and meaningful to students than other frameworks of analysis; it also serves as a model for evaluating the actual operation of our political system, a task I have tackled in the concluding portion of each chapter entitled "Assessment," which reflects my own personal values and points of view.

I have also been deliberately eclectic in my choice of approaches and materials, which cover the spectrum from the latest findings in political socialization and voting behavior to historical research into the intentions and purposes of the Founding Fathers. I have always been puzzled by persons who are fascinated by the political development process in other nations but who view anything that happened in our own country prior to the 1960s as irrelevant. Without some understanding of our political past, students lack a needed perspective on how American democracy has changed over time.

As far as style is concerned, I have been most concerned with immediacy and clarity. Chapters begin with a dramatic incident or development—the riot in Detroit, the hippies, the release of the Pentagon papers—designed to demonstrate in graphic terms the operating principles and problems of our political system. Following this, I discuss basic concepts needed to understand the subject matter of the chapter—rights "in" and "from" government, public opinion, political socialization, power structure, and the like. I have tried to make these explanations clear and precise without resorting to professional jargon.

I have omitted two features of most texts which I think are not meaningful to beginning students: footnote citations to scholarly works and extensive bibliographies. In their place I have substituted a limited number of footnotes that explain and expand on basic points made in the text itself and for each chapter a short list of selected readings on the subjects under discussion. To facilitate the student's use of these books, I have grouped them by topic, following the order of presentation of the material in the chapter itself.

The general content and organization of the book is necessarily similar to that of most texts, but it does have some unique features. For instance, because there are so many one-party areas in the country where the nomination process is tantamount to election, I have devoted an entire chapter (8) to that subject; it also contains a full explanation of the legal and political complications of presidential-nomination contests with which so few Americans are familiar. Chapter 13 provides the student with a basic understanding of law and our legal system, including recent efforts to furnish justice to the poor; this lays the groundwork for an analysis of the federal court system in the following chapter.

I have also treated civil rights and civil liberties differently from most texts. Rather than incorporate all these matters in one chapter, I have placed them within broader subject areas to which they relate. The discussion of First Amendment freedoms immediately precedes an analysis of the methods citizens use to influence public officials; voting rights are included within a discussion of the electoral process; rights of the accused are examined as part of the judicial process; and civil rights are dealt with in a chapter on race relations.

Rather than try to cover all the myriad functions and policies of American government, I have focused my attention on three areas: race, poverty and welfare, and foreign and military policy. These are the most troublesome problems our society faces; in addition, they are particularly relevant to the basic theme of the book: democratic theory. These subjects not only involve key values such as social and economic equality and national security but also raise problems of the participation of disadvantaged groups in the democratic process and the adequacy of that process for defining and pursuing our national interest in the international community.

Many persons have assisted me in one way or another with this book. Professor George A. Peek, Jr. first interested me in the basic course at the University of Michigan, and Nelson Polsby encouraged me to write a text on the subject. My colleagues at the University of Missouri have all supported my efforts; especially helpful have been Frederick Spiegel, David Leuthold, Robert Karsch, Lloyd Wells, Soon Sung Cho, Herbert Tillema, Thomas Barrow, Robert Sharlet, and particularly Arthur Kalleberg, with whom I have discussed normative political theory over the past ten years; he also assumed the chairmanship of the Political Science Department to allow me to finish this book and then facilitated its completion. William Eads, Robert Spurrier, and William Reid did yeoman service as Research Assistants. Alma Bennett, Head of the Social Sciences Division of the University of Missouri-Columbia Library, assisted my searches in a wide range of sources. Barbara Coleman, Stanley Fike, Mrs. Rosemary Ginn, and Andrea Lowenstein provided me information on the 1972 presidential primaries. Ronald Nelson's sharp editorial pencil made the book shorter, clearer, and more precise; Carl Beers and Gerald Papke helped flag my spirits when I became discouraged with the immensity of the venture. I have been assisted by the constructive criticism of A. Lee Brown of Grossmont College, Donald Freeman of the University of West Florida, Joel B. Grossman of the University of Wisconsin, Sam W. Hawkins of San Jacinto College, Robert L. Lineberry of the University of Texas, Norman R. Luttbeg of the Florida State University, Michael K. O'Leary of Syracuse University, and Samuel Huntington and James Q. Wilson of Harvard University.

Mrs. Linda Deming, Dinah Drane, and Sonja Gozum all struggled with my handwriting in typing the manuscript, as did my wife Joan, who also assisted with editorial work on the book.

While all these persons and others too numerous to mention have helped with this book, I alone am responsible for any errors in interpretation and fact.

Richard A. Watson

Contents

PROMISE AND
PERFORMANCE
OF AMERICAN
DEMOCRACY

CHAPTER 1

Democratic Government

Hippies in Golden Gate Park, San Francisco, at the 1967 "Be-in." (United Press International)

A MERICANS WILL REMEMBER the late 1960s and early 1970s as the years of the hippies. The movement reached a peak in February 1967 when the world's first "Human Be-in" was staged in Golden Gate Park, San Francisco, where 10,000 participants churned and chanted to folk-rock music, while a passing parachutist floated into their midst. That summer, college students flocked to the birthplace of hippiedom to "turn on, tune in, and drop out," according to the message preached by one of the headmasters of the movement, former Harvard professor Timothy Leary. Sporting beards and long hair, bedecked with beads and bells, the hippies took over the Haight-Ashbury district of San Francisco.

Behind their bizarre antics lay a deadly serious rejection of the dominant values of middle-class America in the 1960s. Primarily members of middle-class families themselves, the hippies refused to accept society's goals as they saw them: an overwhelming emphasis on the amassing of worldly goods by means of cutthroat competition. For the hippies, "getting ahead" in reality meant becoming victims of the "rat race." They deplored the hypocrisy of America's claim of equal rights for all citizens amidst the reality of racial slums, and they scoffed at the nation's proclamations of peace as it fought a bloody and violent war with a tiny country half a world away.

In place of the phony values of the "square" world, hippies sought to create their own sense of what is important in life. Individuals were to be left alone to do as they saw fit, "to do their thing," free of the control of parents, teachers, and bosses. People were urged to explore not outer space but "inner space," in order to understand themselves and to develop deep and meaningful relationships with their fellow men. Beauty was to be found not in expensive gadgets but in the everyday, simple things of life. Above all, hippies were expected to love everyone, and peace, not violence, was to govern human affairs. "Flower power," the hippies' symbol of beauty, peace, and love, was to save the world.

The hippies rejected not only middle-class values but also the major social groups that ran America, the "establishment," as they called it. Teenagers, rebelling against parents who failed to understand them, ran away from home; university students dropped out of school, charging that their courses were dull and remote from the really important things in life. Hippies left churches they claimed were more interested in building sleek new edifices in the suburbs than in caring for the needs of the city's poor. They rejected companies and labor unions that provided only meaningless jobs offering no sense of satisfaction. Finally, they defied the United States government itself by burning draft cards and refusing to pay taxes to support the war in Vietnam.

For hippies the way to cope with the "sickness" of "straight" society was to withdraw from it, to "opt out." Soon, however, hippies began to develop social groups of their own. "Tribes" (extended family units with as many as twenty-five people) lived together, sharing room, board, and other expenses; parents taught their children, and free courses were offered by hippie writers and artists. The Diggers (named after seventeenth-century English farmers who lived in cooperative communities) ran a "free store" where people helped themselves to second-hand clothing, records, and jewelry; they also served a meal every afternoon in Golden Gate Park. A co-op steered hippies to available jobs such as carrying mail for the United States government. Outsiders from the square world also stepped in to offer needed assistance to the hippies. A free clinic, manned by volunteer doctors, nurses, and pharmacists from nearby San Francisco General Hospital, treated their psychological and medical problems—"bad trips," malnutrition, and infectious diseases. Lawyers offered free legal advice on problems with landlords, school officials, and draft boards.

In time, the hippie movement spread as colonies sprang up along Sunset Strip in Los Angeles, in New York's East Village, and in urban centers across the nation. Seattle developed a food cooperative and free clinic manned by long-haired doctors; a nonprofit "people's" garage was established in Albuquerque. Still other hippies sought refuge from the complexities of urban living by founding communes in remote rural areas in which members worked together to produce for themselves the very essentials of life: food, shelter, and clothing.

Termed the "alternative society" because it provides many citizens with a real choice as to how to live their lives, the hippie movement represents an interesting development in the values and social institutions of modern America. For the student of our society in general and of the government in particular, it points up some essential facts of life in America in the last half of the twentieth century.

THE GENERAL NATURE OF GOVERNMENT

The hippie movement demonstrates first of all that no individual today can exist in isolation; people must form groups to meet their needs. For all his claims of individualism, the hippie, like the square, finds it necessary to organize groups to provide services. Typically he lives in a tribe, sends his children to classes taught by others, may look to the co-op to find jobs, and drops by a free store for articles he needs or fancies. Moreover, because his needs vary, so do the organizations he establishes: the tribe helps to satisfy his sexual desires and provides a setting for the rearing of his children, while free schools and stores help fulfill his educational and economic wants. American society today is a group society, and even the hippie who turns his back on our traditional organizations—the family, secondary schools and universities, companies and labor unions—finds it necessary to create other similar groups of his own—tribes, free schools, co-ops, and stores.

The hippie experience demonstrates at the same time that we do not have to belong to *particular* groups. People can and do break ties with traditional organizations—families, schools, churches, as well as companies. Similarly, the hippie who becomes disillusioned with the movement can leave it to return to the square world. In short, membership in most social groups in our society is voluntary.

GOVERNMENT AS A UNIQUE
SOCIAL INSTITUTION

There is one organization in society, however, in which membership is not voluntary, the *government*. As long as a hippie remains in the United States, he, like everyone else, will be a part of that organization. True, he can leave the country and renounce his citizenship (indeed, every presidential year some disgruntled citizens vow to move to Canada or Mexico if a certain candidate is chosen), but that is a far more serious step than breaking ties with other social groups, and very few persons are willing to take such action. And even if they do, they will come under the control of another government. There is no real escape from government as a social institution.

Furthermore, the government is different from other groups in its capacity to require people to obey its commands, that is, its laws. Although a hippie can escape the rules and regulations laid down by his family, church, or boss, he does not so easily ignore military duty or taxes. If he does, the government can impose serious penalties on him; at the least, he will have to pay a fine; more likely he will receive a jail sentence; and if the infraction is serious enough, such as desertion in the midst of military combat, the government can exact the supreme penalty of death.

The sanctions the government can impose on an individual affecting his property, his liberty of movement, and ultimately his life are available to no other organization in society. The government has a monopoly on the lawful use of force. Other groups and individuals do resort to violence from time to time (hippies, for example, have been attacked by teenage gangs), not because they are given that right by society at large, but rather because they take the law into their own hands. Only the government's use of force is considered *legitimate*, in the sense of proper and right, by most people in a society.

It is this legitimacy that permits the government to control human affairs. People obey a law for other reasons than the fear of force. They may agree with its provisions, that is, believe that the law benefits them personally. Or they may feel that, although they do not actually want to obey a law (such as serving in the armed services), it is necessary for the security of the nation. Persons may even disagree with a particular regulation but respect it because it was passed by public officials only after opponents (including perhaps themselves) were given the chance to express their views. Moreover, as we shall see in Chapter 5, individuals also develop a basic loyalty to their government and are willing to obey its commands simply because of their general support for that government.

It is doubtful that a government can endure if it depends only on the use of force. Even the most authoritarian regime relies on at least the passive consent of its people. Thus public officials rule not by force alone, but also by the legitimacy and authority that the people in a society accord them.

THE INEVITABILITY OF GOVERNMENT

A major goal of the hippie movement—letting people alone to do their thing—is not new. The Digger colony, founded in Great Britain in the seventeenth century and the utopian communities located at Brook Farm, Massachusetts, and New Harmony, Indiana, in the nineteenth century were established for the same purpose. Yet they did not survive, a fate that very early befell a number of hippie colonies in the United States.

The evidence about why such colonies have failed to last is that they have been based on too optimistic a view of human nature. The assumption that people are basically good and can be counted on to cooperate voluntarily and to control their behavior in the interests of others has not turned out to be realistic. Few, if any, individuals are so "beautiful," so imbued with love of their fellow man that they can live together in natural harmony without the use of coercion to require them to respect the rights of others. Even if such a harmony can be achieved within small groups of individuals, it is unlikely that other members of society will permit them to opt out of their general responsibilities of paying taxes, serving in military forces, and respecting health and sanitation regulations. Thus, even if some persons can escape legal coercion from members of their group, the larger society will impose rules and regulations on them.

BASIC DIFFERENCES AMONG GOVERNMENTS

Although all societies have governments, they differ in vital respects. Totalitarian regimes, like those that formerly existed in Fascist Italy and Nazi Germany, as well as the present governments of the Soviet Union and Communist China, try to control virtually all human activities: how families shall raise their children, the kinds of churches they may attend (if, indeed, they are permitted to attend at all), what books and newspapers can be published, what goods will be produced at what prices. Other "free" or "limited' governments, such as those of the United States and Great Britain, let private individuals or groups make such decisions. In short, societies differ in the role government occupies in the total life of the people.

Another major difference among societies is the part that ordinary citizens play in the governing of the nation. In some countries they have little influence over who their political leaders are or the kinds of decisions those leaders make. In other nations the citizenry plays a major role in choosing their officials and determining what actions they take on major political issues. This type of government is *democracy*.

The United States is one of the major democracies in the world. In analyzing our own government, it is, therefore, helpful to determine how closely it approximates the *theory* of democracy. And by theory of democracy I mean the basic principles on which a democratic political system operates as well as the values and assumptions associated with it. By first ascertaining how such a government functions and what ideals it fosters if it is truly democratic, and then comparing the American experience against that standard, we focus on the major theme of this book: the promise and performance of American democracy.

THE GENERAL NATURE
OF DEMOCRACY

The word democracy is derived from two Greek roots, *demos* which means people and *kratia* which connotes rule. Thus literally, democracy means rule by the people. For a society to be democratic, then, a large number of its people must enjoy the right to have some say over important decisions that seriously affect their lives. To express it another way, democratic government is based on the consent of the governed. Viewed in this way, democracy is concerned with *how* political decisions are made, the *procedure* by which ordinary people participate in the making of such decisions.

While democracy is most often defined in terms of *how* governmental decisions are made, it is also associated with the *content* of those decisions. In other words, democracy involves not only the process for making public policies but also the *results* of the process. Democratic governments by definition produce policies that foster certain basic democratic *values* such as liberty, equality, and justice.

The underlying idea, of course, is that if a large number of people participate in the making of governmental decisions, those decisions will be ones that produce liberty, equality, and justice for the great bulk of citizens. Therefore, democracy is also based on certain *assumptions about human nature*, namely, that the ordinary person is rational enough to use his political influence for the purpose of fostering those values.

While there is agreement on these general features and beliefs of democracy, there are differences of opinion on their specifics. For example, what constitutes participation or "some say" over government decisions by ordinary citizens? Is it sufficient that they be able to choose public officials who make decisions, or must the citizens themselves have more direct influence over the content of policies? If so, how much influence, and in what manner is it to be exercised? What is meant by the term "equality"? Are we talking about political equality, legal equality, economic equality, or what? How far does the rationality of the average person go? Must he be able to determine himself what kind of policy is needed to bring more liberty or equality in a society? Or is it sufficient that he can judge between policies suggested by others?

There are no definite answers to any of these questions, and reasonable people equally committed to democracy differ over them. In this respect, there is one general *theory* of democracy, but there are many *theories* about specific procedures, ideals, and assumptions associated with a democratic society. Nonetheless, it is possible to discern certain general types of democracy that have prevailed in certain countries in different historical eras.

ATHENIAN DIRECT DEMOCRACY

Athens, a city-state in ancient Greece with some 300,000 inhabitants, is known as the cradle of democracy. There in the fifth century B.C., a society developed with institutions and beliefs that were clearly democratic. Today, we would refer to the Athenian system as "direct" democracy because all adult, male citizens (women, slaves, foreigners, and free men under twenty years of age were excluded) were permitted to play an important part in the governance of the community. And in fact a significant number of eligible citizens actually did play a role.

POLITICAL TECHNIQUES AND INSTITUTIONS

All adult, male citizens in Athens belonged to the Assembly, a town-meeting type of gathering that met ten times a year to conduct public business. This body, however, was too large and met too infrequently to handle all the political problems of the city-state; much of the real governance was in the hands of a 500-man Council that, in turn, divided itself into ten committees to expedite the consideration of problems. In addition, there were large juries composed of citizens who heard and decided legal controversies.

The system was not pure direct democracy in the sense that the average citizen could participate in each and every political decision in Athens; nonetheless, he played a significant part in many of them. Although the Council and its committees initially handled many problems, major issues came back to the Assembly for final disposition. That body, for example, gave its approval to declarations of war and negotiations of peace, the forming of alliances, the levying of direct taxes, and the like.

Officeholding by ordinary citizens was widespread. The 500-member Council was drawn by lot from persons elected by small geographical units, *demes*, the equivalent of our wards, townships, or parishes. Service on the Council and in most other political posts was typically for one year, so positions rotated from one person to another quickly. The large juries, ranging in size from 200 to 500 persons, were also drawn by lot from a panel of 6000 citizens selected each year. Because different juries were assigned to sit in particular courts, many juries were operating simultaneously. Such a system clearly called for broad participation by citizens: about one in six held some political office in any given year.

The operating principles of Athenian democracy were also distinctly democratic. The give-and-take of spirited debate and extensive discussions were the prevailing means of exploring and clarifying public problems. The final decisions in both the Assembly and the juries were reached by majority vote.

VALUES AND ASSUMPTIONS

Underlying the political institutions and operating principles of Athenian society were certain values that expressed what its citizens felt were the important things in life. Foremost of these was the belief that a citizen could achieve happiness only through *participation in the life of the community*. Only by doing so could he fully develop his personality. He was expected to attend to family and business affairs, but these were not to interfere with his duties to the broader community. His loyalty to the city-state was expected to supersede his private concerns and his attachments to less inclusive groups.

Political equality was another ideal of Athenian democracy. All citizens, regardless of their social station or financial situation, were given equal opportunity to participate in the political life of the community. To insure that the poor could afford to take part in political affairs, most offices were paid; in some instances, individuals were even compensated for attending sessions of the Assembly.

Along with political equality went a *respect for the law*. The Athenian had great faith in the procedures by which the Assembly, Council, and popular juries reached their decisions, and he was inclined to follow those decisions once they were made. For the Athenian the rule of law was distinctly Greek, as contrasted to the edicts of arbitrary rulers under which barbarians were forced to live.

The whole political system was predicated on a great faith in the essential *rationality* of the ordinary citizen. Athenians attributed no special political competence to persons of higher social or economic standing in the community. Nor did they have particular regard for the expert; they rather extolled the virtues of the "happy versatility" of the average citizen, what we would term today the ability of the "amateur." Although Athenians did not expect everyone to originate public policies, they considered each man a sound judge of policies. The belief in man's rationality was also reflected in the discussions and debates that characterized the Athenian political process. The faith that a wise law or good institution could bear the scrutiny of many minds was a basic assumption under which their democracy operated.

Athenian government was thus direct democracy in which a large sample of citizens participated in decisions of the Assembly, while also exercising control over actions of the Council through the Assembly. At the same time, a great number of citizens served on the Council and even more sat as members of the large juries.

Such political institutions have had little application throughout history. In the long period following the decline of Athens (which fell largely as a result of military encounters with its neighbors), people were governed by kings, merchant-princes, generals, religious leaders, aristocrats, or nobles. When democracy was revived in the form of direct citizen involvement in decision-making, it was confined to small units like Swiss cantons and New England town meetings.

A town meeting in New England about 1870: direct democracy in action. (Culver Pictures)

The governance of large countries such as Great Britain and the United States required a different form of democracy. The general type of government that developed in these nations in recent centuries serves as the major example of democracy in the modern world. It is known by many names: *Western* democracy for the geographical location of the countries in which it originated; *constitutional* democracy for its emphasis on limiting government through legal means; and *liberal* democracy for its concern with the liberty of the individual. I will refer to it simply as Western *representative* democracy for its source and for the basic technique it utilizes to implement the ideal of government by the people.

WESTERN REPRESENTATIVE DEMOCRACY

Representative democracy is a system of government in which ordinary citizens do not make governmental decisions themselves but, instead, choose public officials to make decisions for them. In modern nations encompassing millions of people, only a relatively few persons hold public positions, especially in the national government. Thus each member of the United States House of Representatives represents almost half a million persons.

Democratic representative government as we know it today first developed in three Western nations: Great Britain, Switzerland, and the United States. In these countries in the late eighteenth and early nineteenth centuries a large number of people first began to select their political leaders. From this narrow base, democracy spread to other Western European nations, as well as the British Commonwealth. Representative democracy, then, is a form of government that is restricted to a relatively small group of nations in recent centuries.

In fact, if full democracy requires that the majority of the population has the right to affect governmental decisions by choosing its leaders, then this type of government is an even more recent phenomenon. Great Britain and the United States did not provide for universal manhood suffrage until the latter part of the nineteenth century, and women were not permitted to vote in national elections until the 1920s. Switzerland did not fully extend the suffrage to women until nearly fifty years later.

POLITICAL TECHNIQUES AND INSTITUTIONS

As previously noted, in a representative democracy ordinary citizens do not govern; rather they choose those who do. Aristotle referred to such a system as the "rule of the few watched by the many." The crucial part of the phrase is not "rule by the few," since under all political systems a small minority of the populace holds major political offices. The key idea is the many watching those few.

Representative democracy, however, requires more than mere watching;

the many must also be able to implement their observations through political action. The system has to give the people control over their leaders, so that the latter can be held responsible for their actions. If the general populace is unable to exercise such control, then the government does not differ from an *oligarchy*, in which political authority is vested in a few persons who are not accountable to the people.

The particular mechanism that representative democracies have developed to keep their political leaders responsible to the general populace is *elections*. Indeed, democratic societies deliberately create insecurity of tenure for major officeholders, who are periodically required to go before the people to have their terms of office renewed. As Walter Lippmann, a perceptive writer and columnist once put it, those "outside" the government pass judgment on those "inside."

If the citizens in a democracy are displeased with what those in public office are doing about major problems facing the society, the remedy is to replace them. Thus a democratic system of government must provide the electorate with competing groups of political leaders. The power of the people is only effective if they have the opportunity *to choose* one group over another.

All democratic societies, then, must develop some means of providing political leaders for the consideration of the populace. The institution that typically fills this need is the *political party*, which puts forward candidates for public office. In order to provide the element of choice for the voters, there must be at least two competing parties that propose candidates. A voter can then choose a candidate from Party A over one from Party B because he feels that the former will do the more satisfactory job in making political decisions that affect his interests. *At least* two parties must be present so it is entirely consistent with the theory of democracy for three or four (or more) parties to offer potential leaders to the voters.

Since no political party in a democracy can be permitted to be the sole provider of candidates for public office, each party must recognize the right of others to compete. The parties must accept one another's existence as a necessity; beyond that, they must be willing to coexist peacefully. Accordingly, the party (or parties) presently in control of a government must allow the opposition party (or parties) to criticize what the leaders are doing and to propose alternative courses of action for the voters' consideration. Moreover, the incumbents must hold elections in which they can be replaced by members of the opposition. Thus, today's majority must be prepared for the possibility of becoming tomorrow's minority.

It is precisely this spirit of tolerance and willingness to allow themselves to be voted out of office that presents the most difficulty for leaders of nations that are first experimenting with democracy. There is a natural tendency for those in political power to consider persons who question their policies, indeed their very right to remain in control of the government, as traitors. We are familiar today with this attitude among leaders of emerging nations like South Korea and Nigeria, but as we shall see later, a similar attitude existed among the early party leaders of our own country. The idea of a "loyal opposition" presupposes a considerable amount of maturity and sophistication in the ways of democracy. It is perhaps best exemplified today in the British system of government, which not only tolerates opposition but actually fosters it by including a post known as her "majesty's loyal opposition." That position, which is occupied by the leader of the party out of power, carries the right to use funds provided by the government to criticize the party in power.

The minority party (or parties) has more than the responsibility of criticizing the policies of the majority and of suggesting alternatives; it also has the obligation to accept the verdict at the polls and to permit the majority party to remain in office until the next election. One of the most eloquent statements of the proper attitude of a losing candidate in a democracy was made by Adlai Stevenson on the occasion of his defeat by Dwight Eisenhower in 1956. (Stevenson had also lost the Presidency to Eisenhower in 1952, and the margin of loss was wider in the second election than in the first.)

> To you who are disappointed tonight, let me confess that I am too! But we must not be downhearted. . . . For here in America, the people have made their choice in a vigorous partisan contest that has affirmed again the vitality of the democratic process. And I say God bless partisanship, for this is democracy's life blood.
>
> But beyond the seas, in much of the world, in Russia, in China, in Hungary, in all the trembling satellites, partisan controversy is forbidden and dissent suppressed.
>
> So I say to you, my dear and loyal friends, take heart—there are things more precious than political victory; there is the right to political contest.

Democracy provides the electoral machinery whereby competing groups of leaders contest for political office by vying for the votes of the public. The winners take responsibility for developing policies to deal with the major problems of society; the losers have the obligation to criticize those policies and the right to use their criticism as a means of attracting enough supporters at the next election to assume political office themselves. The majority (the general populace) has the responsibility of deciding which of the competing minorities will be permitted to govern until the next election.

Democracy does not just require competition between minorities who seek to govern with the consent of the people: individuals must be permitted to become candidates for public office themselves and, if elected, to serve. The system must thus be open to everyone regardless of his social or economic status.

Beyond elections, which occur periodically, a democratic society must provide means of continual communication between the leaders and the general populace so that personal views on public issues can be transmitted to those who make major political decisions. There is no obligation on those in political power to carry the suggestions into effect, but citizens must have the right to have their viewpoints heard.

Although individuals can express their attitudes on various matters, to be effective they must join with other like-minded persons to form groups that can communicate their demands to decision-makers. The institution that democracies have developed to transmit demands to those in political power is called an *interest group*. Even these groups are likely to contain only a small proportion of the total population, but they do enable a public office-holder to gain some understanding of how a number of persons in a common situation—say, businessmen, laborers, or farmers—feel about such matters as taxes, wages, or farm prices. Moreover, because communication is a two-way process, interest groups not only press *demands* on decision-makers, but also transmit proposals of political leaders to their memberships, which serve as potential sources of *support* for the proposals.

Just as parties compete in a democratic society to place their men in public office, so interest groups vie with one another to influence public policy. If the system is operating properly, they check and balance one another's efforts so that no one group or small number of groups dominates the political process. All kinds of groups representing persons with different social and economic backgrounds and concerns should be able to make themselves heard effectively by officials who make crucial governmental decisions.

The public officials who make the decisions in representative democracies are more diverse and specialized in training than were those who held office in Athenian democracy. Although members of the general public still serve on juries in courtroom controversies, they decide on the facts of the case only, while judges with extensive legal training rule on questions of law. Specialists also serve in the executive arm of the government. Only the legislature remains as the branch of the political "amateur," and as in the Greek Assembly, decisions are typically made by majority vote.

While representative democracy does support majority rule, at the same time it protects the rights of minorities. Representatives of minority viewpoints are permitted to be heard and to criticize the opinions of the majority. Moreover, the system provides the opportunity for present minorities to become future majorities.

Minorities in a democracy, however, enjoy other rights besides that of eventually turning themselves into a majority. As indicated below, certain fundamental rights are protected from infringement by public officials even when they are acting with the support of the majority. The protection comes through constitutions and courts that limit what the government can do. It also derives from attitudes and political customs that determine the proper way for the majority to act towards minorities.

Thus far we have discussed how representative democracies go about making political decisions. But democracy is more than a set of procedures; it also involves values that the procedures are designed to foster and protect.

VALUES

The single most significant idea in democratic thought is belief in the *basic integrity of the individual*. This overriding concern is best expressed in the command of philosopher Immanuel Kant to "treat all individuals, not merely as a means to an end, but as an end in and of themselves." In this view all persons are entitled to consideration simply because they are human beings. As such, they possess dignity and moral worth that everyone is obligated to respect.

One of the consequences of this concern is the belief that the government, or the state, exists for the individual, not the individual for the state. This idea is captured in the Declaration of Independence, which proclaims that men "are endowed by their Creator with certain unalienable rights," and that "to secure these rights, Governments are instituted among Men, deriving their just powers from the consent of the governed." Government does not create these rights; rather it is created by men to safeguard their natural rights.

This idea of the proper relationship between the individual and his government may seem too idealistic, yet it continues to be an important part of the democratic creed. David Lilienthal, the first director of the Tennessee Valley Authority, one of the nation's outstanding public servants with a wealth of experience in practical, everyday affairs, expressed the same basic thought in testimony before a Senate Committee:

> I believe, and I conceive the Constitution of the United States to rest, as does religion, upon the fundamental proposition of the integrity of the individual, and that all government, and all private institutions, must be designed to promote and protect and defend the integrity of the individual.

Another major value of democracy is *liberty*. Liberty involves a person's freedom to select his own purposes in life, together with the means to accomplish those purposes. Obviously, neither of these liberties is absolute. Society, acting through the government, will impose reasonable restrictions; it will not permit a person, for example, to choose to become the world's most skillful thief. Or even if he selects a lofty aim for himself, say the presidency of a great corporation, he will not be allowed to deal violently with rivals who stand in his path. There is a difference between liberty and licence, which is the *unrestricted* freedom to choose one's purposes and methods. Society will not let the hippie or anyone else do his thing if it interferes with the rights of others or even, in some cases, if it harms himself.

Nonetheless, in the ideal democratic society such restrictions are minimal, and citizens retain the liberty to develop themselves to the fullest extent of their capacities.

Liberty carries with it the idea of *privacy*, the freedom to be left alone. Individuals have the right to their own thoughts and their own property, and the government cannot force them to share such personal attributes with their fellow citizens or with the government itself. Again, of course, privacy is not absolute; for example, an individual will be required to pay his share of taxes to provide government services—military and police protection, education, and the like. Nonetheless, democracy maintains as many private preserves for the individual as possible. Democracy thus involves freedom *from* as well as freedom *to*.

Another major value of democracy is *equality*. There are, however, many kinds of equality. The one that is most often accepted as part of the democratic creed is *political equality*. This involves the right of all adult citizens to vote for their political officials, with each vote counting as one and only one. Everyone is also equally entitled to seek and, if he is successful, to serve in public office. Political equality applies to other, nonelectoral activities as well, such as the opportunity to form interest groups or to discuss and debate political issues.

Equality not only relates to participation in influencing or making governmental decisions; it also involves being subject to those decisions. Thus everyone is entitled to *equality under the law*. In other words, the law is to be applied impartially without regard to the identity or status of the individual involved. Few persons quarrel with this concept.

Somewhat more controversial than political and legal equality is the concept of *social equality*. It has as its basis the idea that people should be free of class or social barriers and discrimination. While many agree on the desirability of this ideal, they disagree on what, if anything, the government should do to require individuals to abide by it. The long battle over racial equality described in Chapter 15 reflects differing attitudes on this basic question.

Economic equality is the most controversial of all democratic concepts, primarily because people attribute different meanings to it. Under a strict interpretation, each person would receive the same amount of wordly goods regardless of his contributions to society. This is what Karl Marx had in mind when he wrote, "From each according to his abilities, [society should take from the individual what he is able to contribute] to each according to his needs [he should receive from society what he has to have to get along in life]." If everyone's needs are basically the same, then each person should receive the same amount of economic wealth.

Although Western democracies have generally favored a fairly wide distribution of wealth, they have not construed economic equality to mean that everyone must obtain the same amount of material possessions. Rather, all persons should have *equality of opportunity*, the chance to develop themselves to the fullest extent of their capacities. But even that concept has different interpretations. Does it mean merely formal opportunity in the sense that positions are open to everyone on the basis of capacity? Or does it require that material conditions be equalized by universally providing basic services (good health care, education, and the like) that are vital to individual self-development? This latter position suggests that, although a democratic society need not insure equality at the end of the development process, it should see to it that people are made equal at the beginning.

One of the reasons Western democracies such as Great Britain and the United States favor the equality-of-opportunity concept is that it permits them to reconcile the two values of liberty and equality. If individuals differ in ability, then to give every person the liberty to develop himself to the fullest extent of his capacities will result in some acquiring more goods than others. In other words, Western democracy gives individuals the *equal opportunity to become unequal.*

ASSUMPTIONS ABOUT HUMAN NATURE

Advocates of representative democracy urge the participation of the average person in government because they believe that people are, for the most part, rational and capable of deciding what is good for them personally. Even if their judgments are not always correct, they are more likely to be so than if an elite makes decisions for them. The democrat assumes that no elite group is wise enough or unselfish enough to rule in the interests of the remaining members of society. The only way to insure that the interests of everyone will be taken into account is to give the bulk of the population the right to influence the basic decisions that affect their lives.

The greatest influence most people have on those decisions is exerted through their choice of candidates for public office. Representative democracy does not, therefore, require that the average person himself make decisions about public problems; it only asks him to determine whether political leaders who do make such decisions are doing so satisfactorily. The populace thus acts as a consumer of public-policy decisions produced by others. As one student of democratic theory, A. D. Lindsay, has suggested, "Only the ordinary man can tell whether the shoes pinch and where." In other words, only the individuals subject to rules and regulations know how they are personally affected by them. To determine this effect, the average man does not have to know how to make governmental decisions any more than he has to be a cobbler to know that certain shoes hurt his feet.

The democrat is skeptical about the possibility of knowing what is absolutely "good" or "true." He takes issue with belief in an objective truth that can be discovered by a special group of individuals set apart from the rest of the populace by intelligence and training. The democrat assumes either that no such absolutes exist or that, even if they do, they cannot be discovered by mortals, however intelligent or educated they may be. For all practical purposes, then, the truth is a relative matter. As Supreme Court Justice Oliver Wendell Holmes put it: ". . . the best test of truth is the power of the thought to get itself accepted in the competition of the market. . . ." By this he meant that in a democracy a variety of ideas and viewpoints can be expressed, and what emerges as the choice of the people is the closest thing to truth that can be achieved.

This lack of certainty about truth renders possible another assumption of democracy, namely, that individuals can *tolerate* viewpoints that differ from their own. Since no one has a private pipeline to eternal verities, a person ought to be able to face up to the possibility that he *may* be wrong about a given matter and the other person may be right. The adherent of democracy assumes that a spirit of give-and-take and a willingness to *compromise* will develop among individuals, enabling them to resolve their differences in a peaceful manner.

The democrat also takes the position that decisions made by a large number of individuals are more likely to be good ones than those made by a few. E.B. White, an American writer, expresses this idea in his statement that "Democracy is the recurrent suspicion that more than half of the people are right more than half of the time." In other words, a majority is more likely than a minority to decide the correct thing to do. But White's statement underscores the tentative nature of democratic faith in the majority.

In fact, the proponent of democracy does not always trust the majority and consequently is not willing to allow it to decide all matters that affect individuals' lives. Minority rights are also to be respected. Democracy evolved in Western Europe and America in the eighteenth and nineteenth centuries from an earlier concept known as *constitutionalism*, which had as a major principle the idea that government should be *limited*. For example, in the United States and Great Britain it makes no difference that over half the population are Protestants: they are not permitted to tell persons of the Catholic or Jewish faith how to worship. Likewise, in democratic nations the individual's right to private property is respected and his personal goods cannot be taken from him even for a public use (as, for example, when a university takes private land to expand its operations) without just compensation. It is precisely this limitation on the scope of government—based on a concern for privacy, as well as limited faith in majority rule—that distinguishes a democratic society from a totalitarian one.

Democracy presupposes neither a wholly optimistic nor a wholly pessimistic view of human nature. It does not rest on the faith of the hippie that people are innately good, "beautiful," or cooperative, nor on the assumption made by some advocates of totalitarianism that the average person is depraved. The democrat's ambivalence toward human nature is aptly expressed in the comment of the late theologian Reinhold Niebuhr that "man's capacity for justice makes democracy possible; but man's inclination to injustice makes democracy necessary."

This combination of political techniques and institutions, values, and assumptions regarding human nature underlies the type of Western democracy we Americans normally associate with our own political system, as well as with the systems of certain nations of Europe and the British Commonwealth. As indicated by the following section, however, not everyone believes that American democracy actually operates in this fashion or even that it should.

CONFLICTING VIEWS
OF AMERICAN DEMOCRACY

Students of our political system differ fundamentally on the basic state of American democracy today. Some view it as a successful, if not the most successful, example of democracy in the modern world, one that has for the most part lived up to its ideals or promises. Others feel that its performance falls far short of its promises and that some of these promises themselves are badly in need of revision.

THE CASE FOR AMERICAN DEMOCRACY

The case for American democracy rests on the basic assessment that our political techniques and institutions operate generally as they should. The leaders of the Republican and Democratic parties compete for the support of the voters by tailoring their proposals to appeal to the wishes of a wide variety of groups that make up the electorate. The winning party, representing a broad coalition of such groups, must continue to keep the preferences of many groups in mind after it assumes office, and if it fails to do so, it can and will be replaced by the opposition party. The fact that the Republican and Democratic parties are so competitive (seldom does the losing party draw less than forty percent of the vote in a presidential election) means that overturns in party control are frequent, and even when they do not actually occur, the possibility that they will keeps the majority party responsive to public preferences.

Between elections, public policy is primarily influenced by the activities of concerned minorities who work through interest groups to make demands on decision-makers. Again, the system is competitive because groups such as business and labor take different views on public concerns and frustrate each other's ambitions. Therefore, no one group or small number of groups dominates the American political process.

American governmental institutions also insure that a wide variety of interests will be taken into account when political decisions are made. Public officials in separate parts of the governmental system are responsive to different groups: for example, the House of Representatives favors the concerns of people who live in rural areas and small towns, while the President is receptive to ethnic groups in the large industrial states. Groups whose interests are not met by the national government can turn to state officials for help. As political scientist Robert Dahl puts it, "The normal American political process is one in which there is a high probability that an active and legitimate group in the population can make itself heard effectively at some crucial stage in the process of decision."

The American political system is, in this view, a highly pluralistic one in which power is distributed widely among many individuals and groups: businessmen, laborers, farmers, blacks, white-collar workers among them. Although some groups have more political assets in the form of money, numbers, and campaigning and propaganda skills than others, all have some political resources—at the minimum, the vote.

The American political system is also open in the sense that people from various ethnic, racial, and social backgrounds can become politically active. Indeed, some groups, notably the Irish, have worked their way up the social and economic ladder by using the political process to further their interests. Eventually one of them may win the highest position in the American political system, the Presidency—as John F. Kennedy did. This process continues as Italians, Jews, and most recently blacks are elected to more and more political offices.

Those with favorable views of American democracy generally recognize that the successful operation of our political system depends primarily on persons who are interested and concerned about political matters. Referred to by various names—political "elites," "activists," or "influentials"—they are the citizens who offer themselves or others as candidates and who campaign for election, who man the major appointive positions in the government, who propose policies for dealing with major problems, and who work through the political process to get their proposals enacted into law. They include not only individuals who hold public office but also those who are outside the formal structure of government in leadership posts in political parties, interest groups, private corporations, and labor unions, as well as newspaper editors, college teachers, and others who are in a position to shape the political opinions of the man in the street.

It is the political moves and countermoves by this broad variety of political elites that make the American political system work as it does. While they compete vigorously with each other, at the same time they appreciate and abide by the democratic "rules of the game" regarding the right of freedom of speech and the press for those who oppose them. They are also personally committed to the major values of a democratic society—the liberty of the individual, the right of privacy, religious freedom, and justice under the law. It is these political activists who are the major carriers of the American democratic creed; they can be counted upon to defend it when

The competing interests in American society can be reconciled, as when Senator Robert Kennedy—seen here with Cesar Chavez, organizer of farm workers in California—took up the cause of the poor. (Gene Daniels-Black Star)

other, less politically aware and educated individuals are willing to deny basic rights to unpopular minorities.

In the final analysis, supporters of American pluralistic democracy feel that it serves well the interests of a wide variety of individuals and groups in our society. Competing elites take the initiative in public affairs, but at the same time they must take account of the interests of ordinary citizens on whom they ultimately depend to support their policies as well as their tenure in public office. The entire process, which takes place within prescribed democratic procedures, has moderated differences among our diverse people and brought the nation social peace as well as social progress.

MAJOR CRITICISMS
OF AMERICAN DEMOCRACY

Although most students of American democracy over the years have tended to support our system, it has also had its share of critics. Particularly in recent years, as social problems—increased violence, racial tensions, poverty, the war in Vietnam—appear to be worsening, the critics have increasingly called into question the operation, ideals, and assumptions of our political system.

One of the major criticisms directed at American democracy is that it simply does not operate as its supporters claim it does. Rather than shape their actions to accord with the wishes of the voters, candidates and office-holders manipulate the attitudes of the populace by clever public relations techniques and the skillful use of the mass media. Republican and Democratic candidates, it is charged, stand for essentially the same policies, which means that voters have no significant choice between them. Moreover, significant minorities—blacks, Mexican-Americans, American Indians, the poor, and the young—are not represented or served by either of the two major parties.

The critics view the making of public policy between elections in essentially the same light. None of the above-mentioned minorities is nearly as effectively organized as are more dominant, affluent groups. As political scientist E.E. Schattschneider has suggested, "The flaw in the pluralist heaven is that the heavenly chorus sings with a strong upperclass accent. Probably about ninety percent of the people cannot get into the pressure system." Moreover, the minorities that are organized do not actually check and balance one another as is generally claimed. Rather, each concentrates on getting what it wants in benefits from government: businessmen are served by the Department of Commerce, organized working people by the Department of Labor, and farmers by the Department of Agriculture. Instead of regulating such groups in the public interest, public officials grant them favors at the expense of the general taxpayer.

Nor do the critics feel that the system is equally open or responsive to all kinds of individuals and groups. Few if any women, blacks, laborers, or members of the lower economic classes sit in Congress, in the executive departments, or on the Supreme Court. Middle- and upper-class persons dominate all three branches of our national government, and those at the state level as well. Moreover, the increasing costs of political campaigns may make it even more difficult for those of limited means to hold elective office in the future, especially in the national government. Thus the pluralist version of American democracy simply does not square with the facts.

Critics of American democracy not only question whether the political process works as its supporters claim it does; they also suggest that a democratic government needs to be judged on other bases than the procedures and methods it uses to reach decisions. Specifically, one must take into account the *content* of such decisions to determine whether they promote the major values of democracy, such as liberty, equality, and justice under the law.

When some observers apply this latter standard to America, they find it deficient in many respects. They are particularly critical of what we have accomplished in terms of developing equality in American life, whether it be social equality for the black, Mexican-Americans, or Puerto Ricans; economic equality for those groups and poor whites, as well; or equal justice under the law for all our disadvantaged citizens. They also question a system of priorities that results in huge military expenditures for ventures abroad at the same time that we are unable to meet the needs of our society at home.

Critics further suggest that we change our traditional theories about Western representative democracy and chart new directions for our political system and society in the modern world: for example, not being satisfied with confining democratic values and procedures to governmental institutions but using them for our other institutions as well. According to this view, corporations should not trade with South Africa because of its racist policies, boards of directors of corporations should include representatives of the consumers, and students should participate in the making of university decisions that affect their lives.

At the same time, we need to reinterpret some of our traditional values such as equality. It is not sufficient that we provide individuals with the mere opportunity to participate politically or to have the law applied impartially to them. We should also see to it that all Americans are provided with the education, training, and necessary resources to make their participation effective—and with access to an attorney to insure that their legal rights are fully protected.

Finally, some critics of American democracy charge that we have been far too willing to accept the view that political elites should run the political system because common people are apathetic about public affairs and are not committed to the democratic rules of the game. According to this view, that position underestimates the possibility of educating the average citizen to appreciate his own political rights, as well as the right of others to oppose his views. Moreover, if the political system is made more relevant to his needs, the common man or "little guy" will take a greater interest in its operation. Working toward that goal will point the American political system to the fundamental purpose for which democracy was originally established: the full development of the individual's personality through his participation in the life of the community.

It is interesting to note that some of the recent criticisms of American democracy reflect a desire to return to the kinds of values and assumptions that underlay direct Athenian democracy. Today's mottoes of "participatory democracy" and the "new politics" have much in common with the Greek precept that the individual should involve himself in public affairs, that he must think not just of his own private interests but also of those of the community at large.

APPROACH AND ORGANIZATION
OF THIS BOOK

The general approach of this book is to analyze the American political system in terms of the democratic procedures, values, and assumptions discussed above. The discussion focuses on the conflicting views of our democracy to determine which better reflects the realities of American political life. In the process, certain basic questions are explored: How have our political institutions actually operated? How successful have they been in achieving our ideals? What assumptions have we made about the political capabilities of the common people and how accurate have such assessments been? Have our institutions, ideals, and assumptions changed much over the course of our political development and, if so, how, and in what direction?

In seeking answers to such basic questions, a common pattern is followed in each of the chapters. First, the fundamentals of the subject are analyzed, with particular attention given to key concepts needed to understand the material that follows (for instance, a constitution is defined and its purposes explained in order to prepare for a discussion of the American constitutional system); concepts are also distinguished from related ones (such as a political party from an interest group). The aim is to get at essentials rather than to get bogged down in factual material unrelated to major ideas.

Most chapters also provide basic information on how our political system has evolved over time. Special emphasis is placed on the early years when our institutions were first being established and on the recent period when so many new developments have occurred in American political life. This approach provides a needed perspective on how American democracy has changed over time.

With concepts and background information established, the major portion of each chapter analyzes how the political institution under study actually works today. Particular attention is focused on current problems relating to its operation in a rapidly changing society. The concluding portion of the chapter assesses the operation of the political institution in terms of the conflicting views of American democracy outlined above.

The book is divided into four major parts. The first analyzes the constitutional framework of American government, together with the values and assumptions underlying that framework. It explores the basic features of American democracy, such as the separation and division of powers, as well as the limitations placed on all levels of government in the interest of individual liberty. This part thus focuses on legal powers and limitations and the role they play in establishing the basic rules of the game within which our political process operates.

The second part concentrates initially on the attitudes of citizens toward the American political system and the ways in which their attitudes are acquired. Succeeding chapters in Part II focus on the kinds of institutions Americans have developed to keep those in political power responsible to the general public and on the extent to which such institutions actually enable the public to influence and control their public officials.

The third major part focuses on the three major branches of government —the Congress, the executive branch, and the courts—which together make the official decisions that are binding on the rest of society. These branches are examined in terms of the kinds of persons who serve in them, the procedures each utilizes to carry on its activities, and the relationships that exist among them.

These three parts thus focus on how the various elements of the American process operate generally and the extent to which they satisfy Dahl's criterion that the system enable every active and legitimate group to make itself heard effectively at some crucial stage in the process of decision. Yet as I cautioned earlier, a democratic government should be judged not only on how it makes decisions but also on whether the decisions it makes foster the major values of a democratic society. The final part of the book accordingly concentrates on three crucial issues in the United States today—the race revolution, the problems of poverty, and the nation's relationships with other countries in the world—and assesses how successfully the government's policies have been in promoting social and economic equality and in safeguarding our national interest and security.

Selected Readings

Two good, brief discussions of the unique nature of government as a social institution are contained in Robert Dahl, *Modern Political Analysis* (Englewood Cliffs, N.J.: Prentice-Hall, 1963), and David Easton, *A Framework for Political Analysis* (Englewood Cliffs, N.J.: Prentice-Hall, 1965).

A classic study of the rise of modern democracy is A.D. Lindsay, *The Modern Democratic State* (New York: Oxford University Press, 1962). An extended treatment of the historical evolution and general nature of democracy is Leslie Lipson, *The Democratic Civilization* (New York: Oxford University Press, 1964).

Two excellent recent treatments of democratic theory are Henry Mayo, *An Introduction to Democratic Theory* (New York: Oxford University Press, 1960), and Giovanni Sartori, *Democratic Theory* (New York: Praeger, 1965). For a critique of the excessive optimism concerning human nature underlying some recent theories of democracy, see Reinhold Niebuhr, *The Children of Light and The Children of Darkness* (New York: Scribner, 1944).

The case for pluralist American democracy is set forth by Robert Dahl in several of his recent studies. Included are *A Preface to Democratic Theory* (Chicago: Phoenix Books, 1963), *Who Governs?* (New Haven: Yale University Press, 1961), and *Pluralist Democracy in the United States* (Chicago: Rand McNally, 1967).

An excellent criticism of Dahl's theory is Jack Walker, "A Critique of the Elitist Theory of Democracy," *The American Political Science Review*, LX (1966), 285–95. For a more extended analysis of the same subject, see Peter Bachrach, *The Theory of Democratic Elitism: A Critique* (Boston: Little Brown, 1967). A more recent article expressing the same general viewpoint is Darryl Baskin, "American Pluralism: Theory, Practice and Ideology," *The Journal of Politics*, 32 (1970), 71–96.

PART I

THE AMERICAN CONSTITUTIONAL FRAMEWORK

T HE CONSTITUTION *of a democratic nation provides the basic principles that determine the conduct of its political affairs. These principles relate to three fundamental aspects of the political system. One aspect has to do with the* functions of the government, *the kinds of activities within public, as contrasted to private, control. The second bears on* procedures, *the manner in which the government carries out the activities entrusted to it. Closely related is the third aspect,* structure, *the particular mechanisms used to execute public functions. Together, these elements constitute the rules of the game by which political authority is exercised in the society.*

Historically, constitutions have been linked to the concept that those in political power should be responsible to the populace for their actions. Thus the constitution becomes the practical means whereby the ruled exercise some control over their rulers. In democratic societies like Great Britain and the United States, constitutions have also been associated with limitations on government, insuring that those in political power—even when they are acting with the consent of the majority—do not interfere with certain fundamental rights. In such countries, the constitution determines not only what the government can *do but also what it* cannot *do; thus the constitution both channels and restricts the exercise of political power.*

In the first chapter we found that public officials make binding decisions in the form of legal regulations that determine what private individuals and groups may and may not do and how they should conduct themselves toward their fellow men. A constitution performs a similar function for public officials themselves by determining what they can and cannot do and what their relationships should be with other officeholders, as well as with the general populace. Reciprocity thus characterizes a constitutional form of government: the people grant public officials the power to enact laws and decrees that vitally affect their lives, but at the same time they control the manner in which that power is exercised.

A constitution, then, establishes legal relationships between leaders and followers; even more basically, it is at the heart of a nation's political process. On the one hand, it shapes that process by determining the rules to be followed in competing for political power. On the other hand, the constitution is itself shaped by the political process, as groups struggle to write the rules of the game to favor their own particular interests.

Our study of the American system begins in Chapter 2 with an analysis of the political context in which our Constitution was created—the circum-stances that gave rise to the calling of the Convention in 1787, the kinds of individuals and groups that participated in its deliberations, and the specific purposes they had in mind in forging the basic document to guide the na-tion's future growth. The latter part of the chapter examines the political beliefs of the Founding Fathers and the constitutional principles they chose to implement those beliefs. Chapters 3 and 4 analyze the part that two ma-jor features of the American constitutional framework—federalism and civil liberties—have played in shaping the continuing struggle for political power in the United States.

CHAPTER 2

The American Constitution

"The Signing of the Constitution." (Brown Brothers)

During the summer of 1787, fifty-five delegates met in convention in Philadelphia to frame a new constitution for a young nation. In the group were many of the leading public figures of the day: the revered wartime commander, George Washington, the "Vesuvius of a man" who, despite his famed temper, presided over the four-month deliberations with fairness and dignity; beloved Benjamin Franklin, the nation's elder statesman (age eight-one), admired like Washington not only in his own country but also in the capitals of Europe; youthful Alexander Hamilton, brilliant prime-mover of events that led to the calling of the Convention; and the diminutive James Madison, "no bigger," someone remarked, "than half a cake of soap," ultimately judged by historians the Convention's "giant."

Political history knows no more revered heroes than this assemblage of distinguished men. Americans of many generations have endowed the Constitution and its framers with divine qualities. Thomas Jefferson called his contemporaries "an assembly of demigods"; one of the latest authors to chronicle these exciting days, Catherine Drinker Bowen, entitles her book *The Miracle at Philadelphia.* Nor has the adulation been restricted to our own citizens: William Gladstone, four-time Prime Minister of Great Britain, once described the Constitution as "the most wonderful work ever struck off at a given time by the brain and purpose of man."

Not all Americans, however, have joined in such veneration of our fundamental document. One outspoken opposition delegate at the Massachusetts ratifying convention, Amos Singletry, had this to say about Jefferson's demigods:

> These lawyers and men of learning, and monied men that talk so finely, and gloss over matters so smoothly, to make us poor illiterate people swallow down the pill, expect to get in the Congress themselves . . . get all the power . . . and then they will swallow up us little fellows, . . . just as the whale swallowed up Jonah.

Less partisan men than "plain-folks" spokesman Singletry have also questioned the purity of the Founding Fathers' motives. Scholars Vernon Parrington and J. Allen Smith viewed the Convention as a reaction against the era of the common man that followed the Revolutionary War; they thus regarded it as a "counterrevolution," an overturn of political power (though this time a peaceful one) by which the conservative, propertied classes recaptured control of the country from radicals like Samuel Adams and Patrick Henry, who had dominated politics in the Revolutionary and immediate postwar eras. A similar stream of thought flows through historian Charles

33

Beard's classic study, *An Economic Interpretation of the Constitution of the United States*, which suggests that the Founding Fathers wrote the Constitution primarily to protect their own property interests. Although written in 1913, Beard's work remains the most controversial analysis of the Constitution, as scholars continue to attack, defend, and qualify his thesis.

I will assess these conflicting interpretations in the concluding portion of the chapter. First, however, we need to examine the circumstances that led to the calling of the Convention and the type of Constitution which the proceedings produced.

THE PRE-CONSTITUTION PERIOD

A constitution provides the basic rules of the game that citizens must follow in competing for things they want from the political process. Such rules—dealing with governmental functions, procedures, and structures—are never entirely neutral: they inevitably favor some persons at the expense of others. To understand the background of the American Constitution, we need to appreciate two major factors: first, the preceding frames of government, the national Articles of Confederation and state constitutions; and second, the economic conditions that created dissatisfaction with the existing governmental arrangements and that led some groups to seek a rewriting of the nation's constitutional framework.

FRAMES OF GOVERNMENT

The Articles of Confederation and the early state constitutions reflected American experiences during the colonial period. Because the colonists attributed their particular troubles to the heavy hand of the London government, they feared centralized political power; as a result, they declared themselves to be independent, not only of the mother country, but, in essence, of one another as well. The Articles of Confederation specifically provided that "Each state retains its sovereignty, freedom and independence, and every Power, Jurisdiction and right" not "expressly delegated to the United States, in Congress assembled."

The functions so delegated to the national Congress were restricted primarily to matters of war and peace (raising an army and navy, entering into treaties and alliances, sending and receiving diplomatic representatives) that wartime experience indicated had to be vested in the nation. Missing, for example, was Congress's power to regulate interstate and foreign commerce, a power the Confederation's framers associated with the abuses of the Acts of Trade and Navigation passed by the centralized authority of Parliament. A similar fear of the tyranny of taxation as practiced by the British against the colonists resulted in the denial of the power to tax to the national government: although it had authority to requisition funds from the states for its expenses, the taxes to pay these requisitions had to be laid by the states themselves. National troops also had to be furnished by the states. Lacking the authority to require the states to meet their obligations (which many did not) or to tax or conscript individuals itself, the national government was denied the means to carry out the few functions entrusted to it. Moreover, the Articles provided little opportunity for changing these arrangements, since all thirteen states had to consent to an alteration in the document.

The British experience colored the colonists' attitude not only toward the distribution of authority between the nation and the states but also toward the particular branch of government that should be entrusted with important political powers. Memories of George III and his emissaries, the colonial governors, led Americans of the Revolutionary period to identify tyranny with the executive; at the same time, they associated liberty with the legislature, the arm of colonial government that represented their interests in battles with the king's governor. They had little use for the judiciary, which had been populated by representatives of the crown.

These attitudes toward the various branches of government are directly reflected in the structures of both national and state governments in the post-Revolutionary period. The Articles of Confederation provided for a legislative body with a single house in which each state had an equal vote. There was no provision at all for independent executive and judiciary branches. In the states, too, the legislature was the dominant branch, even to the point of choosing most of the governors: only four states had a chief executive elected by the people. The state judiciaries were also generally weak, frequently appointed by the legislature, and typically given limited powers.

Beyond their particular fears of the national government and the executive, Americans in the Revolutionary era also had a profound distrust of political power in general. The Articles of Confederation and state constitutions provided checks on even the favored legislative bodies of the day. Terms of legislators were short, one year only in the national Congress and most of the states; Rhode Islanders were even more wary of officeholders, allowing their representatives only six months between elections. And for the popular legislator, there was an additional limitation of forced rotation —for example, under the Articles of Confederation no person "was capable of being a delegate for more than three years in any term of six years"; similar provisions plagued ambitious state legislators. As for the unpopular delegate, the voters need not endure him even during his short term, for the national Articles and many state constitutions gave the electorate the power of recall at any time. As a final check on arbitrary government, state constitutions established bills of rights insuring fundamental liberties like freedom of speech and conscience, and trial by jury.

In time, a reaction set in against this legislative, semidirect democracy.

The simple necessities of executive government required the national Congress to create departments of diplomacy, war, and finance, and to appoint eminent men like Robert Livingston, John Jay, and Robert Morris to head their activities. British occupation of New York required that state to develop a strong governorship free of legislative dominance in order to handle its military and civilian affairs. And in Massachusetts the voters adopted a constitution that departed radically from the strong legislative-democratic model. Conceived by John Adams, who favored a "mixed' government representing various social interests, it provided for a popularly elected house of representatives and an "aristocratic" senate apportioned on the basis not of population but of taxable wealth. Moreover, it included a popularly elected governor (eligible to succeed himself) with substantial powers, including that of vetoing legislative acts, and an independent judiciary. The New York and Massachusetts constitutions were important not only for their influence on other states but also because they constituted alternative models to which the Founding Fathers would ultimately turn in their deliberations at the Constitutional Convention.

While alterations were thus being made in the structures of both the national and state governments in the pre-Constitution period, attempts to change the allocation of powers between the two levels of government were continually frustrated. Before Maryland had even signed the Articles of Confederation, Congress submitted an amendment to the states to allow it to levy a duty of five percent on imported goods; the amendment failed of adoption because one state, Rhode Island, refused to ratify. Similar efforts to grant Congress authority to regulate foreign and interstate commerce and to require states to comply with requisitions of men or money owed to the national government foundered on the unanimous-consent requirement for amending the Articles. Financial affairs of the national government had reached such a sad state that its total income in 1786 was less than a third of the interest due on the national debt. Meanwhile, seven states exercised the power to issue money, with the result that the new nation even lacked a common currency; nine states even retained their own navies. Thus the United States in the pre-Constitution period lacked authority over fundamental concerns of any viable, sovereign nation: finances, commerce, and external affairs. Yet as the following section indicates, it was precisely these matters that were of greatest salience to many Americans of that time.

ECONOMIC CONDITIONS

Like many of the newly emerging nations in today's world, the United States in the 1780s faced a major period of adjustment following the successful revolt against Great Britain. Within a few years after the close of the Revolutionary War in 1781, Americans were experiencing an economic depression. Accounts differ about how serious conditions actually became: some historians suggest that the young nation tottered on the edge of an economic abyss that threatened its very existence; others claim that the critical period was very short-lived and that the United States was well on the way to recovery by the time the Convention met in Philadelphia in mid-1787. There is general agreement, however, that the economic downturn did not affect all groups in the same way. Small farmers and the few hired laborers of the day took little of the impact, while persons in commerce and finance were hit the hardest.

One of the ironies of the success of the Revolution was that, while it brought relief from burdensome taxes imposed by the mother country, it also ended the favorable position of American businessmen in international commerce. After the War, in place of the preferential trade treatment and the assured markets they had enjoyed in the British Empire, merchants faced an economic threat from British manufacturers who dumped their goods on the American market. Infant businesses naturally found it very difficult to compete with the products of well-developed British industries; moreover, under the Articles of Confederation the national government lacked authority to levy import duties on British merchants to protect the domestic market. Thus, having thrown off the political yoke of Great Britain, the United States was threatened with being shackled by the economic power of the mother country.

Nor was the commercial competition faced by American merchants restricted to foreign sources alone. Domestic rivalries also developed as states levied duties, not only to raise needed revenue, but also to protect local interests against out-of-state competitors. Particularly disadvantaged by such duties were those states with no seaports of their own. Madison suggested that "New Jersey between Philadelphia and New York was like a cask tapped at both ends, and North Carolina between Virginia and South Carolina was like a patient bleeding at both arms." Lacking the authority to levy duties on imports or to regulate interstate commerce, the national government was thus powerless either to erect a tariff barrier to protect American industries against the British or to break up the obstacles to free trade within the nation.

Another major group adversely affected in the postwar period were creditors who financed both private and public ventures in the young nation. Individuals who were debtors used the political process at the state level to lighten the burden of their debt in various ways. One technique involved enacting "stay" laws to postpone the due date of obligations past the time originally provided for in the promissory note. Another, similar type of legislation permitted a debtor to declare bankruptcy, pay off his obligation at less than the face value, and begin his financial life anew with a clean slate. Yet another advantage for debtors—and disadvantage for creditors—was the issuance of cheap paper money by state legislatures; this inflationary practice allowed obligations to be paid off with money that was worth far less in purchasing power than the currency originally borrowed.

Even more financially frustrated than private creditors were those who had lent the nation money to fight the Revolutionary War. No method existed for collecting on public securities issued by a government that lacked the financial ability to pay off its debts. Similarly affected were wartime veterans who lent, not money, but a more precious commodity, their services, for which they were to be later compensated by proceeds from government bonds.

Although the United States had theoretically achieved an independent status in the family of nations as a result of the War, in actuality numerous challenges to sovereignty persisted after the conclusion of hostilities. Inimical Indian tribes continued to inhabit lands in the West, so that veterans found their claims to such lands no more realizable than the worthless bonds they were issued for their wartime services. Beyond this, the Spanish closed the mouth of the Mississippi to all shipping, and the supposedly vanquished British troops refused to withdraw from certain northwestern forts until claims of British creditors were honored.

GROUP RIVALRIES
AND THE MOVEMENT FOR A CONVENTION

In the situation described above, the groups particularly aggrieved by the postwar situation were those involved in commerce and finance—manufacturers, merchants, shipowners, and public and private creditors. The professional classes—lawyers, doctors, newspaper editors—viewed matters from the perspective of their clientele, and that perspective was shared by former soldiers who felt cheated out of their rightful claims for services rendered in the cause of nationhood. All in all, these groups comprised a potent array of individuals longing for a change in the unfortunate circumstances in which they found themselves. Later, after the Constitution had been framed, these disparate elements were to be welded into an effective group working for its adoption under the name of "Federalists."

Although these groups were for the most part concentrated in the cities, some rural Americans also found their interests jeopardized by the postwar conditions. These were the commercial farmers who produced a surplus of crops which they wanted to dispose of in interstate and foreign markets. Typically large holders of fertile lands, with slave labor and locations on river arteries that linked them to the outside world, they found common cause with merchants whose futures were also linked to commerce.

Arrayed against the nascent Federalists in the economic and political rivalries of the day were those Americans who were not dependent on trade for their livelihood. The small subsistence farmers, scratching out a living on poor soil remote from river valleys, who produced crops entirely for their own families or who marketed their small surpluses in nearby localities, formed the core of the group that were basically satisfied with life in the postwar period. Also included in its ranks were small businessmen, artisans, and mechanics (the small laboring class of that day), and debtors who welcomed governmental assistance in their eternal struggle to keep one step ahead of their creditors. It was their coalition of interests, labeled "Anti-Federalists," that eventually led the fight to defeat the ratification of the Constitution.

The Federalists as a group were wealthier and better educated and held higher-status occupations than their antagonists, who tended to be lower-class, obscure men of modest means. Although the leadership of the Anti-Federalists included such prominent Americans as George Mason, Richard Henry Lee, Patrick Henry, and George Clinton, they could not match either in numbers or in fame those who, like Washington, Hamilton, and Madison, lent their skill and prestige to the Federalists' cause. There were also major differences between the two groups of leaders: the Anti-Federalists were "locals," persons with interests and influence in their own states, while the Federalists were "cosmopolitans," individuals with national reputations who were oriented to the world beyond their immediate communities. The latter enjoyed friendships across the breadth of the young nation, many bred by the camaraderie of common wartime experiences. A number of rich Federalists also acquired their wealth late compared to the established Anti-Federalists like George Mason who, hailing from an old Virginia family, regarded George Washington as something of an upstart. Washington and Hamilton, by propelling themselves up the social and economic ladder through astute marriages, contributed to their *nouveau-riche* image among local Anti-Federalist notables.

These, then, were the opposing leaders and interests that were to vie over the writing and ratification of the Constitution. The nascent Anti-Federalists were essentially satisfied with existing governmental arrangements, while those who were later to become Federalists sought to overturn them in favor of a constitutional system that would provide relief from their mounting problems.

Two events converged in the fall of 1786 that enabled the Federalists to convert their desires into successful action. One was a meeting at Annapolis, Maryland, convened to discuss problems of interstate trade and the possibility of adopting a uniform system of commercial regulations. When only five states showed up, Hamilton and Madison seized the opportunity to issue a report to the Continental Congress suggesting that a commission be assembled the following May to "render the constitution of the federal government adequate to the exigencies of the Union." The other event was the outbreak of an armed revolt in western Massachusetts; farmers there took to arms in response to an effort by the state to take their property for failure to pay taxes and debts in the "hard" money of the time. Although Shays' Rebellion (named for its leader Daniel Shays) was put down, it badly frightened many Americans who regarded it as a threat not only to property rights but also to the very existence of government. Among such men was the most popular American of them all, George Washington. Appalled by the news that a former officer in his army had brought the state of Massachusetts to the brink of civil war, Washington lent his great prestige to the movement for the Convention. The following February the Congress called upon the states to send delegates "for the sole and express purpose of revising the Articles of Confederation." All except ever-recalcitrant Rhode Island, where the debtor clique completely controlled the state, eventually responded, although the North Carolina delegation did not arrive until July, some two months after the deliberations first began.

THE CONSTITUTIONAL CONVENTION

PERSONNEL: THE FOUNDING FATHERS

In terms of the economic, social, and political divisions described above, the most important feature of the Constitutional Convention was that the overwhelming proportion of the delegates were would-be Federalists. Even though the Anti-Federalists matched or even exceeded their opponents in numbers among the general populace, they sent only a few of their men to the deliberations. This failure is puzzling since the state legislatures of the day, which in many instances were the chosen instruments of the debtor forces, were also entrusted with selecting delegates to the Convention and so they could have packed their delegations with Anti-Federalists. The best indications are that they did not do so for two reasons. One is that some of the Anti-Federalists did not want to dignify the constitutional assembly with their presence; a case in point was Patrick Henry who stayed away because he "smelt a rat." The other is that they thought it was not important to attend since the Convention was restricted to revising the Articles of Confederation; moreover, they could always ultimately block any undesirable changes in the Articles because such alterations had to be approved by all the states. In any event, several persons who later opposed the Constitution refused their commissions to the Convention, a decision lamented by one of them, Richard Henry Lee, who later wrote, "The non-attendance of eight or nine men who were appointed members of the convention, I shall ever consider as a very unfortunate event to the United States."

A sprinkling of future Anti-Federalists did attend the Convention (including George Mason of Virginia, Elbridge Gerry of Massachusetts, Luther Martin of Maryland, and Robert Yates and John Lansing of New York), but they were badly outnumbered by their opponents, and even they belonged to the elite element of their group. The nation's subsistence farmers, who constituted the rank-and-file support of the Anti-Federalist cause, were represented by only one delegate, a backwoods yeoman from Georgia. Since such farmers were the most numerous economic group in the nation at that time, the Convention's delegates were decidedly not a cross section of American life.

In fact, an analysis of the backgrounds of the members of the Convention indicates that they were definitely an elite group. Of the fifty-five delegates, thirty-four were lawyers; most of them held college degrees, nine of them from universities abroad. To their educational attainments, they added a wealth of practical political experience. Over three-fourths of them had served in the Continental Congress; many had participated in the writing of the Declaration of Independence and were active in state politics of the period. Learned men, seasoned in political struggles in the past, they represented the cream of the young nation. Some foreign political leaders of the day, not normally given over to praising the newest member of the family of nations, conceded that the group matched in talents any which the most advanced European nations could muster.

Although almost all the fifty-five delegates took an active role in the proceedings, in a gathering of this size certain individuals naturally stood out as the major leaders of the Convention. Without a doubt, by far the most influential delegate was James Madison. Like a schoolboy preparing for an important examination, Madison spent the months preceding the Convention poring over treaties on government, including accounts of the constitutions of the republics of Greece and Rome, sent to him from Paris by Thomas Jefferson. The labors of the Convention's "egghead" were not to be in vain—his grasp of historical materials, plus the practical experience he had enjoyed in state and national politics, enabled him to play a creative role in the deliberations. As the author of the Virginia Plan, the first major proposal to be presented to the Convention, Madison became the leader of the movement to draft a constitutional scheme that would break radically with the principles of the Articles of Confederation. At the same time, Madison was a man of large enough character to compromise his ideas in the interest of solidarity. Madison's contributions to the Constitution transcended the Convention itself; he was a key figure in both the pre- and post-Convention maneuverings, and his diary constitutes the major historical source of information on the four-month-long proceedings. By any standard, Madison well deserves the epithet, The Father of the Constitution.

Next in importance to the giant from Virginia were two delegates from Pennsylvania, James Wilson and Gouverneur Morris. Both in physical appearance and personal style they were poles apart: Wilson, a solid Scotsman, aged forty-four, a shrewd lawyer with a penetrating, logical turn of mind, earned the title of the "unsung hero of the convention"; Morris, eleven years younger, a tall glamorous figure (considered by the ladies of the day "as very handsome, very bold, and very impudent"), possessor of a biting wit, became the convention's marathon talker, speaking on more occasions than any other single delegate. Their views on human nature also diverged sharply: Wilson placed great faith in the common people, while Morris regarded them with an aristocrat's distrust and disdain. But despite such differences, they had more vital commonalities: both were friends of a strong national government headed by a potent Chief Executive, and both were major figures on key committees of the Convention—Wilson, the one on Detail, and Morris, those on Style and Postponed Matters. Their convergence of views and their positions of power at the Convention permitted Wilson and Morris to shape both the contents and the phraseology of the document that ultimately emerged.

Two other figures, George Washington and Benjamin Franklin, contributed in an entirely different way to the eventual success of the Constitution. Neither had the slightest effect on its substance. Not until the final day did Washington address the Convention, but he did not miss a single session in his capacity as presiding officer; Catherine Drinker Bowen suggestively writes that "the spirit of compromise sat on his shoulder like a dove." The assumption that Washington would be the nation's first Chief Executive gave the delegates the confidence to create an office with great legal and political potentialities; his mere presence at the Convention made Americans in general feel easier about the entire affair. The aged Franklin had long since passed the peak of a political creativity that had formulated the Albany Plan of Union more than thirty years before the Convention. Moreover, few of his junior colleagues were inclined to adopt his Convention proposals because they considered him to be something of a radical, too naive in his enthusiasm for the good sense of the common people. But his famed wit cooled tempers during the course of the heated debates, and he closed the proceedings on a benedictory note. Looking at the president's chair, Franklin observed that during many points in the long deliberations he had been unable to decide about the course of the sun painted there. "But now," he pronounced, "I have the happiness to know it is a rising and not a setting sun." In the ratification campaign that followed, no two Americans contributed more toward speeding the adoption of the Constitution than the young nation's greatest heroes, Washington and Franklin.

As with most human events, the Convention also had its failures. Most disappointing was Alexander Hamilton. Outnumbered in his own New York delegation by Yates and Lansing (sent to the Convention by Anti-Federalist Governor George Clinton to keep an eye on Hamilton), he was also out of political step with the bulk of the delegates. His support for a life-tenured Chief Executive and Senate smacked too much of the British model of King and House of Lords, with which the late colonists were all too familiar. Thus, ironically, the conservative ideas of the youthful Hamilton were as uncongenial to the Convention's thinking as the radical proposals of the aged Franklin. At one point Hamilton left the convention in frustration; for all he accomplished, he might just as well never have showed up at all. Ultimately he was to atone for his failure by joining with Madison, his partner in the pre-Convention maneuverings, in successfully campaigning for its subsequent adoption.

Accounts of the great debates of the Constitutional Convention frequently obscure the substantial agreement that existed among the delegates on a number of features of the new government. The authority of the national government to raise revenue by taxing imports and to regulate interstate and foreign commerce was accepted by the delegates, even the Anti-Federalists. The Convention proposal that most clearly reflected the attitudes of that group, the New Jersey Plan, vested such vital functions (along with those previously provided for in the Articles) in the national government. The same plan permitted Congress to act against states that failed to honor financial requisitions; it also granted the federal executive the authority to "call forth the powers of the confederated States" to enforce national laws and treaties against resistant states. Thus the very issues that had raised such difficulties between the nation and the states under the Articles of Confederation presented no serious conflicts at the Convention. Of course, the absence of the most independent and antiunion state of the thirteen, Rhode Island, undoubtedly contributed to this harmonious state of affairs.

Nor were there serious differences at the Convention over the general structure of the national government. Most delegates concurred with Jefferson's assessment of the Virginia experience with legislative supremacy that "173 despots could be as oppressive as one" and that "concentrating all powers in the same hands was precisely the definition of despotic government." They were also mindful of the fact that under the Articles of Confederation the Congress had been forced to develop crude substitutes for the missing executive and judicial arms of the national government. The delegates were thus agreed upon the necessity of creating a government with three separate branches.

The greatest single cause of disagreement among the delegates was the general issue of nation-state relations. The conflicting proposals for dealing with this basic issue, and the way in which they were ultimately compromised, will be discussed in detail in Chapter 3 on federalism.

Closely connected to the issue of nation-state relations was the question of how the states would be represented in Congress. The Virginia Plan provided for a two-branch legislature, the first branch to be elected by the people, the second to be chosen by the first from persons nominated by the state legislatures. The representation of a state in both branches was to be based on its financial contributions or population. Thus the Plan would have been advantageous to the large, wealthy states from which it drew its major supporters. In contrast, the New Jersey Plan would have retained the Confederation's one-house legislative body with its equality of state representation. It was backed by delegates that wanted essentially to retain the confederation system, as well as those who favored a strong national government but did not want to see it dominated by the large states. Ultimately the Convention adopted a bicameral legislature—one house representing population, the other the states on an equal basis—as the best solution to the representation dilemma. Labeled the "Connecticut Compromise" because the delegates from that medium-sized state worked so diligently for its acceptance, it became the most famous of the accommodations developed to bridge the differences among the various delegates.

The Convention eventually compromised a series of issues that divided its members. Equally crucial for the new government as representation was the composition and method of selection of the executive branch. As will be spelled out in detail in Chapter 11, the presidential office that ultimately emerged from the deliberations differed greatly from the one contemplated in early Convention proposals.

Divergent views of the North and South on slavery were also compromised in Convention decisions to permit the continuation of the trade until 1808 and to count slaves as three-fifths of a free person for purposes of determining both the representation of a state in the lower house of the Congress and its share of direct taxes that were based on population. In addition, the desire of Southerners for free trade (as producers of raw materials like cotton they wanted to ship goods to Britain in return for her finished products) led them to support a two-thirds vote for navigation acts as a means of protecting themselves against tariffs favored by Northern manufacturers. While the Convention was unwilling to go this far in deferring to Southern interests, it did agree to a prohibition against export taxes.

This give-and-take process of the Convention has led one close student of the subject, Max Farrand, to label the Constitution a "bundle of compromises." A number of factors contributed to the willingness of the delegates to search for, and achieve, accommodations of their differences. Many genuinely believed that the new nation was on the brink of a dissolution that would divide the country into three separate parts, northern, middle, and southern; to fail in their purpose was thus to return the United States to chaos and eventual extinction. Moreover, since most of the delegates were Federalists, they agreed on the necessity of making radical changes in nation-state relations and on the essential structure of the national government. Their consensus on fundamental principles thus permitted the delegates to reach compromises on the particular application of those principles. Compromise was also fostered by the delegates' early decision to keep the proceedings secret: operating free of public scrutiny and pressures permitted them to change their minds and modify their stands in the process of groping for proximate answers to the nation's difficult problems.

But these very conditions that promoted agreement at the Convention itself were precisely the same ones that threatened to make the subsequent ratification process so difficult. Far from seeing the nation as about to disintegrate, the Anti-Federalists viewed difficulties under the Articles of Confederation as both manageable and temporary in nature. While the Anti-Federalists were generally absent from the constitutional deliberations, they were well-represented in the general population and the state legislatures. And the very secrecy that promoted cooperation among the delegates themselves created resentment and suspicion among those denied access to, and information about, the proceedings. Thus the delegates who worked so hard to create a new constitutional framework faced major obstacles in their final task—getting the rest of the nation to accept the product of their labors.

THE RATIFICATION CAMPAIGN

Before the delegates even left the Convention, they made decisions designed to facilitate the adoption of the proposed Constitution. They chose to ignore the unanimous-consent requirement for amending the Articles; instead, they provided that ratification by nine states would be sufficient for the Constitution's adoption. In this way they avoided the possibility that a state like Rhode Island—which had refused even to send delegates to the Convention—could block their efforts. The fear that state legislatures would refuse to accept a Constitution that reduced their powers also prompted the delegates to substitute elected state conventions as the ratifying bodies. Such a procedure provided the Federalists with at least an opportunity for victory, since they could influence the selection of the delegates as well as the course of the state convention deliberations. Cloaking their real purposes in the rhetoric of democracy, the framers claimed that such a ratification process would more directly involve the people than would the use of state legislatures. Surprisingly, the old Continental Congress, which had much to lose under the new constitutional system, forwarded the Convention's instructions to the states for action.

Having manipulated the rules of the ratification game to favor the Constitution's adoption, the Federalists set out to transform their opportunities into realities. They worked to get themselves and their sympathizers elected as state-convention delegates (twenty-five of the thirty-nine delegates who signed the document were so chosen), developed strategies for convention proceedings, and set out to sell the general public on the virtues of the new Constitution. In doing so, the Federalists were able to trade upon a number of political advantages they held over their opponents: prestigious leaders like Washington and Franklin, whose endorsement alone was worth thousands of votes; continental figures whose contacts across states and regions provided a communications link for the various state and local campaigns; and the bulk of the nation's phrase-makers—newspaper editors, lawyers, teachers, ministers—who could spread the Federalist propaganda by word of mouth and printed page. In addition, they had one vital asset that their

opponents lacked completely: a positive program to sell. Placed in the difficult position of favoring some changes in the Articles of Confederation, but
having no concrete plan to substitute for it, the Anti-Federalists were forced
to adopt a negative, defensive stance in the ratification battle. Meanwhile,
the Federalists argued that rejecting the Constitution would mean a return
to the chaotic situation under the Articles.

Having written the ratification rules and rallied their resources, the Federalists turned to the practical problem of winning support for the Constitution in the nine states necessary for ratification. Some, like Delaware and
New Jersey, burdened with heavy tax and debt loads or plagued by interstate duties, could be counted on for ready support, as could vulnerable
Georgia, described by Washington as having "Indians on its back and Span-
iards on its flank." Others, notably Rhode Island, offered little hope for the
Federalists. Four states were particularly important because of their size
and political strength: Massachusetts, New York, Pennsylvania, and Virginia. Should any of these major states fail to ratify, even a legally constituted union of nine or more states would be a shaky one.

The activities of the Federalists in these four crucial states reveal the
variety of tactics they used in order to win state-convention support for the
Constitution. Threatened with loss of control of the Pennsylvania legislature in upcoming elections, they pressed for immediate action calling for
delegate elections. When Anti-Federalists tried to thwart this move by ab-
senting themselves so as to deny a legislative quorum, they were uncere-
moniously dragged back to the chamber, thrust into their seats, and declared present for the crucial vote. The Federalists won two-thirds of the
convention seats, and although they failed to convert a single Anti-Federalist
in the deliberations that followed, their margin held intact in the final convention vote. This early victory (only Delaware acted sooner than Pennsylvania) in the nation's second most populous state, helped to start the
campaign bandwagon rolling.

Five states had ratified the Constitution by the time the Massachusetts
convention was held. When an early straw vote of the delegates indicated
that the Federalists were in the minority, they set out to win over two of
the state's favorite sons to their cause—Samuel Adams and John Hancock.
Ultimately it was necessary to make a political deal with Hancock; in return
for his endorsement of the Constitution, the Federalists promised to support
him for the Vice Presidency under Washington or, in the event that Virginia failed to ratify, for the Presidency itself. The Bay State Federalists
also made an important concession on the content of the Constitution: a
promise to have the first Congress initiate amendments to add a Bill of
Rights to the document. Massachusetts' ratification of the Constitution with
a specific recommendation to this effect established a precedent that other
states would follow.

The ratification battle in Virginia was crucial, even though the necessary
nine states had approved the Constitution by the time the Dominion State

convention met. For the first time, the Anti-Federalists had outstanding delegates capable of matching wits with the opposition: Madison, with the able assistance of young John Marshall (later to become Chief Justice of the Supreme Court), defended the Constitution against the criticisms of Patrick Henry, George Mason, and President-to-be James Monroe. The most influential Virginian of them all, George Washington, was not at the convention, but his known support of the Constitution (he even converted to the Federalist cause Governor Randolph, who had refused to sign the document at the national convention) swayed enough of the uncommitted delegates so that the result was a vote of eighty-nine to seventy-nine.

Like Virginia, New York had its share of able Anti-Federalist leaders, including Constitutional Convention delegates Lansing and Yates, and Governor George Clinton. But the recent Virginia decision; the series of newspaper articles authored by Hamilton, Madison, and John Jay under the title of *The Federalist Papers*, explaining and defending the Constitution; Hamilton's threat that New York City would secede from the state to join the Union if the state failed to ratify; and, perhaps most important of all, the prestige of Washington and Franklin, brought the Federalists a narrow convention victory (thirty to twenty-seven) and New York into the fold as the eleventh state to ratify. North Carolina and eventually even reluctant Rhode Island (which also feared the secession of its major city, Providence) were later to make ratification unanimous. The pangs of the formation and adoption struggle were over; a new nation was born.

The above analysis of the political and economic conditions of the pre-Constitution period, the groups favoring and opposing the Constitution, and the process by which it was formulated and adopted provides some important clues to the intentions and motives of the men who established our constitutional framework. Before we can fully assess them or the Constitution itself, however, we must examine the political beliefs of the Founding Fathers and the techniques and institutions they chose to implement those beliefs.

THE POLITICAL PHILOSOPHY
OF THE FOUNDING FATHERS

The fifty-five individuals at the Convention spanned the political spectrum from elitists to worshippers of the common man. Yet the greater part of the group was committed to the same general scheme of values and made similar assumptions about the nature of man. The delegate who most clearly articulated the common views was James Madison. In the eighty-five *Federalist Papers* in general and Number 10 in particular, he set forth in plain and succinct terms the fundamental theory of the Constitution. Even though *The Federalist* was written as a political document for the ratification campaign in New York State, it remains to this day the best single source for the Founders' philosophy.

In reading *The Federalist*, it becomes obvious that the democratic value that Madison cherished the most was liberty, an individual's being able to choose reasonable goals for himself and the means to reach those goals. He assumed that one such goal would be the acquisition of private property. Because of what he termed "the diversity in the faculties of men," that is, differences in their individual abilities, Madison reasoned, however, that some persons would succeed in acquiring more worldly goods than would others. This being the case, government must protect property interests because they reflect innate differences in individual capacities. Madison thus embraced the view of English political philosopher John Locke that, because individual intelligence and effort are involved in gaining property, it represents an extension of the human personality.

For Madison, property was not only a value to be protected but also a factor to be appreciated if one was to understand the basis for natural divisions among mankind. In *Federalist Paper* 10 he suggested that society is divided into various *factions*, which he defined as "a number of citizens, whether amounting to a majority or a minority of the whole, who are united and actuated by some common impulse of passion, or of interest, adverse to the rights of other citizens, or to the permanent and aggregate interests of the community." While conceding that the causes of factions are numerous, including differences of opinion over religion and government, Madison stated that "the most common and durable source of factions is the unequal distribution of property. Those who hold and those who are without property have ever formed distinct interests in society. Those who are creditors and those who are debtors, fall under a like discrimination."

Thus Madison's idea that property ownership was the major source of di-

James Madison (far left), John Jay (center), and Alexander Hamilton, authors of *The Federalist Papers*. (Culver Pictures)

visions in society paralleled Karl Marx's analysis more than half a century later. Unlike Marx, however, Madison had no desire to remove divisions by converting private property to common ownership among individuals because such differences reflect the "the diversity in the faculties of men." Moreover, the government was not to wither away as it does in Marxist theory; instead, for Madison, it was the major institution to referee the natural conflicts that develop among various factions in society. In fact, the government provides the legal framework within which factions may compete politically in such a way that no major interest can extinguish another.

Since removing the *causes* of factions would be both unwise (factions are desirable) and impossible (they are also rooted in human nature), Madison set out to construct a system of government that would control the harmful *effects* of factions. As he viewed the matter, minority factions presented no difficulty since the majority of society could always protect itself through voting down their "sinister views." The real problem arises when one faction constitutes a majority of the population. As Madison himself put the issue: "To secure the public good and private rights against the danger of such a faction, and at the same time to preserve the spirit and form of popular government, is then the great object to which our inquiries are directed."

CONSTITUTIONAL PRINCIPLES
OF THE FOUNDING FATHERS

Given the human impulse to pursue selfish interests, Madison saw little hope in either morals or religion as effective checks on the appetites of men. Since "men are not angels," society itself must create a series of obstacles to blunt and divert the opinions and wishes of the majority that threaten private rights and the public good. This aim can best be accomplished through a republican form of government, in which the people elect representatives to make binding decisions, as contrasted to a pure democracy, in which they make such decisions themselves. This is so for two reasons. First, a representative government provides for a "refinement and enlargement of public views" by passing them through a chosen body of citizens whose knowledge of the public good is superior to that of the general populace. Second, because representative government permits effective rule to be exercised over a larger and more populous territory than town-meeting government, it brings under its control a greater variety of people and interests than pure democracy does. This system thus makes it difficult to construct a majority from a large number of groups: because of communication problems, such interests are often unaware of their common motives, and even if they are aware, they find it difficult to work together politically to exercise their will over minorities or the general public.

But Madison was not willing to trust to general principles of republicanism alone to contain the majority. He wanted to build additional controls within the governmental framework itself to protect minority rights. Reflecting his view of human nature, he suggested that "ambition must be made to counteract ambition." In other words, selfish persons occupying different political positions must be deliberately pitted against one another in the struggle for power. In the course of frustrating one another's ambitions, they indirectly protect the liberties of minorities and the general public.

SEPARATION OF POWERS

A major feature of Madison's scheme to make "ambition counteract ambition" was the doctrine of the separation of powers, which he borrowed from a Frenchman, Montesquieu. That political thinker concluded from his studies that the liberties the English people enjoyed were attributable to the fact that political power under their constitutional system was not centralized in the hands of one person or clique but was rather distributed among the legislative, executive, and, to a lesser degree, the judicial branches of the national government. Thus Montesquieu associated tyranny with the concentration of political power and liberty with its dispersal.

The separation of powers might more accurately be termed a separation of processes. That is, each of the three branches or arms of the government carries on a separate portion of the total political process: the legislature has the primary responsibility for making the laws; the executive for putting them into effect; and the judiciary for interpreting them. This distinction is similar to Aristotle's idea of the deliberative, administrative, and adjudicative processes used in making political decisions.

The doctrine, however, does not call for a *total* separation of process. Although each of the three branches has the *major* responsibility for one of these processes—that is, making, executing, or interpreting laws—each participates to some degree in the principal activities of the others. For example, under our system of government, the Congress has the primary responsibility for enacting legislation, but the President is authorized both to recommend measures to the Congress and to veto laws actually passed by that body. Similarly, the Senate can affect the President's execution of the laws by failing to approve his nominees for major positions in the executive branch. Likewise, Congress can affect the courts' interpretations of the laws by determining the kinds of cases they can hear.

By participating in one another's processes, the three branches are in a position to *check and balance* one another's influence and political power. A branch can assert and protect its own rights by withholding its support for the essential activities of a coordinate arm of the government. Thus the President may threaten to veto a piece of legislation as a means of preventing Congress from interfering with the operations of the executive branch. But since the three branches are dependent on one another, the system of shared processes ultimately forces them to cooperate in their mutual activities.

The two principles—separation of process, and checks and balances—complement each other to achieve the desired effect in the political system. The former principle provides that no branch can usurp an activity that is the *primary* responsibility of another; the latter allows the three arms of the government to counteract one another's influence. The end result is a decentralization of political power. Figure 2–1 illustrates the relationships among the governmental branches that the Founding Fathers favored.

But more than a partial separation of process is necessary to make Mon-

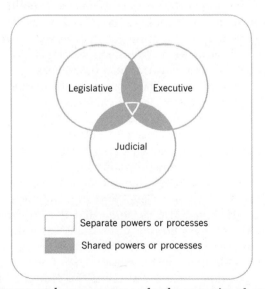

FIGURE 2–1   Governmental arrangements under the separation-of-powers doctrine.

tesquieu's principle operate effectively. He also called for a *complete* separation of governmental *personnel*. In other words, the same persons who occupy the legislative seats of government cannot also serve in the executive or judicial branches. (Our system does not permit congressmen to hold executive or judicial positions, and executives and judges are also similarly restricted.) To allow such a practice would concentrate all political powers in the same hands, the very definition of tyranny.

Another aspect of the doctrine reflected in the American system is the separation of *constituency*. That is, essentially different groups of people choose the personnel of the three branches. As originally conceived, the President, for instance, is selected by an independent group of electors, none of whom can be congressmen; senators are chosen by state electors; and congressmen are elected by smaller local publics. Although members of the national courts are nominated by the President and confirmed by the Senate, no one branch chooses them; moreover, once appointed and confirmed, they enjoy life tenure. Thus the personnel of the three branches have largely separate and independent bases of political support and power.

MIXED GOVERNMENT

There is good reason to believe that the Founding Fathers provided separate constituencies not only because they wished the branches of the national government to be independent of one another but also because they wanted them to represent different kinds of social and economic interests. Ideas expressed in *The Federalist Papers*, plus the similarities between the structure of the national government and that of Massachusetts, which John Adams helped to develop, indicate that Adams as a political thinker influenced the Constitution, even though he was in London at the time of the Convention. In particular, his commitment to a "mixed" government—that is, one representing both property and numbers of people—is reflected in some of the major provisions of our constitutional framework.

Although the Constitution nowhere provides for property qualifications for either officeholders or voters, it is significant that originally the House of Representatives was the only political body directly elected by the people. (The direct election of senators was not authorized until the ratification of the Seventeenth Amendment in 1913.) The other major offices were somewhat insulated from the general populace. As Figure 2–2 indicates, according to the original document, members of the Senate were two, the President three, and the Supreme Court four steps removed from direct control of the people. (It should also be noted that the Founding Fathers gave the House of Representatives no role in choosing members of the Supreme Court.) In addition, the longer *terms* of senators (six years), the President (four years), and Supreme Court members (life) would make them less subject to public pressures than members of the House of Representatives.

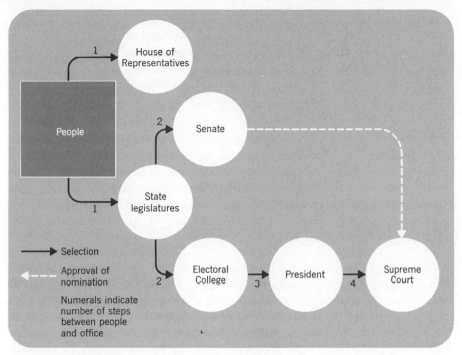

FIGURE 2–2 Relationship between the people and the selection of various office-holders of the nation under the original Constitution.

And because fewer persons were to be chosen for the other three political bodies, their positions would be more prestigious than seats in the lower house of the national legislature. This, in turn, would have the effect of attracting more able persons to them, and since property ownership was considered reflective of natural ability (Adams and Madison agreed on this point), such men would be those of economic substance from the upper social classes.

In all probability, the Founding Fathers expected the House of Representatives to represent the interests of the many in society, the common people who owned no private property of any consequence. It would be the democratic, popular branch of the government. On the other hand, the Senate, with a smaller, more prestigious membership, insulated somewhat from popular control both by its indirect method of selection and longer term of office, would represent the few in society with substantial possessions. It would constitute the oligarchic division of the legislative body.

It is somewhat more difficult to discern the exact intentions of the Founding Fathers regarding the kinds of interests the President and the Supreme Court were to represent in the governmental system. One interpretation calls for their standing above the many-few conflict as guardians of the general interest, promoting unity and justice in society. Another suggests that they were expected to join forces with the Senate to protect the interests of the propertied few against the excesses of the popular legislature. Given Madison's concern with safeguarding both the general interest and minority rights against the evils of a majority faction, it is probable that the President and Supreme Court were expected to serve both purposes.

THE DIVISION OF POWERS

Madison conceived of one final check on the majority, which we will examine in detail in the next chapter, the division of power between the national government and the states. His major concern is reflected in *Federalist Paper* 10: "The influence of factious leaders may kindle a flame within the particular states, but they will be unable to spread a conflagration through the other states."

Thus Madison's system for checking the evils of faction was to create a series of dikes to interfere with the free flow of majority will. First, majority interests are *filtered* by the actions of their elected representatives who have more refined views on the public good than the voters themselves. Second, the wishes of the majority are *diluted* because republicanism allows the expansion of the sphere of government to take in a wide variety of interests. Moreover, the geographical distribution of powers under federalism *contains*, or *segregates*, the evil effects of a faction. Finally, the majority will is *diverted* into many channels by the joint effects of the division and separation of powers. As Madison himself put it in *Federalist Paper* 51:

> In the compound republic of America, the power surrendered by the people is first divided between two distinct governments, and then the portion allotted to each subdivided among distinct and separate departments. Hence a double security arises to the rights of the people. The different governments will control each other, at the same time each will be controlled by itself.

This then was the type of political system the Founding Fathers had in mind for the new nation. As the following section shows, however, vast changes have since occurred in our constitutional framework.

CHANGING THE AMERICAN CONSTITUTION

A constitution necessarily reflects the interests and values of those groups responsible for its original formulation. In time, however, new groups arise that are dissatisfied with the *status quo*, the existing distribution of values, and quite often they seek to rewrite the rules of the democratic game to change that distribution. The press of events and the emergence of different attitudes on the part of leaders and the populace in general also require alterations in a nation's fundamental framework. Every democratic system of government must provide methods for bringing about such modifications peacefully or risk the danger that frustrated individuals and groups will turn to violence to accomplish their ends. Thus the question is not whether a democratic constitution will be changed, but rather what particular form such change will take.

FORMAL AMENDMENTS

One important method of changing the American Constitution has been the formal amendment process. Amendments can be enacted either by a two-thirds vote in both houses of Congress or by a national convention called for by legislatures in two-thirds of the states. (This latter method has never actually been used.) Amendments so initiated must then be ratified either by three-fourths of the state legislatures or by conventions in three-fourths of the states. (Only the Twenty-first Amendment has been adopted by this latter procedure.) By 1972 Americans had added twenty-six changes to the original document by means of the formal amendment process.

In analyzing the formal amendments, it is helpful to understand the particular types of alterations they made in constitutional principles—that is, whether they affected the functions, procedures, or structure of the government—and which level or levels, national or state, were involved. Even more important is an appreciation of the particular groups involved in the amendment process and of the kinds of values they sought to implement through a change in the rules of the game.

The Anti-Federalists, who were primarily responsible for adding the first ten amendments to the Constitution, were concerned with civil liberties, protecting individuals against arbitrary governmental action affecting rights of speech, press, and religion, or the taking of their lives, freedom, or property in criminal proceedings. The first nine amendments place limits on the procedures that the national government may use in such matters. The Tenth Amendment reflects the Anti-Federalists' preoccupation with preserving the powers of the states against encroachment by the national government. The amendments thus reflect political beliefs that are much different from those of the Founding Fathers, who were most concerned with guarding property rights against the actions of state governments.

Many of the remaining amendments reflect still another major value of a democratic society: equality. The Thirteenth, Fourteenth, and Fifteenth relate to race, while the Nineteenth, Twenty-third, Twenty-fourth, and Twenty-sixth govern the voting rights of, respectively, women, residents of the District of Columbia, persons who live in jurisdictions that levy a poll tax as a condition for voting, and young people between eighteen and twenty-one. They are thus designed to allow formerly disadvantaged groups to participate in the political process and, through the Thirteenth and Four-

Some amendments to the Constitution were the result of a long, arduous struggle. The women' suffrage movement began in 1848; in the early 1900s these suffragettes were still soliciting support; their efforts were not successful until the passage of the Nineteenth Amendment in 1920. (Brown Brothers)

teenth Amendments, the social and economic life of American society. It should be noted that this group of amendments affects primarily the states, not the national government.

Two other amendments, the Seventeenth and the Twenty-second, also relate to political participation. However, they affect the suffrage rights of all qualified voters, not particular groups. The former amendment, dealing with the direct election of senators, extends the rights of voters to choose members of the upper house of the national legislature; the latter, which affects the length of term of President, limits their right to choose a man they desire for the Presidency more than twice. The two amendments are based on somewhat different assumptions about human capacities: the Seventeenth expresses faith in the electorate's ability to choose good senators; the Twenty-second evidences a fear that the voters may fall victim to the entreaties of a demagog.

Four of the amendments—the Eleventh, Twelfth, Twentieth, and Twenty-fifth—bear no particular imprint of group influence or political philosophy. They rather relate to changes brought about by the press of particular historical events and affect primarily the structure and procedures of all three branches of the national government.

The one other amendment, the Sixteenth (the Eighteenth and Twenty-first dealing with alcoholic beverages cancel each other out), establishes the procedures the national government may follow in levying an income tax; it provides that the government may do so without allocating the tax on the basis of population of the individual states. Although the amendment does not directly favor or disadvantage any group, the revenue measures developed by the Congress have some potential leveling effects economically since the wealthy are taxed at a higher rate than the poor.

OTHER METHODS
OF CONSTITUTIONAL CHANGE

Although important changes have been made in the American Constitution by means of formal amendments, only twenty-six have made it past the extramajority* hurdles created by the amendment process, and ten of these came at once. Thus in a period of some 180 years (ignoring the Eighteenth and Twenty-first which counterbalance each other), formal alterations in the Constitution have been made on only sixteen occasions.

But the formal amendment process does not begin to tell the full story of the vast changes that have occurred in the functions, procedures, and structure of the American political system over that period. As we shall see in Chapter 14, the Supreme Court has been responsible for significant innovations through its power to interpret the Constitution. Within the last twenty years, shifts in its definition of the "equal protection of the laws" clause of the Fourteenth Amendment have revolutionized race relations in this nation and altered the composition of both the House of Representatives and state legislatures. Thus changes in the direction of more social and political equality in American life have come through judicial interpretation as well as formal amendment.

ASSESSMENT

As we piece together the various bits of evidence on the intentions of the Founding Fathers—the economic and social conditions of the day, the ma-

*A majority is one over half. An extramajority is greater than that proportion, typically two-thirds or three-fourths.

jor provisions of the new Constitution, and the philosophy articulated in *The Federalist Papers*—it becomes clear that two concerns were paramount in their thinking. One was national unity, the necessity of drawing together through an effective political union the states that threatened to go their separate ways in the period immediately preceding the Constitutional Convention. In this respect the United States was faced with the same major problem that preoccupies the leaders of the emerging nations in the world today, namely, providing some sense of national identity for a people divided along lines of economic interests or regional loyalties. Such divisions, or "factions" as Madison called them, threatened the very existence of the American political system.

The other major concern of the Founding Fathers was the protection of private property against the incursion of majority rule. For property ownership was linked with their most cherished value, that of liberty, the right of each person to develop himself to the fullest extent of his capacities. It is significant that while the preamble of the Constitution refers to the "blessings of liberty," it nowhere mentions "equality." In fact, *The Federalist Papers* specifically refer to "the equal division of property" as a "malady" and express concern over the "leveling spirit" of men.

Debates over which of these concerns, national unity or property rights, was most important to the Founding Fathers are meaningless, since the two issues were inexorably linked in their thinking. They felt a young nation could not survive in a situation of interstate commercial rivalries, uncertainties involving the collection of debts, and a worthless currency. Similarly, attempts to determine whether their prime motivation in writing the Constitution was to protect their own personal property interests or to promote the public good miss the point that, for the Founding Fathers, there was no real difference between the two inducements. They believed that the ownership of property gave men a "stake" in society and hence made them better citizens; moreover, like most individuals, they tended to identify their own interests with that of society as a whole.

The constitutional movement did represent a reaction against some of the democratic values and assumptions of the Revolutionary period. Ironically, the same political philosopher, John Locke, provided some of the major ideas for both. But whereas the earlier era espoused Locke's concepts of majority rule and legislative supremacy, the Founding Fathers rather stressed his concern with property rights and his recognition of executive prerogatives. Thus different aspects of Locke's philosophy were borrowed for dealing with differing conditions in the two periods of national development.

The events of the pre-Constitution period tempered the essential optimism concerning human nature that characterized the earlier era. Even such a great admirer of the common man and the legislature as Thomas Jefferson referred to the 173 despots in the Virginia legislature. It was thus experience, rather than a radical shift in leadership, that brought about a change in the dominant thinking of the two eras. For essentially the same men were involved in both: Jefferson and Adams, the major architects of the Declaration of Independence, both heartily approved of the new Constitution, while James Wilson, a major figure at the Convention, signed the Declaration. Moreover, some of the Founding Fathers had endorsed the Articles of Confederation or served in its national legislature. Although some new leaders did emerge in the constitutional period, no genuine "counterrevolution" occurred whereby one group of Americans completely replaced another. Rather, some of the key men changed their minds about the kinds of political institutions that were needed to channel human weaknesses (as well as virtues) to achieve the public good.

In place of legislatively dominated governments of the Articles of Confederation period tied closely to the public by short terms, forced rotation in office, and recall, the Founding Fathers sought to substitute the concept of a political system with three rival branches, differentially removed from direct public control. They favored a "mixed" government that would reflect the interests of both the few with property and the many without. Although they did not embrace the principles of semidirect democracy, they turned their backs on either monarchy or oligarchical control of society by members of the upper class. They created the most democratic system of the day, as evidenced by the refusal of Catherine the Great of Russia to recognize the new government because of its radical nature.

An analysis of the American constitutional system thus indicates that the original rules of the game were written primarily by groups interested in protecting property rights and avoiding what they considered to be the harmful effects of direct democracy. Their most cherished value was that of liberty. The major changes that have been made in the original constitutional system over the years have come from groups particularly solicitous of civil liberties as against property rights, and from those persons who desire to open up the democratic process to additional groups in society. In place of the liberty that was so valued by our nation's founders, equality has become the dominant concern in our recent constitutional development.

Selected Readings

The classic study of the Constitutional Convention is Max Farrand, *The Framing of the Constitution of the United States* (New Haven: Yale University Press, 1913). A recent interesting account of the event written in a journalistic style is Catherine Drinker Bowen, *Miracle at Philadelphia* (Boston: Little, Brown, 1966). Another excellent analysis, Clinton Rossiter, *1787: The Grand Convention* (New York: Macmillan, 1966), also contains valuable background information on the events leading up to the calling of the Convention that is not present in the above selections.

In addition to Rossiter, other good sources on the economic, social, and political conditions that surrounded the calling of the Convention are David Smith, *The Convention and the Constitution* (New York: St. Martin's Press, 1965), and Alpheus T. Mason's edited work with commentaries, *The States' Rights Debate* (Englewood Cliffs, N.J.: Prentice-Hall, 1964). The latter work, along with Jackson Turner Main, *The Antifederalists: Critics of the Constitution, 1781–1788* (Chicago: Quadrangle Books, 1961), contains valuable information on the opponents of the Constitution. Bowen, Rossiter, Mason, and Main also touch on the campaign for the ratification of the Constitution.

The most controversial interpretation of the motives of the Founding Fathers is Charles Beard's classic study, *An Economic Interpretation of the Constitution of the United States* (originally published in 1913; reissued, New York: Free Press, 1965), which suggests that they wrote the Constitution primarily to protect their own property interests. Two recent criticisms of Beard's work are Robert Brown, *Charles Beard and the Constitution* (Princeton: Princeton University Press, 1956), and Forest McDonald, *We the People* (Chicago: University of Chicago Press, 1958). Main, in his work cited above, basically defends the Beard thesis.

There are a number of good sources on the political philosophy of the Founding Fathers. Included are Hamilton, Jay, and Madison, *The Federalist*, Smith's book cited above, and Paul Eidelberg, *The Philosophy of the Constitution* (New York: Free Press, 1968). Another work that touches on the subject as part of a larger historical study of values in American society is Seymour Lipset, *The First New Nation* (New York: Basic Books, 1963).

CHAPTER 3

Federalism

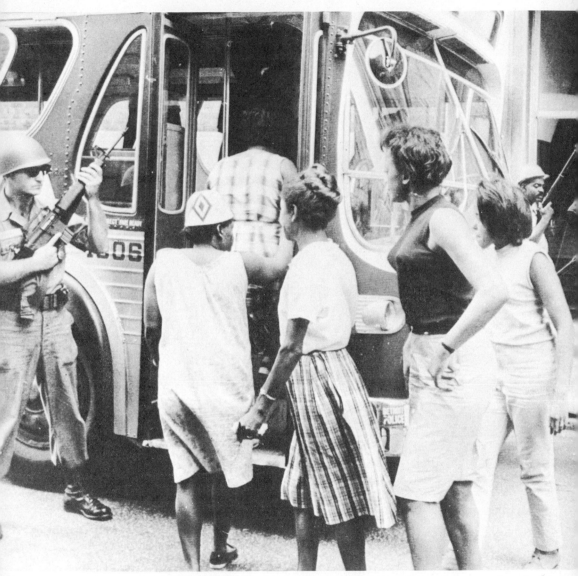

In the aftermath of the Detroit riots, a National Guardsman oversees the transfer of women arrested during the rioting. (United Press International)

IN THE EARLY MORNING HOURS of Sunday, July 23, 1967, the Detroit police raided a "blind pig" (after-hours drinking club) on Detroit's West Side, arresting seventy-three Negro customers and the bartender. Angered by rumors of police brutality, a crowd stoned officers and nearby stores; in the looting, fire-setting, and plundering that followed, property damage and personal injuries mounted. Just one week after order had finally been restored in Newark, New Jersey, Detroit was experiencing the worst riot in the nation's already turbulent summer.

Early the following morning, faced with the inability of local and state police to cope with the situation, Governor George Romney of Michigan turned to the national government for assistance. Attorney General Ramsey Clark advised Romney that before United States troops could be sent legally into Detroit, he, as governor, would have to request them. Romney agreed to do so. However, over twenty hours passed between the time of their early-morning telephone conversation and President Johnson's order dispatching national troops into the riot area shortly before midnight of July 24.

Both sides blamed the other for the delay. Romney charged that by refusing to send troops immediately, President Johnson had "played politics, during a period of tragedy and riot." Clark replied that although he originally talked to the governor at about 2:30 A.M., Romney had not formally "requested" the troops as required by applicable statutes until about 11:00 A.M. (instead he had merely recommended they be sent). Romney also expressed resentment over the President's statement in an address to the nation that he was acting because of the inability of local authorities to restore order; national officials countered that such language was necessary to legally justify the commitment of federal troops. State and national officials also disagreed on whether Romney had vacillated about the need for outside forces to deal with the situation.

To many Americans, and particularly Detroiters, it seemed incredible that in a time of crisis officials should haggle over which forces should be used to quell the riot and the precise language that the governor should use to call for assistance. Why be so solicitous of the rights of local authorities? Why not simply send in national law-enforcement officials at the first sign of trouble as would happen in most other countries of the world?

To make some sense out of the Detroit situation, we need to determine why political officials in the United States are so committed to the delicate and difficult task of dividing political power among the various levels of our government system. To understand the sources of this attitude, we must examine the origins of the American concept of division of power, the particular circumstances that resulted in an act of genuine political creativity: the establishment of the world's first federal system of government.

EARLY EFFORTS TO DIVIDE POLITICAL POWER

Working out proper relationships between central and local authorities has been a persistent problem in American statecraft. In fact, the issue predates the establishment of the nation. When the delegates assembled in Philadelphia in 1787, it was not the first, but actually the third, time Americans had endeavored to solve the thorny problem of dividing political functions and authority between different governments.

THE BRITISH EMPIRE

The first American experience with the issue occurred while the colonies were still a part of the British Empire. Although the authorities in London never conceded that the colonies enjoyed any rights or powers except those that were granted to them by the mother country, over the years a division of authority had been worked out that gave the British control over foreign affairs, war and peace, and overseas trade, and left to the colonists the exclusive right to tax themselves, to raise troops, and to run their own schools, churches, and land systems. This accommodation ended, however, with the termination of the French and Indian War in 1763. Abandoning the colonial policy that British statesman Edmund Burke referred to as one of "salutary neglect," the government of George III embarked on a new program designed to exercise far more extensive control over American affairs. Dissatisfied with the inability of some of the colonies to provide adequate military forces during the encounter with the French, the British decided to use their own troops to provide order in the colonies and to make the residents bear their share of the financial burden of these military forces, along with the debt the London government had incurred in the course of fighting the war. Further, the colonists would be required to provide funds from which royal governors and judges would be paid. (Earlier colonial legislatures had developed a practice of withholding monies for the salaries of the King's representatives as a means of forcing concessions from them.)

The new British policy shattered the traditional division of authority between the mother country and the colonies. Having grown accustomed to their own military forces, Americans resented the presence of British soldiers in their midst. Equally if not more galling were the series of revenue measures the British enacted to enable the colonies to assume their new financial responsibilities. Such activities invaded another touchy area formerly reserved for local authorities; moreover, the particular objects of the new taxes—wine, molasses, and tea, as well as newspapers, deeds, liquor permits, diplomas, and other legal papers which, under the terms of the infamous Stamp Act, required revenue stamps—struck at what colonists regarded as the necessities of life. Rallying around the basic constitutional principle of "no taxation without representation," Americans began to resist these British encroachments into their military and financial affairs in a series of actions that were to culminate in the Revolutionary War. Thus the British failed to solve the delicate problem of balancing central control and local self-government within their Empire; it remained for Americans to tackle the issue themselves.

THE ARTICLES OF CONFEDERATION

As discussed in Chapter 2, the high hopes of Americans for establishing a viable government of their own foundered within a few years after the close of the Revolutionary War in 1781. As with the British experience, the major flaw in the governmental system created by the Articles of Confederation was its failure to provide a satisfactory division of political functions and power between different governments. Reacting to the centralized control of London over trade, taxes, and troops, the authors of the Articles denied the new national government effective control over these vital matters; it was granted no power to regulate foreign and interstate commerce, and it was forced to depend on the states for the financial requisitions and troops so vital to the central government's existence. Thus as overcentralization proved to be the undoing of the British Empire in the colonies, so excessive decentralization led to the failure of the first American effort to deal with national-state relationships. The calling of the Constitutional Convention, however, provided the young nation's political leaders with one more opportunity to devise a workable method of balancing the interests of both the central government and the parts.

THE CONSTITUTION

Although the Empire and Articles experiences ended in failure, they provided the Convention delegates with some object lessons. Alexander Hamilton stood virtually alone at the Convention in favoring the adoption of the British system of extreme centralization. His proposals to grant central authorities the power to pass "all laws whatsoever" and to allow them to appoint state executives who, in turn, could veto state laws died a quick death on the floor, despite Hamilton's eloquent pleas and arguments on their behalf. Also missing from the Convention was any appreciable sentiment for preserving absolutely intact the extreme decentralization under the Articles; persons with this general attitude (including some who were actually elected as delegates) were generally not present at the proceedings.

Although the delegates avoided the extremes that led to past failures to deal with central-local relations, they nonetheless differed on several basic issues relating to the division of political power in the new nation. Their views diverged sharply on the scope of the functions to be entrusted to the national government. They also disagreed on the kinds of controls that the two levels of government should be able to exercise over each other's activities. And perhaps most fundamentally, they differed on the very basis of authority over the central government: should it represent the people of the whole nation or should the states remain as sovereign units possessing ultimate legal authority?

Two plans introduced at the Convention reflected disparate attitudes on such issues. The first, the Virginia Plan, so named because it was introduced by Governor Randolph of that state (Madison was its actual author), represented the "Nationalist" approach. Although it did not go as far as Hamilton's proposal to give the central government the right to pass "all laws," the plan did authorize it to legislate when the states were "incompetent" to do so or when their individual legislation would interfere with the "harmony of the United States." Further, the national legislature would be given the power to negate any state law it deemed contrary to the national Constitution. According to this plan the new government rested on popular sovereignty: representation in both legislative branches would be based on population or financial quotas rather than state equality, and the plan was to be ratified by the people in state conventions.

The opposing views of delegates committed to protecting state sovereignty were reflected in the New Jersey Plan, advocated by William Paterson of that state. Known originally as the "Federalist" proposal (as we shall see subsequently, a more appropriate name would have been "Confederationalist"), it proposed that limited changes be made in the Articles of Confederation. Although the plan did grant the national government authority over commerce and taxes, along with the power to act against states that failed to meet their requisitions or to obey national laws, no national powers could be exercised without the consent of an indefinite number of states. Moreover, the plan retained equal representation of states in the national legislature and required that amendments to the Articles obtain the approval of all the state legislatures.

Neither the Nationalists nor the Federalists had sufficient support to prevail at the Convention, and it remained for a third group, the Unionists, to play the key role in breaking the deadlock. Committed above all to preserving the union of states, they labored to compromise the differences between the two plans. Attacking the most basic issue that separated the contending factions, namely, the method of representation in the national legislature, the Connecticut Compromise offered a half loaf to each: the House of Representatives would be based on population, while states would be represented equally in the Senate. This decision served the practical purpose of mediating large-state–small-state conflicts; it also met the sovereignty issue by proposing that the national government represent both the people and the state governments.

The Connecticut Compromise paved the way for subsequent actions that resolved Nationalist-Federalist differences on a number of issues. Although the latter group succeeded in defeating the Virginia Plan proposal granting the national legislature a veto over state legislation, the delegates took a series of subsequent actions that favored the national government. A clause establishing the supremacy of the national Constitution, laws, and treaties over conflicting state constitutions and statutes was adopted. Moreover, by providing for appeal from state to federal courts on those matters (Jefferson made this suggestion in a letter to Madison from Paris), the delegates placed ultimate authority over such issues in an agency of the central government. The Convention also adopted a clause granting Congress power "to make all laws necessary and proper for carrying into execution" the enumerated functions assigned to it. As we will see later in this chapter, this language paved the way for the indefinite expansion of the specific powers of the national government. Finally, the Convention undercut the basis of state sovereignty by providing that the Constitution would take effect when approved by nine states and that ratification could be accomplished by elected delegates in state conventions rather than by state legislatures.

Thus the give-and-take process of the Convention culminated in a division of powers in the new nation that differed both from the centralized systems of the Empire and the Virginia Plan and from the decentralized arrangements of the Articles of Confederation and the New Jersey Plan. The delegates had somehow fashioned a middle ground that avoided what Hamilton had claimed could not be avoided, having the general government "swallow up" the states, or "be swallowed up by them." Madison explained in *The Federalist* that the new government depended "partly upon the states and partly on the people." Although the Founding Fathers did not realize it at that time, they developed an entirely new means for dividing power between levels of government, a system that came to be known as federalism.

MODELS OF DIVIDING POLITICAL POWER

Although societies employ a variety of methods to divide political power among governmental levels, it is possible to group the arrangements into three general categories: confederative, unitary, and federal systems. In understanding what federalism is, it is helpful to first analyze what it is *not*, that is, to see how it differs from the other two models of divided political authority.

CONFEDERATION

One system was employed by name under the Articles of Confederation. Assuming the people to be the ultimate source of political authority, one can illustrate the allocation of powers under a confederation as in Figure 3–1. The figure indicates that in a confederation, the people grant political power over certain concerns to the governments of the component parts of the political system. These governments as a group, in turn, delegate power over certain of these concerns entrusted to them to the central government. In a confederation the scope of powers granted to the governments of the component parts is generally broad and covers all those activities that people feel should come under the control of public, as against private, authorities. In contrast, the scope of powers of the central government is typically narrow and is restricted to only those matters that the component parts feel must be handled by the large and geographically more inclusive unit of government. For example, under the Articles of Confederation the functions of the national government were restricted to concerns of war and peace, while the state governments exercised broad authority over the remaining activities entrusted to political authorities.

Under a confederation the people grant no political power directly to the central government; a corollary of this restriction is the inability of that government to exercise direct legal control over the people. As suggested by Figure 3-1, the central government typically must depend on the governments of the component parts to enforce its authority over even those relatively few concerns entrusted to it. Thus under the Articles of Confederation the national government had the power to raise an army and to levy certain taxes. Yet it could not exercise direct control over individuals to enforce that authority; rather, it was dependent on the state governments to provide requisitions of money and troops. The national government also had to depend primarily on state courts to enforce its laws.

Two other features are usually associated with a confederation. One is the right of a component government to withdraw voluntarily from the larger union when it feels that its interests are not being served by the more in-

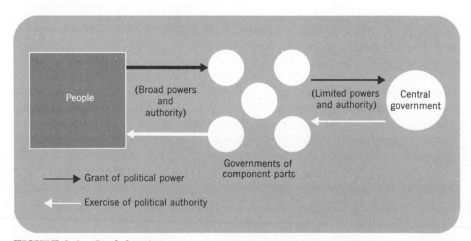

FIGURE 3-1   Confederation.

clusive unit of government. The other is the requirement that all the component parts of the union consent to any change in the division of powers between the two levels of government. Thus under the Articles of Confederation the national government could not be granted the power to levy import taxes because a single state (Rhode Island) refused to consent to an amendment granting this additional power to the central government.

A modern-day example of a confederation is the United Nations. In this body, of course, the nation-states (United States, Soviet Union, and so on) are the component governments, while the United Nations itself is the central political unit. The organization possesses the basic features of a confederation: the UN exercises only those powers granted to it by its members; its governmental authority is narrow compared to that retained by the nation-states; it depends on voluntary contributions of money and military forces of individual countries for its operations; it cannot enforce its provisions on individuals; and nations are free to withdraw from it at any time (as Indonesia did temporarily some years ago). Although the consent of two-thirds of the member nations is sufficient to ratify proposed changes in the charter of the organization, that two-thirds must include all the permanent members of the Security Council (United States, Soviet Union, United Kingdom, France, and China).

UNITARY GOVERNMENTS

Diametrically opposed to a confederation as a means of dividing political power between levels of government is a *unitary* system. As Figure 3–2 indicates, the people grant power over their activities to the central govern-

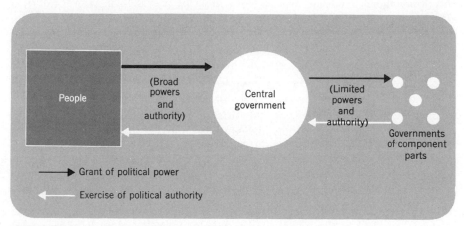

FIGURE 3–2   Unitary system.

ment which, in turn, delegates authority over some of these activities to the component parts. The powers retained by the central unit (like those kept by the parts in a confederation) are usually more extensive or more important than those it grants to the lower political units. Moreover, the governments of the component parts may enforce their decrees on individuals only if they are authorized to do so by the central government.

A historical example of a unitary system of government was the British Empire in the period preceding the Revolutionary War. The colonial governments controlled only those activities granted to them by the mother country; they were likewise dependent on London for authority to enforce their laws. The British did not think it necessary to obtain the consent of the colonies before intervening in military and financial affairs formerly entrusted to the colonists, nor did the mother country recognize the right of the colonies to declare themselves independent of the British Empire. On the contrary, the Revolutionary War was fought for the purpose of forcing Americans to remain under that authority.

Most of the countries in the world today have unitary governments. So do the individual states of our own nation. The arrangements between these latter governments and their lesser units are essentially unitary; the states determine what functions will be granted to local governments (counties, cities, villages) and decide whether these political entities can create their own agencies or must rely on those of the states to control individuals. Nor can the lower units generally block changes in state-local relationships or legally withdraw from the jurisdiction of the state government.

FEDERALISM

At the time of the Constitutional Convention, the term "federalism" did not carry the definite meaning we ascribe to it today. In the early stages of the proceedings, "federal" was used to describe a system in which political power was concentrated in the states. As previously mentioned, those who backed the New Jersey Plan were known as "Federalists," while the supporters of the Virginia Plan called themselves "Nationalists." This is the sense in which Oliver Ellsworth of Connecticut (a major figure in the development of the Connecticut Compromise) used the term when he said that the new government was "partly national, partly federal." During the ratification campaign, however, the title of Federalists was taken over by proponents of the Constitution like Madison and Hamilton, who favored a strong national government, while those who opposed its adoption because they felt it violated states' rights became known as Anti-Federalists. Thus a failure to grasp fully the possible variations in nation-state relationships (including the unique nature of the government they themselves had created), plus the desire to capitalize politically on the favorable image of the word "federal" created in the minds of the people, contributed to the loose, and often contradictory, meaning that the Founding Fathers ascribed to the concept of federalism.

When a political scientist uses the term federalism today, he refers to a system in which political power is divided between the central government of a country and the governments of its component parts so that each level is legally independent of the other within its own sphere of activity. In the American system neither the national government nor the government of an individual state depends on the other for its source of political power. The same is true of other federations in the world. Although the names of the component parts of given nations differ, the principle is the same: provinces of Canada, cantons of Switzerland, and länder in West Germany, all have independent bases of power from their national governments. Figure 3–3 indicates the relationships that exist under a federal political system.

Thus under a federal system each level of government is legally independent of the other. Each receives its grant of powers directly from the people. Each, in turn, has the concomitant right to exercise political authority over the people within its own sphere of activities without depending on the consent of the other level of government.

A federal system also has two other essential characteristics. First, both levels of government must participate in decisions to change the division of powers between them. Thus in the American system both the Congress and the states are involved in amending the federal Constitution. Second, the component parts are not free to leave the union voluntarily as may parts of a confederation. The major legal issue that precipitated the American Civil

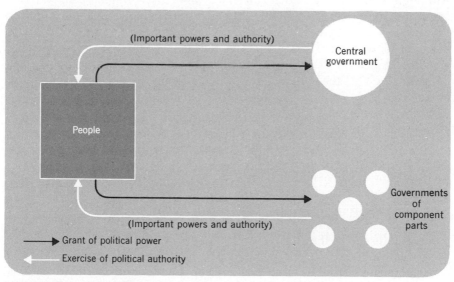

FIGURE 3–3   Federation.

War was precisely this: the Southern states took the position that they had the right to secede from the Union; Lincoln and the Northern states disagreed. The issue was settled militarily on the battlefield, and subsequently the Supreme Court gave its legal blessing to the result by stating that "the Constitution, in all its provisions, looks to an indestructible Union composed of indestructible States." In the late 1960s a similar state of affairs developed in Nigeria: Biafra sought to pull out of the federation and the central authorities used force to prevent it from doing so.

It should be emphasized that differences between confederative, unitary, and federal forms of governments are legal in nature. A division of political power occurs in all three. Moreover, considerable variations in the allocation of powers exist within each of the major systems. As weak as the national government was under the Articles of Confederation, it was granted more political power than the United Nations has today. Both France and Great Britain have unitary governments, but counties and towns exercise more important powers in the latter because of the British tradition of local self-government, as against the historic patterns of centralism in France. Nevertheless, the powers that central authorities in London grant local governments in Britain today, they can legally withdraw tomorrow. Such a possibility is not present in a federation. In fact, federations utilize a series of institutions to safeguard the independence of both levels of the governmental system.

INSTITUTIONAL SAFEGUARDS OF FEDERALISM

Although the Founding Fathers did not realize that they had created a new form of government (the word "federal" does not appear in the Constitution), the give-and-take process at the Convention led to the establishment of a number of devices and institutions that have come to be associated with a federal system of government because they are designed to protect both political levels in the system. Many such practices have been consciously borrowed (with some modifications, of course) by other nations, such as Canada and Australia, that have created federations similar to the one first developed by the United States.

The basic device the Founding Fathers used to distribute powers in the American system was a *formal written constitution*. Because they feared political power, they sought to curb its possible excesses by distributing it among different branches and levels of government, each of which was assigned definite responsibilities in the constitutional system. By spelling out in some detail the respective spheres of authority of the national government and the states, they hoped to protect the domain of each from invasion by the other. Other nations seeking to benefit from the American federal experience have likewise used written constitutions to distribute political powers among the central government and the component parts.

Federations can and do differ, however, on the particular means they use to divide political power. The American approach is to assign certain specific powers to the national government and to reserve all remaining powers to the states. (The details of this division of powers will be discussed subsequently in this chapter.) Canada uses precisely the opposite technique of delegating particular powers to its provinces and permitting the Dominion (national government) to enjoy residual authority. Still other federations, for instance, West Germany, assign certain specific powers to one level of government and other specific powers to the other level. Whatever approach is used, the emphasis in all federations is on dividing political power so that important responsibilities are granted to both levels of government.

Since the two levels receive their respective powers from the written constitution, another practice logically follows in a federal system: *both* levels must participate in the formal process for altering that constitution. Otherwise one of the governmental levels could change the original division of powers in its favor. Under the American Constitution the Congress initiates amendments, either by its own action or in response to a call from the state legislatures for a convention to consider proposed amendments. (This latter procedure has never been used to date.) The states, in turn, must ratify amendments through their legislatures or by conventions before they become effective. Similarly, in Australia and Switzerland the component parts (states and cantons, respectively) must approve amendments to their formal constitutions.

Another institution generally associated with a federal system is an *umpire* to settle disputes that inevitably arise between the two levels of government. No matter how carefully the language of a constitution is drawn, situations arise in which it is not clear from the division of powers which level of government is entitled to undertake a particular activity. In many instances, of course, the difficulty is unavoidable: constitution-framers cannot be expected to foresee all future developments—such as the rise of the modern corporation or the invention of television—and provide for them accordingly. Thus some agency must be provided for allocating new governmental responsibilities between the central unit and the component parts. Typically in a federal system the ultimate authority for settling such nation-state disputes rests with the highest court in the land, such as the United States Supreme Court. (Switzerland, however, refers such issues to the people.)

Most federations also provide some protection for the states in the political process, generally a special house of the national legislature in which the component parts are represented as units. The purest form of this practice is absolute equality of representation as in the American and Australian senates. Other federations such as Canada give larger provinces more representation in their senates than smaller ones, but the disparity is not as great as it would be if population alone were the sole criterion.

Typically federations create two separate sets of political institutions to carry on the constitutional responsibilities of the central government and those of its component parts. Each has its own legislative, executive, and judicial branches of government operating directly on individual citizens, and these two sets of institutions generally function independently of one another. In rejecting both Hamilton's proposal for having the national government appoint state governors and the New Jersey Plan's provision whereby state executives could remove their national counterpart, the Founders established the autonomy of the personnel of both levels of governments. They also refused to adopt the Virginia Plan proposal that the Congress be empowered to negate state laws and guaranteed the territorial integrity of the individual states by providing that boundaries could not be changed without the permission of the states' own legislatures.

By creating general governmental institutions like those described above, federal nations seek to maintain a balance between the central government and the parts. Whether such a balance is actually preserved, depends on how such institutions work out in practice.

LEGAL SAFEGUARDS
OF AMERICAN FEDERALISM

The operation of legal safeguards in the American federal system has been affected by two major factors: first, the method by which powers are divided in the Constitution between the national government and the states; and second, how the Supreme Court has interpreted this division of powers in major cases.

THE DIVISION OF POWERS
UNDER THE NATIONAL CONSTITUTION

Article I, Section 8 of the Constitution delegates certain specific, enumerated powers to the Congress. Included in its jurisdiction are such varied functions as regulating interstate and foreign commerce, raising an army and navy, controlling the currency, and establishing post offices and roads. Congress is also granted the power to levy taxes to pay the debts and provide for the defense and general welfare of the nation, as well as the authority to borrow money on the credit of the United States. At the very end of Article I, Section 8, there appears an important clause granting Congress the power "to make all Laws which shall be necessary and proper for carrying into Execution the foregoing Powers. . . ." With this statement the Founders sought to expand the authority of the national government beyond those matters specifically listed in that section. In other words, they wanted the national government to have implied, as well as expressed, powers.

The national Constitution makes no specific grant of powers to the states.

In fact, in its original form, the document made no mention at all of state prerogatives. By implication the framers intended that all powers not granted to the national government would remain in the states. However, uneasiness among Anti-Federalists over leaving states' rights to implication alone led to the adoption of the Tenth Amendment, which expressly provided that "The powers not delegated to the United States by the Constitution, nor prohibited by it to the states, are reserved to the states respectively, or to the people."

The general sources of political powers of the American states are their own constitutions. Although their powers (and limitations) vary somewhat, the states in general possess "police power" enabling them to pass laws for the "health, safety and morals" of their people. This broad grant of political authority means that unlike the national government, a state government need not depend on a specific grant of power authorizing a particular function; unless an activity is specifically forbidden by the national or its own state constitution, or is considered by state courts to be an "unreasonable" use of the police power (such as permitting men, but not women, to drive motor vehicles), they are free to legislate on it.

The resulting division of powers—whereby the national government can exercise specific enumerated powers and implied powers therefrom while the states are free to take advantage of the general police power—results in a broad area of *concurrent* powers. For example, both the national and the state governments are entitled to raise taxes to finance their activities. At the same time, the Constitution provides for settling possible conflicts that may arise between their operations. Article VI, paragraph 2 declares that if state laws or constitutional provisions are at variance with the national Constitution, laws, or treaties, the latter prevail because they are considered "supreme."

This, then, is the basic method of distributing governmental powers in the American federal system. Since the constitutional language is broad and general, however, and since new situations have arisen which the framers could not possibly have foreseen, the Supreme Court has had to act as umpire in legal disputes involving specific nation-state relationships. In deciding such disputes, the Court has had to interpret the meaning of certain key clauses of the Constitution.

THE SUPREME COURT AS INTERPRETER
OF THE DIVISION OF POWERS

The Court has had occasion to define a number of powers granted to the national government by the Constitution, three of which have been particularly crucial in shaping its jurisdiction: the "necessary and proper" clause; the power over interstate commerce; and the authority to tax and spend for the general welfare. In addition, the Court's interpretation of the Tenth Amendment has affected nation-state relationships.

The "Necessary and Proper Clause." The national government was organized for only a year when Secretary of the Treasury Alexander Hamilton submitted a broad economic program to the Congress proposing the establishment of a national bank. Because he had some doubts about its constitutionality, President Washington turned for legal advice to two perennial antagonists in his cabinet, Alexander Hamilton himself and Thomas Jefferson. The former maintained that although the national government was granted no specific authority to establish a bank, "the necessary and proper" clause of Article I, Section 8 gave it the implied power to do so. Pointing out that Congress was authorized to raise money by taxation or by borrowing, Hamilton reasoned that the creation of a bank was a "convenient" means for keeping such monies. He thus interpreted "necessary" to mean "convenient" or "appropriate." Jefferson took the opposite position that the word "necessary" should be strictly construed to mean "indispensable." Since the establishment of a national bank was not indispensable to the safeguarding of federal funds (they could be deposited in state banks, for instance), then it lay beyond the authority of the national government.

Ultimately, Washington accepted Hamilton's arguments over those of Jefferson and signed the national bank bill into law. About a quarter of a century later, the bank again became a constitutional issue. The state of Maryland taxed a branch of the national bank within its borders; on the instructions of its officials, its cashier, James McCulloch, refused to pay the tax on the grounds that this constituted state interference with a legitimate activity of the national government. When the Maryland Supreme Court decided in favor of the state, the ruling was appealed to the United States Supreme Court. The case, *McCulloch* v. *Maryland*, raised the basic issue of federalism first argued in the Washington administration: does the national government have the right to create a bank?

A battery of famous lawyers of the day argued the case before the Court. The major figure representing the United States was Daniel Webster; his courtroom opponent was the well-regarded Luther Martin of Maryland. The legal arguments were essentially the same as those made previously by Hamilton and Jefferson. Chief Justice John Marshall, a staunch Federalist and friend of a vigorous national government, not surprisingly ruled in favor of that government. In doing so, he adopted Hamilton's interpretation of the necessary and proper clause. Necessary meant "appropriate," not "indispensable" or "absolutely necessary," as Jefferson and Luther Martin maintained. The national government had the authority to create a bank because it was an appropriate means for exercising its power to raise monies.

This early judicial test of the powers of the national government resulted in a liberal interpretation of its authority and opened the door to its expansion of activities through the use of implied, as compared to express, powers. Yet two specific powers expressly granted to Congress—authority over interstate commerce and the right to tax and spend for the general welfare —have proved to be even more important bases for national power.

Interstate-Commerce Power. The constitutional issue concerning the interstate-commerce power is essentially the same as that of the "necessary and proper" clause: how liberal or strict an interpretation to give the phrase. The same John Marshall who interpreted the latter clause liberally in the historic *McCulloch* v. *Maryland* of 1819 used essentially the same approach for the commerce clause five years later in the landmark case of *Gibbons* v. *Ogden.* In that instance he ruled that the national government had the authority to license the operation of boats on the waters of New York State because these passenger vessels were involved in interstate commerce, which he construed broadly to cover all "intercourse" between the states. In so doing, Marshall rejected the argument that interstate commerce should be limited to "traffic" involving only the buying and selling of goods.

Over the course of American constitutional history, justices of the Supreme Court have differed over which activities should be considered interstate commerce. When Congress began to use the powers increasingly to regulate (rather than to promote) the operations of American business, members of the Court who were opposed to governmental intervention in economic affairs narrowed the scope of such regulations by holding that only those activities directly involved in interstate commerce—such as transportation and communication—were subject to the jurisdiction of the Congress. This strict construction of the interstate-commerce power meant that that body could not regulate the manufacturing and mining of products or their local sale or distribution. This interpretation of the commerce clause was dominant in the waning years of the last century and into the third decade of the present one. In the 1940s, however, the Court changed the test from whether an activity is *involved* in interstate commerce to whether it economically *affected* such commerce. Using this approach, the Court in *Wickard* v. *Filburn* (1942) justified the national government's even regulating what a farmer fed to his own chickens on the reasoning that this activity economically *affected* the interstate market for wheat. This decision and others that have followed have led students of constitutional law to conclude that, given the interdependent nature of American society today, there is virtually no activity that the Court will consider beyond the scope of the commerce power.

The Power to Tax and Spend for the General Welfare. Like the "necessary and proper" clause, the power of the national government to tax and spend for the general welfare provoked an early debate between two of the nation's prominent leaders, this time Hamilton and Madison. Both, of course, were supporters of a strong national government at the Convention, and together they wrote the bulk of *The Federalist Papers.* Yet Madison subsequently parted company with his co-author on the proper interpretation of the taxing and spending power. Madison considered that function to be ancillary to the enumerated powers of the Congress; in this view, the national government can tax and spend only for those activities over which it was given specific authority. Hamilton argued that the power was in addition to, and hence independent of, the enumerated ones; in other words, Congress can tax and spend monies for functions that it could not otherwise control. The issue was ultimately resolved by the Supreme Court in favor of Hamilton's view.

A series of other constitutional questions relating to the taxing and spending power have also been decided to favor the national government. The Supreme Court will no longer inquire into the motive behind the enactment of a tax; thus Congress can use it as an indirect method of regulating an activity (such as a tax on gambling) as well as for the purpose of raising revenue. Moreover, the Court will not make a judgment about whether Congress's use of the taxing and spending power in particular instances is in "the general welfare" or not; nor will it interfere with the right of Congress to establish conditions under which the monies it appropriates can be spent. The result is that the taxing and spending power of the Congress has been converted into a kind of national police power, since most government activity involves the expenditure of money.

Thus the two powers that the Founding Fathers thought most crucial to the operation of a national government—interstate commerce and taxation —have been the major bases for the constitutional expansion of national activities. At the same time, another key constitutional question of that early era—the relationship between national and state powers spelled out in the Tenth Amendment—has also played a major part in the continuous struggle over the division of political authority in the American system.

The Tenth Amendment. Constitutional questions raised by the Tenth Amendment concern its effect on the scope of national powers. Those friendly to an energetic central government have maintained that the Tenth Amendment is redundant: it merely expresses what was implied in the original document, that the states enjoy constitutional authority over any matter neither delegated to the national government nor forbidden to the states. The Amendment in no way diminishes or restricts the activities of the national government that are based on its express or implied powers. Those opposed to strong centralism contend that the Amendment limits the scope of national power by preventing the central government from exercising its otherwise legitimate powers if they impinge on matters of state and local concern. Some Supreme Court justices have also been inclined to read the word "expressly" into the Amendment with respect to delegated powers (no such word appears in the Constitution although it did in the Articles of Confederation) so as to negate any idea of implied powers of the national government. Since the 1930s, however, this position has lost favor among the justices so that the Tenth Amendment is now considered the redundancy that the early friends of a strong government maintained it was.

The effect of these judicial interpretations has been legal support for virtually any activity in which the national government chooses to become involved. This support, coupled with judicial checks over state actions that affect matters of national concern (states may not, for example, "burden" commerce through regulations that curtail interstate business activities, nor may they tax the operations of the national government), is evidence that the Supreme Court has had a nationalizing influence on American federalism. The legal checks of federalism have thus not operated (in recent years at least) to maintain a balance in our political system; they have rather favored the interests of the national government over those of the states.

Some advocates of states' rights in the United States have ascribed this favoritism to the nonneutrality of the Supreme Court in federal-state disputes. Rather than an umpire in such conflict, it is a member of the national team. To counteract this advantage, the Council of State Governments (an organization of state officials) some years ago proposed a constitutional amendment creating a Court of the Union to be composed of the chief justices of the highest courts of the fifty states, with authority to overrule the decisions of the United States Supreme Court on nation-state issues. Nothing serious came of the proposal, nor of a companion measure permitting state legislatures to amend the national Constitution without the concurrence of national officials. Fortunately for the states and their supporters, other safeguards have operated to protect their interests in the American federal system.

POLITICAL SAFEGUARDS
OF AMERICAN FEDERALISM

Although the actions of the United States Supreme Court (particularly since the 1930s) have expanded the legal powers of the national government, the interests of the states have nonetheless been protected by our political processes. One reason for this development is the fact that, as lesser geographical units, the states are represented in the national government. Beyond their equal representation in the Senate, the Constitution requires that members of the House of Representatives be residents of the states they serve. (By political custom, they are also residents of the congressional district they represent.) These provisions, plus the legal control states exercise over the nomination and election of their senators and House members (we will explore how this control operates in Chapters 8 and 9), mean that the states possess considerable potential influence over the national legislature.

This potential is converted into actual influence by the realities of the American political party system. One of the cardinal facts about our parties (the general subject will be treated in Chapter 7) is that they are highly decentralized; power resides at the state and local, rather than the national, level. The choice of candidates for the House and Senate is determined not by the national committees of the parties but primarily by state and local party organizations. Moreover, the money for political campaigns comes not from the treasury of national headquarters but from the contributions of local groups and individuals.

Since House members and senators are familiar with these basic facts of political life, they are solicitous of the interests of the districts and states they represent, as reflected in their concern that national legislation either positively benefit their areas or at least not injure them. Thus congressmen from urban districts and states typically seek aid for the cities, while those from areas whose businesses are threatened by foreign trade (such as states with textile mills) push for tariffs or quotas on the importation of competitive goods from abroad. This solicitude of individual legislators for state and local interests is further buttressed by important organizational features of the Congress: informal arrangements and understandings provide for committee seats to be assigned to representatives of the areas most vitally concerned with the work of the committee. Thus congressmen from working-class districts populate the committees concerned with labor legislation, while those from farming areas sit on the agricultural committees of the House and Senate.

Nor is the concern of congressmen for states and localities restricted to the legislative process. As overseers and financial providers of the activities of the executive branch (this matter will be treated fully in Chapter 12), congressmen are in an excellent position to insure that the interests of their districts and states are taken into account. Thus key congressional leaders and committee chairmen can exercise considerable control over where a military base is located. It is no accident that so many defense and space installations have been located in Texas and Georgia in recent years: Texans Lyndon Johnson and Sam Rayburn (former Senate Majority Leader and Speaker of the House respectively) and Georgians Walter George and Carl Vinson (chairmen of the Senate and House Armed Services Committees) used their influence to benefit their state and local economies. (Recently some congressmen have exerted the opposite kind of pressure, working to prevent the location of antiballistic missile sites in their districts out of fear that such complex weapons might malfunction or make their areas prime targets for enemy nuclear attacks.) All congressmen also spend a considerable portion of their time acting as liaison agents between individual constituents and executive agencies to see to it that "their" people are treated fairly.

Thus the two legislative houses of the national government, which reflect state and local interests, counterbalance the nationalizing influence of the Supreme Court in the American federal system. At times the legal and political processes come into direct conflict, as they did in the 1950s over the issue of tidelands oil. Both the national government and the states involved claimed title to valuable oil deposits located in submerged lands off the shores of Texas, Louisiana, California, and other coastal areas. After a lengthy period of litigation the Supreme Court ruled that the national government owned the disputed lands. The Congress, however, ultimately resolved the issue in favor of the states by passing legislation which deeded the valuable lands to them. On another earlier occasion in the 1940s, the Supreme Court ruled that the national government had authority over insurance companies because of the interstate nature of their business transactions; Congress subsequently passed legislation permitting the states to continue to regulate insurance companies.

The legal aspects of American federalism thus permit the Congress to undertake virtually any activity it wishes, but political forces tend to make it receptive to the interests of states and local areas. Together these factors have shaped the nature of the political system that has evolved in the United States.

THE GROWTH OF LOCAL, STATE, AND NATIONAL GOVERNMENT

An analysis of governmental developments points to one overriding pattern: the growth of activities at all levels of our political system. Local, state, and national governments are doing more today in providing services and regulating the actions of their citizens than they have ever done in the past: their total expenditures rose from under $2 billion in 1902 to some $260 billion in 1967, the last year for which actual figures are available. Therefore, any assessment of American federalism must be based on the *relative* activity of the various levels—that is, how much the national government is doing in public affairs at a given time compared to state and local political units. A good measure of the relative activity is the proportion of total expenditures made by the three political levels. Table 3.1 shows such figures for various years of this century.

The most striking over-all trend shown by Table 3.1 is the comparative

TABLE 3.1   Proportions of Total Governmental Expenditures Spent by Federal, State, and Local Governments, 1902–1967 (Figures in Percentages)

| Levels of Government | Year | | | | | | | | | |
	1902	1913	1922	1927	1932	1938	1948	1954	1962	1967
Federal	34	30	40	31	33	44	62	67	58	59
State	8	9	11	12	16	16	13	11	14	15
Local	58	61	49	57	51	40	25	22	28	26

Source: Frederick C. Moser and Orville F. Poland, *The Costs of American Governments* (New York: Dodd, Mead, 1964), Table 3.2. The 1967 figures are derived from the 1967 Census of Governments.

increase in the activities of the national government during the first half of this century. This development is most noticeable in three historical periods: the first is from 1913 until 1922, essentially World War I and its aftermath; the second is 1932 to 1938, the period of the New Deal response to the Great Depression; and finally, the most dramatic change of all, in the period from 1938, the beginning of the military build-up for World War II, to 1948, the first full postwar year for which expenditures are available. All told, the federal share of governmental expenditures doubled in the period from 1902 to 1954.

These increases in the activities of the federal government are related to certain key factors during the first half of this century, particularly war and depression. Military matters have, of course, always been the paramount concern of the national government, so it is not surprising that wars should augment federal activities. The Great Depression, however, resulted in a change in traditional public attitudes against having the national government assume an active role in economic crises. As conditions worsened, neither private enterprise nor local and state governments proved capable of dealing with the unemployment problem; therefore, people turned to the national government to get the country back on its feet. Armed with power over the currency, the banking system, and the regulation of interstate economic activities; supported by a good tax base (the Sixteenth Amendment, ratified in 1913, enabled the Congress to tap an excellent source of revenue —incomes of individuals),* and guided by the powerful political leadership of President Franklin Roosevelt, the national government in the 1930s embarked on a series of new programs designed to lead the country to recovery. Thus the felt needs revealed by the military and economic crises in the first half of this century plus the fiscal and political capacity of the national government to meet these needs altered the division of governmental activities among the three levels of our federal system.

Table 3.1 also indicates that the comparative increase in government spending at the national level has been accompanied by a sharp decline in local expenditures. The latter stood at almost three-fifths of total governmental outlays in 1902; in 1954, they constituted just over one-fifth of the composite figure. The level of government least affected by over-all trends has been the states: although their share of total expenditures increased somewhat during this century, state governments have continued to run a distant third to both the national and local governments in the spending of public funds.

Table 3.1 demonstrates another basic fact of American federalism: the comparative activities of the three governmental levels have stabilized since

---

*Prior to the Amendment, the tax had to be apportioned among the states on the basis of population, and since income is not related to population, the tax could not be administered.

the end of World War II. The military demands of the Korean conflict resulted in an increase in federal spending between 1948 and 1954, but this increase was not nearly so marked as were those associated with the two World Wars. In the period (1962–1967) when the country became increasingly involved in the hostilities in Vietnam, no basic change occurred in the basic pattern of American federalism.

The over-all balance in American federalism since World War II has resulted from increased spending of the national government, particularly for national defense, offset by burgeoning state and local expenditures for major domestic programs such as education, highways, welfare, and health. From 1948 to 1967 federal spending for defense-related matters rose from $28 to $98 billion; meanwhile, domestic expenditures of the national government increased less sharply from $19 to $55 billion. In the same two decades, however, state and local governments stepped up their expenditures drastically to meet pressing domestic needs—from $20 billion in 1948 to $107 billion in 1967. The end result of these developments in the late 1960s was that, while the national government was expending some three of every five dollars used for all public purposes, state and local units were spending a slightly larger figure—two out of every three dollars—of government outlays for domestic programs alone.

Federalism produces a complex mix of governmental levels, as evidenced in this view of Newark, New Jersey. In the right foreground a spur of the federally financed Interstate Highway system crosses a navigable river, which is under the jurisdiction of the Army Corps of Engineers. In the center are the low white buildings of a branch of Rutgers, the State University of New Jersey. At left rear and right center are municipal housing projects. (Charles Rotkin-P.F.I.)

This information on governmental expenditures reveals the basic dimensions of American federalism in the twentieth century: an over-all growth in federal activities, especially relating to military and economic crises, accompanied by the continuing vitality of state and local units undertaking increased responsibilities for the nation's domestic needs. But we cannot justifiably conclude from these gross figures that the division of functions in our political system has been simple, with the national government concerned almost entirely with military and foreign policy, while the states and local units go their own ways, raising public money and spending it on matters of exclusive concern to themselves. Instead, as the following section indicates, the governmental process of American federalism has been far more complex, involving close relationships among the various levels.

COOPERATIVE FEDERALISM

Students of American federalism frequently refer to recent developments in the system as a "new" federalism or, sometimes, a "cooperative" federalism. By this they mean that we no longer have three separate levels of government that undertake distinct functions and operate independently of one another; instead, they all share in carrying out various public functions.*
Another dimension of the new federalism is that the various political levels no longer view each other as "rivals" for public support and the exercise of political power; rather, they regard themselves as "partners" in the great enterprise of government.

Cooperative federalism may have become more prominent in the United States in recent years, but it is not entirely "new." Even before the Constitutional Convention, the Congress passed a statute of 1785, supplemented by the Northwest Ordinance of 1787, which granted designated sections of public lands to the states for educational purposes. Thus the national government financially assisted the states in establishing primary and secondary schools, long considered in the United States to be one of the most basic local functions. Subsequently, Congress provided funds to both the states and local governments to develop internal improvements such as roads, canals, rivers, and railroads. During the Civil War a national law was enacted that has had a major impact on higher education in the United States; the Morrill Act donated lands to the states, the proceeds of which were to be used to establish colleges devoted to instruction in agriculture and mechanics. The "A and M" colleges prominent in the Middle and Far West thus owe their existence to the willingness of the national government to concern itself with traditional state matters.

These early grants involved a resource that the national government had

*The late political scientist Morton Grodzins likened our system not to a layer cake but to a marble one characterized by an intermingling of colors in vertical and diagonal strands representing the mixing of functions at all levels.

in abundance: land. Toward the end of the nineteenth century a shift occurred in the substance of grants from land to cash. Moreover, the nature
of the grants changed from one-shot affairs to continuing appropriations
made on an annual basis. This new form of subsidy is the grant-in-aid, familiar to the student of modern federalism in the United States.

FEDERAL GRANTS-IN-AID

Development. Although a few federal grants-in-aid were established before 1900 (for example, in 1887 the Congress provided the first continuing
cash grant to assist states in establishing agricultural experiment stations),
they are primarily a twentieth-century development. The grants are closely
linked with a major fiscal development: the enactment of the income tax
amendment in 1913. With the major new source of revenue available to the
national government, and a President (Woodrow Wilson) and Congress
willing and able to involve the national government more extensively in the
economy than their predecessors had been, federal grant-in-aid expenditures increased from some $5 million in 1912 to almost $34 million in 1920.
Not only were familiar objects of nineteenth-century subsidies favored (the
Smith-Lever Act of 1914 established the agricultural extension program,
and vocational education and highways also drew major financial support),
but the Congress provided the beginnings of modern assistance programs
with provisions for maternal and child health.

The Republican administrations of the 1920s and early 1930s continued
and improved the existing federal grant-in-aid program. However, no significant new starts were made during the twelve years between the Wilson
and Roosevelt terms. In contrast, the New Deal ushered in a different era in
grant-in-aid programs. Ignoring the advice of many of his advisers to let
the national government itself administer burgeoning new programs in welfare, health, employment security, and public housing, President Roosevelt
chose instead to funnel such expenditures through lesser political units. As
a result, during the period from 1932 to 1939, grant-in-aid expenditures
swelled from some $200 million to almost $3 billion. Two significant departures from the Wilson years were also apparent: a shift in emphasis in
the programs from rural to urban needs and the channeling of some of the
assistance directly from the national government to local units, bypassing
the states in the process. For example, cities became the direct recipients of
federal aid in public housing.

The outbreak of World War II brought a temporary decline in federal
grant-in-aid programs as the national government harbored its resources for
military necessities. Beginning in 1948, grant expenditures began to rise
again, but it was not until 1954 that they reached their prewar level of some
$3 billion. During the remainder of the Eisenhower administration, grant
monies increased as the Republicans sought to counter the centralization of

domestic programs in Washington. Also, consistent with that party's philosophy, the administration was concerned not to bypass the states in favor of direct grants to cities.

The decade of the 1960s witnessed a major surge in federal aid programs similar to that of the 1930s. Grants more than quadrupled, from some $7 billion to over $30 billion in the period from 1961 to 1971. A major increase occurred in the Johnson administration (some two dozen new "Great Society" programs were inaugurated in 1964–65 alone) and continued during the Republican administration of Richard Nixon. Programs tended to concentrate on the problems of the large metropolitan areas of the nation (central cities and suburbs) and ranged broadly in welfare, economic development, education, and race relations. They brought still another feature to the evolution of federal grants-in-aid: some, such as the Community Action Program in the antipoverty field, bypass not only the states but even local governments in favor of private groups that receive funds and, in some cases, help administer the programs.

The development of the federal grant-in-aid program in the United States has thus had a major impact on government expenditures and revenues during this century. Federal outlays during the period mushroomed from $3 million in 1902 to $30 billion in 1971. By the latter year, one of every seven dollars the national government spent was allocated to some federal grant-in-aid program. If domestic programs alone are considered, the ratio rose to almost one in three. Such expenditures, in turn, added a cumulative total of $140 billion to state and local funds in the period from 1964 to 1971. By the latter year such grants constituted about one-fifth of all state and local revenues.

Characteristics. As previously indicated, one of the distinguishing features of federal grants-in-aid is that they generally involve cash payments (one exception is the surplus agricultural commodities used in the school lunch and social welfare programs) authorized by Congress on a continuing basis or for a specific period of years. The distinction between continuous- and specific-term grants has tended to be a legal one, however; Congress normally extends the short-term grants when their original authorization period has expired, so in actual fact they too are continuous. In other words, once enacted, few grant-in-aid programs have been terminated. Groups favored by such grants have used their political influence to prevent that occurrence. Thus the number of grant programs has swelled as new ones have been added to old ones.

The new programs have seldom been integrated with those already in existence. Instead they have developed as separate programs. The outcome of this process is a proliferation of programs, each of which is designed for fairly narrow purposes. For example, there are various categories of public-assistance programs: those for the aged, the blind, mothers with dependent children, and the like, each of which operates independently of the others.

A recent count of federal aid programs indicated that there were over 160 of them, administered by nearly twenty-five departments and 125 bureaus of the national government.

Categorical grants vary considerably in method of distribution to state and local governments. A few, like some to vocational education, are "flat" grants, allocated in equal or minimum amounts to political units without any financial contributions by the units themselves. Most grants-in-aid, however, require states or localities to "match" federal funds by furnishing some of their own money for the program. But even in matching grants, there are various formulas for determining the specific allocation of funds between levels of government and the amount of money to which each political unit is entitled. Some are based purely on population, while others, including some in primary and secondary education, take into account the financial needs and capabilities of the recipient governments. In the latter instance, the federal share of the grant is higher for political units with a large number of citizens requiring assistance, as well as for those with limited tax resources, than it is for those without such handicaps. A few programs, particularly in public welfare, are "open-ended" in that the federal government provides a certain percentage of the state contribution. This arrangement has a built-in incentive: the more a state spends on a program, the more federal monies it receives.

Federal grant-in-aid programs also impose other conditions for states or localities besides a financial contribution, such as the establishment of a single state agency to administer a given program or the use of a merit system for the employees of all agencies receiving federal money. Furthermore, the federal government agency administering a grant program is entitled to review and supervise the work of the recipient agency and to audit its expenditures.

Administrative Improvements. As the grant-in-aid programs have multiplied in recent years, they have produced major problems of coordination and control for all parties involved in their administration. Some of these problems are centered within a single level of government; the administration of the wide variety of aid programs located in the twenty-five departments and 125 bureaus of the national executive branch is a case in point. The compartmentalization of grants into myriad agencies sometimes means that the federal left hand does not know what the right hand is doing: the Public Bureau of Roads develops highways in urban areas that displace low-income groups who are a major concern to federal officials in the Department of Housing and Urban Development. A similar confusion arises in agencies at the state and local level, since each agency has its closest relationships with the federal bureau in the same functional program—health, education, welfare, and so on. The end result is that officials entrusted with viewing over-all public needs—legislators (senators and congressmen, their state counterparts, and city councilmen) and executives (the President, governors, and mayors)—have difficulty controlling the activities of specialized agencies and establishing priorities among them.

The other major type of administrative problem involves relationships among the three levels of government in the American political system. State officials complain that they are not properly informed and consulted by their federal counterparts in the formulation of administrative rules and practices relating to grant-in-aid programs, and that the red tape and delay in the forwarding of federal funds hampers their operations and prevents them from executing their programs as efficiently as they might. State governors, legislators, and administrators also oppose the recent trend in some grant-in-aid programs to bypass the states in favor of direct relationship with local governments. And political officials at all levels are concerned about an even more recent development, noted above: dispensing federal grants to private persons and groups who also play a major role in their administration.

A growing recognition of such problems by supporters as well as critics of federal grants-in-aid has led to concerted efforts in recent years to confront these problems. Lyndon Johnson's emphasis on what he termed "creative" federalism—that is, working out better relationships among officials at all levels of the federal system—resulted in some changes in the administration of federal grants-in-aid. The Congress sought to improve the coordination of federal urban programs by providing, in the Demonstration Cities and Metropolitan Development Act of 1966, that a metropolitan-wide planning agency screen all applications of federal grants relating to urban development projects in that metropolitan area. The Intergovernmental Cooperation Act of 1968 provides for periodic review by Congress of grant-in-aid programs lacking a termination date and calls for presidential coordination of federally aided development programs.

Recent developments also reflect a particular concern for problems of state governments. The Intergovernmental Cooperation Act of 1968 directs federal agencies to speed up the dispersal of funds to state agencies; it also requires federal officials, upon request, to furnish the governor or legislature of a state with information on the amount and purpose of each grant to that state or its localities. A recent amendment to the Economic Opportunity Act of 1964, which originally created the Antipoverty Program, permits each governor to veto projects within his state. The Intergovernmental Personnel Act of 1970 provides grants to state (as well as local) governments for improving their personnel administration and training programs and permits their employees to work at another level of government for two years without losing any benefits (retirement, sick leave, and the like).

Block Grants. The most basic administrative reform sought in the federal grant-in-aid programs in recent years is the *"block" grant*. This approach has two major purposes: to channel federal grants-in-aid through state governments rather than directly to local governments or private groups; and to permit state officials to allocate funds for some broad purpose—such as health, education, or welfare—rather than have the federal government delineate specific limited purposes for grants. The block-grant approach has been utilized by Congress in the fields of health care, juvenile delinquency, and law enforcement. Typically, under such legislation, applications for federal grants must be approved by a state agency that develops a comprehensive plan for spending monies under the broad purposes of the governing act.

The block grant has become a controversial topic among persons interested in federal grant-in-aid programs. It has drawn particular support from state governors and legislators, as well as Republican officials at the national level. Big-city mayors and administrators of the present categorical grant system, along with Democrats who have supported that system over the years, generally oppose the approach on the grounds that state officials siphon away funds that should go to urban areas and spend the grants for the wrong purposes. The battle between these contending groups has been particularly evident in the administration of the 1968 Omnibus Crime Control and Safe Streets Act, with critics charging state officials with distributing too much money to suburban police departments instead of to high-crime areas of the cities and with failing to allocate sufficient monies for courts and correctional institutions. When the Act was renewed in 1970, it provided that no state plan be approved for funding by federal officials unless it allocates an adequate share for areas of high-crime incidence; moreover, it earmarked twenty percent of the funds for corrections.

President Nixon incorporated the block-grant approach in his 1971 State of the Union Message, which called for consolidating some 105 federal aid programs into six broad-purpose ones dealing with urban development, rural development, education, transportation, job training, and law enforcement. To finance these new programs the President suggested taking $10 billion from the existing grants-in-aid (one-third of the total) and adding $1 billion in new funds. There was no immediate action on this proposal.

NEW FUNDING METHODS
FOR DOMESTIC PROGRAMS

Many students of American federalism now conclude that there are fundamental defects in the grant-in-aid system that cannot be remedied by administrative improvements, even those as drastic as the block-grant approach. Instead of using federal grant-in-aid programs to channel the superior tax resources of the national government to states that lack the revenues to meet their domestic problems, they propose dealing more directly with the problem by redirecting the distribution of tax revenues. Although the proposals differ on how this goal can best be accomplished, they all seek to make the states financially independent of the national government.

Tax Offset. One major method for improving the fiscal independence of the states is the tax offset, a device that has already been used to encourage states to enact death and unemployment-insurance taxes, and which is now being proposed for a more lucrative source of revenue: personal incomes of individuals. It would allow taxpayers in states that levy an income tax to claim a substantial amount of their tax payment (say forty percent) as a credit against their federal income tax. Thus if a person paid $200 in state income tax, he could subtract $80 from his federal income tax. This procedure would enable states to levy higher state taxes on their citizens' incomes without adding the entire increase to the total burden of the taxpayers. With this option open to them, states could then raise more of their own revenues and spend them as they see fit rather than depend on the federal government for allocations through a grant-in-aid program.

Revenue-Sharing. Another technique for redistributing fiscal resources that has gained wide support in recent years is revenue-sharing. This proposal calls for the national government to continue to levy income taxes but asks that it share a percentage of these revenues with the states.* The plan thus resembles the block-grant proposal, but it is even more favorable to the states, for the return of revenues is automatic—that is, the states are not dependent on congressional legislation. Moreover, they have complete discretion in spending the funds and are not limited by even the broad purposes spelled out in block-grant legislation.

Originally proposed in the early 1960s by Walter Heller, Chairman of President John Kennedy's Council of Economic Advisers, income-sharing has become popular with a wide variety of public figures of divergent political views. Thus both Barry Goldwater, the conservative Republican Senator from Arizona, and Hubert Humphrey, the liberal Democratic Senator from Minnesota, have announced their approval of revenue-sharing. So has President Nixon, who suggested in the same 1971 State of the Union Message in which he proposed the $11 billion block-grant program that an additional $5 billion from federal revenues be allocated to the states with no strings attached about how the money should be spent.

Revenue-sharing, however, has also had its share of political opponents, including Wilbur Mills of Arkansas, the Democratic Chairman of the House Ways and Means Committee (which considers taxing and spending matters), and the ranking Republican member, John Byrnes of Wisconsin. Mills has objected to revenue-sharing on the grounds that it is unwise to allow states to spend money they don't raise and that the moneys are unlikely to be apportioned to areas that most need them. He has proposed, instead,

---

*While states can and do tax individual incomes, they are disadvantaged by the fact that federal authorities acted first and taxpayers are reluctant to burden their incomes further. Proposals for state taxes are frequently referred directly to the people, who often vote them down. The federal government need not follow this procedure.

exploring other alternatives for improving state finances, including letting the national government take over costs of welfare programs now borne by the states, extending the tax credit device to state income taxes, and allowing the national Internal Revenue Service to collect state taxes (to be returned to them), thereby saving states the costs of collecting taxes themselves.

These proposals indicate some dissatisfaction with today's cooperative federalism. They raise an even broader issue: to what extent is our present federal system meeting the needs of American society today?

ASSESSMENT

If majority rule is the most important feature of democracy, there is no doubt that our federal system is essentially undemocratic. It permits interests that are in the minority nationally on some issue, but in the majority at the state level to have their way on the matter, at least for a period of time. As William Riker has pointed out, the classic instance is the way in which Southerners have utilized the rationale of states' rights to pursue their own policies on race relations over the years.

Yet the federal system has not operated to give the states a permanent veto on any issue. As we shall see in Chapter 15, the South has been unable in recent years to prevent all three branches of the national government from pursuing policies favoring blacks and from having these policies applied in the states. The legal powers of the national government, plus its revenue sources, are such that virtually no issue is beyond its scope, provided national officials have the political will to deal with it.

There is also no question that other minorities have been protected by American federalism over the years. Business concerns and wealthy individuals have frequently been able to dominate state governments so as to prevent regulation and the payment of taxes at a level necessary to meet public needs for education, welfare, health, and highways. Yet the post-World-War-II record of some states is impressive. New York and California in particular have pioneered in higher education and mental health. Indeed, both of them have budgets that exceed that of the national government in the years immediately preceding World War II. Although the other states cannot match the record of these two giants, half of the fifty states in the late 1960s had combined state-local expenditures exceeding a billion dollars annually. States are also increasingly funneling financial assistance to localities; presently such total grants exceed those that state governments themselves receive from the national government. And as evidence of increased activity at the lower levels of the federal system, taxes and indebtedness have risen faster on the state and local levels in recent years than on the national level.

Beyond this, public services have been improved in all states, including the less-advanced and poorer ones, by the operation of federal grant-in-aid programs that stimulate state efforts and insure that some minimum level of services will be provided to citizens wherever they may live in the United States. In addition, the federal government has recently acted to force states into adequate regulation of matters some have slighted too long; for instance, congressional legislation in air pollution, meat inspection, and disclosure of full credit information to consumers requires states to bring their controls up to national standards by a certain date or face the consequences of a federal take-over of those problems.

The division of powers under our federal system also means that it does not always respond to the need for positive action. The Detroit incident described at the beginning of this chapter is a clear case of how dividing political power can contribute to inaction in a time of crisis. Neither Governor Romney nor President Johnson wanted to take responsibility for what each deemed to be an unpopular course of action, calling for the use of federal troops. The governor sought to make it appear that it was the President's decision to order them into the city; the President was just as concerned that it be made clear that he was sending in federal troops only because the governor needed them and specifically requested their presence. Thus federalism offers the possibility of "passing the buck" to officials at other levels of the political system; such a procedure can prove costly in circumstances that demand governmental action.

Federalism can also serve the ulterior purposes of persons who seek to prevent action on a given problem. For example, in recent years some individuals and groups unfavorable to low-cost housing developments have opposed certain federal programs on the grounds that the responsibility for the projects should be local, knowing full well that the community itself would not or could not make the financial sacrifice necessary to resolve the issue. Thus a basic principle of federalism—in this case, that problems should be handled at the grass roots level—can be used to masquerade the real motives of those who invoke the rhetoric of federalism: preventing any level of government from taking a course of action they oppose.

Although federalism can lead to negativism, recent experiences in the United States also indicate that it can have precisely the opposite effect. Groups unable to get one level of government to handle a problem can shift their efforts to another. This tactic has been successfully pursued since the 1930s by those who have persuaded the Congress to undertake urban problems that state governments refuse to act on. At times, groups have used both political levels to advantage. A case in point is public welfare legislation: having persuaded Congress to establish welfare programs, interested persons subsequently persuaded states to supplement and expand federal services in this field.

The charge that federalism is inherently negative is refuted by the rapid expansion of public activities at all levels of the American system. More-over, developments in cooperative federalism indicate that a system of di-vided powers can operate in a positive fashion to meet public needs. Prob-lems in American federalism today no longer turn so much on the issue of which government will undertake a particular activity as on the question of how the various political levels will be utilized to accomplish our na-tion's purposes. Increasingly, our federation has evolved into a system wherein the national government appropriates monies and establishes broad guidelines for programs which the states and localities administer on a day-to-day basis. A similar pattern is becoming prevalent within the states as they provide increased financing for programs (as in education) that local authorities administer.

At the same time, cooperative federalism, or what some term the federal partnership, does not mean the end of conflict within the system. Political officials at all levels will continue to struggle over the specific arrangements of the partnership: what policies will be established with respect to govern-mental programs? how will they be financed? and who will have the major say over their operation? Thus the give-and-take of the political process that led to the initial establishment of the American federal system con-tinues to shape its character two centuries later.

Selected Readings

For a general discussion of the issues involved in dividing political power in a society, see Arthur Maass, *Area and Power: A Theory of Local Government* (New York: Free Press, 1950). The book is particularly valuable in providing an ana-lytical and theoretical treatment of the subject.

The classic study of the general principles of a federal system of government, together with the institutions and social, economic, and political conditions asso-ciated with such a form of government, is K.C. Wheare, *Federal Government* (London: Oxford University Press, 1953). Two other edited works that treat of many facets of federalism in various nations of the world are Arthur MacMahon, *Federalism, Mature and Emergent* (Garden City, N.Y.: Doubleday, 1955), and Valerie Earle, *Federalism: Infinite Variety in Theory and Practice* (Itasca, Ill.: Peacock, 1968). A particularly valuable essay in the latter book is the one by William S. Livingston, "Canada, Australia, and the United States: Variations on a Theme." For a provocative, critical analysis of federalism, see William Riker, *Federalism: Origin, Operation, Significance* (Boston: Little, Brown, 1964).

Two books are particularly helpful in giving an understanding of the establish-ment of American federalism. One is Arthur Holcombe, *Our More Perfect Union* (Cambridge: Harvard University Press, 1950), Chapter 2. The other is an edited work by Alpheus T. Mason, *The States Rights Debate: Antifederalism and the Constitution* (Englewood Cliffs, N.J.: Prentice-Hall, 1964).

Two excellent sources of information on the political philosophy underlying American federalism are Hamilton, Jay, and Madison, *The Federalist*, and, in the Maass book cited above, Chapter 7, "The Founding Fathers and the Division of Powers," by Samuel Huntington.

For analyses of the role of the Supreme Court in settling legal disputes of federalism see, in the Earle book cited above, "The Role of the Court," by Alpheus Mason, and Samuel Krislov, *The Supreme Court in the Political Process* (New York: Macmillan, 1965), pp. 80–95.

Two general treatments of federalism written primarily for the lay reader are William Anderson, *The Nation and the States, Rivals or Partners?* (Minneapolis: University of Minnesota Press, 1955), and Leonard White, *The States and the Nation* (Baton Rouge: Louisiana State University Press, 1953). The former is pronational, while the latter is more favorable to the states.

A broad treatment of federalism in the United States is Morton Grodzins, *The American System: A New View of Governments in the United States* (Chicago: Rand McNally, 1966). This book was edited by one of his former students, Daniel Elazar, after Grodzins's death. Subsequently, Elazar wrote his own general treatment of American federalism entitled *American Federalism: A View from the States* (New York: Thomas Y. Crowell, 1966). Both books treat of a wide variety of topics and are particularly strong on the historical dimensions and political aspects of American federalism. For a recent analysis of federal-local relations, see Roscoe Martin, *The Cities and the Federal System* (New York: Atherton, 1965).

A number of publications have been written in recent years on the subject of federal grants-in-aid. An excellent treatment of the subject is Deil S. Wright, *Federal Grants-in-Aid: Perspectives and Alternatives* (Washington: American Enterprise Institute, 1968).

Finally, there are many good studies dealing with specific problems of federalism made by public agencies. One series of reports was issued in the 1950s by the Commission on Intergovernmental Relations appointed by President Eisenhower. Another series of very helpful reports has been published in recent years by the Advisory Commission on Intergovernmental Relations, an agency established in 1959 to make continuous analyses of problems of American federalism.

CHAPTER 4

Civil Liberties

Washington police arrest members of the Vietnam Veterans against the War on the steps of the Supreme Court, April 1971. (United Press International)

AMONG THE MORE DRAMATIC FEATURES of American political life in recent years have been the demonstrations against the war in Vietnam. Several held in Washington, D.C. have resulted in confrontations between protesters and law enforcement officers. In October 1967, 50,000 persons gathered at the Lincoln Memorial, while some of their number tried to occupy the Pentagon; eventually close to 700 demonstrators were arrested. In November 1969, 250,000 individuals converged on the nation's capital, with the Justice Department and the South Vietnamese embassy serving as their major assembly points; although this demonstration was more peaceful than the 1967 event, 150 persons were arrested for disorderly conduct at these two sites.

These two incidents, however, were dwarfed by the series of demonstrations involving hundreds of thousands of Americans (including 2300 Vietnam War veterans) that were held over a two-week period in the spring of 1971. This time the major focus of the protests was the Capitol Building, as protestors concentrated on persuading Congress (many of them had given up on influencing the Nixon administration's conduct of the war) to help bring American troops home immediately. Different tactics were also resorted to by some demonstrators who tried unsuccessfully to block traffic into the District of Columbia as a means of preventing government employees from getting to their jobs. Mass arrests also ensued, with 13,000 persons being taken into custody by District of Columbia police between April 24 and May 7.

These incidents symbolized not only the growing split in America over the conduct of the war, but also divergent attitudes on the legitimacy of the demonstrations and the means police use to deal with them. Richard Nixon called the 1967 march on the Pentagon "the most disgraceful incident in the history of the United States" and later praised the way in which the District of Columbia police handled the mass arrests in 1971. Referring to a newspaper editorial headline, "Democracy by Demonstration is a Risky Business," that appeared at the time of the 1969 protests, Mike Mansfield, Majority Leader of the Senate, countered that "Democracy is a risky business and that's one of its strengths." Reacting to the 1971 mass arrests, Democratic Senator Edward Kennedy of Massachusetts told a college dinner gathering: "The city may have been a safe place for cars," but "it was an unsafe place for citizens. If they happened to be going out for coffee, or to class, or getting off the bus at the wrong time in the wrong place, and happened to be young, or bearded, or in casual clothing, or to have the wrong facial expression, they found themselves under arrest."

There is no easy answer to the question of which of these attitudes better comprehends and represents the true democratic tradition. Still, an analysis of the national experiences with basic human rights and the part the American Constitution has played in protecting those rights may help to illuminate the age-old issue of liberty versus authority in a free society.

LIBERTY AND AUTHORITY
IN AMERICA

Shocking as these antiwar demonstrations have been to many Americans, they are not the first political protests held in Washington, D.C. Various groups have taken their grievances to the nation's capital: Coxey's army of the unemployed in the 1890s; Ku Klux Klansmen in the 1930s; ex-soldiers in the Veterans' Bonus March during the Hoover Administration; marchers for Negro rights organized by A. Philip Randolph, first in 1943 and again two decades later in the summer of 1963; and participants in the Poor People's Crusade of 1968. In each instance national authorities faced the difficult task of allowing citizens the liberty to peacefully assemble and petition their government for the redress of grievances (rights guaranteed to them by the First Amendment) and, at the same time, of assuring order and maintaining the authority of the government.

Both liberty and authority have exerted powerful, and divergent, influences on our nation's development. Many of the early settlers came to America for religious liberty, the right to worship God as they saw fit rather than as prescribed by the dictates of an established church. At the time of the Revolutionary War, Patrick Henry proclaimed his choice, "Give me liberty or give me death," and a century later the country fought a bloody civil war over the liberty of the black man. Yet the place of authority in the American political tradition is reflected in the colonists' initial reluctance to use violence to overthrow British rule and our people's continuing attachment to law and order and the attendant legal system inherited from the mother country.

Indeed, the classic problem of all democratic societies is how to reconcile liberty and authority. Madison grasped the essential nature of the issue for constitution-builders when he stated in *Federalist* 51, "In framing a government which is to be administered by men over men, the great difficulty lies in this: you must first enable the government to control the governed; and in the next place, to control itself." Lincoln pointed up the same problem for those seeking to preserve constitutional order. Calling upon Congress in July 1861 to support a series of measures he deemed necessary to the nation's survival, he posed the rhetorical question, "Must the government, of necessity, be too strong for the liberties of its own people, or too weak to maintain its own existence?"

Democratic governments must somehow preserve political authority at the same time that they promote the liberties of their people. The issue becomes not a matter of liberty *or* authority but of liberty *and* authority. For without the minimum conditions of order, individual liberties are meaningless; concomitantly, perfect order is present only in the deadening security of a prison. The crux of the issue is, how much liberty and how much authority? How can a free and secure society achieve a balance between these two values?

Even if a democracy manages to strike a delicate balance between individual liberty on the one hand and governmental authority on the other, another knotty problem remains: how can it also resolve conflicts that arise because the exercise of certain liberties by some persons impinges on different rights claimed by others? A classic case is the newspaper editor who, in the course of enjoying freedom of the press, publishes information relating to a crime that jeopardizes the right of the accused to a fair trial. To assess this issue properly, we must spell out what we mean by civil liberties and examine the kinds of specific freedoms that Americans enjoy.

THE NATURE
OF OUR CIVIL LIBERTIES

USE OF THE TERM

Unfortunately, there is no agreed-upon definition of civil liberties. Some persons use the term to refer only to those freedoms that are protected against infringement by the government, not by private individuals. This is correct historical usage since civil liberties did develop, initially in Great Britain and later in the United States, in the context of the relationship of the individual to the state. In recent times, however, civil liberties problems in the United States have involved the issue of safeguarding such freedoms against violation by private individuals. In fact, the government is now frequently interposed to protect individual freedoms against private infractions.

A closely related issue is the source of civil liberties. Again, the traditional view is that they originate in constitutional provisions alone. Yet a number of fundamental rights now enjoyed by Americans stem not from our basic document but from statutes passed by Congress. For example, the historic Civil Rights Act of 1964 protects minority groups from discrimination in a number of areas—schools, jobs, and public accommodations among them. Moreover, the Act forbids discrimination by both governmental agencies and private individuals.

There is also confusion over the terms civil liberties and civil rights. Some persons use them interchangeably (I will do so in this book); others restrict the latter to issues involving discrimination against any minority group; still others simply equate civil rights with Negro rights. This last, highly limited usage has been prevalent in the United States in recent years, but it is worth keeping in mind that the first ten amendments of the Constitution are referred to as the Bill of Rights, and none of them deals with problems of race.

However the term civil liberties is defined, it covers a broad spectrum of freedoms in America today. Included are such diverse matters as the First Amendment freedoms of religion, speech, press, assembly, and petition; the rights of the accused in criminal cases; the protection of private property; the right to vote; and freedom from discrimination not only in political matters but also in certain economic and social activities. The growth and expansion of such rights constitute one of the major developments of the modern age.

RIGHTS "IN" GOVERNMENT
AND RIGHTS "FROM" GOVERNMENT

It is helpful to distinguish between two major types of liberties protected by the American Constitution, those "in" government and those "from" government. The former relate to participation in the political process. The most obvious such right is voting; however, Americans can affect what the government does in other ways as well. For example, the First Amendment freedoms of speech, press, assembly, and petition permit individuals to communicate their ideas on public issues to governmental officials, as well as to their fellow citizens.

Rights "in" government may properly be viewed from the standpoint not only of the individual who enjoys them but also of the government, which is their ultimate beneficiary. As noted previously, democratic societies assume that there is no one discoverable political truth and that the closest we can come to this ideal is to adopt what emerges as the political choice from the marketplace of ideas. Thus the exercise of the franchise, together with the ancillary rights of speech, press, assembly, and petition, are essential to the operation of a democratic form of government because they become the means for achieving one of the major aims of constitutionalism: holding the rulers *responsible* to the ruled.

The other major aim of constitutionalism is *limiting* the scope of government, walling off areas of human activity from governmental interference. Rights "from" government, then, relate to the private preserves that individuals enjoy against the state. A primary example is freedom of religion, which is safeguarded by the First Amendment. Another is the sanctity of an individual's house (a reflection of the traditional British concept that a man's home is his castle), as well as his person, papers, and effects, against unreasonable searches and seizures. The Second through the Eighth Amendments of the Constitution all serve to protect an individual's property, his freedom of movement, and his life, by providing that he may not be deprived of those attributes by the government except under carefully prescribed conditions. For example, his property may be taken by the government for public use only if he receives just compensation. A person may be fined, imprisoned, or even put to death for committing a crime, but only after the government has followed definite procedures designed to safeguard his interests.

Rights "from" government are thus related to a basic democratic value, that of privacy, what former Supreme Court Justice Louis Brandeis once referred to as "the right to be left alone—the most comprehensive of rights and the right most valued by civilized man." In the 1965 case of *Griswold* v. *Connecticut* the Supreme Court used this general concept as the basis for declaring unconstitutional a state statute that prohibited the use of contraceptives by married couples. The justices held that individuals enjoy a right to marital privacy even though it is not spelled out in so many words by the first eight amendments of the constitution. (The Ninth Amendment, it should be noted, provides that "the enumeration in the Constitution, of certain rights, shall not be construed to deny or disparage others retained by the people.") Thus the Court has been willing to go beyond the rights detailed in the Constitution to recognize additional freedoms related to the idea of privacy.

The American Constitution clearly provides a variety of rights designed to keep the government both responsible to the people and limited in its intrusion into their personal affairs. Yet as the following section indicates, the framers of that fundamental document were not convinced that it should spell out such guarantees. Those provisions of the Constitution with which today's citizens are most familiar—the Bill of Rights—were afterthoughts for most of the Founding Fathers.

THE ADOPTION
OF THE BILL OF RIGHTS

Those who took the initiative in calling the Constitutional Convention were primarily concerned with protecting property rights from threats of state governments. In contrast, they gave virtually no consideration to safeguarding civil liberties from actions of national authorities. When George Mason (a major author of the Virginia Declaration of Rights) proposed near the end of the Convention that a committee be appointed to prepare a Bill of Rights for the document, Roger Sherman replied briefly that the various states already had bills of rights and, therefore, one for the national government was unnecessary. The delegates quickly sided with Sherman on the issue, and Mason's motion failed to draw support from a single state. With the exception of the idealistic (and nonbinding) language of the Preamble referring to "Justice" and "the Blessings of Liberty" and the few restrictions on Congress in Article I, Section 9, the original Constitution emerged from the Convention with few safeguards for civil liberties.

In the ratification campaign the absence of a Bill of Rights became one of the major targets for those opposed to the Constitution. Even Adams and Jefferson, who favored its adoption, were unhappy that the framers had not included a statement of rights. Hamilton said that none was necessary since the national government possessed certain enumerated powers only and thus had no authority to invade individual liberties; Wilson argued that enumerating rights would be dangerous because any not expressly listed would be presumed to have been purposely omitted. And Randolph held that listing rights was futile—"You may cover whole skins of parchment with limitations, but power alone can limit power."

The proponents of a Bill of Rights eventually had their way, however: several of the states ratified the Constitution with the express understanding that the first order of business for the first Congress would be the drawing up of a Bill of Rights to be submitted as amendments to the Constitution. Acting under a moral rather than legal obligation, Washington in his first inaugural address asked Congress to give careful attention to the demands for such amendments, and Madison took the leadership in coordinating the suggestions of state ratifying conventions and introducing them into the House. Congress pared down the list of proposals, and ten were eventually ratified. Both Anti-Federalists and Federalists gained from the process: the former saw their initial support for a Bill of Rights vindicated while the latter gained additional popular support for the Constitution they authored.

Proclaiming such a series of rights in a written document is one thing; observing them in actual practice is another. As Roger Sherman warned, "No bill of rights ever yet bound the supreme power longer than the honeymoon of a new married couple unless the rulers were interested in preserving the rights." The following section assesses the historical record of national officials in the United States in safeguarding civil liberties.

THE RECORD
OF THE NATIONAL GOVERNMENT
ON CIVIL LIBERTIES

The long-term record of the national government in protecting civil liberties is generally good, comparing favorably with that of most other democracies in the world. However, there is one major blot on that record which we will examine in depth in Chapter 15: the treatment of the American Negro. That issue has persisted throughout our history, but there have also been certain eras when the fundamental freedoms of other Americans as well have been placed in jeopardy by national officials.

THE ALIEN AND SEDITION ACTS OF 1798

The basic guarantees of the Bill of Rights that had been added to the Constitution in the early 1790s were in jeopardy before the end of the decade. As we will see in Chapter 7, some of the major allies in the writing and adoption of the Constitution came to an early parting of political ways: Hamilton, Washington, and Adams emerged as leaders of the Federalist party, while Madison and Jefferson founded the opposition Republican organization. The bitter partisan rivalry between the two, augmented by Federalist fears that radical ideas of the French Revolution were being carried by French immigrants to America and fostered here by pro-French Republican leaders, led to the enactment of major legislation to put down internal threats to the new republic. Included were laws granting the President the right to deport aliens whom he considered to be dangerous to the nation, as well as a sedition statute making it a crime to speak or write against either the President or members of the Congress with the intent of defaming those officials or bringing them into contempt or disrepute.

Fortunately for the nation, President Adams had no enthusiasm for the Alien laws, and he did not actually expel any foreigners of French descent, although some did leave the country in anticipation of trouble. The Sedition law, however, was enforced: twenty-five men were arrested and ten eventually jailed or fined, including one congressman. Editors of the Republican press were singled out as special targets of the Sedition law, and Federalist judges applied and interpreted the law with blatant partisanship. Federalist officials handpicked the jurors, and courts frequently deprived the accused of his legal right to use the truth of his objectionable statements as a defense.

The Alien and Sedition Acts (the latter in particular) proved to be detrimental to the new nation's attempt to balance order and security with freedom and liberty. Many Federalist officials overreacted to the threat of internal subversion and showed little appreciation of the role of legitimate dissent and an opposition party in a democratic society. Fortunately, this invasion of the First Amendment freedoms of speech and press was cut short when the Republican party swept into political power in 1800 by soundly defeating the Federalists for the Presidency and the Congress.

THE CIVIL WAR PERIOD

The severest test of the national government's ability to meet Madison's criterion of controlling both the governed and itself came during the Civil War. This time President Lincoln and his party faced, not the remote possibility that a foreign ideology would be successfully imported to America, but rather a severe internal crisis based on bitter differences over a genuine domestic issue: the fate of slavery in the territories. Nor was there any question of the disloyalty to the Union that prevailed in the Border States. Southern sympathizers there spied on Northern forces, recruited for the enemy, and committed sabotage. Others in the North, who wanted a peaceful solution to the conflict, did not actively assist the South, but they did try to impede the Union's prosecution of the war by discouraging enlistments, promoting desertions, and circulating disloyal literature.

President Lincoln responded with a series of drastic actions that invaded a number of fundamental American freedoms. He suspended the writ of habeas corpus, whereby citizens are entitled to have officials holding them in custody come before a judicial officer and show good cause why they are confined. When Chief Justice Taney ruled that the suspension was illegal because only Congress, and not the President, had that right, Lincoln ignored the judicial decree on the grounds that he did have constitutional authority, and even if he did not, his action was justified to preserve the Union. Throughout the war, suspected individuals were taken into custody by military authorities, some had their property confiscated, and others served long sentences—all without the traditional safeguards provided by the regular courts. Moreover, this brand of military justice was even meted out to civilians in areas where the regular civil courts were open; only after the war was over did the Supreme Court rule in the famous *Milligan* case that such a procedure was unconstitutional. Beyond this, the President issued decrees censoring the mails and newspapers in the interest of national security.

There is little question that many traditional rights "in" and "from" government that Americans enjoy during peacetime were denied them during the Civil War. But never before (or for that matter since) had the government been under such a severe threat. Lincoln himself put the question to the Congress whether the traditional right to habeas corpus should be observed in wartime: "Are all the laws but one to go unexecuted, and the government itself to go to pieces lest that one be violated?" That is, does not the survival of the government which is necessary for the enforcement of all laws, justify the violation of one of them in an emergency? This basic question of the status of civil liberties in time of war has continued to confront the nation in the twentieth century.

THE WORLD-WAR-I ERA

World War I was the first time the United States mobilized the entire society for a military conflict. President Wilson was given broad authorization over the economy by Congress, along with the authority to control the foreign-language press in the United States and the power to censor the mails. Congress itself passed two major pieces of legislation designed to safeguard the national security against internal enemies. The Espionage Act of 1917 made it a crime to interfere with the military draft or to encourage insubordination in the armed services; the more comprehensive sedition law passed the following year also established punishments for utterances and printed matter that were disloyal to, or abusive of, our form of government or the Constitution.

Federal authorities exercised their new authority by banning certain

newspapers from the mails and by arresting over 1500 persons for disloyalty. The Justice Department under the leadership of the infamous A.
Mitchell Palmer made illegal raids and arrests, seized private property, and
held persons without bail. Singled out as particular targets were German-
Americans, as well as labor leaders, Socialists, and Communists who were
considered sympathetic to the Bolshevik Revolution in the Soviet Union. In
fact, the Red Scare that followed the war resulted in more indiscriminate
violations of civil liberties than did the anti-German sentiment during actual
hostilities. Equally as reprehensible as the Justice Department's own performance (if not more so) was its toleration of the activities of ultrapatriotic private groups that assisted in ferreting out the nation's enemies. One
such group, the American Patriotic League, with a quarter of a million
members, was actually officially sponsored by the Department of Justice
and equipped with badges for its vigilante activities.

Like the 1798–1800 period, the dark age from 1918–1920 was brought to
a close by the election of a new party in the latter year. With the coming to
power of the Republicans, Palmer no longer enjoyed a base of operations.
Ironically, the new President, Warren G. Harding, not known for his devotion to liberal causes, pardoned Socialist leader Eugene Debs, who had been
given a long prison sentence for exhorting an audience to "resist militarism
wherever found."

WORLD WAR II AND AFTER

Like their predecessors in previous wars, President Roosevelt and Congress during World War II exercised vast powers over the domestic as well
as the war front. Generally speaking, however, political authorities were
much more solicitous of civil liberties than had been the case in either the
Civil War or World War I. In place of A. Mitchell Palmer, the nation had,
as its chief legal officer, Francis Biddle, a man committed to personal liberties. As a result there were no wholesale raids on groups suspected of disloyalty by either the Department of Justice agents or by private vigilante
groups. By the 1940s German-Americans were no longer a distinct ethnic
group and thus were not subject to the bitter attacks they had suffered in
the previous war. Nor were Americans of Italian background suspect, since
many Italian citizens were not sympathetic to the war.

One group, however, became the object of blatant discriminatory treatment in World War II: American citizens of Japanese ancestry living on
the West Coast. False newspaper stories of sabotage supposedly committed
by Japanese-Americans in Hawaii at the time of Pearl Harbor, plus wild rumors that information on ships leaving the West Coast was being conveyed
to waiting Japanese submarines, helped develop public hysteria that the
Nisei (second-generation Japanese-Americans) presented a great danger to
national security. President Roosevelt, the Congress, and the military chiefs
joined in developing a series of regulations against the Nisei: initially they

The most severe threats to our civil liberties have occurred during a war or a period of intense domestic concern with foreign subversion. (Above) Japanese-Americans in an evacuation center, 1942. (Below) Senator Joseph McCarthy, shown with his aide Roy Cohn. McCarthy capitalized on anxieties about communist influence after World War II to mount a campaign of political terror. (Above: Brown Brothers; below: Pix)

were subjected to a curfew; later they were banned from wide areas on the Coast; and ultimately tens of thousands were taken from their homes and transported to relocation centers in interior states such as Utah and Colorado. A sensationalist press; unscrupulous persons who bought up property of the departing Nisei (estimates of their losses were later set as high as $400,000,000); a commanding general who said "It is better to have this protection [segregation of the Japanese] and not to have needed it, than to have needed it and not to have had it"; plus the reluctance of the Attorney General and the majority of Supreme Court members to question matters of "military necessity" during a war—all contributed to what one student of the subject has called our "worst wartime mistake." Ironically, the facts ultimately showed that there was not a single act of sabotage committed by a Japanese-American either in Hawaii or on the West Coast during the entire war, and the 442nd combat team of the Fifth Army in Italy, which included mainland Nisei, became one of the most decorated American units in military history.

Like the post-World-War-I era, the period after World War II was also characterized by a Red Scare in America. Again it was related to anxieties about the Soviet Union. Disillusioned with the aggressive tactics in Eastern Europe of a former ally, the fall of China to the Communists in 1949, and the outbreak of the Korean War the following year, Americans became concerned with the Russian threat to our national interests. At the same time, revelations of activities of some Communist sympathizers within the government during the 1930s and 1940s raised fears of internal subversion. An atmosphere of fear and distrust permeated the nation as congressional investigating committees probed into the backgrounds and associations of suspected persons, and the executive branch screened millions of its employees under the loyalty programs of the Truman and Eisenhower administrations. In the process, persons were discharged from government positions on dubious evidence provided by faceless accusers; similarly, witnesses badgered by congressional inquisitors suffered loss of reputation and often jobs as well, simply on the basis of their appearance before investigating committees of the House and Senate. The period, known as the "McCarthy" era because it was dominated by the politically ambitious and unscrupulous senator from Wisconsin, Joseph R. McCarthy, came to a close when he eventually came into conflict with such traditionally conservative organizations as the Army and Senate. Despite its brevity, however, the period of the late 1940s and early 1950s will be remembered as one of the darkest hours for civil liberties in the nation's history.

As one analyzes the eras when the national government put traditional freedoms into jeopardy, it becomes clear that they coincide with one of two basic situations: war or a period of domestic unease caused by fears of the spread of radical political ideas and of subversion by foreign agents and disloyal citizens.

CONSTITUTIONAL RESTRICTIONS
ON STATE VIOLATIONS
OF CIVIL LIBERTIES

Early in our constitutional history, the states rather than the national government showed the greater concern for civil liberties. Jefferson and Mason drafted Virginia's Declaration of Rights shortly before the Declaration of Independence was signed. In it they set forth the same general tenets that were later echoed in the more famous document: men are entitled to certain inherent rights of life, liberty, property, and the pursuit of happiness. Moreover, the Virginia Declaration spelled out in much greater detail than the national one the basic freedoms of the press and religion, and the right to a jury trial that were safeguarded against action by Virginia officials. Other jurisdictions followed suit, with the result that all the early state constitutions either contained a separate bill of rights or incorporated similar provisions as part of the basic document.

When the first Congress turned to the development of a Bill of Rights, its primary attention was focused on the national authorities for obvious reasons: this was the level of government that persons concerned with civil liberties feared, and in any event state officials were restricted by their own constitutions. At one point the House did propose an amendment prohibiting states from infringing on the right to trial by jury in criminal cases or on rights of conscience, speech, and the press, but the measure was defeated by the Senate. Although the first ten amendments nowhere stated specifically that they there were to apply to the national government and not the states (the First Amendment does read, however, "Congress shall make the law," and presumably this phrase is to be read into the amendments that follow), this was undoubtedly the intention of the persons who drafted them in the early 1790s, and four decades later the Supreme Court so ruled in *Barron* v. *Baltimore* (1833).

What the Senate and the Court initially refused to do—that is, to utilize the first ten amendments to restrict state as well as national authorities—has largely come to pass today as a result of a number of decisions of the Supreme Court. In 1925 the Court held in *Gitlow* v. *New York* that freedom of speech and the press are such fundamental rights that they should be construed as "liberties" protected by the Fourteenth Amendment from impairment by states. Subsequently, by similar judicial reasoning, all the other First Amendment freedoms have been added to the liberties so protected. To date the Court has been unwilling to say that the Bill of Rights applies *in toto* to the states, but, as we will see in Chapter 13, virtually all the procedural safeguards set forth in Amendments Four through Eight, which federal authorities must respect in criminal cases, have now been held to bind state officials as well in proceedings against persons accused of violating state laws. Thus the afterthought of the national Constitution—the first ten amendments—has become a major source of rights "in" and rights "from" government at the state level, while state constitutions—which served as inspirations for the Bill of Rights—have proved to be less effective in protecting civil liberties.

THE RECORD OF STATE GOVERNMENTS ON CIVIL LIBERTIES

It is, of course, difficult to assess the record of the various jurisdictions in the United States over the years in safeguarding civil liberties. Experiences naturally vary not only from one historical era to another but also from state to state. Still, we can conclude that as a whole the record of the states is not as good as that of the national government. For one thing, in a number of areas relating to civil liberties, the actions of state and local officials touch the life of citizens far more significantly and consistently than do those of national authorities. The states are primarily responsible for establishing the conditions for the most fundamental right "in" government: voting, for national as well as state officials. In addition, the rights of the accused in criminal cases are mainly affected by actions of state and local policemen, prosecutors, and judges; the number of possible violations of federal criminal statutes is minuscule compared to potential transgressions at lower political levels. Finally, Madison's statement that the national government would have to restrain state governments by protecting local minorities against local majorities has turned out to be remarkably prophetic. Federal efforts to improve the treatment of the Negro minority in Southern states is the classic example of that development, but it also applies to other minority groups, such as Orientals on the West Coast and Mexicans in Texas, who at one time were subjected to discriminatory state laws relating to the ownership of property, marriage, getting jobs, and the use of public facilities.

Nor have the states and localities been free of ultrapatriotic crusades in response to war or perceived threats of internal subversion. In many instances their zeal has equaled or exceeded that of the national government. Public names of German origin were changed and German-language classes and books banned in schools and communities all over the United States during World War I. The first Red Scare was epitomized at the state level by the expulsion of five Socialists from the New York legislature in 1920, and the second by the flurry of teachers' loyalty oaths and investigations by little Un-American Activities committees that occurred in the late 1940s and early 1950s.

The fate of civil liberties at both the national and state levels thus depends on a number of crucial factors: the general climate of the times; the attitudes and actions of executive and legislative officials who occupy public positions that affect personal rights; and the role courts assume in protecting civil liberties. The remainder of this chapter focuses on how these matters have affected our most fundamental freedoms: those set forth in the First Amendment. Elsewhere in the book we will examine other basic rights relating to voting (Chapter 9), procedural safeguards in criminal trials (Chapter 13), and equal opportunity for the American Negro (Chapter 15).

FREEDOM OF RELIGION

Americans, who enjoy freedom from governmental interference in religious matters, frequently assume that this right has been traditional since the Puritans fled England in the early 1620s and came to Massachusetts to escape the dictates of the official Anglican Church. The facts of the matter, however, are that the Puritans proceeded to establish a church of their own —the Congregational—and forced all inhabitants to follow its religious precepts. Other colonies followed a similar practice, and as late as the Revolutionary War most of them had established churches.

The established churches that prevailed before the Revolution did not survive long in the postwar period. The Virginia Declaration of Rights of 1776 contained an article on religious freedom drafted by Patrick Henry, and three years later the Anglican Church there was disestablished. A proposal favored by Patrick Henry and George Washington to make all Christian churches state religions of equal standing and to support them by taxation was rejected in favor of the preference of Madison, Jefferson, and Mason for the separation of religious and civil affairs. As this policy was enunciated in the famous Virginia Statute of Religious Liberty of 1786, "no man shall be compelled to frequent or support any religious worship, place or ministry whatsoever." This general attitude towards church-state relations also became dominant in other states as the proliferation of religious sects made it the only practical course of action to pursue.

Religious freedom also became a national policy. It was written into the Northwest Ordinance of 1787 providing for the governance of those territories, and that same year was implemented in the constitutional clause prohibiting the use of a religious test as a requirement for public office (Article VI). Finally, religious freedom was guaranteed in the First Amendment's provision that "Congress shall make no law respecting an establishment of religion, or prohibiting the free exercise thereof."

Historically the Bill of Rights served as a check on the national government only, and therefore actions of state and local officials on religious matters were not affected by the provisions of the national Constitution. In 1940, however, in the case of *Cantwell* v. *Connecticut*, the Supreme Court extended the principle of its previously mentioned 1925 decision on free speech (it is so fundamental that it should be construed as a "liberty" safeguarded by the Fourteen Amendment) so as to make it also applicable to the states. With this decision, the First Amendment protection of free choice in religion, which had been of little constitutional importance up to that time (few activities of national authorities touched on religious matters), became a matter of great concern as state and local actions affecting religious freedom began to be challenged in the federal courts.

It should be noted that the relevant First Amendment provisions contain two separate concepts: (1) the government cannot by law establish religion, nor (2) can it prohibit the free exercise of religion. Thus public authorities cannot take either positive or negative action with respect to religious matters. Although these two concepts are somewhat related, for the most part they convey distinct ideas and have been so treated by the courts. For these reasons, we will examine them separately.

PROHIBITION AGAINST
THE ESTABLISHMENT OF RELIGION

The first major case in which the Supreme Court directly articulated the concept of separation of church and state was *Everson* v. *Board of Education*, decided in 1947. The case arose in New Jersey, where, pursuant to state law, a local school board reimbursed parents for costs they incurred in transporting their children to parochial schools. Since the Court by this time had ruled that religious liberty was protected against state action by the Fourteenth Amendment, the issue in the case was whether such expenditure of funds constituted the establishment of religion.

The majority opinion written by Justice Hugo L. Black interpreted the principle of the separation of church and state to mean that neither the federal nor a state government can pass laws which "aid one religion, aid all religions, or prefer one religion over another." Nor can either levy a tax to support any religious activity. He went on to adopt Jefferson's thesis that there must be a "wall of separation" between church and state, even though no such language appears in the First Amendment itself. (Jefferson used the famous phrase in 1802 in a letter to a religious group explaining his interpretation of the First Amendment.)

But having enunciated what appeared to be a strict interpretation of church-state relations, Justice Black and the majority of the Court nevertheless held that the reimbursement of parents did not violate the wall-of-separation principle and hence was constitutional. They took the position that the use of public funds for transportation did not aid religion or the church, but rather benefited the children by contributing to their safety. Four judges dissented from the majority opinion. Justice Jackson said that the majority view reminded him of Byron's heroine, Julia, who "whispering 'I will ne'er consent'—consented." Another contended that the child-benefit theory employed by the majority could be employed with equal justification for other expenditures for parochial schools, including teachers' salaries, buildings, equipment, school lunches, textbooks, and so forth, since all ultimately benefit the child who attends the school.

The Supreme Court has remained divided on the issue raised by the *Everson* case. Both groups of justices agree on the general principle that there should be a separation of church and state, but they differ on how it should be applied to the expenditure of public funds to aid parochial schools. Those upholding such expenditures do so on the basis of the child-benefit theory, while those who consider the expenditures a violation of church-state relationship take the position that assistance to parochial schools financially benefits the churches which establish them, since otherwise these churches (or the parents that support them) have to absorb the costs themselves. To date the former group has generally prevailed, as the Supreme Court has sustained financial aid for nonreligious textbooks used in parochial schools; as yet it has not ruled on whether state or local expenditures for other purposes, such as buildings and equipment, violate the Fourteenth Amendment. In one instance, however, the justices have drawn the line on public expenditures for parochial schools: in 1971 the Court invalidated, as "excessive entanglement" of church and state, laws of Pennsylvania and Rhode Island that permitted public funds to be used to pay part of the salaries of instructors in parochial schools teaching non-religious subjects.

Behind the dispute over the application of the child-benefit theory to expenditures for parochial schools lies a more fundamental difference in attitude concerning the role that such schools can and should play in a democratic society. Those who support expenditures for parochial schools take the position that they are important for the education of a large number of students in our society, and that without them the public schools would be forced to absorb more students, with a consequent rise in educational costs. They also point out that, as the Supreme Court held in a 1925 case, *Pierce* v. *Society of Sisters*, parents have a legal right to send their children to parochial schools, and if this right is to become meaningful, then some assistance for those schools is needed to relieve the double financial burden of parents who now must pay taxes for public schools that their children do not attend. Finally, the parochial schools are not viewed as raising serious religious problems in American society because they devote most of their activities to educating students in secular rather than sectarian subjects.

Those who oppose public expenditures for parochial schools take the general position that public schools have had an important democratizing influence by bringing together children of various religious backgrounds in their formative years. They regard the separation of children in the schools on the basis of religion as undesirable, particularly since religious differences are often related to ethnic, social, and economic distinctions among individuals. They, therefore, do not want to see the government take any action that may foster parochial schools at the expense of public ones. They feel that if parents want to send their children to church-supported rather than to public schools, they should bear the financial burden of that choice themselves and not expect the rest of society to assist with it. Finally, they believe that it is not possible in the educational process to draw clear distinctions between sectarian and secular matters and that religious points of view have an effect on how nonreligious subjects are taught.

The Supreme Court has been faced in recent years with another issue relating to the establishment of religion: whether public schools themselves may foster religious exercises in any way. In a 1948 case, *McCollum* v. *Board of Education*, the Court held that school officials in Illinois violated the establishment clause by permitting religious leaders to come to the school during the regular hours to conduct religious classes for students whose parents desired that they receive such instruction. (Other students were given a study period during that time.) Subsequently, however, in *Zorach* v. *Clauson* (1952) the Court held that a similar practice in New York was constitutional because the instruction took place off school property. Dissenting judges argued that where the instruction took place was unimportant and that the use of New York's compulsory school-attendance law to promote religious instruction during regular school hours constituted an establishment of religion.

Recent cases indicate that, while the Court will tolerate religious instruction held off school property during the school day, it will not permit school authorities to conduct religious exercises. In *Engel* v. *Vitale* (1962) the justices declared unconstitutional a practice in New York State of reciting during the regular school period a prayer composed by state officials. That the prayer was religiously neutral, favoring no sect or creed ("Almighty God, we acknowledge our dependence upon thee and we beg thy blessings upon us, our parents, our teachers, and our country"), and that the prayer was voluntary, so students who objected to it did not have to participate in the ceremony, made no difference to the justices. The following year, the Court, in *Abington Township School District* v. *Schempp*, outlawed the reading of the Bible or the recitation of the Lord's Prayer in the public schools. In both cases there was only one dissenter, Justice Potter Stewart, who declared that none of these practices constituted the establishment of religion.

As with the issue of financial aid to the parochial schools, important policy differences exist between those who favor and those who oppose religious exercises in public schools. The former argue that majorities as well as minorities have rights, and it is no great burden on the students who do not want to participate to remain quiet during the ceremonies. The opposition takes the position that the failure to participate in such exercises tends to brand the individuals involved as "odd balls" in the eyes of their fellow students, and that, in any event, religious instruction should be left to other institutions in society—the family and the church—that are better able to offer it than the public schools, which are designed to provide secular education.

Beyond differences about whether a particular practice is wise or unwise for good church-state relationships in a free society, there is also fundamental disagreement over what the Founding Fathers meant to prohibit as regards the establishment of religion. One general line of thinking is that they merely wanted to prevent governmental officials from preferring one religion over another. Under this interpretation the national government (and now state or local ones) can financially support religious activities or foster them in other ways so long as they do not discriminate among various sects and churches in the process. A stricter interpretation of the establishment clause is that those who wrote it into the First Amendment desired to prohibit public officials from undertaking activities that would promote any or all religious groups. Under this reasoning the clause is designed to prevent discrimination not only among religious groups but also between religious and irreligious ones. Thus persons who do not believe in a Supreme Being and agnostics who have doubts about His existence are also meant to be protected by the establishment clause.

Whatever the historical merits of these two interpretations may be, we do not have a complete separation of church and state in the United States. Financial support for religion exists in the form of salaries paid to chaplains that serve the spiritual needs of members of Congress, the service academies, and military forces. Indirect financial assistance is also provided to churches in the form of exemption from the payment of taxes on property used for religious purposes, a practice that has recently been declared constitutional by the Court. Nor have we removed all vestiges of religion from our public life. Even though the Supreme Court has banned prayers from the public schools, they are still used to open sessions of Congress and the Supreme Court, and each year since 1952, under congressional authority, the President has declared a National Day of Prayer. Finally, the phrase "in God we trust" appears on both our coins and paper money, and during the Eisenhower administration the words "under God" were added to the Pledge of Allegiance to the Flag.

It remains to be seen how many (if any) of the above practices will eventually be successfully attacked as unconstitutional. With the exception of the holding of religious exercises in the public schools, to date public authorities (including Supreme Court justices) have not been inclined to a strict interpretation of Jefferson's concept of a wall of separation between church and state.

THE FREE EXERCISE OF RELIGION

Cases involving the free exercise of religion reached the Supreme Court prior to those relating to the establishment of religion. The first major case,

Reynolds v. *United States,* arose in the late 1870s over the Mormon practice of plural marriages. Congress passed a law against polygamy in the territories, and the issue posed by its action was whether this law violated the First Amendment clause prohibiting the national government from interfering with the free exercise of religion. In its decision the Court made a clear distinction between religious beliefs and actions stemming from those beliefs. Thus, the justices reasoned, Mormons could hold the belief that God permits men to have as many wives as possible, but they had no right to implement their belief because it violates social duty and order.

In other instances, however, the Court has permitted religious groups to act on their beliefs even though in so doing they affect the rights of others. A classic series of cases arose in the 1930s and 1940s as a result of activities of members of the Jehovah's Witnesses sect. Acting on the belief that each member of the group is a minister and has the duty to spread the gospel, Witnesses distributed and sold religious literature in the public streets without complying with state and local laws relating to permits, fees, or taxes. The Court upheld their activities and also sustained the right to pass out religious tracts door to door in residential areas. In sustaining such actions the Court balanced the religious liberty of Jehovah's Wittnesses to propagate their faith against the right of individuals to privacy—that is, the freedom of individuals not to be bothered by persons seeking to convert them to religious beliefs—and found the former to be more important.

Another line of cases relating to the free exercise of religion turns on the issue of whether public authorities can force persons to take actions that run counter to their religious beliefs. Two landmark cases in the early 1940s put to constitutional test the practice in some states of requiring students as a part of daily exercises to salute the flag under penalty of being expelled from school. In the first one, *Minersville School District* v. *Gobitis* (1940), the Supreme Court upheld the statute on the grounds that if the legislature felt that the ritual instilled patriotism in children and thus promoted national unity, the Court ought not to interfere with that judgment. Just three years later, however, in *West Virginia State Board of Education* v. *Barnett,* the Court overruled the earlier decision under the reasoning that public officials could not compel students to utter words which they did not believe. In so ruling, Justice Roberts held that under our Constitution, no official can prescribe what is orthodox in politics, nationalism, or religion and force others to confess to such beliefs. Under such circumstances a person has the right to remain silent.

Still another related issue is the observance of days of rest. In a 1961 case, *McGowan* v. *Maryland,* the Supreme Court upheld the constitutionality of Sunday-closing laws against attacks that they denied freedom of religion to individuals who closed their stores on Saturday in keeping with their beliefs. In so doing, the Court held that, although Sunday was originally celebrated as a day of rest for religious reasons, it is now a secular holiday, set aside for recreation and family activities. Thus closing laws are no longer related to religious beliefs. The Court also pointed out that persons who celebrate Saturday as a religious holiday are free to close their stores on that day. While recognizing the potential economic burden (their stores would then be closed on both Saturday and Sunday), the justices held that this is merely the indirect effect, and not the purpose, of a law regulating secular activity.

Thus the Supreme Court has tried to balance the religious rights of the individuals against the interests of other individuals and of society generally. As the following section indicates, the justices have struggled to achieve a similar equilibrium with respect to other vital First Amendment freedoms.

FREEDOM OF EXPRESSION

In addition to freedom of religion, the First Amendment spells out a number of other rights with which Congress may not interfere: freedom of speech and the press, the right of peaceful assembly, and the right to petition the government for a redress of grievances. Together they constitute means by which individuals or groups express their views and communicate them to one another, as well as to their public officials. Insofar as such expressions relate to public issues, they are rights "in" government, enabling citizens to try to influence public decisions. When they pertain to nonpublic affairs and concerns, however, they are rights "from" government, for they protect the freedom to communicate views on private matters.

The Supreme Court has recently recognized another related freedom, that of association, even though no such right appears in the language of the First Amendment itself. In protecting a Southern chapter of the National Association for the Advancement of Colored People from a state law requiring it publicly to divulge its membership, the Court ruled, in *NAACP v. Alabama* (1958), that "freedom to engage in association for the advancement of beliefs and ideas is an inseparable aspect of the 'liberty' assured by . . . the Fourteenth Amendment which embraces freedom of speech." The Court did not restrict this freedom of association for public issues only; it rather said that "it is immaterial whether the beliefs sought to be advanced by associations pertain to political, economic, religious, or cultural affairs." Thus freedom of association is to be added to other First Amendment rights. (Because the case involved not only the right to associate but also the right to keep group membership lists confidential, the decision also indicates the Supreme Court's concern with the issue of privacy.)

Like religious freedom, those First Amendment liberties relating to expression did not become a matter of major concern for the Supreme Court until relatively recent times. The earliest threat to these liberties posed by the Alien and Sedition laws of 1798 ended with the Federalist loss of political power in 1800, and no freedom-of-expression matter reached the Court during the Civil War era. It was not until 1919 that the highest tribunal first directly faced an issue of free speech, in a case (to be discussed below) concerned with antiwar activities during World War I. As we shall see, this general problem of reconciling freedom of expression with national security has continued to be a major concern of the Court in the post-World-War-II era as well. In the 1960s civil rights and anti-Vietnam protests presented the Court with still other vital issues involving First Amendment liberties.

Before discussing decisions in these areas, it will be helpful to analyze the general approaches the Court has adopted in seeking to reconcile the right of personal expression with society's concern for order and authority. With these approaches, in mind, we will then examine how the Court has applied them to specific situations concerning national security and political protest.

GENERAL APPROACHES TO THE ISSUE

Of the various approaches to the issue of freedom of expression, the one advocated by former Supreme Court Justice Hugo Black is the most *absolute*. Black argued that the Founding Fathers wanted the words of the First Amendment to be taken literally; the phrase that Congress shall make "no law" abridging the freedom of speech or of the press means just that—national authorities (and presumably state ones as well) cannot take any action that interferes with the free expression of views. Justice Black even went so far as to suggest that the First Amendment means that libel and slander actions (suits brought by private individuals against others who have defamed their character or reputation through written or oral statement) cannot be brought in federal courts. He was also unwilling to have restrictions placed on newspaper comments on criminal cases even though these comments jeopardize the right of the accused persons to a fair trial.

While Justice Black held absolutist views regarding the constitutional sanctity of the oral and printed word, he did not extend this attitude to conduct or action. For example, he did not recognize picketing as an absolute right, even though the Supreme Court ruled in *Thornhill* v. *Alabama* (1940) that it is a form of symbolic speech and is thus entitled to the protection of the First Amendment. Moreover, Justice Black took a rather conservative position on the methods by which speech can be implemented. He stated that freedom of speech does not mean that a person can express himself whenever, wherever, and however he pleases. In line with this reasoning, he contended that one person cannot use another person's private property to exercise freedom of expression, and that there are even limits on the utilization of public property for such a purpose. Thus Justice Black believed the First Amendment protects absolutely the *content* of speech but not the *manner* by which it is expressed.

A similar general view on freedom of expression was advocated by the late philosopher Alexander Meiklejohn. His attitudes, however, derived not from the historical meaning of the First Amendment itself but from the logic of *self-government*. He argued that freedom of expression is important not only for the individual but also for society; it is not just his right to speak that is involved but also society's obligation to hear what he has to say. The only way to assure that a free society will arrive at good decisions is to see to it that all viewpoints are considered, no matter how wrong or dangerous we may consider some of them to be. Meiklejohn suggested that it is not a question of balancing intellectual freedom against public safety, rather, that freedom is the bulwark of public safety.

The major difference between Black's and Meiklejohn's views is that Black would apply his absolutist approach to expressions relating to both public and private concerns, while Meiklejohn would restrict his to public affairs. Thus the philosopher, unlike the judge, would not bar private libel and slander suits and would tolerate other reasonable restraints on utterances not relating to "community-thinking" or "self-government." Like Black, Meiklejohn would allow restrictions to be placed on the manner in which speech is expressed. For example, the government may suspend utterances until order is established, so that all views may be heard. As he himself expressed it, "When the roof falls in, the moderator may, without violating the First Amendment, declare the meeting adjourned."

Two other general approaches to freedom of expression concern the posture the Supreme Court should take in passing on speech and allied rights. We will examine the general role of the Court with respect to judicial review in Chapter 14; it is sufficient for our purposes here to say that judges differ on the extent to which they should interfere with the actions of legislators and executives on the grounds that they are unconstitutional. Some argue for an "activist" role for the Court, requiring judges to scrutinize carefully the activities of other public officials and to invalidate those that violate what they conceive to be constitutional principles; others feel that Supreme Court justices should assume a "nonactivist" role by presuming the actions of legislators and executives to be constitutional and seldom substituting their constitutional judgments for judgments of those officials.

Those who adopt a *preferred-position* approach to the expression issue (the position is generally associated with former Supreme Court Justices Harlan Stone and Wiley Rutledge, but other judges have also followed it) believe that when such rights become involved in litigation, the Court should take an activist role in reviewing the actions of legislators and executives. The reason is that the First Amendment freedoms are so basic to maintaining the openness of our political system and society that they deserve special or preferred treatment by the courts over other issues. Thus the Court should carefully scrutinize actions of public officials relating to freedom of expression at the same time that it presumes that their activities regulating economic affairs are constitutional. The basis for this special solicitude for rights of free expression is that such rights are particularly important for unpopular minority groups that frequently cannot protect their interests in the political processes of the legislative and executive branches. The special phrasing of the First Amendment (the Congress "shall make no law" respecting religion and expression) further justifies the Court's looking carefully at governmental regulation of such matters rather than presuming them to be constitutional.

The difference between the preferred-position approach and the views advocated by Black and Meiklejohn is thus one of degree. The latter two argue that political authorities cannot place *any* restrictions on the content of political expressions, while those who adopt the preferred-position approach are willing to permit some restrictions, but only under very special circumstances. All three approaches evidence a special solicitude for First Amendment freedoms and require that they be granted a special place in our constitutional order of values.

The man most critical of all the above approaches was former Supreme Court Justice Felix Frankfurter. He was a "nonactivist" who felt that judges should be very reluctant to substitute their constitutional judgments for those of legislative and executive officials on all kinds of issues, including those pertaining to expression. He attacked the preferred-position approach to the problem as a "mischievous phrase" that "attempts to express a complex process of adjudication by a deceptive formula"; he also rejected the absolutist positions of Black and Meiklejohn as doctrinaire. In place of such approaches Frankfurter called for a pragmatic "*balancing*," that is, a case-by-case weighing of competing values, and the exercise of judgment in deciding when restrictions on freedom of expression are warranted in order to protect society's interest in order and authority, or the rights of other individuals or groups. Thus Frankfurter rejected the idea that freedom of expression is either an absolute value or one that is to be necessarily preferred over other legitimate interests.

Although these general approaches to freedom of expression reflect important basic attitudes towards this vital issue, they have not proved to be very helpful in dealing with the wide variety of pertinent cases that have come to the Supreme Court in the last half-century. Although Justice Douglas has moved closer to Black's position in recent years, no other justices have been willing to adopt an absolutist approach. The preferred-position and balancing approaches have been expressed in opinions from time to time, but both reflect a general mood rather than a usable guideline. Thus the former merely suggests that restrictions on freedom of expression are only constitutional under unusual circumstances without indicating what those circumstances are; the latter calls for a balancing of interests without determining the specific interests to be balanced and the weights to be assigned to each.

In attempting to develop more usable guidelines, the Supreme Court has turned to another type of attack on the problem. Rather than look at the issue from the standpoint of the historical meaning of the First Amendment, the logic of self-government, or a general philosophy concerning the role of the Supreme Court vis-à-vis legislators and executives in the protection of free speech, some judges have placed the issue on an *empirical* basis. In doing so, they have utilized certain basic tests relating to the actual consequences of given expressions.

TESTS OF THE CONSEQUENCES
OF EXPRESSION

The judge most prominently identified with analyzing freedom of expression on the basis of consequences was Justice Oliver Wendell Holmes, Jr. In the *Schenck* case of 1919 referred to earlier, which involved the indictment of a Socialist for violating the World War I Espionage Act by circulating antiwar leaflets to members of the armed forces, the celebrated jurist spelled out the test to be applied in free speech cases. Rejecting an absolutist approach by suggesting that no man had the constitutional right to falsely shout fire in a theatre, Holmes stated:

> The question in every case is whether the words are used in such circumstances and are of such a nature as to create a clear and present danger that they will bring about the substantive evils that Congress has a right to prevent. It is a question of proximity and degree.

In this particular case Justice Holmes upheld the conviction on the basis that the antiwar actions did create a *"clear and present danger"* to the prosecution of the war, an evil that Congress had the right to prevent. Later that same year, however, in a dissenting opinion in *Abrams* v. *United States*, Holmes held that restrictions on the publication of pamphlets which attacked the sending of an American expeditionary force to Russia were unconstitutional because the circumstances failed to fulfill the requirements of the test.

The key to the test proposed by Holmes is the meaning of the words "clear" and "present" as they are used in conjunction with danger. Some persons construe the former to mean "obvious"; Holmes himself never defined "clear" with any exactitude, but he seems to have had in mind the "probable effect" of the speech. Equally crucial to the application of the test is the interpretation of the word "present." Holmes stated his meaning with considerable precision in the *Abrams* case, in which he said it was a danger that "imminently threatens immediate interference with the lawful and pressing purposes of the law." In any event, the test is considered favorable to freedom of expression, since it places the burden on those that seek to limit expression to demonstrate that restrictions are necessary to prevent the imminent occurrence of an evil that will probably result from the utterance involved.

In contrast with the "clear and present danger" test is the *"bad tendency"* rule, first utilized by the Supreme Court in *Pierce* v. *United States,* decided just one year after the *Schenck* opinion. Again, Socialists were convicted for distributing antiwar pamphlets, but in this instance there was no indication that any of this literature reached members of the armed forces or had an immediate effect on the war. Even so, the Court upheld the conviction on the ground that the action might eventually have a tendency to cause insubordination and disloyalty among the troops. In so ruling, the Court lifted from those doing the restricting the burden of proving that the speech in question would probably result in an immediate evil, and substituted the less onerous requirement of demonstrating that the utterances *might tend* to bring about an evil sometime in the future.

Finally, in 1950 the Supreme Court developed a third empirical standard for evaluating the constitutionality of restrictions on freedom of expression; this standard has come to be known as the *"gravity of the evil"* or *"sliding scale"* test. In the 1950 *Dennis* case (we will examine this case in detail below) Justice Vinson ruled that "the Court must ask whether the gravity of the evil discounted by its improbability, justifies such invasion of free speech as is necessary to avoid the evil." Thus the decision added a new dimension to the issue: the nature of the evil to be avoided. If the evil is grave enough—such as the violent overthrow of the government by force—then one need not demonstrate that the expression to be regulated will probably result in the immediate occurrence of the evil. However, if the evil to be presented is not so grave—such as a local disturbance—then those seeking to regulate expression must show that it will probably and imminently bring about the disturbance. Although the Court did not say so, it seemed to be suggesting that if the evil is serious enough, the "bad tendency" test is to be employed; if the evil is not so serious, the "clear and present danger" standard is applicable.

Although the empirical tests provide more definite guidelines for analyzing freedom-of-expression issues than do the preferred-position and balancing approaches, they leave unanswered a number of major questions. For example, in the "clear and present danger" test, to *whom* is the occurrence of the evil to be "clear"—the Congress, the President, or the jury that tries the case? What is meant by "present"—tomorrow, next month, next year? In the "gravity of the evil" test, how grave is "grave", and what criteria does one take into account in deciding that question?

The plain fact of the matter is that verbal formulas cannot capture all the complexities of social situations, and judges must ultimately exercise considerable discretion in deciding freedom-of-expression issues. They look at the total circumstances of the particular case before them. Thus it may make a difference *who* made the statement in question—a college freshman or a major official of the Communist party? *When* the statement is made may well be the crucial factor in the Court's thinking—in the midst of a war or threat of war, or during a period of relative calm in international affairs? *Where* the words were said may well be determinative—in a university graduate seminar or at a mass meeting containing militant groups opposed to the speaker's point of view?

Therefore, we need to look at the broad environment and the events associated with particular freedom-of-expression issues if we are to understand the nature of such issues and the considerations that are taken into account in dealing with them. In the remaining portions of this chapter we will focus on some of the major areas in which the important problems of free speech have arisen in recent years.

THE COMMUNIST THREAT

One of the more perplexing problems for American society in the post-World-War-II era has been the perceived communist threat to national security. In Chapter 17 we will examine the foreign policy aspects of this issue; we focus here on the domestic side of the problem as it relates to internal subversion.

One approach is that of the classic civil libertarian who argues that in a free society all viewpoints must be expressed and that democracy has little to fear from such a policy. As the poet John Milton put it, "Let truth and falsehood grapple. Whoever knew truth put to the worse in a free and open encounter?" In the same vein is the philosophy of Thomas Jefferson that a free society should be able to withstand the severest criticisms of its political institutions. Such an approach leads to the conclusion that our society need not concern itself with the activities of communist groups unless they resort to actual acts of violence. Regulating them may even have the unfortunate consequence of driving the groups underground, making it more difficult to counter their philosophy with our own and to scrutinize their activities which may lead to violence.

Those who favor the regulation of communist activities in this country argue that this particular group does not fit the classic case of the political opponent or dissenter. For one thing, they claim, communists do not believe in or follow one of the most fundamental tenets of democracy: the use of peaceful means to reach political decisions. Since they fail to abide by the rules of the game in a free society, democracy need not extend them rights traditionally accorded to members of the loyal opposition. Beyond this, communists do not seek the relative truth that is the goal of a free exchange of ideas; they have already decided what absolute truth is and distort matters that do not fit their preconceived ideas. Rather than come out in the open to state their unpopular views and to identify themselves as heretics traditionally do, they conspire behind the scenes, using "front" organizations and legitimate groups to masquerade their real purposes and identity. They are not native dissident groups but rather serve foreign powers such as the

Soviet Union; although they may not yet have resorted to violence, they are preparing for the day when the time is ripe to do so. All such assumptions logically lead to the necessity of regulating communists in this country.

At the time of World War II, this latter position won the day. The national government, as well as many states, embarked on a program of regulating communists. Inevitably, some of the major issues ended up in the Supreme Court as that tribunal struggled with the problem of reconciling freedom of expression with the interests of national security.

The Smith Act. The Smith Act, technically known as the Alien Registration Act, was passed by Congress in 1940. In addition to its provisions on aliens, it forbade the advocacy or teaching of the overthrow of any government in the United States by force or violence, the organization of groups having such purposes, and conspiring to commit such acts. In addition, it contained a clause which prohibited "knowing" membership in any group advocating forcible overthrow of government.

The Smith Act was not originally aimed at the Communist party but rather at the greater enemy in 1940, fascism. Yet the language of the Act dealing with violent overthrow of government fitted the nation's major postwar rival, international communism. In 1948 the government secured convictions against eleven major officers of the American Communist party for conspiring to teach the overthrow of the government by force, as well as conspiring to form groups advocating such an overthrow. The accused appealed and the Supreme Court ruled on the matter in the famous *Dennis* case in 1951.

The Court upheld their convictions and the constitutionality of the Smith Act itself on the basis of the "gravity of the evil" test. In so ruling, the Court found that the defendants intended to overthrow the government "as speedily as the circumstances would permit" and that the government did not have to wait until "the putsch is about to be executed" before acting to preserve itself. Following the *Dennis* case similar indictments were obtained under the Smith Act for nearly 150 other, lesser Communist officials.

The first major judicial check on prosecutions under the Smith Act occurred in the *Yates* case, decided by the Supreme Court in 1957. The opinion drew a distinction between the advocacy of the abstract doctrine of revolution (as contained in the writings of Marx, Engels, and other communist theoreticians) and the advocacy of action now or in the future. The Court construed the Smith Act to refer to advocacy of action rather than mere belief. The Court also held that the portion of the Smith Act outlawing the organization of groups advocating or teaching revolution applied only to the act of establishing the Communist party in the United States in its modern form in 1945; prosecutions for that crime were no longer possible after 1948 because of a three-year limitation on suits of this nature. The *Yates* case not only freed the Communist officials involved but also

made it difficult for the government to prosecute other persons for violations of the Smith Act, for the reasons that participation in the formation of
the American Communist Party in 1945 was no longer subject to legal action and that convictions for individual advocacy of revolution had to be
based on evidence of incitement to violent action against the government.

One other potential basis for Smith Act prosecution of Communists remained: the membership clause making it a crime to belong to an organization knowing that it has a revolutionary purpose. In the *Scales* case decided
in 1961, however, the Supreme Court construed "knowing" membership to
mean not passive or paper affiliation but personal activity in a group's efforts
directed toward the violent overthrow of the government. Although the
Court ruled that the government had met the test in the present case, this
strict construction of the Smith Act made it difficult to prosecute other individuals on whom the necessary evidence was lacking.

The end result of the major Smith Act cases was that the Supreme Court
upheld its constitutionality but at the same time, through a process of judicial interpretation, made it difficult for the government to meet the standards of proof necessary for successful prosecutions under its provisions.

The McCarran Act. In the midst of government prosecutions under the
Smith Act in 1950 Congress passed an anticommunist statute known as the
McCarran Act or the Internal Security Act. Its major approach to the problem of internal subversion posed by the communists was to expose their
organization and members and to remove communists from vital positions
in American life. Under the provisions of the Act, "communist action" organizations (defined as those "substantially dominated, directed or controlled by . . . the world communist movement"), as well as "communist front"
organizations (those similarly influenced by "communist-action" groups),
were required to register with a Subversive Activities Control Board composed of five members appointed by the President with senatorial approval.
If any group believed by the Attorney General to fit either category failed
to register, he was empowered to petition for a hearing before the Board;
if it found that the group was a "communist action" or "communist front"
org.-nization, the Board had the power to compel registration. The Act required affected organizations to indicate on mailed publications and on
radio or television programs they sponsored that the information was being
disseminated by a communist group. Members of these organizations were
to be notified of the action taken against their groups and given the opportunity to prove before the Board that they had no association with them.
Individuals considered to be members of such organizations were barred
from government employment, work in a defense facility, and the use of a
passport.

The government's attempt to utilize the McCarran Act proved to be even
more frustrating than its efforts under the earlier Smith Act. After a series

of inconclusive legal skirmishes, the Supreme Court, in the 1961 case *Communist Party* v. *Subversive Activities Control Board*, upheld the Board's finding that the Communist party was a "communist action" organization and should be required to register and divulge its officers and members. You will recall the 1958 Supreme Court ruling that the NAACP did not have to provide similar information to Alabama officials; however, in the Communist party litigation Justice Frankfurter used the "balancing" approach to arrive at the conclusion that society's interest in national security outweighed the private right of association. (Presumably the cases could also be distinguished on the basis that the purposes of the NAACP were legal whereas those of the Communist party were not.)

The government's initial victory turned out to be a temporary one, however. Efforts to force the party to register failed because officers of the organization would have to register for the group, an act in violation of the clause of the Fifth Amendment that forbids compelling a person to incriminate himself. An attempt to force certain individuals to register as members of the Communist party was declared unconstitutional in the 1965 case of *Albertson* v. *Subversive Activities Control Board*. The Supreme Court further limited the usefulness of the McCarran Act by declaring invalid those portions denying members of the Communist organization the right to travel with a passport (*Aptheker* v. *Secretary of State*, 1964) and the right to work in a defense industry (*United States* v. *Robel*, 1967).

In 1967 Congress amended the Internal Security Act to meet some of these difficulties. It removed the requirement that communist organizations or individuals be forced to register and provided that the Subversive Activities Control Board hear such cases on petition from the Attorney General. However, there have been few actions filed under the amended Act. As with the Smith Act prosecutions, the government has found it difficult to use the McCarran Act effectively.* This limitation, coupled with improved Soviet-American relations in the 1960s, makes the internal subversion issue less salient today than it was in the recent past. There has been a shift to other kinds of problems relating to the First Amendment freedoms, problems we will now discuss.

POLITICAL PROTESTS

The dominant domestic political problem in the United States in the 1960s was the civil rights revolution, a topic we will examine in Chapter 15. During the last half of the decade the war in Vietnam emerged as the major issue in foreign policy. Political protest was an important part of both

---

*The Supreme Court also frustrated state actions in the field of internal subversion by ruling in *Pennsylvania* v. *Nelson* (1952) that states cannot prosecute persons for sedition against the United States because the national government has "pre-empted" this problem itself.

developments. In the civil rights movement, protests were leveled against the entire structure of segregation and discrimination in the United States; the antiwar protest had as its main targets the military, along with Congress and the executive branch as epitomized by the demonstrations described at the beginning of this chapter.

The protests over civil rights and the war in Vietnam involved different purposes and methods. In some instances protesters sought to stay within the law, as did most of those involved in the various demonstrations in the nation's capital; however, others, such as those who tried to occupy the Pentagon in 1967, deliberately chose to violate regulations knowing full well they would be arrested for doing so.

This latter type of protest, known generally as civil disobedience, has been most prominently identified in the United States with Martin Luther King and the antisegregation movement. Borrowed from Mahatma Gandhi who used civil disobedience successfully against the British in India (Gandhi himself had borrowed the technique from an earlier American protester, Henry Thoreau, who refused to pay taxes used to prosecute the Mexican War), it is based upon the philosophy that individuals need not obey laws they consider to be unconstitutional or immoral. Rather, as a matter of conscience and in order to communicate their disapproval of such laws, they are obliged to disobey them. At the same time, if persons follow the doctrine of civil disobedience, as taught by leaders like King and Ghandi, they are expected to use passive resistance, not violence, as a tactic and to be willing to accept the legal consequences of punishment for violating laws if their validity is upheld by the courts.

Civil disobedience in the United States in recent years has taken two major forms. In some instances, protesters have deliberately broken a specific law to which they object; thus blacks sat in at southern lunch counters in violation of segregation statutes in order to show their disapproval of those laws. On other occasions, dissenters have violated laws to which they did not specifically object in the course of registering their displeasure with other concerns: an example of this method is the attempt of some protesters to interfere with the flow of traffic into Washington, D.C. in the spring of 1971 in order to publicize their views on the war in Vietnam.

The Supreme Court has never condoned civil disobedience as a means of registering dissent, yet its use by political protesters has raised fundamental constitutional issues for the Court. For example, the disobedience of segregation statutes brought into question the constitutionality of such laws, a matter we will examine in Chapter 15. In addition, deliberate violations by protesters of regulations regarding the use of public property, along with innocent infractions by others not committed to the idea of civil disobedience, have forced the Supreme Court to determine how far political officials can go in restricting the actions of demonstrators without interfering with their constitutional right of free expression. We examine this latter issue next.

In the early phase of the civil rights movement, Negro youths gather at a Chattanooga lunch counter in 1960 to stage a sit-in. (United Press International)

Civil Rights Demonstrations. The most fundamental freedom-of-expression issue raised by recent civil rights demonstration cases concerns the kinds of limits that may constitutionally be imposed on the place and manner in which political protests are conducted. A 1963 case, *Edwards* v. *South Carolina*, involved a demonstration held on the grounds of the state capitol by Negroes protesting discrimination practices. Police ordered the crowd of 200 protesters to disperse and, when they failed to do so, arrested them for breach of the peace. The Supreme Court reversed their convictions, emphasizing that the demonstrators were peaceful, that their protest had not interfered with pedestrian or vehicular traffic into the capitol area, and that it had not resulted in a threat of violence either from the demonstrators themselves or from the crowd of onlookers. The Court further held that a state may not make criminal the peaceful expression of unpopular views, even though such views may anger some persons who hear them.

Other recent cases have sustained the use of public property for demonstrations, provided they are peaceful and do not interfere with the operation of the facility. In a 1966 case, *Brown* v. *Louisiana*, the Supreme Court upheld a sit-in at a public library by five black adults protesting segregation of this public service. The majority opinion written by former Justice Abe Fortas stressed that the defendants had the right to protest the segregation of public facilities by "silent and reproachful" presence in a place "where the protestant has every right to be." Four judges dissented in an opinion written by Justice Black, arguing that the Negroes were expressing their protest in an inappropriate and unauthorized place, since they had no right to be there after they had completed their business.

Although Justice Black's views did not prevail in that instance, they did in the 1966 case of *Adderly* v. *Florida*, which concerned a demonstration of 200 college students outside a county jail. Their convictions for violating a trespass law were upheld by Justice Black and four of his colleagues on the grounds that the students had no right to be on a part of the jail grounds that was set apart for security purposes and not open to the public. In so ruling, Black held that the state, like a private individual, has "the power to preserve the property under its control for the use to which it is properly dedicated." The opinion also contained the statement, typical of Justice Black, that people who engage in protest do not have the right to do so "whenever, however, and wherever they please." Three other judges joined Justice Douglas in dissent, arguing that a county jail housing political prisoners is an obvious center for protest and that the students had not upset the jailhouse routine.

Anti-Vietnam Protests. The anti-Vietnam cases that have reached the Supreme Court have not involved demonstrations by large numbers of people but, rather, protests by individuals. Typically they have risen from acts of disobedience and defiance directed against the war and the military, such as the burning of draft cards and the wearing of black armbands. The major legal issue raised by these cases is what constitutes permissible *symbolic* speech, since political views are expressed through conduct rather than words.

In the first major case of this nature, *United States* v. *O'Brien*, decided in 1968, four young men were convicted for burning their draft cards in violation of a federal statute making it a crime to destroy or mutilate such a card. Justice Warren, speaking for the majority of the Court, sustained their convictions on the grounds that not all conduct can be labeled speech just because the person engaging in it intends to express an idea and that the use of draft cards contributed to the administration of the Selective Service System. He held that acts of dissent can be punished if the government has "a substantial and constitutional interest in forbidding them, the incidental restriction of expression is no greater than necessary, and the government's real interest is not to squelch dissent."

The Supreme Court held, however, in a 1969 case, *Tinker* v. *Des Moines Independent Community School District*, that local school officials could not punish students for violating regulations against wearing black armbands to protest the war in Vietnam. Justice Fortas held this conduct to be "closely akin to pure speech," and pointed out that it had not resulted in any substantial disruption or material interference with school activities. Justice Black in dissent expressed his usual sentiment that a person does not have the constitutional right to express himself whenever, wherever, and however he pleases, and also objected to transferring the power to control pupils from school officials to the Supreme Court.

Thus recent Supreme Court cases dealing with both civil rights and anti-Vietnam protests have forced the Court to come to grips with freedom of expression evinced through conduct rather than through words. The civil rights instances have focused on the problems that mass demonstrations held on public property pose for the use of the property and the maintenance of order. The anti-Vietnam cases have involved the possible effects that defiance of legal regulations have on the conduct of war and the upholding of general respect for political authority.

ASSESSMENT

The Supreme Court has assumed a major role in recent years in protecting First Amendment freedoms. It has ruled that these freedoms apply to state governments and has declared unconstitutional a number of state actions abridging these freedoms. The Court has been more reluctant to declare actions of national officials unconstitutional, but it has interpreted congressional statutes so as to protect freedom of expression.

The Court's solicitude for rights "from" government is evident in its handling of freedom-of-religion cases. While it has agreed to allow some subsidies to parochial schools, it has struck down attempts to conduct religious exercises in the public schools. Moreover, religious minorities like the Jehovah's Witnesses have been granted both the liberty to proselytize for their beliefs on one hand and the freedom not to have to violate them (as, for example, by saluting the flag) on the other. A right of association has also been recognized by the Supreme Court and applied to groups pursuing private as well as public purposes.

Another area of litigation, not treated earlier in this chapter, which reflects the Court's concern for rights "from" government relates to the distribution of obscene literature (since 1957 there has been on the average one such case a year before the Court). Although it has held that these materials are not entitled to the constitutional protection of the First Amendment, it has placed a major burden on those seeking to limit the distribution of such literature to demonstrate that it is indeed obscene. The Court has thus held that the material in question must satisfy *all* the following tests: (1) the work taken as a whole (not selected portions of it alone) must be prurient, shameful, and morbid; *and* (2) it must be patently offensive to prevailing standards in the adult community; *and* (3) it must be utterly without redeeming social importance. The end result of the application of such strict tests has been that relatively few literary works are subject to restriction, so that adults at least have gained great freedom to read whatever they choose. (The Court has applied less strict standards to materials made available to juveniles.)

The right to participate in government through freedom of expression relating to public affairs has also expanded. Supreme Court decisions restricting the application of the Smith and McCarran Acts have served to remove threats to freedom of speech, press, and association created by the Red Scare after World War II. More recently the Court has expanded freedom of expression by adopting a generally liberal attitude toward civil rights demonstrations and anti-Vietnam protests.

Another area not previously noted in which the Supreme Court has recently acted to expand liberty of expression concerns comments regarding public officials. In the landmark 1964 case of *New York Times Company* v. *Sullivan,* the Court overruled a libel judgment against the newspaper for printing a full-page advertisement by Negro clergymen, charging local officials in Montgomery, Alabama, with conducting a "wave of terror" against civil rights demonstrators. Although some of the material contained in the advertisement proved to be false, the Court held that the public officials could not recover because the printed statement was not made with "actual malice"—that is, with knowledge that it was false, or with "reckless" disregard of whether it was false or not.* In adopting this position, the Court reasoned that "debate on public issues should be uninhibited, robust, and wide-open, and that it may well include vehement, caustic and sometimes unpleasantly sharp attacks on government and public officials." The Court went on to state that "the constitutional protection of freedom of speech and press does not turn on the truth, popularity, or social utility of the ideas and beliefs which are offered." The decision might well be construed as an adaptation of Professor Meiklejohn's approach on freedom of expression relating to public affairs.

The combination of civil liberties set forth in our Constitution and a liberal interpretation of them by the Supreme Court has thus provided our citizens with the potential means to participate broadly in the political process. Constitutional provisions and Court rulings, however, merely provide the opportunity for political participation and establish the legal rules under which the struggle for political power takes place. In the final analysis, the way the political process works in actual practice depends on a number of other factors, including the political opinions of citizens and the institutions

*The Court has recently extended this same test to apply to comments about a candidate for public office (as well as someone serving in office).

they develop to make these opinions heard by public officials. It is to these subjects that we now turn.

Selected Readings

One of the better histories of constitutional developments in the United States, including civil liberties issues, is Alfred H. Kelly and Winifred A. Harbison, *The American Constitution: Its Origins and Development* (New York: Norton, 1963). The classic legal study of freedom of speech during the period from 1920 to 1940 is Zechariah Chafee, *Free Speech in the United States* (Cambridge: Harvard University Press, 1942). A broad social and political analysis of human rights in America from World War I until the early 1960s is found in John Roche, *The Quest for the Dream* (New York: Macmillan, 1963).

The historical evolution of church-state relations in the United States is treated in Alan Grimes, *Equality in America* (New York: Oxford University Press, 1964). Philip Kurland, *Religion and The Law* (Chicago: Aldine, 1962), analyzes Supreme Court cases pertaining to religion.

Two recent analyses of the role of the Supreme Court in free speech cases and the approaches used to resolve such issues are Martin Shapiro, *Freedom of Speech: The Supreme Court and Judicial Review* (Englewood Cliffs, N.J.: Prentice-Hall, 1966), and Samuel Krislov, *The Supreme Court and Political Freedom* (New York: Free Press, 1968). Justice Black's views on free speech are contained in a compilation of his statements edited by Irving Dilliard under the title, *One Man's Stand for Freedom: Mr. Justice Black and the Bill of Rights* (New York: Knopf, 1963). Alexander Meiklejohn sets forth his opinion of freedom of expression in *Political Freedom: The Constitutional Powers of the People* (New York: Oxford University Press, 1965).

The issues involved in the attempt to control communist internal subversion in the United States in the late 1940s and early 1950s are treated in Harold Chase, *Security and Liberty: The Problem of Native Communists 1947–1955* (Garden City, N.Y.: Doubleday, 1955). Philosopher Sidney Hook sets forth his views on the difference between legitimate and illegitimate opposition in a free society in *Heresy, Yes, Conspiracy, No* (New York: John Day, 1953).

Paul Kauper discusses recent judicial trends in such areas as church and state, obscenity and censorship, and freedom of association in *Civil Liberties and the Constitution* (Ann Arbor: University of Michigan Press, 1962). Milton Konvitz treats these same First Amendment issues in his study, *Expanding Liberties: Freedom's Gains in Postwar America* (New York: Viking, 1966). A brief analysis of the problems posed by protests and demonstrations is contained in a book by former Supreme Court Justice Abe Fortas, *Concerning Dissent and Civil Disobedience* (New York: New American Library, 1968).

Supreme Court decisions are published in official volumes of the *United States Reports*. A brief yearly analysis of major decisions appears in the December issue of *The Western Political Quarterly*. A more extended treatment of such cases is published each year in the November issue of *The Harvard Law Review*.

PART II

POPULAR CONTROL

As EXPLAINED IN *Chapter 1, the most distinctive feature of democratic government is that citizens have a major voice in determining the public decisions that vitally affect their lives. In pure direct democracy people arrive at those decisions themselves; however, in modern political units encompassing millions of individuals, responsibility for lawmaking must be vested in a small minority of the populations the political officeholders. The fundamental issue in a representative democracy thus concerns the amount and kind of influence that the general populace exercises over the policy-making of public officials.*

One possible solution would be to maximize the influence of the mass over political decisions. In effect, the duty of those in public office would be to find out what the majority of the people want to do about a public issue, such as the war in Vietnam, and then enact their wishes into law. Representatives thus would act as the agents of the people by converting their sentiments into public policy. Such a process would require the average person to take an interest in, and be informed about, political matters, and also to be rational enough to know what course of action should be taken to deal with the problems of his society. Given that condition, his wishes would be respected—and indeed courted—by those in public office.

At the opposite extreme, the public could play a minimal role in the enactment of governmental policy. Essentially the people in a democracy would have only one task: to elect public officials and let them make major political decisions without being hamstrung by the opinions of the general populace. This view would be predicated on the belief that the mass of people has neither the interest nor the capacity to deal with political problems in any meaningful way. Therefore, those that do—the ones who hold political office—should have no obligation to heed their desires.

Neither view fits the realities of the situation in the United States. Communication between the people and those who hold office is in fact a two-way process: the public presses certain demands on political decision-makers and provides support for them and their actions; in turn, those in office respond to demands of the people in some respect, while also seeking their support to take initiatives of their own on public policy matters.

The following five chapters explore the nature of public attitudes on political issues and how such attitudes are channeled to political decision-makers. Chapter 5 analyzes the general substance of the political views of citizens, how they are acquired, and the various outlets that exist for expressing attitudes through the political process. Chapter 6 focuses on the major means for expressing views between elections: the interest group. Chapters 7, 8, and 9 examine the role that political parties and the electoral process play in registering public preferences to political officials.

CHAPTER 5

Public Opinion, Political Socialization, and Political Participation

Huddling during a session before the Senate Foreign Relations subcommittee hearings on the ABM system are: General Earle Wheeler, chairman of the Joint Chiefs of Staff; John Foster, Pentagon director of the defense research; and Melvin Laird, Secretary of Defense. (Wide World Photos)

O NE OF THE MOST CONTROVERSIAL ISSUES of the late 1960s and early 1970s was the development of an ABM (antiballistic missile) system for the United States. In the last year of the Johnson administration Congress authorized the Sentinel system, which provided for the deployment of weapons around major cities as a defense against nuclear attack. Strenuous objections to such installations led President Nixon in March 1969, his second month in office, to shift to the new Safeguard system, under which ABMs would be located in sparsely settled areas to protect Minuteman missile bases.

Despite this change in the ABM program, it became the first major issue of the new Nixon administration. Both proponents and opponents of the ABM considered it not only a matter of great importance for our national security, but also an initial test of political strength between the Republican President and the Democrat-controlled Congress. Executive officials appeared before congressional committees to defend the program, and supporters and critics of the ABM debated it on Capitol Hill. Meanwhile, television and radio, newspapers and newsmagazines gave intensive coverage to the controversial issue. Suspense over it grew as polls of congressmen indicated that the vote on Nixon's program would be extremely close in the Senate: in fact, some commentators predicted that it would end in a tie, with Vice President Spiro Agnew being required to use his power as presiding officer of the chamber to break the deadlock. Ultimately, in August 1969, the ABM issue ended in a victory for President Nixon, as the Senate voted to support his program by a razor-thin 51 to 49 margin.

Three times in the period from late March until mid-July 1969, the Gallup Poll* asked a sample of American adults whether they favored or opposed the ABM program as submitted by President Nixon. Table 5.1 indicates the results of those polls.

Thus the heated debate between forces engaged in vigorous campaigns for and against the ABM had little effect on the attitudes of the American public even though the issue was receiving intensive coverage in the mass media. At the end of that period about three of every five Americans were still uninformed or undecided about the ABM. To understand the possible reasons for this situation, it will be helpful to analyze the nature of the po-

---

*The poll, so designated because George Gallup has been closely associated with it over the years, is conducted by the American Institute of Public Opinion. The organization interviews some 1500 American adults—chosen at random—as a representative cross section of the national population and draws its conclusions about the entire populace from this sample.

TABLE 5.1 Gallup Poll Results, 1969, on ABM (Figures in Percentages)

Response	March 28-31	May 16-19	July 11-14
Favor	25	24	23
Oppose	14	14	18
Undecided	1	2	1
	40	40	42
Unaware of program or have not made up mind	60	60	58
Total	100	100	100

Source: American Institute of Public Opinion.

litical attitudes and opinions of the American people, and how such attitudes and opinions are formed.

THE NATURE OF PUBLIC OPINION

Probably no concept has presented more difficulty for students of popular government than public opinion. The late V.O. Key, Jr., a political scientist who pioneered in the study of the subject, once remarked that "to speak with persuasion of public opinion is a task not unlike coming to grips with the Holy Ghost." Problems arise in understanding public opinion because individuals seldom define adequately what they mean by "public." Moreover, they fail to spell out the various kinds of matters to which public opinion is directed.

When a political scientist uses the term "public," he has in mind a group of people outside the formal structure of government. In other words, he is referring to private citizens, not those who hold political office. Thus public opinion refers to attitudes that members of the mass of people, not the few who exercise legal authority, have on certain matters.

The public, however, does not include every citizen. It is a fiction to suggest that all Americans have an opinion on most subjects. As indicated above, even though the ABM controversy was spotlighted by the mass media over several months, only about two-fifths of our citizens formed any opinion on this vital issue. This lapse may be attributed in part to the technical nature of the subject, but other polls have shown Americans to be uninterested in other major issues that cannot be explained away on that basis. In November 1953 only about one-third of American adults interviewed in a Gallup Poll expressed an opinion on what should be done about the Taft-Hartley law regulating labor-management relationships, even though that matter was less technical than the ABM and had been a prominent public issue for a number of years. (Businessmen and Republican candidates generally supported the Act, while labor and Democratic hopefuls opposed it.)

If the public does not include all citizens, it must involve enough persons to have an impact on the political process. Yet a public is not composed of any precise minimum number of opinion-holding individuals because the effectiveness of opinions depends on how intensively they are held and the political resources and skills of those who hold them. Key's definition that public opinions are "those opinions held by private persons which governments find it prudent to heed" comes as close as possible to expressing the basic elements of the concept because it focuses on the influence of public attitudes on official decision-making.

The student of government naturally concentrates on political opinions. He would not normally be interested, for example, in analyzing the opinions of Americans on the best methods of raising children, a topic of concern to a sociologist. Once a matter takes on political relevance, however, the political scientist becomes interested. When President Nixon proposed that the national government subsidize child-care centers so that mothers with dependent children could earn outside income, public attitudes on working mothers became a major concern to the student of the American political process.

Frequently, studies of public opinion consider only mass attitudes towards particular political issues such as the ABM and the Taft-Hartley Act. Yet other kinds of political matters bear on relationships between the people and governmental officials in a democratic society. Most basic of all are the feelings of citizens towards their country and the legitimacy of its government, that is, whether they feel loyalty to the nation and accept its political system as the proper vehicle for making decisions that vitally affect their lives. The latter issue involves public attitudes towards the constitutional order—the functions, procedures, and structures of their government —or what I have been calling the rules of the game. Without public support—either as a positive allegiance to the fundamentals of the system, or at least as a negative acquiescence to them—the delicate act of governing becomes impossible, and all other political matters are irrelevant.

The feelings people have toward government officials themselves also determine whether the public will accept their decrees as legitimate and binding. Again, public support, active or passive, of such decrees must exist if the political process is to be effective in a society. In a democracy like the United States the selection of major public officials through free elections in which the mass of people participate and the ease of removing and replacing the officials at reasonable intervals provide a basis for general acceptance of their rule.

Assuming public support of the nation, its form of government, and its leaders, other factors bear on the amount and kind of influence that citizens exercise over governmental decisions. One basic consideration is the extent to which they identify psychologically with particular groups, such as political parties or social, economic, or geographical divisions in the population, and shape their political views accordingly. Another is their reaction to the personalities of candidates for office. Such matters, along with views on specific issues, help to determine the ways in which political attitudes and preferences of the general public influence both the choice of personnel and the policies of the government.

Viewed in the broadest context, then, public opinion refers to opinions of private individuals that affect the operation of the political system. Yet the particular concerns to which such attitudes are directed are crucial: the nation and its constitutional system, its major decision-makers, political parties or other social groups in the population, political candidates, and issues of public policy. Moreover, there is no one political "public"; rather, there is a series of "publics," separate groups of people with opinions on different matters. On some, such as the kind of political system they favor, the public may consist of most individuals in a society; on other, more specific topics, such as what should be done about a special policy issue such as the ABM, the public may well consist of a very limited number of persons.

Ultimately, of course, the importance of "publics" in the political process depends not only on their size but also on the ways in which they channel their views to those in positions of political authority. Before turning to that topic in subsequent chapters, however, we need to examine the substance of individual political opinions and the methods by which they are acquired.

THE FORMATION
OF POLITICAL OPINIONS

Teaching citizens proper attitudes and information about their government has long been a concern of political philosophers, as evidenced by Plato's views on the importance of civic education in the Greek city-state. Only very recently, however, have scholars begun to conduct empirical examinations into the ways in which individuals actually come to acquire their political attitudes. The learning process is called *political socialization.*

Like public opinion, political socialization is given different meanings. Some persons equate it with the study of how children acquire their political attitudes. Others restrict political socialization to the acquisition of the prevailing values and beliefs of the society, not deviations from them. In other words, they focus on how leaders instill a respect for the *status quo* in citizens. Here, however, we will interpret political socialization more broadly to mean the process by which individuals acquire all kinds of political attitudes (unfavorable as well as favorable to the existing political system) over a period of time that includes adulthood as well as childhood. Moreover, we will look at not only the individual who acquires political attitudes but also the agencies which shape those attitudes.

THE DEVELOPMENT OF POLITICAL OPINIONS

Guided by theories of psychologists, psychiatrists, and sociologists that emphasize the crucial importance of the formative years in molding a person's attitudes and beliefs, students of political socialization have focused most of their attention on the development of political opinions in children. They find that people begin to develop some awareness of the political world when they are quite young.* This earliest political orientation generally takes the form of strong patriotic feelings toward their country, as children react favorably towards symbols like the flag. The political system itself is personified for them primarily by the major officials. They first become aware of government executives at the top and bottom levels of the system—at the national level, the President; at the local, the mayor or the policeman. The identity with the government, as with the nation itself, is generally positive; that is, children by and large look upon the President, mayor, or police chief as a "good" person who "helps" people and "gets things done." They also feel that they should respect and obey such individuals. Thus a child's early orientation to the political system is essentially one of allegiance and support.

A young child is also inclined to find his own particular place in the political world he has become aware of. In particular, he seeks to identify with a group, to associate himself with some persons in society—and to distinguish himself from others. He may form an early psychological attachment to a political party. Indeed, children as young as seven already regard themselves as Republicans or Democrats; they also come to think of themselves as white or black, rich or poor, Protestant or Catholic. These identifications with social and economic groupings, like those with political parties and the nation and its political system, have deep emotional underpinnings, and therefore they tend to persist throughout subsequent stages of an individual's political life.

Later, as the average person approaches or enters his teens, his conception of the political world begins to change. He becomes more critical in his thinking and is less likely to think that the President, mayor, or police chief is all-benevolent and all-powerful. These figures no longer personify and dominate his view of the political system as they did; the older child is aware that they share the running of the government with other groups, such as the Congress, the Supreme Court, and the local city council. He also adds the state level of government to his view of the political system. Furthermore, he begins to develop some notion of what concepts like "democracy" and "communism" mean, though typically his views on such matters are superficial or, in many instances, erroneous.

*Most studies deal with school-age children but some have discovered the beginnings of political attitude in preschoolers.

Young people are trained in the political attitudes of the social system in which they live, like these children reciting the pledge of allegiance in class. (Robert Smith-Black Star)

Towards the end of childhood, an individual becomes even more politically sophisticated. He begins to associate differences between being a Republican and a Democrat, particularly in terms of the social and economic groups (business, labor, rich, poor, black, white) that each party favors. He also develops reactions to political personalities. Moreover, public policy issues, particularly those of a general nature, like race relations and the war in Vietnam, become matters of concern to the older child. In addition, he may have ideas of how such problems should be handled by those in public office. He may also develop a better understanding of democracy and its procedures—majority rule, minority rights, and the like.

Information on the political socialization of adults is sparse. We have no studies of particular individuals over a period of time that enable us to spell out in any detail how political attitudes of persons change after they reach maturity. What evidence is available indicates that political learning continues as the individual is exposed to new experiences in life, such as getting a job, raising a family, moving to other areas of the country, or associating with people and groups that differ from those he previously knew.

Thus political socialization is a developmental process. In the early years, a person's political orientation is general, positive, and based on strong emotional attachments towards nation, government, and officials. Later on, as an individual becomes more knowledgeable and discriminating, he may develop expectations of what public officials should do about particular social issues. In short, his attitude toward political leaders changes from offering unqualified support to making demands.

This is not to suggest, however, that all individuals follow this pattern. For example, one study found that children from Appalachia, a region characterized by poverty and physical isolation, are less favorably disposed to the President than those from more affluent urban areas of the Northeast and Midwest. Moreover, everyone does not acquire political attitudes at the same pace: children from wealthier and better-educated families are more knowledgeable and discriminating about political matters than are those of a similar age from poorer circumstances. As a rule, boys develop political interests and sophistication faster than girls do; young people of both sexes with high IQs politically outdistance their less intelligent classmates. Nor is everyone's eventual level of development the same. Some never proceed past the early stage of generalized emotional attitudes towards the political system, while others develop a keen interest in trying to analyze political issues and events objectively.

It is difficult to determine precise reasons for differences in the development of political opinions of various individuals. One obvious factor, however, is the variation in associations with the key social groups that shape political orientations.

AGENCIES AFFECTING POLITICAL OPINIONS

A vast number of influences affect a person's political opinions. Some of them, like the family, are felt early in his life, while others, such as work groups, affect his political orientation as an adult. Some of the agencies of political socialization are primary groups in which he has close face-to-face relationships with the same individuals over a considerable length of time—again, the family is the prime example. Others are secondary groups like labor unions or employers' associations, in which contacts among members are more limited and frequently involve, not a continuing common core of individuals, but rather a range of different persons over time.

Family. By far the most potent group in shaping individual political attitudes is the family. It exercises its major effect on a person during his most impressionable years, he has his closest emotional ties with it, and it influences his political attitudes during the time when other agencies have not yet begun to affect them. In fact, the family enjoys a virtual monopoly over an individual's political attention during his early years in life.

The family shapes the most basic aspects of an individual's political opinions. A child who respects his parents is inclined to transfer this feeling to other authorities outside the family, such as the President. He will also imitate his parents' political opinions and behavior: if they think and speak well of the President, the child too will tend to favor him. Parents who do not hold the Chief Executive in high regard may keep their adverse feelings to themselves to avoid undercutting the child's respect for authority. If so, their child also will develop a favorable image of the President.

Parents also affect another basic feature of the child's early political attitudes: his identification with a political party, as well as with social and economic groups. Young children are very likely to identify with the same political party as their parents, particularly if the parents share strong partisan attachments. If there is a difference of opinion between the two parents about political parties, then their children may avoid the delicate problem of choosing between the mother's and father's views by declaring themselves political independents. Children also acquire from their parents a sense of identity with religious, racial, or social groups and so learn to think of themselves as Jews, blacks, or laboring-class people.

One of the more interesting questions raised by the rebellion of many children against parents is whether this rejection manifests itself politically. That is, do children consciously deviate from the political views of their parents as a means of expressing their general hostility to their elders? The limited evidence available on the subject indicates that political rebellion occurs only when political matters are highly important to the parents. Otherwise, the child gains no psychological value by adopting a different party identification from the parents'; he can reject and punish them more effectively on matters that mean more to them—by refusing to go to their church or into the father's business. Deviation from the political views of parents is more likely to result, not from general hostility towards their elders, but rather from the differing experiences of the two generations. We will explore this matter further in the discussion below.

Public Schools. Another major organization that shapes political attitudes is the public school, which like the family has its major impact during the early years of an individual's life. One of the major reasons why societies establish schools is to transmit values to the young; therefore, teachers instill in students favorable attitudes toward their country and government. Thus symbolic exercises like saluting the flag, singing patriotic songs, and honoring the nation's heroes engender positive feelings towards the nation and its system of government. Teachers, like parents, try to develop a respect for authority, and children are inclined to transfer their respect of classroom supervisors to political leaders.

There are, however, some major differences in the shaping of political attitudes between the home and school. In the interest of maintaining good relationships with all kinds of parents, teachers are generally careful not to

appear to favor one political party over another. If the schools are to fulfill
the function of promoting harmony among children from various kinds of
economic and social backgrounds (as many people feel they should), then
teachers must also strive to avoid partiality towards any such groups. Thus
unlike the family, schools do not generally shape a child's orientation towards his particular niche in the political world.

In the secondary and high schools the curriculum typically contains instruction on civics or the problems of democracy. Yet often such courses
have relatively little impact on the political opinions of most students, partly
because by the time a student takes such courses, his basic political attitudes are already formed. Even so, children who have not been exposed to
political matters in the home (most likely among the poor and uneducated)
may be influenced by instruction on civil duties to vote and to respect the
rules of the democratic game regarding the toleration of opposing viewpoints.

Other factors besides the curriculum shape students' political attitudes.
Teaching techniques employed by particular instructors may have an impact: students acquire an understanding of the democratic process from the
instructor who encourages debate and questioning in the classroom, in contrast to the authoritarian taskmaster who runs his classes with an iron hand.
Extracurricular activities also influence political attitudes of students as they
learn to govern themselves in voluntary clubs and organizations. The way
in which principals and other school authorities treat children and the kinds
of rules and regulations developed by school boards regarding attire and
personal appearance affect students' attitudes toward authority in general
and political authority in particular. Thus the total social setting of the public school shapes political attitudes.

College. Many young people who go on to college (some seven million
were enrolled in American institutions of higher learning in the fall of
1970) experience a marked change in political attitudes. Colleges generally
encourage a critical approach to problems, and courses are much less likely
to defend the *status quo* than are those taught in the public schools. College faculties, particularly those in the social sciences, tend to be liberal in
their political orientation (that is, they favor greater public concern with
social problems in general and the plight of disadvantaged groups—blacks
and the poor—in particular), and some students who come from politically
conservative families are influenced by their values.

Other factors may be even more important in changing the political attitudes of college students. Going away from home is a major social disloca-
tion for many students, for it involves breaking with families and the values
learned from them and becoming exposed to ideas of other persons with
backgrounds quite different from their own. Particularly important at this
point is the influence of their *peers*, that is, their contemporaries. While

peers, of course, shape students' political attitudes earlier than college years, classmates are particularly influential at this time because students live together and are in constant association with one another. This common situation of breaking with the past and close physical proximity, plus easy communication among college students, is conducive to their forming distinct attitudes and values, including ways of looking at the political world.

Other Peer Groups. As he becomes an adult, a person's political attitudes may be influenced by other peer groups, such as churches, lodges, and ethnic groups. The extent of that influence depends on a number of factors: how important political concerns are to the group; how closely its members agree on such matters; whether the individual himself thinks it is proper for the organization to be involved in political issues (some persons, for example, feel that churches should not take political stands); and how closely the individual identifies with the group. Thus an individual who belongs to a politically active labor union composed of like-minded members, who approves of the activities, and who thinks of himself as a "union" man is likely to be strongly affected by the political beliefs of his fellow union members.

It is also possible for individuals to have their political attitudes shaped by groups to which they do not belong. Thus a white liberal who is sympathetic with the plight of the underdog in society may identify with the National Association for the Advancement of Colored People or with black groups in general, so that he favors government programs that benefit Negroes even though he personally does not benefit from them. Such groups are called *"reference groups"* or sometimes *"reference symbols"* because they provide guideposts from which individuals take their social and psychological bearings. Of course, reference groups or reference symbols can be negative as well as positive: the self-made business man may be against a proposal he believes will benefit labor unions or social welfare organizations because he has unfavorable images of such groups.

The Mass Media. Another agency in our society with a potential for shaping political opinions is found in the mass media, comprising television, radio, newspapers, and magazines. In fact, many political observers in the United States in recent years have expressed increasing concern that those who control the media are able to manipulate political attitudes of the population at will, that Madison Avenue techniques projected over the tube result in a nation of political puppets. Undoubtedly, the mass media do have an appreciable effect on political attitudes, particularly reactions to the personalities of candidates, but there are a number of built-in limits on the long-term influence of the media.

One such factor is the nature of the messages carried by the media. Most television programs, for example, are nonpolitical. Advertisers who pay the high costs of television time want the maximum audience for their dollar;

since most people are far more interested in being entertained than they are in being informed on public affairs, few programs with political content are sponsored by private companies or groups. Under regulations of the Federal Communications Commission, networks and individual stations themselves, of course, do carry a certain amount of "public affairs" programs, but most of these are not controversial (such as the astronauts' trips to the moon), because the owners of the stations do not want to antagonize viewers and because they have an obligation to provide free "equal time" to those with opposing viewpoints. For these reasons, few stations have taken advantage of the opportunity provided by regulations of the Federal Communications Commission to carry editorial comments, instead confining their news broadcasts to fairly objective accounts of the facts of political developments.

In newspapers, as on television, much of the content is nonpolitical, for editors seek to avoid antagonizing their readers and advertisers. Although editorial pages do print controversial viewpoints, relatively few readers examine these columns. (The comics, sports, and social and financial sections are likely to capture more interest.) Some news magazines, notably *Time*, *Newsweek*, and *U.S. News and World Report*, do carry a great deal of political information, but the readership of such publications is fairly limited.

Even the minimal political content of the mass media has less effect on individuals than may be supposed. Communication depends, after all, not only on the messages sent but also on the messages received. Some persons screen out political information entirely because they have no interest in it; a television viewer, for instance, may turn off the set or turn his attention to other matters when political comments are carried on the air. Others select only the messages they want to hear: thus the liberal may read *The New Republic*, the conservative, *The Chicago Tribune*. Still others actually misperceive what they hear or read; they interpret an editorial or other political comment to mean what they want it to mean, not what the conveyor of the message is trying to say.

Students of the mass media have discovered something else that bears on their impact on political attitudes; there often is a "two-step" or "multi-step flow" in the communication process. That is, many messages do not reach the average citizen directly because he is not interested enough to expose himself to them; instead, they are transmitted to him indirectly via "opinion leaders" (party and interest group officers or local "influentials" such as lawyers, doctors, bankers, and teachers) who are especially attentive to the media and who discuss their content with less-informed individuals. In the process, of course, these transmitters alter the messages in keeping with their views and biases.

The end result of all the above factors is to minimize the independent influence of the mass media on individual political opinions, especially those that persist over a period of time. Those persons who pay the most attention to the media are the very ones who already have well-established political views; those with vague and insubstantial opinions that offer the greatest potential for change are least likely to expose themselves to whatever political content the media do carry. Thus generally the media serve to maintain the *status quo* in political opinions rather than to change them.

Political Events and Experiences. Two other factors that shape political attitudes, particularly in the adult years, are political events and experiences, which may even serve to change early political beliefs of an individual. Thus the outbreak of a war or the loss of a job may call into serious question the trust he developed in childhood for the President; a charge of police brutality or his own treatment by a rude officer may also raise doubts about the benevolent view he once held of the local policeman. On the other hand, his previously acquired attitudes may shape the way he views present political developments; he may believe his nation's involvement in a foreign war is a just cause simply because he trusts the judgment of the President on such matters, or because of his childhood appreciation for the policeman he may dismiss the charges of police brutality as ridiculous.

Studies of political socialization have illuminated the ways in which individuals acquire their political beliefs, but many areas have not been adequately explored. For example, most studies have focused on middle-class white children, and we have comparatively little information on the acquisition of political beliefs by disadvantaged children in our society, particularly those who live in Northern black ghettos. It is doubtful that they acquire the feelings of trust for the policeman that white children in middle-class neighborhoods do. Nor do we know much about how children from impoverished rural areas react politically to the hopeless world that surrounds them.

Nor have we fitted together the series of influences that shape a person's political attitudes over the course of a lifetime. Under what circumstances will adult experiences and group associations serve to consolidate early political opinions, and what conditions will result in a fundamental change in those opinions? In this connection it is interesting to speculate why some young people today, particularly those in college, depart radically from the political beliefs of their parents? Is this a consequence of the questioning attitude instilled in the students by their instructors? Or have dramatic events like the war in Vietnam and urban riots graphically demonstrated the naivete of their early trust of political authorities? Or do they see the world in the light of present political events (an ugly war against a backward people, the hopelessness of the ghetto) while their parents see it in terms of the salient occurrences in their formative years (a just war—World War II—against powerful dictators, the recovery of the nation from depression)?

POLITICAL ATTITUDES
OF AMERICAN CITIZENS

Although we have not determined with any precision how political views of individuals change over the course of their lives, we can analyze the general nature of the views held by Americans. As previously suggested, public opinion does exist on a variety of political subjects, including basic orientations towards the nation and to the government and public officials which are vital to the very existence of a political system. Public reactions to the vital issues of the day also shape the public policies political leaders develop to meet them. The remainder of this chapter and all of Chapter 6 treat those aspects of public opinion that affect the everyday operation of our government. Attitudes towards political parties, social and economic groups, and political personalities that relate so closely to the periodic electoral process are discussed in later chapters.

ATTITUDES TOWARD THE NATION

The strong sense of loyalty to the nation that children in the United States develop very early in their lives persists in adulthood. A 1948 survey sponsored by the United Nations showed that 96 percent of Americans questioned felt that their nation would give them the best chance of leading the kind of life they wanted to lead; no other nation received as great a vote of confidence from its citizens.* While Americans were more critical of their country a quarter-century later, a nine-nation survey taken by Gallup-affiliated organizations in 1971 indicated that fewer Americans (12 percent) than citizens of the other nations questioned, said they would like to settle in another country.† (The countries Americans would most like to go to were Australia, Canada, Great Britain, and Switzerland; the group most desirous of emigrating were persons with college training between the ages of 18 and 29.)

ATTITUDES TOWARD THE
AMERICAN POLITICAL SYSTEM

Surveys of public attitudes taken in the United States, Great Britain, West Germany, Italy, and Mexico during 1959 and 1960 by Gabriel Almond and Sidney Verba also reflect the favorable opinion Americans have of their government. When asked what things about their country they were most

---

*Comparable United Nations surveys in other countries produced the following percentages: Australia, 83; Britain, 51; Norway, 50; Mexico, 45; France, 43; Italy, 36; Netherlands, 31; and Germany, 30.

†The percentages in the other countries were: Great Britain, 41; Uruguay, 32; West Germany, 27; Greece, 22; Finland, 19; Sweden, 18; Brazil, 17; and the Netherlands, 16.

proud of, 85 percent of those questioned in the United States cited some feature of their political system, such as the Constitution, political freedom, or democracy. By way of comparison, 46 percent of the Britons, 7 percent of the Germans, 3 percent of the Italians, and 30 percent of the Mexicans prized aspects of their government or political tradition. As indicated by Table 5.2, citizens of these nations were more inclined than Americans to emphasize other aspects of their countries.

The general attitudes evinced towards our political system raise a related concern: to what extent does the American public subscribe to the basic tenets of democracy discussed in Chapter 1? Are there any differences among our citizens in such matters?

ATTITUDES TOWARD DEMOCRATIC
PRINCIPLES AND VALUES

It will be recalled that democracy is based on certain operating principles. In particular, as it has developed in Western nations like the United

TABLE 5.2   Sources of National Pride (Responses by Nation in Percentages)

Characteristic	Nation				
	U.S.	U.K.	Germany	Italy	Mexico
Governmental, political institutions	85	46	7	3	30
Social legislation	13	18	6	1	2
Position in international affairs	5	11	5	2	3
Economic system	23	10	33	3	24
Characteristics of people	7	18	36	11	15
Spiritual virtues and religion	3	1	3	6	8
Contributions to the arts	1	6	11	16	9
Contributions to science	3	7	12	3	1
Physical attributes of country	5	10	17	25	22
Nothing or don't know	4	10	15	27	16
Other	9	11	3	21	14
Total percentage of responses*	158	148	148	118	144
Total percentage of respondents	100	100	100	100	100
Total number of cases	970	963	955	995	1,007

*Percentages exceed 100 because of multiple responses.

Source: Gabriel Almond and Sidney Verba, *The Civic Culture* (Princeton: Princeton University Press, 1963), p. 102.

States, democracy employs certain techniques and procedures of governance. Included among them are the concepts of majority rule and minority rights. Thus the question arises whether American citizens really believe in these two basic principles.

We have limited information on the subject, but one study of citizen attitudes in two cities—Ann Arbor, Michigan, and Tallahassee, Florida—made a number of years ago by two political scientists, James Prothro and Charles Grigg, indicated overwhelming public support for both principles. A sample of registered voters in each of these communities was asked whether every citizen should have an equal chance to influence public policy; they were also questioned about whether they agreed with the statements that the minority should be free to try to win majority support for these opinions. The rate of agreement on these statements ranged from 94.7 to 98 percent.

Agreeing on abstract principles is one thing; applying the principles to particular situations is another. When the citizens of the two cities were asked their opinion toward a number of concrete questions that required them to make such an application, the responses shown in Table 5.3 resulted. The table shows that on none of the ten statements does agreement on the democratic responses reach the 90 percent figure that was associated with the four more abstract principles pertaining to majority rule and minority rights. On only three statements (3, 7, and 9) do three-fourths or more of the respondents agree on the democratic response.

At the same time, the table indicates that the responses of the voters to the questions vary with education and income, as well as with the community in which they live. Persons with more education and income in both cities tended to give more democratic responses than did less educated and less affluent persons, as did residents of the northern city as a whole in comparison with those in the southern community. Of the three factors, education was the most important in differentiating between respondents. Yet even the more highly educated voters achieved the 90 percent figure on only one statement (7), and on three propositions (2, 5, and 10), less than half gave the democratic response.

Another survey of democratic attitudes of a nationwide sample of American adults conducted by Herbert McCloskey generally confirmed the findings of Prothro and Grigg. In none of the 12 sepcific statements submitted to them relating to democratic rules of the game (principles of fair play, respect for legal procedures, and the rights of others) did the national sample achieve a 75 percent level of agreement. However, when McCloskey put the same questions to a sample of 3000 political influentials drawn from the delegates and alternates who attended the Democratic and Republican presidential nominating conventions in 1956, he found that they achieved a 75 percent agreement on 8 of the 12 specific statements.

McCloskey also tested the attitudes of the general public and the political influentials toward a major value of a democratic society—equality. As with his analysis of beliefs in the democratic rules of the game, he developed a list of concrete statements that required the respondents to apply the principles of political, social, and economic equality to specific situations. Table 5.4, which gives the responses of the two groups, indicates that neither members of the general public nor the political influentials achieved much agreement on these statements relating to political, social, and economic equality. Compared to the public, the influentials tended to take more equalitarian stands on political and social matters but were less likely to support the idea that the government should mitigate economic inequalities by providing the basic necessities of life for all individuals.

TABLE 5.3   Percentage of "Democratic" Responses to Basic Principles of Democracy among Selected Population Groups

		Education†		Ann	Talla-	Income‡	
Statements	Total N=244	High N=137	Low N=106	Arbor N=144	hassee N=100	High N=136	Low N=99
Majority Rule							
1. Only informed vote*	49.0	61.7	34.7	56.3	38.4	56.6	40.8
2. Only taxpayers vote*	21.0	22.7	18.6	20.8	21.2	20.7	21.0
3. Bar Negro from office*	80.6	89.7	68.6	88.5	66.7	83.2	77.8
4. Bar Communist from office*	46.3	56.1	34.0	46.9	45.5	48.9	43.0
5. AMA right to bloc voting**	45.0	49.6	39.2	44.8	45.5	45.5	44.4
Minority Rights							
6. Allow antireligious speech**	63.0	77.4	46.5	67.4	56.6	72.8	52.1
7. Allow socialist speech**	79.4	90.2	65.7	81.3	76.8	83.8	73.7
8. Allow Communist speech**	44.0	62.9	23.5	51.4	33.3	52.2	36.7
9. Bar Negro from candidacy*	75.5	86.5	60.2	85.6	58.0	78.6	71.1
10. Bar Communist from candidacy*	41.7	48.1	30.3	44.1	38.2	44.8	34.4

*For these statements disagreement is recorded as the "democratic" response.

**For these statements agreement is recorded as the "democratic" response.

†"High education" means more than 12 years of schooling; "low education," 12 years or less.

‡"High income" means an annual family income of $6000 or more; "low income," less than $6000.

Source: James Prothro and Charles Grigg, "Fundamental Principles of Democracy: Bases of Agreement and Disagreement," Journal of Politics, 22 (1960), p. 285.

TABLE 5.4 Political Influentials versus the Electorate: Responses to Items Expressing Belief in Equality

Items	Percentage Agreeing	
	Political Influentials (N=3020)	General Electorate (N=1484)
Political Equality		
The main trouble with democracy is that most people don't really know what's best for them.	40.8	58.0
Few people really know what is in their own best interest in the long run.	42.6	61.1
"Issues" and "arguments" are beyond the understanding of most voters.	37.5	62.3
Most people don't have enough sense to pick their own leaders wisely.	28.0	47.8
It will always be necessary to have a few strong, able people actually running everything.	42.5	56.2
Social and Ethnic Equality		
We have to teach children that all men are created equal but almost everyone knows that some are better than others.	54.7	58.3
Just as is true of fine race horses, some breeds of people are just naturally better than others.	46.0	46.3
Regardless of what some people say, there are certain races in the world that just won't mix with Americans.	37.2	50.4
When it comes to the things that count most, all races are certainly not equal.	45.3	49.0
The trouble with letting certain minority groups into a nice neighborhood is that they gradually give it their own atmosphere.	49.8	57.7
Economic Equality		
Labor does not get its fair share of what it produces.	20.8	44.8
Every person should have a good house, even if the government has to build it for him.	14.9	28.2
I think the government should give a person work if he can't find another job.	23.5	47.3
The government ought to make sure that everyone has a good standard of living.	34.4	55.9
There will always be poverty, so people might as well get used to the idea.	40.4	59.4

Source: Herbert McCloskey, "Consensus and Ideology in American Politics," *The American Political Science Review*, 58 (June 1964), p. 369.

Thus Americans support in a general way their political system, as well as the rules of the game and values of democracy. They are less likely, however, to agree on the application of general democratic principles to specific situations. Finally, there are differences among our citizens, the well-educated and politically influential ones being more likely to support democratic principles.

ATTITUDES TOWARD POLITICAL LEADERS

The childhood trust in public officials characteristic of American children also persists among adult citizens. For example, 83 percent of the Americans questioned in the five-nation survey previously referred to expected to be treated as well as anyone else if they had to take a tax-regulation or housing problem to the government office concerned. The same question drew the following percentages of favorable responses from the citizens of the other four countries: Great Britain, 83; Germany, 65; Italy, 53; and Mexico, 42. Thus only the British expressed as much confidence in their public officials.

Additional evidence of the support our political leaders enjoy is provided by a series of annual Gallup polls on the question of whom Americans admired most. Since Dwight Eisenhower went into office in 1953, the incumbent President of the United States has ranked first among men each year, with the single exception of 1968 when Lyndon Johnson was second in public esteem to former President Eisenhower. Moreover, since 1952 the most-admired woman has been either the current or past First Lady, again with an exception in 1968 when the wife of another leading political figure, Robert Kennedy, won the poll.

Besides the President, other men the general public respects tend to be political figures. For example, in 1970, of the ten most admired men, only two (Billy Graham and Pope Paul VI) were not from political life. Included in the top ten that year were Edward Kennedy, Spiro Agnew, Edmund Muskie, Lyndon Johnson, Ronald Reagan, Hubert Humphrey, and Harry Truman.

ATTITUDES ON POLICY ISSUES

Among the major problems facing the nation in recent years three frequently mentioned by adults polled by the Gallup organization have been Vietnam, civil rights and race relations, and the high cost of living. Thus the matters of great concern to the American people involve domestic issues of economics and civil liberties, as well as a vital foreign-policy problem plaguing a succession of Presidents. An analysis of attitudes on these vital problems illuminates the nature of public thinking on issues of primary concern to our citizens.

One proposal in the polls for fighting the high cost of living was to freeze prices and wages at their current level until the conclusion of the Vietnam war. In October 1970 when Americans were asked if they thought that would be a good or poor idea, the results shown in Table 5.5 were obtained.

TABLE 5.5   Support for Wage and Price Controls (Figures in Percentages)

Categories of Respondents	Good Idea	Opinion Poor Idea	No Opinion
Nation	46	43	11
By Education			
College	39	54	7
High School	47	42	11
Grade School	50	32	18
By Income			
$15,000 and over	43	50	1
10,000–14,999	43	49	8
7,000– 9,999	48	41	11
5,000– 6,999	48	43	9
3,000– 4,999	49	32	19
Under $3,000	49	31	20

Source: American Institute of Public Opinion, October 1970.

The American public as a whole was fairly evenly divided on the matter. People with diverse educational backgrounds felt differently about the proposal: more college graduates opposed it than persons with a grade school education. Income revealed a similar but less marked pattern of variation in responses. The poll also indicated that individuals with little education and low income were more likely to have no opinion than those with higher academic and economic attainments.

Another Gallup poll, taken in February 1970, on withdrawing all American troops from Vietnam revealed that the public was less closely divided on this issue. Nationally, 35 percent favored the step, 55 percent opposed it, and 10 percent had no opinion. Again, however, education and income made a difference, with the categories of college-educated persons and those earning more than $10,000 a year considerably more opposed to pulling out our troops than persons at the lower levels of the educational and income scales. The latter groups once again were most likely not to have formed an opinion on the issue.

Attitudes of Americans on the race issue were tapped in March 1969 by a Gallup poll that asked Americans if they would vote for a well-qualified man their political party nominated for President if he happened to be a Negro. As Table 5.6 indicates, three factors affecting attitudes on this issue

Education and class differences affect attitudes on policy issues. (Above) Construction
workers supporting the government's Vietnam policy attack a young anti-Vietnam dem-
onstrator. (Below) A few days later, when students engaged hard-hats in peaceful discussion of their differences, both sides agreed that violence is futile. (Above: Wide
World Photos; below: United Press International)

TABLE 5.6   Willingness to Vote for a Negro for President (Figures in Percentages)

Categories of Respondents	Opinion		
	Yes	No	No Opinion
National	67	23	10
Education			
College	79	14	7
High School	71	21	8
Grade School	49	36	15
Age			
21–29	77	14	9
30–49	72	20	8
50–over	58	31	11
Region			
East	74	14	12
Midwest	71	20	9
South	52	39	9
West	74	20	6

Source: American Institute of Public Opinion, March 1969.

were education, age, and region of residence. Persons with a college education, under 30, from areas outside the South were most likely to answer yes.
Level of education again affected the formation of an opinion on the subject.

These polls indicate some important characteristics of public attitudes on
policy issues. One is the effect of different social backgrounds on individuals' opinions. Particularly notable is the effect of education. College graduates, for instance, tend to oppose government intervention in the economy,
but they are hesitant to see the country forsake its commitments to other
nations; they also tend to be tolerant on the race issue.* The great reluctance with which the President finally inroduced wage and price controls,
as well as the general policies the national government has pursued in recent years in fostering internationalism and preventing racial discrimination,
may mean that public officials pay particular attention to the views of well-
educated persons on such matters.

One possible reason for that extra attention is that many less well-
educated citizens have not formed an opinion on the most vital problems of

*Previous polls of attitudes on similar issues show the same pattern of preferences. The
1956 election-year study of the Survey Research Center of the University of Michigan
indicated that persons from upper-status (professional and business occupations) were
less likely to favor the government's helping people get doctor's and hospital care at low
cost than were those from lower-status (unskilled and agricultural) jobs. The former were
less likely than the latter to say that the nation was too involved in world affairs or
that the national government should stay out of the question of sending white and black
children to the same schools.

the day. When issues become more complex—such as the ABM program of the Nixon administration or the Taft-Hartley law governing labor-management relations—the general public's interest and information becomes even more limited. Some students of the subject have suggested that on most issues only about one-fifth of the American public is concerned with the matter. In formulating public policy, it is more meaningful for officials to look at the views of the "attentive public"—those who are knowledgeable and concerned about a particular problem—than it is to try to divine a majority will that does not exist. Concerned persons are likely not only to have a viewpoint on a public issue but also to feel intensely enough to do something about it.

Doing something about a public issue means participating in the political process. As the following section indicates, people undertake a variety of political activities, but some are more politically active than others.

POLITICAL PARTICIPATION

In a sense, everyone participates in the political process, if only in a passive way. As we saw in Chapter 1, one of the unique features of government is that all persons are subject to its commands and benefit from its operations. Thus people obey laws, pay taxes, and gain advantages from the order and security provided by public officials.

ACTIVE POLITICAL PARTICIPATION

When we talk of citizen participation in a democracy, however, we have in mind some kind of active involvement in the political process. This involvement may take many contrasting forms. It may entail private communication, as when an individual calls a public official on the telephone, writes him a letter, or pays him a personal visit. Or the communication may be public, as when a citizen sets forth his views in a letters-to-the-editor column of a newspaper. Another major distinction in type of involvement can be made between electoral activities—voting, attending party rallies, contributing financially to a candidate's campaign—and nonelectoral ones—organizing a letter-writing campaign on an issue, or joining an interest group. Yet another pair of categories contrasts continuous day-to-day activities undertaken within the normal operation of the political process and isolated episodes such as the mass demonstrations in Washington, D.C. described in Chapter 4. There are even differences in the methods used in demonstrations: some are legal and peaceful, while others are deliberately illegal and violent.

Lester Milbrath, a close student of political participation, uses still another basis for categorizing political actions: the amount of effort (time, money, and the like) that a given activity entails. Thus the citizen who turns on his television set to listen to a political speech makes a small political investment compared to one who serves in public office. In between these extremes are a variety of activities that run the gamut from voting to becoming a candidate for political office.

As might be expected, the number of persons who participate in a particular activity varies with the degree and personal costs of involvement. Most people listen to a political speech or vote at some time or another; relatively few run for a political office. Relationships also exist among various political activities. If a person engages in a fairly demanding one, such as holding office in a political party, chances are that he will also be involved in a less onerous one, such as attending a political rally.

Using this hierarchy of political actions as his criteria, Milbrath divides American adults into three major categories. One group he calls political "apathetics": they are totally uninterested in political matters and don't participate in even minimal activity, such as listening to political speeches. Milbrath estimates that about one-third of our adult population falls into that category. Another 60 percent he terms political "spectators": they seek political information, vote, discuss political matters, try to influence others into voting a certain way, and display their political preferences by bumper stickers or campaign buttons. The remaining 7 percent are the political "gladiators" who contribute time or money to political campaigns or run for office themselves.*

Thus individuals vary greatly in the extent to which they participate in political activities. What is it that disposes certain people to become politically involved and others to be unconcerned about the political world about them?

FACTORS AFFECTING
POLITICAL PARTICIPATION

Milbrath's analysis indicates that essentially the same factors are associated with various types of political activities, particularly those relating to political campaigns. These factors are of three major types: 1) personal (especially psychological) attributes of the individual, 2) his social position, and 3) the general political setting in which the participation takes place.

Persons who participate most extensively in political affairs are those who are psychologically interested in politics, that is, those who have intense feelings on an issue, a political candidate, or a political party. They also have confidence in the worth of their political views and feel politically efficacious, believing that political officials will listen to their views and take them into account. (In fact, individuals who have confidence in their gen-

*Milbrath draws his analogy from the roles played at a Roman gladiatorial contest: the "gladiators" actively engage in battle, while the "spectators" have the power to decide their fate. The "apathetics" are those that don't even bother to come to the arena for the contest.

eral abilities and who are sociable tend to transfer these attitudes over into the political arena.) Some other citizens who have no great personal interest in political affairs nonetheless feel that they have a civic duty to participate politically, at least to vote.

Certain social factors are also associated with political participation. Social class affects political actions: the well-educated are highly conscious of political matters and develop the confidence to deal with them; the affluent see a financial stake in politics; lawyers and teachers have important intellectual and social skills that are transferable to the political arena. Other social conditions also correlate with participation: people from urban areas are more active than rural residents; men tend to become more politically involved than women; Jews are somewhat more inclined to participate in politics than are Catholics, who, in turn, are more active than Protestants.*

Finally, the general political environment shapes political participation. Individuals who live in areas where politics has traditionally been an important activity or where political contests are close tend to be drawn into the campaign process more actively than people who reside in areas of low political interest and competition.

ASSESSMENT

The overwhelming proportion of American citizens support our nation, its form of government, and major public officials. However, they hardly meet the model of the Athenian citizen, highly interested and actively involved in political affairs. Rather, they tend to be apathetic or passive spectators of what is going on in the political process. Few become active in political campaigns or are interested or knowledgeable about major political issues.

There is, however, a minority of political activists in the United States who are concerned about public issues and who take the time and effort to participate in the campaign process. The factor that is most closely related to both political interest and political participation is social-class background, particularly the amount of formal education a person has. The well-educated not only participate more, but they also have a greater appreciation for the rules of the game and the values of democracy.

There are certain advantages in the fact that persons who know little about issues and do not understand the democratic rules of the game do not participate more in the political process. Otherwise, uninformed opinions would be transmitted to political officials. There is also a danger that the rights of minorities and democratic values in general would not be pro-

---

*A number of recent studies indicate that the backgrounds of student protesters strongly parallel those of persons involved in more traditional political actions: they tend to come from upper-middle-class professional parents (frequently the mother also has a career) who live in urban areas. A disproportionate number of them have a Jewish heritage.

tected. Viewed in this light, democracy is best protected by the present system whereby the political activists bring their knowledge and understanding of procedures to bear on the problems of governing our nation.

Yet there is also danger in the present situation. There is no assurance that the politically apathetic will always remain so: they may, for example, become exercised over a controversial issue such as communism or race relations and suddenly enter the political arena in support of leaders and policies that may be highly undemocratic. Also, there is no guarantee that upper-class activists will always take into account the interests of lower-class apathetics.

An ideal solution to the problem would be to politically educate everyone to protect his own interests and to understand the democratic rules of the game. Political-socialization studies provide some evidence that disadvantaged persons can be given a greater appreciation of democratic procedures and values in high school civics courses. Yet it would be naive to assume that such courses alone can accomplish miracles. It is much more realistic to think that political socialization must take place through many social institutions and at various stages of an individual's life. Moreover, we must face the fact that some persons will never become politically interested and involved, however much we may want them to do so.

There are some signs, however, that changes in our society may result in increased political interest and participation on the part of more Americans. It is significant to note that the conditions that are most closely associated with political understanding and involvement are also those that are becoming more prevalent in the United States. Thus more citizens today are attending college, moving to urban areas, going into the professions, and becoming part of the middle class. Also, with all their limitations, the mass media, particularly television, are providing political information to persons who have never before been exposed to it.

Another factor also bears on political participation: the extent to which our political institutions effectively channel the concerns of citizens to public officials. It is to this general subject that we now turn.

Selected Readings

An early study with remarkable insight into the psychological aspects of public opinion is Walter Lippmann, *Public Opinion*, first published in 1922 and reissued more recently as a paperback (New York: Free Press, 1965).

The best modern treatment of the role that public opinion plays in the American political system is V. O. Key, Jr., *Public Opinion and American Democracy* (New York: Knopf, 1961). Using survey data on political attitudes of the American public, the author traces the linkages between such attitudes and decision-making by public officials. A good short analysis of public opinion, with particular emphasis on how such opinions are formed, is Robert E. Lane and David A. Sears, *Public Opinion* (Englewood Cliffs, N.J.: Prentice-Hall, 1964). A book relating public opinion to democratic theory is Bernard Hennessy, *Public Opinion* (Belmont, Cal.: Wadsworth, 1965).

An analysis of the political socialization of elementary school children which pointed the way for other studies is Fred Greenstein, *Children and Politics* (New Haven: Yale University Press, 1965). Other major works in the field are Robert Hess and Judy Torney, *The Development of Political Attitudes in Children* (Chicago: Aldine, 1967), which focuses on the psychological aspects of political development, and David Easton and Jack Dennis, *Children in the Political System* (New York: McGraw-Hill, 1969), which emphasizes the way poltical attitudes learned early in life contribute to the stability of the American political system. A book incorporating data on political socialization in Jamaica as well as the United States is Kenneth Langton, *Political Socialization* (New York: Oxford University Press, 1969). An excellent general treatment of the subject, which synthesizes the findings of a number of studies and places them within a meaningful analytical framework, is Richard Dawson and Kenneth Prewitt, *Political Socialization* (Boston: Little, Brown, 1969).

A pioneering study of political attitudes of citizens in the United States, Great Britain, West Germany, Italy, and Mexico, is Gabriel Almond and Sidney Verba, *The Civic Culture* (Boston: Little, Brown, 1963). Based on survey data, the analysis focuses on basic orientations of individuals in these five countries towards their government and the role they expect to play in its operation. Two analyses of citizen attitudes on democratic principles and values are James Prothro and Charles Grigg, "Fundamental Principles of Democracy: Bases of Agreement and Disagreement," *Journal of Politics*, 22 (1960), 276–294, and Herbert McCloskey, "Consensus and Ideology in American Politics," *The American Political Science Review*, 58 (1964), 361–382.

A monthly publication of the results of public opinion polls on a variety of subjects is the *Gallup Opinion Index* (Princeton, N.J.).

Two excellent books that draw together a large number of studies treating various facets of political participation are Robert Lane, *Political Life: Why People Get Involved in Politics* (New York: Free Press, 1959), and Lester Milbrath, *Political Participation: How and Why Do People Get Involved in Politics?* (Chicago: Rand McNally, 1965). For an analysis of various aspects of one type of activity, student protest, see *The Annals of the American Academy of Political and Social Science*, 395 (May 1971).

CHAPTER 6

Interest Groups

Mothers marching outside the White House to protest the ABM program. (United Press International)

ALTHOUGH THE ABM CONTROVERSY described in the previous chapter had little meaning for the average American, it was of vital concern to a number of "attentive publics." Starting with a handful of scientists in Chicago who objected to the deployment of weapons in that area, opposition burgeoned in other urban communities as concerned citizens held mass meetings, picketed, and wrote their congressmen in protest. These actions helped influence President Nixon's decision to move the ABMs out of population centers and into rural areas.

A number of groups were opposed to any form of the ABM, however. Included were twenty-five church, peace, and disarmament organizations that joined forces in calling an Action Conference on National Priorities in the nation's capital to publicize their grievances with weapons policy. Another group, the Council for a Livable World, asked its members to contribute two percent of their income to support the campaigns of anti-ABM senators. Meanwhile, the National Committee for a Sane Nuclear Policy distributed bumper stickers proclaiming "ABM is an Edsel" [the Edsel was a Ford-produced automobile that flopped in the 1950s], and Jerome Wiesner, former scientific advisor to President Kennedy, helped prepare a book setting forth technical difficulties and dangers of the weapon. Elements of organized labor also joined the "anti" forces as the United Auto Workers, under Walter Reuther, opposed the ABM, claiming that it drained funds from needed domestic programs, while the United Mine Workers viewed the issue in light of their larger concern over the use of nuclear energy to replace fossil fuels like coal.

At the same time the pro-ABM forces rallied governmental officials in support of the program. Top administrators, led by Secretary of Defense Laird, appeared on television and before private groups to allay fears about the reliability of the ABM. The Department of Defense conducted briefings for interested congressmen and representatives of the mass media and worked closely with defense contractors in explaining the merits of the ABM.

Private groups also united forces to support the Nixon administration on the ABM issue. Three of the major ABM contractors (General Motors, General Electric, and Lockheed) contributed to the American Security Council, a private organization that published a pro-ABM booklet and report signed by Dr. Willard Libby, a Nobel-prize-winning chemist. The United Brotherhood of Carpenters and the International Brotherhood of Electrical Workers, unions that would have members employed on site construction, carried favorable reports on the ABM in their union magazines.

In addition, a newsletter of the conservative Liberty Lobby alleged that the Communist party was "orchestrating a massive drive against the Safeguard System."

The incident illustrates the variety of organizations that can become involved in public issues in American society and the kinds of motives—moral, economic, political—that prompt their actions. It also illustrates the diverse techniques that groups in the United States use in attempting to influence decisions made by public officials. Before examining such matters further, however, it will be helpful to consider a fundamental question: what do all interest groups have in common?

NATURE OF INTEREST GROUPS

An interest group is any collection of individuals with a shared attitude on some matter who make certain claims or demands on others in society with respect to that matter. It should be noted that not every group fits this definition. People who have red hair, or who earn $10,000 or more a year, or who are members of the Jewish faith share something, have certain characteristics in common. (Sociologists call these categorical groups.) But these common characteristics may or may not produce a common viewpoint.

Shared attitudes develop among people who have a common interest in a particular subject; typically they interact with one another over it. Thus people who like symphonic music may meet as a group to listen to records or to attend concerts. Or they may work together to sponsor a visit of a touring orchestra. Such a group does not qualify as an interest group, however, unless it meets the second requirement of the definition: that it make some claim on other people. If they demand that a local radio station stop playing nothing but rock music and devote certain hours to classical concerts, they are acting as an interest group.

In many instances the claims that interest groups make on others do not involve the political process. If the symphony-lovers merely try to influence radio station owners to play their preferred music, they do not qualify as a political interest group. But if the group demands that the Federal Communications Commission (an agency of the national government that grants licenses to radio stations) force every station to devote a certain percentage of air time to symphonic music under pain of losing its license, it is acting as a political interest group. This is the kind of interest group that is of primary concern to the student of government.

Typically symphony-lovers in the United States do not turn to the political process to further their interests, but there would be obvious advantages if they did. A radio station owner that refuses to cooperate voluntarily in playing symphonic music might do so under threat of losing his license. Moreover, symphony-lovers might persuade their city council to subsidize a local orchestra by using public funds to make up any deficit the group might incur. In doing so, they would be taking advantage of the government's ability to take money from individuals who do not necessarily like orchestral music and use it for the enjoyment of those who do. Thus public officials are particularly helpful to groups because they can do what private individuals cannot: issue commands people will consider legitimate and utilize the taxing and spending power to benefit some persons at the expense of others.

Political interest groups have available two basic approaches for attempting to influence public officials. They may seek *positive* benefits, such as requiring radio stations to play symphonic music or convincing city councils to subsidize a local symphony orchestra. Or they may try to *prevent* the government from taking an action; for instance, those who do not appreciate symphonic music may try to stop public officials from pursuing either of the above policies. Groups that are generally satisfied with the present distribution of values attempt to preserve the *status quo* by taking defensive actions in the political arena. The two approaches are not mutually exclusive, however, and groups frequently pursue both simultaneously: at the same time that music-lovers are attempting to influence the city council to subsidize a local symphony, they may try to prevent the use of public money to support a baseball team.

Interest groups also attempt to accomplish their purposes through private channels. Although labor unions exert extensive influence in government, they also make demands on employers and the general public through strikes and picketing. Other groups also seek to satisfy their demands by dealing directly with private individuals and organizations; students have sought to bring about major changes in universities through negotiation, as well as confrontation, with school officials. We will examine the activities of one of these groups—the Students for a Democratic Society—later in the chapter.

Thus interest groups attempt to achieve some of their objectives by private means and others through political channels. This is one of the characteristics that distinguishes an interest group from a *political party*, which focuses its activities almost entirely on political processes. In addition, the primary methods by which interest groups and political parties attempt to accomplish their purposes differ. Political parties seek to staff governmental positions by running candidates for office; interest groups typically attempt to influence the actions of whatever officials are in office.

This distinction is a matter of emphasis only; the division of political labor between the two kinds of organizations is not complete. As we will see in Chapter 9, some persons who participate in political party activities are concerned with issues and support a party or its candidates primarily because of their stands on such issues. Conversely, some interest groups try to influence the selection of political office-holders because they believe that certain persons will be more likely than others to pursue sympathetic courses of action. Yet the primary purposes of the two types of organization differ. Political parties *always* run candidates for office, and frequently issues are not a major factor in campaigns. Interest groups typically try to influence public officials on issues in which the group is concerned; quite often they make no attempt to determine who is chosen; and they *never* (at least in the United States) run a candidate for office under the label of their own organization.

A final note is in order on the name *pressure group*, an older term for interest group, often used in disapproval by persons who think of such groups as selfish, irresponsible organizations seeking special privileges for their members. Yet some groups have members who devote themselves to causes that benefit others; many white persons, for instance, belong to the National Association for the Advancement of Colored People because they sympathize with the problems of blacks. The word "pressure" implies that such groups use improper means—force, bribery, threats—to achieve their purposes. But, as described later in this chapter, the techniques by which interest groups attempt to wield political influence vary greatly and include methods like conveying factual information to political officials, which can hardly be said to constitute "pressure" in the sense in which that term is normally used. To avoid any emotional connotation or inaccurate characterization of what the groups I am discussing actually are or do, I use the more neutral and descriptive term "interest group."

INTEREST GROUPS
IN AMERICAN SOCIETY

Americans have long been known as joiners. Alexis de Tocqueville, a young French nobleman who came to America in the 1830s and wrote a perceptive analysis of American society, *Democracy in America*, had this to say on the subject:

> The Americans of all ages, all conditions and all dispositions constantly form associations. They have not only commercial and manufacturing companies in which all take part, but associations of a thousand other kinds, religious, moral, serious, futile, restricted, enormous or diminutive. The Americans make associations to give entertainments, to found establishments for education, to send missionaries to the antipodes. Wherever at the head of some new undertaking you see the government of France or a man of rank in England, in the United States you will be sure to find an association.

Tocqueville's impressions of the part associations played in American society during the Jacksonian era are generally confirmed by recent studies of voluntary groups in the United States. The Five-Nation study referred to in the last chapter showed that Americans are more likely to join voluntary associations than are citizens of the other countries studied: 57 percent of our citizens were members of some such organization, compared to 47 percent of Britons, 44 percent of Germans, 30 percent of Italians, and 24 percent of Mexicans. Significantly, the 1970 edition of the *Encyclopedia of Associations* lists more than 15,000 national associations covering a wide variety of interests.

At the same time Tocqueville's statement is undoubtedly too sweeping. Not *all* Americans today (not in all probability in his time either) belong to voluntary associations; in fact, almost half do not belong to even one. Moreover, there are marked differences in membership among people of different "conditions." The comparative survey showed that fewer than one-half of Americans with a primary school education (or less) belonged to a voluntary group, compared to four-fifths of those who attended a college or university. Other studies also show that the number of organizations a person belongs to varies with his social and economic background. A 1952 investigation by the Survey Research Center at the University of Michigan indicated that over half of professional people were members of three or more voluntary organizations; for unskilled workers, the figure was one in twenty.

The student of government, of course, is particularly interested in political associations, those that turn to the political process to accomplish at least some of their purposes. There are no precise statistics on how many of the more than 15,000 voluntary groups reported in the *Encyclopedia of Associations* are political in nature, but those listed as pursuing, say, hobbies, athletics, and horticulture probably accomplish most of their objectives through private rather than public channels. Three of the four groups most often mentioned by Americans in the Five-Nation study were religious, social, and fraternal organizations (the fourth was trade unions), which again probably seldom use political means to accomplish their purposes. In fact, in that same study, only about two in five Americans reported that groups they belonged to got involved in political affairs.

Even those groups that do use political means differ in the extent to which they do so. Thus some become politically involved only on rare occasions, while others do so almost constantly. Groups also vary with respect to the scope of their political activities. Some turn to government to accomplish a broad range of purposes; others restrict their political involvement to one major issue.

Historically, economic groups have been most frequently involved politically in a broad range of issues. At the very outset, commercial cliques (manufacturers, merchants, ship-owners, and large farmers) and noncommercial ones (small businessmen and farmers, artisans and mechanics) contended over the writing of the Constitution and Madison himself considered the major differences among men to be based on the distribution of property. The following discussion focuses on the three major economic groups that have been most prominently involved in the American political process over the years: business, labor, and agriculture.

BUSINESS INTEREST GROUPS

The first national organization representing a variety of businesses was established in 1895 in response to an economic depression. Taking the name *The National Association of Manufacturers*, the group initially had a positive goal of promoting trade and commerce but soon shifted to the negative aim of counteracting the growing strength of organized labor. During the 1930s the NAM came under the control of large firms; it remains the major spokesman for big business today. Its 14,000 membership consists of firms and individuals engaged in manufacturing; it also has "cooperating" members (financial institutions and transportation companies with close relationships to manufacturers) that contribute financially to the organization. Its major policy goals are counteracting the power of organized labor (although the organization now accepts the general principle of labor unions); lowering individual and corporate taxes; preventing extensive government regulation of business; and promoting free enterprise in the United States and other nations of the world.

The NAM never claimed to represent state and local chambers of commerce, or a large number of trade associations operating at the regional and national level. In 1912 the Taft administration sponsored a meeting of such groups from various parts of the nation to establish an organization that would legitimately speak for the general business community. At that meeting the *Chamber of Commerce of the United States* was born. Today it consists of 4000 chambers of commerce and trade associations, plus 34,000 business firms and individuals with an underlying membership of more than 4,500,000 firms and individuals. Since its membership is broader than that of the NAM, its officials can speak more legitimately for the entire business community; however, because the chamber represents such a wide range of businesses, frequently it cannot take stands on certain important issues. For example, the Chamber has avoided enunciating a definite position on reciprocal trade (exchanging goods between countries with little or no duty) because some members fear competition from companies abroad while others want to export goods free of foreign duties. The general political goals of the Chamber parallel those of the NAM: counteracting the power of organized labor, reducing taxes and government regulation, and promoting the virtues of a free economy.

A third business interest group with somewhat different policy goals than those of the NAM and the national Chamber is the *Committee for Economic Development*. Founded in 1942 by persons who felt that business groups had been too negative towards the New Deal without developing positive economic programs of their own, the organization played a major role in the enactment of the Full Employment Act of 1946 under which the national government assumed the responsibility of promoting high employment, high production, and economic growth in the American economy. In keeping with this greater appreciation for the role of government in the affairs of the nation, several of the major leaders of the CED have occupied top positions in Washington: most notably one of the founders of the organization, Paul Hoffman, served as the first Director of the Economic Cooperation Association, which dispensed financial aid through the Marshall Plan to European nations after World War II. Favoring greater economic cooperation with other nations, the CED also played a major part in the establishment of the International Monetary Fund and the World Bank.

For much of American history, business groups dominated the political system. The depression of 1929, however, shook public confidence in the business community, which failed to prevent the passage of major New Deal legislation. The general prosperity after World War II restored some of that confidence so that business organizations once again became more politically effective. Even so, they have never regained their former preeminence in public affairs, in part because other groups—particularly their traditional rival, labor—have become better organized politically.

LABOR INTEREST GROUPS

American workers have faced major obstacles in organizing themselves. Owners have traditionally regarded attempts to influence working conditions as an improper intrusion into their own prerogatives, and for many years public officials (particularly judges) supported that position. American laborers themselves have frequently regarded their employee status as temporary until they could acquire enough capital to start their own businesses; they have also failed to develop a sense of working-class consciousness. Many citizens have also associated labor organizations with the violence used by working classes in some European countries. American workers have had to take these conditions into account in creating groups to represent their interests.

The first successful national labor organization, *The American Federation of Labor* (established in 1886), reflects the adaptation of a European concept of working class to the American environment. Its organizational base was skilled craftsmen—carpenters, bricklayers—who exhibited a sense of pride and solidarity. The economic goals of the AFL were essentially conservative: the union used the governmental process in a negative way, primarily to seek protection against court orders forbidding strikes, rather than for positive benefits in the form of minimum wages, public housing, or social security for its members. (In 1932, three years after the beginning of the Great Depression, the AFL still opposed unemployment insurance for workers on the grounds that such payments constituted governmental interference in concerns that should be left to management and labor.) The group's political tactics were similarly cautious: following the advice of the organization's founder, Samuel Gompers, to "defeat labor's enemies and reward its friends," the union avoided blanket endorsement of candidates of either major political party, including those running in presidential elections.

The growth of mass industries (coal, steel, and automobiles) in the 1920s and 1930s created unskilled jobs rather than openings in the skilled crafts; the appropriate organizational units for the new giant concerns were industry-wide unions joining all steelworkers, all autoworkers, and the like. The AFL leadership, however, was not eager to bring a flood of unskilled workers into the organization to threaten the dominance of skilled craftsmen, and so refused to permit workers in the mass industries to be organized permanently along industrial lines. This decision led John L. Lewis, head of the United Mine Workers, to leave the organization and form a new national union known as the *Congress of Industrial Organizations.*

The CIO sought much broader and more positive political goals than the AFL. Its leadership favored minimum wages, public housing for low-income groups, social security, and other measures associated with the New

At a union meeting, literature is passed out for study in a program aimed at political education. (Werner Wolff-Black Star)

Deal of Franklin Roosevelt. (In contrast, as late as 1938, the AFL leadership supported, only with the greatest misgivings, legislation providing for minimum wages in interstate businesses.) The CIO leaders also differed markedly in background from the top men in the older organization: younger and better-educated than their AFL counterparts, they felt more at home with the intellectuals who formed an important part of the Roosevelt administration. The CIO also departed from the cautious political policy of the AFL by establishing a Political Action Committee in 1944 to work for the reelection of Roosevelt.

This division in labor's ranks contributed to the movement's inability to prevent the passage in 1947 of the Taft-Hartley Act, a law placing restrictions on union activities. Eventually this outside threat from labor's traditional enemy—big business—forced the craft and industrial unions together so that the two organizations merged in 1955 as the *AFL-CIO*. However, tensions developed between the organization's new president, George Meany (former head of the AFL), and Walter Reuther, president of the Industrial Union Department of the new organization, who previously headed the United Auto Workers of the CIO. Besides the personal power struggle between the two men, they also differed in policy: Reuther charged that the organization was not involving itself in broad social causes he favored, such as ending racial segregation in all areas of American life (including the construction industry, which traditional AFL unions dominate). Differences in style between Meany, a cautious man with limited verbal abilities, and Reuther, called by many the "Billy Graham of Labor," also created personality clashes between them.

Ultimately the break came in 1968 as Reuther's union, the United Auto Workers, left the AFL-CIO and shortly thereafter joined forces with another major ex-CIO union, the Teamsters (this union, led by Jimmy Hoffa, had been expelled in 1957 for alleged ties with gangsters and a misuse of union funds by its officers), to form a new group called the *New Labor Alliance*. Soon a third body, the International Chemical Workers Union, joined the organization. Boasting a membership of some four million, the new group dedicated itself to a Reuther-inspired program calling for broad social and economic reforms and to an effort to forge links with the youth of America and the intellectual community.

The result of these developments is a weakened labor movement. Besides the New Labor Alliance, other important elements of organized labor (in particular the railroad workers) lie outside the AFL-CIO. Thus labor speaks with a divided voice. Moreover, all labor organizations together today represent less than one-fourth of the civilian work force.

Cross currents are operating in the labor movement today. Automation in industry has eliminated blue-collar jobs of employees who traditionally have joined unions. On the other hand, the growth of white-collar positions in our economy creates organizational problems for labor, since employees in these positions have generally had middle-class aspirations and have not felt the need to be unionized. Yet labor organizers have begun to make inroads into white-collar ranks, especially among government employees and school teachers. Other potential targets for unionization include migrant farm workers, service employees (hospital workers and the like), office clerks, and employees of the burgeoning new industries of the South where organized labor has traditionally been weak.

AGRICULTURAL INTEREST GROUPS

The farmer has traditionally been considered a rugged individualist who, by hard work and diligence, can supply the necessities of life for himself and his family without depending on others. Whatever the romance, in fact, the commercialization of agriculture in the years after the Civil War made the farmer dependent on a number of other groups: manufacturers of agricultural machinery, railroads that transported his crops to distant markets, concerns that provided storage facilities, as well as a variety of "middlemen"—flour millers, grain operators, wholesalers, and retailers—who intervened between him and the consumer.

American farmers initially sought negative political goals, particularly the regulation of rates charged by railroads and grain elevators. In time they turned to the pursuit of positive benefits for themselves. *The American Farm Bureau Federation* developed from a program established by the national government in 1914 to educate farmers in new agricultural techniques. County farm bureaus, established by states to cooperate with extension agents of the United States Department of Agriculture in demonstrating such techniques, formed state chapters, and eventually a national federation was set up in 1920. Also supporting the federation were the state land-grant colleges that had traditionally carried on programs in agricultural research.

During the 1920s to 1930s the Federation joined forces with other farm groups to pursue a broad program that included getting the national government to guarantee the farmer a "fair" price for his produce.* Bills providing such assistance were vetoed by Republican Presidents Coolidge and Hoover, but a price-support program was ultimately enacted during the administration of Franklin Roosevelt.

Since the end of the 1930s, however, the experience among farm groups has paralleled that of the labor movement: the major agricultural organizations have come to speak for different, and in many cases, competing interests. The American Farm Bureau today represents primarily the wealthy large farmer of the Midwest corn and hog belt, as well as cotton planters of

---

*The price is generally referred to as "parity," meaning the dollar figure needed to maintain a balance between what a farmer has to pay for things he buys and what he can sell his crops for. Thus if the cost of items a farmer purchases goes up, so should the price he is paid for his products.

the South. Although the group took the initial leadership in the development of a price-support program for basic crops, today it favors a reduced role for government in agriculture and a free market for determining the level of food prices. The members are mostly prosperous farmers who benefit from the economies of large-scale farming and who can now compete effectively in such a market; moreover, withdrawing price supports from small farmers forces many of them out of agriculture, thus removing economic rivals of the large-farmer clientele of the Farm Bureau.

The primary voice of the less advantaged farmer today is the *National Farmers' Union*. This group, which draws its support from wheat farmers of the Plains states who are particularly vulnerable to vagaries of the weather (particularly droughts), favors a high level of government support for farm products and the provision of cheap credit. In recent years the NFU has also fought for legislation to protect migratory farm workers. The organization proclaims itself the champion of the dirt farmer, the man who devotes his life to farming as a way of life, rather than what the NFU calls the corporation farmer (represented by the Farm Bureau), who looks at farming strictly as a business.

Located somewhere between the Farm Bureau and the NFU in terms of clientele and general goals is the *National Grange*. Today the organization has its major base of support among dairy farmers in the New England, Middle Atlantic, and Pacific states. Less militant than the other two farm organizations, the Grange has moved closer politically in recent years to the NFU, primarily because it opposes the Farm Bureau's ultimate goal of abandoning governmental farm support programs.

Like labor, agriculture is experiencing a decline in its organizational potential because of technological developments. Mechanization and improved fertilizers mean that fewer farmers are needed to raise the nation's food supply. As a result, more and more people have left the farm in recent years to seek employment in the cities. (In 1960 our farm population was between fifteen and sixteen million; by 1969, it had fallen to between ten and eleven million.) Furthermore, farmers are not much inclined to join interest groups. In 1970 the largest of the three major groups, the Farm Bureau, claimed almost two million members; the Grange had 800,000; and the NFU, 250,000 members respectively. Only about one in four farmers belonged to any of the major farm organizations.*

The three general interest groups that have traditionally been most active politically continue to be so today, but they no longer dominate the American political scene as they once did. This decline in relative importance is due in part to their own difficulties described above; however, it also stems

---

*A fourth general agricultural interest group established in 1955 is the *National Farmers' Organization*. Concentrated primarily in Missouri and Iowa, it has tried unsuccessfully to withhold products from the market until a satisfactory price is received from food processors and purchasers. The group does not publish its membership size.

from the fact that a number of new interest groups have become better organized and more active in public affairs.

MAJOR CONTEMPORARY INTEREST GROUPS

Groups representing professional interests have become increasingly involved in public affairs. Doctors, for instance, have been organized into a national interest group, *The American Medical Association*, since 1847, but this association has turned more and more to the political process recently to further its aims. The activity has been largely negative, principally involving efforts to *prevent* the government from undertaking a broad program of health care for citizens through compulsory health insurance. On the other hand, the AMA, together with other groups involved in public health (hospital administrators, nurses, and the like), has acted positively to seek government aid for research grants and the construction of hospitals. Another professional interest group that has become increasingly involved in national politics of late is the *National Educational Association*, representing over a million school administrators and teachers. The fruits of its labor, as well as those of many other groups (such as the American Federation of Teachers) interested in all levels of the school system, are evidenced by the drastic increase in the amount of federal funds allocated for education in recent years: in the early 1960s it totaled to about $2.5 billion; by the early 1970s the figure had swelled to over $13 billion. Thus increased demands in health and education have brought new groups into prominence in public affairs.

Technological developments, along with increased American involvement in international affairs since World War II, have also moved other groups to the political forefront. An *ad hoc* group of scientists, alarmed by dangers associated with the development of the atomic bomb, is credited with influencing Congress in 1946 to establish a civilian agency, the Atomic Energy Commission, to control the manufacture and distribution of nuclear energy in the United States. The *Federation of Atomic Scientists* (now known as the *Federation of American Scientists*) has continued to exercise influence over the nation's nuclear program. In addition, the high level of government spending for national defense in the postwar period stimulated the formation of an informal coalition of interested groups: private companies seeking defense contracts, military officers protecting the interests of their branch of the service, labor unions involved in defense work, and congressmen promoting defense installations in their districts to further the local economy. Referred to by President Eisenhower in his farewell speech to the nation in 1961 as the "military-industrial complex," this coalition has been said to have a major influence on foreign policy, a topic we will consider in Chapter 17.

Among the many other interest groups that have become increasingly important in American political life in recent years have been those motivated by moral concerns, as epitomized by the John Birch Society and the Students for a Democratic Society. We will examine these two groups later in this chapter. First, however, let us analyze the internal operation of interest groups, as well as the ways in which they traditionally attempt to influence public policy.

INTERNAL OPERATION
OF INTEREST GROUPS

In theory, at least, interest groups are internally democratic in the sense that the rank-and-file members have a say over policy decisions, as well as the selection of officers. A small voluntary group operating at the local level takes the form of direct democracy, with its periodic meetings as the equivalent of the Greek Assembly or the New England town meeting. Officers serve the group by presiding over such meetings and carrying on the group's activities between them. Interest groups that are important in national politics, however, encompass thousands, or even millions, of members who are organized on a nationwide basis. Given their size, these organizations use institutions and procedures of representative democracy that permit a relatively few persons to act on behalf of the entire membership.

Most national interest groups have similar means for governing themselves. A national convention attended by delegates chosen at the state and local level usually meets once a year to pass on major policy matters and to select the persons who will be responsible for carrying on the activities of the organization between conventions. The latter group generally consists of an executive body composed of elected officials that meets periodically to discuss group affairs. (This body, in turn, often selects a permanent staff headed by an executive secretary who carries on the day-to-day activities of the organization.) Thus the operating principles of interest groups are democratic in form, and the few who handle the organization's affairs are held responsible to the many through representative institutions and procedures.

As a matter of fact, however, internal governance in most interest groups works in precisely the opposite way: an active minority runs the organization and the rank-and-file members exercise relatively little control over their activities. Conventions held once a year attended by persons who have limited knowledge of the details of the group's operations can hardly be expected to serve as a meaningful check on the actions of the group's leadership. Typically the convention adopts the leaders' policy proposals with relatively little debate. Elections at the conventions also generally result in acceptance of the leadership's nominees for office. In fact, it is not uncommon for the same individuals to be elected year after year without significant opposition: the United Mine Workers, for instance, had no seriously contested election for its presidency for almost half a century—from 1926 until 1969 when the incumbent president, Tony Boyle, beat off a challenge to his leadership by another official of the organization, Joseph Yablonski.*

A number of factors contribute to this internal situation. For one thing, the active minority has certain advantages in dealing with the rank-and-file membership. Besides a greater knowledge of the group's affairs, the experience the leaders gain in office helps them develop managerial and political skills that few regular members can match. They are also in a position to dominate the group's affairs in various ways: by appointing the "right" persons to key committees; by determining what views will be carried in the organization's newspaper (referred to generally as the "house organ") that is distributed to all members; and by seeing to it that group's finances are used for the proper purposes. Thus power over personnel, the pen, and the purse enable the officers and staff of most interest groups to control their organization's activities.

Also contributing to the active minority's dominance is the fact that checks and balances are not built into the internal goverance of most interest groups. Generally no organized opposition (like a political party) exists to field a slate of candidates against the incumbent leadership and criticize what it is doing. (Some groups have regulations forbidding members from conducting campaigns or holding behind-the-scenes meetings to line up support for elected officials; others have an informal understanding that such activities will not occur.) Nor is there a contending group of permanent officeholders present (such as a legislative body) to counter the ambitions of the ruling clique. Thus the concept of competing elites that operates in public democratic bodies is generally absent in private interest groups.

The situation described above characterizes *most* interest groups in the United States, but, of course, the active minority cannot always control all organizations: the International Typographical Union, for instance, has had two separate groups (or "parties") vying for leadership within the organization for years. Moreover, splits sometimes occur within a group's leadership: David McDonald, for many years the president of the Steel Workers of America, ultimately lost his post to another officer of the organization, Walter Abel. Nor does the leadership of an interest group succeed entirely in imposing its policies on the rank-and-file membership: not all doctors subscribe to the AMA's fears over socialized medicine, and many state and local chapters of the AFL-CIO have failed to implement the desegregation edicts of the union's national headquarters.

---

*Yablonski was fired from his union position after he entered the presidential contest, but a federal court ordered his reinstatement. Three weeks after the election he was killed. The federal government subsequently sued to have Boyle's election set aside on the grounds that there were irregularities in the voting.

Most interest groups, however, are able to reach substantial agreement on the organization's political goals and policies. The following section discusses the techniques they utilize to try to influence public officials to adopt those policies.

INFLUENCING PUBLIC POLICY

In order to accomplish its primary purpose of influencing public policy, a political interest group seeks "access" to official decision-makers, that is, the opportunity to present its point of view to them. For an interest group, however, access means more than mere contact with decision-makers; it also connotes a willingness to consider the group's views, whether or not the official ultimately decides to adopt them.

The process by which interest groups seek access to public officials is called *lobbying*. The term originated in the practice common to interest group representatives of frequenting the lobbies of government buildings in order to contact officials. Those who did so were referred to as "lobbyists" and the activity itself became known as "lobbying."

Lester Milbrath, a close student of the subject, defines lobbying as a process by which someone (the lobbyist) communicates with a governmental decision-maker* to try to influence what he does (or does *not* do) about a particular matter. Milbrath confines lobbying to communications made on behalf of someone else: a citizen who acts solely for himself concerning some public policy is not usually considered a lobbyist.

LOBBYISTS

As Milbrath suggests, interest groups make various arrangements to have their views presented to national officials. Large trade associations that have major offices in Washington, D.C. typically use executive officials of the association as lobbyists, as do national labor unions which are headquartered there. Groups with offices elsewhere must depend on a "Washington representative" to handle their lobbying; these persons normally handle the political affairs of a number of organizations. Some law firms located in Washington not only carry on a standard legal practice before the courts but also represent clients on essentially political matters before legislative and executive officials. In addition, individual "lobbyist-entrepreneurs," who specialize in particular matters not requiring legal expertise, farm out their services to groups on a fee basis.

Whatever the arrangement, interest groups look for persons who possess

---

*Although interest groups seek access to all three branches of government, the means by which they try to influence judges are much different from those they use on legislators and executive officials. We will examine the techniques they utilize before the courts in Chapters 13 and 14.

information and skills that make them effective lobbyists. Ex-senators and former members of the House of Representatives (along with former members of their staffs) are knowledgeable about particular legislation and also understand the complexities of the legislative process and enjoy contacts with former colleagues. As former legislators they have the right to go on the floor of the legislative chambers, a privilege that supposedly gives them an advantage in influencing legislation, particularly at the crucial time of a vote.* Despite these advantages, however, more lobbyists come from the executive than the legislative branch in Washington. The former has a far larger number of former employees than the latter to draw from, and as we will see in Chapter 12 more and more crucial decisions are made by administration officials. Therefore, individuals knowledgeable about a given government agency are invaluable to organizations with business before it.

The skills of two professions, law and journalism, are particularly helpful to lobbyists. Lawyers are able to analyze the provisions of legislation, as well as executive regulations. Persons trained in writing and public relations work can utilize those skills effectively in communicating with decision-makers, members of their own organizations, and the general public—all targets of lobbying activities as discussed below.

Lobbying is not a profession for which people specifically prepare themselves. Most individuals go into the work by happenstance. Serving a stint as a lobbyist for a business organization is often part of the broad training of executives. Labor lobbyists are typically people who have previously demonstrated their political and verbal skills in the work of a union. Former employees of the legislative and executive branches are often sought as lobbyists by interest groups who have observed them in their previous capacities.

Even though lobbyists do not specifically point towards that career, most of them enjoy the work and continue in it. Particularly rewarding is the sense of accomplishing something for their organization, the opportunity to interact with other people, and the challenge involved in preparing and defending an argument supporting their group's point of view. Pay and working conditions are also good, particularly for those lobbyists who represent business and professional groups.

TYPES OF LOBBYING

Lobbyists utilize a variety of approaches in communicating viewpoints to decision-makers. Some involve direct contacts with public officials; others utilize intermediaries to try to influence such officials. The former method is called *direct* lobbying, the latter, *indirect* lobbying.

*Former House members, however, are forbidden to go on the floor if they are in the employ of an organization that is interested in the particular legislation under consideration.

Direct Lobbying. The lobbyist who is trying to influence Congress has a variety of options open to him. Since, as we will see in Chapter 10, the fate of legislative proposals largely depends on congressional committees that initially consider them, lobbyists appear before those committees to express their group's viewpoint on pending legislation. This approach permits the lobbyist to reach a number of influential legislators at one time. It also allows his group to get its views on record, since a transcript of committee hearings is made and distributed to concerned parties (including members of the interest group, who are thus furnished with proof that their lobbyist is working on their behalf).

Lobbyists, however, rate direct personal communications with individual congressmen or senators as a more effective technique of persuasion than appearances before committees. Congressmen are frequently absent from committee meetings, or they have their minds on other matters while testimony is being taken. A personal visit to a congressman assures attention and is more likely to convey the impression the lobbyist thinks the individual legislator is important enough to warrant special consultation.

The above techniques are applicable to direct communications with officials of the executive branch. Government agencies also hold official hearings to take testimony of private groups, and lobbyists frequently call on executive officials to discuss problems of their clients.

Indirect Lobbying. Lobbyists work through intermediaries to try to influence decision-makers. Congressmen and top executive officials with busy schedules depend heavily on their assistants to keep them briefed on legislative and executive matters. Therefore, lobbyists who are able to persuade staff members of the merits of a client's point of view may be able to reach a major public official through his trusted employees.

Lobbyists often find it advantageous to work through other persons who enjoy special relationships with a decision-maker they hope to influence. Personal friends of officials, of course, may provide an entrée, but even more helpful in reaching senators and representatives are their constituents, particularly those who are in a position to affect their political careers. If a lobbyist is able to get a heavy contributor to a congressman's campaign or a newspaper editor who supported him for election to adopt his interest group's point of view and convey it to the elected official, he is virtually ensured that it will be well-received.

Lobbyists frequently use intermediaries to contact congressmen and executive officials who are not generally sympathetic to their organization's political goals. By working through neutral individuals, not only do they avoid rebuffs, but they also hope to counteract any prejudice that might prevent their group's case from being examined by public officials on its merits. Lobbyists also use intermediaries as a means of increasing the number of people concerned with a particular issue. By widening the public, they seek to increase the political support for (or opposition against) a program of concern to their group.

One natural source of political support for a lobbyist is the membership of the organization he represents. Individual members often are not aware of the stands their lobbyist takes in Washington, but they can be made aware of them through letters from the leadership or through the organization's newspaper. Thus the United Brotherhood of Carpenters and the International Brotherhood of Electrical Workers used their union newspapers to carry favorable accounts on the ABM as a vital weapon for defense. Similarly, the American Medical Association ran stories in its weekly journal for years against "socialized medicine."

Lobbyists frequently enlist the aid of members of groups they represent to try to influence public officials. One technique is to get an individual to write his congressman or the executive officials involved, expressing his views. A flood of mail can serve to alert a decision-maker of the importance an issue has for some segments of the American public. At the same time, experienced public officials are able to detect a contrived letter-writing campaign stimulated by a lobbyist. Letters with identical wording, those sent on the same day, as well as those coming in disproportionate numbers from a particular area of the country, are not likely to have much influence on a public official. The wise lobbyist advises members of his organization to express their views in their own words and seeks to solicit letters written at different times from various parts of the nation.

Besides letter-writing, other possibilities for using group members include getting them to talk to congressmen and senators when they are back home campaigning or visiting, having individual members call on their congressmen when they are in Washington, and perhaps most effectively of all, calling a conference in the nation's capital to let the lawmakers know firsthand how concerned individuals and groups feel on a particular issue.

A further broadening of the public involves getting diverse interest groups to join forces in the effort to influence congressmen and executive officials on a particular matter. This approach indicates to politicians that an issue is of concern to more than an isolated segment of the public. Groups that join political forces in this way are frequently drawn together as natural economic allies: defense contractors worked together with the carpenters' and electrical workers' unions to win congressional support for the ABM because, despite their differences over labor-management problems, all of them stood to benefit economically from development of the weapon. Business interest groups also take on the political battles of their customers: certain railroads, for instance, have opposed the importation of oil from abroad because so much of their freight business comes from coal companies that are hurt competitively by the rival fuel.

Beyond immediate interests that lead groups to join forces on a particular issue, there is an increasing tendency for certain organizations with divergent interests to adopt each other's political causes. Thus the Chamber of

Commerce of the United States typically sides with the American Farm Bureau Federation on agricultural policy questions, while the latter takes the Chamber's side on business issues before the Congress. Similarly, the AFL-CIO and National Farmers' Union tend to end up on the same side of most political issues. This form of "logrolling"* or exchange of support, has obvious political advantages for all parties concerned, but the practice also develops because members of various interest groups share certain fundamental values and political attitudes. Thus "liberal' organizations like the United Auto Workers, the National Farmers Union, the Americans for Democratic Action, and the Federal Council of Churches generally advocate that the national government develop programs to help the disadvantaged. "Conservative" groups such as the National Association of Manufacturers, the American Farm Bureau Federation, the American Legion, and the Young Americans for Freedom prefer that the poor and deprived help themselves, or if outside assistance is necessary, that it come from private groups or state and local governments. Such opposing ideologies frequently result in two general constellations of interests, those that support and those that oppose governmental programs to change the *status quo* in favor of underdog groups in American society.

Besides rallying the support of members of their own organizations and forming alliances with like-minded groups, lobbyists in recent years have turned their attention to an even more inviting target for indirect lobbying: the general public. If an interest group can make enough people sympathetic to its desires and persuade them to convey their sentiments to those in public office, then it has achieved a major strategic objective: getting other people to lobby for it.

The effort to shape public attitudes on issues takes different forms and involves various strategies and groups. Frequently, lobbyists use members of their own organizations to influence the general public. In the fight against "socialized medicine" some years ago, the leadership of the American Medical Association got doctors to distribute literature and to talk to their patients about the matter. The organization capitalized on the layman's tendency to respect his own physician and to regard him as an expert on health issues.

As another technique the testimony of independent authorities can be presented to persuade the public of the merits of a particular view. As we saw, both the pro- and anti-ABM forces used this technique: the American Security Council published a booklet signed by a Nobel-prize-winning chemist supporting the weapon, while the other side countered with a publication by a former science advisor to President Kennedy setting forth his objections to it.

Yet another tactic is to operate through an organization whose name con-

---

*This term is usually used to describe the practice whereby legislators back each others' bills to their mutual support.

ceals the true identity of its supporters. Some years ago a group called the Small Business Economic Foundation was formed purportedly to speak for the views of the modest entrepreneur. On investigation, it was determined that among the small businesses behind the organization were United States Steel, Goodyear Tire and Rubber, the Texas Company, and a number of other firms of comparable size. This same attempt to capitalize on symbols to which the public responds favorably* is reflected in the title of an organization called the Committee for Constitutional Government, which is backed primarily by a number of conservative business groups in the United States. It has a counterpart, The Public Affairs Institute, through which liberal groups, particularly certain labor unions, convey their views to the public.

Interest groups also use the mass media to transmit ideas in ways that camouflage their true source: letters-to-the-editor columns of newspapers frequently carry statements signed by individuals that in actuality are drafted by lobbyists. A similar practice is the preparation of "canned" editorials. The harried editor of a weekly newspaper who must handle all aspects of the paper's operation may welcome prepared statements on public issues that save him the effort of writing original editorials—especially when the material expresses his own viewpoint and is better organized and written than anything his busy schedule would permit him to develop. (Both parties benefit from such an arrangement: the editor is made to look like a perceptive and critical analyst of public issues, and the interest group gets its views purveyed without the public's knowing their real source.)

Television is another natural outlet for interest groups that seek to shape public attitudes on controversial issues. When President Kennedy outlined his program on medical care for the aged on national networks, a representative from the American Medical Association responded shortly thereafter with the physicians' case against the program. Standing alone in a bare studio, the AMA spokesman sought to convey the image of the solitary citizen battling to preserve his liberties against the organized forces of the national government and the awesome power of the Presidency.

Thus lobbying has become increasingly complex and sophisticated over the years as interest-group representatives have zeroed in on a broader array of targets and utilized a greater variety of techniques in their quest to influence public policy. Whereas communications were once directed essentially to legislators, lobbyists have now broadened their efforts to the executive branch of government where more and more key decisions affecting

---

*An additional advantage in using such titles is the possibility that the organization will be considered an "educational" group by the government, thus qualifying it for certain tax advantages or exempting it from registering under federal legislation regulating lobbying.

private groups are now being made. At the same time, they have expanded their activities to take in various intermediaries—including the general public itself—which can assist them with their lobbying efforts. Their techniques have also undergone change as interest groups employ modern methods in influencing public attitudes through the mass media.

Along with such changes has come a supplementary activity: keeping communication channels open to decision-makers so that when future lobbying takes place, it will be effective. In other words, lobbyists seek to create good relationships with legislative and executive officials to insure that their messages to them will be well-received. They also strive to develop a generally favorable impression with the American people so they may benefit from that impression when they later try to exert influence on behalf of their group.

OPENING COMMUNICATION CHANNELS

In a democratic society the relationship between public officials and interest groups is a two-way process: private groups not only press demands on officials; they also serve as potential bases of support for them. Thus lobbyists can keep communication channels open to congressmen and members of the executive branch by undertaking activities of value to them.

The most basic support an interest group can provide any public official is to help him get into office in the first place. If he seeks an appointive office, the group's representatives can use whatever political influence they have to see to it that persons responsible for the appointment are made aware of the man's qualifications and the high esteem in which he is held by that organization. As will be discussed in Chapters 12 and 14, many interest groups become involved in appointments to major executive posts and seats on the federal bench; in the process they try to persuade the President, who makes the nominations, and the Senate, which must confirm his nominees, to choose men who will be receptive to their organizations' political views.

Interest groups are also in a position to provide important political support for a man who is running for an elected office. This support can take many forms: making financial contributions to his campaign; providing information or writers for his political speeches, along with audiences for them; running favorable publicity for the candidates in the house organ, besides endorsing him publicly; or helping to get voters registered and to the polls to vote in his behalf. In addition, an interest group can help him in the nomination process (discussed in Chapter 8) and in the general election (analyzed in Chapter 9). The earlier the group provides an individual political support, and the more extensive that support is, the more likely he is to grant access to the representatives of that organization.

Yet there are also political dangers involved for the interest group that commits itself to a would-be official. If he fails to be appointed or elected, it is not likely that the group will have access to his opponent. Moreover, it is by no means certain that an organization can deliver its members' votes in an electoral contest: despite organized labor's endorsement of the Democratic presidential candidate, Adlai Stevenson, in 1952 and 1956, many rank-and-file workers voted on both occasions for his opponent, Dwight Eisenhower. Or even if a group can persuade its members to support a particular candidate, they may be so widely scattered geographically that they don't have much of an impact on the election. The group must also consider the possibility that if it throws its active political support one way, its political enemies may be stimulated to enter the contest on the other side. Thus an organization's representatives must weigh the advantages and disadvantages of active political involvement in behalf of a particular political party or candidate.*

Whether or not an interest group decides to try to play a role in the selection of public officials, it typically performs important services for those who are already in office. Included are the furnishing of factual information and, if the official desires it, the writing of speeches to be given before his constituents. Lobbyists can also provide officials with ready-made audiences through their own membership and can rally their support for measures favored by the officials. Such services are designed to make a public official grateful and incline him to be receptive to future lobbying.

Another technique for keeping channels open to public officials is entertainment, or the "social lobby." Frequently the general public is treated to newspaper exposés that play up such socializing as though it were the only form of lobbying. Undoubtedly this tactic is successful with some national officials, yet most of them are so busy that they harbor the few moments they can spare from the pressures of their job for their family and close personal friends. The social lobby may be more successful in state capitals, where legislators are away from their families during the week and hence have more time for (and less family scrutiny of) social activities.

Lobbyists are frequently pictured as stealthy figures with little black satchels stuffed with money that they disperse as bribes to win favorable decisions from congressmen and officials of the executive branch. Although bribery may occur on occasion, instances of it have rarely been proven, despite the vigilance of the Washington press corps. In 1956 lobbyists of an oil company were accused of offering Republican Senator Francis Case of South Dakota a $2500 campaign contribution (which he rejected) to influence his vote on a natural gas bill. Bribery charges were brought but subsequently dropped against two lawyers involved in the affair; however, they

---

*One technique employed by some groups is to contribute financially to more than one candidate or to have various leaders or members support different would-be officials. Then, presumably, no matter who wins, the organization has access.

did plead guilty of violating the Federal Regulation of Lobbying Act of 1946 discussed below. As a result of the incident, President Eisenhower vetoed the bill, even though he originally favored it. The repercussions from the event (in which there was no suggestion that Senator Case acted improperly in any way) demonstrate the peril to lobbyists of establishing questionable relationships with persons in positions of political authority.

Lobbyists also try to keep communication channels open to the American public in order to shape basic attitudes that are favorable to their respective groups. One approach is to work through the schools to promote particular textbooks: business prefers those that support the free enterprise system, while labor looks with favor on books that emphasize the dignity of work and the contributions that unions have made to American life. Groups from both camps frequently send materials to teachers for use in the classrooms. Some have gone so far as to subsidize the writing of textbooks favorable to their general point of view on public issues. Another technique is "institutional advertising," which seeks to sell a political point of view as well as a commercial product. For years a Cleveland corporation, Warner and Swasey, has run an advertisement in *Newsweek* magazine setting forth a conservative viewpoint on economic and other issues.

A more subtle way of keeping channels open to the American people is through publicizing activities that reflect credit on a group. A number of years ago certain chain stores in California faced the possibility that a tax on their operations passed by the legislature would be approved in a referendum set for a year later.* A public relations firm determined that their unfavorable public image could dispose the voters to support the tax. With the assistance of the firm, the stores launched a campaign publicizing a plan to improve their employees' wages and working conditions. They also cooperated with peach-growers in helping to absorb an unforeseen surplus of their crop. In addition, the chains offered to close their businesses on Sundays if independent stores would do likewise. A poll taken immediately before the referendum indicated a change in public attitude towards the chain stores, and the electorate subsequently voted down the proposed tax decisively.

Many interest groups today do not wait for an issue to develop before attempting to shape public attitudes; they rather work constantly to create a reservoir of good will toward their organization from which they can draw when the occasion arises. Public relations men see to it that favorable publicity about a group's members is released: when business executives and labor leaders head up Red Cross drives and United Fund campaigns or offer their services voluntarily in building a Boy Scout camp or fixing up a church, news of their philanthropic activities is not hidden under a bushel

---

*Laws passed by legislatures in most states can be referred to the voters for approval or rejection in referendum elections.

but instead is displayed widely to the American people. Thus groups seek to keep the channels open to the general public as a means of ensuring that when they do want to lobby on issues that concern them, their communications will fall on receptive ears.

LEGAL REGULATION OF LOBBYING

Lobbying is regarded in the United States as a legitimate method for influencing public policy. It has been granted constitutional sanction as coming within the basic rights of free speech and petition guaranteed by the First and Fourteenth Amendments to the Constitution. Congress has, however, placed two types of restriction on lobbying: 1) certain limits on the kinds of activities interest groups may engage in; 2) requirements that lobbyists and organizations disclose their identity as well as certain basic facts about their operations.

One type of lobbying that is clearly considered beyond the rules of the game is bribery. Federal laws make it a crime for persons to offer a congressman "anything of value" for the purpose of buying his vote or otherwise trying to influence his official actions. Congressmen who accept such offers are also subject to criminal charges. The difficulty with enforcing the law is that it is virtually impossible to prove that a favor was tendered for the purpose forbidden by the Act. (For example, it does not constitute bribery for a lobbyist to promise a congressman future political support in order to influence his vote on legislation.) Most students of the subject consider this legislation ineffective in preventing questionable dealings between interest group representatives and congressmen.

The role of lobbies in making financial contributions to political campaigns is limited by law. We will explore the subject of campaign finance in Chapter 9; it is sufficient for the present to note that certain organizations (corporations and labor unions) are prohibited from making any direct campaign contributions in federal elections and other groups face limitations on the amount of contributions they may make.

With these exceptions, interest groups are free to lobby at will. But Congress has taken the position that its members, as well as the American people, have the right to know who is supporting and opposing legislation and that financial arrangements of lobbyists and interest groups with business before the national legislature ought to be a matter of public record. Thus lobbying activities are not to be prohibited but, rather, illuminated.

Although lobbyists for certain groups were singled out by Congress in the 1930s and made to disclose information about themselves and their clients (included were lobbyists for public-utility holding companies and shipping firms, and representing foreign governments), it was not until 1946 that a law was passed requiring similar information of lobbyists and interest groups in general. Enacted as part of a broad statute dealing with the reorganization of Congress, the Federal Regulation of Lobbying Act requires any person (or group) hired by someone else for the "principal purpose" of influencing congressional legislation to register with the Secretary of the Senate and Clerk of the House and file quarterly reports on his receipts and expenditures for lobbying. Organizations that collect money to engage in such activities but do not hire themselves out as lobbyists for someone else are required to file similar financial information with the Clerk of the House.

It is generally agreed that the law contains so many loopholes that it has not been effective. Groups ostensibly affected by the Act avoid its applicacation by arguing either that they spend their own funds for lobbying rather than soliciting them from outside sources or that the outside funds they do collect are not raised for the "principal purpose" of influencing Congress. Lobbying directed to executive agencies or the general public is not covered by the law, nor is testifying before legislative committees.

The law also leaves it up to groups themselves to determine the portion of their total lobbying expenditures that needs to be reported; as a result, organizations with large financial outlays claim to spend very little, arguing that most of it goes for research and public information (which are not covered by the statute) rather than direct personal contact with congressmen. Finally, even the information that is reported is virtually worthless, since no agency is empowered either to investigate its truthfulness or to assure that violations of the law are enforced. Until such time as these deficiencies are rectified (to date, Congress has been unwilling to do so), the Act will fail to accomplish its major objective: disclosure of activities of major lobbyists and interest groups in the United States.

Despite the lack of effective legal regulation of lobbying, however, Washington observers agree that most persons tend to respect certain informal rules of the game in attempting to influence public policy. Aside from matters of individual conscience, lobbyists naturally desire to protect their reputations with their colleagues and, even more importantly, with public officials. If a lobbyist provides false information to an official and is found out, he will certainly lose the very thing he works so hard to achieve: access to that individual. In all probability, the official will also tell others of his unfortunate experience, so that the lobbyist will find himself cut off from a number of important persons who make vital decisions affecting his group. Thus the denial of access is a powerful deterrent to lobbyists who may be tempted to engage in improper activities in seeking to influence public decisions.

Access is important, however, only to those lobbyists who attempt to work within the present governmental system in affecting public policy. Yet a number of persons in recent years have sought to bring about great changes in American society but have despaired of accomplishing their goals through the ordinary political processes. They have instead turned to "extremist" interest groups to achieve their purposes.

EXTREMIST INTEREST GROUPS

Typically the term "extremist" is applied to groups without definition. Two frames of reference are common. One relates to the *purposes* of the group: the goals sought by its members differ greatly from those of the great bulk of citizens in the society around them. Thus a group in the United States that wants to take private property from individuals and place it under public ownership may be said to have an extremist view on property ownership. (In another society, this attitude might be shared by most citizens, in which case it would not be an extremist view.) The second frame of reference relates to the *means* by which a group seeks to accomplish its purposes. Thus an organization that openly advocates violence to achieve its ends is considered to be operating beyond the rules of the American game, and so is labeled extremist. Frequently the two frames of reference are linked, since it is unlikely that groups can accomplish goals radically different from those sought by most citizens in a society without resorting to extreme means to achieve them. Not all groups fit both categories, however: various socialist societies in the United States over the years have favored extremist economic goals (at least by American standards) without advocating or resorting to violence to reach them. Their commitment to peaceful means has meant more to them than a desire to see major changes in the economic organization of American society.

Extremist groups have haunted American history—witness the Ku Klux Klansmen who took the law into their own hands in dealing with racial conflicts in the South and the vigilantes who maintained order extralegally on the American frontier. Recently there have developed in the United States a number of groups that are committed to both extremist goals and extremist means to accomplish them. Their distinguishing feature is their devotion to broad, basic ideals. Rather than focus attention on fairly narrow matters that affect specific interests of their own members, they have instead concerned themselves with basic moral values, as they conceive them, that should apply to society in general. Unhappy with the present state of affairs in the United States, they have sought underlying reasons for society's ills, as well as means to cure them. In diagnosing defects and prescribing remedies, the members of each group have necessarily established certain tenets that are basic to any set of beliefs: a number of assumptions concerning human nature—that is, convictions about how good, bad, rational, irrational, competent, or incompetent the average person is.

An interesting aspect of the recent activities of extremist groups in the United States is that both sides of the political spectrum, the left as well as the right, have been involved. Although the opposing groups share a common concern about the failure of our society to adhere to certain basic moral values that they feel are important, members of the left and the right do not agree on what those moral values are and the reasons why our citizens do not live up to them. Moreover, they differ over the kinds of policies that should be adopted to set things right, as well as the means to be used to get those policies adopted.

THE RADICAL RIGHT

In the late 1950s and early 1960s a number of anticommunist organizations became politically active in the United States. Although they had different memberships, their political beliefs were essentially the same and they used similar means to implement those basic beliefs. As a group they were labeled the "Radical Right." The best-known of these organizations was the John Birch Society; because it is typical of the others, we will focus our attention on it.

Founded in 1958 by Robert Welch, a candy manufacturer and one-time member of the Board of Directors of the National Association of Manufacturers, the organization was dedicated to stopping what Welch conceived to be a communist take-over of the nation. To symbolize that threat, the society was named for a young Baptist missionary, who, while serving as an American intelligence officer in World War II, was killed by Chinese communist guerrillas ten days after the defeat of Japan in August 1945. Welch considered Birch the first victim of "World War III," a confrontation in which first the nations of Eastern Europe, then China, and later Cuba were lost to powers hostile to the nation's basic interests.

Welch and his followers were also aggrieved by a number of domestic developments—racial integration, welfare programs, the banning of religious exercises in the schools, high taxes, civil rights demonstrations, the "coddling" of criminals, and other changes in what they considered to be the traditional American "way of life." In fact, for the Birchers, these developments in foreign and domestic policy were closely linked: a giant conspiracy was responsible for both. Hard-core communists, their sympathizers, and well-meaning persons duped by their devious designs, were all part of a movement to take over American society and deliver it to their masters in Moscow or Peking. In pursuing their evil schemes, these groups worked not only through the government, but also the major private institutions; the churches, the schools, and the mass media had all been subverted by the communists. A major threat to America came, therefore, from within.

This being the case, Welch and his followers set out to counteract the communist threat through the same channels. The media were to be used to alert the American people to the real nature of communism and its conspiratorial methods. Welch proposed the establishment of reading rooms, similar to those employed by Christian Scientists, where people could be educated on such matters. The Society itself developed a series of publications, including a monthly journal entitled *American Opinion*, to carry the true word on communism to its members, as well as to a larger audience.

Local chapters were urged to make sure that the public schools and libraries carried books on the dangers of communism and that churches heard ministers who were alert to the Red Peril. Finally, the Society provided financial and other support for political candidates who were dedicated to fighting communist influences in government. Thus the John Birch Society practiced indirect, grass-roots lobbying, along with the tactics of keeping channels open to decision-makers.

Welch, however, also encouraged his members to pursue tactics usually considered to be beyond the rules of the democratic game. Birchers were advised to heckle opposition speakers by planting themselves in the audience and raising pointed questions suggesting that those on the platform were communists. Persons suspected of communist leanings were singled out for threatening phone calls late at night, while merchants who sold goods from communist countries—such as Polish hams and Hungarian brooms—were subjected to the harrassment of having cards placed under the merchandise carrying the message, "Always buy your Communist products at _____."

In a famous book entitled *The Politician* published in 1963, Welch himself attacked prominent political leaders of our nation as members of the communist conspiracy. Included were George Catlett Marshall, Army Chief of Staff in World War II, who was charged with being "a conscious, deliberate, dedicated agent of the Communist conspiracy." Also identified as serving the communist cause was a former President of the United States. "With regard to . . . Eisenhower," Welch wrote, "it is difficult to avoid raising the question of deliberate treason." The latter statement lost Welch support among many followers, but he defended it as necessary to expose the enormity of the communist threat.

Welch argued that it was necessary to "fight fire with fire" and that therefore Birchers should, when possible, employ the tactics of the enemy. One device typically used by communists is the creation of "front organizations" designed to accomplish a political goal without identifying the persons behind it. Birchers accordingly founded an organization entitled "The Movement to Impeach Earl Warren" and purchased billboard space to attack the Chief Justice as a traitor. (Welch himself contributed to the movement by sponsoring an essay contest for college students with awards going to those who gave the best reasons for Warren's impeachment.) Other practices the Society borrowed from the communists included maintaining the secrecy of its membership and keeping centralized control over the organization (Welch himself chose local chapter leaders), which Welch defended as necessary to prevent communists from infiltrating his organization.

Thus both the beliefs and the tactics of the John Birch Society were extremist. The values cherished by Welch and his followers—individualism, the rights of private property, and a concern for the spiritual needs of man —are shared by many Americans, but few regard them as the moral absolutes that Birchers do. Nor do most Americans agree with the Society that virtually all the recent developments that have occurred in the United States since the New Deal—social security, unemployment compensation, labor legislation, welfare programs, and the like—are "socialistic" or collectivist ventures that are leading the nation inexorably down the road to a communist dictatorship.

Even political conservatives in America do not share the beliefs of the Society. They are willing to accept reasonable restrictions on free enterprise, and while they do not agree with many of the policies the government has pursued at home and abroad, they attribute the policies to the misjudgments of political leaders rather than to a deliberate conspiracy to undermine the American way of life. Finally, no responsible conservative would share Welch's view (espoused in *The Blue Book*, one of the publications of the society) that democracy is "merely a deceptive phrase, a weapon of demagoguery" and "a perennial fraud." Welch's preference for a "republic," in which a few natural leaders, endowed with special qualities of moral insight and courage, would rule, is clearly too elitist for the mainstream of American conservatism.

The halcyon days of the John Birch Society and the Radical Right came to an end in the middle of the 1960s after the disastrous defeat of Barry Goldwater in the presidential election of 1964. About that time, however, new groups from the opposite end of the political spectrum began to make their influence felt in American society.

THE NEW LEFT

The "New Left" is the label attached in recent years to those who have protested injustices in America and have demanded that society be radically restructured to end them. The word "new" is included in the label to distinguish the movement from the communist groups in the 1930s that constituted the "Old Left." Unlike their predecessors, the members of the New Left do not agree on a coherent political philosophy, such as Marxism, with a blueprint of what society should become. Rather they reflect a general mood of dissatisfaction with the nation's values and social institutions and a commitment to taking action to change them—even though they cannot predict exactly what form the new society will take. The group most prominently identified with New Left was the *Students for a Democratic Society.**

The SDS was formed in 1962 by a group of college students who met at Port Huron, Michigan, and adopted a manifesto setting forth the guiding principles of the organization. Drafted by Tom Hayden, a graduate student at the University of Michigan, the "Port Huron statement" defined the ma-

---

*Another group associated with the New Left was the Student Nonviolent Coordinating Committee that took action in the 1960s against racial segregation in the South. I will discuss that group in Chapter 15.

jor purpose of the organization as "the establishment of a democracy of individual participation governed by two central aims: that the individual share in the social decisions determining the quality and direction of his life; that society be organized to encourage independence in men and provide a medium for their common participation."

In many respects the general SDS indictment of American society parallels that of the hippies discussed in Chapter 1. They charged that we have become too materialistic, worshipping things rather than caring about individuals, and that our major social institutions—the government, schools, corporations, labor, unions—are huge bureaucracies, cold, impersonal organizations that rob people of their essential dignity and worth as human beings.

A number of specific injustices deeply disturbed members of the Students for a Democratic Society. They charged that American society is thoroughly racist, as reflected in the treatment of Negroes and other minority groups at home and in interference with the internal concerns of helpless peoples abroad, notably in South Vietnam and the Dominican Republic. National policies are also militaristic: the nation wastes its youth on imperialistic wars and spends billions on defense hardware at the same time it ignores the desperate needs of the cities and the poor. Universities pay no heed to the problems of blacks or of students in general; they prefer to allocate their precious resources to research on military weapons and on esoteric courses with no relevance for the social problems of American society.

For the SDS the answer to such problems was not to escape an immoral society by "opting out" of it as the hippies do, but rather to restructure social institutions so that they will serve human needs. Most members saw little hope for changing those institutions by a process of gradual reform from within; the Establishment—governmental leaders, university presidents, corporation executives, and the like—would never permit this to happen. The only way to bring about necessary alterations in American society is to use drastic methods to destroy its existing institutions and to substitute new "counter governments" or "counter organizations" in their place.

The methods employed by the SDS varied greatly. In some instances its members stayed within the rules of the democratic game by utilizing peaceful sit-ins and marches to protest injustices. Some, however, harassed speakers, prevented companies involved in defense work from conducting job interviews on campuses, disrupted classes, and occupied university buildings to get officials to accede to their demands. On some occasions property was damaged (as when the President of Columbia University had his desk ransacked), and physical force was used by some militant members of the SDS to remove university administrators from their offices. Most extremist of all were the tactics of the militant "Weatherman"* faction of the SDS: in Oc-

*The group took this name from a line in Bob Dylan's song, *Subterranean Homesick Blues*: "You don't need a weatherman to tell which way the wind blows."

tober 1969 they staged "Days of Rage" demonstrations in Chicago during which they destroyed property and charged police lines.

The use of such tactics clearly differentiates SDS adherents from political liberals who also seek to eliminate injustices in American society but who work through regular channels and within the conventional rules of the democratic game. In fact, the SDS reserved its most bitter criticism for liberals who, they charged, pay lip service to equality, individualism, and democracy, all the while tolerating racism and manipulating people to win political support through false promises and token benefits.

Within less than a decade after it was established, the SDS virtually disappeared from the American political scene. The beginning of the end came at the organization's annual convention in 1969 when the group divided into warring factions: the National Officer Collective under the leadership of Mark Rudd, leader of the 1968 Columbia University revolt, and representatives of the Progressive Labor Party, a clique that labeled itself as "Maoist" and that was committed to the communist doctrine of class warfare. The "Days of Rage" demonstrations led by the Weathermen alienated moderate members who quit the organization by the thousands. In early 1970 the na-

During their "Days of Rage" in Chicago in 1969, helmeted Weathermen smash store windows with sticks. (United Press International)

tional headquarters was closed and hard-core militants went underground to plot violent revolution against the Establishment.

Thus the John Birch Society and the Students for a Democratic Society shared a deep dissatisfaction with the values and goals of American society, and a willingness to use extremist means to implement their demands for change. As previously indicated, however, most American interest groups seek to channel the desires of their members to political decision-makers through the regular processes of government. How well, in fact, do they perform this basic function in American society?

ASSESSMENT

Interest groups clearly make a valuable contribution to the American political system. By channeling demands of citizens to those in positions of public authority, they inform leaders on what people in various segments of our society think about important public issues. They also educate officials by providing them with factual information and arguments relating to vital issues. Although each interest group naturally presents its own side, legislative and executive officials are able to examine a wide range of views and can balance the merits of one against another in making decisions.

One major weakness in American interest groups is that not everyone benefits equally from them. Well-educated persons from the upper social classes are more inclined to join organizations than are the less educated and the poor. Beyond the matter of representation, business and professional organizations have more financial resources to spend on lobbying than do other interest groups. They also benefit from their prestige and the deference accorded their members by office-holders and the general public as well. The result is that upper- and middle-class Americans are more likely to have their demands satisfied than are less-advantaged persons.

Yet the have-nots in American society are better organized today than they formerly were, as is evidenced by the number of interest groups representing blacks, welfare mothers, tenants, and the like, that have been formed in recent years. What these groups lack in the way of financial resources is at least partially compensated for by their numbers and the efficacy of direct action techniques such as political protest marches and sit-ins. Moreover, these groups have been aided by the sympathy that many people in public office, as well as significant elements of the American public, have for their claims. (In fact, many Americans, particularly young people, have worked actively with such groups to help them organize for political action.) The outcome has been the enactment of a number of laws benefiting social and economic disadvantaged persons.

Another major aspect of interest groups that deserves comment is their internal operation. The form of their governance is democratic but the practice is oligarchical. Members typically have little control over their leaders, and competing internal elites do not frustrate one another's ambitions.

There are, of course, certain political advantages in that situation. Long-term leaders who are knowledgeable and experienced about group affairs are able to effectively represent the interest of the members in the political arena. Being cohesive and disciplined also assists an organization in combating its political rivals and in speaking with a united voice.

The danger in the internal situation, however, is that group leaders will pursue their own interests rather than those of the general membership. This has happened, for example, in certain labor unions where officers have misused moneys (especially in the administration of pension funds) and have also made arrangements with employers that benefited them but not the rank-and-file members. In some instances, moreover, group leaders promote political goals that have little appeal for the general membership.

Describing the problem of the internal governance of interest groups is much easier than figuring out ways to improve it. It seems unrealistic to expect such organizations to develop opposition candidates, together with other institutions and techniques that operate in public bodies: almost none has done so to date. Government regulation of certain aspects of internal governance—such as requiring disclosure of financial affairs and insuring that elections of officers are honest—has been utilized, especially with respect to labor unions. Even so, there are limits to how much public authorities should intervene in the affairs of private organizations in a democracy.

There are, however, some mitigating circumstances. Rival organizations do exist in some instances, so that a person who is not satisfied that the leadership of one organization is adequately representing his interests can join another. Furthermore, as the following chapters indicate, demands and preferences can be channeled to decision-makers through agencies and means besides interest groups, such as political parties and elections.

Selected Readings

The most comprehensive treatment of interest groups is David B. Truman, *The Governmental Process: Political Interests and Public Opinion* (New York: Knopf, 1951). Emphasizing the theoretical aspects of group behavior, it stimulated a number of studies in the 1950s on the role of interest groups in our society and today is still considered the classic work on the subject. Other good recent studies supplementing Truman's work are Harmon Zigler, *Interest Groups in American Society* (Englewood Cliffs, N.J.: Prentice-Hall, 1964), and Abraham Holtzman, *Interest Groups and Lobbying* (New York: Macmillan, 1966). The latter book also analyzes the activities of interest groups in Great Britain and Italy and compares them with those operating in the United States.

Tocqueville's perceptive analysis of voluntary associations in the United States is contained in his classic study, *Democracy in America*, edited by Phillips Bradley (New York: Knopf, 12th ed., 1954).

Analyses of the organizations and purposes of major interest groupings in the United States are included in the Truman and Zigler books cited above. Other excellent treatments of the subject are V.O. Key, Jr., *Politics, Parties and Pressure Groups* (New York: Thomas Y. Crowell, 5th ed., 1964); J.W. Peltason and James M. Burns, *Functions and Policies of American Government* (Englewood Cliffs, N.J.: Prentice-Hall, 2nd ed., 1962); and R. Joseph Monsen, Jr., and Mark W. Cannon, *The Makers of Public Policy: American Power Groups and Their Ideologies.* (New York: McGraw-Hill, 1965).

For an analysis of the internal operation of interest groups in terms of democratic theory, see Grant McConnell, "The Spirit of Private Government," *The American Political Science Review*, LII (1958), 754–770. For general treatments of the subject of the internal governance of interest groups see Chapter 2 of Holtzman and Chapters V, VI, and VII of Truman. Two excellent studies of the internal operation of specific interest groups are Oliver Garceau, *The Political Life of the American Medical Association* (Cambridge: Harvard University Press, 1941), and Seymour Martin Lipset, Martin Trow, and James S. Coleman, *Union Democracy: The Internal Politics of the International Typographical Union* (New York: Free Press, 1956). The former discusses the methods by which the leadership of the American Medical Association dominates its affairs; the latter examines the unusual "two-party" system of the ITU that results in alternative groups of leaders being offered the rank-and-file membership.

The general treatments of interest groups cited above include analyses of the techniques by which interest groups attempt to influence the making of public policy. The best empirical study of the characteristics of lobbyists who operate in the nation's capital and the means they use to communicate their desires to congressmen is Lester W. Milbrath, *The Washington Lobbyists* (Chicago: Rand McNally, 1963).

Two good collections of articles treating of right-wing groups in the United States are *The Radical Right*, edited by David Bell (Garden City, N.Y.: Doubleday, rev. ed., 1964), and Robert A. Schoenberger, *The American Right Wing* (New York: Holt, Rinehart and Winston, 1969). Both contain treatments of the John Birch Society. A similar book dealing with the New Left, including the Students for a Democratic Society, is the volume edited by Paul Jacobs and Saul Landau entitled *The New Radicals: A Report with Documents* (New York: Random House, 1966). Treatments of both the New Left and the Radical Right are included in the March 1969 issue of *The Annals of the American Academy of Political and Social Science* entitled "Protest in the Sixties."

Two books that stress the contributions of interest groups to American democracy are those cited above by Truman and Milbrath. Those critical of the narrow perspectives of such groups are E.E. Schattschneider, *The Semisovereign People: A Realist's View of Democracy in America* (New York: Holt, Rinehart and Winston, 1960), Grant McConnell, *Private Power and American Democracy* (New York: Knopf, 1966), and Theodore Lowi, *The End of Liberalism: Ideology, Policy, and the Crisis of Public Authority* (New York: Norton, 1969).

CHAPTER 7

Political
Parties

Delegates to a state Democratic convention typify the middle-class, middle-aged members who, by their power in party organization, contribute to students' critical views of political parties. (Wide World Photos)

IN SEPTEMBER 1796, six months before the end of his second term as President, George Washington announced to the American people his decision to eliminate himself as a candidate in the upcoming election. His famous Farewell Address set forth his hopes and fears for the young republic. What troubled Washington most was the possibility that it would be destroyed by the "baneful effects of the spirit of party." For he saw parties, particularly those based on geographical divisions, as threatening not only to national unity but also to popular government itself.

Almost two centuries later, at the end of the turbulent decade of the 1960s, a Gallup poll of American college students revealed the same mistrust of political parties. As Table 7.1 indicates, they ranked lowest of nine major American institutions in the estimation of the students. Statistically, not even one student in five rated political parties excellent or good, compared to two out of three who were favorably disposed towards universities. For a college generation not known for its satisfaction with institutions of higher learning, the poll pointed up how critical students are of political parties.

That today's vocal and critical young people would find themselves in agreement on a key political matter with the nation's chief father figure— a charter member of the American Establishment—is perhaps ironical. What is even more ironical is that despite Washington's attitude, the first democratic political parties in the world developed right here in the United States. In fact, they were already in existence at the time of the Farewell

TABLE 7.1 How Students Rate American Institutions

Institutions	Responses (in Percentages)		
	Excellent	Good	Total Favorable
Universities	12	56	68
Family	23	35	58
Business	12	44	56
Congress	7	49	56
Courts	6	40	46
Police	6	34	40
High schools	4	33	37
Organized religion	7	26	33
Political parties	2	16	18

Source: The Newsweek Poll—The Gallup Organization, Newsweek (December 29, 1969), p. 43.

Address. Moreover, they have persisted: the Democratic party, indeed, is the world's oldest political party. Further, as indicated in Chapter 9, most Americans today identify with either the Republican or the Democratic party.

Such conflicting attitudes indicate that the national experience with parties has been ambivalent. Americans created a major political institution that exists in all democratic societies in the world, yet many of them have great misgivings about the value of what they created. Why this is so is not clear, but exploring a number of questions may help to explain the situation: what is a political party and what part should it play in the governance of a free society? what are the major characteristics of political parties in the United States? and what have they actually contributed to the political system and to American society in general?

THE NATURE
OF POLITICAL PARTIES

Students of government have experienced as much difficulty in defining a "political party" as they have had in explaining what is meant by "public opinion." Particularly confusing has been the failure of political scientists to identify the specific features of a political party that distinguish it from other political agencies linking the general public to political officials.

POLITICAL PARTIES, INTEREST GROUPS,
AND FACTIONS

The writings of some of the Founding Fathers illustrate the same problems of definition. In *Federalist Paper* No. 10, Madison uses three separate terms to describe divisions in society. One is "faction," a concept we explored in some detail in Chapter 2. Another is "interest," which he calls the most durable source of factions, using as illustrations a manufacturing interest, a mercantile interest, and the like. Elsewhere in the same selection, the Father of the Constitution refers to conflicts of rival "parties." Washington's Farewell Address is similarly vague: his condemnation of the "spirit of party" seems to reflect an unhappiness with the general state of divisiveness and bickering among citizens rather than an attempt to single out a particular kind of political agency, the party, for criticism.

A student of government today has different things in mind when he uses these three terms. A *political party* is a group of persons who run candidates for public office under a label. It is this activity that distinguishes a party from an "interest," or what we would today call an *interest group*. Members of the latter do care about who holds office and may try to influence voters' decisions: business groups tend to support Republican candidates who they feel are generally sympathetic to their policies, while labor unions favor Democratic ones for the same reason. But neither group offers its name to persons seeking office: no one runs under the banner of the United States Chamber of Commerce or the AFL-CIO.

Frequently, if inaccurately, political parties are distinguished from interest groups on other grounds, such as the number of persons associated with each. Typically, political parties do attract more supporters than interest groups: far more people identify with either the Republican or the Democratic party in the United States than belong to the Chamber of Commerce or the AFL-CIO. But the same is not true of minor political parties. Only about 52,000 persons voted for the Socialist-Labor candidates for President and Vice President in 1968, as compared with the more than thirteen million Americans who belonged to the nation's largest labor organization that year.

Nor can political parties necessarily be distinguished from interest groups on the basis of their purposes. Not all political parties have as their primary goal the capture of public office. Witness the succession of minor parties that have appeared from time to time in American politics. Although some members of these parties undoubtedly thought their candidates had a chance to win, most members have worked through these organizations as a means of registering their political demands. They have reasoned that even if their party could not win, because of the publicity given its goals during the course of the campaign or the electoral threat posed to the two major parties, their demands might receive more attention than if they worked only through interest groups. As we will see subsequently, many policy proposals of minor parties have eventually been adopted by officeholders and the major parties, evidence that such political calculations of minor party backers have been vindicated.

On the other hand, not everyone who supports a political party does so because of its policies. Many individuals develop a psychological attachment to a particular party at an early age and, as discussed in Chapter 9, back its candidates without regard to their stand on issues. Some persons participate in party activities because they expect to be rewarded with some concrete benefit, such as a job or other political favor. Others enjoy the excitement of party activities or the social contacts with other participants.

In brief, the crucial factor that distinguishes a political party from an interest group is neither size nor purpose; it is, rather, the *method* each chooses to make its influence felt in the political arena: a political party is the only organization that runs candidates for office under its label.

It is also necessary to distinguish a political party from a faction. Historically, factions preceded political parties; they were groups of individuals who joined together on an *ad hoc* basis to win some political advantage for themselves. Thus certain individuals in England worked as a group to influence the King or to control the Parliament. After the advent of elections to choose public officials, factions formed around particular individuals or families (such as the Clintons in New York State) to contest for political posts. In the days of a restricted electorate and relatively few elective offices, these factions were able to control elections fairly effectively. As a greater number of individuals gained the right to vote, however, and as more and more offices became elective, it became necessary to organize electoral efforts more extensively and to place them on a more permanent basis. Particularly important was the task of identifying candidates so that voters could tell who represented which group. It was then that factions took the crucial step that turned them into political parties: running candidates for office under a common label.

The term "faction" is still used today, primarily to designate groups that are part of a larger political entity. Sometimes it is employed to describe portions of an interest group, such as the National Office Collective and Progressive Labor Party factions of the SDS described in the last chapter. More often the term is used to designate some grouping within a political party based on a particular personality, philosophy, or geographical region. Thus we speak of the Daley faction of the Illinois Democratic party (after the powerful Mayor of Chicago), the conservative faction of the Republican party, or the Southern faction of the national Democratic party. In this sense, faction is synonymous with "division" or "wing."

A faction typically centers around some political personality, local political elite, or occasionally a particular political issue. Factions generally lack the features of a major political party—a permanent, well-organized structure and a symbolic relationship with their followers—that enable parties to transcend particular personalities or issues. For this reason, factions are less likely to persist over a series of elections than are parties.* They also frequently operate behind the scenes rather than out in the open, because they lack the legitimacy of political parties in that people are not willing to grant them the right to run candidates for office. In any event, they do not do what I have suggested is the hallmark of a political party: running candidates for public office under a given label.

MEMBERSHIP IN AMERICAN POLITICAL PARTIES

Another difficulty in dealing with political parties is the problem of identifying its members. Most Americans do not go through the formality of joining a political party and paying dues to it as is common in interest groups and in many European political parties. Thus the Socialist party of France or the American Farm Bureau Federation of the United States can state that it has so many members, but the Republican and Democratic

---

*Exceptions do exist, particularly in certain Southern states. For instance, former Senators Harry Byrd of Virginia and Huey Long of Louisiana dominated the politics of their states for years; even after they died, their respective followers continued to be associated together as members of the Byrd and Long factions.

parties cannot. When we speak of those who belong to our two major parties, whom are we talking about?

One way to decide who should be considered members of a party is to
determine the ways in which various individuals are involved in the kinds
of party activities Milbrath demarcated. We could start with the following
general categories:

1. *Party leaders*: the individuals who hold major positions in the party,
   such as the chairman and members of the national, state, or local
   committee.
2. *Activists*: persons who work extensively in party affairs, raising money,
   recruiting candidates, making speeches for candidates, attending rallies, and canvassing voters.
3. *Supporters*: those who support the organization by donating money to
   the party or its candidates and by displaying labels, buttons, and
   bumper stickers.
4. *Voters and identifiers*: those who regularly vote for the party's candidates in elections or who, when asked, say they consider themselves
   a Republican or a Democrat.

Although this approach does make some important distinctions, it also
has some major limitations. First, the somewhat arbitrary categories may
not reflect the actual influence various persons have in party affairs. Many
activists, for example, swing more actual weight in party matters than those
in formal party positions. Second, the realities of political life are such that
no one remains in a category on a permanent basis: an individual may become an activist in one election because of his interest in a particular candidate or issue, whereas in the next contest he may be merely a supporter
or even an ordinary voter. In which group should he then be placed? Finally, the categories do not include everyone who is associated with a party.
The prime example is a senator, congressman or state representative, or
executive official. Although a person in one of those positions does not hold
an official party post, he is elected under the party label or is appointed to
his position primarily because of his relationship to a particular party. Moreover, in the course of his official activities he is expected to reflect the views
of his party. He may thus be considered a party representative.

Aware of such difficulties, V.O. Key and Frank Sorauf identified three
major divisions of political parties associated with different activities and
different persons who participate in them. The three are:

1. *The party organization*: those who are active in party affairs, whether
   they hold an official party post or not. These are the individuals who
   carry on the major campaign activities of the party, contributing their
   time, money, skills, and effort.
2. *The party in the government*: those who hold official positions in the

legislative and executive branches and, as indicated above, are considered to be party representatives.

3. *The party in the electorate*: those who have a more casual relationship with the party—the supporters, voters, and identifiers.

These categories point up a major characteristic of political parties: they are broad-based and undertake a variety of activities. When we speak of the Republican or Democratic party, we need to identify the particular facet of party affairs and the specific group of individuals we are talking about. For a party itself encompasses a wide range of functions in a democratic society.

FUNCTIONS OF POLITICAL PARTIES

What do parties do? Some of their functions are specific and observable, such as recruiting candidates. Other functions are general and intangible, such as contributing to the peaceful settlement of disputes in society. A party's action may have a very specific intention, as when it runs a candidate with a particular ethnic background for office in order to attract the votes of members of that ethnic group. Yet a given action may also have a

Vice President Agnew greets the Republican faithful at a $100-a-plate dinner in St. Louis. (Wide World Photos)

significant byproduct—in this example, giving members of the minority group a feeling of importance, a sense of belonging to the society and an allegiance to its government. In talking about party functions we must also distinguish between things that parties *should* do, if they operate according to democratic theory (as discussed in Chapter 1), and the things that they *actually succeed in accomplishing*. We must also delineate those functions that are characteristic of all parties compared to those that are peculiar to only some.

One function that all parties perform is running candidates for public office under their label. Sometimes party leaders themselves actually go out and induce persons to become candidates. Political candidates are also recruited in other ways, however. An individual may be approached by an interest group or by acquaintances to seek public office. Or he may be a self-starter, deciding himself to become a candidate. Ultimately, however, he must run under some party label if he hopes for any success, at least in national and most state elections.*

In addition to providing political leaders, parties take the initiative in policy matters. The party in the government in particular helps to identify the major problems—social, economic, and political—that require the attention of the citizens of a society. As President Kennedy stated, it is the responsibility of these party leaders to lay the unfinished business of America before its people for discussion and action. Besides setting an agenda, party leaders have the obligation of recommending specific programs to help mitigate the problems they have identified.

Leaders of the party in the government also have the responsibility of using their influence to see that policies are implemented. The majority party organizes the legislative and executive branches of government so that programs they favor can be enacted into law. The minority party (or parties) has the function of criticizing the programs of the majority and of proposing alternative solutions to social problems.

Thus the major functions of political parties relate to three aspects of the the political process: providing leadership through participation in elections; identifying problems and proposing programs to deal with them; and organizing and managing the government. There is little question that, of the three, the first is paramount. It is also the function on which American political parties have concentrated. Our two major political parties have

---

*Many local elections are nonpartisan in the sense that no label appears on the ballot. Judges in some states and state legislators in Minnesota and Nebraska are also elected in this way. The rationale behind nonpartisan elections is that by removing party labels from the ballot, "politics" is removed from the selection process. Studies indicate, however, that the political affiliations of the candidates are known by many voters anyway; moreover, removing party labels from the ballot doesn't eliminate politics—it just *changes* the politics so that interest groups and newspapers (rather than the traditional parties) become influential in recruiting and backing candidates.

been somewhat less concerned than European political parties, for example, with developing concrete social programs; they have also been less success-ful in organizing the legislative and executive branches of government so as to enact party programs into law.

American minor political parties have also been deficient in regard to these latter two aspects of the political process. Although a variety of them have developed specific proposals for dealing with particular problems (witness their plans for removing the evil influence of alcoholic beverages, for dealing with currency problems, for giving relief to the farmer, and for controlling the trusts), they have not dealt with the broad range of issues demanding public attention. Nor have third parties performed the govern-ing function. They have lacked the power to organize the political branches, and in most cases their representation has been so limited that they have not even been able effectively to criticize the proposals of the major parties.

These activities of political parties produce certain side effects that bene-fit individuals, groups, and the entire society of a democratic nation. The party helps to structure the voting choice of many citizens. As we will see in Chapter 9, most individuals are unwilling to put in the time and effort to study the issues and the candidates' stands on them. Nor are they generally familiar with the background and abilities of the aspirants for public office. Lacking such information, voters find it difficult to cast their ballots. For them the party serves as a point of reference, a guide to which is the best-qualified candidate and the one who is most likely to approach problems from their own general point of view. As imprecise as such guidelines are, they nonetheless provide clues for distinguishing the "good" guys from the "bad" guys in a large number of American electoral races.

For some individuals the party serves as more than a point of reference in voting; it also helps to meet their economic, political, and social needs. The classic case is the traditional American political machine of the latter part of the last century and early years of the present century; whatever else can be said of them, the machines helped assimilate immigrants into American society by furnishing them with the necessities of life, finding them jobs, educating and socializing them in the ways of our political sys-tem, and sponsoring social activities for them. Few persons today in the United States are so dependent on party organizations or receive so many benefits from them; nonetheless, many individuals continue to derive sub-stantial satisfactions—psychological, social, and economic—from participat-ing in party affairs.

Like interest groups, political parties also channel the views and demands of individuals and groups to public officials. But rather than *articulate* par-ticular desires as interest groups do, major political parties *aggregate* mul-tiple demands, that is, combine them and accommodate their differences. Parties do so because if they hope to win power at the polls (some minor parties may not), they must develop broad-based programs that appeal to a wide variety of groups. Working out accommodations among diverse—and at times conflicting—demands of various groups enables the party to satisfy enough persons to win control of key governmental positions.

Finally, the activities of political parties contribute to the stability of the political system and of the larger society. A personal identification with, and commitment to, a political party helps create a sense of allegiance to the government. The process whereby parties reconcile and accommodate a broad spectrum of views and demands assists in the settlement of conflicts in society and in the development of significant areas of agreement among citizens of various backgrounds and perspectives. The creation of such a consensus, in turn, permits political parties to provide, and citizens to accept, the most basic feature of a democratic society: the pursuit and maintenance of political power by peaceful means and, when the populace desires it, the transfer of that power into other hands.

These, then, are the functions of political parties. Not all parties discharge them equally well; in fact, some parties do not perform a number of these functions at all. Nor are political parties the only organizations that carry on such activities: interest groups, factions, and *ad hoc* groups also participate in recruiting candidates, organizing campaigns, and proposing public policies. It is even conceivable that a democratic society might not need political parties at all, that other institutions might be developed in their stead. The fact remains, however, that no democratic nation has ever done so: all have depended on political parties to perform these vital functions. The remainder of this chapter focuses on the oldest party system in the world: our own.

THE DEVELOPMENT
OF AMERICAN POLITICAL PARTIES

If there was any one matter on which the political leaders discussed in Chapter 2 were agreed, it was that the nation should not divide itself into warring political camps. Madison and Washington were particularly concerned lest divisions imperil the national unity at a time when the young republic was fighting for its very existence against disruptive forces of geographic and economic rivalries. Hamilton, who had little faith in the common man (at one time he told Jefferson that the "people" were a "great beast"), quite naturally had no use for political organizations that would enable the public at large to influence decisions that he felt were better left to persons of superior intellect and training. Even Jefferson, who *did* place great trust in the masses and their ability to be educated politically, did not regard parties favorably: he declared in 1789 that, "If I could not go to heaven but with a party, I would not go there at all." Instead, he assumed that political officials would respond to currents of public opinion without the necessity of channeling public attitudes through political parties. Yet within less than a decade after the creation of the national government under the Constitution they all favored, all four became key figures in the establishment of rival political parties.

What precipitated the formation of the two parties was the economic program that Hamilton, as the first Secretary of the Treasury in the Washington administration, proposed to the Congress in 1790. Designed to promote manufacturing and commerce and to place the new government on a sound financial basis, the plan called for a number of controversial measures, including the assumption by the national government of debts owed by the states as well as the creation of a national bank. Madison, who was serving in the Congress, opposed the assumption of debts on the grounds that many Southern states had already paid theirs off and should not be taxed to help satisfy the obligations of Northern states. Jefferson, who was serving in the Washington administration as Secretary of State, worked out a political compromise whereby the debts would be assumed by the national government in return for the location of the capital in the South, specifically what was to become Washington, D.C. But Jefferson was unwilling to consent to the creation of a national bank (he regarded it as a dangerous monopoly that would benefit only mercantile interests, not the farmers for whom he had such admiration) and joined forces with Madison in trying to defeat the proposal in the Congress. Hamilton's supporters prevailed, however, and the bank was authorized in 1791.

A number of other domestic issues contributed to the growing split between the former political allies. Hamilton's economic program called for financial measures that clearly favored the industrial sections of the nation: a tax on foreign goods (a tariff) was levied not only to raise revenue for the national government but also to protect American manufacturers and merchants from foreign competition. Farmers who purchased manufactured goods bore the brunt of the tax since prices on foreign commodities were raised to cover the amount of the tariff. Even more vexing to them was the excise tax on liquor. While Eastern distillers could pass on the tax to their consumers, it was a direct levy on farmers who made liquor for their own use. Some frontiersmen in western Pennsylvania refused to pay the tax, intimidated government collectors, and dealt drastically with those who assisted revenue officers. Ultimately an insurrection known as the Whiskey Rebellion broke out there in 1794, and Washington sent a military force over the Alleghenies to put down this threat to the legitimacy of the new government.

While domestic economic concerns thus contributed to a growing split between the contending forces, ideology and foreign policy widened the cleavage. The eruption of the French Revolution in 1789, coupled with the outbreak of hostilities between the new revolutionary regime and Great Britain some four years later, polarized Americans. The followers of Jefferson viewed the French Revolution as a logical extension of our own, with the common people of both nations removing the political yoke of the upper classes. Hamiltonians agreed with the British statesman Edmund Burke that the stability of society was threatened by the excesses of the French mob. Hamilton's belief that the affairs of state should be entrusted to the national aristocracy was completely at odds with Jefferson's faith in the basic equality of man and his disdain for the nobility.

Injected into this general ideological climate was the highly controversial agreement negotiated with the British in 1794 by the Washington administration. Although the Jay Treaty (so named because John Jay was the American negotiator) did settle some major controversies with the British (they did agree, for example, to withdraw troops from forts in the Northwest), it failed to satisfy two basic American grievances: compensation for slaves that the British had carried away during the Revolution and the impressment into British service of American sailors who were serving on ships the British seized for trading with the French. Overnight the treaty became the target of bitter attacks by the anti-Hamiltonians (their favorite curse was "Damn John Jay! Damn everyone who won't damn John Jay! Damn everyone who won't put out lights in his windows and sit up all night damning John Jay!"), and it was necessary to throw the great prestige of Washington into the political battle to win its approval in 1795.

Out of this series of controversies over domestic issues, ideology, and foreign policy, the Federalist and Republican parties were born. The former, with Hamilton as the initiator of policies and Washington as the popular leader around whom men could be rallied, had formed by the early 1790s and soon had candidates running for Congress under its label and voting in the legislature in favor of the Hamiltonian programs. Jefferson's resignation from the Washington administration at the end of 1793 over the national bank issue paved the way for the establishment of the opposition, who came to be known as the Republicans. Although Jefferson returned to his home in Monticello, Madison remained in the Congress and organized the party so well that by the middle of the decade an antiadministration block in the Congress was voting together consistently; soon congressional candidates were being identified with the party as well. With the retirement of Washington at the end of his second term, the party rivalry spread to presidential politics when Adams, the Federalist candidate, narrowly defeated Jefferson, the Republican, in 1796.

During the next four years the partisan battle became even more intense. Direct taxes were levied on three major property sources of farmers, who supported the Republican party—land, houses, and slaves. The passage of the Alien and Sedition laws and their partisan application against Republicans (particularly newspaper editors) by Federalist judges served to deepen the partisan schism in the young nation. The stage was thus set for the crucial presidential election of 1800, in which the Republican ticket of Jefferson and Burr decisively defeated the Federalist team of Adams and Charles

Pinckney at the polls and the Republicans gained control of both the Senate and the House of Representatives.

Thus within a decade the United States had gone through crucial stages of political development. Many had viewed Washington as a "patriot king" who would rule in the interests of all the people, but it soon became apparent that there were major differences among groups that could not be settled by a neutral political figure, no matter how fair-minded or popular he might be. It also soon became apparent that traditional electoral organizations—factions based on local or state political personalities—would not be sufficient to capture control of the Congress and the Presidency: to sponsor and help identify candidates for the growing electorate, permanent, visible, and broadly based organizations would have to be created. And so the world's first democratic political parties were established in the United States. When the Federalists, however begrudgingly, relinquished control of the national government to the Republicans in 1800, another political first was achieved: the peaceful transfer of power from one party to another. Orderly, nonviolent competition has continued to characterize the American party system ever since.

GENERAL NATURE
OF PARTY COMPETITION

Political scientists distinguish three types of electoral situations: one-party, two-party, and multiparty. In the first, representatives of one political party hold all or almost all the major offices in the government. This condition may prevail where only one party is legally permitted to run candidates—as in Nazi Germany and Fascist Italy between the two world wars and in Communist China and the Soviet Union today—or where opposition parties are legally recognized but, for one reason or another, only one party is successful in election contests—as in Mexico, where the Institutional Revolutionary Party has won election after election for over forty years despite the fact that other groups like the National Action Party field opposition candidates. In the United States the Democratic party held a similar monopoly in most Southern states from the end of the Reconstruction period following the Civil War until recently. In a one-party system, if electoral competition exists, it involves only factions within the dominant party.

Under a two-party system, two and only two political parties have a reasonable chance to control major political offices. Both parties seek total political power, but neither is able to eliminate its rival at the ballot box. Each party is capable of capturing enough public positions to govern, but the opposition party continues to draw a sufficiently large vote to threaten the party in power. The result is that those in control of the various governments must take public wishes and sentiments into account lest they lose out to the opposition party at the next election. Moreover, the system works best if the opposition threat is realized from time to time, so that the two parties alternate in governing at reasonable intervals of time. According to Leon Epstein, a student of comparative political parties, only six nations have two-party systems: Australia, Austria, Canada, Great Britain, New Zealand, and the United States.

Under a multiparty system, three or more parties compete effectively for political offices, and none of them expects to win control of the government on its own. Rather, representatives of a combination of parties share the major positions of public authority. Generally, multiparty systems operate in countries with a parliamentary form of government, wherein the legislative body chooses the major leaders of the executive branch. Typically a coalition is formed of parties that together control a majority of the seats in the legislature; these parties in turn divide up the cabinet seats among persons from their respective organizations. Examples of nations with a multiparty system are France and Italy.

Only the one- and two-party systems have operated to any significant extent in the United States. Minor, or "third," parties* have appeared from time to time, but they have had relatively little success in winning political office, particularly at the national level. Yet, as the discussion later in this chapter indicates, they have nonetheless had some important political effects in the United States.

AMERICAN PARTY COMPETITION
AT THE NATIONAL LEVEL

THE HISTORICAL RECORD

As we have seen, the United States within a few years of its establishment had an operating two-party system. Although the Federalist Adams edged out the Republican Jefferson for the Presidency in 1796 and his party also managed to win control of the House of Representatives (at that time senators were chosen by state legislatures), the Republicans swept them from power in both branches in 1800. After that crucial election, the Federalist party continued to operate nationally for the next decade and a half, but it never again gained control of either the Presidency or the House. The demise of the party has been ascribed to a number of causes: the split in the party organization created by differences between Adams and Hamilton; an elitist political philosophy that prevented Federalist leaders from expanding membership to less-advantaged individuals and from organizing at the grass-roots level; and the pro-British attitude of many Federalists (particularly in New England) during the War of 1812, which served to associ-

*This is the term typically used for minor American parties, but it would be more precise to designate them as "third," "fourth," or "fifth" parties depending on their relative electoral strength.

ate the party with disloyalty to the nation. The party disappeared completely from the national scene around 1816.

There then followed a period of one-party government. This so-called "era of good feeling" culminated in James Monroe's virtually unanimous election as President in 1820. After that, however, competition broke out within the Republican party as "factions" formed around John Quincy Adams and Andrew Jackson. Gradually these factions developed into genuine parties: the followers of Adams became known as the National Republicans, those of Jackson as the Democratic Republicans. In the late 1830s the National Republican party was replaced by the Whigs; when in 1840 the Whig candidate, William Henry Harrison, defeated the incumbent President Martin Van Buren (who now ran under the label of the Democratic, rather than Democratic Republican, party), true two-party competition returned. It continued into the middle 1850s when the Whig party disappeared, only to be succeeded by another group, the Republican party which ran its first presidential candidate, General John Frémont, in 1856. Since that date, the Democratic and Republican parties have dominated American politics in the oldest continuous two-party competition in the world.

The Republican and Democratic rivalry over the years clearly meets the requirements of a two-party system. In the 112-year-period from 1856 through 1968, the Republicans were successful in sixteen presidential elections, the Democrats in twelve. The competition every two years for control of the House of Representatives has been even closer: both parties won exactly the same number of elections, twenty-eight. In this century alone, the results are also close: through 1968 each party captured the White House on nine occasions, while the Democrats enjoyed a twenty-to-fourteen edge in contests for the control of the lower branch of Congress. Thus both Republicans and Democrats have been able to win political power in both the executive and legislative branches of the government.

Besides winning control of the national government, both parties have managed in defeat to win a substantial portion of the popular vote. "Landslide" presidential elections—those in which the winning candidate gets more than sixty percent of the vote—have occurred only three times in this century: Warren Harding's victory in 1920, Franklin Roosevelt's in 1936, and Lyndon Johnson's in 1964. Contests for the House of Representatives since 1900 have been even closer. Only once, in the postwar election of 1920, has the losing party (the Democratic) won less than forty percent of the total votes cast. Thus the party out of power has retained enough popular support to constitute an electoral threat to the party in power.

As for the alternation of parties in power, the record has been mixed. In their century-long rivalry, the Republicans and Democrats have generally been able to oust each other from office at fairly frequent intervals, although there have been some notable eras of one-party dominance. The newly formed Republican party controlled the Presidency from Lincoln's election in 1860 until Cleveland won the office for the Democrats in 1884. The latter party, in turn, held the office over a twenty-year span from 1932 until 1952, with Franklin Roosevelt's four consecutive elections followed by Truman's upset victory in 1948. There have also been extended periods of one-party control of the House of Representatives. The Republicans maintained majorities for sixteen years three separate times—1858–1874, 1894–1910, and 1916–1932; twice the Democrats dominated the Chamber for several consecutive sessions, from 1932–1946 and again after 1954. Although these periods deviate from the pattern of frequent alternation of parties in office, on balance the American system at the national level must be considered a two-party affair. The near-equality of Republican and Democratic victories, the fairly close division of the popular vote, and the considerable degree of alternation in power clearly place the system in that category.

REASONS FOR THE NATIONAL
TWO-PARTY SYSTEM

Political scientists have long puzzled over the question of why a given country has a one-, two-, or multiparty system. There is no ready answer because it is difficult, if not impossible, to demonstrate that certain social, economic, or political conditions actually "cause" the formation and operation of a given party arrangement. Yet it is possible to investigate the kinds of conditions that are associated with particular party systems and to deduce logical reasons for these associations.

Historical Factors. One reason for the original formation of that system was the early division into two general groups over political issues facing the young nation. As we saw in Chapter 2, two broad constellations of interests appeared in the battle over the Constitution: the Federalists representing the manufacturers, merchants, shipowners, and commercial farmers who were dependent on trade for their livelihood; and the Anti-Federalists speaking for the subsistence farmers, artisans, and mechanics who were not. This same general split persisted over the Hamiltonian economic program, with the commercial classes rallying to its support and agricultural interests generally opposing it.* This basic breach widened further when the large landowners (who supported the Constitution and Hamilton's early program) subsequently became disenchanted with the Federalists because the Jay Treaty provided them with no compensation for the slaves the British carried away during the Revolution. Thus the two parties, the Federalists and the Republicans, represented two disparate groups: the former, the

*Not all individuals, however, followed this pattern: Madison and Jefferson supported the Constitution, but founded the Republican party. Still, most proconstitutionalist leaders supported the Federalist party, while the anticonstitutionalists became Republicans.

business and commercial elements of the nation that tended to be concentrated in the North, particularly along the coasts; the latter, the agricultural interests that predominated in the South and in the interior, along the "frontier."

Two broad constellations of interests have continued to characterize our party division. In the period of Jacksonian democracy, the Western-frontier forces were allied against Eastern monied interests. As the slavery issue became more salient, the East-West schism was replaced by a new sectionalism, arising from conflicts between the North and South. This cleavage, based on differences in the economies of the two regions (the industrial Northeast versus the more rural South), the memories of the Civil War, and the problems of race, persisted through the first third of this century. In fact, the period from the Civil War until the 1920s was characterized by *sectional* politics—the Republican party based in the Northeast and the Democrats in the South, with both vying for the support of the West and Midwest, which held the balance of political power.

Beginning in late 1920s a new dimension was introduced into American politics by increasing urbanization. This development caused a breakup of sectional unity as industry increasingly located on the West and South. The result was the development of *class* politics, as the Republicans gathered the support of the upper and upper-middle economic groups, while the working class, together with ethnic groups (especially immigrants from central and southern Europe and their children) and Negroes (who had traditionally been wedded to the Republicans since the Civil War) increasingly moved into the Democratic camp. The pattern continues to prevail today, but it is further complicated by the reemergence of race as a major issue in American politics: more Southerners, together with some working-class whites and ethnics, have begun to cast their votes in presidential elections for Republican candidates (whom they perceive as being less pro-Negro than Northeastern and Western Democrats).

This historical sketch of party divisions is admittedly simplified (we will examine the nuances and complexities of elections and voting patterns in more depth in Chapter 9), but it does indicate that the two parties have been able to develop broad coalitions of groups and that between them they have managed to absorb and aggregate the major interests in our society. Unlike many European nations, we have not developed a number of major parties, each representing a fairly narrow range of groups and concerns.

Consensus. Another factor that has contributed to the American two-party system is the considerable consensus that has existed on the fundamental goals of our society and the major means for reaching these goals. Most Americans have shared the views of Locke and Madison on the importance of individual self-development, including the right to acquire private property. There has been little sentiment for vesting the ownership of the means of production in public ownership, a common goal elsewhere. This being so, the dispute between the parties has focused not on whether there should be private property or not, but rather on how it should be distributed. The Republicans have tended to represent the interests of the haves and the Democrats the have-nots who want to become haves. Certainly this division has not been absolute, but as historian Charles Beard expressed the idea some years ago, "The center of gravity of wealth is on the Republican side, while the center of poverty is on the Democratic side."

Agreement on fundamentals extends beyond economic matters to political and social concerns as well. Thus Americans have been committed not only to the private enterprise system but also to our basic political institutions. No sizable group has ever advocated another form of government, such as monarchy, which many Frenchmen have proposed over the years. Because a feudal system never existed in the United States, there has been no aristocratic social class to establish an oligarchy to protect its privileges as has happened in other countries. Finally, religious divisions that have plagued many societies and spawned a variety of parties have played no meaningful role in American politics. As suggested in Chapter 4, the early decision to separate matters of church and state has prevented that result here.

This agreement on fundamentals has meant that American society has not been rent by the variety of basic cleavages—economic, political, and social —around which multiple parties have clustered in other nations. Keeping religion out of the politics, for example, has meant the absence of Catholic and Protestant parties or of groups supporting and groups opposing the subsidizing of religious institutions, an issue that has divided parties in France and Italy. Nor have we had significant monarchist or socialist parties. Instead, American parties have generally split on only one significant issue—how economic goods and privileges should be allocated among the population—and two parties have been sufficient to represent opposing views on that issue.

The economic nature of party differences has also made compromise possible in the American political system. Although individuals may not see eye to eye on the matter of who should have how much of the good things of life, conflicts in viewpoint are not irreconcilable. The issue is not an either-or proposition; everyone can receive something in terms of material comforts. Our great natural resources and expanding economy have made it possible to distribute economic benefits to ever more people without threatening the interests of those who already have considerable possessions. Few significant groups have found it necessary to go outside our two major parties to protect their economic interests.

Electoral Rules. The rules of the democratic game are seldom, if ever, neutral; they tend to favor some interests over others. One factor that has permitted the American two-party system to survive—and, indeed, to flourish

—is that certain features of our electoral system give the major parties advantages over third parties. We will examine the electoral process in detail in Chapter 9; for the moment, it will be sufficient to note the two points most relevant to our party system.

The way we elect our President favors a two-party system. In nations with a parliamentary form of government under which the chief executive (the Prime Minister or Premier) is chosen by the national legislative body, a minority party can become a part of a coalition that controls a majority of the legislative seats and may have one of its leaders chosen for that post. As will be explained in detail in Chapter 9, however, to win the American Presidency a candidate must win a majority of the electoral votes, which means that he must have a large proportion of the popular vote. Third parties do not achieve that success, and as a consequence they have not survived: a party that cannot capture control of the highest office, the Presidency, cannot be a major force in the nation's politics.

Our method of electing congressmen also favors the two major parties. Although most states elect several representatives to the House of Representatives (only Alaska, Delaware, Nevada, Vermont, and Wyoming send one) they are not chosen under a system of multimember constituencies and proportional representation as in many European countries. Under that electoral system, voters select a number of representatives, and the seats are allocated to the parties on the basis of their share of the popular vote. If Missouri, say, which is entitled to ten members of the House of Representatives, used such a system, a minor party that won twenty percent of the popular vote would have two of its candidates sitting in Washington as representatives of that state. Under the single-member district method used by Missouri and other states, the Show-Me State is divided into ten separate House districts and voters cast their ballots only for the candidates for the one representative of their particular area. The winner is the contestant who gains a plurality of the votes (that is, more than any other candidate) for that district. Under this arrangement a minor party whose candidate draws twenty percent of the popular vote in any or all the ten districts does not gain any representation in Washington, since under our two-party system that proportion would not constitute a plurality of votes. As with the presidential contest, our single-member district, plurality method for choosing congressmen operates under a "winner-take-all" principle; thus losing minor parties receive no electoral rewards for their efforts.

Natural Perpetuation of the Two-Party System. One final factor that supports the two-party system in the United States is that certain built-in mechanisms tend to make it self-perpetuating. As we saw in Chapter 5, children develop an attachment to a political party at an early age. This psychological identification, which they acquire primarily from their parents, tends to deepen during the course of their adult lives. In a society where the two major political parties have been dominant for over a century, the citizens, in overwhelming proportion, naturally learn to think of themselves as Republican and Democratic. In other words, traditional party patterns, plus the political-socialization process by which attitudes are passed on from one generation to another, combine to perpetuate the two-party system in the United States.

Our two-party system also serves to concentrate the political leadership of the nation in the Republican and Democratic parties. Persons aspiring to political positions know that unless they can use one of these labels, they have little chance of succeeding in their quest for public office. Thus political talent is attracted towards the two major parties and away from minor parties, which typically back losing candidates.

The two-party system also perpetuates itself by channeling political conflict into two major outlets, the organization in power and the one out of power. Support for, and opposition to, the government and what it is doing, polarizes around two party groups. Under this arrangement citizens who are unhappy about the current state of affairs not only vote against the present office-holders but also give their support to candidates of the other major party, which serves as the only real political alternative to the party in power.

COMPETITION AT THE LOWER LEVELS OF GOVERNMENT

Students of American politics who speak of a two-party system are referring primarily to electoral competition at the national level. What about the lower levels of government? Table 7.2, developed by Austin Ranney, which classifies the state party systems on the basis of competition for the governorship and both branches of the state legislature in the period 1956 through 1970, indicates that only twenty-eight of the fifty states had a two-party system during that time. Of the remaining twenty-two states, fifteen leaned toward political control by one of the two major parties, and the other seven were clearly dominated by the Democrats. Thus only a little over one-half of the states during the period under analysis had party systems resembling that of the nation as a whole.

Further down the levels of the American political system, electoral contests become even less two-party in nature. The overwhelming proportion of the some 3000 counties in the United States are dominated politically by one of the two major parties, as are municipalities that use partisan ballots to elect their officials: typically, the large central cities are controlled by the Democratic party, while suburban communities, particularly those populated by the well-to-do, favor the Republicans.

TABLE 7.2 The Fifty States Classified According to Degree of Interparty Competition, 1956–1970

One-Party Democratic	Modified One-Party Democratic	Two-Party		Modified One-Party Republican
Louisiana (.9877)	North Carolina (.8332)	Hawaii (.6870)	New Jersey (.5122)	North Dakota (.3305)
Alabama (.9685)	Virginia (.8235)	Rhode Island (.6590)	Pennsylvania (.4800)	Kansas (.3297)
Mississippi (.9407)	Florida (.8052)	Massachusetts (.6430)	Colorado (.4725)	New Hampshire (.3282)
South Carolina (.9292)	Tennessee (.7942)	Alaska (.6383)	Michigan (.4622)	South Dakota (.3142)
Texas (.9132)	Maryland (.7905)	California (.6150)	Utah (.4565)	Vermont (.2822)
Georgia (.9080)	Oklahoma (.7792)	Nebraska (.6065)	Indiana (.4450)	
Arkansas (.8850)	Missouri (.7415)	Washington (.0647)	Illinois (.4235)	
	Kentucky (.7170)	Minnesota (.5910)	Wisconsin (.4102)	
	West Virginia (.7152)	Nevada (.5742)	Idaho (.4077)	
	New Mexico (.7150)	Connecticut (.5732)	Iowa (.3965)	
		Delaware (.5687)	Ohio (.3837)	
		Arizona (.5663)	New York (.3835)	
Scale:		Montana (.5480)	Maine (.3820)	
1.0000 = Completely Democratic		Oregon (.5387)	Wyoming (.3537)	
.0000 = Completely Republican				

Source: Austin Ranney, "Parties in State Politics," in Herbert Jacob and Kenneth N. Vines, *Politics in the American States* (Boston: Little, Brown, 2nd ed., 1970), p. 87.

FACTORS AFFECTING COMPETITION
BELOW THE NATIONAL LEVEL

Interestingly enough, some of the very same factors that are associated with the national two-party system have had precisely the opposite effect at lower levels of the American political system. As Table 7.2 makes clear, the trauma of the Civil War that split the nation into the Republican North and the Democratic South, created one-party politics within each of these regions. All seven of the one-party Democratic states fought on the side of the Confederacy, while eight of the ten modified one-party Democratic states were either Confederate or Border states. The only exceptions are New

Mexico and Oklahoma—and these were settled originally by Southerners. Of the five modified one-party Republican states, three supported the Union, while the two Dakotas had immigrants mainly from the Union states. Thus more than any other single historical event or issue, the Civil War shaped state partisan politics in a mold that still existed in the post-World-War-II era.

The race issue has been particularly instrumental in shaping the one-party Democratic politics of the Southern states, for it has suppressed natural economic divisions in the electorate there that might have led to a competitive party system. For a short period in the early 1890s, it appeared that the Populist party (to be discussed later in this chapter) might be the vehicle for an alliance between blacks and poor whites against the Bourbons, the upper-class planter group that had traditionally controlled Southern politics. When that possibility occurred, the latter protected their interests by using the race issue as a means of splitting the poor whites from their natural economic allies, the blacks. This ploy, coupled with the demise of the Populists after the presidential election of 1896, restored Southern politics to its traditional one-party mold with the Bourbons in political command. The Democrats continued to use the race issue to brand the Republican party as the political enemy, the party of treason, with which no true Southerner would have any association. Moreover, differences with the rest of the nation, particularly the North, over racial matters (as well as economic issues, such as a low versus a high tariff) tended to drive Southerners together, with the Democratic party serving as an instrument for regional unity.

Other factors have also operated to preserve the one-party politics of states and localities. Just as traditions and political socialization have perpetuated loyalties so that, over-all, nationally a two-party system persists, so have they continued the one-party inclinations of staunch Northerners and Southerners. Political leadership has also been channeled into regionally dominant parties, as ambitious candidates have taken the only practical route open to political office. As we will see in Chapter 9, the rules of the electoral game have also been manipulated to favor the prevalent party at the state level. State legislatures have drawn single-member districts in contests for their own seats (as for the national House of Representatives) to favor candidates of the dominant party. In addition, these legislators have passed laws giving all the state's electoral votes in presidential elections to the candidate that wins a mere plurality of the popular vote. In this fashion, the traditional majority party in one-party states has been able to deny a struggling minority vital political offices or influence that is so desperately needed if it is to successfully challenge the traditional one-party control of the state.

Although these factors help to explain the lack of party competition at the state and local levels in the United States, they fail to account for the twenty-eight states listed in Table 7.2 that do have two-party systems. A number of these, particularly in the Northeast, are highly urbanized states with a diversified economy and a population composed of many ethnic, religious, and social-class groups. Thus the changes in these highly industrialized states in the direction of class politics—upper-class suburbanites and residents of the small towns and rural areas aligned against working-class and ethnic groups in the central cities—have supplanted the one-party politics promoted by the Civil War.

There are in the two-party group, however, a number of Western states that are not urbanized, such as Alaska, Idaho, Montana, Nebraska, Utah, and Wyoming. Their two-party systems appear to be associated with two other factors. As newer states, they have not been so greatly affected by the memories of the Civil War. Also, they have been populated by persons from other parts of the country, both North and South, which has meant that political traditions (including partisan ones) have not been very important in shaping their politics. Indeed, the variety of settlers has provided a partisan mix and a competitive two-party system.

PATTERNS OF STATE COMPETITION

Even though states with one-party systems have no meaningful electoral contests between the candidates of the major parties, they are not totally without political competition. The nature of the competition is simply different, occurring within the framework of the dominant party: the focus of electoral combat shifts from the general election to the nominating process. In one-party states, particularly those of the once-solid Democratic South, more voters participated in the primary contest of the majority party than cast their ballots for the candidates of both parties combined in the general election. When the primary was over, people knew who would hold office for the next term, since the dominant party's candidate had little to fear from his rival in the general election. Thus one-party politics substitutes intraparty struggle for interparty competition.

States with one-party systems, however, differ significantly among themselves. V.O. Key, Jr., in his classic study of politics in the American South in the 1940s, *Southern Politics in State and Nation*, distinguished two separate patterns of intraparty competition. One is *bifactionalism*, wherein contests within the majority party between two identifiable groups persist over a series of elections. Good examples of bifactionalism are the previously noted Byrd–anti-Byrd and Long–anti-Long splits in the Virginia and Louisiana Democratic parties that continued after the death of both leaders, as the contending groups took on an identity that transcended the particular personalities involved. A student of politics in the New England states, Duane Lockard, has found a similar situation in Republican Vermont between the supporters and opponents of the long-powerful Proctor family there.

The second of Key's basic patterns of intraparty competition is *multifactionalism*. He applies this term to Florida and Arkansas (Lockard to Maine), where several factions typically vie for the top state offices. In such a situation factional alliances among political leaders are loose and often change from one election to another. Moreover, virtually everyone fends for himself as each candidate builds his own personal organization.

Key and others have concluded that, of the two kinds of intraparty competition, the bifactional type provides the voter with the more meaningful choice. Typically in a multifactional race, each candidate does well in his own geographical area, gaining what Key calls "friends and neighbors" support. In these situations elections turn on the appeal of the hometown boy rather than on differences between candidates over social, economic, and political issues. Bifactional competition is more likely to reflect such differences—as it has, for instance, in Louisiana where the Long faction has generally championed the interests of the dirt farmer and other economically disadvantaged groups (including blacks) against the business community and wealthy planters that have constituted the major support of the anti-Long faction. Even where such clear liberal-conservative differences do not exist (they have been less apparent, for example, in Virginia between the Byrd and anti-Byrd factions), bifactionalism creates the potential for such a division. In any event, deciding between two major candidates for each office is less confusing to the voter than trying to distinguish among a large number who cannot be characterized on the basis of their association with different economic or social groups.

This is not to say, however, that bifactionalism offers the voter the same choice as a two-party system does. Quite often factions do not run a complete slate of candidates as do the major parties. Even when they do, not all voters know which particular candidates are associated with each of the two factions, since no designations appear on the ballot. As previously stressed, parties offer voters what factions cannot: a label on the ballot that helps to identify which candidate belongs to which electoral group.

One final pattern of state party politics combines elements of both one- and two-party competition. John Fenton, a student of the Border states (Kentucky, Maryland, Missouri, and West Virginia), suggests that they have three identifiable political groups that are increasingly vying for political power. Two operate as factions within the Democratic party: a liberal wing with its principal political support among labor, blacks, and ethnic groups from the urban areas; and a conservative counterpart with its major base in the Bourbon class. In addition, an opposition has grown in recent years among traditional Republicans from the mountain areas of these states,*

---

*During the Civil War, persons from mountainous areas who owned no slaves sided with the North. Many of these areas have remained as pockets of Republican strength over the years.

new arrivals from the North, and residents of the burgeoning suburbs. Fenton sees this three-way competition not only as the prevailing pattern in these states but also as the wave of the future in the South as states in that region take on more of the characteristics (growing industrialization and a more potent political alliance between Negroes and organized labor) of the Border states.

Thus American party competition in the United States has been of either the one- or two-party type. The former has prevailed in cities, counties, and about half the American states. The latter has been prominent in the remaining states and in contests for national political offices. We have not had meaningful multiparty competition at any level of the American political system. Minor parties have continued to exist in the United States, however, and although they have never captured a significant number of national offices and have seldom been successful in states and localities either, they have nonetheless had considerable impact on American politics—enough so that it is worth considering their record in some detail.

MINOR AMERICAN PARTIES

There has been a wide variety of minor, or third, parties in American history. Some, like the Anti-Masonic party of the 1830s, contested a single presidential election and disappeared almost immediately from the political landscape. Others, like the Socialist party, have fielded candidates in a hopeless electoral cause over a number of years. The Prohibition party has zeroed in on what members regard as the tragic flaw in the national well-being, while the Communist party has sought to overhaul the entire economic and political structure of a basically "decadent" society. The Progressives of the early part of this century genuinely expected to capture key offices and succeeded to some extent in doing so; the leaders of the Vegetarian party have accepted political realities and run presidential candidates for publicity. But despite these differences, minor parties have one thing in common: a feeling that certain values and interests they think important are not being properly represented by the two major parties.

GOALS AND TYPES OF MINOR PARTIES

Some of the minor parties have promoted ideologies that are entirely foreign to the nation's traditional beliefs—notably the parties that were introduced into the United States from Europe but failed to adapt to our essentially free-enterprise economic environment. Included in this general category are the Socialist party, which advocates public ownership of basic industries but is satisfied with moving toward its goal gradually through the workings of parliamentary democracy; the Socialist Labor party, which also seeks to eliminate the capitalist system through essentially peaceful, but not too clearly defined, means; and the American Communist party, with close ties to the Soviet Union, which has not ruled out violence as a method to bring about a classless society.

Of the three, the Socialist Labor party has been the most long-lived, running presidential and vice-presidential candidates in every election since 1896. On the other hand, the Socialist party has been by far the greatest vote-getter, polling close to a million votes in 1912, the first election in which it competed, and combining with the Progressive party in 1924 to give their joint candidate, Robert La Follette, almost five million votes. After 1932, however, it never again commanded a significant electoral following, and ceased running presidential candidates after 1956. Meanwhile, the forays of the Communist party into American electoral politics have been both sporadic and uniformly hopeless.*

The most successful minor parties in the United States have, like the Marxist ones, protested economic injustices. Rather than tracing their origins and ideologies to foreign sources, however, they have been indigenous and have proposed programs that remain within the American consensus of a free-enterprise system. Included in this category are two groups of the past century, the Greenback party that ran candidates in the 1870s, and the Populists that came into prominence in the 1890s. The former called for assistance to debtor farmers by way of issuing more cheap paper money; the latter proposed an expansion of the money supply in the form of free and unlimited coinage of silver, along with gold, at a ratio of sixteen to one, as well as a graduated income tax, the public ownership of railroads, and other measures designed to break the financial hold of the industrial East over the producers of raw materials in the West and South.

Twentieth-century minor parties have continued this tradition of sounding the call for reform while staying within basic institutions to achieve them. In 1912 former Republican President Theodore Roosevelt headed the Progressive party, which attacked abuses of both economic and political power in the United States. To correct the former, the party proposed governmental control over monopolies; for the latter, it urged adoption of such "direct democracy" devices as the initiative (allowing citizens to propose legislation), the referendum (referring laws to the voters for an ultimate decision), and the recall (permitting citizens to oust unsatisfactory officeholders between elections). Later on, as previously indicated, another minor party adopted the label of the Progressives and joined with the Socialists in backing Robert La Follette for President in 1924. This group's concern for the problems of the farmer paralleled that of the Populist party a quarter-century earlier, but in addition it spoke for the laboring man who wanted the right to organize. Thus the two Progressive parties of the first quarter of

---

*The party ran presidential candidates from 1924 through 1940 and again in 1968. Its highest vote total was 100,000 in 1932 (compared to Franklin Roosevelt's 23,000,000); in 1968, its supporters numbered slightly over 1000.

Third-party candidate George Wallace is greeted by admirers during the 1968 presidential campaign. (United Press International)

this century* expanded economic protest beyond the rural areas of the West and South to the urban areas of the Northeast.

The race issue has also recently spawned some new developments in party competition. In 1948 a group of dissident Southern Democrats walked out of their party's presidential nominating convention over the issue of civil rights, formed a States' Rights Democratic party, or Dixiecrat party, and nominated J. Strom Thurmond of South Carolina and Fielding Wright of Mississippi as President and Vice President. Rather than use that label on the ballot for the selection of presidential electors (this matter will be explained in detail in Chapter 9), they chose instead to offer them as the "official' Democratic nominees in Alabama, Louisiana, Mississippi, and South Carolina, a tactic that paid off with victories in those four states. Twenty years later, a third party with similar views on the race issue headed by George Wallace, ran candidates under the label of the American Independent Party. Although its candidates, Wallace and vice presidential nominee Curtis LeMay, appeared on the ballot in all fifty states, they prevailed only

*Still another party using this name ran Henry Wallace for President in 1948. Its major emphasis, however, was on foreign affairs, in particular, a more conciliatory policy toward the Soviet Union.

in five in the South—Alabama, Arkansas, Georgia, Louisiana, and Mississippi.

Third parties have also operated in state and local elections. The Socialists have elected mayors in Milwaukee, Wisconsin, and Hartford, Connecticut. Even before the Farmer-Labor party of Minnesota merged with the Democratic party in the 1940s, it had won the governorship of that state on its own. In New York the American Labor Party and more recently the Liberal party, operating under provisions of that state's electoral laws that permit an individual to be the nominee of more than one party, have contributed to the elections of candidates in the Empire State. The former combined with the Republicans to elect Fiorello La Guardia as mayor in 1937, and thirty years later the latter joined electoral forces with the same major party to put John Lindsay in that post. In other instances, the Liberals have come to the assistance of the Democrats, as they did when Herbert Lehman nosed out John Foster Dulles for the Senate in 1949, and in 1960 when John F. Kennedy won a close victory over Richard Nixon in the state. Yet another New York minor party, the Conservatives, elected their own candidate, James Buckley, to the United States Senate in 1970.

For the most part, however, third parties in states and localities have met the same fate as those operating on the national scene: little success in winning public office and frequently a short political life. The absence of strong minor parties at the top level of the American political system has made it difficult for such groups to operate effectively at lower echelons as well. For the two national political parties have determined which parties can also compete in state and local political arenas.

EFFECTS OF MINOR PARTIES

At first blush one might conclude that third parties have been of little significance in American politics. Judged by the major criterion for evaluating parties—namely, their electoral victories—the record of such parties could hardly be less impressive. None has won the major prize in the American political system, the Presidency, and few have even managed to capture much in the way of other political offices (the most successful, the Populists, won a few seats in the House, three governorships, and hundreds of local posts). Generally speaking, they fail to win any electoral votes at all in the presidential election (the most earned was Roosevelt's eighty-eight in the 1912 election). Since the Civil War only four have gained more than ten percent of the popular vote for President: the Populists in 1892, the Progressives in 1912, the Progressives in 1924, and the American Independent Party in 1968.

The significance of minor parties, however, is greater if they are viewed from another perspective: the effect they have had on the two major parties in the United States. In some instances, such as the presidential election of 1912, their presence on the ballot has contributed to taking victory from one party and giving it to another. Even though this may not have been the only reason for Taft's defeat that year, it certainly was a major factor in bringing a Democratic candidate into the White House for the first time since the early 1890s. In other instances, minor parties have made a differ- ence in individual states where the vote between the candidates of the two leading candidates was close. Richard Nixon's popular-vote margin over Hubert Humphrey was less than the size of the vote for George Wallace in no less than seventeen states in 1968.

Besides affecting the division of the vote at election time, minor parties frequently have an impact on the general policy orientation of the major parties. One of the two may clearly borrow the ideas of a third party—as in 1896 when the Democrats under William Jennings Bryan took over the po- sition of the Populists on free and unlimited coinage of silver. In the process the Democratic party was pushed to the left and its differences with the "sound-money," gold-standard policies of the Republican party became more apparent. A similar phenomenon occurred in the aftermath of the Progres- sives' show of strength in 1912 and 1924, for the Democratic party absorbed some of the basic ideas of Roosevelt and La Follette (such as the regulation of large corporations and the promotions of labor interests) for which the Republicans had little concern. It is precisely this kind of process that has led to the demise of many minor parties, as they find their programs and followers siphoned away by one of the two major parties. Many third-party supporters are not distressed with this result, however, since it means that the rationale for the party's formation no longer exists; the two major par- ties are now representing values and interests they formerly ignored.

Finally, third parties play a role in the composition of the two major parties. When the Wallace Progressives of 1948 fielded candidates that ad- vocated a more conciliatory policy with the Soviet Union, they drained away from the Democratic party some of its supporters who agreed with that position. At the same time, they pushed back into the party fold some traditional Democrats, particularly Catholics, who had been alienated by the nation's close relationship with Russia during the Democratic adminis- trations of war years. Thus differences among the various factions of the principal parties—in particular the majority party, which wins elections be- cause it represents such a wide variety of interests—may result in the defec- tion of a group that feels it is losing out in basic conflicts over key issues within the national party. This analysis would help explain the formation of the Progressive party from the ranks of the Republicans in 1912, and the Dixiecrats and the American Independent party from the Democrats in 1948 and 1968 respectively. Moreover, the process may eventually lead to the migration of such groups to the other major party, with the minor or- ganization as a half-way house used enroute to the new party home. Recent cases in point are former Dixiecrats, including political leaders like Strom Thurmond, who have now affiliated themselves with the Republican party.

ASSESSMENT

Generally speaking, the historical record of American political parties has been a good one. Established in the very early years of the republic, they became the world's first permanent electoral organizations, models that other democratic countries have emulated. Another measure of their success is the persistence of our party system for almost two centuries.

The success of American political parties has been due in large part to the favorable environment in which they have been located. A general American consensus on basic social, economic, and political values and institutions has spared our parties the problem of trying to represent and reconcile deep cleavages on such matters, cleavages that have plagued party leaders in other societies. Our expanding economy has also made it possible for a wide variety of groups to satisfy their demands through the rival parties without having the rivalry become an all-out, do-or-die struggle.

American political parties, in turn, have contributed to the successful operation of our democratic institutions. Both have recruited and backed many able men for public office. In addition, the close competition that has existed between the two major parties over the years, together with their representation of different economic and social interests, has provided voters with significant choices of personnel and policies.

On the other hand, American political parties have also had some notable failures. Their inability to deal with the race issue resulted in a bloody civil war. The race issue and the memory of that war have continued to confuse party divisions over the years and spawned one-party politics in many areas, thereby denying the voters a meaningful choice between rival candidates and policies.

An assessment of American political parties must necessarily be limited at this point because we have not yet examined in any detail the way the parties actually perform some of their most basic functions. In Chapters 8 and 9 we focus on their role in the electoral process. In subsequent chapters we will analyze the part that the party in the government plays in the making of public policy.

Selected Readings

Particularly helpful for discussions of the nature of a political party and of how it differs from other groups linking the general populace to political leaders are Chapter I of Leon Epstein, *Political Parties in Western Democracies* (New York:

Praeger, 1967), and Austin Ranney's selection, "The Concept of 'Party'," that appears in a book edited by Oliver Garceau entitled *Political Research and Political Theory* (Cambridge: Harvard University Press, 1968).

The functions political parties play in various kinds of societies are analyzed in Sigmund Neumann, *Modern Political Parties* (Chicago: University of Chicago Press, 1956). Their role in underdeveloped countries is treated in Gabriel Almond and James Coleman, *The Politics of Developing Nations* (Princeton, N.J.: Princeton University Press, 1960), and in Almond's subsequent study with G. Bingham Powell, *Comparative Politics: A Developmental Approach* (Boston: Little, Brown, 1966). The best analyses of the part they play in American politics are V.O. Key, Jr., *Politics, Parties and Pressure Groups* (New York: Thomas Y. Crowell, 5th ed., 1964), and Frank Sorauf, *Party Politics in America* (Boston: Little, Brown, 1968). The latter book has a thoughtful discussion of what is meant by a "function" of a political party.

The best treatment of the original establishment of political parties in the United States is William Chambers, *Political Parties in a New Nation: The American Experience* (New York: Oxford University Press, 1963). It is especially valuable in distinguishing parties from factions and in indicating how the transition from the latter to the former took place. Two good studies of American parties in the Jeffersonian era are Noble Cunningham, *The Jeffersonian Republicans in Power: Party Operations, 1801–1809* (Chapel Hill, N.C.: University of North Carolina Press, 1967), and James Young, *The Washington Community, 1808–1828* (New York: Columbia University Press, 1966). The latter extends beyond the Jeffersonian years and focuses broadly on politics in the nation's capital. A good series of selections dealing with various stages in the growth of American parties is contained in a book edited by William Chambers and Walter Burnham, *The American Party System: Stages of Political Development* (New York: Oxford University Press, 1967).

Epstein's book cited above has an excellent discussion of various types of party competition, as does an article by Hugh McDowell Clokie, "The Modern Party State," *The Canadian Journal of Economics and Political Science* (May 1949), 139–157. Good discussions of two-party competition at the national level in the United States, including the reasons associated with that particular type of party competition, are included in the Key and Sorauf books cited above.

V.O. Key's classic work, *Southern Politics in State and Nation* (New York: Knopf, 1949), is an excellent study of the patterns of politics in the one-party South. He subsequently published another analysis of the politics of other parts of the nation in *American State Politics: An Introduction* (New York: Knopf, 1956). Two of Key's students have analyzed party competition in other regions of the United States: John Fenton in *Politics in the Border States* (New Orleans: The Hauser Press, 1957), and *Midwest Politics* (New York: Holt, Rinehart and Winston, 1966); and Duane Lockard in *New England State Politics* (Princeton, N.J.: Princeton University Press, 1959). Austin Ranney has a chapter on party politics in Herbert Jacob and Kenneth Vines, *Politics in the American States: A Comparative Approach* (Boston: Little, Brown, 1965).

Chapter 10 of Key, *Politics, Parties and Pressure Groups* cited above, is an excellent analysis of minor parties in the United States.

CHAPTER **8**

The Nomination Process

Richard Nixon acknowledges his nomination in Miami, 1968. (Fred Ward/Black Star)

It was election night, November 8, 1960, and the American people were keenly following the closest presidential contest of this century. In early evening, as the returns from the Eastern industrial states began to come in, John Kennedy, the Democratic candidate, jumped off to an early lead over his Republican rival, Richard Nixon. Soon it became apparent that most of the Southern states would remain loyal to the region's traditional party, so that by 10:30 p.m. (EST) some commentators were predicting that Kennedy might win by four or five million votes and capture over 400 of the 537 electoral votes. But at that precise moment the tide turned; first, key Midwestern states and, later, Western ones came into the Nixon column. By 3:00 a.m. Kennedy edged towards the winning figure of 267 electoral votes, but the closeness of the contest in several key states kept the outcome in doubt until midmorning of the ninth; when the doubt was resolved, Richard Nixon appeared on television to give his concession speech. The final tally showed the young Senator's popular-vote margin over the Vice President to be less than 113,000 votes out of almost 69,000,000 cast.

Two years later Nixon attempted a political comeback at the state level: he ran for governor of his home state, California, against the Democratic incumbent, Pat Brown. This time he lost by an embarrassing 300,000 votes of just over 4,000,000 cast. To make matters worse, the morning after the election he lashed out at the assembled members of the press with his famous exclamation, "You won't have Nixon to kick around any more because, gentlemen, this is my last press conference." Within the week the ABC television network aired a special show entitled "The Political Obituary of Richard Nixon."

Humiliated and at loose ends, the former Vice President set about picking up the pieces of his life. Advised by friends to seek a change of scenery and attracted by the lure of the capital of the legal world, Nixon moved his family to New York City where he joined a prominent Wall Street law firm. Soon he was enjoying what he had never before achieved in life: an income exceeding $200,000 a year; membership in the most exclusive social clubs in the nation's largest city; and, most important, the feeling that he could match wits with the finest legal talent in the land.

But even this success was not enough for a man who had spent virtually his entire adult life in the public service; before long, Nixon began to edge his way back into the political arena. Despite his feeling that Senator Barry Goldwater would be swamped in the presidential election of 1964, he introduced the candidate at the Republican convention and campaigned dutifully for him that fateful fall. More importantly, Nixon took the leadership in "Congress '66," a group that campaigned across the nation for Republican congressional candidates that year. When the GOP effort was successful, it redounded to the political credit of the former Vice President.

From that base Nixon made his own personal comeback. In January 1967 the nucleus of the "Congress '66" group held its first planning session to put their candidate in the White House. The organizers assessed Nixon's chances at the Republican national convention—some eighteen months away—and decided to withhold announcement of his candidacy in order to let the Michigan governor, George Romney, who also aspired to the Presidency, play the role of front-runner. Meanwhile, names for a "Nixon for President" committee were to be assembled and money gathered for the demanding nomination and election campaigns that lay ahead.

The following year Nixon swept to victory in every presidential primary he entered. He was nominated on the first ballot at the Republican convention. And the morning following election day, it was he who watched his rival, another Vice President, Hubert Humphrey, concede the victory on television. As in the election eight years before, the result was close: Nixon's margin over Humphrey was just over half a million out of some 73,000,000 votes cast. To paraphrase Mark Twain's remarks regarding his own mortality, the rumors of the political death of Richard Nixon had been greatly exaggerated.

Even though few persons in politics experience the extreme highs and lows of Richard Nixon's career, they must all pass through the crucible of the electoral process in which a free people tests its political leaders. The process is particularly demanding for those, like Nixon, who seek the highest office in the land, but aspirants to the Senate, the House of Representatives, and, to a lesser extent, state and local offices are often put through a grueling procedure before the people make a choice. To top it off, the procedure involves two separate tests of political strength. First, as discussed in this chapter, a candidate must win his party's nomination; then he must emerge victorious in the general election, a subject we will examine in Chapter 9.

PURPOSE AND IMPORTANCE OF THE NOMINATION PROCESS

As we saw in Chapter 7, one of the major functions of political parties is to present alternative groups of candidates for the electorate's consideration, thereby structuring the voter's choice and making his task more manageable. To do so, however, each party itself must have some method of deciding which person is to wear its label for each office. That method is the nomination process.*

*Even in nonpartisan elections, some method is generally used to narrow down the number of candidates. Typically, if no person receives the majority (one over half) of

Although the selection of a candidate by political parties is important in all democratic political systems, it is particularly so in the United States. For one thing, we elect to public office far more officials than any other nation in the world (a recent estimate set the numbers at about half a million), not only because our population is large but also because Americans have been little disposed toward appointive political positions. The "Jacksonian Revolution" (associated with President Andrew Jackson), which swept the nation in the 1830s and 1840s and left lasting marks on politics, was based on faith in the common man and in his ability to choose his political leaders wisely. As a result we traditionally elect many officials, particularly at the state and local levels, that are appointed in other democracies.

Another basic feature of our politics that contributes to the importance of the nominating procedure is the large number of one-party areas in the United States. As previously noted, in such constituencies the significant competition involves opposing candidates and factions within the dominant party; the locus of the struggle is thus not the general election but the process by which the party chooses its candidates.

Finally, the nomination process is important even where genuine two-party competition exists, because our parties provide the voter with such a limited choice: he must pick between the Republican and Democratic candidates unless he is willing to back a third-party candidate who, he knows, will rarely be successful in American politics. In contrast, in a multiparty system a range of candidates is available for consideration in the general election. Thus American citizens have a special incentive for taking an interest in the nomination process so as to avoid being presented with an undesirable choice in the general election.

As the following section shows, this problem has been a matter of concern over the course of the nation's political history as citizens have continued to seek improvements in the operation of the nomination process.

EVOLUTION
OF THE NOMINATION PROCESS

Political parties appeared early in the history of United States, and so did the need to develop some means of choosing candidates to run under their labels. Races for local offices, as well as for state legislatures and the House of Representatives, presented no real difficulty, since they involved a limited number of voters. Therefore, parties simply held caucuses, that is, meetings of their most active supporters, to nominate candidates.

Selecting candidates for statewide offices presented more problems, how-

---

the votes in the initial election, a second election is held involving the two top runners. A recent example occurred in the 1969 Los Angeles mayoralty contest. A Negro councilman, Thomas Bradley, who led all fourteen candidates on the first ballot, did not receive a majority vote and was beaten in the run-off by the incumbent mayor, Sam Yorty.

ever. Given the transportation of the day, it was difficult to assemble politicians from all over a state to choose a party's candidate for governor. Moreover, even if such a group could be convened, it would be too large and unwieldy to function efficiently. Of course, nominating the President and Vice President, with their national constituency, presented the same problems in exaggerated form.

THE LEGISLATIVE CAUCUS

The parties soon moved to a more appropriate method of choosing nominees for state- and nationwide offices: the *legislative caucus.* Under this method a party's members in state legislatures and the House of Representatives assembled to choose, respectively, candidates for statewide office and for President and Vice-President. By the turn of the nineteenth century, this procedure was in general use at both the state and the national level.

The legislative caucus made a lot of sense in the early stages of party development. State legislators and congressmen were already convened in one location, and since they were few in number the nominating task was manageable. Moreover, legislators were likely to be highly knowledgeable about potential candidates from all parts of the political unit in question. Thus members of the party in the government were logical agents to choose candidates representing large constituencies.

There were, however, obvious defects in King Caucus, as the institution was popularly known. For one thing, it violated the separation-of-powers principle of the Constitution to have members of the legislative body play a key role in determining the occupants of major executive positions. The provisions of the Virginia and New Jersey Plans to allow Congress to choose the President had been rejected by the Constitutional Convention. Yet now the legislative caucus threatened to bring the parliamentary system in the back door via the nomination process. This possibility eventually became near-actuality when the Republican legislative caucus in effect chose Madison and Monroe as Presidents of the United States during the era of one-party politics.

The legislative caucus also proved to be deficient in representing various party elements. For example, when a party lost an election in a legislative district, state or congressional, that area was not represented in the decisions of the party's legislative caucus. Although this defect was eventually remedied by permitting local party leaders from such areas to sit in the caucus, a more fundamental flaw remained: interested and knowledgeable citizens who participated in party activities at the grass roots level (especially in campaigns) had no direct say in nominations. The legislative caucus thus became too limited and centralized a group to make key decisions for parties that were increasingly local in organization and increasingly dependent for political victories on active members who did not hold legislative posts.

The fate of the legislative caucus is exemplified by what happened to the Republican congressional caucus in 1824. No fewer than five candidates emerged that year with support from various elements of the party. Only one-fourth of the Republican legislators attended the caucus, and in the general election that followed, no candidate received a majority of the electoral votes. As a result the election was thrown into the House of Representatives; to make matters worse, that body chose not Andrew Jackson (the candidate with the greatest number of popular and electoral votes) but John Quincy Adams, who benefited from a political deal with Henry Clay, one of the five nominees, who threw his support in the House to Adams in return for being named Secretary of State. This unfortunate combination of events discredited King Caucus as a means of nominating a presidential candidate.

After 1824, presidential nominations swung briefly to the state level: the Tennessee legislature chose Jackson for the 1828 campaign, and other "favorite son" candidacies followed as John Quincy Adams and John Calhoun were put into nomination by Massachusetts and South Carolina. But if the legislative caucus had proved to be too centralized for the political necessities of the day, selection by individual states was too decentralized for selecting a nationwide official. What was needed was some process that would represent party elements in various parts of the country and at the same time facilitate the nomination of a common candidate by these diverse groups.

THE CONVENTION

The nomination method that emerged to meet these needs was a national party convention composed of delegates from various states. It was not a major party but a minor one, the Anti-Masonic party, that pioneered the way in 1830. The National Republicans (who, like the Anti-Masons, had no appreciable representation in Congress, and thus could not have used the legislative caucus effectively even if they had wanted to) called a similar convention the following year. So did the Democratic Republicans under President Jackson, who saw a convention as an ideal means for getting his handpicked candidate, Martin Van Buren, chosen by the delegates as Vice President.

Although the Anti-Masons disappeared from the political scene almost immediately, they left the national convention as a legacy that the major parties have used since 1840 to nominate their presidential candidates. Moreover, as we will examine in more detail below, their model contained two basic features that have persisted to this day: the selection of delegates by each state through whatever means it deems appropriate, and the allotment of delegates to states on the basis of the size of their congressional delegations (senators and members of the House of Representatives).

For a number of years the convention became the dominant means of nominating candidates at both the state and the national level. Delegates to state conventions were chosen either directly by party members in their localities (towns, cities, or counties) or, more often, by county conventions whose delegates themselves had been selected by party members in smaller local units. The state convention, in turn, selected candidates for statewide office and also chose the state's delegates to the national presidential convention. The system thus allowed rank-and-file members of the party to participate in the choosing of delegates but left the nomination process itself in the hands of the delegates. Viewed in the way we analyzed political parties in the last chapter, actual candidate-selection lay with the party organization, that is, those who were most active in party affairs.

In time, however, disillusionment with the convention set in. Critics charged that instead of representing various elements of the party, the convention was the instrument by which a small clique controlled the nomination process for private purposes. These critics pointed out that the convention system lent itself to manipulation at various stages of the process: *ad hoc* meetings to choose delegates were frequently called without proper notice to all interested parties, and such meetings could be packed by ineligible participants; contests between rival delegations from a particular area were common, and the convention that ultimately ruled on the disputes frequently did so unfairly or without full knowledge of the facts; finally, the convention proceedings themselves placed in the hands of the presiding officers great powers over such key matters as the recognition of speakers, ruling on motions, and the taking of votes. Rather than eliminate the injustices of convention rules, however, foes of the convention chose instead to develop an entirely new means for nominating officials that would give the general public a greater role in the process. The method they chose was the direct primary.

THE DIRECT PRIMARY

The direct primary permits voters themselves to decide who will be nominated for public office. In contrast to the convention system, whereby the voters *indirectly* decide who will be nominated by choosing delegates who actually make the nomination decision, in the primary voters select the nominees themselves.

The direct primary in the United States is chiefly the product of this century. Although it was actually used before the Civil War in some localities and was adopted voluntarily by the Democratic party in several Southern states in the post-Reconstruction period when it became apparent that the nomination process there was in effect the election, the movement to make the primary mandatory developed in the early 1900s. It became a part of the general Progressive movement that called for taking government out of the control of the political bosses of the day and placing it where it belonged—in the hands of the people.* Under the leadership of Robert LaFollette, Wisconsin in 1903 passed the first law for a statewide, direct primary. Other states soon followed suit, and by 1917 all except a few used it for most party selections. Today the direct primary is utilized by all fifty states for some, if not all, nominations.

Nominations in the United States have thus become progressively democratized as the selection of candidates has passed legally from the party in the government to the party organization and, ultimately, to the party in the electorate. Even so, as the rest of this chapter will indicate, the process differs from one office to another. Presidential candidates, for instance, continue to be nominated by national conventions rather than by a popular primary. In addition, primary laws themselves vary, so that candidates chosen by this general method do not all face the same rules of the game. And finally, aside from the legalities of the nomination process, political forces shape the particulars of various electoral contests.

NOMINATING THE PRESIDENT

No other political candidate faces the range of obstacles that confront a man with presidential ambitions. The rules that govern the nomination process for him are infinitely more complex than those for congressional aspirants or state and local politicians. But even more important, presidential-nomination campaigns place demands of time, energy, resources, and planning on candidates and their staffs that dwarf the efforts required of any other office-seeker.

THE ALLOCATION
OF NATIONAL-CONVENTION DELEGATES

A presidential candidate starts out with a well-defined goal in mind: he must win a majority of the votes at his party's national convention in order to be nominated for the Presidency. In 1972 for Republicans 674 votes out of 1346 were required; for the Democrats the comparable figures were 1509 and 3016.

Although the numbers of their convention votes differ, both parties use the same general principles in deciding how many votes each state is entitled to. Specifically, they use the size of a state's congressional delegation (the number of representatives plus the two senators) as the basic figure, to which are added "bonus" votes assigned on the basis of how well the state supported the party's candidates in recent elections. The Republicans

---

*In addition to the popular primary, other "direct democracy" devices proposed by the Progressives included the initiative, referendum, and recall procedures referred to in the last chapter.

take into account not only state voting for their last presidential nominee but also for governors, senators, and candidates for the House of Representatives. In contrast, the Democrats distribute their bonus votes to states strictly on the basis of voting in recent presidential contests.

The allocation of convention votes thus reflects three factors: status as a state (the small states receive the same number of votes based on their two senators as the large states); population (the large states receive more votes based on their membership in the House of Representatives than the small states do); and party support (the extent to which the state has supported the party's candidates in recent elections).*

THE SELECTION OF DELEGATES

In zeroing in on the needed number of convention votes, a candidate must also take into account how delegates are selected. Both parties leave that matter to the individual states, and, as might be expected in a nation of great political diversity, selection methods vary greatly.

A candidate seeking to garner delegate votes must look at the various selection methods with certain basic questions in mind. First, who is primarily responsible in a given state for choosing the delegates—party activists (what we have called the party organization) or rank-and-file voters (the party in the electorate)? Second, to what extent does the choice of delegates depend on their own personal preferences for President? That is, do they run with the understanding that they favor and will definitely support a particular candidate at the convention, or may they use their own discretion in deciding whom to vote for? Third, does the rank-and-file voter have an opportunity to register his preference for President, and if so, how, and with what result? Fourth, if a state does permit voters to register their preferences, must a candidate enter the contest, or can he choose not to put his popularity to a direct test in that state?

Presidential Primaries. For 1972 there were over twenty scheduled presidential primaries permitting voters to choose delegates to the national conventions.† However, there are great variations in these primaries with respect to the delegates' commitments to candidates. California, for instance, provides for running slates of delegates—that is, groups of persons who are pledged to vote for a particular candidate at the convention. Some states

---

*Population is also reflected indirectly in some aspects of the party support criterion: for example, in 1972 the Democrats took into account the number of popular votes a state cast for the Democratic presidential nominees in 1960, 1964, and 1968. The Republicans assigned one extra convention vote for each 4000 votes cast in each congressional district for the Republican nominee for President in 1968 or Republican nominee for Congress in 1970, and one more vote for each 12,500 votes cast for the same officials in each district.

†This was the situation in December of 1971 when this book went to press. The number is up appreciably from 1968 when fifteen political units (fourteen states plus the District of Columbia) authorized presidential primaries.

permit delegates to run as individuals and do not require them to commit themselves to a particular candidate. Rather, they may simply indicate on the ballot whom they "favor," or they may even run as "uninstructed" delegates so that they are entirely free to vote as they desire at the national convention.

Most of the states with presidential primaries conduct simultaneous presidential preference polls, which are separate and distinct from the selection of delegates. Voters in those primaries that elect delegates thus have two separate tasks: to select the delegates to the national convention from their state and to register their own preferences for the nomination. At times, these separate decisions result in a conflicting expression of voter attitudes. In the 1968 New Hampshire Democratic primary, President Johnson won forty-nine percent of the presidential preference poll votes compared to forty-two percent for Senator Eugene McCarthy of Minnesota; in the same primary, voters chose twenty delegates "pledged" to the Senator and four who were designated on the ballot as being "favorable" to the President. All twenty of the McCarthy delegates ultimately voted for him at the 1968 national convention, as they could have done even if President Johnson had not withdrawn from the race, since the results of the preference poll in New Hampshire are not binding on the delegates.

The result in New Hampshire is not peculiar to that state alone: it can also happen in some other states where the preference poll is advisory only.

Eugene McCarthy campaigning in Manchester, New Hampshire, before that state's presidential primary in March 1968. (Charles Harbutt/Magnum)

TABLE 8.1   Presidential Primaries, 1972

Political Unit	Type of Primary
New Hampshire	Nonbinding preference poll. Elected delegates who may be pledged or favorable to candidate.
Florida	Binding preference poll.** Slates of delegates chosen by candidate or by party rule.
Illinois	Nonbinding preference poll. Elected district delegates with presidential preference; at-large delegates elected or chosen by state convention as determined by state central committee.
Wisconsin	Preference poll. Delegates submitted by candidates winning in districts and statewide.
Rhode Island	Nonbinding preference poll. Elected delegates who may be pledged or unpledged.
Massachusetts	Binding preference poll.* Elected district delegates; at-large delegates submitted by state committee but may be opposed to another slate. Delegates may express candidate preference.
Pennsylvania	Nonbinding preference poll. Elected district delegates who may state willingness to be bound by preference poll; at-large delegates chosen by state committee.
District of Columbia	Election of officially unpledged delegates who often make candidate preferences known.
Indiana	
Alabama[a]	
Ohio	Binding preference poll.* Delegates chosen by state convention.
	Preference poll. Elected delegates must state 1st and 2nd candidate preferences and may also pledge to support winner of preference poll.
Tennessee	Binding preference poll.** Delegates chosen by conventions.
North Carolina	Binding preference poll* with convention votes allocated among top 4 candidates. Delegates chosen by conventions.
Nebraska	Nonbinding preference poll. Elected delegates who run pledged or unpledged. Pledged delegates bound to candidate.**
West Virginia	Nonbinding preference poll. Election of unpledged delegates.
Maryland	Binding preference poll.** Elected district delegates who may indicate preference. At-large delegates chosen by district delegates.
Oregon	Binding preference poll.** Elected delegates who may indicate candidate preference or be uncommitted.
California	Elected slates of delegates who may be pledged to candidate or be uncommitted.
New Jersey	Nonbinding preference poll. Elected delegates who may be pledged or unpledged.
New Mexico	Preference poll in which voter expresses preference for candidate or none of names shown. Delegates chosen under party rules apportioned between 2 top candidates in preference poll or 1 candidate and unpledged category. Pledged delegates bound.*
South Dakota	Election of slates of pledged or unpledged delegates. Pledged delegates bound.***
New York[a]	
Arkansas[a]	

[a]Full information unavailable as of December 1971.

*Bound at National Convention for one ballot or until released by candidate.

**Bound at National Convention for two ballots, or until candidate receives less than 35% of Convention votes (20% in Tennessee), or until released by candidate.

***Bound at National Convention for three ballots, or until candidate receives less than 35% of Convention votes, or until released by candidate.

Consent of Candidate	Convention Votes†† Democratic	Republican	Primary Date
Not required. Can withdraw.	18	14	March 7
Not required. Entry by Selection Committee.† Withdrawal by noncandidacy affidavit.	81	40	March 14
Required.	170	58	March 21
Not required. Entry by Selection Committee.† Withdrawal by noncandidacy affidavit.	67	28	April 4
Required.	22	8	April 11
Not required. Entry by Secretary of State† or state committee chairmen. Can withdraw.	102	34	April 25
Not required. Can withdraw.	182	60	April 25
Not required.	15	9	May 2
Required.	76	32	May 2
	37	17	May 2
Required.	153	56	May 2
Not required. Entry by Secretary of State.† Withdraw by failing to pay filing fee.	64	32	May 6
Not required. Entry by Board of Elections.† Withdrawal by noncandidacy affidavit.	49	26	May 4
Not required. Entry by Secretary of State.† Can withdraw.	24	16	May 9
Required.	35	18	May 9
Not required. Entry by Secretary of State.† Withdrawal by noncandidacy affidavit.	53	26	May 16
Not required. Entry by Secretary of State.† No provision for withdrawal.	34	18	May 23
Required.	271	96	June 6
Not required. Can withdraw.	109	40	June 6
Not required. Entry by Selection Committee.† Withdrawal by failing to pay filing fee.	18	14	June 6
Not required.	17	14	June 6
	278	88	June 27
	27	18	June 20

†On basis that candidacy is generally advocated or recognized nationally (typically in news media).
††Tentatively set by National Committees as of the end of 1971.

In some states the delegates to the national convention are required to vote for the candidate who wins the preference poll. Even in these the delegates are typically bound only for two ballots at the convention.

For the presidential hopeful who manages to puzzle his way through this array of primary provisions and to weigh their implications for his candidacy, one other major legal consideration remains: does a particular state have a contest he can avoid if he wants to or will he be forced by state law to run? In some states with primaries a candidate is protected in that he must consent to having his name entered in the contest. However, in others, his name is put on the ballot automatically by state officials if his candidacy is generally advocated or recognized by the national news media. In some instances an unwilling candidate may simply withdraw his name; in others the only way he can get off the ballot is to sign an affidavit that he is not a candidate for the Presidency; in others, he cannot withdraw at all. Table 8.1 incorporates the above information about the states with presidential primaries scheduled in 1972.

Nonprimary Selection. As if presidential primaries were not enough trouble, a candidate also needs to concern himself with how delegates to the national convention are chosen in the remaining states. Most often delegates are selected by state conventions composed of party representatives chosen at lower political levels, typically the congressional districts. A state convention generally selects these district delegates themselves to represent that portion of the state's contingent that is based on the size of its membership in the House of Representatives. It then chooses others to serve as "delegates-at-large" (those to which the state is entitled because of its two senators and its bonus votes for supporting the party in recent elections). In some states, however, the state central committee* selects the delegates-at-large.

However the selection procedures in the nonprimary states may vary, the important fact from a candidate's point of view is that the choice of delegates is firmly in the hands of what we have referred to as the party organization. Most states choose their congressional-district delegates in party conventions; only in a few jurisdictions are they selected by rank-and-file voters. Moreover, even in those states the "at-large" delegates are controlled by the state party organization. Thus in New York State in 1968 delegates favorable to Senator McCarthy were chosen by the voters in sixty-two of the 123 congressional-districts; however, of the sixty-seven delegates-at-large picked by the state central committee, only fifteen were favorable to the Senator's candidacy.

*State committees vary in composition. They are usually built upon lower electoral units such as counties or state legislative or congressional districts. Committee members are typically chosen in conventions or primaries, but in some states lower-level party officials themselves (particularly county chairmen) serve as ex-officio members of such committees.

The rules of the game for the selection of state delegates to the national convention thus grant influence to both rank-and-file voters (the party in the electorate) and activists (the party organization). Although the latter are clearly favored in nonprimary states and exercise considerable control even where there are presidential primaries, most candidates cannot afford to ignore their standing with the general electorate. For delegates to the national convention wish not only to choose a candidate they personally favor but also to nominate a man who can beat his rival in the general election. Therefore, as we will see in the following sections, each presidential hopeful conducts a campaign for the nomination designed to convince the delegates that he is the man most likely to lead the party to victory in November.

THE NOMINATION CAMPAIGN:
THE POOL OF CANDIDATES

Although many persons entertain presidential ambitions (the bug is considered to be virtually incurable once it strikes), comparatively few are seriously considered as potential nominees by the two major parties. Those that are, possess what is generally called "political availability," that is, they have the characteristics and experiences that supposedly make them attractive candidates both to activists and to the general voting public. There is, however, no definite check list of job qualifications for the Presidency. About the closest one can come to determining what particular characteristics and experiences put an individual in line for a presidential nomination is to look at past candidates. But even this approach poses some difficulties, since the attitudes of political leaders and the American public change over time.

Writing on the subject in 1959, Sidney Hyman listed nine "tests" for a presidential hopeful based on standards that had been applied to nominees over the years. It is instructive to consider whether the informal qualifications he found for the office until that time continued to operate during the 1960s, a period of profound change, when six additional nominees were chosen by the two parties. Hyman's criteria were the following:

1. He must first have had some official connection with the governmental process in an appointive or elective post.
2. Nominating conventions show a clear preference for state governors.
3. A candidate is preferred who comes from a state which has a large electoral vote and which does not have a one-party voting record.
4. Candidates have been favored who come from the big Northern states to the exclusion of Southerners.
5. Conventions will choose only men who are in fact, or who can be made to appear, hospitable to the claims of many economic interests in the nation.
6. Presidential candidates, like the English Crown, are expected by nomi-

nating conventions to present an idealized version of all that is felicitous in home and family life.

7. In defiance of the fact that the majority of Americans live in great urban centers, candidates are preferred who come from small towns.
8. Candidates are preferred who come from English ethnic stock.
9. Nominating conventions have raised an extra-constitutional religious test by their decisive preference for Protestant hopefuls.

The one criterion that clearly stood the test of time is the first. All the nominees—the Republicans, Nixon (twice) and Goldwater, as well as the Democrats, Kennedy, Johnson, and Humphrey—had been prominent in public service. Although Nixon did not hold an office at the time he was nominated in 1968, he had first come to Washington in January 1947 as a young (thirty-four) congressman, and he subsequently held public office until 1960 when he was defeated by Kennedy. As we saw earlier, he next tried for the governorship of California in 1962 and continued to be active in party affairs during most of the intervening years until he was nominated again in 1968.

Kennedy, who had begun his career in Washington the same day as Nixon as an even younger (thirty) congressman, had no significant career in private life at all, spending six years as a representative and another seven as a senator before running for the Presidency. Johnson and Humphrey had both gone into public service after short teaching careers. Of the five nominees, only Goldwater, who became a senator at forty-four, had spent any significant portion of his life in a private pursuit, his family's department store business. Thus the experience of the 1960s would, if anything, strengthen Hyman's first test; indeed, it could be amended to read that a candidate must have a "long-term connection with elective posts in the national government."

In fact, we can be even more precise and identify two national offices as stepping stones to presidential nomination in the 1960s. All five nominees acquired their major reputation while serving as United States senators; three of the five also served as Vice Presidents. Although Lyndon Johnsons' service in that office was not a true apprenticeship for the nomination since he succeeded to the Presidency on the death of Kennedy and then was nominated in 1964 as the incumbent, Nixon and Humphrey both occupied the post when nominated.

What is particularly interesting about the experiences of the 1960s is not only that all five nominees were former senators but also that in the Democratic party in 1960 and again in 1968 *all* the serious contenders were serving in the upper chamber. These included Humphrey, Johnson, and Stuart Symington in 1960, and Robert Kennedy and Eugene McCarthy in 1968.*

*All the major contenders for the 1972 Democratic nomination at the time this book went to press were also senators.

No major candidate in that party came from the traditional recruiting ground for Presidents that Hyman identified in his second test, the state governorship. Only in the Republican party in the 1960s did governors appear as presidential hopefuls, and they were limited both in number and in the seriousness of their candidacies. Nelson Rockefeller of New York made noises as a contender in all three presidential years, but without much success, and frequently with little concerted effort. William Scranton of Pennsylvania and Ronald Reagan of California made belated attempts to stop Goldwater and Nixon in 1964 and 1968 respectively, while Governor George Romney of Michigan withdrew from the race in the latter year before the first presidential primary was held in New Hampshire.

Other tests mentioned by Hyman also apparently failed to impress party leaders in the 1960s. John Kennedy's candidacy in 1960 violated the traditional preference for Protestants, and once he had succeeded, people seemed not to notice that two of the major Democratic contenders in 1968, Robert Kennedy and Eugene McCarthy, were of the Catholic faith. Nor did Republicans seemed concerned in 1964 that Senator Goldwater, although an Episcopalian, came from a Jewish background on one side of his family.* The related traditional preference for English stock did little to deter the nomination of the two Irish Kennedys or Goldwater with his Russian genealogy.

Traditional geographical factors mentioned by Hyman also had limited effect on presidential nominations in the 1960s. Past preferences for nominees from Northern, two-party states with a large electoral vote failed to prevent the candidacies of Arizonan Goldwater, Texan Johnson, or Minnesotan Humphrey. (Sixteen states had more electoral votes than Minnesota in 1968, and three had the same number, ten.) And even though all five nominees were born in small towns, Whittier (the birthplace of Nixon) and Brookline (that of Kennedy) were close to large cities (Los Angeles and Boston respectively). As for the others, Goldwater and Humphrey lived their young adult years in the cities of Phoenix and Minneapolis.

The remaining two of Hyman's tests also had less application in the 1960s than in the past. Goldwater, far from being hospitable to many economic interests, was clearly identified with the business community, both in his own private family interests and in his philosophy concerning the limited role that government should play in economic affairs. Nixon also had close ties to business interests in southern California, especially early in his political career; moreover, immediately prior to his nomination in 1968 he was a senior partner in a Wall Street law firm that represented many of the major corporations in the United States. On the other hand, Humphrey had firm

---

*An amusing story made the rounds in 1964 to the effect that when the Senator was refused admittance to a golf course because of his religious background, he demanded the right to play nine holes on the rationale that he was only half Jewish.

political links with organized labor throughout his entire life in the public service.

As for a felicitous family life, all five nominees at least give an outward appearance of domestic bliss. However, a perennial contender for the Republican nomination throughout the 1960s, Nelson Rockefeller, divorced his wife of over thirty years in 1963 and remarried a much younger woman, a divorcee whose previous husband won custody of the children of that marriage. This succession of events was generally thought to have harmed Rockefeller's chances for the nomination in 1964 (some attributed his narrow loss to Goldwater in the California primary that year to the birth of a son to his second wife just three days before the balloting, which served to remind voters of his recent marital problems), but it was assumed that by 1968 most Americans had either forgotten about the matter or had become more understanding of it.

Thus the 1960s demonstrated that presidential hopefuls no longer need to concern themselves too seriously with religious, national-origin, geographical, and family matters that once stood in the way of aspirants.* Nor did they necessarily have to be governors to become a candidate. On the other hand, a new set of informal qualifications seemingly emerged for those who entertain realistic expectations of winning their party's nomination. They should, above all, be well-known political figures with considerable experience in public life. Even though this qualification does not necessarily eliminate governers, it does mean that other offices, in particular a senate seat and, to a lesser extent, the Vice Presidency, provide the kind of visibility to party leaders and the general public that astute candidates can turn to their political advantage.

There are several possible reasons why senators have suddenly become prime presidential prospects. One is that they receive a great amount of coverage in the mass media, particularly network television, which focus more closely on national news and events in Washington than on happenings in the states. Beyond this, the nation's increasing involvement in foreign affairs naturally places the Senate in the public's eye because of the influential role the upper chamber plays in the conduct of relationships with other countries. Governors, in contrast, have no responsibilities of consequence in this area of public affairs, and frequently they do not appear as well-versed in such matters as they should be. Furthermore, state chief executives have been placed in a difficult position in recent years, caught between conflicting public demands to tackle major domestic problems (schools, mental health, highways, and the like) and at the same time to hold the line on taxes; the result has often been unpopularity and short

*Of course, these considerations have never been absolute. Al Smith, nominated by the Democrats, was an Irish-Catholic, while Grover Cleveland was a bachelor who never denied fathering a child out of wedlock.

terms of office. Such a record is hardly calculated to endear a man to party leaders looking for a political winner.

Recent vice-presidential experiences also help explain why that post has become a more important launching pad for higher office.* As national figures, Vice Presidents have benefited in recent years because Presidents began to give them duties that not only were meaningful but also resulted in increased exposure to both party leaders and the general public. Eisenhower, for instance, virtually turned over the job of political campaigning and forging ties with Republican party professionals around the nation to Nixon; to a lesser extent Johnson permitted Humphrey to continue to cultivate the friendships he had long enjoyed with Democratic chieftains. Both men also traveled widely abroad as representatives of the country and received the publicity that naturally attends such globe-trotting in the nation's behalf.

Thus the typical candidate of the 1960s differed considerably from his predecessors. It would be premature to suggest that the backgrounds of the six presidential nominees of the 1960s will necessarily be duplicated in the years ahead. Yet the tendencies noted here appear to derive from certain basic trends. The development of a more common culture and the nationalization of American life in general brought about by improved means of communication and transportation quite naturally have led to minimizing the importance of parochial concerns, such as the religious, ethnic, or geographical background of a candidate, and to upgrading the experiences he has had in the national political arena.

There is also some indication that party leaders in the United States no longer do what Lord Bryce suggested in his classic study, *The American Commonwealth*, written in 1888: choose mediocre men whose lack of opinions on controversial issues make them politically acceptable to the broadest combination of voters. Instead, one party selected Goldwater in 1964, another Humphrey in 1968, men who were identified with conservative and liberal views at virtually the opposite ends of the traditional political spectrum. And, to a lesser extent, the other three candidates—Kennedy, Johnson, and Nixon—were also connected with national political issues, such as, respectively, the French-Algerian war, social-welfare legislation, and a tough stand on law and order in American society.

Another piece of evidence on the growing importance of national forces in presidential politics is the changing attitude of party leaders toward defeated candidates. American history has generally relegated the losers to political oblivion (exceptions were two Democrats: Grover Cleveland, who won in 1884, ran again but lost in 1888, and was renominated and reelected

---

*Prior to Nixon's nomination in 1960, the last incumbent Vice President who was nominated for the Presidency was Martin Van Buren, who was chosen in 1836 while he was the second man to President Andrew Jackson.

in 1892; and William Jennings Bryan who was nominated in 1896, 1900, and 1908), yet in the twenty years after World War II three defeated candidates were selected a second time by their parties: Dewey by the Republicans in 1948, Stevenson by the Democrats in 1956, and Nixon by the GOP in 1968. Recent political experience thus indicates that if a defeated candidate does not lose by too wide a margin and if he takes certain key actions (discussed in the following section), he may well have another chance to head his party's ticket.

If even a defeated candidate has a fair chance at renomination, a winner has a virtual monopoly of his party's nomination the second time around. In this century no incumbent President who sought another term of office has been denied renomination. Even Herbert Hoover, hardly the nation's most popular political figure during the depression years, was chosen to lead his party again in 1932 against the Democrats. Moreover, Vice Presidents who have succeeded to the Presidency on the death of their predecessors have all been renominated by their party in this century—Theodore Roosevelt and Calvin Coolidge by the Republicans, Harry Truman and Lyndon Johnson by the Democrats. It is interesting to note, however, that none of the former Vice Presidents sought a second successive full term. Roosevelt retired in 1908 (he attempted a political comeback against President Taft in 1912 but failed); Coolidge "chose not to run" in 1928 (some students of the era claim, however, that he actually wanted to be renominated and was bitterly disappointed when his party took him at his word); while Truman and Johnson withdrew in 1952 and 1968 (their exact reasons are unknown, but both had been challenged and embarrassed politically in the New Hampshire primary by, respectively, Estes Kefauver and Eugene McCarthy).

PRE-CONVENTION STRATEGIES:
EARLY MANEUVERINGS

A basic fact of political life that presidential candidates face today is that they must make a concerted effort to win the nomination. No longer can they sit back and let others drag them reluctantly into the contest. Nor can they wait too long to make their bid. Typically an aspirant begins his planning for the nomination quite early. As previously mentioned, Richard Nixon and his supporters held their first strategy session in January 1967, a year-and-a-half in advance of the Republican convention.

A decision to begin planning for the presidential nomination, however, is not necessarily announced publicly. A candidate may want first to assess his chances of success by sounding out party leaders on his candidacy or to test the reaction of voters by having private public opinion polls taken comparing his popularity with that of prominent rivals. He may also want to see whether he can acquire the vast sums of money necessary for the race ahead. If the assessments are not favorable, he may prefer not to risk the chance of defeat and simply decide to take himself out of contention. He can do so somewhat more gracefully, of course, if he has not committed himself publicly in the first place.

Even if a man has definitely decided to seek the nomination, he still may not want to announce his candidacy immediately. For one thing, such a step may encourage other aspirants to forge political alliances against him because they regard him as the front-runner. In addition, an announced candidate must face demands to commit himself on a broad range of controversial issues. This necessity prompted Richard Nixon to withhold announcement of his own candidacy in 1967 in order to let George Romney be exposed to the media and the public. The strategy proved to be a wise one, for the Michigan governor was unable to cope with incessant pressure from representatives of the press and television to state his policies on Vietnam. Romney's unfortunate explanation for his change of views on the matter—that he had been previously "brainwashed" by the American military and diplomatic leadership there—is credited with ending his chances for the presidential nomination in 1968 and with putting Richard Nixon in the driver's seat.*

Observers of nomination politics, however, do not require formal announcements of candidacy to know who is maneuvering for a presidential bid. Almost immediately after losing his try for the vice presidential nomination in 1956, John F. Kennedy began accepting speaking engagements outside his own state of Massachusetts. Edmund Muskie, who was nominated for Vice President by the Democrats in 1968, pursued a similar strategy following his and Hubert Humphrey's defeat. Such aspirants frequently appear before audiences of the party faithful; the wise candidate also attempts to gain more exposure to the general public as well. Suddenly he begins to appear with some regularity on television programs like "Meet the Press" and "Face the Nation"; he may also write articles for popular magazines. Some may even find time to produce books such as Kennedy's *Profiles in Courage* or Nixon's *Six Crises*. A trip abroad may also serve to keep the candidate in the news and, if he has not had much experience in foreign affairs, help counteract the charge that he is not knowledgeable in this vital area which consumes so much time of the American President.

Not all candidates, however, face identical problems in cultivating party leaders and the American voter. Prominent senators and incumbent Vice Presidents, whose duties place them in the public eye, do not have to work as hard at making themselves politically visible as do state governors, comparative newcomers to national public life, and those persons not presently holding a public office. Since the defeated presidential candidate (called

---

*George McGovern's public announcement in January 1971 that he was a candidate for the Democratic nomination in 1972 is unusual. A forthright man, McGovern also knew he had to make himself better known to the American public and that his announcement might help him do that, as well as gather the money needed for the race.

the titular leader) is most likely to be in the latter category, it is especially important that he keep his political fences mended by maintaining contact with both national and local party leaders and helping to pay off the party's debt, to which his defeat is thought to contribute.* A titular leader who hopes to be renominated also generally speaks out on public issues as a means of conveying the impression that he remains the leader of the party out of power.

The activities described above are a part of the early maneuverings for the nomination. In the early months of election year, however, some candidates publicly announce their intention to seek the Presidency. For it is then that those who plan to enter the presidential primaries must begin to get their campaigns organized: the first such contest in New Hampshire has traditionally been held in mid-March with Wisconsin's coming in early April. (In 1972 New Hampshire had the first primary, held on March 7th.)

CAMPAIGNING IN PRESIDENTIAL PRIMARIES

Every candidate faces the basic strategic question of whether to enter the presidential primaries. Winning has two potential advantages. One is that the candidate will pick up delegates in the states he carries. Since many delegates come from states that have presidential primaries, the contests represent a sizable block of potential votes at the convention. As previously explained, many of these delegates either are uncommitted to a candidate or have only a short-lived commitment. Thus a candidate may win a series of primaries, as Democratic candidate Estes Kefauver did in 1952, only to see the ballots cast at the convention for another candidate.

A much greater benefit for the candidate than the legal commitment of delegate votes is that victories in a number of such contests may convince delegates in states without primaries (as well as uncommitted delegates in primary states) that he has great popular appeal with the voters. Because delegates generally want to pick a winner, they may support him at the convention. Thus the indirect effect of presidential primaries on delegates from many states is more important than their direct consequences in the particular states in which primaries are held.

For some candidates the question of whether to enter the presidential primaries is academic: they must do so in order to have any chance to win the nomination. This is true of those who have no significant support from key party figures, particularly delegation chairmen from large states who influence how their states' sizable blocks of votes are to be cast at the convention. Thus both Estes Kefauver in 1952 and John Kennedy in 1960 made an early decision to enter the Democratic primaries because they had no

*The relationship between lack of money and political defeat is a chicken-and-egg proposition. Candidates who appear to be losing have trouble raising money, which, in turn, helps to make the expectation of their defeat a self-fulfilling prophecy. The losing party typically ends up with a deficit.

standing with the party professionals. The former was a political neophyte who, as chairman of a Senate committee investigating crime, embarrassed Democratic leaders in industrial states like Illinois where organized crime was rampant; the latter was also a political independent whose youth and Catholicism were regarded by the "pros"—some of whom who were Catholics themselves—as insurmountable barriers to his election as President. For Kefauver primary victories had little effect; the convention delegates proceeded to nominate Adlai Stevenson who had not entered a single contest. But for Kennedy they were the means by which he convinced the reluctant professionals to choose him to lead the party.

If, on the other hand, a candidate has significant support from party leaders, he may choose not to enter the primaries and still win the nomination. Adlai Stevenson in 1952 and Hubert Humphrey in 1968 both prevailed over candidates who had entered and won the primaries. Yet the circumstances of both years were unusual. Because few Democratic candidates in 1952 were anxious to contend with the probable Republican nominee, Dwight Eisenhower, Kefauver ran unopposed in the primaries; as a result his victories were hollow and failed to prove his popularity. Stevenson for his part did not enter the primaries most probably because he did not want the nomination; he was certainly reluctant to accept it at the convention. In 1968 Humphrey was prevented from entering some of the primaries because President Johnson did not withdraw from the race until the last day of March. Moreover, Robert Kennedy was assassinated immediately after his victory in the California primary; had he lived, he might have wrested the nomination from Humphrey at the convention.

The dominant trend in nomination politics, especially since World War II, has been for successful presidential candidates to enter the primaries. Particularly in the party out of power, there is normally a factional fight for the nomination, with the contestants battling it out in the presidential primaries. In the postwar period, whenever the Democrats held the Presidency, all the Republican nominees proved their popularity in this fashion: Dewey in 1948, Eisenhower in 1952, Goldwater in 1964, and Nixon in 1968. When Eisenhower occupied the White House, the successful Democratic candidate—Stevenson in 1956 and Kennedy in 1960—pursued the same course of action.

Primaries are less crucial in the party that controls the Presidency. As previously mentioned, Stevenson and Humphrey both won the nomination without entering a single one. More typically, however, candidates enter the primaries of the party in power, but the contests are not meaningful, particularly when the incumbent is seeking reelection. Both Truman in 1948 and Eisenhower in 1956 were successful in the primaries. In 1964 Lyndon Johnson won several contests, generally as a write-in candidate; in addition, in others state political figures served as successful stand-ins for him, primarily against challenges to his party leadership from Governor Wallace of Alabama. In 1960 Richard Nixon, the heir apparent to the Republican nomination, who had no appreciable opposition, nonetheless found it advisable to enter a series of primaries.

In the postwar years presidential primaries have become virtually a "must" for candidates. A number of prominent aspirants in the out-party who chose to ignore the primaries failed in their bid for the nomination, including these Democratic hopefuls—Governor Averell Harriman of New York in 1956, Senators Symington of Missouri and Lyndon Johnson in 1960—and these Republicans—Governor William Scranton of Pennsylvania in 1964 and Rockefeller of New York in 1968. It would appear that today both the general public and political leaders expect candidates to prove their vote-getting abilities in the presidential primaries.

For the serious presidential contender today, then, the crucial question is not whether he should go into the primaries; rather, it is which particular ones he should enter. In choosing among the contests that are held over the relatively short period from March until early June, the candidate must balance the desire to demonstrate support for his candidacy in a number of states with the need to limit his campaign efforts so that he does not spread himself too thin. He should thus avoid entering too few primaries as Nelson Rockefeller did in 1964 (he was a serious candidate in only three, two of which he lost), or too many, a mistake that Estes Kefauver made in 1952 and again in 1956.

The candidate naturally wants to go into those primaries he thinks he has the maximum chance of winning. Sometimes geographical considerations play a role in his choice. In 1960 John Kennedy entered the New Hampshire election partly because the state is next to his home base of Massachusetts which he could draw upon for campaign workers, particularly over the weekends. For a similar reason, Hubert Humphrey chose to bypass the New Hampshire primary in 1960 in favor of Wisconsin, which borders his home state of Minnesota. Political and social factors also influence the candidates' selections of contests. That same year Humphrey considered West Virginia a favorable state for his candidacy because he thought (wrongly, as it turned out) that its depressed economy would make its citizens receptive to his long liberal record of favoring governmental assistance to the disadvantaged.

In some instances, however, a candidate may deliberately choose to enter a primary that is not considered advantageous to his candidacy in order to demonstrate that he has a broader public appeal than is generally recognized. John Kennedy went into the West Virginia primary in 1960 to prove that a Catholic could win in a state in which the population was ninety-five percent Protestant. Similarly, his brother Robert entered the Indiana primary in 1968 to show that he could win over a potent state organization that was backing a popular governor, Roger Branigin. Both risks proved to be good ones that advanced the candidacies of the Kennedy brothers.

Primary options for presidential hopefuls today are not as great as they were at one time. The trend in recent state primary laws of entering a person automatically in the race if his candidacy is generally advocated or recognized by the national media and making it difficult for him to withdraw tends to force candidates to contest in such states. Moreover, candidates are increasingly expected to demonstrate their strength in various parts of the country.

Different considerations tend to force the candidates into other presidential primaries. The time when they are held is an important factor. The earliest contest, traditionally in New Hampshire, generally attracts most of the major contenders because it constitutes the first test of popular sentiment. On the other hand, California has become a serious battleground because it provides a late indication of voter preferences.

One of the trends emerging from recent primary results is that victories in the later elections are the most important. Stevenson lost to Kefauver in several early contests in 1956, but his later successes in Florida, Oregon, and California paved the way for his eventual nomination. Similarly, Goldwater's victory in California in 1964 is credited with insuring his successful candidacy and eliminating Nelson Rockefeller from contention.

Thus states with primaries that virtually force candidates into the contest, as well as those with early and late election dates, generally play an important part in preconvention campaigns. Yet there are no hard and fast rules operative here. Neither John Kennedy in 1960 nor Richard Nixon in 1968 entered the California primary for a reason that sometimes deters presidential hopefuls: not wanting to challenge favorite sons (Governors Pat Brown and Ronald Reagan in these two instances) or to run the risk of splitting the state party.

The candidate who makes judicious choices and campaigns effectively in primaries so that he either sweeps them all or wins some key contests, especially late in the election year, goes a long way towards establishing his claim for the presidential nomination. Not only does he demonstrate popularity in these states, but also through his victories he gains more favorable ratings in nationwide public opinion polls. (The process works both ways, that is, candidates who improve their standing in the polls frequently begin to do better in the presidential primaries.) The wise candidate, however, does not put all his efforts into the primaries; he also works to garner as much support as he can from other sources as well.

GATHERING DELEGATE SUPPORT
IN STATES WITHOUT PRIMARIES

Although the attention of the media and the general public focuses on presidential primaries, the fate of the candidate also depends on how effective he is in lining up the support of delegates from states without primaries (as well as those whose primaries do not bind their actions at the convention). The time has passed when a presidential hopeful could wait until delegates showed up at the convention itself to try to influence their votes. Instead, the trend in recent years has been toward laying the groundwork for delegate support long before the convention convenes.

A classic strategy for garnering support was followed by the Kennedy forces in 1960. At an initial meeting in late October 1959 (some nine months prior to the Democratic convention), the candidate's brother Robert assigned state delegations to the assembled supporters: John Bailey was to take New England and upstate New York; he was also to work with the candidate's father, Joseph Kennedy, in New York City and northern New Jersey; brother Ted was given responsibility for the Mountain states; Robert himself was to take the South; and the candidate was to negotiate with favorite sons in Ohio, Pennsylvania, Michigan, and California. All soon began to make the necessary contacts, and in the late spring and early summer of 1960 John Kennedy himself crisscrossed the nation visiting with undecided delegates and attending state conventions.

Before the next presidential election the Goldwater forces made even more extensive efforts to corral delegate support for their candidate. As early as 1961 volunteer groups under the leadership of Clifton White marked out on a map each state with its delegate count and procedures. When the party meetings in the precincts, counties, and congressional districts were held, Goldwater workers were there to see that delegates favorable to their candidate were chosen. They also made sure that the state conventions that chose the delegates-at-large to the national convention picked those who supported the Arizona Senator.

The Nixon forces in 1968 also benefited from early delegate support. Because of his long service to the party, the former Vice President could already count on a good many adherents when his initial planning session was held in January 1967. At that time the planning group was able to determine that 603 votes would be delivered at the convention if he held the South. A year-and-a-half later, on June 1, 1968, Nixon himself insured that he would: a meeting in Atlanta with Strom Thurmond of South Carolina, John Tower of Texas, and other Republican leaders led to a pledge of Southern support at the convention in return for certain commitments on Nixon's part to promote a strong defense policy and to take Southern interests into account in matters of school desegregation and federal appointments.

Thus the presidential candidate today pursues two separate preconvention strategies: entering the presidential primaries and lining up delegates in other states as well. If he does his job well, he may have gained the necessary support for the nomination before the convention meets. Still he cannot be sure until then whether the promises of votes to him will be kept. Moreover, the convention serves other purposes for the man who has his eye on the White House.

THE NATIONAL CONVENTION

The convention is important to the presidential candidate for two major reasons. First, whatever may have transpired beforehand, it is that body which makes the actual nomination. Second, the convention provides opportunities for the candidate to strengthen his chances to win the general election the following November.

A number of decisions that precede the balloting on presidential nominations can have significant effects. In some instances, the location of the convention is important.* Illinois Governor Adlai Stevenson's welcoming speech to the Democratic delegates assembled in Chicago in 1952 is credited with influencing their decision to nominate him that year. In 1968 the events growing out of the confrontation between protesters and Mayor Daley's police in that same city contributed to Hubert Humphrey's defeat in the general election.

Also important in some instances are contests between rival slates of delegates from states where there have been disputes in the selection process. In 1952 opposing groups favoring Taft or Eisenhower showed up at the Republican convention from some Southern states. The National Committee decided by a majority vote to seat most of the Taft delegates, and the convention Credentials Committee (composed of two delegates from each state) supported the decision. Even so, adroit manipulation of the rules of the convention, plus the control of large-state delegations, enabled the Eisenhower forces to overturn the decision of the two committees on the floor of the convention.

On several occasions in recent years the Democrats have also had disputes over the seating of delegations. Most of these credentials contests have involved either the unwillingness of Southern delegates to sign a loyalty oath to support the party's nominee in the general election or disputes on the openness of the selection process to Southern blacks. The rules for the 1968 Democratic convention provided that persons who could not support the nominee should withdraw from the convention and that no delegations would be seated from states where the selection process deprived citizens of the right to vote by reason of race or color. Violations of these rules led to the replacement of all members of the "regular" Mississippi delegation and half of those from Georgia.†

*This decision is made officially by the National Committee composed of one man and one woman from each state chosen by the state's delegation at the last national convention. (The Republican Committee also includes the chairman of each state party.) For the out-party, the chairman of the National Committee has the greatest say in the matter; for the in-party, the President does.

†The conflicts do not always involve the South, however. The McCarthy forces in 1968 unsuccessfully challenged several Northern delegations on the grounds that irregularities occurred in meetings at which delegates were chosen.

Such incidents also point up another matter of vital concern to a candidate, namely, the rules for both delegate selection and voting at the convention. In 1968 McCarthy supporters moved to change the traditional "unit" rule of the Democrats whereby states can require all delegates to vote for the candidate favored by the majority of the delegation. The Humphrey people joined with the McCarthyites in defeating Southern attempts to maintain the rule. In addition, the convention agreed to abolish the unit rule at every level of the delegate-selection process in 1972.

Another major decision is the writing and adoption of the party platform. Although these documents have traditionally been ridiculed as meaningless promises the party does not intend to keep or as vague phrases produced by the necessities of compromise, the fact of the matter is that many delegates have taken them seriously. In 1948 some Southern delegations walked out of the Democratic convention because they felt the platform was too liberal on the issue of civil rights; twenty years later the delegates of the same party debated the Vietnam plank of the platform before a nationwide television audience in an amazing display of self-criticism by the party in power.

Republicans have also had their share of platform disputes. In 1960 Nelson Rockefeller threatened to lead a floor fight over the platform unless it committed the party to stronger programs for national defense and civil rights. To avoid that possibility, Richard Nixon agreed to the Rockefeller demands and used his influence to get the changes included. At the 1964 convention the Goldwater forces adopted the opposite tactic: they refused to make any concessions to party liberals like Governors Rockefeller and Romney on such issues as civil rights and political extremism.

For potential presidential candidates, credentials contests, the adoption of rules of procedure, and the party platform, all provide tests of strength, as well as opportunities for forging the kinds of political alliances necessary to win the nomination. They have other effects as well. Rockefeller, for instance, had no hope of winning the nomination himself in 1960, but he concentrated on the platform as a means of commiting his party to public positions on civil rights and national defense that he favored. The statement of party principles may also influence the general election campaign, since party leaders who oppose such matters may not be inclined to work too hard in the party's behalf. Republican Governors Rockefeller and Romney did little to help the Goldwater cause in 1964, and many Democrats opposed to the proadministration plank on Vietnam in the party's 1968 platform did not bestir themselves in the general election campaign that year.

Although the candidate must concern himself with such matters during the early stages of the convention, he and his supporters must work at the same time towards the most crucial decision of the assemblage: the balloting that normally occurs on the third or fourth day of the proceedings. In the interim, plans are laid for that fateful roll-call vote. Presidential hopefuls appear before caucuses of state delegations to solicit support. Polls are taken of delegates so that candidates know how many votes they can count on and from whom they might pick up additional support. Individual delegates are also wooed. In 1960 Edward Kennedy retained contacts with the Wyoming delegates he had worked with the previous spring and was in their midst when the state's votes put his brother over the top on the first ballot. That same year Richard Nixon arranged to have his picture taken with each delegate at the Republican convention.

The kind of strategy a candidate employs in the balloting for the nomination depends on the amount of delegate support he has. If he is the front runner, he concentrates on holding the votes he has been promised and in picking up any additional ones he needs to win a majority on the initial ballot. To this end he and his workers use the bandwagon technique—that is, they argue that since he is going to win the nomination anyway, delegation chairman or individual members who are smart politically will come out now for his candidacy and not wait until the matter has already been settled. The candidate, it is suggested, will take early support into account in the future when he is in a position to do political favors. Franklin Roosevelt did so quite specifically after he was elected in 1932 by determining whether a person seeking a political position was for him "before Chicago."

Candidates with weak delegate support attempt to counter the bandwagon technique with strategies of their own. They typically encourage delegates who do not support them to cast their ballots for favorite sons or other minor candidates. The important thing is to hold down the vote for the front runner on the first roll call. Candidates also attempt to forge alliances to stop the leader. They may agree, for example, that at some point in the balloting, the one who falls behind in the voting will throw his support to the other. The difficulty with making such an arrangement, however, is that frequently minor candidates may have greater differences between themselves than either has with the leader. The only alliance that might conceivably have stopped Richard Nixon at the 1968 Republican convention would have been one between Nelson Rockefeller and Ronald Reagan. Yet given their divergent views on vital issues of the day, plus Rockefeller's failure to support Goldwater in 1964 (Reagan had made the best speech of that campaign in his behalf), the two governors were hardly a compatible political combination.

The front runner, as well as minor candidates, hold forth various enticements in bargaining with possible political supporters. Some persons are interested in getting the party to take a particular stand in the platform. Others have more tangible concerns: a senator or governor may seek the candidate's support in his own campaign; another political leader may have his eye on a cabinet post. Although a presidential candidate himself may refuse to make such commitments so that he can go before his party and the electorate as a "free" man beholden to no one, his supporters do not

A fish-eye view of convention hall. John Bailey, Chairman of the National Committee, officially opens the proceedings. (United Press International)

The 1968 Democratic convention. (United Press International)

A party stalwart. (Dennis Brack/Black Star)

A Kansas delegate with varied enthusiasms. (Wide World Photos)

Georgia delegate Julian Bond declines the nomination for Vice President on the grounds of being too young. (United Press International)

The convention's choices. (United Press International)

hesitate to make promises on such matters. One delegate to the 1960 convention claimed to have been the nineteenth person to whom the Kennedy forces offered the Vice Presidency!

The actual selection of the vice presidential nominee is the final decision of the convention. Although in theory the delegates make the choice, as a matter of political custom they allow the presidential nominee to pick his own running mate. On rare occasions the nominee may decide not to express a preference of his own and permit the convention to make an open choice, as Adlai Stevenson did in 1956. Typically, however, the presidential nominee confers with leaders whose judgment he trusts, and when he makes his decision on the matter, the word is passed to the delegates. Even though some may resist a particular vice presidential candidate, the presidential nominee generally gets his way. Franklin Roosevelt threatened to refuse to accept the presidential nomination in 1940 unless Henry Wallace was chosen as his Vice President. In 1960 John Kennedy insisted on Lyndon Johnson as his running mate against the objections of some liberal elements of the party, including his own brother, Robert. Thus, in effect, the Vice President is the winning presidential candidate's first political appointment.

Various considerations underlie the choice of a vice presidential candidate. Traditionally there has been an attempt to balance the ticket, that is, to select a person who differs in certain ways from the presidential nominee himself. For example, the two may come from separate parts of the country. The Democratic party often chooses Southerners to run with presidential nominees from other, two-party areas—the Kennedy-Johnson ticket in 1960 was such a combination. The Republicans fielded a similar team in 1968 when Maryland Governor Spiro Agnew was selected as the vice presidential candidate because of his acceptability to Republican leaders from the South like Strom Thurmond. In other instances the balance is between liberal and conservative factions, with the segment of the party that loses the presidential nomination being offered the Vice Presidency as a consolation. A case in point was the selection of the conservative governor of Ohio, John Bricker, as the running mate for the more liberal Republican Thomas Dewey in the 1944 election. Balancing the ticket in these ways is designed to broaden its appeal so as to strengthen the party's chances in the general election.*

There are indications, however, that presidential candidates are giving consideration to how the vice presidential candidate will perform in office. The trend towards assigning the second in command important responsibilities has led some candidates to choose as their running mates persons with whom they feel they can work effectively. This factor apparently led

*Carried to the extreme, the balancing principle would lead to the selection of a candidate who differs in many respects from the presidential nominee. One wag suggested in 1960 that what Richard Nixon needed for a running mate was a Negro nun from the South who was president of a labor union!

Hubert Humphrey to select Edmund Muskie to share the ticket with him in 1968. The senator's views on a variety of public issues (including Vietnam) paralleled those of Humphrey; moreover, the presidential nominee also admired Muskie's effective work in the Senate, where the Vice President had also served with distinction. The possibility of succession to the highest office (we will discuss this matter in Chapter 11) has also led Presidents to choose running mates whom they felt would be best able to step into their shoes should anything happen to them. There is evidence that John Kennedy regarded Lyndon Johnson as the most capable leader among his rivals for the presidential nomination in 1960.

Of course, these factors are not mutually exclusive. It is possible to choose a man for the second place on the ticket because of more than one of these considerations. Thus Kennedy chose Lyndon Johnson not only because he regarded him as an effective political leader, but also because he calculated that Johnson's presence on the ticket and his campaign efforts in the South would help the Democratic party's chances in that region.

With the choosing of the vice presidential nominee, the last major decision of the national convention is completed. The final night of the proceedings is given over to acceptance speeches. This is a time for attempting to bring back together the various candidates and party elements that have battled each other during the long preconvention campaign and the hectic days of the convention itself. Typically, major party figures are expected to come to the convention stage to pledge their support for the winner in the campaign that lies ahead. At times, however, personal feelings run too high and wounds fail to heal sufficiently for a show of party unity. Major figures of the liberal wing of the Republican party in 1964 and many McCarthyites among Democrats in 1968 (including their candidate himself) refused to endorse the chosen nominees, at least immediately. Thus the convention does not always achieve one of its major objectives: rallying the party faithful for the coming general election battle.

For the presidential candidate, the nomination process is a long and arduous effort involving complicated legal arrangements for the selection of delegates and voting at the convention itself, as well as difficult strategic decisions of a highly political nature. For the congressional candidate, the path to the nomination is less complex, from both legal and political standpoints. Nevertheless, he too must take into account a variety of factors as he maps his campaign to win his party's nomination for the Senate or House of Representatives.

THE NOMINATION
OF CONGRESSMEN

Although senators and members of the House of Representatives are national officials in the sense that they enact laws that govern the entire nation, they are more commonly considered to be representatives of smaller geographical units. This being so, their method of selection is left, under the Constitution, to the individual states. How a congressman gains his party's nomination, therefore, depends on state law.

PRIMARY LAWS

Most states nominate both senators and members of the House by means of a direct primary. There are, however, differences among primaries, which span the months from late winter to early fall. Most are "closed," that is, restricted to voters who are affiliated with a party, as evidenced by declaring their affiliation when they register to vote or by pledging that they have supported the party's candidate in the past, that they do so now, or that they will in the future. Some states, however, have "open" primaries that allow a voter to choose which party's primary he wants to vote in, and a few use a "wide open" primary that permits a person to vote in one party's primary for some officials and in another for different officials. In most states the plurality candidate, the one receiving the largest number of votes, wins the nomination. In the remaining states (primarily in the South) a majority vote is needed to win; if no candidate receives a majority on the first ballot, a runoff election is held between the top two vote-getters.

While most states let the party in the electorate choose congressional candidates, a few grant that right to party activists by using state conventions to nominate senators or members of the House of Representatives. Other states use a combination of the party organization and the party in the electorate to nominate candidates. In some of these jurisdictions official endorsement of candidates by the state central committee or state party convention precedes the primary; in others the process is reversed: the convention is used to choose a candidate in the event that the top vote-getter in the primary does not receive the requisite proportion of votes (usually thirty-five percent).

The congressional aspirant thus faces a variety of legal requirements in seeking his party's nomination. The political factors affecting his candidacy, however, are even more diverse and complex.

THE POLITICS OF CHOOSING
CONGRESSIONAL CANDIDATES

It is far more difficult to discuss the naming of congressional candidates than the nomination of the President. For one thing, students of politics have focused more of their attention on the Presidency. Moreover, even if a researcher has data on the politics of some individual congressional nominations, he cannot properly conclude that these are necessarily typical of 535 races for the national legislature (100 Senate and 435 House). Nonetheless, the limited information we have on the subject reveals certain basic political patterns in congressional nominations.

Senatorial candidates have generally been drawn from two major pools: state governors and members of the House of Representatives. State legislators constitute a third, but less frequent, source of senatorial aspirants. The national executive branch has also become a good recruiting ground for senators: former Vice President Hubert Humphrey returned to a Senate seat, and Abraham Ribicoff, one-time Secretary of Health, Education and Welfare, went to the Senate after serving in that post; John F. Kennedy's presidential assistants, Pierre Salinger and Theodore Sorensen, also ran for the upper chamber, although unsuccessfully. Of late, celebrities like movie star George Murphy and astronaut John Glenn have become senatorial candidates. The position of United States senator is so highly prestigious that it attracts persons from all areas of public life.

The same cannot be said of the House of Representatives. Few governors or officials of the national executive branch are likely to consider a position there as a move up the political ladder. Sitting senators naturally have no interest in the less prestigious House, and even those that are defeated for reelection are more likely to seek some other position—a governorship, a place in the national executive branch, or employment as a lobbyist—than to run for the more parochial lower chamber of Congress. So where do members of the House come from? Primarily from state legislatures and from county or city posts. Some House aspirants, indeed, have no previous political experience at all.

Congressional candidates are recruited in various ways. Some are self-starters who take the initiative on their own. At other times party leaders, other senators or congressmen, interest-group representatives, or personal friends stimulate a candidacy. However the process is initiated, it usually involves those groups eventually. In other words, a candidate who first decides to seek congressional office on his own will try to determine how much support he can rally from these various sources. For without help from at least some of them, he is unlikely to have the resources necessary for the nomination and election contests that lie ahead.

The extent to which state and local party organizations become involved in congressional nominations varies. In states that use a party convention either to officially nominate or to screen congressional candidates, an aspirant must generally win the support of party leaders if he is to have a chance for the nomination, especially for the Senate. He must also do so in non-convention states where strong party organizations make a practice of committing resources (mainly workers and money) in the primary. Thus most potential Democratic senatorial aspirants in Illinois simply do not run if they cannot win the support of Chicago's Mayor Daley. Although few states in the nation have such a potent party organization as his, the support of political activists is essential for a congressional nomination in other urban areas as well.

In some instances, however, the support of party organizations is not crucial for congressional nominations. In states like California and Wisconsin, laws prevent official party organizations from endorsing candidates in the primary.* Even where no such legal restrictions exist, party organizations or individual party leaders may think it wise to remain neutral in intraparty contests in order to avoid antagonizing unendorsed candidates, some of whom may eventually win despite the lack of organizational support. Finally, party support in contests for the House of Representatives is hampered because in many states there are no official party organizations for congressional districts, only for counties and the state. All these circumstances force congressional candidates to build their own personal organizations of workers and financial contributors for primary campaigns.

If assistance in many congressional primaries is minimal from state and local party groups, it is virtually nonexistent from national party officials and leaders. As a matter of political custom, congressional nominations are considered state and local concerns into which national leaders should not intrude. Even as popular a political leader as Franklin Roosevelt was unsuccessful in his attempt in 1938 to purge certain Southern congressmen in the Democratic primaries because they had voted against his liberal legislative proposals. Most Presidents consider it politically unwise to try to unseat congressional incumbents of their party. Not only do defeats in those primaries result in a loss of presidential prestige; they also make political enemies of the victors upon whom the Chief Executive may have to depend for support of his legislative program.

About the only congressional primaries in which national leaders are likely to intervene are in those areas where the other party controls the seat or where the incumbent in their own party is not running for reelection. In such circumstances the President or other national officials may encourage an individual to enter the primary and even go so far as to offer him financial assistance to do so. For example, in 1970 national Republican leaders persuaded Attorney General John Danforth of Missouri to seek their party's senatorial nomination against the Democratic incumbent, Stuart Symington. Even in these cases, national officials are wary of intraparty squabbles and generally support only candidates who are acceptable to most, if not all, important party leaders. Most instances of national party intervention involve contests for the Senate rather than for the House, because individual senators are more important politically to the President than the more numerous members of the lower chamber.

One final fact of political life is that most congressional primaries are not competitive, in part because most congressional elections, particularly for the House of Representatives, are not competitive. Candidates of the minority party in an area do not normally battle vigorously for the honor of

*Sometimes extralegal groups are organized to get around this restriction. The California Republican Assembly and California Democratic Clubs have endorsed candidates in primaries of their respective parties for years.

going down to defeat in the general election. On the other hand, candidates of the majority party might be expected to be more plentiful; however, if the incumbent himself is seeking reelection, challengers in his own party generally have little chance against him. Previous campaign experience, close relationships with voters, greater knowledge of issues, and other assets give the veteran congressman almost insurmountable advantages over his opponents. Recent estimates indicate that, on the average, of incumbent representatives, only one percent is defeated for renomination.

Senatorial nominations are more competitive than those for the House. The prestigious nature of the position draws candidacies even in the state's minority party, and the majority party naturally has a good share of contested nominations. Incumbent senators, however, tend to be fairly successful in hanging on. In the twenty-five years after World War II, an average of only two senators per election year failed to be renominated.

Even though congressional nominations are generally noncompetitive, spirited battles do occur at times, particularly when the incumbent is not seeking reelection, or when he is considered politically vulnerable for some reason. The reasons may include his age, his status as one-term congressman with comparatively little seniority and campaign experience, or a change in the district he has been representing so that a new constituency with a different electorate is created.

For the congressional or presidential candidate, the nomination process constitutes the first of the two hurdles he must clear if he is to hold public office. For those in competitive situations with the opposition party, the general election campaign ahead may be even more trying than the one he has just completed. Before turning to that subject, however, we should assess the nomination process.

ASSESSMENT

Permitting the voters (what we have called the party in the electorate) to choose congressional candidates in a direct primary opens up the nomination process to far more persons than participate in a convention dominated by the party organization. Thus the present system is more democratic than it formerly was and avoids the irregularities and chances for manipulation so often associated with the choosing of delegates and the convention proceedings themselves.

Yet the direct primary has not lived up to the expectations of its proponents. Voting turnout is typically low in primaries, averaging about thirty-five percent of the potential electorate. Many of those who do vote do not appear to be very knowledgeable about the candidates (particularly when there are a large number of them), and as a result extraneous factors enter into the electorate's decision. Persons with well-known names have been nominated for high office even though their political experience was limited and they did not represent the attitudes of either party leaders or the rank-and-file voter. In Ohio in 1962 a political neophyte named Richard D. Kennedy, who ran his primary campaign on a program of segregation, won the Democratic nomination for congressman-at-large; state party leaders, including the Governor, Mike DiSalle, refused to back him in the general election, which he lost decisively to the Republican nominee, Robert Taft, Jr.

Another major problem of direct primaries, particularly in recent years, is that they often favor the candidate who has a great deal of personal wealth. In 1970 Howard Metzenbaum, an obscure political figure known by few Ohio voters, used his personal fortune to launch a TV blitz campaign that enabled him to defeat the well-known astronaut, John Glenn, for the Democratic senatorial nomination.

One possibility for improving the nomination of congressmen is to adopt the procedure, already used in a few states, of having the party organization endorse particular candidates (and having that endorsement shown on the primary ballot) or to use a convention to narrow down the list of candidates to a few from which the voters in the primary would choose. This combination of methods permits the superior knowledge of party activists concerning the qualifications of candidates to be taken into account initially and at the same time insures that a broader group of voters will make the final selection of the candidate.

The greatest criticism of the nomination process, however, has been leveled at our system of choosing presidential candidates. Charges have been made over the years that these nominations are made in smoke-filled rooms by a few party leaders with little or no thought given to the wishes of the party in the electorate. Particularly resented in recent years was Hubert Humphrey's nomination by the Democrats in 1968 even though he did not enter a single presidential primary.

Actually, however, the nomination of the President has become a much more democratic process than it used to be. As previously indicated, the situation in 1968 was an unusual one: virtually all the nominees, particularly in the post-World-War-II period, have proved their voter appeal in the presidential primaries. Moreover, with the exception of Barry Goldwater in 1964, all the recent nominees (including Humphrey) either led or ranked very high in polls of party members' preferences at convention time. The increase in state presidential primaries between 1968 and 1972, a growing number of which virtually force candidates into the contest, makes the nomination process even more of a popular one than it has been in the past.

Under these circumstances there is no necessity of adopting a nationwide primary to choose presidential candidates. Such a procedure would make campaigning exceedingly expensive and place even more of a premium on personal wealth or access to necessary funds from interest groups or affluent individuals. It would also be too demanding and physically exhausting on candidates, particularly if they were forced into a runoff in the event that no candidate received a majority of the votes cast in the original primary. If that proved necessary, candidates would be faced with making three nationwide campaigns (including the general election) within a relatively short period of time.

A more promising approach to changing the present system for nominating the President is in the reform of the national convention system itself. Both political parties initiated changes in 1972 designed to open up the selection process more to young people and women; they have also sought to provide fuller information to rank-and-file voters on delegate-selection procedures and to lessen the domination of party professionals over the choice of delegates, especially those serving at large. New rules of the Democratic party also provide for more regularized proceedings in credentials contests, including the holding of open hearings on such matters by impartial officers experienced in the law, particularly in fact-finding and procedural due process.

Thus the rules of the game for the presidential nomination are in a process of revision. As the following chapter indicates, those that apply to the presidential election are also the subject matter of current debate.

Selected Readings

For an excellent general treatment of candidate selection in democratic political systems see Leon Epstein, *Political Parties in Western Democracies* (New York: Praeger, 1967). Very helpful treatments of the nomination process in the United States are contained in V. O. Key, Jr., *Politics, Parties and Pressure Groups* (New York: Thomas Y. Crowell, 5th ed., 1964), and Frank Sorauf, *Party Politics in America* (Boston: Little, Brown, 1968).

A monumental study of the presidential-nomination contests in 1952, which contains detailed information on delegate selection in the various states, is Paul T. David, Malcolm Moss, and Ralph M. Goldman, *Presidential Nominating Politics in 1952* (Baltimore: John Hopkins University Press, 1954). A one-volume condensation of the above study was published by David, Goldman, and Richard Bain under the title of *The Politics of National Party Conventions* (Washington, D.C.: Brookings Institution, 1960). This book was subsequently revised and condensed by Kathleen Sproul as a Vintage paperback (New York: Random House, 1964). Another excellent study of the subject is Gerald Pomper, *Nominating the President: The Politics of Convention Choice* (New York: Norton, 1966). A good analysis of presidential primaries and the role they play in the nomination process is James W. Davis, *Presidential Primaries: Road to the White House* (New York: Thomas Y. Crowell, 1967). An excellent factual treatment of the 1968 conventions was published by Congressional Quarterly Service of Washington, D.C. under the title *The Presidential Nominating Conventions, 1968*.

Treatments of presidential nominations are also included in broader studies that cover the general election process as well. One very good study is Nelson W. Polsby and Aaron B. Wildavsky, *Presidential Elections: Strategies of American Electoral Politics* (New York: Scribner, 1968). Theodore White's three classic studies of *The Making of the President* (*1960, 1964,* and *1968*) (New York: Atheneum) are highly readable accounts of the nomination and election campaigns in these three election years. Another journalistic and exhaustive analysis of the latter by three reporters of the *London Sunday Times*, Lewis Chester, Godfrey Hodgson, and Bruce Page, is *The American Melodrama: The Presidential Campaign in 1968* (New York: Viking, 1969).

Studies of congressional nominations are very limited. Chapter 16 of the Key book cited above contains basic information on the subject. An excellent comparative study of ten congressional campaigns in 1962 in the Bay Area of California is David Leuthold, *Electioneering in a Democracy: Campaigns for Congress* (New York: Wiley, 1968).

A major criticism of primaries is in V. O. Key, Jr., *An Introduction to State Politics* (New York: Knopf, 1956). The David, Polsby, and Pomper books cited above all contain evaluations of the presidential nomination process.

CHAPTER 9

Elections and Voting Behavior

The public watches Nixon during the historic television debates with Kennedy in the 1960 campaign. (Cornell Capa/Magnum)

I N HIS ACCEPTANCE SPEECH to the Republican convention in late July 1960, Richard Nixon made a vow to the American people: "I pledge to you that I, personally, will carry this campaign into every one of the fifty states between now and November eighth . . .". Within ten days of that announcement, the candidate had already visited six states, including a hop across the Pacific Ocean to Hawaii. Despite an injury that kept him out of action for two weeks and the urging of his staff to use that as a reason for not keeping his vow, Nixon persisted: in the closing days of the campaign, while his opponent, John Kennedy, was barnstorming through populous Illinois, New Jersey, New York, and the New England states, the Republican candidate took precious time to fly north to Alaska. Before the campaign was over, Nixon was to exhaust himself by making 150 major speeches in 188 cities, where some ten million Americans saw him in the flesh.

In 1968 Nixon conducted an entirely different kind of campaign. Republican strategists calculated that twenty-one states in northern New England, the farm belt, and the Rocky Mountain region were safely in the Republican column and, therefore, to all intents and purposes could be ignored. Nixon did not even visit Kansas, nor was money spent there; as one campaign aide put it, "If you have to worry about Kansas, you don't have a campaign anyway." Nixon himself drew up a list of nine competitive states in the Midwest, Middle Atlantic, and Border states plus five New Southern states (North Carolina, Virginia, Texas, Florida, and Strom Thurmond's South Carolina) in which to concentrate his campaign efforts. Furthermore, in 1968 Nixon did not play down the use of television as he had eight years before; instead, he built his campaign around this medium as the means of reaching a maximum number of people without exhausting himself with excessive personal appearances.

The 1960 and 1968 campaigns ended with different results. Although the two-party division of the nationwide popular vote was remarkably similar (Nixon lost the first election by about 100,000 votes and won the second one by a little over 500,000), the electoral college count was not. In 1960 the Republican candidate carried twenty-six states, but only two of the very populous ones, California and Ohio; as a result, he lost decisively to Kennedy in the electoral vote, 303 to 219. In 1968 Nixon expanded his base to thirty-two states, including key places like Illinois, Missouri, and New Jersey that he had lost eight years before; this time he won over Humphrey in the electoral college 301 to 191.

These experiences of Richard Nixon point up the calculations that candidates have to make in American presidential elections. In laying their campaign plans, they must make choices about how to concentrate their efforts to realize their major objective: winning the 270 electoral votes necessary for victory.*

THE ELECTORAL COLLEGE

One of the supreme ironies of the American political system is that the electoral college now governing the most important *popular* election contest was designed for precisely the opposite purpose. In fact, it was a distrust of the ability of the common man to choose the nation's highest political official (Constitutional Convention delegate George Mason suggested that to allow the people such a choice made no more sense than "to refer a trial of colors to a blind man") that led the Founding Fathers to create the electoral college in the first place. They had already ruled out selection by Congress for two reasons: because that method violated the separation-of-powers doctrine, and because the delegates could not choose between state-unit voting, which favored the small states, and joint action of the two chambers, which benefited the large states with their greater voting power in the House of Representatives. To protect the interests of the national government, the delegates also rejected a proposal that the state legislatures choose the President.

Having decided against both popular election and selection by legislative bodies, the delegates proceeded to adopt an entirely new plan put forth by one of their own committees. The proposal provided that each state legislature choose, by whatever means it desired, a number of electors (none of whom could be congressmen or hold other national office) equal to its total of senators and representatives in Congress. The individual electors would assemble, at a fixed time, in their respective state capitals and cast two votes for President. These votes were then to be transmitted to the nation's capital, to be opened and counted in a joint session of Congress. The person receiving the largest number of electoral votes would be declared President, provided he received a majority; if no candidate received a majority, then the House of Representatives, voting by states (one state delegation, one vote), would choose the President from among the five candidates receiving the highest number of electoral votes. After the choice of the President was made, the person with the next highest number of electoral votes would be declared Vice President. If two or more contenders received an equal number of electoral votes, then the Senate would choose the Vice President from among them.

This complicated procedure reflected certain values and assumptions

---

*The electoral college consists of 538 electoral votes, 435 for the membership of the House, 100 for the Senate and 3 electoral votes for the residents of the District of Columbia, provided for by the Twenty-third Amendment.

about human nature that are enunciated in *The Federalist Papers.** As mentioned above, the Founding Fathers felt that the average person did not have the ability to make sound judgments about the qualifications of the various presidential candidates; therefore, this crucial decision should be left to a small group of electors—a political elite who would have both the information and wisdom necessary to choose the best men for the nation's two highest offices. Since the electors could not be national officeholders with connections to the President, they could approach their task without bias; because they assembled separately in their respective state capitals rather than as a single body there would be less chance of their being corrupted by evil men or exposed to popular ferment; and because they were convened for a single purpose only, to be dissolved when their task was completed, the possibility was eliminated of tampering with them in advance or rewarding them with future favors.

Although philosophy largely shaped the presidential-selection process the delegates adopted, so did a recognition of political factors. Some of the delegates evidently did not expect the electors to be entirely insulated from popular preferences on presidential candidates. They rather anticipated that each state's electors would cast one vote for a "native son," some locally popular political figure, and the other for a "continental character," an individual with a national reputation that they, as members of the political elite, would be aware of, even though he might not be well-known to the average citizen of their state.† It was also expected that after George Washington the electoral votes would be so widely distributed that few candidates would receive a majority, and, therefore, most elections would ultimately be decided by the House of Representatives. The electors would thus serve to "screen" (today we would say "nominate") the candidates, and the House would choose (elect) the President from among them. The same large-state–small-state conflict that was settled by the Connecticut Compromise on the composition of the Senate and House was also involved in the plan the delegates worked out for the selection of the Chief Executive. In the initial vote by the electors the large states had the advantage, since the number of each state's votes reflected the size of its House delegation. If no candidate got a majority, then in the secondary selection the small states were favored, since the contingent vote was by states, not by individuals, in the House of Representatives.

Subsequent events, however, soon nullified both the philosophical and

*The particular selection is Number 68, which is generally attributed to Alexander Hamilton. It is difficult to determine whether the views expressed represent the attitudes of a majority of the Convention delegates or primarily those of Hamilton, who was more elitist than most of the others.

†Evidence for this assumption is provided by Article II, Section 1 of the Constitution, which states that at least one of the two persons for whom an elector votes must not be an inhabitant of his own state.

political assumptions underlying the Founders' vision of the electoral college. The formation and organization of political parties in the 1790s proceeded at such a rapid pace that by the election of 1800 the electors no longer served as independent men exercising their own personal judgment on candidates' capabilities; they rather acted as agents of political parties and the general public. In fact, party discipline was so complete that all Republican electors in 1800 cast their two votes for Thomas Jefferson and Aaron Burr. Although it was generally understood that the former was the Republican candidate for President and the latter for Vice President, the Constitution provided no means for the electors to make that distinction on their ballots. The result was a tie in electoral vote between Jefferson and Burr; neither won a majority (one over half), and the matter was thrown into the House of Representatives for a final decision. Ironically, the Federalists, despite their major defeat in the congressional elections of 1800, still controlled the lame duck Congress (which did not go out of existence until March 1801) and, therefore, were in a position to help decide which Republican would serve as President and which as Vice President. At the urging of Alexander Hamilton, who disagreed with Jefferson on policy matters, but distrusted Burr personally, some of the Federalist congressmen eventually cast blank ballots, which permitted the Republican legislators to choose Jefferson as President.

One result of this bizarre chain of events was the ratification in 1804 of the Twelfth Amendment stipulating that electors cast separate ballots for President and Vice President. The amendment also provided that, if no presidential candidate receives a majority of the electoral votes, the House of Representatives, balloting by states, will select the President by majority vote from among the three (rather than the five) candidates receiving the highest number of electoral votes; if no vice presidential candidate receives a majority of electoral votes, similar procedures are to be used by the Senate in choosing between the two persons with the highest number of electoral ballots.

Other changes in the selection of the President soon followed, but these came not by way of constitutional amendments but rather as political developments that fit within the legal framework of the electoral college. Thus state legislators, who were granted the power to determine how electors should be chosen, began vesting this right in the general electorate. By 1804 a majority of the states had done so.

Another matter left to the discretion of the states, how their electoral votes would be counted, soon underwent change. Initially states were inclined to divide the vote by congressional districts: the candidate who won the plurality of the popular votes in each district received its electoral vote, and the remaining two electoral votes (representing the two Senate seats) were awarded to the statewide popular winner. However, legislatures soon began to adopt the "unit," or "general ticket," rule whereby all the state's electoral votes went to the candidate who received the plurality of the state-wide popular vote. Two political considerations prompted this decision: it benefited the state's majority party, which did not have to award any electoral votes to a minority party that might be successful in individual congressional districts; it also maximized the influence of the state in the presidential election by permitting it to throw all its electoral votes to one candidate. Once some states adopted this procedure, others, wanting to maintain their political effect on the presidential contest, felt that they had to follow. As a result, by 1836, the district plan had vanished and the unit system reigned supreme.

One other major political development of the era changed the nature of the presidential-election contest: the elimination on a state-by-state basis of property qualifications for voting. As discussed later in this chapter, by the early 1840s white manhood suffrage was virtually complete in the United States. Thus the increasing democratization of American political life is reflected in the procedure for choosing the most important public official. Yet the formal provisions of the electoral college remain the same today as they were in 1804 when the Twelfth Amendment was adopted. The popular vote for the President has simply been grafted on to a system initially designed to place his selection in the hands of a select few.

This graft produces results that violate some of the major tenets of political equality. Not every person's vote really counts the same: the influence he has in the election of the President depends on the political situation in his particular state. For many Americans who support a losing candidate in their state, it's as though they hadn't voted at all, since under the general ticket system all the electoral votes of a state go to the candidate who wins a plurality of its popular votes. Other citizens who live in populous, politically competitive states have a premium placed on their vote because they are in a position to affect how large blocks of electoral votes are cast. Nor does the electoral college insure that the candidate who receives the most popular votes will win the Presidency: John Quincy Adams in 1824, Rutherford B. Hayes in 1876, and Benjamin Harrison in 1888 went to the White House even though they trailed their political opponents, Andrew Jackson, Samuel Tilden, and Grover Cleveland.

The requirement that a candidate win a majority of the electoral votes or have the election decided by the House of Representatives also violates the idea of political equality. In 1948 Harry Truman defeated Thomas Dewey by over 2,000,000 popular votes, but if some 12,000 people in California and Ohio had voted for Dewey rather than the President, the election would have been thrown into the House of Representatives for a decision. The same thing could have happened in 1960 if some 9000 persons in Illinois and Missouri had voted for Nixon instead of Kennedy and again in 1968 if about 50,000 persons in Missouri and New Jersey had cast their ballot for Hubert Humphrey rather than President Nixon. Permitting the House of

Representatives, voting by states, to select the President of the United States is not consistent with the "one man-one vote" principle.

The 1968 election also illustrates another danger of the electoral college system: an elector need not cast his ballot for the candidate who wins the plurality of votes in his states. Had Nixon failed to win a majority of the electoral votes, third party candidate George Wallace would have been in a position to bargain with him. Wallace could have asked his electors (forty-five*) to cast their ballots for Nixon which would have given the latter enough electoral votes so that the election would not go into the House. While Wallace's forty-five electoral votes would not have been enough to give Humphrey a majority of the electoral votes (even if the Vice President had carried both Missouri and New Jersey), the Alabama governor could have tried to bargain with the Vice President by offering to use his influence with Southern representatives to get them to choose him over Nixon.

These problems have created a great deal of dissatisfaction with the electoral college over the years. The sentiment for changing it has increased recently, particularly in wake of the above-noted elections of 1948, 1960, and 1968 in which a switch in votes of a relatively few persons in key states would have sent the selection of the President into the House. Yet while there is widespread agreement on the necessity for changing the electoral college, there is marked disagreement over what form that change should take. Three basic plans have been suggested as substitutes for the present system.

The first, known as the *district plan*, proposes that we return to the method the states used early in our history under which the presidential candidate who received the plurality vote in each House district would receive its electoral vote, with the remaining two electoral votes going to the statewide popular winner. If no candidate received a majority of the electoral votes, senators and representatives, sitting jointly and voting as individuals, would choose the President from the three candidates having the highest number of electoral votes. Its major supporters have been congressmen and private groups from rural areas such as the Farm Bureau. If the plan were adopted, the crucial areas would be the some seventy-five politically competitive congressional districts where the two major parties traditionally divide the vote fifty-five to forty-five percent.

A second proposal, known as the *proportional plan*, would divide each state's electoral votes in proportion to the division of the popular votes: if a candidate received sixty percent of the popular votes in the state, he would receive sixty percent of its electoral votes. A plan of this nature introduced by Republican Senator Henry Cabot Lodge of Massachusetts and Demo-

---

*Although Wallace actually earned forty-five electoral votes, he received forty-six because one elector in North Carolina (which went for Nixon) cast his vote for the Alabama governor.

cratic Representative Ed Gosset of Texas passed the Senate in 1950, but failed to be enacted by the House. The plan would eliminate the present advantage of the large states in being able to throw all their electoral votes to one candidate and has, therefore, been opposed by many of their legislators, including John Kennedy when he was a senator from Massachusetts. One possible consequence of a proportional division of the electoral votes would be a fairly even split between the two major candidates so that neither receives a majority; hence there would be a greater likelihood of elections being thrown into Congress for decision.*

The third plan, *direct popular election* of the President, has picked up major support in recent years, especially since its recommendation in 1967 by a special commission of the American Bar Association. In addition, it has been endorsed by such politically disparate groups as the Chamber of Commerce of the United States and the AFL-CIO. In 1969 the House passed a constitutional amendment providing that the President (and Vice President) be elected by a minimum of forty percent of the popular vote and, if no candidate received so large a vote, that a runoff be held between the two front runners. The Senate failed to pass the amendment, however, despite the efforts of its major sponsor, Birch Bayh, Democrat of Indiana. A more recent proposal by Republican Senator Robert Griffin of Michigan and former Democratic Senator Joseph Tydings, Jr. of Maryland called for eliminating the runoff election (in the event that no candidate receives 40 percent of the popular vote) and urged that if a candidate receives a majority of the electoral votes, he be named President or failing that, Congress, sitting jointly and voting individually, choose the President from the two candidates receiving the largest number of popular votes.

We will assess the merits of these various plans, along with the present system, at the conclusion of this chapter. We next consider the rules for electing congressmen.

RULES FOR CONGRESSIONAL ELECTIONS

Unlike presidential aspirants congressional candidates do not face complex rules about how special types of votes are determined and counted, an unusual proportion of the vote necessary for election, or contingency procedures if they do not achieve that proportion. All they need to do is win a plurality of the popular votes. Moreover, senatorial aspirants, as well as House candidates in the five states that have only one representative (Alaska, Delaware, Nevada, Vermont, and Wyoming), have an easily de-

*Most of the proportional plans have suggested lowering the winning electoral-vote requirement from a majority to forty or even thirty-five percent to avoid the possibility of having the election go to the House. They have also proposed that, if no candidate receives the requisite proportion of electoral votes, the two houses, meeting jointly and voting as individuals, choose the President.

fined constituency—the whole state population. But those who seek a seat in the House from the other forty-five states face a very real problem: how are the geographical limits of their constituency to be determined? What rules of the game govern that decision?

The Constitution provides that members of the House of Representatives be apportioned among the states according to population. In order to keep the allocation of House seats current with changes in state populations, an enumeration of national population every ten years was prescribed, a practice that has been followed each decade since 1790.

The Constitution does not establish a permanent size for the House of Representatives, leaving the matter to Congress. Beginning with sixty-five members, the House gradually expanded over the years until it reached the size of 435 in 1912 after New Mexico and Arizona came into the Union. Congress has generally maintained the membership at that figure since then.*

Holding the size of the House of Representatives constant in the face of national population growth has resulted in an increase in the average number of persons represented by each congressman. In 1912 the figure was just over 200,000; in 1970 it was nearly 500,000. Apportioning the permanent House membership among the various states means that after each census, each state gains, loses, or stays even depending on how its population changed in relation to the national average in the preceding decade. In 1970 eleven seats were exchanged: five Southwestern and Western states gained seats in the House of Representatives, while nine others in the Midwest, East, and South lost.

Thus the provisions of the Constitution pertaining to apportionment and the laws of Congress establishing the size of the House of Representatives together provide the means for determining how many representatives each state is entitled to. For the congressional candidate, however, an even more salient issue remains: what method will be used to distribute congressional seats within a state?

LEGISLATIVE APPORTIONMENT
OF CONGRESSIONAL SEATS WITHIN STATES

For the first half-century of the nation's existence, each state was free to determine how congressional seats were to be apportioned internally. Many states elected their representatives at large, much as they allocated electoral votes for presidential candidates. Congress itself, however, reacted differently to the two situations: it permitted states to make their own decisions on electoral college matters but in 1842 intervened in legislative apportion-

*When Alaska and Hawaii were admitted into the Union in the 1950s, two representatives (one for each) were temporarily added to the House membership. After the 1960 census the membership was again reduced to 435.

ment by requiring that members of the House of Representatives be chosen in separate, "single-member" districts.

Although single-member districts have the virtue of making individual legislators responsible to a limited number of constituents, they are also subject to the vice of having their boundaries drawn to favor certain groups over others, typically by distributing voters so as to maximize the political influence of a state's majority party. (A state legislature draws the boundaries of its own legislative districts, as well as those of the state's congressional districts.) This feat is accomplished by concentrating voters who support the minority party in a few legislative districts, allowing their candidates to carry those constituencies by wide margins, or by spreading them fairly evenly and seeing to it that they are outnumbered by the majority party's supporters in the districts concerned. Both techniques have as their purpose minimizing the minority party's (and hence maximizing the majority party's) number of district victories.

The common result is legislative districts of strange shapes. Some are noncontiguous; others, while contiguous, are long, thin strips, not compact entities. In fact, one state legislative district in Massachusetts that resembled a salamander was responsible for the coining of a word, gerrymander (the Democratic governor at the time was Elbridge Gerry), that is used to describe the technique by which legislative district boundaries are manipulated politically.

Gerrymandering can benefit not only the majority party but also other kinds of political interests. Incumbent legislators manipulate boundaries of districts to protect themselves against electoral challengers from within their own party. Sitting state legislators as well as congressmen avoid political battles against one another by maintaining the boundaries of their districts in the face of population shifts within the state that call for redistributing. This latter technique, known as the "silent" gerrymander, leads to the third abuse of legislative districts: different-sized constituencies. Areas that lose population are overrepresented in that their state legislators and congressmen represent relatively few people; regions that gain residents are underrepresented since their representatives have extra-large constituencies. Thus the silent gerrymander tends to benefit rural areas with dwindling numbers and to work to the disadvantage of urban localities with burgeoning populations.

For a number of years Congress gave an indication that it was aware of these abuses and that it might try to prevent them in congressional districts. The Act of 1842 that first required states to choose members of the House of Representatives by single-member districts provided that they consist of "contiguous territory"; in 1872 a requirement was added that House districts contain an "equal number of people"; in 1901 Congress went a step further, adding a stipulation that the districts be "compact." All three requirements—contiguity, compactness, and equality of population—were subsequently included in the Reapportionment Act of 1911.

There is little evidence, however, that Congress really intended to enforce the regulations. In 1901 and again in 1910 it rejected attempts to deny House seats to persons on the grounds that their districts did not meet federal standards. When a new Reapportionment Act was passed in 1929, none of the three requirements was included in its provisions. It was obviously asking too much to expect congressmen, many of whom themselves came from malapportioned and gerrymandered districts, to commit political suicide by changing the system from which they benefited.

As the nation became urbanized, the silent gerrymander produced more and more unequal legislative districts. The disparities were particularly pronounced at the state level, where constitutional provisions granted local units (such as towns and counties) representation in the state legislature, frequently without regard to their size. In 1960 the most populous district of the California State Senate had 422 times as many people as the smallest one. At the national level, the differences were less marked; even so, the ratio between the largest and smallest congressional districts in Texas that same year was four to one. Yet neither state legislatures nor successive Congresses were disposed to change the situation. Representative Emanuel Celler of New York introduced a bill in 1951 seeking to reinstitute the former requirements of contiguity and compactness for congressional districts and to require that they not vary in size more than 15 percent from each state's average district population; he failed to rally the support of his colleagues. Faced with the unwillingness of legislative bodies themselves to remedy the situation, aggrieved parties turned to the courts for assistance.

THE SUPREME COURT AND REAPPORTIONMENT

Attempts in 1930s and 1940s to use the federal courts to rectify unfair congressional districts ended in failure. In a 1932 case, *Wood* v. *Brown*, involving redistricting in Mississippi, the Supreme Court ruled that although the 1929 Reapportionment Act had not specifically repealed the contiguity, compactness, and equal-population provisions of the 1911 Act, its failure to mention these requirements specifically made them no longer applicable to congressional districts. In a 1946 suit, *Colgrove* v. *Green*, the Court considered a new approach to the problem: the plaintiff (a political science professor at Northwestern University) argued that the disparity in Illinois's congressional districts violated the Fourteenth Amendment provision forbidding states to deny persons the "equal protection of the laws." The Court, with Justice Frankfurter writing the majority opinion, refused to grant relief on the grounds that legislative apportionment is a "political" problem whose remedy lies not with the judiciary but with state legislatures and Congress.

By the 1960s, however, the composition of the Court had changed so that Frankfurter's nonactivist philosophy (that judges should be reluctant to substitute their constitutional judgment for that of legislative or executive officials) no longer prevailed. In a 1962 case, *Baker* v. *Carr*, the Court held that legislative reapportionment was not a "political" question and, therefore, federal courts could hear such matters. Several landmark cases followed. In the 1964 decision in *Westbury* v. *Sanders*, the Court invalidated unequal congressional districts in Georgia; citing the language in the Constitution providing that representatives be apportioned among the states according to population and that they be chosen by the people of the several states, the justices ruled that "as nearly as practicable, one man's vote in a congressional election is to be worth as much as another's." (The opinion was popularly condensed to "one man, one vote.") The same year, in *Reynolds* v. *Sims*, the Court held that the "equal protection of the laws" clause of the Fourteenth Amendment requires that state legislative districts also be substantially equal and that seats in both houses of a bicameral state legislature must be apportioned on the basis of population. At the end of the decade, in a 1969 case, *Kirkpatrick* v. *Preisler*, the Court invalidated congressional districts in Missouri, even though the disparity between the largest and smallest was slight (the largest had about 445,000 residents, the smallest, around 420,000) on the grounds that all variations in size, however small, must be justified by the state or shown to be unavoidable.*

POLITICAL REPERCUSSIONS AND EFFECTS
OF THE APPORTIONMENT DECISIONS

Few decisions of the Supreme Court have had more immediate repercussions than those dealing with legislative apportionment. State legislatures throughout the country were forced to reapportion themselves, as well as draw new congressional districts. Hundreds of law suits have been filed challenging the validity of both old and new legislative districts. And Congress and the state legislatures have sought ways to avoid some of the effects of the reapportionment decisions. Most objectionable to state lawmakers has been the requirement that both houses of the state legislature be based on population. The late Senator Everett Dirksen of Illinois sought to initiate a constitutional amendment to allow one house to be based on some other criterion (such as geographical units), but it failed to pass the Senate. Subsequent attempts to initiate such an amendment through actions of the state legislatures have also been unsuccessful.

To date, the decisions have been highly successful in rectifying the disparities in populations of both state-legislative and congressional districts.

*Since the 1960 population of Missouri was about 4,320,000, the ideal figure for each of its 10 congressional districts was 432,000. The largest and smallest districts varied about 3 percent above and below that figure.

But they have scarcely touched the other abuses of "gerrymandering": drawing noncontiguous and noncompact districts with strange shapes to benefit particular groups. Thus it is possible for a state legislature to distribute residents equally among districts but still benefit the majority party or an incumbent legislator. A recent practice is to add suburban dwellers to an essentially rural constituency but to keep their number sufficiently small so that the rural residents still dominate the district. Candidates still have to contend with this situation in running for state legislatures and Congress.

The provisions of the electoral college and those that govern the election of congressmen affect the kind of contests that are waged by candidates for the major offices in the American political system. The following sections analyze the dynamics of campaigns for those offices.

THE GENERAL NATURE OF POLITICAL CAMPAIGNS

A political campaign may be defined simply as the activities of a political candidate (and those working for him) that are designed to motivate other citizens to take the time and effort to vote, and to vote for him. Voters' minds are not, of course, blank pieces of paper on which campaign activities are written. Rather, the political socialization process described in Chapter 5 has already left the average person with certain political opinions and ways of looking at the political world around him. The key to securing votes, then, is somehow to trigger a person's key political dispositions so that they result in decisions to vote for the candidate concerned.

In Chapter 5 we saw that people have political opinions on a variety of matters. Some are quite general, determining whether a society will be governable at all—namely, the attitudes of individuals toward their country, its constitutional system, and the right of public officials to make binding decisions that vitally affect their lives. Other opinions are more specific, relating to the particular persons who should be entrusted with carrying on the day-to-day activities of the government and the kinds of public policies they should pursue. Included in this category are attitudes on political personalities, issues, and events. These, along with personal identifications with political parties and social, economic, or geographical divisions in the population, have most relevance for the key question facing the voter at election time: which of the alternative candidates should he choose?

During a campaign a candidate can try to affect the voter's perceptions of these matters. For example, he can project himself as having a *pleasing personality* with the kinds of traits that the average person admires in his leaders. In modern lingo, he can try to project an "image" to the public that is most attractive and believable.

If he is from the majority political party, he will obviously emphasize his *party label.* If not, he may prefer to play down party affiliation and instead suggest that the voters should select the "best man." Or he may try to appeal to voters who are unhappy with their party's candidate by arguing that his opponent does not really represent that party anyway, that he, not his opponent, is the one who actually stands for the principles that their party has traditionally espoused over the years. Thus Richard Nixon could tell Southerners that he, not Humphrey, represents their views on states' rights.

Another obvious possibility is to associate himself with major social, economic, or geographical *groups.* Thus a former businessman is in a position to woo the votes of members of the United States Chamber of Commerce. But even if he is not a member of any such groups, a candidate can indicate what he has done in his political career to further their interests. He can also solicit the endorsement of their leaders.

Although relatively few voters have the interest or inclination to study the *issues* carefully and to support specific policies, a general public stance on a problem will often elicit a positive response from concerned individuals. Thus a candidate's pronouncement that he is for "law and order" may trigger deep-seated fears of crime in the streets and at the same time offer a vague assurance that he will somehow be able to handle the problem. Closely allied with this approach is the ploy of associating oneself or one's party with favorable *political events,* such as peace and prosperity, and the opposition with unfavorable ones, like war and depression.

By manipulating political objects and symbols and by playing on fears and hopes, a candidate seeks to tap basic political attitudes of the electorate in such a way that they will perceive him as the one who best represents them and their needs. But to do so the candidate must somehow *communicate* with the electorate and get his personality and views before it.

One way to communicate during a political campaign is to go before the people in a series of personal speeches and appearances. In state and local races a candidate can hope to reach a significant proportion of the electorate in this fashion, but it is increasingly difficult to do so in contests for the House of Representatives and virtually impossible in senatorial and presidential elections. Even the herculean efforts of Richard Nixon in 1960 reached only ten million of the nation's then 180 million inhabitants. Today's candidates must utilize the mass media—television, radio, and newspapers—to reach so large an audience.

Vital to all political campaigns are two final ingredients, *people* and *money,* people to communicate a candidate's message calling for votes and money to pay for the campaign costs. Anyone who has too little of either is unlikely to do well in a modern political campaign, particularly for major national offices.

Thus a political campaign involves a complex combination of popular appeals, communicated by various means to voters through the utilization of manpower and money. As a student of political campaign, David Leut-hold, suggests, it is a process in which a candidate and those who assist him acquire a number of resources and use them so that they can be converted into votes. Because such resources are limited, difficult decisions must be made on the best means of gaining and utilizing them to achieve the maximum effect on voters.

Thus a candidate and his staff must wrestle with a series of key decisions. Should he emphasize his own qualifications and approach to public problems, or should he attack his opponent and his opponent's programs? Should he agree to a debate? Is it best to emphasize his party label, or will that antagonize independent voters? Should he discuss issues, and if so, which ones should he single out for most attention? Which social and economic groups offer the best potential support for his candidacy, and how should he go about appealing to them? How much of the campaign budget should go to television, as compared to newspaper advertisements or radio broadcasts? Which are better—volunteers or paid political workers? Should campaign money be raised from a relatively few "fat cats," or from a large number of small donors?

Not only are such decisions difficult, but they must often be made when the candidate and his staff lack full information on which to make a judgment. At the time Mr. Nixon originally agreed to the television debates in 1960 with Mr. Kennedy, the decision made a lot of sense. After all, he had built his political reputation on successful debates with congressional opponents and with Chairman Khrushchev in the famous exchange in Moscow over the relative virtues of the Soviet and American economic and political systems; moreover, he had used television very effectively in 1952 in his famous "Checkers" speech in which he answered charges that he had a political slush fund.* On the other hand, Kennedy was not known for either his forensic talents or his facility before the TV cameras. It was only *after* the first debate that the full circumstances could be known: fatigue and lack of preparation were to result in a bad night for Nixon, while superb coaching by his staff and an unusually calm demeanor for the often-nervous Kennedy enabled the young senator to put on the best public performance of his career. Yet Monday morning political quarterbacks would point afterwards to this decision to debate as the one that cost Nixon the 1960 election.

Because it is difficult to foresee contingencies and also because so much information must be gathered and so many activities coordinated, many political campaigns are not unlike some military battles where participants seem to go off aimlessly in all directions simultaneously. The over-all management of campaigns demands leaders with superb administrative skills

*The speech was so named because in the course of describing his limited financial resources (his wife wore a cloth coat, not a fur one) the vice presidential candidate referred sentimentally to one of his family's prized possessions—their dog, "Checkers."

who can put together and utilize information on such diverse matters as voting patterns in past elections, public attitudes on issues, and the best format for a television presentation.

Traditionally, political campaigns in the United States have been devised by candidates, their personal advisors, and party leaders on the basis of intuitive judgments and experiences in successful contests of the past. Beginning in the 1930s in California, however, public relations firms that had developed advertising programs for private businesses began to transfer their propaganda skills to persuading the public to vote for certain political candidates or propositions put to the voters in referendums. Both parties have used professional firms of this type since the 1952 presidential election, and subsequently more and more senators and congressmen sought their services. Some companies work for candidates of only one political party; others are "guns for hire," available on a first-come-first-serve basis.

These firms can provide a wide variety of services for a political candidate: they take public opinion polls, inquiring into voter attitudes on issues as well as their reactions to the candidate and his opponent; they research past voting patterns and political preferences of various social, economic, and geographical groups; they write speeches, plan press conferences, and oversee the use of mass media. Beyond that, firms will even plan and manage the over-all campaign, budgeting funds and directing the use of personnel. Some have even entered into domains formerly reserved for the candidate and party leaders: raising funds and recruiting workers for the campaign.

Although all political campaigns face the basic problem of acquiring resources and converting them into votes, the particulars differ. Republicans, for example, typically have more access to the mass media and money than do Democrats, who, on the other hand, have the edge in campaign workers, particularly from organized labor. Then, too, the type of appeal a candidate makes in his campaign, as well as his prospects for gathering resources, depends on whether he is an incumbent or a representative of the party out of power. Finally, the particular office sought significantly affects the entire process: a presidential campaign differs from a race for Congress.

PRESIDENTIAL CAMPAIGNS

As the world series of politics, a presidential campaign entails far more time, effort, and money than any other political contest. To take one rough measure of its dominance, the Citizens Research Foundation (a private nonpartisan group that analyzes all aspects of campaign expenditures) estimated that in 1968, when the total cost of *all* political activities was $300 million, $100 million was spent on the presidential race alone—one-third of the total to elect one man!

MANIPULATING POLITICAL APPEALS

Because so much public attention is focused on the presidential contest, the personalities the aspirants project are especially important. Each party strives to create a composite image of the attractive attributes of its candidate. Yet the image must be believable. Thus the elderly Dwight Eisenhower was pictured as a benevolent "father," whereas the youthful John Kennedy was epitomized as a man of vigor. (Robert Kennedy once remarked that the major contribution his brother made to America was to make the people feel young again.)

Frequently presidential candidates take their opponent's image into account in shaping their own. In 1960 Richard Nixon painted himself as the man of maturity and experience to counteract Kennedy's emphasis on youth and aggressiveness. Similarly, in 1964 Lyndon Johnson pictured himself as the candidate of moderation, hoping thereby to point up the extremeness of some of Senator Goldwater's statements and views.

Besides shaping their own image to take account of their opponents', candidates can directly attack the opposition candidate to put him in a bad light with the voters. In 1964 Senator Goldwater advocated that field commanders be given the right to use tactical nuclear weapons in an emergency; the Democrats took advantage of his statements to paint him as trigger-happy. To the Goldwater slogan "In your heart, you know he's *right*," the Democrats countered with, "In your heart, you know he *might*" [order the use of nuclear weapons].

Not all candidates, however, think it is politically wise to attack an opponent. Franklin Roosevelt, for example, thought that doing so only served to give him free publicity. Moreover, there is always the chance that voters will resent the tactics or that they may open the way to counterattacks by the opposition. A classic case occurred in the presidential campaign of 1884. Seeking to take advantage of the accusation that the Democratic candidate, Grover Cleveland, had fathered a child out of wedlock (an accusation Cleveland himself never denied), Republicans composed the campaign ditty, "Ma! Ma! Where's my Pa? Gone to the White House, Ha! Ha! Ha!" The Democrats responded with a slogan that sought to remind voters of the charges of political dishonesty directed against the Republican candidate, James G. Blaine: "James G. Blaine, the continental liar from the state of Maine." Thus the voters that year were presented with a dilemma: should they favor Cleveland, whose private life was morally questionable but whose honesty in public life had never been challenged, or should they vote for Blaine, whose family relationships were idyllic but whose conduct in public office made him seem risky? One of Cleveland's supporters offered a solution: "We should elect Mr. Cleveland to the public office which he is so admirably qualified to fill, and remand Mr. Blaine to the private life which he is so eminently fitted to adorn."

Generally speaking, however, candidates spend more time trying to pro-

The Republican candidate found supporters on President Johnson's home ground but failed to carry the state. (Seheler/Black Star)

ject a favorable image of themselves than to cast an unfavorable light on their opponents. Thus in 1968 Nixon focused his attention on refurbishing his own former portrait as a humorless and overly aggressive political in-fighter. In touching up the picture he strove to present a "new Nixon" who could laugh at himself (he acknowledged being "an electoral college 'drop-out' who had flunked debating") and who had somehow matured and be-come more humane over the intervening eight years since he last ran for the Presidency.

Candidates deal with their party label in different ways. Given the Demo-crats' status as majority party since the days of Franklin Delano Roosevelt, it is not surprising that their candidates generally play up party affiliation and that their opponents do not. Thus John Kennedy stressed during the 1960 contest that he stood "where Woodrow Wilson stood, and Franklin Roosevelt stood, and Harry Truman stood," whereas "his opponent stood" with McKinley, Taft, Harding, Coolidge, Landon, and Dewey. (Kennedy neglected to mention Lincoln, Teddie Roosevelt, or Dwight Eisenhower.) Nixon, in contrast, urged voters to ignore party labels and to vote for the "best man," the man with experience in foreign affairs who had stood up to Khrushchev and bested him in the kitchen debate in Moscow.

Although such tactics did not succeed for Nixon, they did for his predecessor. Dwight Eisenhower was able to project the image of a kindly, warm man, a father figure who was above party. His Democratic opponent, Adlai Stevenson, tried without much effect in 1952 to force voters to associate Ike with the Republican party and the men who would surround him if he were elected President. He thus likened Ike's situation to that of the Duke of Wellington, who in the course of reviewing his troops is reputed to have explained, "I don't know how they affect the enemy, but they sure scare the hell out of me!"

Whether a candidate represents the majority or the minority party, prominent political figures in it must support his campaign. In 1964 Goldwater's candidacy suffered (although it is unlikely that he could have won the Presidency in any event) from the fact that leading Republicans like Governors Rockefeller and Romney and Senator Kenneth Keating of New York disassociated themselves from their party's presidential nominee and conducted independent campaigns of their own. Senator Eugene McCarthy's lukewarm and belated endorsement of Hubert Humphrey in the last stages of the 1968 campaign did little to help the latter avert his narrow defeat that year.

Presidential candidates also attempt to rally members of important social groups to their cause. Typically a campaign organization itself has separate divisions designed to appeal to women, youth, older citizens, nationality groups, business, labor, and the like. Candidates and their staff must decide which groups to appeal to in particular, taking into account the size of the group as well as its geographical concentration, the likelihood that its members will be receptive to the candidate, and the extent to which appeals to certain groups will alienate others.

The classic case of the latter dilemma occurred in Nixon's 1960 campaign. Initially, he hoped to win a number of Negro votes (Ike had done well with blacks in 1952 and even better in 1956), for he capitulated to Rockefeller's demands for more liberal platform provisions on race relations. Early in the general election campaign, however, he visited Atlanta, where he received what he termed "the most impressive demonstration he had seen in his fourteen years of campaigning." After that, Nixon vacillated between trying to woo the black vote and appealing to white Southerners. When Martin Luther King was jailed in Atlanta for refusing to leave a restaurant table, Nixon took no action; in contrast, Kennedy made a quick decision to take a campaign aide's advice to telephone Mrs. King and express his concern. King's father, who before the incident had been a Nixon supporter, switched to Kennedy, a move many observers credit with giving Kennedy enough black votes in close states like Illinois to win the election. Eight years later Nixon pursued an entirely different tactic: he made a concerted effort to appeal to white Southerners and made no bow at all in the direction of the Negro community. In contrast, Hubert Humphrey appealed to blacks and made no overtures to white Southerners.

Although presidential candidates talk a lot about discussing the issues, as a matter of fact they seldom do so in any detail. (In 1968 the *New York Post* remarked testily, "Mr. Nixon has published a collection of positions he has taken on 167 issues. It seems a pity he could not have made it a round 170 by adding Vietnam, the cities, and civil rights.") The candidates usually do focus on major problems in American society, but only in very general terms. Typically a catchy slogan is used by the out-party to link the one in power with unfortunate political events; hence the "Korea, corruption, and communism" brand was stamped on the Democrats by Republicans in 1952. The party in power responds in kind, as when the Democrats defended their record with the plea to voters, "You never had it so good."

It is this kind of general attack and defense that characterizes most presidential campaigns. The party out of power has the advantage of associating all the ills of American life with the administration; the latter is in the position of claiming that all the nation's blessings have resulted from its leadership. The candidate who is in the most difficult situation is the nonincumbent nominee of the party in power; recent examples are Nixon in 1960 and Humphrey in 1968. Both served as Vice Presidents in administrations whose policies they did not fully endorse. Nixon, for instance, did not believe Eisenhower was doing enough in space exploration and national defense; Humphrey opposed the bombing of North Vietnam when it was first initiated in 1965. Yet both hesitated to criticize an administration in which he had served. Humphrey's inability to disassociate himself from the Johnson administration's approach to Vietnam is considered to be one of the major reasons for his defeat in 1968.

Not only are the issues framed in general terms in presidential campaigns, but also few concrete suggestions are made for handling them. Thus Kennedy urged in 1960 that he be given the chance to "get the nation moving again," but he was very vague about what specifically he would do to move the nation forward. Nixon was even more nebulous in 1968: he refused to spell out his plans for dealing with the major issue in American political life, Vietnam, on the excuse that if he did so, he might jeopardize the Paris peace talks that were being held to try to settle the problem.

In manipulating a variety of political appeals, candidates typically attempt to develop a *general theme* that will incorporate a wide variety of matters and leave the voters with some over-all impression of the campaign. Sometimes the theme focuses on the candidate himself, as did Humphrey's slogan, "He's a man you can trust." Or it may be essentially an appeal to a wide group, like Nixon's "Forgotten Americans" who did not break the law, but did pay their taxes, go to work, school, and church, and love their country. At other times, the theme is directed at issues and political events ("Korea, corruption, and communism" or "peace and prosperity") or a general call for action ("We've got to get the nation moving again"). Once the theme is established, a candidate tries by constant repetition to get the electorate to respond emotionally to it. His success in doing so, however, depends on another important aspect of presidential campaigns: the means by which political appeals are communicated to the American voter.

COMMUNICATING WITH THE PUBLIC

No other aspect of political campaigns has undergone more change than the means of communicating political appeals to the voters. First radio in the 1920s and then, even more importantly, television in the 1950s have revolutionized campaign techniques and rewarded candidates who have been able to master their use. Franklin Roosevelt's radio skills did much to counteract the newspaper support given his Republican opponents; John Kennedy's adept use of television, particularly in the television debates, was a key factor in his 1960 victory over Richard Nixon. Nixon's triumph in 1968, in turn, is attributed at least in part to his ability to use the medium more effectively than he had eight years before.

In fact, some campaign observers consider Nixon's use of television in the 1968 campaign as the most successful exploitation of the medium to date. Calculating that long speeches on TV fail to sustain the interest of the voters, his advisers convinced him to utilize two other approaches: short, sixty-second spot announcements during popular programs like Rowan and Martin's "Laugh-in" and appearances before panels of citizens who asked questions to which Nixon could seem to reply in a spontaneous fashion. To guard against possible embarrassing questions, both the makeup of the panels and the questions themselves were carefully screened by his advisers. To make the show even more interesting, former football coach and television personality Bud Wilkinson received the questions and lateraled them on to the candidate.

Nixon's use of television also deliberately avoided two pitfalls that had plagued him in the past: debates and interrogation by newspaper and television representatives. Even though he himself had urged as recently as 1964 that all presidential candidates should be willing to debate (that year he wanted Johnson to provide needed exposure to Goldwater), it was decided in 1968 that under no circumstances would Nixon debate Humphrey. (Initially the excuse given was that Wallace, the third-party candidate, would thereby be granted a nationwide audience; however, after the Alabama governor voluntarily withdrew from participation, Nixon still refused to face the Democratic candidate.) The use of panels of citizens to interro-

gate the candidate on his views also enabled him to avoid the more searching (and unscreened) questions of the members of the press whom Nixon
felt had generally been hostile to him.

Television possesses several advantages over the other mass media. First,
it requires less effort to watch the screen than to read a newspaper. Second,
it has now become the major source of political information for most Americans. And third, people are more inclined to believe what they see on television than what they read in the newspapers or hear on the radio. The il-
lusion of being there on the spot (few are aware of the possibilities for
staging a scene or event) helps create the feeling of political reality.

Radio and newspapers continue to be used, however. Nixon's 1968 campaign included five-minute excerpts on radio from his acceptance speech
before the Republican convention; his manager, John Mitchell, considered
them so successful that he said if he had it to do over again, he would
spend more money on radio time. Advertisements in newspapers offer the
potential for visual effects; in 1960 the Democrats used pictures of their
handsome candidate and his attractive wife in sixty percent of their ads.

Thus the mass media offer the candidate a wider audience than could be
reached in the past. They also enable him to make direct contact with the
public, and hence to bypass to some degree groups formerly relied on.
Among such groups are political party workers who have traditionally carried the campaign to the voter. Yet as the following section indicates, it
would be premature to write off those workers as a political relic of the
past.

MANPOWER AND MONEY

Interpersonal contacts remain an important instrument in shaping people's political decisions. As previously explained, there is frequently a two-
step or multistep flow in the transmittal of political information, so that the
views expressed in the mass media are filtered through opinion leaders before they reach the average voter. Beyond that, personal contacts are particularly vital in getting many persons to make the most basic political decision: whether to vote at all. Sometimes the only thing that will overcome
the apathy of a citizen is the dogged determination of someone who sees
to it that he gets himself registered to vote and then takes him to the polls
to do so.

That service has traditionally been provided by political party workers,
particularly those who labor for party machines* As suggested in Chapter
7, machines operated by a rule of *quid pro quo*: in return for his vote, an
individual was often given a job, furnished with the necessities of life, educated politically, and given social outlets for his energies. Particularly vul-

*The word "machine" was used because of the efficiency with which party organiza-
tions "delivered" automatic votes.

nerable were immigrants who desperately needed assistance in becoming assimilated into the American way of life. Indeed, they provided the major clientele for the old-style party worker.

The political machine, however, has been on the decline in the United States for the last thirty or forty years. A number of factors have contributed to its demise: the passage of restrictive laws cutting off the flow of immigrants; the provision of welfare and other regular governmental programs that have filled the needs formerly met through the informal largesse of the political boss; the enactment of legislation eliminating political appointments in many public service jobs and placing them under the civil service; the general prosperity of the country, which has made low-paying public jobs less attractive than those available through the private sector of the economy; and the increased educational level of the populace which has made more and more citizens self-reliant and independent in political matters.

The traditional political machine still exists in some cities of the nation (Richard Daley's Chicago is the prime example), but it is no longer the powerful force it once was in American politics. Moreover, even where it exists, it tends to have more effect in state and local races than in national elections. Even so, many observers attribute Hubert Humphrey's defeat in Illinois in 1968 to the failure or unwillingness of Mayor Daley to rally the party faithful to his cause.*

Aside from the classic political boss, party organizations in general are not nearly so potent as they are typically pictured to be. The standard organization chart shows a military-type chain of command proceeding from the precinct workers (the privates) up through ward leaders, and county and state officers to, finally, the national chairman of the party (the general). All presumably are working around the clock on party affairs. The realities of the situation are that many party posts are not even filled (particularly in the minority party), and those that do hold positions seldom stir themselves to do the hard and time-consuming chores that are crucial in getting out the vote: polling the precinct to see who is registered and who is not; discovering the party preferences of the people living there; and figuring out what can be done to get the "right" people to the polls on election day.

In the absence of potent party organizations, modern presidential candidates have turned to other means to get out the vote. In recent years organized labor has helped to carry out that vital function, chiefly to the benefit of the Democrats. In 1968 the AFL-CIO, working through its Committee on Political Education,* claimed to have registered 4.6 million voters,

*Before the Democratic convention, Humphrey wrote to Mayor Daley requesting that the protesters be given permits to demonstrate and halls in which to gather, but Daley did not even bother to reply.

printed and distributed over 100 million pamphlets, operated telephone banks in 638 localities, sent out over 70,000 house-to-house canvassers, and provided almost 100,000 volunteers on election day to get people to the polls. Of course, this effort was extended on Hubert Humphrey's behalf and is credited with helping eventually to swing into line a number of workers who initially planned to vote for George Wallace.

Another form of political organization that has become increasingly prominent in recent years is the *ad hoc committee* for a particular presidential ticket. Typically designated along the lines of "Citizens for Johnson-Humphrey" (sometimes the presidential candidate's name alone is used), they are designed to attract the support of persons who may not be willing to work with the traditional party organizations. They may appeal, for example, to people who consider political parties outdated or meaningless but who favor a particular candidate because of his personal magnetism or his stand on issues. They also can be valuable in winning the support of people who generally support the opposition party or are political independents. Also, in many instances, even fairly potent state and local organizations will not expend efforts in behalf of a presidential candidate either because they regard him as a loser who will hurt the party ticket (many Republicans took this attitude towards Goldwater in 1964, as did some Democratic leaders toward Humphrey four years later) or because they feel that who gains the Presidency is not nearly so important for their interests as who wins the county sheriff's race. (Sheriffs not only control some patronage positions—deputies and jail custodians—but also determine the extent to which laws against gambling, prostitution, and the like are enforced.)

The well-run presidential campaign should be able somehow to draw on all these sources of campaign workers. Some, however, tend to regard each other with mutual disdain. The "Citizens for" types often think of regular party workers as political hacks who are in politics only for their own materialistic interests and who will support any party candidate, no matter what his personality, character, or stand on issues may be. The party worker, in turn, often regards the citizens' group workers as "station wagon" types who come out of the political woodwork every four years to campaign for a particular candidate, but who show no concern for the long-range prospects of the party and no loyalty to it as an institution. Squabbles among local, state and national party organizations are also common since each feels that election races at its particular level are most important. All these groups are rivals for the same prerogatives and resources—for example, visits by candidates and financial donations.

*Like corporations, labor unions are forbidden by federal law to contribute money to either the nomination or the election of the President, Vice President, or member of Congress. COPE was created as a separate organization to which union members can contribute voluntarily (union dues may not be used) for political activities.

Like manpower, money is a resource that affects the entire campaign process; without a generous supply of it, political appeals cannot be properly communicated to a sufficient number of voters. The need is particularly intense in presidential elections, which involve a nationwide electorate. Strategists must wrestle with two questions: how can it best be raised, and how can it be allocated most effectively among the many activities of the campaign?

Traditionally both parties have gathered their campaign funds from a relatively few large donors, often referred to as "fat cats." It is simply much easier to collect a sizable amount of money in that fashion; seeking small donations from a large number of people requires considerable time and effort, whether by mail or by personal solicitation. Both the Republicans in 1964 and the Democrats in 1968, however, benefited from a new, less demanding approach: at the end of campaign television programs, viewers were asked to send in donations, which they promptly did, to a much greater extent than anticipated.*

Generally speaking, Republican candidates have more financial resources than do Democrats. (In 1968 reported Republican expenditures in the general election campaign exceeded the Democrats' by a three-to-two margin; the Nixon-Agnew team spent twice as much on television and radio broadcasts than did Humphrey and Muskie.) This advantage is credited to the traditional appeal of the GOP to the business community, which not only has vast financial resources available but is also skilled in the techniques of fund-raising. (Quite often the Republicans establish a *special* campaign organization designed to get out the vote, which operates independently from the rest of the campaign organization.) Recently, however, organized labor has begun to expend considerable sums on political campaigns (reportedly over $7.5 million in 1968), and since virtually all of this goes to Democratic candidates, the margin between the two parties is not as great as party figures of spending alone would suggest.

The importance of money in political campaigns is a matter not only of *how much* but also of *when.* Availability is particularly crucial in buying television time for the last stages of the campaign. In September 1964, when Goldwater money was scarce, the Republican finance chairman decided to cancel all advance time spots that had been booked for the last ten days before election day; in late October, when money began to pour in, the precious TV time had been preempted. (The Republicans ended the campaign with the largest campaign surplus on record, coupled with one of its largest electoral deficits.) In 1968 the Humphrey forces suffered a similar fate. When $500,000 in extra funds was turned up in the last week of the campaign, they were unable to buy any television time in California be-

*Many politicians regard donations as valuable not only from a financial standpoint but also from an electoral one, because they act as an incentive for contributors to turn out to vote for a candidate in whom they have invested money.

cause state and local candidates had previously purchased it. (Unlike the Republicans four years before, however, they had a final deficit of some eight million dollars.)

CONGRESSIONAL CAMPAIGNS

We have less reliable data on congressional than on presidential campaigns. Nonetheless, from the limited information available we can detect certain basic similarities and differences between the two types of contests.

The general campaign process itself is similar, of course. The congressional candidate makes the same basic political appeals involving his own personal image, his party label, pleas for group support, general positions on issues, and the development of a campaign theme. He also seeks the best means to communicate his appeals and the best use of money and manpower to do so. To that end, he acquires and allocates scarce political resources for conversion into votes.

There are, however, important differences. Perhaps most basic is the great advantage an incumbent enjoys over a challenger. First of all, he is likely to be running in a one-party district whereas a candidate for the Presidency has to compete for a more diverse nationwide constituency. (As we saw in Chapter 7, the race for senators is competitive in only one-half of the states; in congressional seats, the figure is even less—about one-sixth.) Second, even if the general party competition in a state or congressional district is close, advantages accrue to the incumbent simply because as a senator or House member he has contacts with many constituents and frequently does favors even for those who normally identify with the opposite party. Because of gratitude for such services, plus a belief that an incumbent may be unbeatable anyway, social and economic groups that generally support the other party are often susceptible to his appeal.

Furthermore, just by being present in his district and in Washington, D.C. between elections, as well as during them, he is a far more familiar figure to the voters than the average challenger is. From his experience in Congress he is well-versed in salient issues, and through mail from constituents and public opinion polls (which most congressmen conduct today), he knows the attitudes of the "folks back home" on such matters. He is also able to exploit the media on a year-round basis through letters to his constituents, newspaper columns, and appearances on local radio and television stations.

The incumbent enjoys two other enormous advantages: superior access to campaign workers and to money. Unlike the presidential candidate someone running for Congress has no pool of regular party workers to which he can automatically turn. Since many states do not have any party organization for congressional districts, individual candidates must build their own personal following. An incumbent can call on those who have helped him in past races, but a challenger who is seeking a congressional seat for the first time must start from scratch.

The challenger is disadvantaged even more in raising campaign funds. Because everyone likes to back political winners, contributors are more likely to put their money on the incumbent. Moreover, from experience in fund-raising the latter develops expertise in the delicate art of dunning people for contributions that few challengers possess. Thus those who seek to oust a sitting congressman generally have difficulty raising the funds necessary to do so, particularly now that the increased use of television (as well as of public relations firms and consultants) has raised the cost of campaigning. As cases in point, the Chairman of the Democratic National Committee, Fred Harris, testified that a senatorial campaign that cost $250,000 in 1964 would require upwards of a million dollars by 1970, and congressional expenditures filed by Florida congressmen in 1968 averaged nearly $100,000 per district. Quite often a challenger must go into debt personally to conduct his campaign; to make matters worse, he generally loses the election.

There are, of course, some exceptions to this pattern. The challenger in a competitive state or district (where the minority party gets forty to forty-five percent of the vote) has more realistic hopes of winning the election and so does not find the task of raising manpower and money as difficult as do challengers in one-party constituencies. In fact, he may be able to get some funds from his party's campaign committees in the Senate and House, which frequently try to allocate them to challengers for closely held seats.

VOTING PARTICIPATION

Political campaigns today involve tremendous investments of time, effort, and money for the candidate and those who participate in them. But as previously noted, only a small percentage of the American public (anywhere from one to seven percent) becomes actively involved in what Milbrath calls political "gladiatorial" activities such as becoming a candidate for office, soliciting political funds, contributing time to a campaign, and the like. The great bulk of Americans are political "spectators" who confine their activities primarily to voting or attempting to talk others into voting a certain way. It is this group that furnishes the "audience" for the campaign as political activists try to affect their voting decisions.

Yet we know relatively little about the effect such activities actually have on the electorate. Winners tend to congratulate themselves on having conducted an effective campaign; losers are inclined to blame their defeat on circumstances they could not control, such as their minority-party status or the superior resources of their opponent which even their best campaign efforts could not overcome. Some studies of recent presidential contests indicate, however, that one-third of the voters make up their minds whom to vote for even before the national conventions are held; another one-third do so during the conventions or immediately afterwards; and the remaining one-third come to a decision during the general election campaign.

The campaign is in truth only one of many factors that shape voters' decisions. Others include long-range political predispositions of individuals and individual perceptions of the immediate contest which may be arrived at independently of the campaign itself. The following sections analyze two distinct aspects of the voting decision: whether to vote and for whom to vote.

Before we can consider who votes and who does not, we have to examine another question: who is eligible to vote? The answer to that question has undergone substantial change in the United States over the years.

THE RIGHT TO VOTE

One of the hallmarks of a democratic society is that, instead of "breaking" heads, it "counts" them. According to democratic theory each person is the best judge of his own interests. Accordingly he must be able to vote for leaders who pursue policies that favor his interests and against those who do not. Everyone, then, should have the right to vote unless for some reason he is incapable of making judgments about his own self-interest.

The franchise in the United States has had a history of expansion, as a series of reasons for withholding the ballot from various groups have been eliminated over the years, either by the states or by the national government. Property qualifications (based on the assumption that the votes of the poor could be bought) disappeared at the state level by the end of the Civil War.* Almost immediately, the battle to enfranchise the Negro (who traditionally had been considered unable to think for himself) began. As described in detail in Chapter 15, this has been the longest and most bitter enfranchisement struggle, one which persists to this day.

The twentieth century has seen the vindication of the voting rights of two other major groups, women and young people. The former ultimately defeated the legal notion that a woman's place was in the home (not in politics), when the Nineteenth Amendment, ratified in 1920, denied states the right to discriminate in voting rights on the basis of sex. Youth won its major victory in the early 1970s: Congress first passed a statute granting eighteen-year-olds the right to vote in national, state, and local elections, and when the Supreme Court ruled that a national law could only affect voting in national elections, the Twenty-sixth Amendment was enacted extending that right to state (and local) elections as well.

Two other voting restrictions were removed in the early 1960s with the passage of the Twenty-third and Twenty-fourth Amendments. The former

*The exception to this development is the requirement in some jurisdictions that voters be property owners in order to participate in referenda on bond issues.

Washington, D.C. voters line up to use the voting machines. (Dennis Brack/Black Star)

granted the residents of the District of Columbia the right to vote in presidential elections, a privilege they had been denied since the nation's capital was located there at the beginning of the nineteenth century. The latter eliminated the payment of poll taxes (in use in five Southern states at the time) as a requisite for voting in primaries and general election contests for the President, Vice President, senators, and members of the House of Representatives. (In a 1966 decision, *Harper* v. *Virginia*, the Supreme Court eliminated the poll tax as a requirement for voting in state elections by ruling that it violated the equal protection clause of the Fourteenth Amendment.)

Several other voting restrictions are still retained by most states. Some relate to special groups which are presumed not to have the intelligence or moral character necessary to cast a ballot. These include prisoners and the mentally incompetent, for example. Persons who are convicted of a crime are denied the right to vote in most states. These disqualifications are temporary, however, and anyone who recovers from the disability has his voting rights restored.*

---

*Another type of temporary disability is alien status; all states today require voters to be citizens.

One voting qualification that has come under attack in recent years is the requirement of lengthy residence in state, county, or precinct. While residency requirements make sense in relation to state and local officials of whom a newcomer might have little knowledge, they are less justified in voting for the President and Vice President. In the 1970 Act that lowered the voting age to eighteen, Congress provided that persons can vote in an election for these officials if they have lived in the place concerned for at least thirty days.

Another major voting qualification that has been imposed by some states is *literacy*. The states differ, however, in the way they measure literacy. Some require minimal efforts such as writing one's name or filling out an application form to vote. Others, like New York, require voters to demonstrate their ability to comprehend certain reading passages. Some Southern states have administered their literacy tests to favor whites over blacks. To obviate the use of literacy tests for that latter purpose, the Congress passed a law in 1965 suspending literacy tests in areas where less than fifty percent of the voting-age population was registered or voted in November 1964. The act was subsequently amended in 1970 to cover areas where a similar situation existed in November 1968. In addition, that same act suspended literacy tests in all states until August 6, 1975.

Thus the trend in the United States has been towards counting more and more heads. As the following sections will show, however, the right to vote and the actual exercise of that right are two separate matters.

POLITICAL FACTORS IN VOTING TURNOUT

Among the factors that affect voting turnout in the United States are the general political circumstances of an election. As shown by Figure 9–1, the political office in contest determines the level of public interest. Although there has been some variation in presidential and congressional voting over the years (the most dramatic being the increase in both between 1948 and 1952), for the most part the basic size of the electorate (the proportion of those over 21 who voted) for each office has remained fairly constant. The real difference in turnout occurs between the two types of elections. In a presidential election year, some five percent of those who vote for the Chief Executive fail to mark a ballot for congressman. (In 1968, that five percent amounted to some seven million persons.) Moreover, in the midterm congressional elections when there is no presidential contest to attract voters to the polls, voting generally is about fifteen percent less than the presidential turnout figure.

A similar pattern prevails in elections for state and local officers. Governors draw more voters to the polls than do state legislators. The further one goes down the levels of government, the smaller the voting turnout be-

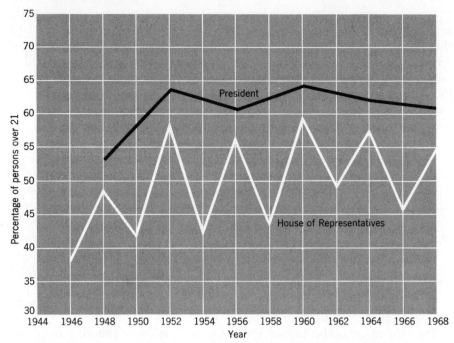

FIGURE 9–1   Voting turnout in elections for President and House of Representatives, 1946–1968. (Source: "That All May Vote," by the Freedom-to-Vote Task Force, Democratic National Committee, December 1969.)

comes: fewer persons vote for a mayoralty candidate than a gubernatorial one. Thus a common argument in praise of grass roots democracy—that the people have more interest in political officers of smaller geographical units —is simply not true, at least to judge by votes.

Why do voters take more interest in certain elections than in others? They may feel that a particular official can have more effect on their lives than others can. (Presidents can affect whether a son is sent off to war; the city council can improve the condition of the streets.) Moreover, contests for higher political positions attract wide public attention simply because candidates use the mass media (particularly television) so much. The networks themselves give more extensive coverage to what they view to be the more significant elections. It may even be that, generally speaking, more attractive candidates run for higher offices and thus stimulate voters' interests in their campaigns.

Voter turnout is also higher in close contests than in one-sided elections. As indicated in Table 9.1, the proportion of voters participating in senatorial and gubernatorial contests tends to increase with the degree of inter-

TABLE 9.1   Voting Turnout* in Senatorial and Gubernatorial Contests, 1966 and 1968

Degree of Party Competition†	Voting for Senator		Voting for Governor	
	Nonpres. Year	Pres. Year	Nonpres. Year	Pres. Year
One-Party	28	48	38	46
Modified One-Party Democratic	38	51	37	58
Modified One-Party Republican	56	67	56	67
Two-Party	58	63	56	69

*Computed as a percentage of persons over 21 years of age.

†States' votes grouped by degree of party competition.

Source: The categorization of states—Herbert Jacob and Kenneth N. Vines, *Politics in the American States* (Boston: Little, Brown, 1965), p. 65 Turnout data—"That All May Vote," The Freedom-to-Vote Task Force, Democratic National Committee, December 1969.

party competition in a state. The same general trend prevails in nonpresidential as well as in presidential years. One other pattern revealed by the table, the relatively high turnout in Republican states, raises another issue related to electoral participation: the extent to which various groups take the time and effort to vote.

GROUP DIFFERENCES IN VOTING TURNOUT

Besides differences in turnout based on the political circumstances, there are also variations among groups in participating in the same elections, as Table 9.2 shows. One significant pattern revealed by the table is that several low-participation groups were formerly denied the franchise: women, nonwhites, poor people (who presumably would have no property or could not pay a poll tax), as well as those with short-term residence. As those under twenty-one begin to cast their votes, they will probably behave similarly to those from twenty-one to thirty who today have a low turnout record.

One possible reason for this pattern of low participation is that some of the "newly" enfranchised may still be affected by public attitudes that originally denied them the right to vote. Thus, even after fifty years, many women (particularly from working-class families) cling to the belief that their place is in the home and that politics is none of their business. Similarly, nonwhites, especially older people who grew up in the South, may feel that they are not able to make good choices between candidates. In

TABLE 9.2   Voting Participation of Various Groups

Group Category	High Participation	Low Participation
Age	The middle-aged	The young (under 30 and the old (over 60)
Sex	Men	Women
Race	Whites	Nonwhites
Class	College graduates Professional persons Wealthy people	Those with grade school only Unskilled workers Poor people
Residence	Westerners Suburbanites Long-time residents	Southerners Rural dwellers Short-time residents
Party	Republicans Strong partisans	Democrats Independents

time such attitudes may change, but there is a lag between the legal elimination of an impediment to voting and the removal of the attitudes and reasoning that underlie it.

Some group differences in voter turnout are rooted in psychological feelings that, as we saw in Chapter 5, affect all kinds of political participation, including voting. The well-educated are more likely to be aware of political developments and the significance they have for their lives than are the poorly educated. In addition, they tend to feel politically efficacious, that is, to have a sense of confidence about the value of their opinions, to believe that people in public office will listen to them; therefore, they think that what they do has an important effect on the political process. Poorly educated persons, on the other hand, are likely to feel that political officials don't care about them or their opinions. General attitudes about other persons also affect voting behavior: those who trust people are more likely to cast their ballots than are those whose cynicism and hostility toward their fellow humans makes them feel politically alienated.

The influence of a group itself is frequently important. Thus if a person belongs to a business organization or labor union whose members talk about political affairs a lot, he is apt to develop an interest of his own in such matters. If so, his political interest will lead him to make the effort to vote. Moreover, even if a person is not interested in politics, he may feel that it is nevertheless his duty as a citizen to vote. Such an attitude is much more likely to exist in the upper and middle classes than it is in the lower class.

If the reasons that prompt certain persons to vote and influence others to remain at home on election day are varied, the factors that shape preferences between competing groups of candidates are even more complex.

VOTING PREFERENCES

The reasons underlying voting decisions have long been of interest to students of democratic politics. Some political philosophers created the model of the rational citizen who carefully studies the major issues that his society faces, decides what public policies are needed to deal with them, and then chooses the candidate whose views on such matters are closest to his own. Viewed in this context, the results of elections turn on the "issues" and the candidates' stands on them. Historians, journalists, and other political observers writing on individual campaigns have similarly tended to focus on issues, along with dramatic events and personalities, as the key factors in election outcomes. They have also been inclined to attribute victory or defeat to campaign strategies.

Survey techniques developed in the United States in the 1930s have made it possible to interview a carefully selected sample of persons on some matter and, on the basis of their responses, to generalize how a much larger group feels about it. These techniques became highly useful for eliciting the reasons behind electoral decisions. Instead of relying on what other persons *thought* the reasons were, it was now possible to get them from the voters themselves. Moreover, rather than focusing on what the voters *should* consider in making voting decisions, the emphasis now turned to what they actually *did* take into account.

In-depth studies of voters' attitudes first began in the 1940 presidential election in a single county in Ohio. Beginning in 1948, and for each presidential election thereafter, the Survey Research Center at the University of Michigan has interviewed a nationwide sample of Americans on how they voted and why they voted as they did. V.O. Key, Jr. also analyzed the results of Gallup polls pertaining to presidential elections over the period from 1936 to 1960. From these rich sources of information, students of voting behavior have been able to enhance their perceptions of electoral preferences. By probing with open-ended questions (those that let the respondent answer in his own frame of reference rather than forcing his reply into preestablished categories), interviewers have been able to gain some insight into the reasons that prompt voters to cast their votes as they do.

VOTING IN PRESIDENTIAL ELECTIONS

Analysts of presidential elections agree that the single most important determinant of voting is the *party affiliation* of the voter. This general psychological attachment, which, as discussed in Chapter 5, is acquired early, tends to intensify with age and increasingly shapes the way in which he votes. For the average person looking for some guide in the midst of the complexities of personalities, issues, and events, the party label of the candidates is an important reference point or clue.

From the late 1940s to the late 1960s, partisanship in the United States remained fairly constant. When asked by the Survey Research Center about whether they regarded themselves as a Republican, Democrat, or independent, most Americans—from seventy-five to eighty percent—identified with one of the two major parties. The Democrats maintained about a three-to-two advantage during this period. In the latter part of the 1960s, however, the number of independents increased. In the 1968 election study by the Survey Research Center, their proportion rose to thirty percent. Indeed, in a Gallup poll of college students in November 1969 over half rated themselves as political independents.

Not only are more Americans of late *saying* they are political independents; significantly, more of them are *acting* that way. Two indexes are the proportions of switchers and ticket-splitters. (The former switch their votes for a given official from one party to another from election to election; the latter vote for candidates of more than one party for different offices at the same election.) V.O. Key's analysis of presidential voting from 1940 to 1960 showed that, on the average, one in six voters switched; the 1968 election study by the Survey Research Center indicated that one in three Americans had switched their presidential vote from that of 1964. Political scientist Walter Burnham, writing in *Transaction* magazine in December 1969, indicates that in 1956 some seventy percent of Americans voted a straight ticket in state and local races; by 1966 only fifty percent did so.

Although party identification continues to be the single most important factor in voting behavior, its influence appears to be declining. It is particularly significant that young people and college-educated voters tend to be political independents. The increase of the numbers of these groups in the population means that they could have a greater potential impact on elections than they have in the past, particularly the eighteen- to twenty-one-year-olds who have so recently acquired the right to vote.

The second most important factor is the individual's reaction to rival *candidates*. If a nominee is attractive enough and inspires enough confidence, he may be able to overcome being the standard-bearer for the minority party. A classic case was Dwight Eisenhower, who was elected as a Republican in 1952 and 1956. Studies conducted during the Eisenhower years clearly indicated that his victories were primarily personal; many persons who were questioned on why they cast their ballots for him mentioned his personality, his character traits, and their confidence in his abilities. Yet, despite his victories in both elections, more Americans continued to identify with the Democratic than the Republican party. Another piece of evidence that Eisenhower's appeal was personal is that fact that the Democrats controlled both houses of Congress during six of his eight years in office (1954–

1960). Even in 1956, when Eisenhower defeated Stevenson more easily than he had four years before, the Democrats won both the House and Senate, the first time the winning party in a presidential election had failed to carry either house of Congress for a century.

A third factor that affects how people vote is political *issues*. Very, very few persons, however, match up to the model of the rational voter mentioned earlier. The Survey Research Center studies point out that, as a matter of strict logic, in order for a person to vote on the basis of an issue, he would have to be familiar with it; the issue would have to be of psychological importance to him; and he would have to be aware of a difference in the candidates' stands on it. The number of citizens who display that kind of interest and knowledge is very limited. Moreover, those who are most likely to identify strongly with a political party take their cues on how they should feel about an issue from the party leaders. Thus Republicans tend to look with disfavor on Medicare, not because they have studied the issue, but because their party spokesmen are generally against it. In other words, the connection between voters' attitudes on issues and their party preference often works in reverse of the rational-voter model.

Although the above description may be generally true of strong party identifiers—or what Key calls "standpatters," those who vote for the same party's presidential candidate in successive elections—it is not so for switchers. These voters, Key found, do tend to turn to the candidate whose stand is similar to their own policy preferences. Thus many persons who voted for Hoover in 1932 but for Roosevelt four years later favored Roosevelt's social security program. In 1940 those who deserted Roosevelt for the Republican candidate Wendell Willkie were inclined to oppose the Wagner Act, favoring organized labor, which Roosevelt backed. Although there is no proof that policy preferences "caused" the switching, at least the voting behavior was consistent with the preferences.

While attitudes on individual issues may influence particular choices, from the evidence of the voting studies very few voters make their decisions on the basis of a consistent set of political beliefs—that is, a related system of values, assumptions about human nature, and views on the role that government should play in society. When asked to explain why they voted for one candidate instead of another, few Americans express their political preferences in even such rough philosophical terms as "liberal" or "conservative." Nor do there seem to be any consistent patterns of preferences on issues: for instance, many individuals who favor governmental programs for the economically disadvantaged oppose plans that benefit social underdogs such as Negroes.

Voters do, however, link parties and issues to some extent. They tend to associate certain *political events* with the party that was in office when they occurred. As a reflection of the memory that the Republicans were in power when the Great Depression began in 1929, voters to this day still believe the

Democratic party will do a better job of keeping the country prosperous. In a Gallup poll taken in July 1970, forty-four percent chose it as being more likely to do so, compared to twenty-nine percent who chose the GOP. And because the Democrats were in power at the inception of World Wars I and II, as well as the Korean and Vietnamese conflicts, Americans have been inclined to consider the Republican party as being more likely to keep the nation at peace. (Whether the two parties actually should bear the blame for their respective crosses is beside the point, as long as the voters *think* they should.)

Another belief of many citizens that affects voting behavior is the conviction that the two parties tend to favor different groups. The Democratic party is thought to be for the "common man," or the "little guy," the Republican for business and professional interests, or persons of "substance." In recent years the Democrats have been seen as the party that benefits blacks, ethnic groups, and Catholics, the Republicans as the party for WASPS (white Anglo-Saxon Protestants). Again, whether these assessments are actually true is not important so long as people think they are and vote accordingly. Table 9.3, which shows voting preferences of various groups in the 1968 presidential election, is consistent with those general conceptions.

It is difficult to isolate any of the above factors as the one that determines how a particular voter casts his ballot. More than one may affect his de-

TABLE 9.3   **Voting by Various Groups for Nixon and Humphrey, 1968***

Group	Nixon	Humphrey
High income	63	29
Middle income	44	43
Low income	19	69
Professional and business	56	34
White collar	47	41
Manual labor	35	50
Union workers	29	61
Negro	5	94
White	47	38
Italian	39	51
Slavic	24	65
Protestant	49	35
Catholic	33	59
Jewish	17	81

*Figures in percentages. Wallace vote not included.

Sources: Gallup Poll, December 1968; *Congressional Quarterly Weekly Report* (November 1968), p. 3218.

cision, especially since some can be linked together. V.O. Key points out that, although FDR's personality was attractive, it alone does not explain his popularity with the voters. Key asks, supposing he had favored a political program entirely different from the New Deal, one that called for the national government's staying out of economic and social problems—would he still have had the voter appeal he demonstrated in several presidential elections? Similarly, in 1952, was Eisenhower chosen because of his personal attributes alone, or did the issue of the Korean War not also contribute to his victory? Thus the voting decision is a complex event subject to a variety of influences. As the next section shows, the office itself also affects the weight and balance of factors underlying voting preferences.

VOTING IN CONGRESSIONAL ELECTIONS

As with nominations and campaigns, we have rather meager evidence on voting in general elections for members of Congress. The limited information available indicates that the same basic factors are at work as in voting for the President; however, differences in the circumstances of the two kinds of races result in some variations in the way and degree to which the influences are felt.

Party identification, the single most important determinant of presidential voting, is even more potent in the choosing of congressmen. One explanation is that fewer persons turn out in midterm congressional elections, and those that do, tend to be the strong party-identifiers who are more involved in political matters. The person with less concern with politics, who may be motivated to vote in presidential elections because of the extensive coverage of the contest in the mass media, is less likely to receive that kind of stimulation from the less glamorous off-year congressional campaign. Party also looms as more important in congressional voting simply because other factors mean less. Congressional candidates are not as visible and well-known as presidential nominees: a study by the Survey Research Center of the 1958 congressional election indicated that only about one of five persons interviewed could name both candidates running in their district; only two in five could name one candidate, and the incumbent (who, it will be recalled, has contacts with voters between campaigns) was likely to be the one with whom they were familiar.

Issues are also less important in shaping voters' decision in congressional than in presidential races. Not only are voters unlikely to be familiar with issues before Congress, but they also display little knowledge of how their congressmen voted or how the opponents stand. Surprisingly, less than half of those questioned by the Survey Research Center in 1958 even knew which party controlled Congress. Thus the link, in presidential elections, between a voter's discontent with an issue or political event and his remedy of voting the party in power out is simply not available for many citizens.

If they don't know which party controls the Congress, they can scarcely use the ballot to wreak electoral revenge on the party that is supposedly responsible for the unfortunate state of affairs.

In summary, the voting decision of each individual is a resultant of various factors: whether he identifies with a political party, and if so, the intensity of his commitment to it; his perception of candidates and issues; his general frame of mind on the state of the nation and the record of the party in power; and the groups he relates to and the extent to which he feels the respective parties and candidates represent the interests of those groups.

VOTING BEHAVIOR AND THE OPERATION
OF THE AMERICAN POLITICAL SYSTEM

The collective decisions of individual voters determine not only the results of the elections but also the operation of the political system. Elections that turn on long-term forces such as traditional party loyalties build stability into the system because representatives of the majority party remain in power over a considerable period of time. Other short-term factors, such as individual candidates or dramatic political events, produce change as the party is turned out of office. Thus our political system contains elements that are conducive to both stability and change, desirable characteristics of any human institution.

In fact, students of American presidential election have categorized them according to different clusters of electoral factors. An election in which the long-term partisan orientation of the electorate results in keeping the traditional majority party in power is a *maintaining* election. The majority party candidate wins primarily because the voters choose him on the basis of their traditional party loyalties. Short-term forces, such as candidates and issues, are present, but rather than determining which party wins, they contribute to the size of the majority party's victory. If they favor that party as they did in 1964 when the Goldwater candidacy redounded to the benefit of the Democrats, the vote margin separating the two major candidates is larger than usual. If short-term forces are in balance as they were in 1948, the vote division approximates the proportion of voters who identify generally with the two parties.

While maintaining elections provide general continuity in governance, others result in change. A *deviating* election occurs when short-term forces sufficiently benefit the minority party that they override the long-term partisan preferences of the electors. A particularly appealing candidate or some favorable issue or event allows the minority party candidate to win with the support of some majority-party members, independents, and a good share of new voters. The electorate does not, however, change its basic party preferences. Examples of deviating elections are those in 1952 and 1956; they were won by the Republican candidate Eisenhower but the commitment of many persons to the major party, the Democrats, was unaltered.*

The election that brings about major political change is referred to as a *critical* or *realigning* election. Such elections involve a major realignment of electoral support among blocks of voters who switch their traditional party affiliation. An unusual number of new voters may also enter the electoral arena and cast their ballots disproportionately for one party's candidate. Unlike the deviating election, the effects of the realigning one tend to persist in the form of durable loyalties to the advantaged party. Political historians usually include five elections in the realigning category: 1800, 1828, 1860, 1896, and 1932.

It is somewhat misleading, however, to identify a single election as realigning. For one thing, it is not always possible to determine at the time of the election whether the new political alignment will persist. For another, the realignment process usually begins earlier and culminates in the election itself. Thus the realignment of 1932 had actually begun in 1928 when the Democratic candidate, Alfred E. Smith, gained significant support from ethnic groups in urban areas; moreover, it continued in 1930 when the Democrats made dramatic gains in the Senate and House of Representatives.

The realignment of partisan forces is associated with changes in social and economic conditions that have not been accommodated within existing arrangements. In the case just cited, the majority Republican party had not concerned itself sufficiently with the needs of immigrant and low-income groups in general from urban areas. The increased movement of this group into the Democratic camp, plus the economic depression of 1929 that affected a wide variety of American citizens, triggered a massive swing to the minority Democratic party by old and new voters alike and ushered in a long period of Democratic rule.

An indication that the parties are not meeting needs of certain groups is the fact that a significant third party movement often precedes the realignment. The rise of the Free Soil party and of the Republican party itself, which began as a third party, eventually culminated in the realignment of 1860; the Populist party played a role in the critical election of 1896; and La Follette's Progressives contributed to the reorganization of American politics that occurred in the late 1920s and early 1930s. The rise of the American Independent party in 1968 may possibly foretell a future party realignment if the majority Democratic party is unable to cope with the race problem that increasingly splits certain key elements of its New Deal coalition: blacks, Southern whites, and Northern working-class whites.

*Analysts of the Survey Research Center refer to an election following a deviating period as a *reinstating* one, because it reinstates the usual majority party in power. An example is the 1960 election when the Democrats returned to power after the two Eisenhower victories. Thus a reinstating election is like a maintaining one in that long-term partisan factors are controlling.

ASSESSMENT

The rules of the game for choosing our nation's highest political figure are archaic and should be changed as soon as possible. As indicated earlier, the electoral college makes little or no sense in the present situation in which the President is expected to be chosen in a nationwide popular election: retaining it means playing a game of electoral roulette which the nation almost lost in three recent elections and can ill afford in the future. A major argument for its retention that John Kennedy used in the 1950s—that its bias in favor of large urban states compensates for the rural bias in the House of Representatives—no longer applies with as much force since the congressional redistricting that has taken place to meet the one-man–one-vote principle.

The direct popular election of the President is superior to the district and proportional proposals. The first would incorporate into the selection of the President the gerrymandering abuses that still remain despite the reappointment decisions—manipulating House district boundaries (including noncompact, noncontiguous ones) to favor particular political interests. Although the proportional system is superior to the present general ticket one, it still does not guarantee what should be guaranteed: that the President be the person who receives the most popular votes.

The major objections to the popular election of the President are that it violates the principles of federalism and discriminates against small states. Yet the principles of federalism we examined in Chapter 3 do not include favoring state interests in the choice of the national executive; states are already given special protection in the composition of the Senate. No state should have special consideration in the selection of the President; he should represent all the American people, no matter where they live.*

As far as the general electoral process is concerned, the average American voter does not meet the philosopher's model of the highly rational citizen who interests himself in the vital issues of the day, analyzes alternative means of dealing with these issues, and then chooses the candidate whose policy views are closest to his own. The voting studies show, rather, that partisan affiliation and candidate appeal are more important in most voting decisions than the candidates' stands on issues.

Yet there is little evidence that the electoral process is a totally irrational one in which devious candidates successfully manipulate voters through the use of the mass media and expensive public relations campaigns. As

*It is interesting to note that under the direct popular election of the President, a small, one-party state might have more of an impact on the election result than a large, politically competitive state. In Nebraska where some 540,000 votes were cast in 1968, Nixon's popular plurality over Humphrey was about 150,000; in New Jersey where almost 2,900,000 voters went to the polls, the President's vote margin was about 60,000.

previously suggested, selective perception operates so that voters screen out many messages that are not consistent with their political attitudes and predispositions. Richard Nixon's presidential campaign of 1968 is reputed to be the perfect example of the use of television for image-building, but his support among the electorate did not rise during the campaign; on the other hand, Humphrey who, because of financial limitations, made far less use of television than Nixon, gained ground on his rival, especially during the latter stages of the campaign. An analysis by *Congressional Quarterly* following the 1970 off-year elections showed that a majority of the senatorial and gubernatorial candidates handled by the nation's nine top media consultants that year went down to political defeat. As one of them, Charles Guggenheim, put it: ". . . where television really has a dramatic effect is in a primary, where there is no opposition [television campaign] and little press coverage."

The fact of the matter is that the American voter does demonstrate considerable rationality when he goes to the polls. The two major parties do have different approaches to public problems. Generally speaking, the Republican party has been solicitous of the interests of business and espoused a program of minimum intervention of the government (especially the national one) into the economy to regulate private interests. The Democratic party, in turn, has (at least since the 1930s) been concerned with the less-advantaged groups and has favored governmental programs to benefit them. Thus the voter who is not conversant with the issues and the proposals of the competing candidates for handling them can look to the two parties as reference points, general guides for identifying who the candidates are and what their group sympathies and general approaches to governmental problems are likely to be. Moreover, there is an increasing number of Americans, including young and well-educated ones, who do not have to depend on such general party clues for guidance: they switch and split their votes among party candidates in a way that is consistent with their policy preferences.

While voters do not generally choose between candidates on the basis of alternative prospective programs that should be followed in the future, they do make retrospective judgments on how the party in power has performed in the past with respect to handling issues and preventing crises. Thus Americans in 1968 who were unhappy with the state of the nation, and the administration's handling of Vietnam in particular, forced the incumbent majority-party President, Lyndon Johnson, not to seek another term and declined to elect his party's successor candidate that year. As the late V.O. Key, Jr. put the case, the electorate is "moved by concern about central and relevant questions of public policy, of governmental performance, and of executive personality."

Voters not only succeed in replacing one group of leaders with another, but they also have some influence on the public policies that are followed by the new administration. Although elections are not "mandates" in the sense that they instruct political leaders what precise policies they should follow, they do at least give the winners a good indication of what the electorate does *not* approve of—they let leaders know "when the shoe pinches." In the 1968 presidential election the voters did not direct Richard Nixon to follow any particular course of action in extricating the nation from Vietnam, but they did give him the general message that he should somehow reach that goal. Nixon himself made it clear after the election that he realized that this was the general policy the American public wanted him to follow and that if he did not, he would have to pay the electoral consequences. By what political scientist Carl Friedrich has termed the "law of anticipated reactions," political leaders thus shape their policies and actions to take account of what they think the public's attitude toward them will be.

Although the American public indirectly affects public policy through the electoral process, the guidelines it establishes for political officials tend to be broad and general, leaving public officials broad discretion on the specific policies they enact into law. The following Part analyzes the process by which those policies are developed by decision-makers in the three branches of our national government.

Selected Readings

An excellent treatment of the evolution and weaknesses of the electoral college is Lucius Wilmerding, *The Electoral College* (New Brunswick, N.J.: Rutgers University Press, 1958). A more recent analysis of the subject is Neal Peirce, *The People's President: The Electoral College in American History and the Direct Vote Alternative* (New York: Simon & Schuster, 1968). A good reference to the reapportionment issue is *Representation and Apportionment* published by Congressional Quarterly Service of Washington, D.C.

Several of the sources listed in the *Selected Readings* for the nomination process treated in Chapter 8 are also helpful for general election campaigns. Included are Chester *et al*, Leuthold, Polsby and Wildavsky, and White's three presidential-year analyses. Two recent studies that focus on the role of the mass media and public relations firms in political campaigns are Joe McGinniss's journalistic best-seller, *The Selling of the President, 1968* (New York: Trident Press, 1969), and Dan Nimmo's scholarly analysis, *The Political Persuaders: The Techniques of Modern Election Campaigns* (Englewood Cliffs, N.J.: Prentice-Hall, 1970).

The first in-depth analysis of voting (made of the presidential campaign in 1940 in Erie County, Ohio) was Paul Lazarsfeld, Bernard Berelson, and Hazel Gaudet, *The People's Choice* (New York: Columbia University Press, 1944). The first two authors published another community study (Elmira, New York) of presidential voting in 1948 with William McPhee, *Voting* (Chicago: University of

Chicago Press, 1954). Two publications growing out of the national studies of the Survey Research Center at the University of Michigan are Angus Campbell, Gerald Guerin, and Warren Miller, *The Voter Decides* (New York: Harper & Row, 1954) and Campbell and Miller's classic study with Philip Converse and Donald Stokes, *The American Voter* (New York: John Wiley, 1960). V.O. Key's analysis of presidential preferences expressed in Gallup polls over the years is *The Responsible Electorate: Rationality and Presidential Voting, 1936–1960* (Cambridge: Harvard University Press, 1966). A recent short treatment of voting behavior is William Flanigan, *Political Behavior of the American Electorate* (Boston: Allyn & Bacon, 1968). A study of voting behavior in congressional elections is Milton Cumming, *Congressmen and the Electorate* (New York: Free Press, 1966).

An excellent study of the groups forming the New Deal coalition is Samuel Lubell, *The Future of American Politics* (New York: Harper & Row, 1950). An analysis of recent political trends by the same author is *The Hidden Crisis in American Politics* (New York: Norton, 1970). Two other interesting studies with differing perspectives on recent partisan coalitions are Kevin Phillips, *The Emerging Republican Majority* (New Rochelle, N.Y.: Arlington House, 1969), and Richard M. Scammon and Ben J. Wattenberg, *The Real Majority* (New York: Coward-McCann, 1970).

The first study analyzing types of presidential elections was V.O. Key, Jr., "A Theory of Critical Elections," *Journal of Politics* 17 (1955), 3–18. Chapter 16 of *The American Voter* and Chapter 5 of Gerald Pomper, *Elections in America* (New York: Dodd, Mead, 1968) contain methods of classifying presidential elections. An excellent extended analysis of realignment is Walter Burnham, *Critical Elections and the Mainsprings of American Politics* (New York: Norton, 1970).

An analysis that links voting behavior to the operation of the American party system is William Chambers and Walter Burnham, *The American Party System* (New York: Oxford University Press, 1967). Among those that relate voting behavior studies to the operation of the political system and democratic theory are Campbell, Converse, Miller, and Stokes, *Elections and the Political Order* (New York: John Wiley, 1966), and Pomper, *Elections in America.*

PART III

GOVERNMENT DECISION-MAKING

ALTHOUGH DEMOCRATIC OFFICIALS PAY HEED *to the attitudes of private citizens on political issues, they make the actual decisions in the form of laws and decrees that bind the entire population. These decisions are the product of a number of factors we will explore in this Part.*

One major consideration is the kind of people who occupy important positions in the government. The particular backgrounds and experiences of an officeholder shape his values and the attitudes he takes on public matters that command his attention. Another related factor that affects his decisions is his perception of his role in government—that is, what he thinks someone in his position should do in a given situation, as well as what he believes others expect of him. These two sets of expectations may differ: a congressman who has studied a bill may feel that it is unwise legislation and he should vote against it, and yet he may sense that his constituents are for the bill and expect him to vote in accordance with their wishes. Under such circumstances, he must decide which course of action to follow.

While the attitudes of individual officials are important, decision-making in all three major branches of our national government tends to be a collective enterprise in which many persons participate. It is, therefore, important to analyze both the formal and the informal structure of each branch in order to determine the relationships that exist among its various officials. In particular, we need to know who exerts the most influence on decision-making and how that influence is exercised. Closely related to structure is the procedure each branch uses to make its decisions, since inevitably procedures favor certain persons and interests over others.

Finally, decision-making in the American political system typically involves more than one branch of government: our separation of powers, or more precisely, separation of processes, is not a complete one. Therefore, it is important to understand the powers each branch wields in the political process and the ways in which officials of the three branches supplement, modify, or nullify one another's actions.

The following five chapters explore these various factors as they relate to decision-making by each branch, as well as actions involving more than one arm of the national government. Chapter 10 examines the Congress, the following two deal with the executive branch, while the final two chapters in this Part focus on the judiciary.

CHAPTER 10

Congress

At a hearing on auto safety of a Senate Government Operations Subcommittee are the Chairman, Senator Abraham Ribicoff; the chief counsel, Jerry Sonosky; and the late Senator Robert Kennedy. (Wide World Photos)

T HE INTERNAL COMBUSTION ENGINE, first developed toward the end of the last century, has had a profound influence on the American way of life. By the early 1970s over 100 million automobiles and trucks (one for every two inhabitants—men, women, and children—in the United States) were driven annually a trillion miles over our highways and streets. Production of these vehicles is the country's largest industry. Dollar sales of General Motors top those of any other American corporation, and the other two of the Auto Big Three, Ford and Chrysler, also rank high among the nation's economic giants. The industry also spawned the two largest labor unions, the Teamsters and the United Automobile Workers. As automobiles go, so does the city of Detroit, the state of Michigan, and the nation.

Motor vehicles also brought their share of grief to the American people. Accidents increased over the years—over a twenty-year period more people lost their lives in automobile mishaps than in all the wars fought in the nation's history—and by the 1970s some 50,000 citizens were killed each year on the highways. Twice as many were permanently disabled, and four million—about one in twenty-five of the nation's drivers—received an injury in a car or truck accident. Billions of dollars were lost in property damages, medical payments, and wages by accident victims. As a result, auto injury and damage cases clogged the courts: in some urban areas, it required four years from the filing of a suit to the rendering of a judgment.

Despite this carnage on the highways, little was done over the years to make automobiles safer. The industry itself shied away from the task. Ford made an effort in 1956 to produce a "safe" car but had a bad sales record that year; the experience convinced manufacturers that safety was bad business, that talking about it made consumers nervous. Moreover, replacing and repairing damaged vehicles was itself a thriving enterprise. Nor were automobile insurance companies disposed to rate automobiles as they did drivers. The government likewise dragged its feet on the issue. The President's Committee for Traffic Safety, first established in the 1950s, was headed by an executive director chosen and paid by the automobile industry.

In the early 1960s, however, certain groups and individuals began to agitate for an end to a "do nothing" policy on one of the nation's greatest health problems. Doctors (who were on duty in emergency rooms of hospitals when accident victims came in for repairs) pushed for action through the American Medical Association and the American College of Surgeons, which established committees to look into the possibility of transferring crash-injury equipment developed for airplanes—seat belts, padded dash

boards—to automobiles. The American Trial Lawyers' Association, representing clients injured in automobile accidents, developed a strategy of
suing not only drivers but also automobile manufacturers on the theory that
defective equipment contributed to the cause of many mishaps. Ralph
Nader, a young lawyer who championed the cause of the consumer, wrote
a best seller, *Unsafe at any Speed,* condemning the automobile industry for
its failure to develop means of cushioning what he called the "second impact," the one that occurs when drivers and passengers are thrown about
inside the car after the initial impact with the other vehicle. Finally, the
cause picked up important governmental allies, among them Senator Abraham Ribicoff, who had led a vigorous campaign for highway safety while
he was governor of Connecticut.

Ultimately such pressures were felt in the political arena. Despite the in-
sistence of the automobile industry that it would develop safety devices
itself, the Johnson administration proposed legislation in 1966 for federal
automobile safety standards, and Congress responded with the passage of a
law directing the Secretary of Commerce to establish such standards for
use on all motor vehicles operating in interstate commerce. The Federal
Highway Safety Bureau (later placed by order of President Johnson in the
new Department of Transportation) was subsequently vested with the responsibility of developing safety requirements to be followed by the nation's
automobile manufacturers. Thus the first battle in what one close observer of
the developments, Daniel Moynihan,* called the "war on the automobile,"
ended in victory for the proponents of safety.

Controversy, as expressed in the give-and-take of the political process, has
continued to characterize the fight to make the automobile a safer vehicle.
The first twenty-three standards proposed by the Bureau met such opposition from automakers (representatives of American Motors claimed they
would put their company out of business) that three were eliminated altogether and fourteen others were amended by executive officials. These
adjustments led Nader to charge a sell-out to the industry and Senator Ribicoff to call for an investigation into why such changes were made in the
original standards. Other standards continued to draw opposition from the
automobile industry, which, in turn, was accused by Nader and others of
jacking their prices up far higher than necessary to absorb the small costs
of installing new safety equipment. Congress meanwhile extended the original Act in 1970, authorizing funds for planning a facility for testing in traffic safety, with the limiting provision that no appropriation of more than
$100,000 could be made without the concurrence of the House and Senate
Commerce and Public Works Committees.

*Moynihan, known best for his role in the development of President Nixon's welfare
program (to be discussed in Chapter 16), was at one time chairman of the New York
State Traffic Policy Committee in the administration of Democratic governor Averill
Harriman.

The "war on the automobile" is only one of many political struggles in which Congress has become involved in recent years. It does serve to point up, however, the way in which the national legislative body performs some of its basic functions.

FUNCTIONS OF CONGRESS

One of the major responsibilities of Congress, as a law-making body, is to pass *legislation* designed to deal with the major problems the people face, such as the large number of deaths and injuries and great property damages sustained in motor vehicle accidents. In doing so, Congress establishes rules and sanctions. In this case, for instance, automobile companies are required to follow certain standards—such as installing seat belts and head rests—when they manufacture motor vehicles to be used on the nation's highways; if they do not, they can be fined or prevented from selling vehicles. As a result of the actions of Congress, then, individuals and groups are forced under pain of legal penalties to do what they otherwise could postpone or never do at all. despite the contentions of the automobile manufacturers that they would develop safety devices of their own and install them in all their motor vehicles, they did not do so until Congress made them take such actions.

There is, of course, nothing inevitable about Congress's recognition of a problem and decision to take actions to meet it. Americans had been killing and injuring each other on the highways for almost a half-century before the national legislature required any safety equipment on motor vehicles. Until then it had been assumed that the problem of vehicular accidents should be approached in other ways: by constructing highways that were well-designed and by regulating licenses to drive. It was only after groups of physicians and lawyers and individuals like Nader and Ribicoff began to charge that the manufacturers should bear part of the blame for highway tragedies, and after the Johnson administration adopted its stand, that Congress became receptive to regulation.

In making its decisions on needed legislation, then, Congress responds to pressures from a variety of sources. Some are private groups and individuals who have a particular concern or interest in a problem and develop ideas about what should be done about it. A political party or candidate may propose legislative action to deal with a particular issue. Frequently the initiative comes from the executive branch. Indeed, it has been estimated that about eighty percent of all laws passed by Congress are originally proposed by the President or some administrative agency. Finally, congressmen themselves develop an interest in particular matters and become advocates of legislation designed to meet what they view as a major societal problem.

Although passing laws to meet societal problems continues to constitute an important function of the Congress, it is no longer as influential in legislation as it was earlier in the nation's history. Not only does Congress now tend to allow, and even to *expect*, the President to take the initiative in major legislative proposals (we will examine this matter in Chapter 12), but it also is less inclined than in the past to make major changes in the content of those proposals.

In fact, Congress increasingly turns over to executive agencies the job of formulating precise rules and regulations for handling particular problems. Thus in the case of automobile safety standards, all that Congress did was to recognize that standards were necessary, but it relinquished the responsibility of devising them. The language of the National Traffic and Motor Vehicle Safety Act of 1966 merely stated that the standards developed by executive officials should be "appropriate" and "practicable," "meet the need for motor vehicle safety," and "be stated in objective terms." Within these broad guidelines, then, the Federal Highway Safety Bureau was granted authority to develop standards it feels are necessary to make motor vehicles safe.

Congress takes this approach to public problems for two major reasons. One is that congressmen cannot be expected to have either the time or the expertise to deal with the intricacies of any of the broad variety of issues they must be concerned with. They can only hope to identify some major problems and suggest general approaches for dealing with them, leaving particular policies to specialized agencies in the executive branch. Thus congressmen as generalists could determine that developing safety standards for automobiles was desirable without having special knowledge of what these standards should be.

The second reason is that congressmen often decide to leave the development of specific policies to executive officials for political considerations. Although everyone agreed on the need for safety devices on automobiles, everyone disagreed on which particular devices or on how long manufacturers should be given to install them. Thus officials in the National Traffic Safety Bureau were caught in the crossfire between the automakers, who wanted them to act cautiously in devising and implementing safety standards in order to allow the industry time to adjust to the new requirements, and critics like Nader and Senator Ribicoff, who demanded that they act quickly to develop strict regulations. Quite naturally, congressmen typically prefer to allow others besides themselves to be exposed to such political pressures.

These developments indicate a shift in the major functions performed by the American Congress. Today it is less a body that develops specific rules regulating the actions of private individuals and groups than one that delegates to the executive branch the authority to develop rules under the supervision of Congress. In other words, Congress is not so much involved in directly controlling the activities of citizens through its own actions as in indirectly affecting the public through determining how administrative officials shall carry on that function. In the process, Congress has become less a body that legislates and more an institution that *controls the administration of governmental activities* performed by executive officials.

As we will examine in detail in Chapter 12, Congress has a number of means of controlling the administration. In the original legislation establishing new governmental programs, it determines broad guidelines for administrative activities. It also has the final say on organizational structure, that is, where in the executive branch the activities will be performed. Moreover, the Senate plays a role in determining who will occupy the major executive positions through its power to confirm or reject the nominees of the President to important government posts. Finally, since the scope and intensity of an agency's actions depend on the funds provided for its operations, Congress has a crucial function because it must first authorize the expenditure of funds and then actually appropriate them.

Nor does congressional control of the administration of a particular program end with its establishment. Legislators continue to oversee the activities of executive agencies. By authorizing operations for a limited period of time (often as short as one year), Congress retains the power of reviewing how effectively the program has been carried out. Annual appropriations also insure that executive officials will be forced to account often for their actions. Congressional investigations into the performance of agencies can expose inefficiencies and mistakes and occasionally lead to the forced resignation of officials who are found to be doing an unsatisfactory job. In recent years Congress has also developed a new means of administrative control: the legislative veto. Under this technique decisions of administrative officials are made subject to the assent of the Congress. Thus when it extended the National Traffic and Motor Vehicle Safety Act in 1970, Congress authorized the Secretary of Transportation to plan facilities for testing in traffic safety but provided that an appropriation of more than $100,000 for them could not be made without the concurrence of the House and Senate Commerce and Public Works Committees.

A third function of Congress is what Woodrow Wilson, in his classic study *Congressional Government* (written in 1885*), referred to as the *informing* function. By this he meant that the national legislative body has the obligation of educating the general public on the major issues and on some of the basic approaches that can be taken to alleviate them. Thus when Congress holds hearings on, say, automobile safety, pollution, or the control of drugs, it is trying to inform the American people (as well as its own members) about these problems and what steps might conceivably be taken to deal with them.

The informing function also has two potential practical effects. One is

*Before going into public life, Wilson was a professor of government. His study of Congress remains one of the most perceptive analyses of that institution ever written.

that an aroused public will force private individuals and groups to take actions on their own. One of the purposes behind congressional inquiries into automobile safety was the hope that manufacturers would inaugurate their own safety programs to avoid having the government enact a mandatory one. The vice president of Ford Motor Company did eventually propose that the industry do precisely that, but by the time the offer was made, the faith of many congressmen in voluntary action had waned.

If timely voluntary action on a problem is not forthcoming, the informing function has still another potential consequence: laying the groundwork for appropriate legislation. Concerned legislators hope that when enough groups are made aware of an issue and of what might be done about it, they will put political pressure on Congress to take action. When Senator Ribicoff conducted hearings on automobile safety, he was seeking to build public support for what he had already determined was necessary to deal with the situation.

In addition to educating the public in general on issues, many congressmen try to keep their constituents informed on a variety of problems, including those of special local interest. Such information typically goes out in the form of mass-produced newsletters, television broadcasts, and government publications. Although the primary motive behind such communications is often promotion of the congressman himself, nonetheless, they do help to keep private citizens informed on matters of public concern.

A final major function of Congress also pertains to relationships with constituents, namely, the *service* task legislators perform for individuals in their state or congressional district who request assistance in dealing with practical problems involving the federal government. For instance, an elderly woman may inquire about her social security benefits or a father may seek help in clarifying his son's draft status or his eligibility for a medical discharge. In performing this function, congressmen act as middlemen between private individuals and the administrative agencies in the executive branch. They help to get individuals in touch with the proper person to handle the problem, put in a good word on their behalf, and see to it that their constituents are well-treated and receive benefits to which they are entitled. Indeed, much of the time of the average congressmen is taken up with personal casework for the folks back home.

The legislative, administrative control, informing, and service functions together constitute the major responsibilities of Congress. Of course, they are not entirely separable, and one frequently has important consequences for another. Overseeing the executive branch, for example, helps to make congressmen aware of additional legislation that is needed to make government more effective. Handling cases of constituents alerts legislators to defects in the procedures of executive agencies that require legislation or stricter administrative control by Congress.

The performance of these functions also has important by-products for society. By serving the needs of constituents, congressmen "represent" their interests and help develop the loyalty and allegiance of individuals to the political system. The give-and-take of the legislative process accommodates and compromises competing demands, and serves to help make the final decision acceptable to the parties concerned. This, in turn, helps to legitimize the political system so that citizens in general are willing to abide by the rules and regulations developed by Congress and executive agencies.

Thus Congress performs a variety of specific functions in the political system that have important side effects for individuals, groups, and the larger society. The following section focuses on the individuals who perform those functions—the American congressmen.

CONGRESSMEN AND THEIR WORLD

Over the years our national legislators have ranked rather low in the estimation of many observers. They are common objects of derision for contemporary political cartoonists who picture them as bumbling, loquacious men of meager talent. Commentators in the past were often no kinder in their estimations. Alexis de Tocqueville, that perceptive French analyst of the Jacksonian period, referred to the "vulgar demeanor of that great assembly." He went on to describe its members as "almost all obscure individuals, village lawyers, men in trades, or even persons belonging to the lower class." To what extent do Tocqueville's comments accurately picture members who sit in Congress today?

BACKGROUNDS OF CONGRESSMEN

Contemporary congressmen resemble those described by Tocqueville in at least one important respect: they do tend to come disproportionately from the legal profession. Although lawyers constitute less than one percent of the adult population in the United States, almost three in every five members of the House and Senate of the Ninety-second Congress (1971–1973) is an attorney.

There are a number of reasons why attorneys dominate Congress. For one thing, the tools of the lawyer's trade—the ability to analyze statutes and administrative regulations, verbal and argumentative facility, and skills in negotiations—are precisely those that are needed by the men who perform the functions of the Congress—legislating, controlling the administration, informing the public, and representing constituents. As a professional man, a lawyer enjoys prestige in his community. Moreover, his professional role is to provide help in various kinds of personal problems. People, then, regard lawyers as natural legislators.

Members of the legal profession themselves also seek legislative positions. In fact, some go to law school in the first place not just to practice but to prepare themselves for a political career. The law is also a "dispensable" profession, that is, it can be fitted in well with service in public life. Indeed, many individuals continue their legal practice even while they are serving in Congress. The late Everett Dirksen for one retained ties and received remuneration from his law practice in Illinois while he was serving as the Republican Minority Leader of the Senate. Although he obviously had little time to draw up contracts or prepare cases for trial, his prestige and contacts brought the firm clients that might have gone elsewhere. Should a lawyer-legislator be defeated for reelection or decide to retire from Congress, he can return to his profession fairly easily, since law does not change as much as fields like medicine or science.

If by "men in trades" Tocqueville meant businessmen, then this characterization also applies today. Next to lawyers, businessmen and bankers constitute the second most numerous group in both the House and Senate: they account for about one-third of the members of the Ninety-second Congress.

The third most prevalent occupational group in today's Congress was not mentioned by Tocqueville: teachers. Almost one in every seven congressmen today was at one time an educator. Included are a number of college professors such as Senators Mike Mansfield of Montana, Hubert Humphrey of Minnesota, Gale McGee of Wyoming, J. William Fulbright of Arkansas, George McGovern of South Dakota, and Mark Hatfield of Oregon.

Tocqueville's description of persons "belonging to the lower class" does not apply today. The occupations of law, business, and teaching clearly have upper- or middle-class status. Another measure of social class, educational background, also reveals how the members of Congress surpass their constituents. Whereas almost one in five persons in the United States today has attended college, nine of ten congressmen have done so.

In social background congressmen as a group fit the stereotype of the male white Protestant. Although more than half the population is female, only about two percent of the members of Congress are women, including only one senator, Margaret Chase Smith of Maine. Although blacks make up eleven percent of the American people, they constitute only two percent of the Congress, including one senator, Edward Brooke of Massachusetts. Finally, a nation that is just over one-half Protestant is represented by a Congress that is three-fourths Protestant.

One comment of Tocqueville merits additional attention, his reference to "village lawyers." Although the phrase seems appropriate to the national legislature of over a century ago, even in today's urbanized America a number of our congressmen grew up in areas of limited population, as studies of political scientists Donald Matthews and Leroy Rieselbach reveal. As Table 10.1 indicates, about seventy percent of senators serving from 1947 to 1957, and over fifty percent of representatives of the Ninetieth Congress (1967–68) were born in rural areas or small towns (those with less than 10,000 population).

TABLE 10.1   Birthplace of Congressmen Compared with Population Distribution*

Size of Place	Senators (1947–1957)		Representatives (1967–1968)	
	Birthplaces	Population Distribution (1900)†	Birthplaces	Population Distribution (1910)†
Rural	52	60	36	54
2,500–4,999	12	4	7	5
5,000–9,999	7	4	10	5
10,000–24,999	8	5	8	6
25,000–49,999	6	4	7	4
50,000–99,999	3	4	6	5
100,000 and over	12	19	26	22
	100	100	100	101
	(N=177)		(N=430)	

*Figures in percentages.

†Census closest to average date of birth of legislators studied.

Sources: Donald R. Matthews, "United States Senators: A Collective Portrait," *International Social Science Journal* 13 (1961), pp. 620–634; Leroy N. Rieselbach, "Congressmen as 'Small Town Boys': A Research Note," *Midwest Journal of Political Science* (1970), p. 325.

The table makes two salient points that are often not fully realized. One is that in both the Senate (1947–1957) and the House of Representatives (1967–1968), it was the rural areas that were *underrepresented*. That is, the proportion of the nation's population born in those areas in 1900 and 1910 (the census closest to the average date of birth of senators and representatives, respectively) was greater than the congressmen born in them. The other point is that, although cities of over 100,000 population were underrepresented in the Senate in the periods studied, they were *overrepresented* in the 1967–68 House. This shift may indicate that legislative reapportionment granting more representation in the House to populous areas is already having some effect on the composition of our national legislature.

TENURE AND CAREER PATTERNS
OF CONGRESSMEN

As we saw in the previous chapter, incumbent congressmen have great advantages in political campaigns. Those advantages (assuming their desire to remain in office) are reflected in increasing tenure over the years. In the early years of this century members of the House of Representatives averaged about six years in office; by the late 1960s, the average tenure was some eleven years. The tenure of senators has also increased over the years since they became directly elected in 1914; by the latter part of the 1960s, over three-fourths were beyond their first term in office.

With this extended tenure, service in the national legislature has become increasingly professionalized and now constitutes a permanent career for many members. Most senators—the major exceptions are those who covet the Presidency—want to spend their entire working life in that position. So do many members of the House, the main exceptions being those who try to move on to the Senate or seek the governorship of their home state. As political scientist Samuel Huntington points out, however, those that seek other offices typically do so before the beginning of their fourth term in the House.

Huntington also points to other consequences of the present system of recruiting and retaining congressmen. One is a decline in interchange of people between the national legislature and the executive branch of government. Between 1861 and 1896 over one-third of the cabinet members had previously served in Congress; from 1897 to 1940 the number declined to less than one-fifth; between 1941 and 1963 it fell further to one-seventh; and in the Johnson and Nixon administrations it stood at a low figure of one-fifteenth. The movement in the other direction is also fairly limited. Relatively few congressmen have previously served in the national administration. They are much more likely to have come from state or local governmental positions. Thus the concept of separation of personnel that we examined in Chapter 2 has been extended beyond the idea that the same persons should not sit in the legislative and executive branches simultaneously; people now seldom serve in both branches at any time in their political careers.

Another result of congressional careerism is that there is relatively little exchange between the national legislature and private industry. Members of the House and Senate typically come to those bodies with considerable background in political office; once there, they generally remain until death or retirement or move to some other public post. In the executive branch, in contrast, officials largely come directly from private pursuits and typically return to them after short terms in office. Thus the movement that takes place between persons in the private world and the executive branch of the national government seldom involves the national legislative body.

CONGRESSMEN AS "LOCAL BOYS"

Another important aspect of a congressman's life is his basic orientation to his local community and state. In a society in which more and more young people never return home after college and where workers and executives move around the country frequently as job opportunities dictate,

Senate and House members retain deep roots in their home soil. Most of them return to their home towns, or at least their native states, after they finish their education and become immersed in political life. (The Robert Kennedys and Theodore Sorensons who seek public office in another state are the rare exceptions to the rule.)* And, of course, once elected, they remain residents as long as they stay in Congress.

In fact, congressmen are creatures of two worlds. One, Washington, D.C., is the locale for two of their major functions, legislating and supervising the executive agencies of the national government. The other, their home area, is the focus of informing and servicing functions for constituents.

Members of Congress retain close ties with their home areas in order to get reelected. To this end, senators and representatives find it wise to spend as much time "back home" as possible, particularly in an election year. For those who live in the East, not far from the nation's capital, extended weekends at home are the rule: many belong to what is known as the "Tuesday-Thursday Club"—that is, they are in Washington the middle three days of the week when the Congress customarily transacts its business and return to their local constituencies during the other four days. But even those from areas more remote from the District of Columbia find it advisable to make it home at least one weekend a month, and in those short periods when Congress is not in session, many of its members are on the road visiting in various parts of their constituency.

Living in two worlds is not an easy task for congressmen. It frequently means separation from their families to avoid taking children out of school They face problems of allocating their time and that of their staff members between Washington and their home base. Increasing numbers of congressmen have home offices manned by a permanent staff member to service the needs of their constituents. The double life of a congressman also calls for adjustment in interests and personal life styles. Back home they are expected to be "folksy," to demonstrate an avid interest in local events and in the progress of their constituent's children and grandchildren; in Washington they are called upon to evince a capacity to deal with domestic and foreign problems in a complex and sophisticated world. It is to this latter world that we now turn.

BICAMERALISM
IN THE AMERICAN CONGRESS

One basic and distinctive feature of the American Congress is that it has two separate and independent chambers. A number of factors contributed to the decision of the Constitutional Convention to divide it so. One was the British legacy; the English Parliament was divided into two chambers, the

*The Constitution requires that senators and House members be inhabitants of the state they represent. By custom, the latter are also inhabitants of the district they serve.

House of Lords and the House of Commons. A second was the bicameralism of many of the colonial legislatures, where the upper chamber was composed of emissaries of the crown appointed by the king or his representatives and the lower consisted of individuals elected by the colonists themselves.

But these traditions were not determinative; after all, the legislature under the Articles of Confederation had been unicameral. Rather, the two-house legislature grew out of the conflicts described in Chapters 2 and 3: the political struggle between large and small states and the legal battle over the issue of whether national legislators were to represent sovereign states or individuals. The "Connecticut Compromise" settled both arguments.

Bicameralism continues to have an effect on the workings of the American Congress. Most nations in the world today have two legislative chambers (two unicameral exceptions are Denmark and New Zealand), but in few places are they equally important. Rather, upper houses in nations like Great Britain and Italy are relics of the days of aristocracy; they are composed of persons who hold life tenure but who have little influence over the legislative process, which is controlled in reality by the popular, lower body. Only in countries like Australia and the United States does the upper house act as a coordinate legislative chamber. And of these few the United States Senate is preeminent, the most influential upper legislative chamber in the world.

The Founding Fathers had distinct purposes in mind for the Senate as compared to the House of Representatives. They created it to protect the interests of sovereign states, a function also served by upper legislative chambers in other federal systems, such as Australia, Switzerland, and West Germany. Beyond this, the Senate was expected to safeguard property interests: the prestigious nature of a Senate seat, it was thought, would attract an aristocratic elite, insulated from popular control by both indirect selection and a long term in office. In contrast, the directly elected House members with two-year terms were to reflect the interests of the many, those with little in the nature of worldly goods.

Linked to the protection of states' rights and property interests was the intention of using the Senate to check on hasty legislation passed by the House of Representatives. (As Washington explained the Convention's decision to the absent Jefferson, delegates provided for two houses to act on legislation for the same reason that they poured their coffee into a saucer—to let it "cool.") Thus the bicameral legislature was meant to serve two major purposes: the representation of different interests and deliberative, careful law-making.

The Founding Fathers also had separate special functions in mind for the Senate and House. The Senate was to pass on the qualifications of the President's nominees to major positions in the national government and it was to play a major role in foreign policy through the power to "advise and consent" on treaties negotiated by the President with other countries. The House was entrusted with the special and traditional prerogative of lower chambers: originating bills to raise revenue.

Having examined the reasons behind the Founder's adoption of a two-house legislature, we now turn to the ways in which the Senate and House carry on their business.

THE NATURE OF POWER
IN CONGRESS

One of the most intriguing and controversial questions about any organization is, who controls it? Americans today seem preoccupied with this basic issue as it pertains to both private and public groups—universities, churches, and corporations, as well as all levels and branches of government. The standard answer, particularly with those who are unhappy with our basic institutions, is that the "establishment," an inner clique, determines the decisions of all of them.

When a political scientist examines the issue of organizational control, he tries to discover who has "power." And by power he means the ability of one person (A) to get another (B) to do his (A's) bidding. The political scientist asks, who can get others to do what he wants them to do even though they personally would prefer not to? Who are the leaders and who are the followers?

A related issue is the question of *how* power is exercised, whether through coercion or by persuasion. Another question is, what is the *source* of power? Does an individual have it because he occupies a particular position in an organization or because he has particular skills in interpersonal relationships?

In Congress power involves the ability to shape major decisions. Thus legislators who successfully initiate, block, or make changes in legislative proposals through their ability to get other congressmen to go along with their desires exercise power. Power can be exerted in other functions of the legislature too. The senators who took the leadership in successfully defeating President Nixon's nominations of Clement Haynsworth and Harrold Carswell to the Supreme Court were also exercising power.

Who exercises power in the American Congress? As political scientist Randall Ripley suggests, there are various possibilities. It may be the persons who hold *elected positions* in the two chambers, such as the presiding officers of the two houses and the party officials chosen by the Democratic and Republican members. If so, we would say that power is *centralized*.

Another possibility is that congressional power is primarily exercised by chairmen of the various standing committees of the Senate and House. In such circumstances, power would be *decentralized*.

Power might not reside in those who hold official positions in the Congress, whether presiding officers, party officials, or committee chairmen. Rather, the organization may be controlled behind the scenes by an inner clique, some of whose members may not occupy any official post at all. Power in that situation would be *informal.*

Finally, there is the possibility that neither the official leadership of the Congress nor any informal group controls decisions but that rank-and-file members are to a great degree their own men. That power would be *individualized.*

With these general considerations in mind, in the following sections we will analyze the exercise of power in the American Congress. Because the situation differs somewhat in the two chambers, the Senate and the House will be examined separately.

POWER WITHIN THE SENATE

There are two kinds of central leaders in the Senate. One is composed of those who preside over the body and exercise essentially ceremonial duties in that chamber. Included in this group are the Vice President of the United States and the Senate President *pro tempore.* The other type of central leader occupies a party position, such as a Majority Leader, Minority Leader, and party Whip. There are great differences in the amount and type of power these two types of leaders exercise in the Senate.

PRESIDING OFFICERS—VICE PRESIDENT
AND PRESIDENT PRO TEMPORE

Under the Constitution the Vice President of the United States is the President of the Senate. As such, he is entitled to preside over it and exercise such duties as recognizing speakers and ruling on points of procedure. He has no vote, however, unless there is a tie among the senators, in which case he can cast a ballot to break it. He can also assign bills to committees, a decision that can be important if a measure could be referred to more than one committee. One, for example, might speed it on its way to passage, while another might pigeonhole it, or bury it, a matter we will examine subsequently in the chapter.

The Vice President is not an important figure in the Senate. Because he is not chosen by the senators themselves, they regard him as an outsider, especially when he is of the opposite political party from the one that controls the upper chamber—the fate of Republicans Richard Nixon and Spiro Agnew in Democratic Senates. Yet even when the Vice President is from the party in control, he is still an outsider to some degree. Lyndon Johnson did not try to run the Senate when he was Vice President from 1961 to 1963 as he had done as Majority Leader in the previous six years. Senate Democrats would have considered the attempt highly improper even though he was an esteemed colleague whose leadership they had accepted in the immediate preceding period.

The President *pro tempore* who presides over the Senate in the absence of the Vice President is not a powerful figure in the Senate either, even though he is selected by the members themselves. The choice is distinctly ritualistic: the party that controls the Senate nominates the person with the most seniority and in a straight-line party vote, he defeats the candidate of the minority party.

Since presiding over the Senate is relatively unimportant, frequently neither the Vice President nor the President *pro tempore* does so. The role is rather assumed by freshman senators of the majority party who take a turn at exercising the responsibility.

MAJORITY AND MINORITY LEADERS

The single most powerful individual in the United States Senate is the *Majority Leader*, who is chosen by the members of the party in control. Although experience in the Senate is an important asset for a would-be leader, it is by no means determinative. Lyndon Johnson, considered by some observers to be the most influential Majority Leader (1955–1961) in the history of the Senate, came to that position during his very first term in office. Democrat Mike Mansfield, Johnson's successor, and William Knowland, the last Republican to sit in that post (1953–1955), were both in the early years of their second term when chosen.

The Majority Leader has a number of rewards with which to affect the behavior of his fellow senators. He can use his influence with the committee that makes assignments to Senate standing committees. Lyndon Johnson's decision to allow freshmen senators to sit on one important committee (previously they had been placed only on obscure ones) helped build a base of political support on which he drew for a number of years. The Leader can also see to it that favored senators get appointed to select committees that take foreign "junkets," that they receive favorable office space, that some governmental installations (post offices, dams, federal buildings, air bases, and the like) are placed in their states, and that private bills they favor (such as allowing a relative of a constituent to come into the country under a special act of Congress) are given favorable consideration.

Even more crucial to the influence of the Majority Leader is his position in the center of the Senate's communications network. As the man responsible for legislative scheduling, he is in a position to know the status of bills: to which committee they have been assigned; what their chances are of being favorably reported out; which senators are for and against them; and when and under what conditions they will be ready for debate and voting on the floor of the chamber. In a confusing system of specialized committees and complex legislative procedures, the Majority Leader is the one man who sees the over-all workings of the Senate. He thus possesses more information on more matters than any other senator, and he can use it to further his influence. Moreover, it is to him that the rank-and-file member must turn for knowledge and advice about particular concerns.

The Majority Leader also acts as the chamber's communication link with the President. The relationship is particularly close if, as is usual, both men are from the same party. Then he is regularly briefed by the man in the White House on the administration's programs and is expected to use his influence to get favorable Senate action on them. He thus becomes a source of intelligence on what the President wants, how keenly he wants it, and what compromises he is willing to accept to get some measure enacted. Information on presidential attitudes is important even when he and the Majority Leader are not from the same party. In developing Democratic legislative proposals in the late 1950s, Lyndon Johnson took into account what President Eisenhower would and would not accept (for example, how many units of public housing at what cost) and scaled down his party's bills to avoid a presidential veto.

The Majority Leader not only conveys presidential wishes to senators, but he also informs the Chief Executive of their attitudes. His colleagues thus expect him to be not just the President's man but theirs as well. Playing

At the center of power in the Senate: Minority Leader Hugh Scott and Majority Leader Mike Mansfield. (United Press International)

both these roles satisfactorily is not an easy matter, but the Majority Leader who does so can do much to cement good relationships between the legislative and executive branches of the national government.

In many respects, the *Minority Leader* parallels his majority counterpart: he is elected by his colleagues; he tends to have experience, but seniority alone is not determinative (Everett Dirksen came to the post during the early years of his second term in the Senate); and he serves as the focal point of communication among senators of the minority party. Because he works closely with the Majority Leader in legislative scheduling, he too is a source of information on the status of bills and their likelihood of being enacted into law.

The Minority Leader also has certain prerogatives that allow him political influence over his colleagues—he can influence committee assignments to some degree—but the rewards he can bestow are not as plentiful as those of the Majority Leader. For example, he has less to say about where governmental installations are located. He is also less likely to have the President's legislative program as a focal point for rallying his colleagues. Even when he does (Republican senators Robert Taft and William Knowland were Minority Leaders during the Eisenhower administration and Everett Dirksen and Hugh Scott held the post during Richard Nixon's tenure), he has difficulty influencing a body controlled by the opposition party. The President may indeed find it politically more profitable to work with the opposition Majority Leader, particularly if the President's own party has relatively few senators compared to the majority party.

WHIPS

Both the Majority and Minority Leaders have assistants commonly referred to as Whips. The term came from the British Parliament, which borrowed it from fox-hunting: the Whip, or "whipper-in," was responsible for keeping the hounds from leaving the pack during the chase of the fox. By analogy, the Whip keeps the rank-and-file members from straying from the party fold; he sees to it that they are present to vote on key legislative measures and to cast their ballot as party leaders desire.

According to Senator Edward Kennedy, who served as Democratic Whip from 1969 to 1971, the name is a misnomer, for the Whip does not have the ability to bring his colleagues into line. He rather serves as a potential communication link between his Floor Leader (this is the term applied to either the Majority or Minority Leader) and the rank-and-file members of his party, letting each know what the other is thinking so that legislative strategy can be planned accordingly.

Even that function is not indispensable to the two Floor Leaders, since they can personally contact the limited number of senators from their party without too much difficulty. When Lyndon Johnson was Majority Leader, he was reputed to have talked daily with every Democratic senator.

To a considerable extent, the situation of a Whip under his Floor Leader is like that of a Vice President under the President: frequently the two who are supposedly serving as a team come from the opposing factions of the party—Republican Thomas Kuchel, for instance, was much more liberal than the Leader, Everett Dirksen, with whom he served. Personal relationships between the two may also be strained, as they were between former Democratic Whip Russell Long of Louisiana and his Leader, Mike Mansfield of Montana. If so, the Floor Leader may simply work around his Whip, as Mansfield did when he appointed four assistant Whips to aid him in the Senate. Like the Vice President's, the Whip's job is what his superior wants it to be: when Edward Kennedy replaced Long in 1969, Mansfield not only used the young senator (whom he admired) to gather information and get Democratic senators to the floor for crucial votes, but he also permitted Kennedy to share legislative scheduling and other leadership responsibilities.

The post of Whip also resembles the Vice Presidency in that it may constitute a stepping-stone upward. Since 1949 three Democrats—Scott Lucas, Lyndon Johnson, and Mike Mansfield—and an equal number of Republicans—Kenneth Wherry, Everett Dirksen, and Hugh Scott—have been promoted to the Floor Leader's position by their party colleagues. Thus the position of Whip has recently become a training ground for the top party post in the Senate.

PARTY COMMITTEES

There are three major groups in each party involved in the business of the Senate: one concerned with the assignment of members to standing committees (the Democrats call theirs the Steering Committee, the Republicans, the Committee on Committees); the Policy Committee; and the Conference, to which all members of each party belong. As we will see, the two parties differ in the way they choose members for the first two committees as well as in the functions the three groups have in party affairs.

The *Democratic Steering Committee* is dominated by the Floor Leader: he not only chairs the body but also nominates all its members, who are automatically approved by the Democratic Conference. Its membership usually includes the Whip and many chairmen of standing committees as well. Sitting members tend to continue automatically on the Steering Committee year after year. Although seniority in the Senate is a major factor in assignments and transfers of members to standing committees, the Floor Leader can influence these decisions. Lyndon Johnson helped arrange good committee assignments for freshman senators and also persuaded Theodore Green of Rhode Island to step down as chairman of the Foreign Relations Committee in order that Johnson's *then* friend, Senator Fulbright of Arkansas, might become its chairman.

The *Republican Committee on Committees* is chaired not by the Floor

Leader but by some other senior senator with good standing among his party colleagues. Except for the chairman, its members rotate every two years. The influence of the Floor Leader on the Committee has also been lessened by the Republicans' tendency in assignments and transfers to standing committees to follow the seniority principle fairly strictly.

The Legislative Reorganization Act of 1946, which created the *Senate Policy Committees*, intended that they would be executive groups entrusted with the planning, development, and implementation of party programs. They have never fulfilled that function, however. The Democratic group has become the creature of the Floor Leader, who chairs it, appoints all its members, and uses it only for advice on the scheduling of legislation. The Republican Policy Committee is more independent, for it is chaired by someone other than the Floor Leader and its members are nominated by the chairman of the Republican Conference and approved by the members of the Conference. It has also been of considerable service to rank-and-file Republicans in doing research, reporting on legislation, and providing them with material for use in their campaigns.

Finally, the *Conferences* of the parties also differ. The Floor Leader, again, chairs the Democratic one; it seldom meets; and when it does, it generally restricts itself to choosing the party leadership. Except when vacancies occur, however, even that is a fairly meaningless function, since the last successful ouster of an incumbent leader by the Democratic Conference occurred in 1913. On the other hand, the Republicans, once more, choose some senator besides the Floor Leader to chair the Conference; they meet as a group more frequently than the Democrats; and they even occasionally pass a resolution favoring a particular piece of legislation, as they did with the Civil Rights Bill in 1964 when all thirty Republicans voted for its passage. Even so, Republicans, like Democrats, shy away from passing Conference resolutions on controversial bills that attempt to bind individual members.

STANDING COMMITTEE CHAIRMEN

A second major source of power within the Senate lies with the chairmen of the seventeen permanent standing committees to which bills are referred for consideration prior to floor action. Over eighty years ago Woodrow Wilson referred to them as "little legislatures" in which the real work of Congress is accomplished. The greater volume of legislation the Congress considers, plus the need for specialization in a more complex and technical society, has made the Senate, and the House as well, even more dependent on the committees today than they were in Wilson's time. Both chambers are inclined to accept the action (or inaction) of standing committees on most legislation.

The standing committees of the Senate deal with a variety of subjects, including such divergent matters as agriculture, banking and currency, the armed services, and foreign relations. Two are concerned with money matters: the Finance Committee, which deals with raising it, and Appropriations, which decides how it shall be spent.

Not all standing committees, however, are of equal importance. The special role the Senate plays in foreign affairs makes the Foreign Relations and Armed Services Committees particularly crucial to the Senate's work. Appropriations is a key committee because the level of expenditures allotted for various governmental programs reflects senatorial priorities and helps to determine how well each program operates. The Finance Committee is significant because it makes decisions about how the tax burden will be distributed among the population.

The committees' pecking order is reflected in their membership. Senior senators with high status among their colleagues are most likely to populate the key committees. Some freshmen senators manage to get on such committees early in their careers: one example is Harry Byrd, Jr., who sat on both the Armed Services and Finance Committees in his first term in office. More commonly, if a seat is open, a senior member is transferred to it from another committee; sometimes a senator gives up one committee chairmanship to accept another one, as the late Democratic senator Richard Russell of Georgia did when he resigned from the top post on the Armed Services Committee to become chairman of the Appropriations Committee.

Although seniority in the Senate is not entirely determinative of committee assignments, seniority on a particular committee does dictate its chairmanship. As a matter of custom, the senator from the majority party who has the longest continuous service on a committee is designated its chairman. Senators from "safe" states that return them to office again and again who choose to stay with a particular committee assignment move automatically up the ladder to the chairmanship when their party controls the chamber. When the Democrats control the chamber, the chairmen tend to be from the South; when the Republicans do, they are more likely to be from the East or Midwest.

The power of the standing committee chairman in the Senate stems from two main sources. One is the preferments he has at his disposal *vis-à-vis* other committee members. The chairman can favor a colleague, for example, by making him the chairman of an important subcommittee and assigning him a good staff and budget for its operations. The chairman can also see to it that a member gets to go on trips the committee makes in connection with its work. Moreover, he can allow a member to become the sponsor of an important piece of legislation, to lead the fight on the floor for its adoption, and to be included as a member of the conference committee assigned to work out any differences between the Senate and the House over the measure.

These activities also relate to the other major power base of a committee chairman: the ability to control the procedures of his own committee and the floor action of the entire chamber on legislation referred to it. As we shall see later in this chapter, the standing committee chairman looms large in the legal and political maneuverings of the legislative process.

THE SENATE "CLUB" OR "ESTABLISHMENT"

Some analysts of the operation of the Senate in recent years have pointed to the existence of an "inner club" or "establishment" as the key group exercising power in that body. Although there has been some disagreement about the identity and number of senators in the group, the general consensus is that it has been dominated by Southern Democrats with considerable seniority. Clinton Anderson of New Mexico, former Senator Lyndon Johnson of Texas, and the late Robert Kerr of Oklahoma and Richard Russell of Georgia are generally considered to be the archetypes of the club members. The power sources of club members vary. Johnson held a central party post; Russell and Anderson gained strength as chairmen of important standing committees; Kerr had no major official position, but he enjoyed high personal status and respect among his colleagues.*

In his classic study, *United States Senators and Their World*, political scientist Donald Matthews points to certain "folkways," or customs, that senators must follow if they hope to become members of the club. As freshman senators they are expected to be seen but seldom heard from. When they do speak, they are to limit themselves to topics on which they are well-informed. Indeed, each senator is expected to develop expertise on a particular subject matter. Neophytes are also expected to be duly respectful of, even deferential to, their elders.

Folkways also bind more experienced senators who hope to join or remain in the inner club. All are expected to do their share of the "nitty-gritty" work of the chamber, the tough mastery of detail of substance and procedure that go into the shaping of legislation. They are expected to be tolerant toward fellow senators who disagree with them on political matters but intolerant of those who attempt to change the basic rules and methods by which the Senate operates. Club types are expected to be fiercely loyal to the Senate as an institution and to remain in it rather than use it as a stepping-stone to the Presidency or Vice Presidency.

If senators follow these folkways, they may eventually make it into the club. Even Republicans and some liberal Democrats have been accepted, although the inner group consists primarily of conservative Democrats. Thus the late Everett Dirksen and Hubert Humphrey have generally been considered members of the establishment.

Those who subscribe to the inner-club theory of Senate control feel that

*He was, however, chairman of the Rivers and Harbors Subcommittee of the Public Works Committee, which determines how such projects are distributed among the states.

definite benefits accrue to its members. For example, they receive more favors in terms of committee assignments, trips abroad, government installations in their states, and the like than do nonmembers. Matthews's study also indicates that legislative proposals they favor are more likely to be enacted into law than are those of "outsiders."

Not all students of the Senate, however, are convinced of the theory because the difficulty of agreeing on who is in the establishment raises a question of its actual existence and because it is doubtful that a group composed of men with such divergent views as Russell and Humphrey could be expected to work together to influence the passage or defeat of vital legislation involving controversial issues of public policy. Some analysts believe that, although an inner group may have controlled the Senate in the late 1950s and even into the 1960s, their power has now been eroded: figures like Johnson, Kerr, and Dirksen are no longer in the chamber, and a new breed of young, aggressive legislators such as Birch Bayh of Indiana, George McGovern of South Dakota, and Charles Percy of Illinois have come into prominence.

Another criticism of the inner-club thesis is that it fails to take into account the various kinds of *roles* that senators can play. Not all choose to be insiders who go along with the group in order to gain the esteem of their colleagues; some prefer to be outsiders who concentrate on winning favor with special interest groups and the general public. Some senators don't measure their success in terms of being on the winning side of a current measure; they may want to champion minority causes or to help lay the groundwork for future legislative triumphs. Congress, after all, has an informing as well as a legislative function, and those who emphasize the former are performing a role essential to the work of the Senate.

THE POWER OF INDIVIDUAL SENATORS

The willingness of the Senate to allow its members to play a variety of roles means that individual senators can exercise considerable power. William Fulbright, in many ways the prototype of the establishment man (a courtly Southerner with rather conservative views on race and economic matters, he has been in the Senate since 1944 and chairs the prestigious Foreign Relations Committee), has made his influence felt primarily as a critic of national policy in Southeast Asia. Other senators who have made their mark primarily as nonestablishment mavericks include William Proxmire of Wisconsin and former Senator Wayne Morse of Oregon.

It is the Senate's tolerance for deviant views that allows individual members to play an important part in the chamber's activities even though they are not part of the "club." In fact, the natural interest that unpopular views engender virtually guarantees good public exposure for the senators involved, for the mass media play up those matters that are controversial and hence newsworthy, as indicated by the publicity given Fulbright's views.

For similar reasons, senators who head up investigating committees, as Estes Kefauver did in the early 1950s, receive notoriety even though they are not a part of the inner group.

The influence of individual senators, however, is not restricted to the maverick or newsmaker. The limited number of senators who must tackle the myriad problems of society forces the body to divide itself into a large number of specialized groups to consider legislation. The restriction on the number of Senate standing committees provided for by the Legislative Reorganization Act of 1946 means that the work is delegated down to subcommittees—no less than 118 for the seventeen permanent standing committees at the beginning of the session of the Ninety-second Congress (1971–1972). By becoming a member, and even more important, chairman of such a subcommittee (frequently the chairman and one or two members make the decisions), a senator can exert power that is felt up the legislative line, for parent committees are inclined to accept with little change the action of their subcommittees, and the entire chamber usually respects the decisions of the standing committees. Thus the subcommittee chairman is able to affect greatly what the Senate does about a particular problem.

An industrious senator can wield considerable influence over legislation even early in his career. During his first term Senator Edmund Muskie became the chairman of two important subcommittees dealing with intergovernmental relations and pollution. He educated himself thoroughly on these problems and soon was acknowledged by senators, lobbyists, and executive officials alike as the expert in these fields. And a diligent senator may not have to wait long to see a pay-off in terms of public policies he favors. Birch Bayh of Indiana steered a controversial constitutional amendment relating to presidential succession through the Senate in his third year; Gaylord Nelson of Wisconsin saw his teacher corps bill enacted within a few years after he entered the Senate; and by the end of his first term Senator Harrison Williams of New Jersey had achieved success with mass transit legislation.

Thus individual senators today can play a meaningful legislative role after a relatively short period of service. With the newness of many of our national problems, the willingness of many a young legislator to educate himself so that he becomes known as the Senate "expert" on some issue enhances his influence. Even members of the minority party can acquire reputations as specialists in a particular area, as Republican Senator Charles Percy of Illinois has in the field of housing.

Power in the United States Senate is thus distributed broadly among a variety of individuals. Before analyzing the major patterns of influence that prevail there, it would be instructive to compare and contrast the situation just described with that of the lower chamber of the United States Congress, the House of Representatives.

POWER WITHIN THE HOUSE
OF REPRESENTATIVES

In some respects the sources and distribution of power within the House and the Senate are quite similar. Yet there are notable differences, especially as regards informal leadership and the role of the individual legislator.

PARTY LEADERS

Unlike the Senate the House has no purely ceremonial figure to preside over its deliberations. Rather, this function is handled by the body's most powerful political figure: the *Speaker of the House of Representatives*. Theoretically chosen as an officer of the entire chamber, he is, in essence, selected by the caucus of the majority party, since this group nominates and then votes for him over the opposing party's candidate. Thus the Speaker is both a House and a party official.

Because this is so, the ceremonial duties of the Vice President and the political powers of the Senate Majority Leader are combined in the office of Speaker. He has the power of recognition, rules on procedural questions, and refers bills to committees. But unlike the Vice President he is not a neutral figure with no vote except in a tie: not only can he vote, but he also can and does leave the chair to lead and participate in debate. Like the Senate Majority Leader he is the floor captain of his party who plans strategy and schedules measures for consideration and action.

The Speaker has generally the same rewards for exercising influence over his colleagues as does his Senate counterpart: assistance in obtaining a favorable committee assignment, appointment to select committees, inquiring into fascinating issues in attractive locations, help with favored private bills, invitations to serve as floor leader for a measure or to preside over the House, and help with a tough political campaign. Like the Senate Majority Leader, too, he is in the center of the internal communication network of the House, as well as being its link with the White House.

Working with the Speaker of the House is the *Majority Leader*. Officially chosen by the majority party caucus, he is often the favorite of the Speaker himself. In any event, his influence in the House will be what the Speaker permits it to be. Generally he assists the Speaker in scheduling legislation, distributing and collecting information of concern to the majority-party members, and attempting to persuade the rank-and-file legislators to go along with the wishes of the legislative party leaders and also of the President, if he is from their party. As a subordinate, however, the Majority Leader frequently has a higher goal in mind: selection as Speaker when the incumbent dies or retires. For Democratic majority leaders of late this aspiration has been realized: four in a row—William Bankhead of Alabama, Sam Rayburn of Texas, John McCormack of Massachusetts, and Carl Albert of Oklahoma—were all promoted to the top spot in the House.

The nominee of the minority party caucus who loses out in the election for the Speakership becomes the *Minority Leader* of the House. His role is essentially the same as it is in the Senate: to work with the Majority Leader in scheduling legislation and to lead the opposition party. He has some influence over committee assignments and the like, but he suffers from the same frustrations of his Senate counterpart: fewer preferments than the majority party can offer and, except when his party controls the Presidency, lack of an external program around which to muster the support of his House colleagues.

The *Majority* and *Minority Whips* have the same general function as they do in the Senate: to serve as a communications link between the party leadership and rank-and-file members and to see to it that the latter are there when crucial votes are taken. This function takes on far more importance in the House than it does in the Senate, however, because the greater number of members in the lower chamber makes it virtually impossible for the party leaders themselves to reach them. (Whereas Lyndon Johnson could be in touch with all members of his party in the Senate in the 1950s, Sam Rayburn, serving as the Speaker of the House at the same time, could not.) Both parties have elaborate organizations composed of representatives (called Assistant Whips) from various geographical areas of the nation who serve as liaison with colleagues from their regions.

There are, however, some differences in the parties' approach to the Whips. The Democratic Whip is appointed by their floor leader with the concurrence of the Speaker, while the Republican Conference (a body to which all House Republicans belong) chooses that party's Whip. As a consequence the Democratic Whip is always part of the party team, a result that does not always occur in the G.O.P. (For instance, when Gerald Ford was chosen Minority Leader in 1965, he backed another candidate against the long-time incumbent Leslie Arends—who had served since 1943—but the Republican Conference continued Arends in office). This difference in selection policy affects the pattern of succession to higher party offices in the House. Democratic Speakers John McCormack and Carl Albert previously served as Whips (as well as Majority Leaders), but no Republican Whip in this century has been similarly promoted.

PARTY COMMITTEES

The party committees in the House parallel those in the Senate: one handles standing committee assignments; another purports to be an executive committee that plans and implements the party program; and the third, composed of all party members in the lower chamber, is supposedly the ultimate source of party decision-making. Again, however, the committees actually perform these functions in varying degrees, and Democrats and Republicans differ in selecting and using them.

The group that handles assignments to standing committees is the most important for both parties. Members of each *Committee on Committees* are chosen by the entire party membership of the chamber, but the party leaders have a major voice in the selection. (The Democrats actually use their members of the House Ways and Means Committee to act as their Committee on Committees.) Both parties also provide for a broad geographical representation on the Committee. The Republicans appoint a member from each state that has at least one Republican representative. When a committee member votes, however, he does so on the basis of the size of his state's Republican delegation. This system tends to favor large states with a considerable number of Republicans sitting in the House. Geographical representation is built into each party's Committee on Committees because members act as spokesmen for the rank-and-file legislators from their area of the country. Thus when a freshman congressman from either party wants to get assigned to a particular standing committee, he attempts to get the man on the Committee on Committees in his area to persuade the entire Committee to award him the desired seat. In most instances, however, persuading the entire Committee on Committees really means influencing the dominant senior members.

In making its decisions on assignments on standing committees, the Committee on Committees takes into account the attitudes of a variety of individuals. The Speaker and other party leaders often make their preferences known, particularly on appointments to important committees such as Rules, Ways and Means, and Appropriations (the next section discusses why these are key committees), and such preferences are generally respected. A standing committee chairman sometimes has a veto power over appointments to his group. The Committee on Committees may also consult with the senior party member of a congressman's state delegation on his qualifications, and on occasion it checks with local party officials and civic leaders concerning his background and abilities.

The other party committees resemble their Senate counterparts. The Republican Policy Committee has been active at times since its creation in 1949 in helping to develop a consensus of rank-and-file members on legislation and in communicating their attitudes to the party leadership. Most recently, however, this function has been assumed by the Republican Conference. In contrast, the Democrats do not even have a policy committee, and its supposed counterpart, the Steering Committee, seldom meets and never steers. Similarly, the Democratic Caucus (the equivalent of the Republican Conference) typically meets only at the beginning of a congressional session and confines itself to organizational matters, that is, to choosing party leaders and the members of the Ways and Means Committee, and to approving the decisions made by that group as the Committee on Committees. Even that function is virtually meaningless, since the Caucus just confirms the existing leadership: no major party official has been ousted from office in this century.

A meeting of the House Ways and Means Committee. (Cornell Capa/Magnum)

STANDING COMMITTEE CHAIRMEN

Committee chairmen occupy the same powerful position in the House as they do in the Senate. They have similar preferments to dangle before committee members: subcommittee chairmanships, appointments to select committees, and the like. They also play a crucial role in committee and floor procedures relating to legislation assigned to their groups. Moreover, they arrive at their lofty position by the same automatic rule of seniority that prevails in the upper chamber.*

Even some of the same committees are crucial in the two houses. Appropriations is as important, if not more so, in the House (compared to the Senate) because of the political custom that spending measures originate in the lower chamber. Similarly, Ways and Means (the counterpart of the Senate Finance Committee) is vital because revenue measures *must* by constitutional edict commence in this chamber and also because, as indi-

*The Democrats have made some exceptions to the rule in recent years. Two Southern representatives were stripped of their seniority for supporting Republican presidential candidate Barry Goldwater in 1964. In 1967 Adam Clayton Powell of New York was ousted as chairman of the House Education and Labor Committee for mismanaging travel and staff funds.

cated above, the Democrats use its membership to man their Committee on Committees.

There are, however, differences in the committee pecking order in the two chambers. Neither the Foreign Affairs nor the Armed Services Committee is as important in the House as its Senate counterpart. On the other hand, the House Rules Committee is a key body because of the crucial role it plays in procedures for scheduling legislation; in contrast, the Senate Rules and Administration Committee (which concerns itself with such vital matters as supervising thc Scnate library and restaurant) is virtually at the bottom of the priority list in the upper chamber.

INFORMAL LEADERSHIP IN THE HOUSE

Observers of the House have been less likely than students of the Senate to impute influence to an inner club or establishment. The most prominently mentioned clique of this type was Sam Rayburn's "board of education," an informal group of changing membership that is reputed to have made major decisions at certain times during the late Speaker's tenure in office. Little has been written about the actual composition of the "board," however, and no such group has existed under other party leaders.

One possible reason for the absence of a House club is that the sheer size of the body makes it difficult for a small group of persons to control it from behind the scenes. While the formal and informal leaders of a small group may be different persons, the more members an organization has, the more difficult contact between them becomes. As a result only those in formal positions of authority have the visibility and communication ties with the general membership necessary to control the organization. These facts of organizational life may help to explain why party leaders and committee chairmen, rather than an informal group, generally exercise influence in the House.

Informal patterns of influence have not been totally lacking in the House, but the size of the body has tended to create several groups rather than a single, dominant one. One is the state delegation, which particularly binds party colleagues but which frequently reaches across partisan lines as well. There are other geographical and ideological groupings. For a number of years a sizable bloc of liberal Northern and Western Democrats have joined together under the title of the Democratic Study Group to research problems, to rally members to be present for crucial votes in the House, and to help to finance liberal Democratic candidates. A smaller, conservative group of Southern Democrats known as the Boll Weevils has also met together frequently as have members of the Wednesday Club composed of liberal Republicans.

THE POWER OF INDIVIDUAL REPRESENTATIVES

The rank-and-file member of the House has less influence in the chamber than does an individual senator. Many congressmen experience a real shock when they leave state and local political circles where they have been influential figures and are swallowed up in the anonymity of national politics. Typically in the early stages of a House member's career, he is an unknown, not only to the general and "attentive" publics but also to most of his colleagues.

Several factors help to explain this situation. One is the difference in the size of the two chambers. As one of 435 persons the rank-and-file House member is simply less visible than a senator, who is one of a hundred. Consider particularly the representatives from populous states like California and New York, with congressional delegations of over forty members, compared to their two senators. In addition, congressmen have been less visible to the public because prior to 1970, House committee proceedings could not be televised as Senate hearings could and were.

It is also more difficult for the average congressman to gain notoriety as a maverick or dissenter than for a senator. Few, if any, become "household names" in the same sense as a Fulbright or a Morse.* Nor is it as easy for the average representative to gain prominence in the legislative process. A subcommittee chairmanship has potential for influence, but there are proportionately fewer such positions available. (In the Ninety-second Congress there were 435 representatives to man 115 subcommittee chairmanships of the 21 standing committees compared to 118 such posts in the 17 standing committees for 100 senators.) In the House, unlike the Senate, many subcommittees are designated simply as number one, number two, and so on, and are given temporary and varied assignments. This practice prevents subcommittee chairmen from developing expertise on a special subject. Committee chairmen are also less likely in the House than in the Senate to allow young representatives to get credit for legislation. If a novice has a good idea for a bill, the senior legislator often takes it and introduces the legislation under his own name.

Faced with all these handicaps, the rank-and-file congressman must struggle to gain some visibility and influence in the chamber. One close student of the subject, Richard Fenno, has suggested that the best way he can do so is to ingratiate himself with some senior party leader or committee chairman so that he becomes his protégé. The senior congressman will then see to it that he gets a committee assignment, subcommittee chairmanship, floor managership of a minor bill, the opportunity to preside over the House, or other privileges. He will serve an apprenticeship following essentially the same folkways as in the Senate: he will be expected to specialize; to do his committee homework; appear on the floor, but speak only in his areas of specialty; and cooperate with party and committee leaders. If he performs these chores satisfactorily over a period of years (and keeps getting reelected), the principle of seniority will give him his just reward: a place in the power structure of the House.

*Republican Congressman Paul McCloskey of California gained notoriety in 1971 but this attention came not as a result of his legislative activities but because of his possible presidential candidacy.

THE DISTRIBUTION OF POWER: A SUMMARY

This analysis indicates that power is not concentrated in either house of Congress. Although major party officials such as the Speaker of the House and Majority and Minority Leaders in both chambers have some means of influencing their colleagues, for the most part persuasion is more effective than coercion (as Everett Dirksen put it some years ago, "The oil can is mightier than the sword."), particularly in their dealings with individuals with seniority and power sources of their own. Thus party leaders in both chambers negotiate with committee chairmen as they would with rival chieftains: the former, working with the President, determine the general nature and scheduling of legislative proposals, while the latter have a large say in their actual content.

There are, as we have seen, some major differences in the way power is distributed in the Senate and the House. There are some influential individuals in the upper chamber who do not have an important formal position; this circumstance exists rarely, if at all, in the House. Moreover, the individual senator is a power to be reckoned with, whereas the rank-and-file member of the House is not. Only when the latter acquires some seniority and special status does he become important in the power structure.

Finally, the patterns of leadership differ between the two parties. In both chambers the Democrats concentrate almost all power in the hands of their Floor Leaders, who use other party officials and committees to further their purposes. The Republicans distribute influence among party officials more widely. It is difficult to determine the reason for this distinction. It might reflect the Republicans' general distrust of political power. It may also be related to a pragmatic feature of politics: the Democrats have controlled both houses of Congress, along with the Presidency, for most of the last forty years and may have found it necessary to concentrate authority in their Floor Leaders as a means of getting legislative proposals of liberal Chief Executives enacted into law.

Closely related to the distribution of power in the American Congress is the question of how it is actually exercised in the course of the legislative process. The following section explores the basic procedures of the two chambers for considering legislation.

CONGRESSIONAL PROCEDURE: RUNNING
THE LEGISLATIVE OBSTACLE COURSE

One outstanding characteristic of Congress is the tortuous process through which most proposals must pass. In a typical session only about one in a hundred proposed measures is finally enacted into law. The other ninety-nine fail to surmount some obstacle along the way.

The procedures of Congress are so complex and technical that only the parliamentarians of the two chambers, plus a few veteran congressmen, grasp their intricacies. Nonetheless, it is possible to outline in general terms the process through which legislative proposals are screened and the kinds of political, as well as legal, considerations that affect their ultimate disposition. There are some differences in detail between the Senate and the House, but the general stages are similar.

INTRODUCTION OF BILLS
AND REFERRAL TO COMMITTEES

The introduction of bills in either chamber is a simple matter: a member merely has a proposal drawn in proper form (a legislative counsel offers assistance with this chore) and introduces it in his name (the actual source of the bill may be the President, an administrative agency, or even an interest group). Since both chambers now permit cosponsors, frequently a measure bears the signature of a number of senators or representatives to indicate that it has considerable support. (Often members from both political parties, different regions of the country, or even different political philosophies—liberal, moderate, conservative—join together as sponsors for that reason.) Similar measures can be introduced simultaneously in the two chambers with the exception that revenue and appropriation bills must originate in the House.

Naturally, some bills are more important and have a greater chance of passage than others; particularly successful are those that are suggested by or have the backing of the President or some executive agency. (These are known as "administration" bills.) Also, a major measure often bears the name of the chairman of the standing committee to which it is referred because its backers calculate that this will insure sympathetic handling both in committee and on the floor.

Generally speaking, deciding which committee a bill should be referred to presents no great difficulty for the presiding officers of the Senate and the House. Even when a measure could be sent to several committees, the sponsor can have it drafted so that it is appropriate to one in particular. Previous decisions on similar bills provide precedents, so that only new types of legislation present any real problem.* In such circumstances, the discretion of the presiding officer is crucial and may help determine the ultimate fate of the bill.

COMMITTEE CONSIDERATION

One student has suggested that the standing committees are the kilns in which legislation is baked, where proposals are sorted, mixed, and molded into form. For most bills, however, they are more like Woodrow Wilson's

*The Senate has a potential way around this problem, however, since a bill can be referred to more than one committee in that chamber.

description of them: "dim dungeons of silence" from which most measures never emerge. (Recent estimates indicate that, on the average, of ten bills referred to committee, only one is reported out favorably.)

In fact, standing committees do not even hold hearings on most bills referred to them. The chairman may simply not schedule any ("carrying the bill around in his pocket" as this practice is referred to), a decision that is difficult to overrule unless a majority of the committee makes a concerted effort to force his hand on the matter. Even then, however, the hearings may have been so delayed that there is little chance of concluding them in time to get the bill reported out and passed before the end of the congressional session.

Bills the chairman and most committee members favor are scheduled for early hearings by the committee or, even more often, by a subcommittee. A variety of witnesses appears at such hearings to give their views on a bill. Typically, these include: officials of the executive branch who have an interest in the legislative proposal (the Secretary of State or Defense will normally kick off hearings on matters of foreign policy); members of Congress from both Houses; and finally, private citizens, particularly spokesmen for concerned interest groups. Both supporters and opponents are provided an opportunity to appear, although the chairman's own attitude on a bill often determines which side is favored in the scheduling of witnesses.

Witnesses generally read a prepared statement setting forth their views and supporting evidence for them, and then face interrogation from the committee members. The kind of treatment an individual receives often depends on how his attitudes on the bill in question compare with those of the committee chairman. Sometimes, however, other committee members will come to the defense of a beleaguered witness, particularly if they are sympathetic with his stand on a matter.

Most analysts of congressional hearings agree that they reveal little factual information to determine how committee members vote. Indeed, most members have pronounced views on the matter before the hearings even begin. Why, then, are they held? Because they do serve other purposes. One relates to the informing function of Congress: media coverage of testimony given in hearings alerts citizens to the bill and to the stands of various groups and individuals. Hearings thus widen the public concerned with the issue.* Hearings also act as safety valves for the losers. Legislative defeat is easier to accept if one has been given the opportunity to state his views, to feel that he has had his day in court.

At the conclusion of the hearings, the subcommittee or committee involved goes into "executive session" (that is, private deliberations) in order to reach a decision about the measure. The members may give it a favorable or unfavorable recommendation, suggest it be tabled, or, more typically,

---

*Not all hearings are public, however. If testimony covers confidential matters (such as national defense) or may injure the reputations of third parties, it may be taken in private.

amend it in any way they desire. The amendment process is usually referred to as the "mark-up" of the bill, since the committee members go over the measure line-by-line to rewrite it. When a subcommittee has the initial consideration of a bill, the parent committee is free to make changes. Generally, however, it tends to go along with the decisions of the subgroup. Bills that are favorably reported by a committee but do not receive its unanimous endorsement are often accompanied by majority and minority reports setting forth the reasons why members favor or oppose its passage.

SCHEDULING BILLS FOR FLOOR ACTION

Senate. There is generally no problem in scheduling for floor action any bills reported by standing committees of the Senate. If a bill is noncontroversial, the chairman of the standing committee may ask for unanimous consent to hear the bill at once, and if no one objects, floor action follows. If a bill is controversial, scheduling is left to the Majority Leader, who works it out with the Minority Leader and, if the Democrats control the chamber, with their Policy Committee as well. He also generally discusses the scheduling of administration bills with the President or executive-agency officials.

In the Senate there are even ways to get bills to the floor that have not been reported out of a standing committee. The most prevalent tactic is to move the bill as an amendment to a measure that is already on the floor for action. Since amendments need not be germane to the general measure to which they are attached (the one exception here is general appropriations legislation), virtually any bill can be rescued from a standing committee. Liberals, for instance, used this technique to bypass the Senate Judiciary Committee chaired by Senator Eastland of Mississippi; one of the early civil rights measures was attached as an amendment to the foreign aid bill.

Another tactic is to place a House-passed measure on the Senate calendar for action without sending it to a standing committee, a maneuver that can be accomplished if a single senator objects to committee referral. It has been used frequently to get civil rights bills already passed by the House to the Senate floor for action without the necessity of having them considered by the Judiciary Committee.

Two other possibilities exist for bypassing Senate standing committees and bringing matters directly to the floor for action. One is suspension of rules, a method which is used primarily for amendments to appropriations bills to which the rule of germaneness does apply. The other is a motion to discharge the standing committee from consideration of a bill already referred to it. Both motions, however, can be defeated fairly easily by a filibuster, a matter we will explore below.

In fact, the possibility of a filibuster acts as a restraint on all four tactics, as does the informal courtesy of reciprocity among senators that standing committees should not generally be bypassed in the legislative process.

Nonetheless, the availability of the nongermane amendment, considering a House-passed measure, and motions to suspend the rules and discharge a committee of a bill makes it likely that a measure favored by a majority of the Senate membership will not be blocked by a standing committee.

House. The relative ease of getting bills to the Senate floor for action is in sharp contrast with the situation in the House of Representatives. Some noncontroversial measures are scheduled in the lower chamber without too much difficulty: included are private bills—typically these involve special claims against the government—and public bills that are unobjectionable. Bills involving any degree of controversy, however, must generally clear the potent House Rules Committee. This group has the power to issue vital "rules" on the scheduling of measures for floor action: whether they should be sent to the floor and, if so, under what conditions—that is, *when* debate should take place, *how long* it should last, whether the bill can be *amended* on the floor, and if so *by whom* (for example, just by the standing committee chairman).

Because it makes such crucial decisions affecting floor action on controversial bills reported by standing committees, the Rules Committee is in a strong bargaining position. It can kill a bill altogether or insist that certain changes be made in its content as the price of scheduling it for floor debate. It has the power to hold hearings of its own on a bill and then to require its proponents on the standing committee to defend it before the House Rules Committee.

In the period from the late 1930s to the early 1960s, the Rules Committee was controlled, under the chairmanship of Howard Smith of Virginia, by a coalition of Southern Democrats and Northern Republicans who used it to kill, delay, and emasculate much liberal legislation. In 1961, at the urging of President Kennedy, Speaker Sam Rayburn succeeded in getting the House to change the size of the Committee from twelve to fifteen; the appointment of two new carefully selected Democrats then gave the liberals a majority on the Committee. This change; the defeat of Smith in a primary fight in 1966; the appointment of other liberals to the Committee in 1967; and the adoption of rules denying the chairman the right to set meeting dates, requiring the consent of the majority of the Committee to table a bill, and setting limits on proxy voting by members—all have served to diminish the Committee's role in frustrating liberal legislative proposals. Even so, it is still a formidable stumbling block to the passage of liberal legislation in the House of Representatives.

As in the Senate there are ways that House members can circumvent a standing committee as well as the Rules Committee. For one, a bill can be discharged from a standing committee after thirty days if there is no report on it, and from the Rules Committee after just seven days of consideration without action. To rescue a bill under the discharge rule a majority of the

House members merely has to sign a petition. However, members are reluctant actually to use this device to enact legislation: between 1910 and 1968 only nineteen bills brought to the House floor in this fashion passed the chamber. Discharge is much more effective as a threat. If the Rules Committee sees that a petition will probably be successful, it is inclined to release the bill in question. By doing so the Committee can exercise some control over the conditions of debate on the floor, whereas if a bill is discharged, no such control is possible.

Another procedure, known as *Calendar Wednesday,* can be utilized to free legislative proposals from the Rules Committee. Each Wednesday, under House regulations, standing committee names are read in alphabetical order; members can call up a bill that has been reported to the Rules Committee but has not been given a rule for floor action. This tactic, however, is generally ineffective and used very infrequently. Indeed, Calendar Wednesday is usually dispensed with by unanimous consent of the House, and even if it is not, it is difficult to dispose of a measure within a single legislative day as required. Between 1950 and 1968, it was used on only two occasions.

Clearly, in the House unlike the Senate, committees are formidable roadblocks to legislative action. In some instances, however, House members appreciate these barriers. Pressures may build up from powerful interest groups to pass legislative proposals the congressmen do not actually favor; the chairmen of the standing and Rules committees (most of whom come from "safe" districts, and hence are fairly invulnerable to such pressures) can then be blamed if the measures never come to the floor for a vote.

FLOOR ACTION

Senate. Debate on the Senate floor tends to be informal, and members are not inclined to adhere closely to even the limited number of rules that govern debates. For example, rules requiring that remarks be germane to the discussion are seldom enforced. Senators are not inclined to challenge a colleague who is speaking off the subject, and if he himself acknowledges that he is doing so, they will usually grant him unanimous consent to continue.

This tolerance for discussion makes the Senate a unique legislative body. It is the only one in the world that has the right of unlimited debate, whereby a senator can speak for as long as he wants to on a measure. On most occasions, however, members do not exercise that right, and debate terminates simply because senators voluntarily stop talking on a bill and proceed to vote on it.

There are ways in which debate may be closed involuntarily in the Senate. One is by a unanimous consent agreement to terminate discussion. Even senators who oppose a bill may be willing to stop debating it because they concede that the majority should be able to work its will on the matter.

In some instances, however, feelings are so high against a particular bill (as on a highly emotional issue such as civil rights) that the minority is willing to use extraordinary means to prevent its passage. In this event members join together to *filibuster* it, that is, to keep discussing it so long that no vote can be taken on the measure. The participation of a number of senators is required since one or a few cannot talk continually for a long period. The technique is usually most effective at the end of a legislative session when time is short and members have other business they need to transact.

There are measures that can be taken to defeat a filibuster. One is to keep the Senate in continuous session so as to wear down the filibusterers. That tactic, however, is often subject to a counterploy: some years ago when Lyndon Johnson attempted to use this technique to break a filibuster against a civil rights bill, the minority retaliated by constantly calling for a quorum (the Constitution requires a majority of body membership to be present to do business), which necessitated many of those favoring the bill to get to the chamber at all hours of the night to keep the Senate in session. Meanwhile, only one of the minority's valiant band—the one talking—had to be there at any one time.

If all these tactics fail, a filibuster can be stopped by a *cloture* motion which terminates debate. This method requires that sixteen senators sign a petition and that two-thirds of those present and voting, vote in favor of the motion. If the motion is passed, each senator may speak for one hour on any one previously proposed amendment after which time the bill must come to a vote.

At first blush it would appear that the cloture motion would be used frequently and, when attempted, would have a fair chance of succeeding. Yet from 1917 (when the cloture rule was first adopted) to 1971, it was tried on just forty-nine occasions, and only eight of these were successful. Of these eight successes, however, four were in the 1960s: one in connection with the Communications Satellite Bill in 1962, the other three on civil rights legislation in 1964, 1965, and 1968.

Several reasons explain why cloture has not been successfully resorted to more often on the Senate. One is that members use the right of unlimited debate with considerable discretion, reserving it only for those measures to which they are violently opposed. Also, senators who are in the majority on an issue are reluctant to invoke cloture because they may want to filibuster future bills that are anathema to them. Then, too, traditions die hard in the Senate. But more importantly, many senators realize that the filibuster is a valuable weapon in thwarting what they feel are increasing encroachments of the President and the executive branch into their affairs.

After debate terminates in the Senate, whether voluntarily or by unanimous consent or through a cloture motion, the chamber moves to a vote on the bill. Prior to final passage, votes are taken on amendments to a bill, some of which are designed to clarify a measure, others to defeat it. In addition, opponents move that the bill be sent back to committee, a tactic which is designed to kill it. In voting on motions, as well as on the final amended bill, there are three possibilities: a voice vote, a division (standing) vote, or, if one-fifth of the members request it, a roll-call vote. The latter, which is reserved for controversial measures, requires each senator to answer yea or nay when his name is called; since the votes are recorded, the public can determine how each member cast his ballot.

House. The House of Representatives does not provide for unlimited debate. The chamber is able to move to a vote on a matter after members have had a reasonable time to deliberate its merits. On the other hand, controversial bills are dealt with in two steps, first by members sitting as the Committee of the Whole House and then as a regular chamber.

The Committee of the Whole device was borrowed from the British practice of the seventeenth century of getting the Speaker (who was the King's man) out of the chair so that members of the House of Commons could act independently of his scrutiny. Although the original purpose is not applicable (the Speaker does, however, as a matter of custom vacate his place as presiding officer), the device is useful today for other reasons. When members are meeting as the Whole House, a quorum of 100 rather than 218 (the majority of the entire membership) is sufficient to do business. In addition, before 1970 actions of members while in the Committee of the Whole were protected from public scrutiny: no roll-call votes were possible and other votes—voice, division, and teller (under the teller arrangement, members favoring and opposing a bill pass through separate aisles)—were not recorded. As a result of a change in the House rules in 1970, however, one-fifth of the Committee quorum (twenty) can ask that clerks record how (as well as whether) members vote on teller tallies. Thus a relatively small number of House members can now force their colleagues to make their votes on measures a matter of public record. Some congressional observers credit this new procedure with contributing to the defeat of the funding of the supersonic transport plane (SST) in 1971 because members had to make their vote known on a measure that was unpopular with many of their constituents. Negative actions taken by the Committee of the Whole are final; affirmative decisions on bills and amendments to them are subject to overruling by the House when it reconvenes as a regular body.

The voting procedures of the House (as contrasted to the Committee of the Whole), are the same as those of the Senate.

RESOLVING DIFFERENCES
BETWEEN SENATE- AND HOUSE-PASSED BILLS

Even if a measure has been able to get by the many roadblocks outlined above, unless it passes both chambers in identical form it still has one major obstacle to surmount: getting the two houses to agree on its content. For most bills this is no great problem. The differences are resolved by action of the chamber that first passes the bill, which simply agrees to changes made in its version by the second chamber.

On controversial measures, however, it is usually necessary to iron out the differences between Senate and House bills through the use of a *Conference Committee* composed of representatives from each chamber. Typically the presiding officers of the two houses both appoint three members, generally the chairman of the standing committee that considered the measure, the ranking minority member, and one other committee member. These individuals meet in executive session to resolve their differences and to recommend a common bill. When agreement is reached (a majority of each chamber's representatives must approve it), it is sent to the respective houses for approval. Neither house can change the Conference Committee version; they must accept it as it is, send it to the Conference Committee for further negotiations, or vote it down completely. Usually agreement is ultimately reached and the bill is ready for presidential action, a matter we will examine in Chapter 12.

VOTING IN CONGRESS

Students of legislatures have long been concerned with the voting behavior of legislators. Traditionally the matter has been examined from a *normative* standpoint: what *should* guide a legislator when his own attitude on an issue differs from that of the majority of his constituents. One view is that, as an elected representative, he is obliged to carry out the wishes of the voters who put him in office regardless of his own outlook. In effect, he is to act as the *agent*, or instructed *delegate*, of the people. An opposing concept, most often associated with the eighteenth-century British statesman Edmund Burke, holds that the representative owes his constituents, not blind obedience to their will, but rather his own independent judgment.* The legislator is, in this view, a *trustee* whom the people elect because they have faith in his native capacities and in his ability to study matters and to arrive at judgments that are better informed than their own. Recent studies of legislative voting, however, have shifted their focus to what a legislator *actually does*, to the particular considerations he takes into account in deciding on bills.

One of the major findings of recent studies is that the traditional delegate-trustee dichotomy is far too simplified and fails to explain the complexities of legislative voting. For one thing, it exaggerates the interest in and information about legislative issues of both constituents and representatives. Most voters are not concerned with measures before the Congress, nor are

---

*Burke delivered an oft-quoted speech to his constituents in Bristol setting forth his views to that effect. It is significant, however, that he subsequently withdrew as a candidate because he felt that he could not be reelected because of these views.

they familiar with how their senators or representatives vote on such matters. On the other hand, congressmen are often unaware of the general sentiments of their constituents who do have attitudes on measures before the Congress. Letters from voters and even replies to questionnaires sent out by congressmen typically come from a relatively small number of individuals whose views are not necessarily representative of those of all the voters. A study by the Survey Research Center at the University of Michigan comparing the attitudes of voters on major economic, civil rights, and foreign policy issues with what their congressmen *thought* their attitudes were, revealed that the representatives misperceived their constituents' opinions, especially on the foreign policy and economic issues.

Moreover, the concept of the model congressman who carefully studies the facts and considerations behind each bill and, with this information in mind, rationally determines his vote is unrealistic. The tremendous volume of business that the Senate and House of Representatives have before them prevents a legislator from engaging in such a time-consuming task. Like the voter, the congressman is seeking shortcuts in the decision-making process and so he looks for certain cues, points of reference, to guide his actions.

Party affiliation has been the strongest influence in roll-call tallies in the American Congress over the years. Although senators and representatives do not vote the party line to the extent that legislators do in, for example, Great Britain, party is more closely associated with voting patterns on a wide range of issues than any other single variable. Party identification thus plays a major part in determining how congressmen vote on legislation, just as it does for the average voter when he faces a choice in a general election contest.

A related influence is the attitude of the *President* toward particular legislation. Congressmen from his party are obviously more inclined to support measures that he favors than are members of the opposition. In 1969, Richard Nixon's first year in office, some two-thirds of the Republican senators voted his sentiments on legislation, while only one-half of the Democratic senators did so. In 1965, after Lyndon Johnson's election when he was enjoying his greatest legislative successes, the situation was just reversed.* There are differences between freshman and veteran legislators in following the presidential lead. That same year, 1965, the seventy-one new Democratic members of the House of Representatives supported Mr. Johnson eighty-two percent of the time, compared to seventy-four percent for all House Democrats. Thus, ironically, Barry Goldwater's resounding defeat in the 1964 presidential contest helped carry into office a bumper crop of

*Each year the *Congressional Quarterly* analyzes congressional voting along certain dimensions such as party and region. Included is a measurement of congressional support for the President on measures he favors. To ascertain his attitudes on legislation, all his messages, press conferences, and other public statements are examined.

Democrats from politically competitive congressional districts, a bonus that contributed to Johnson's success with the "Great Society" Program.

Partisan differences within Congress, as well as between Congress and the President, by no means entirely determine the voting in the national legislature. For example, in 1969 there was a bipartisan majority on about two-thirds of the roll-call votes: in other words, Democrats and Republicans voted on the same side of issues twice as often as on the opposite side. In addition, Mr. Nixon's desires prevailed on about three-fourths of the measures on which he took a stand, even though the opposition party controlled both the Senate and House. Clearly, then, we must look to other considerations besides party to help explain the voting patterns in roll-call tallies.

One general influence to look at is a legislator's *constituency*. Senators and representatives from the *same state* tend to vote alike on many measures. Moreover, *region* helps explain congressional voting patterns. Over the last three decades, the major split among Democrats in both houses has been between Northern and Southern states.* (In 1969 this division was reflected in forty percent of the roll-call votes in the Senate, and in thirty-two percent in the House.) There has been less of a regional cleavage within the Republican party, but some division has existed between legislators from the coastal areas and those from the interior of the country, particularly on foreign policy. In addition to regional differences, some divisions have existed in both parties between members from *urban* constituencies and those from *suburban* and *rural* areas.

Thus constituency modifies party influences on voting in the American Congress, resulting in common interests across party lines. The most obvious example is the Conservative Coalition of Republicans and Southern Democrats that has formed against Northern Democrats on a variety of issues since the late 1930s. In 1969 this coalition formed on twenty-seven percent of the roll-call votes and prevailed in seventy-one percent of those. Less well-known, but still influential, is the liberal combination between Northern Democrats and Republicans, particularly from New England and the Middle Atlantic states. Because of these coalitions, the outcome of many crucial votes in Congress turns on the extent to which the two minority groups in the two parties (the Southern Democrats and the Eastern Republicans) vote by party or by constituency.

Finally, there are instances in which neither party nor constituency appear to determine how a congressman votes on a particular issue. Lewis Froman compared voting on reciprocal trade legislation over a ten-year period by legislators from constituencies that changed their congressman (but not the party he represented) with those who stayed in office over that

*The *Congressional Quarterly* classifies the following as Southern states: Alabama, Arkansas, Florida, Georgia, Kentucky, Louisiana, Mississippi, North Carolina, Oklahoma, South Carolina, Tennessee, Texas, and Virginia. The other thirty-seven states are designated Northern.

time; his study indicated that the attitudes of an individual congressman can make a difference, for the voting on the issue by the representative from the stable districts was more constant than that by the congressmen from the more changeable constituencies.

Thus a congressman voting on a legislative measure is not unlike a voter casting his ballot in an electoral contest: he responds to a variety of cues or, in some cases, political pressures. In some instances all influences may guide him in the same direction. If a measure is favored by the President (who is of his party), his party leadership in the chamber, and key interest groups and party leaders in his own constituency, and if it is also consistent with his own personal political philosophy and preferences, then he has no problem on how to vote. But if there is a conflict among these various cues, he must make a choice among them, which will depend on various factors: how urgently the President and legislative leaders want the bill to be passed (or defeated), how important the measure is to important political groups in his constituency, and how strongly he feels about the matter himself. (The University of Michigan study cited above showed, for example that congressmen are likely to respond to party cues in voting on social welfare measures, to the President on foreign policy issues, and to their constituents on civil rights matters.) His choice may also turn on when the vote takes place: a senator, for example, may be willing to vote against the attitudes of important groups in his constituency early in his term, but not during an election year.

In fact, congressmen have considerable discretion in voting. Very few of their constituents—only the attentive publics, such as interest groups and party leaders—are familiar with their voting records, and even these few are concerned with only some issues. As long as a representative avoids voting against the wishes of his electorate on a matter of great concern to them (one from the Deep South, for example, favoring liberal civil rights legislation), he may expect to be returned to office without too much difficulty. As the University of Michigan researchers concluded, rather than peering over their congressman's shoulder closely when he votes on most issues, constituents are generally looking the other way.

ASSESSMENT

There is little question that the Congress tends to be a body designed to block legislation rather than to facilitate it. A number of factors contribute to this situation: the conservative *status quo* orientation of many legislators, particularly representatives from small communities; the use of the seniority rule for choosing committee chairmen, which tends to place in these positions older men from safe districts, many of which are located in sparsely populated areas of the South and Midwest; the power that such committee chairmen wield over the consideration of bills; and the procedures of the two chambers, especially the role that the Rules Committee of the House and the filibuster in the Senate play in obstructing floor action on proposed legislation. The many obstacles a bill must surmount before it is enacted into law gives the advantage to its opponents: they can kill it at a number of places along the way in either chamber (as well as the conference committee), while its proponents must work up a majority sentiment in its favor at each hurdle (and in the case of overcoming the filibuster, an extra-majority vote).

Certain reforms would do much to rectify the above problems and to make the Congress more democratic. The ability of the dominant party to steer legislation through both houses would be enhanced by having the standing committee chairmen chosen on the basis of service and loyalty to the party rather than as a result of seniority alone. The rank-and-file members, especially in the House, could also be given more of a role in the manning of party and standing committees, as well as in the development and scheduling of the party's legislative program. Partisan and bipartisan majorities would also have their legislative wishes facilitated if the power of the House Rules Committee were restricted and the filibuster eliminated by making it possible for the majority of the senators to cut off debate on the floor.

Virtually all the above reforms could be put into effect if the majority of the representatives and senators were willing to change the present rules and customs accordingly.* One can only conclude that most congressmen like the situation the way it is. Granting the majority party greater power over the affairs of the House and Senate flies in the face of two dominant facts about American parties: they are composed of factions with different philosophies and bases of power, and power lies at the local and state, not the national, level of the party organization. It is, therefore, unrealistic to expect congressmen from various geographical areas always to follow the lead of the legislative party, especially when their constituents, not national party leaders, determine their political fortunes through control over the nomination process and campaign finances.

It is somewhat more difficult to determine why individual senators and representatives (particularly the latter) have not demanded more of a voice in decision-making in their respective houses. Perhaps young rank-and-file members simply lack the confidence and know-how to challenge the existing leadership, and by the time they acquire these attributes, they themselves have been members long enough to be in line for leadership positions. As far as procedural rules are concerned, many congressmen like the fact that certain legislation does get buried and that they can blame others for it; also, the filibuster enables them to protect interests they favor as well

---

*One exception is the use of the filibuster as a means of preventing changes in the rules of the Senate, including alterations in cloture itself.

as thwart what many of them feel is too much presidential and executive-agency influence in legislative business. In other words, the present rules and customs are there because they provide the individual congressman with a measure of independence from both his constituents and his natural political rivals.

There are some recent indications, however, that Congress is beginning to respond to the interests of rank-and-file members as well as the general public. The Democrats in the House agreed in 1971 to limit the number of legislative subcommittee chairmanships that one man can hold; Republicans in the Senate that same year took similar action with respect to ranking minority positions on standing committees. Both changes are designed to spread such posts among a greater number of congressmen. House Democrats also provided that committee recommendations on chairmen and members are to be debated by the Democratic Caucus on the demand of ten members. The secrecy of teller voting in the House has been eliminated, and provisions have been made for opening committee business meetings and hearings to the public (unless a majority of the committee members votes otherwise) and for making roll-call votes of standing committees more readily available. Although these measures fall short of major congressional reform, they do provide some evidence of greater congressional sensitivity to charges of domination by senior members and of excessive secrecy in legislative proceedings.

Selected Readings

For an excellent analysis of traffic safety and policies developed to meet them, see Daniel Moynihan, "The War Against the Automobile," *The Public Interest* 3 (1966), 10–26.

A classic study of Congress is Woodrow Wilson, *Congressional Government: A Study in American Politics* (Boston: Houghton, Mifflin, 1891). Two good recent treatments of the legislative process at both the national and state level are Malcolm E. Jewell and Samuel C. Patterson, *The Legislative Process in the United States* (New York: Random House, 1968), and William J. Keefe and Morris S. Ogul, *The Legislative Process: Congress and the States* (Englewood Cliffs, N.J.: Prentice-Hall, 1968). A good short treatment of Congress is contained in Nelson W. Polsby, *Congress and the Presidency* (Englewood Cliffs, N.J.: Prentice-Hall, 1964). An excellent general study of Congress containing chapters on various topics by different authors is David B. Truman (ed.), *Congress and America's Future* (Englewood Cliffs, N.J.: Prentice-Hall, 1965). The chapter entitled "Congressional Responses to the Twentieth Century," by Samuel P. Huntington, gives an excellent overview of the personnel, structure, and functions of the Congress. For an expanded analysis of the same general topics with particular emphasis on the latter, see John S. Saloma III, *Congress and the New Politics* (Boston: Little, Brown, 1969).

The world of a senator is graphically portrayed in Donald R. Matthews, *U.S. Senators and Their World* (Chapel Hill: University of North Carolina Press, 1960). Two excellent treatments of the life of a member of the House of Representatives are Charles L. Clapp, *The Congressman: His Work as He Sees It* (Washington, D.C.: The Brookings Institution, 1963), and Clem Miller (ed. by John W. Baker), *Letters of a Congressman* (New York: Scribner, 1962). An analysis of the tenure of House members over the years is T. Richard Witmer, "The Aging of the House," *Political Science Quarterly* 79 (1964), 526–538.

A journalist's description of the Senate's inner club is William S. White, *Citadel, The Story of the U.S. Senate* (New York: Harper & Row, 1957); for one by a senator himself see Joseph S. Clark, *The Senate Establishment* (New York: Hill and Wang, 1963). Randall B. Ripley, *Power in the Senate* (New York: St. Martin's Press, 1969), is a balanced scholarly treatment of the same topic. For an analysis of the role of the party in the House of Representatives see Ripley's *Party Leaders in the House of Representatives* (Washington, D.C.: The Brookings Institution, 1967).

The best recent treatment of congressional procedure is Lewis A. Froman, Jr., *The Congressional Process: Strategies, Rules, and Procedures* (Boston: Little, Brown, 1967).

Two excellent analyses of voting patterns in Congress are Julius Turner, *Party and Constituency: Pressures on Congress* (Baltimore: Johns Hopkins University Press, 1951), and David Truman, *Congressional Party: A Case Study* (New York: John Wiley, 1959). A good short treatment of the subject is continued in Lewis A. Froman, Jr., *Congressmen and Their Constituencies* (Chicago: Rand McNally, 1963). An analysis based on survey data of attitudes of both congressmen and their constituents is Warren E. Miller and Donald E. Stokes, "Constituency Influence in Congress," which appears in Angus Campbell, Philip E. Converse, and Miller and Stokes, *Elections and the Political Order* (New York: John Wiley, 1966).

A major academic criticism of Congress is James MacGregor Burns, *Congress on Trial: The Legislative Process and the Administrative State* (New York: Gordian, 1966). Two congressmen most often associated with attacks on the two chambers are Senator Joseph Clark and Representative Richard Bolling. The views of the former are set forth in *Congress: The Sapless Branch* (New York: Harper & Row, 1965) and of the latter in *House Out of Order* (New York: Dutton, 1965). A good defense of Congress is Ernest Griffith, *Congress: Its Contemporary Role* (New York: New York University Press, 1951). Thoughtful analyses of the issue of reform are contained in Froman's *The Congressional Process* and Saloma's work cited above.

An excellent publication for keeping abreast of current developments in Congress and in American politics in general is the *Congressional Quarterly Weekly Report*.

CHAPTER 11

The Executive: Continuity and Development

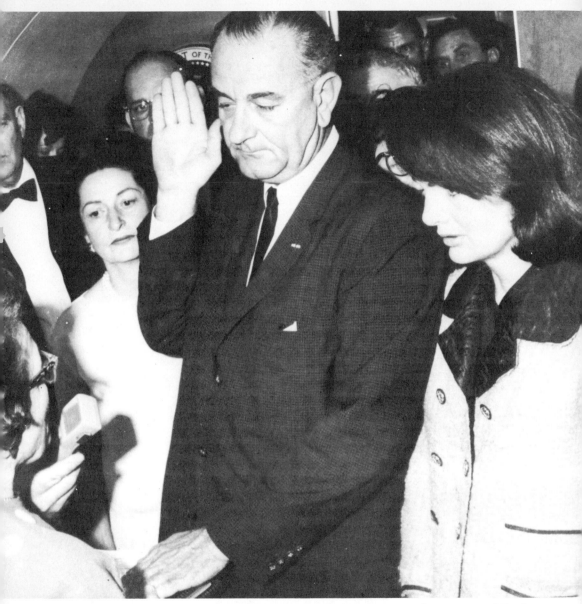

Lyndon Johnson takes the oath of office, November 22, 1963, in the presence of President Kennedy's widow. (United Press International)

IN THE EARLY 1960s bitter internal battles in the Texas Democratic party between factions led by Governor John Connally and Senator Ralph Yarborough had reached such proportions that they threatened to cost the 1964 Democratic ticket twenty-four precious electoral votes that the Kennedy-Johnson team had won by a narrow margin four years before. With reluctance President Kennedy agreed to go to the Lone Star State in the fall of 1963 to appear at speaking engagements with the Governor, the Senator, and the man most politically embarrassed by the squabbles—Lyndon Johnson—in order to restore unity to the divided state party. For the young President, however, there was one bright spot to the trip: his wife, Jackie, had agreed to go along. Besides personal companionship, her elegance (Kennedy himself helped pick her wardrobe for the trip) and her fluency in Spanish were viewed by Governor Connally and others as valuable assets on the campaign trail.

Not everyone was enthusiastic about the trip, particularly the visit to Dallas, the last stop on the tour. Adlai Stevenson, then Ambassador to the United Nations, who had been assaulted there the previous month by right-wingers, considered warning the President not to go but changed his mind at the last minute. Others, however, did advise against it. Senator Fulbright of Arkansas, who had been subjected to bitter attacks by the *Dallas News* the year before, pleaded with Kennedy to bypass the city. The ranking United States Attorney there advised Vice President Johnson that the Dallas political climate made a presidential visit unwise. Even the evangelist Billy Graham tried to pass on his sense of unease about the trip to Kennedy through a mutual friend, Senator George Smathers of Florida.

Despite such misgivings, the trip went well as the young President and his wife were greeted by enthusiastic crowds in San Antonio, Houston, and Fort Worth. Even Dallas gave him a warm reception by friendly throngs lining the streets used by the motorcade between the airport and the Trade Mart where the Chief Executive was scheduled to address a noonday luncheon on Friday, November 22. At 12:29 P.M., some six minutes away from the Trade Mart, Governor Connally's wife, who was riding in the same car as the President, turned to him and exclaimed, "You sure can't say Dallas doesn't love you, Mr. President." Kennedy smiled in reply, "No, you can't."

One minute later, just after the President's car had passed by the Texas School Book Depository, a sharp sound rang out. Jackie Kennedy thought it was a motorcycle noise; the Dallas Chief of Police mistook it for a railroad torpedo. But it was a rifle shot, and it had found its mark: the President was wounded in the lung and throat, though not fatally. Seconds later, however, another shot tore into his brain.

371

There followed a chain of dramatic and bizarre events: a secret service agent riding in another car with Vice President Johnson ordered him to "Get down!" and hurled him to the floor of the back seat; the motorcade sped to Parkland Hospital four miles away, where the President was admitted and pronounced dead within half an hour; when the Dallas County medical examiner insisted on performing an autopsy, Kennedy aides used physical force to get the body out of the hospital for the trip back to Washington, D.C.; and a federal judge, Sarah Hughes, was located and at 1:39 P.M. (one hour and ten minutes after the fatal shot) administered the presidential oath inside Air Force One to the new Chief Executive, Lyndon Johnson, standing beside the dazed Jacqueline Kennedy. Meanwhile, Lee Harvey Oswald, an ex-marine who had lived in Russia and was married to a Soviet citizen, killed a Dallas policeman and was captured in a theatre; by 3:30 P.M. police interrogation had linked him with the assassination. Two days later, as Oswald was being transferred from the Dallas municipal building to the county jail, he was shot fatally by Jack Ruby, a Dallas nightclub owner.

No event in human history had ever been made known so quickly to so many persons. Within six minutes of the shooting the news was being broadcast on local radio; by 1:00 P.M. two-thirds of the American people knew of the assassination. For the next four days Americans sat transfixed before their television sets as the networks covered the subsequent events, along with imaginative background stories. Moreover, the coverage was beamed to people around the world; some ninety-nine percent of the people in Athens, Greece were reported to have watched or listened to the funeral service on Monday, November 25.

No other event has had so much personal impact on so many individuals as did the President's assassination. A study of the reaction to the tragedy by the National Opinion Research Center at the University of Chicago revealed that four of every five Americans felt physical discomfort on hearing the news; over fifty million suffered from insomnia; and half of all the nation's fathers said they cried once or more during those fateful days. A New York news dealer put a sign on his stand, "Closed because of a death in the American family."

The event also shocked people around the world: London teenagers wept in the streets; in Berlin, 60,000 persons gathered to express their sorrow; and Charles de Gaulle told a friend that people were crying all over France, as though the American President were a member of their own family. On hearing of the news, Nikita Khrushchev interrupted a trip to return to Moscow; Andrei Gromyko, one of the toughest Russian leaders, was seen weeping as he left the American embassy in Moscow. Ultimately representatives of ninety-two countries (including de Gaulle himself) gathered in Washington, D.C. for the President's funeral.

The events testify to two dominant characteristics of the modern American Presidency. One is the continuity of the office: in all the confusion of those tragic days, the nation's governance was assured as Vice President Lyndon Johnson took over the leadership of the nation immediately and without incident. The second is the great importance the Presidency has acquired not only for Americans but also for people in all parts of the world.

THE CONTINUITY
OF THE PRESIDENTIAL OFFICE

Although Americans took for granted the Vice President's succession to the office upon the death of John Kennedy, many political systems do not provide machinery to determine in advance who will become the leader of the nation if something happens to the incumbent. When Joseph Stalin suddenly died of a heart attack in March 1953, a power struggle ensued in the Soviet Union before Khrushchev eventually took over sole leadership of the nation. For over twenty years of communist control of China, speculation has continued about who will become the political leader upon Mao Tse-Tung's death. The succession to power is thus generally a major problem in totalitarian societies, but even democratic nations do not always take account of the problem: Great Britain, for example, has no official designated to succeed immediately to the Prime Ministership.

In contrast, the United States Constitution (Article II, Section 1), together with an act of Congress passed in 1947, provides that in the event of the death of the President, his resignation, or his removal from office,* the Vice President shall succeed to the office. If he cannot (for example, if Mr. Johnson had been killed by the assassin too), the Speaker of the House of Representatives would, after resigning his office, become President. If he could not do so, succession would go to the President *pro tempore* of the Senate and then to the cabinet officials, beginning with the Secretary of State and on down the line in chronological order of the establishment of the executive departments. Thus barring a major disaster that simultaneously eliminated many high government officials (the President, Vice President, Speaker of the House, President *pro tempore* of the Senate, plus cabinet officials), the continuity of the presidential office is assured under our political system.

The Constitution, including the Twenty-fifth Amendment (1967), also provides for another difficult situation that has troubled the nation several times: the disability (sometimes called inability) of the President. (The most serious instances of presidential inability were President James Garfield's confinement to bed for eighty days until he ultimately died of an

---

*No President has ever resigned, nor has any ever been removed, though Andrew Johnson almost suffered that fate. The House voted impeachment charges against him, but the Senate failed by one vote of the necessary two-thirds majority to find him guilty of such charges.

assassin's bullet, Woodrow Wilson's incapacity for 280 days following a stroke he suffered on a speaking tour to win support for the League of Nations, and the 143-day recovery period after Dwight Eisenhower's heart attack.) If, for example, President Kennedy had been wounded, not killed, by the assassin, and had been unable to discharge the powers and duties of the office, Vice President Johnson would have temporarily assumed them. In such circumstances the Vice President serves as Acting President until the President declares that he is able to resume the powers and duties of the office. However, should the Vice President and the cabinet (or some other body designated by Congress) declare that the President is unable to resume such powers and duties, Congress ultimately decides the issue. If both President Kennedy and Johnson had been disabled, then temporary succession to the office would have followed the same line as that for permanent succession.*

The Twenty-fifth Amendment also provides for another problem that the nation has faced nine times: a vacancy in the office of the Vice President. Now, if that should occur, the President would nominate a new Vice President who must be confirmed by a majority vote of both houses of Congress. As a result of this Amendment, it is unlikely that succession to the Presidency will go beyond the Vice President unless something happened to both officials simultaneously, in which case the succession described above would take effect.

Thus the continuity of the presidential office is much more assured today than it was earlier in the nation's history. The remainder of the chapter analyzes the kind of office that was originally established by the Founding Fathers, together with the changes that have occurred in it over the years.

THE ESTABLISHMENT
OF THE PRESIDENCY

As we saw in Chapter 2, the experiences under the Articles of Confederation had demonstrated vividly that the national government could not carry on executive activities through legislative committees. Therefore, those who gathered in Philadelphia were convinced that the new government required some kind of separate executive branch. They did not agree by any means, however, about what the nature and powers of the executive should be.

There was even some question of establishing a monarchy: as John Jay put it in a letter to George Washington, "Shall we have a king?" Of the

*The Twentieth Amendment provides for a similar succession if the President-elect dies before he takes office, if no President is chosen by the beginning of the term (as, for example, when no candidate receives a majority of the electoral votes and the House has not yet chosen the President from among the three top candidates), or if the President-elect fails to qualify for the office (if he were under thirty-five years of age, for example).

fifty-five delegates at the Constitutional Convention, however, only Hamilton seemed willing to seriously consider the British model, which he considered the "best in the world." Others either opposed it on principle or recognized, as John Dickinson of Delaware put it, that a monarchy was "out of the question." The American experience under George III and the colonial governors sent as emissaries of the king had created a climate of opinion that excluded any kind of monarchy, however limited it might be.

There were, however, other American models to consider: the state governorships of the day. For the most part these were weak offices overshadowed by state legislatures, but there were two exceptions: New York and Massachusetts both provided for independent governors vested with important political powers. That the governors of these two states served effectively without endangering political freedom convinced many of the delegates that a strong Chief Executive accountable to the people was not to be equated with a tyrannical king or colonial governor.

Two disparate concepts concerning the nature and powers of the national executive emerged. One was the idea of a "weak" executive whose primary function would be to put into effect the will of the legislature. To this end, a plural executive would be established, or even if one man did head the branch, a powerful council would share his powers and hold him in check. The Congress would choose the Chief Executive for a limited term; moreover, he could not be reappointed immediately and would even be subject to removal by the legislative body during his term of office. The powers of the executive would be limited and in essence delegated to him by Congress, which would also make appointments to the executive branch and exercise the treaty- and war-making powers. This concept of the office provided for no executive veto of laws passed by the Congress.

At the other extreme was the idea of a "strong" executive, independent of the Congress, exercising important functions in the new government. Under this concept a single Chief Executive, chosen by some means other than legislative appointment, would have no limit placed on his tenure. If he were to be removable at all, it would be only for certain definite, enumerated reasons, and then only after impeachment by a judicial body or the legislature. His powers would be derived from the Constitution and not be subject to legislative interference. He would appoint judicial and diplomatic officials and participate in the execution of foreign affairs, including the making of treaties. He would have a veto over legislation passed by Congress, a power he would exercise either alone or in conjunction with the judiciary. Finally, either there would be no executive council at all, or if one did exist, it would merely be an advisory body whose actions would not bind the Chief Executive.

In the initial stages of the Convention it appeared that the delegates would create an essentially "weak" executive. The New Jersey Plan called for a plural executive chosen by Congress; members would be eligible for a single term and be removable by the national legislative body on application of the majority of the executives of the states. Federal officials would be empowered to execute federal laws and to direct, but not take command of, military operations. The Virginia resolution provided for an executive (it was vague on whether the executive was to be single or plural) chosen by the Congress and with no right to hold a second term. The powers were limited to executing national laws and implementing rights vested in Congress by the Confederation. Thus neither of the two major plans before the Convention envisioned a strong Chief Executive.

In the course of the Convention's deliberations, however, the office was strengthened. A decision made early by the Committee of the Whole to provide for a single executive was a major victory for the friends of a strong Presidency. Subsequent Convention decisions—to which the work of the key Committees on Detail and on Style (James Wilson was a key figure in the former, and Gouverneur Morris in the latter) contributed—eventually led to an independent Chief Executive with considerable political powers.

The Presidency created by the Convention resembles in many respects the strong-executive model described earlier. He is chosen by some method other than legislative appointment (electoral college), is eligible to succeed himself, and can be removed only for specific causes (treason, high crimes, and misdemeanors), and then only upon the vote of two-thirds of the members of the Senate. He is not dependent on the Congress for his authority; rather, specific powers are granted to him by the Constitution. In addition, as a result of the efforts of Gouverneur Morris, he is given broad undefined authority by the opening sentence of Article II: "The executive Power shall be vested in a President of the United States of America."

At the same time, the President does not enjoy all the prerogatives of the strong-executive model. Although he has the veto power, it is not absolute, since his action can be overridden by a two-thirds vote in each of the two houses of Congress. Moreover, his appointment power is subject to the approval of the Senate, as is his authority to negotiate treaties. Thus although the Founding Fathers did not create a council that shares all the Chief Executive's powers with him, they did grant the upper chamber of the national legislature a check on certain presidential actions.

Why did the Convention move from an essentially weak concept of the executive to a final version that closely fits the strong-executive model? Individual delegates certainly played a part in the outcome. The efforts of Pennsylvanians Wilson and Morris (who had also helped create the strong New York governorship), Rufus King and Elbridge Gerry of Massachusetts, Charles Pinckney and John Rutledge of South Carolina, Alexander Hamilton of New York, and others, helped shape the Convention's decisions all along the way. George Washington, too, was a key figure in the process even though he never spoke to the issue personally. Pierce Butler, a delegate from South Carolina, described that contribution in a letter written after the Convention completed its deliberations: "Nor . . . do I believe that they [the President's powers] would have been so great had not many of the members cast their eyes toward George Washington as President, and shaped their ideas of the powers to be given to a President by their opinions of his virtue."

Other factors also played a role in the final decision. Because the powers of the Congress were increased as compared to those of the former Confederation legislature, some delegates came to the opinion that a strong executive was needed to counterbalance the new legislative body. As political scientist Joseph Kallenbach has pointed out, there is even some indication that during the course of the proceedings an alliance was formed between the supporters of a strong Chief Executive and delegates from the small states, an alliance that furthered the interests of both groups. Evidence of a coalition is particularly noticeable in the recommendations of the Committee on Postponed Matters and Unfinished Business granting the President and Senate joint responsibilities in the appointment of executive officials and the making of treaties, and making the Senate, rather than the Supreme Court, the trial body in impeachment cases. It is also worth noting that both the President and the small states benefit from the electoral college arrangement: the President is selected initially by a process that does not involve the Congress directly, but if no candidate receives an electoral majority, the House, voting by states, not individuals, chooses the Chief Executive.

Controversy over the executive continued after the convention adjourned. George Mason of Virginia, one of the delegates who refused to sign the Constitution, charged that the provisions relating to the Presidency would prove to be a device for an "elective monarch"; this sentiment was shared by Luther Martin of Maryland, who also left the document unsigned. Moreover, some state-ratifying conventions proposed that the first Congress initiate amendments restricting the President's eligibility for reelection as well as limiting certain of his powers. Unlike the situation with respect to a Bill of Rights, however, Congress declined to act on any of these proposed amendments. Washington's presence in the highest office in the land undoubtedly helped to allay fears over the possible abuse of executive power.

Certain amendments to the Constitution do change the executive article somewhat: the Twelfth, on the choosing of the President and Vice President; the Twentieth, pertaining to the beginning of their term; the Twenty-second, which limits the tenure of the Chief Executive; and the Twenty-fifth, about presidential disability and succession. Yet the essential constitutional framework of the presidential office remains as it was created almost two centuries ago. Most of the vast changes in the Presidency since that time have arisen, not from formal legal alterations in its structure, but rather from informal political customs and precedents.

THE GROWTH OF THE PRESIDENCY

One of the dominant trends in American political life has been the growth of the Presidency. The legislative and judicial branches of the national government have also increased in power and influence over the years, but not at the same pace. Thus the separation of powers is similar to the division of powers as described in Chapter 3: all branches (like all levels of government) have augmented their political authority, but some have done so more than others.

Although the over-all trend has been in the direction of a more powerful Presidency, growth has not been constant. The office occupied by Grant was not as potent as that of Lincoln. Conditions in American society, the people's reaction to them, and the personal qualities of particular incumbents have affected the functions and influence of the Presidency.

CONDITIONS AND FACTORS AFFECTING
THE GROWTH OF THE PRESIDENCY

In defending a single Chief Executive in *The Federalist Papers*, Alexander Hamilton emphasized what he termed "energy" as a desirable characteristic of good government. He went on to suggest that energy was particularly associated with the executive, as compared to a legislative body. As he put it: "Decision, activity, secrecy and despatch will generally characterize the proceedings of one man in a much more eminent degree than the proceedings of any greater number; and in proportion as the number is increased, these qualities will be diminished."

More than any other single factor this axiom of human behavior so clearly put by Hamilton explains the growth of presidential power and influence. The need for "decision, activity, secrecy and despatch" has become increasingly necessary to a leading power in an interdependent world. If military action is contemplated, the President as Commander-in-Chief of the armed forces has a crucial role to play in decisions on committing American troops. Such decisions need to be made not only with "despatch," but with secrecy.

Even without military action the President plays a dominant part in foreign affairs in general. As we will see in Chapter 17, he has a number of powers—such as the negotiation of treaties that require senatorial approval and of executive agreements that do not, the initiation as well as the breaking off of diplomatic relationships with foreign governments, and the choosing of representatives abroad—that make his voice the crucial one in foreign affairs. Moreover, as in military matters, diplomacy requires a certain amount of secrecy. As the late British scholar Harold Laski expressed it, "Diplomatic negotiations are like a proposal of marriage; they must be made in private even if the engagement is later discussed in public."

The President's role in crises, however, is not confined to military and foreign affairs. To an increasing extent the American people have demanded that the national government "do something" about economic depressions, social problems such as race relations, the plight of the cities, and other pressing concerns. Once again such expectations have enhanced the influence of the Presidency, for a President can move swiftly and forcefully to help counteract mass unemployment, send troops to assist in integrating the schools, or deal with major riots such as the one in Detroit in 1967. Thus the Presidency has grown in power and influence as the American people have accepted the concept of the positive state, that is, one in which the government—particularly the national one—plays a major role in meeting (and hopefully, on occasion, even preventing) the many crises of our troubled society.

Hamilton's conviction that a large assembly of men have trouble in taking decisive action has been borne out by the experience of the American Congress. As he suggested, the problem becomes greater as the number is increased; this is precisely what happened as the number of senators and representatives grew from 26 and 65 respectively in the first Congress to 100 and 435 today. The present American political system makes it especially difficult for legislators to move quickly on problems. The variety of viewpoints represented by congressmen from different kinds of constituencies in a large and diverse country prevents the national legislature from making the rapid decisions that are called for in a crisis. Also contributing to congressional sluggishness are the way power is distributed within the two chambers and the predominance in positions of authority (especially the chairmanships of standing committees) of senior legislators from safe districts who are inclined to support the *status quo* rather than to respond to demands for change in society. Because the Congress often cannot, or will not, act decisively when the occasion demands, people turn to the President to do so.

Hamilton may not have foreseen another development that has led to the expansion of presidential power and influence: the democratization of the selection process for Chief Executive. (Given his distrust of the common man, he certainly would have disapproved of the development.) The shift from choice by elites in the various states to a national popularity contest has given the President a nationwide constituency that no other officeholder (except his political inferior, the Vice President) can claim. As a result he is the most visible figure in American politics and the one official from whom the public expects action and leadership. Because the President is accountable at the ballot box to the American people as a whole, he can claim them as his following and as support for his policies.

All these conditions have contributed to the natural growth of the Presidency, uninhibited by the constitutional provisions relating to the office.

The indefinite phraseology of the opening sentence of Article II of the Constitution—"The executive power shall be vested in a President of the United States"—has been, in effect, a grant of broad authority for bold and innovative ventures. Supplementing this general grant of presidential power are other clauses—for instance, "he shall take Care that the Laws be faithfully executed"—on which Presidents can draw for legal justification of their actions. Woodrow Wilson may have exaggerated the situation somewhat when he claimed in 1908 (five years before he occupied the Presidency himself) that the Chief Executive "has the right in law and conscience to be as big a man as he can," but few students of the Presidency would deny the great potential of the office.

Wilson's observation points up still another major factor in the development of the Presidency: the important part that individual Presidents have played in the process. Neither the natural conditions conducive to the increase in presidential power and influence nor the legal potentialities of the office in themselves guarantee decisive actions. The crisis that both James Buchanan and Abraham Lincoln faced was virtually identical. Buchanan, however, took the position that he was powerless to prevent secession whereas Lincoln took bold steps to try to counter it.

"STRONG" PRESIDENTS
AND THE GROWTH OF THE OFFICE

Those men who have contributed in a major way to the growth of the office are generally called "strong" or "great" Presidents, or as Edwin Hargrove has recently termed them,* Presidents of "action." These terms imply certain kinds of behavior. A strong President does not wait for the Congress to take the leadership in political matters but initiates his own actions on major problems. He does not shrink from political conflict with the Congress, and he protects the executive branch from undue interference by the legislature. Moreover, a strong President leads not only the Congress but also the American people, charting new directions in public policy. Finally, he uses the full powers of the office and, if the need arises, stretches those powers to accomplish his purposes. A strong President leaves an office that is a more powerful institution than the one he inherited; he establishes procedures and customs that successors tend to follow.

Students of the Presidency do not all agree about which Chief Executives have had such a major impact on the office and American society in general that they should be labeled "strong" or "great," but there is a general

---

*Hargrove's term represents an attempt to be more neutral in categorizing Presidents; in this spirit he uses the phrase "of restraint" rather than "weak" or "small" for the less assertive ones. It is important to keep in mind that "strong" is not necessarily to be equated with "good": a President can exercise power effectively, but for the wrong purposes.

consensus on at least seven men.* The following discussion focuses on the contribution these individuals have made to the expansion of the Presidency into the world's most important political office.

George Washington. Because George Washington was the first person to occupy the Presidency, whatever he did established precedents for his successors. He himself clearly recognized his situation; within two weeks after his inauguration he expressed the opinion that ". . . things which appear of little importance in themselves . . . may have great and durable consequences from having been established at the commencement of a new general government." With this thought in mind, Washington embarked upon his Presidency determined not only to meet the needs of his times but also to insure that no action of his would jeopardize the faith that the people had placed in his leadership or in the high office he occupied.

Before Washington retired voluntarily after his two terms, he had taken firm control of his administration and established precedents that would affect the conduct of the executive branch for generations to come. Although the Constitution nowhere mentions a presidential cabinet, Washington soon turned to his group of department heads for advice on political matters. (In so doing, he expanded his constitutional right to gather their individual opinions in writing on subjects relating to the duties of their offices; the expansion encompassed soliciting their oral judgments as a group on any matter he put before them.) By forcing Secretary of State Edmund Marshall to resign because of his views opposing the Jay Treaty, he established the precedent that department heads should be loyal to the President's policies.

The Washington administration also saw the rise of legislative leadership by the executive. The broad economic program authored by Secretary of the Treasury Alexander Hamilton and steered through the Congress by his efforts paved the way for the close liaison established by subsequent executive department heads with the Congress. Although the initiatives in this case were more the product of Hamilton than of Washington, the latter lent his prestige and political support to the efforts, thus providing an example that subsequent Presidents would follow in getting public policies enacted into law.

In foreign policy Washington moved quickly to establish the prerogatives of the President. He received Citizen Genêt as an emissary from the new French government, setting the precedent that the President has the right to receive ambassadors and to grant diplomatic recognition to foreign countries. When the Senate delayed his efforts to get its advice on treaty negotiations with certain Indian tribes by referring the matter to committee,

*In addition to the seven discussed here four other Presidents—John Adams, James Polk, Grover Cleveland, and Harry Truman—are most often mentioned as "strong" Chief Executives.

Washington stalked out of the chamber in anger, vowing never again to bring such a matter to the Senate. Since that date no President has sought that body's counsel on the negotiation of a treaty, despite the constitutional instruction that he "shall make such treaties with its advice."* When the House of Representatives demanded that he present papers pertaining to the negotiation of the Jay Treaty, he refused to do so on the grounds that the Constitution granted the lower chamber of Congress no authority in such matters.

It is difficult to overemphasize the importance of Washington to the existence of the new government that was struggling to achieve legitimacy among a divided people, many of them suspicious of the Constitution and of a presidential office which Patrick Henry said "squinted toward monarchy." On occasion Washington lent his great prestige to the maintenance of "law and order" in the new republic, as he did in sending troops against the farmers of Western Pennsylvania who threatened to rebel at paying an excise tax on liquor. (On the approach of the military force the rebel force disintegrated.) Yet Washington's temperate approach to public affairs was demonstrated vividly in the same incident when he pardoned two of the ringleaders of the Whiskey Rebellion who were convicted of treason. With all his initiatives in conducting domestic and foreign affairs and in asserting and protecting the prerogatives of the executive branch, he remained a constitutional and republican official. At a turbulent time in the life of a new nation, when conditions were ripe for the kind of monarchical rule that prevailed in most countries of the world, this was an astonishing achievement.

Thomas Jefferson. The most significant contribution of Thomas Jefferson was to put the President into the role of political party leader. Using the Republican party members in the Congress as his medium, he proceeded to dominate the political affairs of the legislature. His control extended to decisions of the party caucus (which, unlike today's counterpart, did exercise significant powers over legislation) and to the appointment and removal of standing committee members, as well as party officials in the Congress. So potent was his leadership that he pushed the drastic Embargo Act of 1807 through both houses in one day. His control was not restricted to crisis situations alone, however. It is a testament to Jefferson's domination that he did not veto a single piece of legislation: no law he seriously opposed was reported out of the Congress during his eight years in office.

Jefferson also epitomized the President who stretches the powers of the office when the occasion demands it. When Napoleon unexpectedly offered

*As a matter of political strategy Presidents often seek the advice of influential individual senators. Woodrow Wilson's failure to consult with prominent Republican senators about the Versailles Treaty is reputed to have contributed to his failure to get it approved.

French lands (the Louisiana Purchase) for a minimal price, he put Jefferson in a quandary: as a believer in a strict construction of the powers of the national government (recall from Chapter 3 that he held the establishment of a bank to be beyond its authority), Jefferson doubted the constitutionality of acquiring foreign territory (in fact, he favored a constitutional amendment on the matter), yet he was torn by fears of losing the chance to consummate such a favorable agreement. Putting aside his constitutional qualms, Jefferson chose direct action. More than one President since that time has decided to act in response to political rather than legal considerations.

Andrew Jackson. Jefferson exercised political leadership by working through his party organization in Congress; Andrew Jackson became a strong President by asserting his independence of the legislative branch. In fact, his administration was characterized by conflicts with Congress. In a battle over the national bank (supported by the legislature, but opposed by Jackson), the President forced the Secretary of Treasury to resign so that he could place a friend, Roger Taney, in office for the purpose of withdrawing funds from the national institution and depositing them in state banks. (The Senate censured him for this action, but he was later successful in having the censure motion lifted.) Similar conflicts also developed over opposition to his nominations. The Senate turned down Martin Van Buren as ambassador to the Court of St. James's; it also refused to sanction Taney's appointment to the Supreme Court on three separate occasions. (Jackson, however, was to have his revenge: Taney ultimately became Chief Justice and in that capacity swore in Van Buren as President.) The full range of Jackson's disputes with the Congress is reflected in his use of the veto: he exercised it on no less than twelve occasions, the first President to use it to any significant degree.

Jackson did not recoil from other kinds of political conflicts. He asserted his independence of the judicial branch by taking the position that the President has as much right as the Supreme Court to judge the constitutionality of legislation. Moreover, when John Marshall issued a ruling with which Jackson disagreed, he invited the Chief Justice to enforce it himself. He also acted decisively to protect the rights of the national government against the states: when South Carolina threatened to secede from the Union if a high-tariff law was enforced, Jackson issued a proclamation declaring the action treasonous and pushed a bill through Congress giving him the power to use force to prevent it. (No other state joined South Carolina, and its officials backed down on their threat.)

Jackson's vigorous actions in defiance of other branches and levels of government were possible because he was the first President with a popular constituency. Chosen not by the congressional caucus but by a national convention reflecting party support at the grass-roots level, Jackson considered himself the "tribune of the people." When he got into conflicts with congressmen, he appealed over their heads to the population at large for support of his policies; to keep control of his administration he instituted the "spoils system" (so named for the idea "to the victor belongs the spoils") to reward his political friends and punish his enemies. Jackson was a key figure in transforming the Presidency from a somewhat elitist office to a popular one.

Abraham Lincoln. The nineteenth-century Presidency reached the full zenith of its powers during the wartime administration of Abraham Lincoln. In fact, some students of the office consider the eleven-week period from the outbreak of hostilities at Fort Sumter, South Carolina, in April 1861 until the new President called the Congress into special session the following July 4 as a time of executive dictatorship. During those momentous weeks Lincoln authorized a series of drastic actions: he called up the militia and volunteers; threw a blockade around Southern ports; expanded the Army and Navy beyond the limits set by statute; pledged the credit of the United States without congressional authority to do so; closed the mails to "treasonous" correspondence; arrested persons suspected of disloyalty; and suspended the writ of *habeas corpus* in areas around the nation's capital. Admitting that most of these matters lay within the jurisdiction of the Congress rather than the Presidency, Lincoln took the position that they were done because of popular demand and public necessity, and with the trust "that Congress would readily ratify them." Thus he deliberately chose not to call the national legislature into special session until he was ready to do so, and then he presented it with accomplished facts.

Although Lincoln's Presidency was most dramatic in those early days of hostilities, he continued to exercise firm control over the war during the entire time he was in the White House. As we saw in Chapter 4, he did not hesitate to control the mails and newspapers, to confiscate property of persons suspected of impeding the conduct of the war, and even to try civilians in military courts in areas in which the regular courts were open. To justify such actions, he appealed to military necessity, asserting that the "Commander-in-Chief" clause and the "shall-take-care" (that the laws be faithfully executed) clause combined to create a "war power" for the President that was virtually unlimited. Lincoln's success in defending that position is demonstrated by the fact that neither the Congress nor the courts placed any significant limits on his actions.

Theodore Roosevelt. An internal domestic crisis shaped Lincoln's Presidency in the middle of the nineteenth-century; for Theodore Roosevelt the office was vitally affected by the emergence of America as a world power at the beginning of the twentieth. Concerned over the rise of Japan as a threat to American interests in the Pacific, Roosevelt sought and obtained a major role in negotiating the Portsmouth Treaty that terminated the Russo-

Japanese War of 1905. In this hemisphere "Teddie" pursued a policy of intervening in the affairs of neighbors to the South when it might further what he conceived to be the national interests of the United States. Troops were sent to Santo Domingo and Cuba for this reason. Even more blatant was Roosevelt's role in fomenting the rebellion of Panama against Colombia so that the United States could acquire rights to build a canal. An avowed nationalist with the desire to expand America's influence in international affairs, Roosevelt ordered the navy around the world as a demonstration of American military might. When Congress balked at the expense, he countered that there were sufficient funds to get the navy halfway there; if the lawmakers wanted the fleet back home, they would have to provide the money for the return trip.

Roosevelt also responded vigorously to the other major development of his era: the rapid industrialization of American life. He had charges pressed against corporations that violated antitrust laws, and he pushed legislation through Congress giving the Interstate Commerce Commission power to lower railroad rates. When coal mine operators in Colorado refused to agree to arbitration of a dispute with their workers, Roosevelt threatened to have army troops seize the mines and administer them as a receiver for the government. He thus became the first American Chief Executive to intervene in a labor dispute who did *not* take management's side. Beyond this, Roosevelt championed major reclamation and conservation projects, as well as meat inspection and pure food and drug laws.

Perhaps most important of all, Roosevelt did much to popularize the Presidency after a third of a century of lackluster leaders. (Of the eight men who served from Lincoln through McKinley, only Grover Cleveland is considered to be at all significant.) A dynamic personality, an attractive family, and love of the public spotlight enabled Teddie to focus the nation's attention on himself and his position. Considering himself (as did Jackson) the "tribune of the people" and the office a "bully pulpit" from which the incumbent should set the tone of American life, Roosevelt was the first President to provide facilities for the members of the press and to hold informal news conferences to link the Presidency with the people.

Woodrow Wilson. No man came to the Presidency with a clearer concept of the office than Woodrow Wilson. A professor of political science who in the 1880s had written a perceptive analysis describing Congress as the dominant political force, Wilson had decided by 1908 (when he wrote another book on the national government) that the Presidency was potentially the more important political institution. (Roosevelt's administration contributed to Wilson's change of mind on the subject.) For Wilson the means by which that potential could be transformed into reality was imitation of the British Prime Minister in leading Congress and the nation at large.

Wilson used various techniques in implementing his Prime Minister concept of the Presidency. A skilled public speaker, he was the first President since John Adams to go before the Congress in person to give his State-of-the-Union message. He held frequent meetings with legislative leaders both at the White House and at a previously seldom-used President's Room in the Capitol. Like Jefferson, he was a powerful party chief who worked through congressional leaders and the Democratic caucus to influence legislative decisions. He also did not hesitate to take his case to the people: on one occasion when special-interest spokesmen made concerted efforts to defeat a low-tariff bill he favored, Wilson made a public statement decrying the fact that "the people at large should have no lobby and be voiceless in these matters, while great bodies of astute men seek to create an artificial opinion and to overcome the interests of the public for their private profit."

These techniques were highly successful as Wilson took the leadership in both domestic and foreign affairs. In his first term in office he pushed through a vast program of economic reform, which included major measures lowering tariffs, raising taxes for the well-to-do, creating a central banking system, regulating unfair trade practices, providing cheap loans to farmers, and establishing an eight-hour day for railroad employees. When the United States became involved in World War I during his second term, rather than prosecute it through unilateral executive action as Lincoln did, Wilson went to the Congress and obtained authority to control the economic, as well as the military, aspect of the war. He was thus granted the power to allocate food and fuel, to license trade with the enemy and its allies, to censor the mail, to regulate the foreign language press of the country, and to operate railroads, water transportation systems, and telegraph and telephone facilities. Only in the latter part of his second term did his leadership falter, when the Senate refused to approve the Versailles Treaty, including its provision for Wilson's dream of a League of Nations. Even that failure, however, helped to pave the way a generation later for the country's acceptance of the United Nations.

Franklin D. Roosevelt. When Franklin Roosevelt came into office in March 1933, business failures were legion, twelve million of his countrymen were unemployed, banks all over the country were closed or doing business under restrictions, and the American people had lost confidence in their leaders as well as in themselves. Counseling the nation in his inaugural address that "We have nothing to fear but fear itself," the new Chief Executive moved into action—a four-day bank holiday was declared, and an emergency banking bill was prepared within seventy-two hours and pushed through Congress within a day's time. During his first one hundred days in office, the nation was to witness a social and economic revolution in the form of Roosevelt's "New Deal" as Congress adopted a series of far-reaching governmental programs insuring bank deposits, providing crop payments for farmers, establishing codes of fair competition for industry, granting labor the right to organize, providing relief and jobs for the unemployed, and creating the Tennessee Valley Authority (a government corporation) to develop that region. With these measures and other programs that followed (Social Security, public housing, unemployment compensation, and the like), Roosevelt was to establish the concept of the "positive state" in America—a government that had the obligation to take the leadership in providing for the welfare of all the people.

Roosevelt did not ignore relations with other countries. Soon after he took office he recognized the Soviet Union diplomatically, embarked on a "Good Neighbor policy" toward South Americans, and pushed through a Reciprocal Trade Program lowering tariffs with other nations. In his second term FDR began the slow and difficult task of preparing the nation for its eventual entry into World War II by funneling aid to the Allies, trading fifty "over-age" destroyers to Britain for defense bases in this hemisphere, and obtaining the passage of the nation's first peace-time draft. As FDR himself put it, after Pearl Harbor, "Old Dr. New Deal" became "Dr. Win-the War," taking over the economic control of the war effort granted him by Congress and establishing the victorious strategy of concentrating on defeating Germany first (rather than Japan). And while the hostilities were still going on, he took the leadership in setting up the United Nations. (Unfortunately, he died before he could see the organization established in 1945.)

Roosevelt was also an innovator whose actions left a major impact on the presidential office itself. Not only was he an effective legislative leader, but he was also responsible for a major reorganization of the executive branch, including the creation of the Executive Office of the President, which we will examine in the following chapter. Most important of all, FDR was the most effective molder of public opinion that the nation has ever known. It was he who pioneered in the use of "fireside chats" over radio to explain his actions to the people. In addition, he raised the presidential press conference to new heights as a tool of public persuasion. As a man who could take idealistic goals, reduce them to manageable and practical programs, and then sell them to the Congress and the American people, Roosevelt had no peer.

Thus a variety of influences have contributed to the growth of the American Presidency: the press of foreign and domestic events, the inability and unwillingness of Congress to assume leadership over such matters, and the actions of strong Chief Executives that established precedents for their successors to draw on. In fact, the public has come to expect all Chief Executives to exhibit the initiatives of Presidents of "action." In the process, the office has become more and more complex and demanding. The kinds of varied responsibilities contemporary Presidents face, as well as the methods they utilize to discharge those responsibilities, are examined in the following chapter.

Selected Readings

There are many accounts of President Kennedy's assassination, but the one on which I have relied most heavily is William Manchester, *The Death of a President, November 20–November 25, 1963* (New York: Harper & Row, 1967).

There are several excellent general treatments of the Presidency. Two of the best recent ones are Joseph Kallenbach, *The American Chief Executive: The Presidency and the Governorship* (New York: Harper & Row, 1966), and Louis Koenig, *The Chief Executive*, rev. ed., (New York: Harcourt, Brace, 1968). Earlier studies included Edward Corwin's legalistic treatment of the office, *The President: Office and Powers, 1787–1948*, rev. ed. (New York: New York University Press, 1948), and two highly readable analyses: Sidney Hyman, *The American President* (New York: Harper & Row, 1954) and Clinton Rossiter, *The American Presidency* (New York: Harcourt, Brace, 1960).

Two studies treating of the problem of presidential disability are Ruth Silva, "Presidential Succession and Disability," in *Law and Contemporary Problems* (Autumn 1956), 646–663, and Richard Hansen, *The Year We Had No President* (Lincoln: University of Nebraska Press, 1962).

The best analysis of the establishment of the presidential office is contained in Chapter One of Kallenbach's book.

Analyses of the reasons for the growth of the Presidency, along with the contributions of individual Presidents, include Chapter One of Corwin, and Chapters Three and Five of Rossiter. An excellent book treating of "strong" Presidents, edited by Morton Borden, is *America's Ten Greatest Presidents* (Chicago: Rand McNally, 1961). A book analyzing three Presidents "of action" and three "of restraint" is Erwin Hargrove, *Presidential Leadership: Personality and Political Style* (New York: Macmillan, 1966).

CHAPTER 12

The Contemporary Executive

The Oval Room office of the President, in the West Wing of the White House. (United Press International)

I$_{\text{N A VERY REAL SENSE}}$ the American President stands at the center of the American political system. As the prime elected official, he is the head of his political party. At the same time he is expected to be the President of all the people, including those who voted against him. As such, he acts as the ceremonial head of the government; in addition, as a leader of a democratic nation, he both reflects and molds public opinion. Moreover, he must not only head the executive branch but also provide legislative leadership. Finally, he plays a dominant part in policy-making in both domestic and foreign affairs.

In this chapter, we will first explore four aspects of the Presidency: party matters, public opinion, legislation, and administration. Then we will look at the interrelationships among these aspects and at the ways in which a President tries to cope with the over-all problems of the office. (The President's part in the making of policy will be analyzed in Part IV.)

THE PRESIDENT AND HIS PARTY

Of the various activities of the President, that of party leader would have been least appreciated by the Founding Fathers, who visualized him as a neutral figure standing above conflict and promoting unity and justice in society. Yet it is expected today that the Chief Executive will be the avowed chief of the party that put him in the White House. It was, indeed, while President Kennedy was conducting party business—trying to restore some semblance of unity to the Texas Democratic organization—that he was cut down by an assassin's bullet.

The President's role as partisan leader involves him in all the major political activities of his party. He is expected to play some part in the election contests for various offices in our political system. As party chief, he also has the responsibility for identifying problems and for formulating programs to deal with them. Finally, the President has a major role in organizing and managing the government as a means of implementing his programs.

THE PRESIDENT AND ELECTORAL ACTIVITIES

Naturally the President's part in electoral activities is most pronounced as far as his own office is concerned. If a President decides to seek reelection, the renomination is normally his for the asking; he dominates every aspect of the convention—location, choice of major officers, party platform, and selection of his running mate—and makes strategic decisions regarding the general election campaign. Even when the incumbent President is not seeking reelection, if he chooses, he can influence the selection of his party's nominees.

American Presidents have also come to play an important part in midterm congressional elections. Even Dwight Eisenhower, who did not enjoy playing the role of partisan leader, gave some forty speeches in the 1954 campaign. President Kennedy took an active part in the 1962 congressional elections until the Cuban missile crisis forced him to cancel speaking engagements and return to Washington. And although Lyndon Johnson did not go on the campaign trail in 1966 (in part because the Vietnam war had made him so unpopular that many congressional candidates preferred that he stay away), the pattern of presidential involvement was restored (in fact, expanded) by Richard Nixon in 1970 when he traveled to more than twenty states on behalf of Republican candidates.

A popular President who does decide to campaign in the midterm elections has the difficult decision of determining which candidates he will work for. Should he concentrate on crucial competitive contests, or should he also assist close political friends who seem to be in no appreciable danger of being defeated but who seek his assistance anyway? Should he campaign in favor of important party figures even though they voted against him on a number of major legislative measures? If the President does not and an ignored man wins anyway, the latter may retaliate with even less support in the future; moreover, if his party's candidate loses, the opposition replacement may be even more opposed to the President's programs.

Because of such unattractive possibilities a President may be tempted to try to pick his party's nominees for Senate and House seats. As we saw in Chapter 8, however, this course of action violates the political custom of local determination. If there is local opposition, the President who gambles on intervention, only to have his protégé lose in a primary fight, risks a decline in political prestige and also the enmity of the winning candidate. For these reasons Presidents typically avoid overt involvement in spirited nomination contests.

If the battle lines in a congressional nomination have not been drawn, however, a President can influence the selection of congressional candidates by taking early action on behalf of certain individuals. President Kennedy, for example, encouraged individuals, such as Joseph Tydings, Jr. of Maryland, to seek a seat in Congress, and President Nixon persuaded some ten Republican members of the House to give up their seats to run for the Senate, where they would be more important politically to him. Thus Chief Executives attempt to build a base of support in Congress by personally recruiting men who share their general views on public affairs. Presidents also work discreetly behind the scenes through sympathetic state political leaders to interest certain individuals in running. They may also use their influence to funnel needed funds to candidates they favor.

Party leader: President Johnson joins the campaign of New York State Representative Joseph Resnick. (Wide World Photos)

A President's ability to affect the persons who are selected for Congress is limited, however. The large number of elections for the House of Representatives (435 every two years) precludes any significant presidential involvement in them. Even Presidents as popular as Dwight Eisenhower find it difficult to transfer popularity to others, especially in a nonpresidential election. In addition, an incumbent congressman is in a very strong electoral position: as long as he keeps his political fences mended with state and local party leaders and with his constituents, he has little to fear from presidential opposition. The difficulties a President faces in midterm elections is reflected in Mr. Nixon's experience in 1970: of the twenty-one Republican senatorial candidates for whom he campaigned in the general election, only eight won.

Yet it would be a mistake to write off the President's role in congressional campaigns as meaningless. In competitive states (as well as some congressional districts) a visit by the Chief Executive, a special public endorsement, or a channeling of funds to his party's candidate may provide the margin of victory. Furthermore, there is some evidence that national issues (as compared to state and local ones) are becoming more important, even in midterm elections, and that the fate of both Senate and House aspirants in many areas may turn on voters' regard for the current administration.

Thus even if the President does not become directly involved in a congressional race, his conduct in office may indirectly affect its outcome.

Despite the potentialities of the President's role as party leader, however, there are considerations that deter him from playing it on all occasions. Voting in the American Congress, as we found in Chapter 10, does not follow strictly partisan lines. President Eisenhower was dependent on votes from Democratic congressmen for many of his programs, particularly in foreign policy. Presidents Kennedy and Johnson also received crucial Republican support on civil rights legislation as a result of the efforts of the Republican Floor Leader in the Senate, Everett Dirksen. The Minority Leader also defended Johnson's Vietnam policies more vigorously than did many Democrats. In such circumstances, it was hardly surprising that neither Democratic President expended any genuine effort to get Dirksen defeated in Illinois.

Other factors also prompt some Presidents to play down their activities in midterm elections. If their party's candidates do not do well, the election may be interpreted as a repudiation of their administration. Campaign rhetoric can also be taken personally by members of the opposition party, making it more difficult for the President to get their future support for his legislative program. The Chief Executive may also be concerned that too much time spent on the campaign trail will create the impression in people's minds that he is not exerting enough effort on other important duties of his office; it may also detract from his image as the leader of all the American people.

Presidents resort to certain tactics to overcome these disadvantages. One is to schedule foreign visits (which emphasize the Chief Executive's nonpartisan role as the entire nation's representative) to coincide with congressional elections: Richard Nixon visited the Middle East and Mediterranean areas in early October 1970. Another is to make use of the Vice President: Spiro Agnew campaigned longer and in more states that year than Nixon did, and it was he, rather than the President, who attacked the opposition candidates in personal terms.* This practice permitted Nixon to take the "high road" in the campaign by stressing issues rather than personalities.

DEVELOPING PARTY PROGRAMS

One area of partisan activity that the President clearly dominates is the preparation of party programs for dealing with major national problems. An incumbent President has the biggest hand in the writing of the party platform at the national convention. He also has the opportunity to identify party issues and programs during the course of the campaign. He may choose to emphasize certain parts of the platform, ignore others, or even

---

*Nixon also let the Vice President handle the sticky job of criticizing Republican Senator Charles Goodell of New York who voted against the President on a number of key issues such as Vietnam and the ABM. Agnew even helped raise money for the victorious Conservative party candidate, James Buckley.

take stands at variance with those contained in the document. The equivocal statement in the 1928 Democratic platform, which stopped short of favoring the abolition of prohibition, was in effect rewritten by the party nominee that year, Al Smith, who openly advocated repeal of the Eighteenth Amendment.

Perhaps the most crucial role the President plays in developing party programs comes through his actions while in office. As we will see later in this chapter, he has the responsibility of initiating legislative proposals to be considered by the Congress. Included among them are programs initially mentioned in the party platform; others may emanate from other sources, including party leaders. The President is also in a position through his own actions to make good on campaign promises, as President Kennedy did in 1962 when he signed an executive order prohibiting discrimination in future housing constructed or financially guaranteed by the federal government.

PARTISAN INFLUENCES IN ORGANIZING
AND MANAGING THE GOVERNMENT

The extent to which presidential programs actually get implemented depends to a considerable degree on his influence over the party in the government. This group is composed of officials in the legislative and executive branches who are either elected under a partisan label or are appointed primarily because of their party activities or because it is expected that they will implement party views on public policy matters.

The President's control over his party in the legislature is distinctly limited. He doesn't have much to do with its composition, since most senators and congressmen are elected independently of him. Moreover, he has comparatively little influence over the organization of his party in Congress. Although some Presidents have played a major role in determining their party's legislative leadership (Thomas Jefferson did, for example), for the most part American Chief Executives have been chary of interfering with the right of Congress to choose its own men. Dwight Eisenhower was forced to work with Senate Republican Leader William Knowland whose views on foreign policy were quite different from his own. During part of John F. Kennedy's administration the Democratic Speaker of the House was John McCormack, a political enemy from Kennedy's home state.

The President does have more influence over the party in the executive branch, a matter we will examine in detail later in this chapter. The only other elected official, the Vice President, is his man, to be used or not as he sees fit. In addition, the President can make appointments to policy-making posts that both reward individuals for their service to the party and permit him to influence the administration of government programs. In particular, his closest political advisers on the White House staff constitute what is, in effect, the President's personal party: of the twenty-eight individuals Nixon appointed when he took office, twenty were key people in his 1968 presidential campaign. Yet the overwhelming number of the some three million civilian employees of the executive branch are neither appointed by the President nor removable by him.

THE PRESIDENT AS HEAD OF STATE
AND LEADER OF PUBLIC OPINION

As explained in Chapter 5, public opinion refers to the attitudes of private citizens that affect the operation of government—general attitudes about the nation, its form of government, and major public officials, as well as particular views of specific political matters, such as social problems and policies for dealing with them.

To a considerable degree the American President is the major focus of each of these elements of public opinion. Like the British monarch our Chief Executive is the symbol, the personification, of the nation and the state. It is the President who inspires feelings of loyalty and patriotism, particularly in times of crises when he becomes the rallying point for national efforts. Thus political friends and foes of Franklin Roosevelt both turned to him for leadership when the Japanese attacked Pearl Harbor in December 1941.

Even though this is a democratic nation, the Presidency is surrounded with the trappings of ceremony and pomp. The inauguration of a President bears certain resemblances to the coronation of a king, complete with the taking of an oath in the midst of notables and the multitudes. Ceremonial aspects of the office include the display of the presidential seal and the playing of "Hail to the Chief" when he arrives at an occasion, along with a round of traditional duties: visiting other nations and entertaining foreign heads of state when they visit Washington, D.C., lighting the giant Christmas tree on the White House lawn, throwing out the first ball at the opening of the baseball season, proclaiming a variety of "weeks" devoted to a host of good causes, and the like. All such activities emphasize the role that the Chief Executive plays in embodying the nation, its government, and its ideals.

Unlike the British monarch, however, the American President not only "reigns" but also "rules." As the nation's leading political figure, he is expected to develop and put into effect controversial policies that are binding on the entire populace. In doing so, he must lead public opinion on vital public issues; at the same time he must respect the broad limits that public attitudes (particularly those of interest groups) place on his actions.

The size and composition of the President's "public" varies with circumstances. He may have virtually the entire nation as an audience for his inauguration or a major speech in time of crisis. But his target may be much smaller, as for an address on a current issue to the annual meeting of a major interest group such as the NAM or the AFL-CIO. The President must even take into account the attitudes of foreign publics on certain matters: one of the considerations that led President Kennedy to stop the shipment of Russian missiles into Cuba by blockade rather than by invasion (see pages 428–430) was his assessment of foreign reaction, particularly in Latin America.

As the most visible political figure in the nation, the President is constantly in the public spotlight. Virtually everything about him—including his golf score, favorite foods and songs, health, and reading habits—becomes a matter of intense interest. In fact, public attention focuses on his entire family. Yet a President cannot depend on public curiosity alone (much of which is trivial) for success in wielding political power. He must establish close ties with a variety of publics in order to convert personal popularity into political effectiveness. Such ties enable him to help mold public opinion, while informing himself about the attitudes of citizens.

PERSONAL TRIPS

One of the earliest means developed for communicating with the American public was the "Grand Tour," first used by George Washington in a two-month trip through the South in 1791. Enduring both the rigors of travel and a surfeit of wining and dining by citizens eager to please the new Chief Executive, Washington found value in the trip. According to his own account of the venture, it both reassured him that the new Federalist government was popular in the South as well as in New England and enabled

Head of state: President Nixon with President Tito of Yugoslavia during an official visit to that country. (Tanjugfoto Belgrade/Pix)

him to learn with more accuracy than he could have gained by any other means the "disposition" of the people.

Modern Presidents have continued the Washington tradition: Johnson and Nixon both spoke of the invigorating feeling they experienced in getting away from Washington, D.C., and establishing contacts with the people in other parts of the country. (Smarting from the political in-fighting in the nation's capital, Presidents find the adulation of crowds a good tonic; it also reassures them that the popularity they enjoyed on the campaign trail has not disappeared.) Many Presidents today find it helpful to extend their travels abroad as evidenced by Eisenhower's trip to eleven nations, Kennedy's tour of Europe with his wife, and Nixon's visit to the Mediterranean area. Such ventures capture the attention of a variety of publics, including the people of the countries visited, ethnic groups at home (Irish-Americans, Italian-Americans, and the like) with ties to those nations, and the general American populace.

Not all presidential trips, however, turn out to be triumphant. The most notable failure was Woodrow Wilson's ill-starred attempt in 1919 to take his case for the Versailles peace treaty and the League of Nations to the American people when these proposals ran into political difficulties in the Senate. He collapsed near the end of the tour and was disabled for a long period. He was particularly discouraged because his efforts went completely for naught: the American people failed to respond to his pleas, and some historians have concluded that not a single senator's vote was changed by his difficult journey.

Presidents contemplating trips, for whatever purpose, face the possibility not only of failure but also, even when successful, of draining away valuable time from other facets of their demanding job. Because of these hazards Presidents in recent years have commissioned Vice Presidents to make journeys for them both at home and abroad. Moreover, leading cabinet members are also frequently dispatched to explain administration policies to interested publics and to get their reactions to such policies.

WHITE HOUSE VISITS, MAIL,
AND PUBLIC OPINION POLLS

In most personal contacts between a President and other citizens, they come to him. Along with meeting public officials a Chief Executive spends much of his day in the White House receiving individuals and group representatives in connection with a variety of matters. (Harry Truman, for example, averaged about 100 such visits a week.) The activities include holding sessions with interest group representatives pertaining to public policy concerns, welcoming delegations of young people who are visiting the capital, and honoring persons receiving the Congressional Medal of Honor as well as those singled out for achievement in letters, the arts, or sports. Such

visits enable the President to create a favorable impression upon his flat-
tered guests, and they also provide him with clues to what is on the minds
of a variety of Americans.

Another source of information is the letters, telegrams, and telephone
calls that pour into the White House from the American people. The volume has varied with the incumbent: Franklin Roosevelt received an average
of 4000 pieces of mail a day, ten times the amount dispatched to Warren
Harding. Particular events, such as the incursion into Cambodia in 1970,
swell the flood. Although the views expressed give the Chief Executive
some idea of public reactions to vital issues (his staff compiles the number
registering pro and con attitudes and analyzes the major reasons behind
them), letter-writers, telegram-senders, and long-distance callers do not
necessarily constitute a cross-section of the American people. Typically they
have intense feelings one way or the other on an issue, and they come disproportionately from the more educated and articulate segments of the
citizenry.

A more reliable barometer of attitudes of the general population is provided by public opinion polls taken by private firms such as the Gallup,
Harris, and Roper organizations. Since the days of Franklin Roosevelt,
Presidents have had an avid interest in such polls because they provide
various kinds of useful basic information. One is the attitude of the public
toward specific issues of public policy, such as the pace of school integration or the proportion of people who are unemployed. Another is the degree of approval or disapproval of his handling of a particular situation,
such as the war in Vietnam. Still another is the public estimate of his over-
all handling of his job, a question that is periodically put to the American
people by the pollsters. Figure 12–1, showing how former President Johnson
fared on this question, indicates a fairly steady erosion of public confidence
in him over the course of the years, with some variation based on public
reactions to specific events.

THE PRESS

Historically the most important medium linking the President to the
American public has been the press. In the early years of the republic there
was a partisan press similar to what prevails in many European countries
today. The Federalists had their party organ, *The Gazette of the United
States*, while the *National Gazette* spoke for their Republican opponents.
The partisan press reached its apogee during the Presidency of Andrew
Jackson when federal officeholders were expected to subscribe to the administrative organ, which was financed in part from revenues derived from
the printing of official government notices.

In the latter part of the nineteenth century, however, the partisan press
began to disappear in the United States, largely because of two develop-

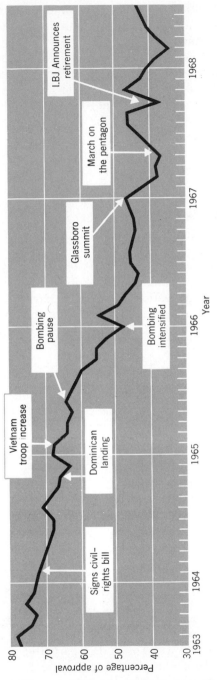

FIGURE 12–1 President Johnson's declining popularity in public opinion polls. (*News week*, January 1969)

ments. One was the invention of the telegraph, which led to the formation of wire services that distributed news to all parts of the country; the information transmitted tended to be standardized and politically fairly neutral to avoid antagonizing the diverse readership of the various newspapers in the country. The other factor was the increased use of the press for advertising by business concerns; this innovation provided newspapers with a secure financial base and lessened their dependence on official notices and other types of party largesse.

The modern press in the United States is nonpartisan in the sense that newspapers are not overtly affiliated with particular parties. There is little question, however, that most of today's newspapers have distinct partisan preferences which they disguise thinly, if at all. *The Chicago Tribune* speaks distinctly for the more conservative elements of the Republican party, while the *St. Louis Post Dispatch* clearly represents the views of liberal Democrats.

It is important, however, to distinguish between the owners and editors of newspapers on the one hand and the members of the working press— reporters and commentators—on the other. Most of the former, representing the interests of management and business in general (on whom they depend for advertising revenue) tend to defend the *status quo* and favor the Republican party. The latter, interested in the world of ideas, are more inclined to want change in American life and are more often attuned to the general philosophy of the Democratic party.

A President must take these realities into account in utilizing the press to further his influence over public opinion. Each has sought to establish useful relationships with reporters who can help or hinder his efforts. Teddie Roosevelt, as we saw, initiated the practices of providing working quarters in the White House for reporters and of granting personal interviews to some of them. Woodrow Wilson later established the regular press conference to which all Washington correspondents were invited.

Over the years the press conference has become a major tool used by Presidents both to influence public opinion and to gauge the public mind as revealed by the questions put to them by reporters from all parts of the country. Each President has used the institution in his own way. Some, like Harding, Coolidge, and Hoover, have required that questions be submitted in advance. (This practice began when Harding was unprepared for a question involving a treaty and gave an erroneous and damaging interpretation of it.) Others, like Franklin Roosevelt, have permitted spontaneous questioning. The frequency of press conferences has also varied widely among Presidents, even within a single administration. In times of crisis Chief Executives have tended to hold few press conferences, in part because they have little time for them, in part because they wish to avoid divulging sensitive information.

The success of a press conference depends on the skills of the President.

Harry Truman, who enjoyed the give-and-take of exchanges with the reporters, nonetheless performed poorly in formal encounters: he tended to
answer questions quickly rather than thoughtfully, and he was unable to
envision just how his words would look in print or how they might be interpreted. Dwight Eisenhower also came across badly. Not only did he have
trouble expressing himself clearly and grammatically, but he also displayed
meager knowledge about many vital issues of the day. In contrast, Franklin
Roosevelt and John Kennedy were masters of the press conference. The former had a keen sense of what was newsworthy and even suggested reporters' headlines for them. He also prepared members of the press for actions
he took on controversial problems by educating them initially with confidential background information; consequently reporters tended to support
Roosevelt's ultimate decisions because they understood the reasons behind
his actions. Kennedy, who served a brief stint as a newspaper man and enjoyed the company of reporters, used his press conferences to great advantage; his ability to field difficult questions impressed not only the members
of the press involved, but also the American public who viewed the proceedings on live television.*

Presidential contacts with the working press have thus changed over time.
Today it is expected that the Chief Executive will conduct some formal
press conferences attended by hundreds of Washington reporters and
watched simultaneously by millions on television. Not all Presidents feel at
ease in that situation, however. President Johnson, who preferred to converse with small groups of reporters, also experimented with informal,
hastily called conferences held in a variety of settings; at times, he led the
assembled press on a brisk walk around the White House. Even Kennedy
did not confine his meetings with reporters to formal press conferences; he
also gave exclusive stories to special reporter friends of his, a practice that
was naturally resented by many other members of the working press.

Presidents also attempt to work through other elements of the press besides the Washington reporters and correspondents. President Kennedy
invited newspaper editors and owners to White House conferences at
which he discussed major public issues. President Nixon, wary of the Washington press corps, chose to experiment with a number of approaches for
establishing contacts with sympathetic elements of the medium—for example, holding briefings before selected editors and executives of news organizations around the country with key officials like Henry Kissinger on hand
to discuss foreign policy problems and decisions, and furnishing editorial
writers around the nation with transcripts of his speeches and comments on
issues.

*Kennedy prepared as carefully for his press conferences as he did for the television
debates during the 1960 campaign: key staff members provided him with questions that
might be asked, together with the information necessary to answer them.

OTHER MASS MEDIA

Radio and television are, of course, available to a President who wants to address the American people directly without having his remarks filtered through reporters or editorial writers. Franklin Roosevelt made effective use of radio for his famous "fireside chats." His resonant voice and effective timing were the envy of professional broadcasters; his facility for discussing complicated social problems in understandable terms won the confidence of the American people in difficult times. He made the first of his chats at

Leader of public opinion: Franklin Roosevelt addresses the nation on radio. (New York Public Library)

the end of his first week in office and continued to utilize them effectively during his twelve years in the White House. At the same time, he was careful not to overuse the technique because, as he put it, ". . . individual psychology cannot, because of human weakness, be attuned for long periods of time to a constant repetition of the highest note in the scale."

Television required new techniques and formats. Dwight Eisenhower hired movie and television star Robert Montgomery to coach him on methods of projecting a favorable image. On one occasion he appeared with cabinet members to convey the idea that his administration was a "team" in which individual specialists joined efforts in the common cause of "good government." Nixon announced the appointment of his cabinet on television as a means of dramatizing the event and introducing the appointees. And John Kennedy, searching for an equivalent of FDR's fireside chat, had major television commentators come to the White House for personal interviews in which he fielded spontaneous questions from the informal comfort of his favorite rocking chair.

Today's President can utilize a variety of media in his efforts to shape public opinion. How effectively he does so will depend on his own communication skills as well as his ability to gauge when and how far he should go in trying to alter public sentiments on controversial matters. To some extent there is a built-in conflict between the President and the media representatives. The former often wants to suppress information that he feels will endanger the nation's security, or at least put his administration in a bad light; the latter, in turn, are eager for news, however sensitive it may be, and have a vested interest in criticizing the President and his associates as a means of stimulating public interest and thereby creating a demand for their services. Virtually every President has complained of unfair treatment by the media, while newsmen have often charged that the President and his team are "managing" the news to further their own political purposes.

A President's relations with his party colleagues, and with the American people, create the potential for public support required of the leader of a democratic nation. However, the decisions he makes either on his own or in conjunction with other public officials depend on the legal powers of his office, as well as his ability to convince other office-holders to act as he desires. His contacts and influence in the three major branches of the national government are thus crucial to the conduct of his office.*

THE PRESIDENT AND CONGRESS

Although the primary responsibility for making the laws is vested in the Congress, the Founding Fathers clearly intended the President to play a vital role in influencing legislation. To that end they granted him certain

*The federal judiciary is more autonomous than the other two branches. It does, however, have certain relationships with them, which we analyze in Chapter 14.

powers through which he might affect legislative decisions, among them giving messages and recommendations to Congress, calling it into special session, and vetoing bills. In some instances, the use of these powers is mandatory: as discussed in detail below, even President Eisenhower, who was not inclined to exercise strong leadership over the Congress, remarked that "the Constitution puts the President right square into the legislative business."

Beyond the legal powers vested in the President, however, certain practices that have developed over the years have increased his influence over the making of the laws. These practices were initiated by individual Presidents who wanted to exercise strong leadership over legislation. But over the years Congress and the American people have come to expect that all Presidents will follow them as part of the political, if not legal, duties of the office.

MESSAGES AND RECOMMENDATIONS

Article II, Section 3 of the Constitution is specific in its language that the President "shall from time to time give to the Congress Information on the State of the Union and recommend to their Consideration such Measures as he shall judge necessary and expedient." Every Chief Executive since Washington has followed his practice of presenting an annual message to the Congress at the beginning of each regular session, but the method of delivery has changed over time. Washington and Adams gave their messages in person, but Jefferson (a notoriously poor public speaker) dispatched a written message, giving as his reasons that such a speech intruded on the privacy of the legislature and that the practice smacked too much of the royal prerogative from which it developed.* This practice continued until Woodrow Wilson surprised Congress and the nation by delivering a message in person shortly after he was inaugurated. Since Wilson's time all Presidents (no matter how meager their speaking skills) have appeared before Congress to deliver the annual state-of-the-union message.

Although the assembled senators and congressmen are the immediate target of the speech, the President has other audiences in mind as well. In a sense, the message is addressed to all the American people, who today can watch the proceedings on television. In fact, the State-of-the-Union Message is beamed to nations around the world via satellite and becomes a matter of interest to political friends and enemies alike. For through this general pronouncement the President indicates the problems that he feels are of concern to American society and suggests policies to mitigate them.

Typically the State-of-the-Union Message contains far more concerns and proposals than the President expects the Congress to deal with; twenty-five

*The message followed the British tradition whereby the king delivered a "speech from the throne" to Parliament. This custom was carried to the New World in the form of pronouncements by colonial governors to the legislatures of the day.

or thirty separate matters may be treated of in the speech. (Covering a wide variety of topics is designed to appeal politically to a broad range of interest groups.) Moreover, the President seldom attempts to distinguish among the problems on the basis of their relative importance. Finally, the policy proposals made in the Message are usually couched in very vague terms. Thus the State-of-the-Union Message is somewhat like a party platform in its comprehensiveness and generality, yet it does represent some screening of policy proposals made in the platform.

Modern Presidents, however, do not restrict their recommendations to Congress to those contained in this message. Instead they adopt the practice, initiated by Woodrow Wilson, of following up this general pronouncement with a series of specially written messages focusing on specific problems and outlining in detail proposals for dealing with them. For example, one message may deal with crime, another with pollution, a third with agricultural problems, and so on. (A commentator remarked that if all the special messages of President Kennedy were laid end to end they would form a veritable Harvard "five-foot shelf" of reading materials.)

A final presidential step in spelling out precisely what should be done about a particular issue is the development of a specific bill. Even though Congress may (and usually does) make changes in the "administration" proposal, the bill enables the Chief Executive to affect ultimate legislative

Molder of legislation: Richard Nixon delivers a State-of-the-Union Message in the House of Representatives to assembled senators, congressmen, and Supreme Court justices. (United Press International)

actions by forcing senators and congressmen to focus initially on what the President thinks should be done about a given problem.

Congress itself has come to realize that large assemblies cannot establish a legislative program that reflects an over-all system of priorities. The program must come from an outside source—the President. (This is true even when different parties control the Presidency and the Congress: rival legislative leaders made it clear to Presidents Truman, Eisenhower, and Nixon that they expected them to propose specific programs, including administration bills.) When Congress passed the Budget and Accounting Act of 1921 requiring the Chief Executive to present a comprehensive plan of suggested expenditures by the various executive agencies (we will examine this matter later in the chapter), it indirectly placed in his hands the job of establishing priorities among governmental programs, since success depends on financing. In recommending expenditures the President is forced to express his preferences among programs. Thus the annual Budget Message is a much better indication of which policies and programs in particular the President favors and how much so, than is his annual State-of-the-Union Message. (Unlike the latter, the Budget Message forces him, in the vernacular, "to put his money where his mouth is.") As a result of the passage of the Full Employment Act of 1946, the President must also give an annual Economic Message to the nation in which he estimates, among other matters, how much money the government may expect to take in from existing revenue measures and how additional monies might be raised should they be needed.

Today's Presidents are thus expected to develop both a comprehensive legislative program reflecting over-all priorities and concrete proposals for dealing with specific problems. Following a practice first developed in the Truman administration, Presidents now have departments include, with their estimates of financial expenditures, information on legislative matters of interest to them. Such information contains actual drafts of bills and the names of other executive agencies interested in the matter. With this systematic inventory of proposals at his disposal a President can better screen and coordinate the legislative concerns of the many agencies of the executive branch.

CALLING CONGRESS INTO SPECIAL SESSION

The President has the constitutional prerogative to convene the Congress —both houses or either one—on "extraordinary occasions." (For example, the President might want to bring just senators together for the purpose of confirming an executive appointment or approving a treaty.) Unlike many state governors, however, he has no power to restrict the agenda of the special session. He thus runs the risk not only that congressmen may ignore what he wants them to do but also that they may decide to take actions he considers peripheral or even opposes.

The use of the power to call Congress into special session has varied. The practice became particularly prominent in the first third of this century, as

Presidents (beginning with Taft) called special sessions shortly after they took office in March of the year in order to get the Congress busy immediately rather than waiting for the then-appointed time of December. The highly productive congressional session held during the first year of the Wilson administration (1913–14) and the famous "Hundred Days" under Franklin Roosevelt were both specially convened by the two Chief Executives.

Since the passage of the Twentieth Amendment in 1933, the President's power to call the Congress into special session has become less important as a tool of legislative leadership. He is inaugurated on January 20, but the two Houses assemble on January 3; therefore, there is no necessity of convening them as did Wilson and FDR when they first took office. Since Congress begins each annual session on January 3, it is ready to receive the President's various messages later in the month. Beyond this, Congress now meets virtually year-round (exceptions are holiday recesses, breaks for national conventions, election-year campaigns, and the immediate postelection period in November and December), so there is relatively little time when the lawmakers are not available for hearing presidential legislative requests.*

Even so, the power to call Congress into special session is still potentially useful as an electoral tactic when one party controls the Presidency and another the Congress. Harry Truman used it effectively in the summer of 1948 when he convened the Republican-controlled Congress after the party's national convention was held and a platform adopted; in so doing, he challenged the GOP legislature to enact the platform's policy proposals into law. He used its failure to do so to great effect in his fall campaign.

THE VETO POWER

More important than the authority to call Congress into special session is the President's veto power, which gives him three options with respect to a measure passed by Congress: (1) He may sign it, thereby making it a law. (2) He may veto the measure by withholding his signature, in which case it (together with an explanatory message) is returned to the chamber in which the measure originated; this nullifies the measure unless each house, by a two-thirds vote, repasses it over his veto. (3) He may take no action so that it becomes a law within ten days unless Congress is no longer in session; if that is the case, the measure is said to have been "pocket vetoed."

Conceived originally by the Founding Fathers as a defensive weapon for the President to protect himself against encroachments into his domain by a powerful legislature, the veto developed into a tool he can use to shape public policy. Franklin Roosevelt vetoed over 600 measures, a record, partly because he was in office longer than any other President, partly because he

---

*The President's discretion *not* to convene Congress is also less important than it once was. Lincoln's tactic of acting on his own in the early months of the Civil War would not be available today.

had strong views on public policy and was willing to use the prerogative to demonstrate his political power; he was known to tell his aides, "Give me a bill I can veto," to let congressmen know they had a President to deal with.

The most important single factor affecting the use of the veto has been political conflict between the Congress and the Chief Executive. The control of the Presidency and the Congress by opposite political parties tends to create the kind of conflict that gives rise to frequent vetoes, as evidenced by the number of times Harry Truman (250) and Dwight Eisenhower (181) exercised the prerogative.*

Actual use is not the only gauge of the veto power's value, for the mere *threat* to use it can be a valuable weapon for a President who wishes to shape pending legislation. By passing the word on which features of a particular bill he finds objectionable and what must be done in order to make it acceptable to him, the President can affect the content of any measure that is sent to him. This tactic does not always work, however. Congressmen may not be willing to scale down measures they favor; moreover, if the Congress is controlled by the opposite political party, its leadership may accept the presidential challenge and force him to veto what they believe is a popular measure. The Democrats in Congress in 1970 sent President Nixon a bill for hospital construction that he vetoed for economy reasons. Not only did they successfully override his veto, but they also charged in the congressional campaign that year that his veto indicated his lack of concern for the health needs of the citizens.

The mere possession of these several legal powers does not, of course, insure presidential success with the Congress. Political factors play a major part in determining how effective his use of his powers will be.

CONDITIONS LIMITING
PRESIDENTIAL INFLUENCE WITH CONGRESS

Every President faces certain basic conflicts with Congress that were built into the constitutional system by the Founding Fathers. Operating on Madison's advice that "ambition must be made to counteract ambition," they deliberately created rivalry between the executive and the legislature by assigning important constitutional powers to each, thus inviting them to compete for political leadership. By granting the rivals independent bases of political power, they insured that each would be capable of protecting its interests.

Their expectations have proved to be very accurate. Since the days when some members of the first Congress began to withstand the attempts of

---

*While Congress can override a presidential veto, over the years only about one in twenty have met that fate. Several of the Reconstruction acts were passed over President Andrew Johnson's veto, and the Taft-Hartley Labor Relations Act and the McCarran-Walter Immigration Act became law despite President Truman's vetoes of them.

Alexander Hamilton (and indirectly of Washington) to push an economic program, senators and House members have resisted presidential efforts to dominate their affairs as well as those of the nation.

Of course, the conflict between the Presidency and the Congress is likely to be even more pronounced if the two are controlled by opposite political parties: added to the natural rivalry between the branches of government is the competition between parties for political leadership. Still, congressmen from a President's own political party frequently engage him in political battle. In fact, as the late British scholar Harold Laski suggested, some members, particularly those in the House of Representatives, have a vested interest in doing so as a means of gaining publicity. So long as the press plays up conflict because it is more newsworthy than cooperation, a congressman who opposes a President will find public attention focused on him. He can then appeal to his constituents by claiming that he is no rubber stamp for the President, that he is battling to protect their interests. Of course, a congressman takes into account the popularity of the President: few Republican senators or representatives picked a fight with Dwight Eisenhower.

Conflicts also reflect differences in constituencies. Since the President has a nationwide vote, he tends to look at public policy issues from a national perspective. A senator or member of the House of Representatives necessarily must be concerned with how a matter affects residents, particularly the "attentive publics", of his state or district. The careers of John Kennedy and Lyndon Johnson gave vivid evidence of the different attitudes appropriate to different offices. As a representative and then a senator from Massachusetts, Kennedy voted to protect key industries in that state (watchmaking, textiles, and the like) from the economic effects of foreign competition. When he became President, the first important piece of domestic legislation he helped steer through Congress was a Reciprocal Trade Act designed to promote commerce between the United States and other countries. Similarly, when Lyndon Johnson represented Texas in the House and Senate, he was not a strong advocate of civil rights; when he assumed the Presidency, however, he successfully promoted several major statutes protecting minority rights and appointed Negroes to major governmental positions, including Thurgood Marshall, the first black man to sit on the United States Supreme Court.*

President Johnson's increased concern with the problems of the Negro stemmed not only from the national perspective of his office but also from a keen appreciation of the number of blacks in the populous states with

---

*When Johnson was the Majority Leader of the Senate, he did assist with the passage of the Civil Rights Act of 1957, but it was a conservative measure compared to the legislation of the 1960s.

many electoral votes. The large-state bias built into the election of the President tends to make Democratic candidates solicitous of groups (blacks, "ethnics," labor union members) that are concentrated in urban areas. But this concern produces political conflicts between these Presidents and Southern congressmen whose constituencies contain fewer voting members of such groups. Southern dominance of standing committees (when the Democrats control the Congress) makes effective legislative leadership particularly difficult for Democratic Presidents.

Constituency differences also result in conflicts between Republican Presidents and congressmen. Even though Eisenhower's popularity enabled the Republican party to capture the Presidency in 1952, he immediately ran into political difficulties with Daniel Reed and John Tabor (representing rural areas in New York and Illinois respectively) who, as chairmen of the House Ways and Means and Appropriations Committees, sought to cut taxes and reduce his budget requests for mutual security. Richard Nixon, who pursued a southern strategy in his quest for votes in 1968, saw his nominations of South Carolinian Clement Haynsworth and Floridian G. Harrold Carswell to the Supreme Court opposed by a number of Republican senators from the North.

Thus the influences of constituencies underlie certain basic executive-legislative relationships that have developed in recent years. Liberal Presidents, of whatever party, generally encounter major political problems when they try to steer legislation changing the *status quo* through the House of Representatives, many of whose members reflect the conservative values of rural and small-town America. There is less difficulty with the upper chamber, because senators from the large states articulate the interests of urban Americans who tend to be somewhat more liberal in their orientation than are people from less-populated areas. Conversely, Presidents who attempt to implement more conservative legislative goals generally experience more opposition from the Senate than from the House.

INFORMAL METHODS OF INFLUENCING LEGISLATION

Such political realities make it difficult for a President to make effective use of his constitutional tools (messages, special sessions, and vetoes), but there are informal methods for influencing Congress. Two sources have already been discussed: party loyalty and public opinion. A President can appeal to his colleagues in Congress to follow the party program and, with senators and representatives who are vulnerable politically, he can threaten to withhold political backing. He can also cultivate the support of the people—particularly "attentive publics"—for his legislative programs and depend on them to exert pressure on congressmen to enact those programs into law.

Personal persuasion is another valuable technique, one with a variety of manifestations: wooing individual congressmen with personal flattery and invitations to them and their wives to social affairs at the White House; making phone calls to key senators and representatives (particularly those who are not publicly committed on an issue) immediately preceding a crucial roll call; and for the President whose party also controls the Congress, holding periodic conferences with the leadership of the House and Senate (Speaker, President *pro tem*, and the Majority Leaders of the two chambers), as well as major standing committee chairmen. Although personal contacts do not necessarily bring a President all the results he desires, they do often win some immediate congressional support for his program and may also create a reservoir of good will upon which he can draw in future attempts at legislative leadership.

Beyond personal persuasion a President does have a certain amount of patronage to use as a bargaining point with recalcitrant congressmen. Franklin Roosevelt deliberately postponed filling government positions in which congressmen were interested until major portions of his legislative program had been enacted into law. Even though fewer public jobs are at the disposal of Presidents today (over the years, more and more have come under Civil Service regulations requiring competitive examinations), modern patronage exists in the form of government contracts and defense installations. Recent Presidents have seen to it that major military bases have been located in the home states of principal congressional leaders and committee chairmen, particularly those from Southern states like Texas, Georgia, Alabama, and Florida.

Presidents who want to exercise strong legislative leadership and who are skillful in utilizing the tools to do so can often persuade Congressmen to enact their programs into law. Particularly successful legislative leaders in this century have been Woodrow Wilson, Franklin Roosevelt, and Lyndon Johnson. Yet each of them benefited from particular conditions of the time that favored their efforts. In Wilson's case there existed a sentiment for progressive domestic legislation among political leaders and "attentive publics" alike when he came to office; moreover, he had large Democratic majorities in the House, and in the Senate a number of liberal Republicans supported his social and economic legislative programs. Roosevelt was elected in a time of crisis when the nation and the Congress turned instinctively to the President for leadership; he also enjoyed large congressional majorities. When Johnson took office, major social and economic legislation delayed for a quarter-century was ripe for enactment; to get it passed he asked Congress to honor John Kennedy's memory by acting speedily on measures the late President had initiated, and he counted on the bumper crop of freshman congressmen elected in 1964 to support his (Johnson's) proposals. Thus the general climate of the times, plus the specific situation in Congress, constitute major factors in a President's legislative success.

THE PRESIDENT AND THE ORGANIZATION
OF THE EXECUTIVE BRANCH

Everyone expects the President to run into difficulties with members of Congress when he tries to influence legislation, for law-making is their major responsibility and his role is subordinate. The administration of the laws is the President's primary task under the Constitution, and accordingly he should have less trouble in controlling the activities of the executive branch. This is not necessarily so. Arthur Schlesinger reports in his biography of the late President Kennedy, *A Thousand Days*, that the resistance Kennedy encountered from executive officials was almost as great as the opposition of congressmen. Kennedy's difficulties were not peculiar to him alone. All Presidents have had similar experiences. The following discussion analyzes the reasons why a President cannot control executive personnel as effectively as he would like.

The organization chart of the national government in Figure 12–2 reveals the formal, legal structure of the executive branch. Essentially the organization is a pyramidical military chain of command. The connecting lines show that the various departments and the independent offices and establishments report to the Executive Office of the President and through it to the Chief Executive. The arrangement of boxes reveals what organizations have the same formal relationship with the President—for example, the White House Office and the Council of Economic Advisers are both located within the Executive Office of the President, and the Tennessee Valley Authority and the Veterans Administration are both in the category of Independent Offices and Establishments.

In reality, however, the informal organization of the executive branch varies greatly from this pyramidical chain-of-command model. As William Moyers, former Assistant to President Johnson, has suggested, a more accurate graphic illustration would be a series of concentric circles with the President in the middle and the various units in the executive branch located on the circles. This model would depict two important aspects of the actual relationships. One is that the President can and often does direct contacts with the various units; all matters are *not* screened through a rigid chain of command before they reach him. The second is that the amount of contact with, and degree of presidential control over, a unit varies, depending on its functions and the President's power over and concern with its operations.

Using the amount of presidential contact and control as the major criterion, it is possible to place the various units in several broad categories. Political and legal considerations shape the nature of the units and their relationships with the President of the United States.

414

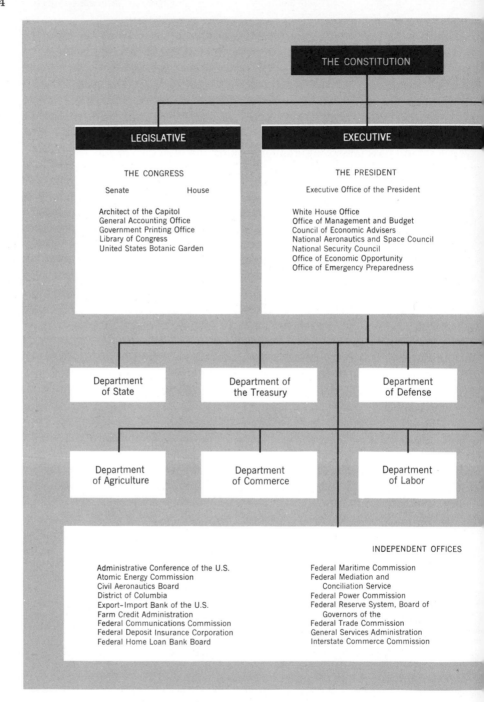

FIGURE 12–2 The government of the United States.

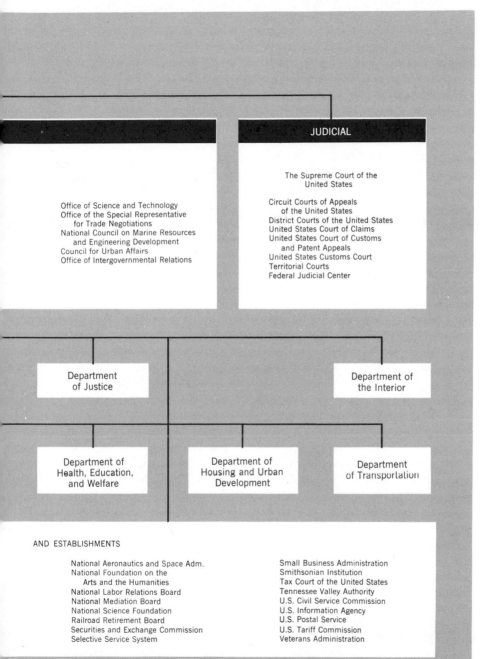

JUDICIAL

Office of Science and Technology
Office of the Special Representative
    for Trade Negotiations
National Council on Marine Resources
    and Engineering Development
Council for Urban Affairs
Office of Intergovernmental Relations

The Supreme Court of the
United States

Circuit Courts of Appeals
    of the United States
District Courts of the United States
United States Court of Claims
United States Court of Customs
    and Patent Appeals
United States Customs Court
Territorial Courts
Federal Judicial Center

Department
of Justice

Department of
the Interior

Department of
Health, Education,
and Welfare

Department of
Housing and Urban
Development

Department
of Transportation

AND ESTABLISHMENTS

National Aeronautics and Space Adm.
National Foundation on the
    Arts and the Humanities
National Labor Relations Board
National Mediation Board
National Science Foundation
Railroad Retirement Board
Securities and Exchange Commission
Selective Service System

Small Business Administration
Smithsonian Institution
Tax Court of the United States
Tennessee Valley Authority
U.S. Civil Service Commission
U.S. Information Agency
U.S. Postal Service
U.S. Tariff Commission
Veterans Administration

THE WHITE HOUSE OFFICE

In the orbit closest to the President are the members of the White House Office, a part of the larger Executive Office of the President. They are, in the phrase of Patrick Anderson, "the President's men": he appoints them without the necessity of senatorial approval, assigns them whatever duties he deems appropriate, and removes them when they no longer serve his purposes. A new Chief Executive means a complete turnover in the composition of the White House Office.

The White House Office is organized to assist the President with his myriad tasks. Included are those assistants who write his speeches, arrange his appointments, plan his trips, facilitate his relationships with the press and other media, and smooth his way in dealings with Congress and political party officials. Others advise him on matters of public policy, such as national security and urban problems. Although their tasks vary, they share a common concern: the welfare of the President. As Theodore Sorensen, former aide to President Kennedy, described their responsibilities: "We were appointed for our ability to fulfill the President's needs and talk the President's language. We represented no man but John Kennedy."

The White House staff is populated with people whom the President knows well personally and in whom he has great trust and confidence. During the Kennedy administration, individuals like Sorensen, who was formerly on his Senate staff, were much in evidence, along with Arthur Schlesinger, Jr., and others from Harvard with whom the President had close intellectual ties. Also represented were political campaign associates like Larry O'Brien. Nixon also apointed to his White House office people he knew intimately, including Robert Finch, a long-time associate from California politics; Bryce Harlow, who served in the Eisenhower White House Office while Nixon was Vice President; and Leonard Garment, a former New York law partner, who was also a major figure in the 1968 presidential campaign.

Flexibility is the major characteristic of the White House Office organization. Presidents Kennedy and Truman had relatively few persons in the Office, on the average of about fifteen; Eisenhower and Nixon generally used about twice that number. Positions also change. For the one traditional Press Secretary, Nixon substituted two: Ronald Ziegler was made Special Assistant for Press Relations and Herbert Klein, who was made Director of Communications for the executive branch, was entrusted with the responsibility of supervising and coordinating public statements made by units throughout the branch.

Presidents feel free to use a single individual in a variety of capacities, switching him from assignment to assignment as they see fit. Theodore Sorensen was a jack-of-all-trades for John Kennedy (the latter referred to him as his "intellectual blood bank"): he wrote the President's speeches, helped formulate his legislative program, and acted as his trouble-shooter on a variety of public-policy issues. William Moyers performed a similarly broad array of duties for Lyndon Johnson, including a short stint as his Press Secretary. In making decisions about the internal organization and operation of the White House Office, the President applies a single criterion: "What is likely to serve my personal interests most effectively?"

OTHER UNITS IN THE EXECUTIVE OFFICE
OF THE PRESIDENT

The other units shown in Figure 12–2 that are located in the Executive Office of the President also have close relationships with him, but their personnel are not so much "the President's men." For example, with the exception of the Director of the Office of Management and Budget (formerly known as the Budget Bureau), their appointments must be confirmed by the Senate. Moreover, while the top officials in these units leave with a change in administration, many lower-level employees remain. Individuals who serve in these posts tend to be specialists in their particular areas of responsibility, not generalists who occupy the positions in the White House Office. (Members of the Council of Economic Advisers are unlikely to be switched to another position in the Executive Office as are White House aides.) The President is less likely to be personally familiar with them and frequently accepts recommendations from others about who would, for example, make a good chairman of the Council of Economic Advisers. Symbolically, White House staff men are generally located in the White House itself while others in the Executive Office are housed in a separate building across the street.

Basic to presidential control of the executive branch is the *Office of Management and Budget*: it gathers estimates from executive units of their proposed expenditures for the coming fiscal year; holds hearings at which officials are required to justify expenditures; and recommends to the President, in light of the total expenditures for a fiscal year, the amounts that should be allocated to each unit. The Office evaluates existing and proposed government programs, taking into account probable costs and benefits, as an aid to the President's assessment of alternative approaches and programs.

The Office also studies the efficiency of the units (for example, how they handle their accounting problems) and makes suggestions for improving and standardizing operations. It gathers and evaluates suggestions from the various units on needed legislation pertaining to their programs and makes this information available to the President in conjunction with his legislative recommendations to Congress. And as an aid to the President in making veto decisions the Office solicits reactions of executive units to legislation already passed by Congress.

Three other units in the Executive Office are especially important in providing advice and helping the President coordinate a wide variety of governmental activities. *The Council of Economic Advisers* (created by the

Full Employment Act of 1946) is composed of three professional economists who advise the Chief Executive on his annual Economic Report to the nation and the economic policies his administration should pursue. *The National Security Council,* established by Congress in 1947 (it includes the President and Vice President, the Secretaries of State and Defense, the Director of the Office of Emergency Planning, and whatever other officials the Chief Executive invites to sit with it) advises the President on the foreign, military, and domestic policy aspects of the nation's security. A comparable body, the *Domestic Council* (created by President Nixon in 1970), consisting of various officials concerned with the country's internal problems, performs a similar integrating function for the President.

A final point should be made about the units in the Executive Office of the President. Although most of them coordinate activities of other organizations, at times they perform programmatic functions of their own.* For instance, the *Office of Economic Opportunity,* which undertakes programs designed to assist the poor and unskilled in our society, was originally located in the Executive Office to indicate President Johnson's particular concern with the task of carrying out some of his major Great Society programs. When President Nixon came into office, however, he transferred some of the operations of the OEO, such as the Job Corps and Head Start programs (we will examine these in Chapter 16), to regular cabinet departments.

THE CABINET DEPARTMENTS

Next in closeness to the President are the eleven departments granted cabinet rank by Congress. The heads of these departments (called Secretaries) are appointed by the President with the consent of the Senate. Rarely, however (only eight times in the nation's history), does the Senate refuse to confirm a President's nominee for a cabinet post; it is his right to choose cabinet officers and to remove them if he is dissatisfied with the way they are performing. When a new President comes into office, an entirely new cabinet team generally comes in with him.†

Although Congress does not generally interfere with the President's selections for the cabinet, other factors place some real limitations on his choices. For one thing, some cabinet posts require special experience and expertise: the Secretary of the Treasury, for example, must have a broad knowledge of financial affairs. The President is also expected to introduce some partisan balance into the makeup of the cabinet. The losing faction at the previous national convention is often permitted to name some cabinet officials: several "Taft men," for instance, were included in Eisenhower's initial cabi-

---

*Students of public administration refer to units that coordinate and assist activities of other units as "staff" agencies; those that undertake substantive programs are known as "line" agencies.
†A Vice President who succeeds to the office on the death of a President is likely to keep the same team for the transition period, as Lyndon Johnson did after John Kennedy's assassination.

Head of the administration: President Eisenhower, at right center, with his cabinet. At far right, Presidential Assistant Sherman Adams. (United Press International)

net. Similarly, both "liberal" and "conservative" elements of a party are usually represented. If a national crisis exists or an election is close, the President may even include members of the opposition party in his cabinet: Franklin Roosevelt's wartime cabinet included two Republicans; John Kennedy and eventually Richard Nixon chose persons of the opposite party for cabinet posts.

A former congressman is usually included, presumably to help the President establish good relationships with that body. Most Chief Executives (including Nixon) consider it politic to include a Southerner in the cabinet; traditionally the Secretary of Interior comes from the western part of the United States where most of the vast public lands under the department's jurisdiction are located. In fact, with the exception of the Departments of State and Defense, each of the departments has a "clientele," that is, particular groups which it serves:* The Commerce Department caters to business, Labor to the working man, and the like. In making appointments to these cabinet positions, the President takes into account the attitudes of interest groups toward the man who is to head the department: he would not, for example, appoint a Secretary of Agriculture who is unacceptable to the farmers of the country.

*The composition of the cabinet reflects the political power of various interest groups: one sign that a group has arrived politically is the establishment of a cabinet-level department to serve its needs.

Thus the President lacks absolute freedom of choice over the makeup of the cabinet. Suggestions for department secretaries come from a variety of sources; many of the persons whom he selects are not personally known to him prior to their appointment. And even though the President has the legal right to remove members of his cabinet at any time, he may hesitate to do so if the individual involved has a strong political following, particularly among the groups which his department serves.

THE INDEPENDENT AGENCIES

The thirty-three Independent Offices and Establishments listed in Figure 12–2 are all "independent" in the sense that they are not part of any cabinet department, but their degree of independence from the President varies. There are three major types of these units.

One type performs a specific function and is headed by a *single individual*; examples are the National Aeronautics and Space Administration and the Veterans Administration. Their relationships with the President parallel those of cabinet departments.* Major administrators are appointed by the Chief Executive with the consent of the Senate and are removable by his action alone. Even so, the heads of these independent agencies frequently stay in office after a new President takes over. General Lewis B. Hershey, for example, served as head of the Selective Service System for a succession of Presidents of both political parties until he retired because of age. Cabinet secretaries do not endure so long, because the President exercises closer political control over them than over the administrators of independent agencies.

Further removed in orbit from the presidential center are the seven *independent regulatory agencies*, which are administered through boards rather than single administrative heads. Included in this category are the Civil Aeronautics Board (CAB), Federal Communications Commission (FCC), Federal Maritime Commission (FMC), Federal Power Commission (FPC), Federal Trade Commission (FTC), Interstate Commerce Commission (ICC), and the Securities and Exchange Commission (SEC). The members of these boards (five on all except the ICC, which has eleven) are less subject to presidential control because they have fixed terms (five to seven years) and cannot be removed by the President except for causes set forth in the statute creating each agency. Moreover, the commissioners' terms are usually "staggered" (that is, overlapping) so that few (if any) expire simultaneously. This combination of lengthy, staggered terms and removal only for cause makes board members relatively free from presidential control and influence.

---

*Some cabinet departments were originally independent agencies that acquired cabinet status when they became more important politically.

The rationale for insulating these commissions from presidential (as well as congressional) control is that they are concerned with regulating activities of major private industries and so should be free of partisan politics that might interfere with objectivity and fairness in the way they are treated. (Most boards are required to be composed of members of both major parties.) The result of this policy, however, is to create a political vacuum into which other forces rush, in particular those groups supposedly regulated by the agencies. Thus the railroads take a great interest in the Interstate Commerce Commission, which regulates the fares they charge and the routes they follow, and television station owners exert influence over the Federal Communications Commission, which determines the conditions they must meet to obtain and retain their licenses.

Included in the third major category of independent agencies are the twenty or so *government corporations*, exemplified by the Tennessee Valley Authority and the newly-created United States Postal Service. Because these agencies perform commercial functions (the TVA builds dams and channels, and produces and sells electrical power, while the Postal Service distributes mail), they are organized along the lines of a private corporation, with a governing board that makes policy for the unit. Like the commissioners of the independent regulatory agencies, the board members of government corporations are appointed by the President with the consent of the Senate and serve long, staggered terms to prevent any one President from controlling the activities of those units. Furthermore, the corporations are less subject to financial control by the President or the Congress than other executive departments and agencies because they are not dependent on annual appropriations for their operations. Rather, long-term appropriations are provided (Congress, for example, is committed to a fifteen-year funding program for the Postal Service); in addition, corporations furnish some of their own financing (the Postal Service uses revenues it generates from its own activities and is also empowered to borrow money by issuing bonds). Government corporations are, therefore, free of the usual process of defending their estimates for the coming fiscal year before the Office of Management and Budget, the President, and the Congress. Although their operations are reviewed annually by all three, since the corporations are not requesting funds, the scrutiny tends to be less severe than for other executive units.

Thus the executive branch is composed of a variety of organizations with different functions and different legal and political relationships with the President. The employees of these organizations collectively constitute the executive-branch personnel of the national government.

EXECUTIVE-BRANCH PERSONNEL

Few groups are subject to more misconceptions than the employees of the executive branch of the national government. Typically called federal "bureaucrats," or members of the federal "bureaucracy,"* they are stereotyped as clerks who spend their time pushing meaningless forms from one side of their desk to another and harassing innocent citizens for private information which they put to improper use or none at all. Most are perceived as working for the Department of Health, Education, and Welfare, and as being located in Washington, D.C.

The realities could hardly be further from the stereotype. The federal service employs persons with a wide variety of occupational skills, about two-thirds of the number in all aspects of private enterprise. In 1968 over 600,000 of the federal employees (about one-fifth of the total) were blue-collar workers; of these some 140,000 operated mobile industrial equipment or did manual labor. Of the white-collar workers, more were filling professional, technical, or administrative jobs than serving as clerks and aides. More than a quarter of a million, for example, were employed in engineering and architecture, medicine and public health, and legal activities.

As Table 12.1 indicates, it is not Health, Education, and Welfare that harbors the most federal employees; it is Defense. The latter has almost twelve times as many employees as HEW. HEW does not even have as many employees as two of the major independent agencies: the Postal Service and the Veterans Administration. These three largest units of the federal government (Defense, Postal Service, and the Veterans Administration) together employed well over two million workers of the some three million civilians that worked for the national government in 1970.

Nor are federal civilian workers concentrated in the area of Washington, D.C., as is commonly supposed: only about 300,000 (about one in nine) lived there in 1968. The rest were located in every state in the country; slightly more resided in California than in the nation's capital. Almost a quarter of a million federal employees lived outside the United States.

Executive-branch personnel fall into two broad categories: those who make a career of the public service and enjoy security of tenure; and those in high political positions in the executive branch who come into office for a limited period and then generally return to private life.

THE CAREER SERVICE

The overwhelming proportion of employees of the executive branch are under some sort of merit system for selection and tenure. Over two million are governed by the rules of the United States Civil Service Commission regulating entrance requirements and general work conditions. In addition,

---

*The term "bureau," which originally referred to a cloth covering the desks of French government officials in the eighteenth century, was linked with "cracy" (rule) to connote an unwieldy organization with cumbersome procedures ("red tape"). A political scientist (or sociologist) uses the term in a neutral sense to describe a formal, large-scale organization that carries on complex operations through a division of labor and a hierarchy of authority.

TABLE 12.1   Number of Civilians Employed by Cabinet Departments and Selected Independent Agencies, January 31, 1970

Unit	Employees
Cabinet Departments	
Agriculture	104,332
Commerce	34,349
Defense	1,251,982
Health, Education, and Welfare	106,481
Housing and Urban Development	14,782
Interior	67,800
Justice	37,091
Labor	10,499
State	41,464
Transportation	62,670
Treasury	95,383
Independent Agencies	
Postal Service*	727,645
Veterans Administration	166,314

*Still designated as Post Office Department as of that date.
Source: Statistical Abstract of the United States, 1970, Table 593.

a number of agencies, because of highly specialized needs, have their own merit systems, notably the Federal Bureau of Investigation, the Central Intelligence Agency, the Atomic Energy Commission, the Tennessee Valley Authority, and the Foreign Service.

A career employee is generally hired from among the three candidates with the highest scores on the examination for a vacant position. Not all examinations are competitive, however; if a job calls for professional or technical skills that are in relatively short supply, it may be filled by someone who gets a minimum score on the examination. And some positions that involve policy-making or confidential relationships with high governmental officials may require no examination at all.

Work conditions are governed by definite rules and procedures. Positions and pay are ranked on the basis of job difficulty, and promotions typically come within a unit as employees work themselves up in the hierarchy of the organization. A career employee can be dismissed only for "cause" after procedural safeguards (hearings and the like) have been satisfied.

Most critics of the system charge that it is essentially negative for it rewards docile functionaries who carefully fulfill its myriad requirements (including filling out countless forms and reports) rather than imaginative persons who relish innovation and experimentation in handling the public's business. Even supporters of the present system concede that, while the salaries for lower- and intermediate-level career employees are competitive with those for similar positions in private industry, pay for upper-level posts is not. As a result the federal government loses too many senior career officials to private companies.

POLITICAL EXECUTIVES

Political executives are those who man policy-making positions, among them officials of the Executive Office of the President, secretaries of cabinet departments, and the heads of independent offices and establishments; they also include second- and third-level officials such as assistant and under secretaries of departments and the heads of certain subsidiary "bureaus," "administrations," "divisions," or "services." All told, only a few thousand persons serve as political executives in the federal government.

Although political executives are relatively few in number, they are vital to the functioning of the government, for they bear the responsibility for converting political goals into concrete programs and results. Because of their role they are seldom technicians or specialists; rather they are "politicians" who spend most of their time dealing with individuals and groups both inside and outside government that can help or impede their mission.

The single most important official to a political executive is, of course, the President, to whom in most instances he ultimately owes his appointment. In turn, the executive's own power to appoint and remove major political officials under him is dependent on support from the President. How his unit stands within the executive branch is also frequently dependent on the actions of the President: as previously mentioned, Richard Nixon by executive order transferred the Head Start Program for preschool children from the Executive Office of the President to a regular Department (Health, Education, and Welfare). He also depends on the President's recommendations for financing and legislative proposals.

Given the vast responsibilities of the President, it is natural that a political executive has relatively few, if any, direct contacts with the Chief Executive. Accordingly, he must spend time cultivating the men around the President, particularly those on the White House Staff and in the Office of Management and Budget. And because the operations of executive units are not autonomous but are closely related to those of other organizations, political executives spend time "touching base" with their counterparts in other agencies of the federal government.

The political executive's job is not limited, however, to establishing relationships within the executive branch; he is equally dependent on the Congress for success. In fact, the legislature shares all the major powers the President has over his organization. The Senate, for instance, can block presidential appointments and so can determine who will and will not man major political positions in the executive branch. Several of the officials on independent regulatory commissions owe their appointments to the support of the late Senator Dirksen of Illinois, who, conversely, also forced President Nixon to withdraw the nomination of Dr. John Knowles as Assistant Secretary of Health, Education, and Welfare for Health and Scientific Affairs even though he was the first choice of the departmental secretary, Robert Finch. Moreover, although Congress has no direct 'power to remove major executive officials, it does have indirect means of doing so. In the late 1950s congressional investigations into the activities of Sherman Adams, President Eisenhower's closest staff aide (who was accused of using his influence on behalf of a personal friend who was later convicted of engaging in improper dealings with the government), put such political pressures on Eisenhower that he ultimately let Adams resign.

Congress also has the last say on two other vital matters for executive units: financing and location in the executive branch organization chart. Although the President requests operating funds, the House of Representatives and Senate ultimately decide how much money will be appropriated. In addition, Congress has authority over the structure of the executive branch. Since the 1940s it has generally delegated to the President the right to reorganize units, but only within certain limits. For example, no cabinet level department can presently be created by executive order; rather, all must be authorized by act of Congress. Congress refused to enact legislation implementing President Nixon's proposal in 1971 that seven existing departments be consolidated into four new ones—Community Development, Economic Development, Human Resources, and Natural Resources. The legislature also reserves the right to veto (usually within sixty days by action of *either* chamber) reorganization plans proposed by the administration. A number of years ago (before the current reorganization law was passed), President Kennedy's attempt to create a Department of Urban Affairs by executive order was vetoed by the House of Representatives.

Thus the political executive is subject to the actions of both the President and the Congress. In a very real sense he must serve two political masters that often disagree on what kinds of things his unit should do and how it should go about doing them. Further, he finds himself in competition with his counterparts in other executive agencies over scarce funds and over jurisdiction. For many years, for instance, the Forest Service in the Department of Agriculture and the National Park Service in the Department of the Interior have vied over the control of vacant lands, particularly in the western part of the United States. Similarly, the Defense Department's Army Corps of Engineers and the Interior Department's Bureau of Reclamation have battled for the right to develop the waterways of the nation.

Under such circumstances a political executive finds it necessary to secure political allies outside as well as inside the formal structure of government. One natural outside source is his "clientele." Thus the Veterans Administration establishes close relationships with the American Legion and the Veterans of Foreign Wars, as does the Office of Education with the National Educational Association, the American Federation of Teachers, and other professional educators. The support of such interest groups can prove useful in the political process.

Another source of natural allies, one within the government, is congressional committees and subcommittees. The head of the Veterans Administration establishes ties with the Veterans Affairs Committees of the Senate and House of Representatives, and the appropriate subcommittees of the Appropriation Committees of the two chambers. Similarly, the Commissioner of Education works closely with the Education Subcommittee of the Senate Labor and Public Welfare Committee, the House Education and Labor Committee, and the pertinent subcommittees of the two Appropriations Committees.

These three-way alliances of executive units, congressional subcommittees and committees, and interest groups have been called "whirlpools of power" and "subsystems" operating within the larger political system. However described, they point to the existence of enduring political relationships that advance common interests. In seeking to expand and improve the services provided by this unit, a political executive serves the interests of its clientele group: a program of better benefits for veterans naturally pleases the American Legion and the Veterans of Foreign Wars. By the same token such a program is usually favorably regarded by the congressional committees and subcommittees involved with veterans' affairs, since senators and representatives generally seek assignments to committees that deal with matters in which they have a personal interest and sympathy.

Many political executives also seek to build a broader basis of outside support than that provided by special interest groups; they look to the general public as well. Perhaps best known for its activities in this regard is the Federal Bureau of Investigation. As many visitors to Washington, D.C. know, the most interesting tour of governmental agencies is provided by the Bureau. It has also succeeded in making itself the subject of many magazine articles, books, movies, and even television series, which extol the virtues of the "G" men. In the process, its director, J. Edgar Hoover, became a Washington legend, virtually immune from control not only by the secretary of the Justice Department, of which the Bureau is a part (witness the difficulties between Hoover and recent Attorneys General, the late Robert Kennedy and Ramsey Clark), but also by the President of the United States.

Not all political executives, of course, experience the success J. Edgar Hoover has enjoyed over the years. Many are frustrated victims of the political infighting that involve rivalries between the President and congressmen, among heads of agencies within the executive branch, and among competing interest groups. Added to their troubles are the members of the press, who have a vested interest in keeping a close watch on their activities. As a result many political executives stay in Washington, D.C. for a relatively short period of time before fleeing for a more tranquil (as well as more lucrative) existence in private life. This high rate of turnover, plus the difficulties of attracting qualified individuals to public service in the first place (many must give up seniority and allied benefits when they temporarily leave their private companies), presents a major personnel problem for the federal service.

If the world of these executives is difficult and frustrating, how much more so is that of the President himself. The following section examines the nature of his problems and the means he has at his disposal to deal with them.

THE PRESIDENT AS DECISION-MAKER

Given the broad scope of the President's activities, it is helpful, as we have done, to examine each of his several roles separately. Yet we need to keep in mind what the early friends of a strong executive saw so clearly: the office is and must be unified. The man who occupies it must, therefore, coordinate and accommodate these various roles if he is to give the nation effective political leadership.

The interrelationships of his various activities present major problems. For one thing, a scarcity of time and political resources means that he must frequently concentrate his attention on certain matters to the detriment of others: when President Kennedy faced problems in West Berlin, the number of his press conferences declined appreciably. In addition, playing one role may have adverse effects on another: a President who undertakes vigorous partisan campaigns in midterm elections may jeopardize his chances of securing support from members of the opposite party in Congress or of maintaining his public image of the nonpartisan leader of the nation. A failure in one aspect of his duties may also erode confidence in his ability to perform others well. After the fiasco at the Bay of Pigs in 1961, when Castro's forces destroyed Cuban political exiles attempting to invade the island with American support, President Kennedy experienced increased opposition to his legislative program. On the other hand, a success in one role may enhance the President's leadership in another: after Kennedy's skillful handling of the Cuban missile crisis (described below), he became generally more effective with Congress.

The President is thus a man with many closely related responsibilities. He must somehow learn to cope with a variety of groups, both inside and outside the government, that affect his political leadership. Termed by political scientist Richard Neustadt the Chief Executive's "constituencies," these groups include the Congress, the bureaucracy, members of his own party, citizens of the nation (especially "attentive publics"), and even people abroad.

In dealing with these forces, the President makes major decisions that vitally affect the people of this nation as well as those around the world. For the Presidency is above all an office calling for great decisions. John Kennedy faced a particularly awesome one in 1962 when it was determined that the Russians were developing missile sites in Cuba. Although the nature of decisions naturally differ from case to case, certain aspects of that incident point up common problems Presidents confront in determining what to do about matters that require their attention.

ELEMENTS OF PRESIDENTIAL DECISION-MAKING

As in any situation requiring a decision, the first step is to *find the facts*. In the early stages of the Russian arms build-up in Cuba in the late summer and early fall of 1962, it was not clear whether the missiles were defensive only or offensive as well. Initially, most officials (including Kennedy himself) assumed that the Soviets would not risk nuclear war by introducing in this hemisphere weapons that threatened the American mainland. Contrary reports by Cuban exiles were discounted initially on the basis that they could not tell the difference between defensive and offensive weapons and that their previous information had not been particularly reliable. Eventually, however, U-2 flights over the island on October 14 produced photographic evidence that a launching pad for offensive missiles had been built; in less than two week's time missiles would be on the pads ready for firing.

Faced with these facts, Kennedy assembled an *ad hoc* committee composed of fifteen individuals holding key positions relating to military and diplomatic affairs, such as the Secretaries of State and Defense, the Ambassador to the United Nations, the head of the Central Intelligence Agency, and the Joint Chiefs of Staff. Also included were White House staff aides; the President's brother, Attorney General Robert F. Kennedy; the Vice President, Lyndon Johnson; and two private individuals who had formerly served as Secretaries of State and Defense. This group, meeting extensively over the days that followed (Kennedy himself did not attend most of the meetings because he did not want his presence to inhibit the discussions), *considered various alternatives*. Doing nothing and making an airstrike to knock out the missiles were two options first considered by the group. In time, a third possibility emerged: throwing a naval blockade (euphemistically called a "quarantine," since a blockade is considered in international law as an act of war) around Cuba to prevent the shipment of missiles and materials associated with them into the island.

Having outlined the alternatives, the executive committee *explored the advantages and disadvantages of each*. The choice of taking no action was quickly discarded on the grounds that allowing the Soviets to get away with such a bold move would threaten the American mainland, upset the present balance of terror between the two nuclear giants, and destroy American credibility as a major power. Although the airstrike proposal backed by the

Decision-maker: John F. Kennedy at the presidential desk. (Cornell Capa/Magnum)

military initially received the most support, in time the quarantine plan advocated by Secretary of Defense Robert McNamara and Robert Kennedy emerged as the preferred course of action. The former alternative had several major disadvantages: it might not effectively destroy the sites, could bring about nuclear retaliation from the Soviets, and would be most unpopular among our allies in Europe and South America. On the other hand, the quarantine avoided immediate war and gave Soviet Premier Nikita Khrushchev time to reconsider his actions. It also left the option of military action open if the quarantine did not work.

Although the *ad hoc* executive committee could and did provide the President with the alternatives and the pros and cons of each, *only he could make the final decision.* He did so, ruling in favor of the quarantine. With the committee's advice, he also set in motion a series of actions designed to *implement* the decision. Interested groups were informed of it, starting with congressional leaders, allies in Western Europe, and ultimately publics here and abroad as the President went on television to explain the dangerous situation and our response to it. Further support for his action was sought by presenting the matter to the United Nations and the Organization of American States. Meanwhile, land, sea, and air forces were alerted in preparation for an invasion of Cuba if all other methods failed.

In the days that followed the world waited anxiously to see what Khrushchev would do. An exchange of letters between him and Kennedy, together with meetings between American and Soviet diplomatic representatives, eventually led to the settlement of the matter: the Soviets ordered their ships to turn back and also dismantled the missiles they had already placed in Cuba. All the while, Kennedy was careful not to push the Soviet Premier into a position in which he would have to choose between total humiliation or launching a nuclear attack; the young President also cautioned all parties not to boast about the outcome. The final resolution of the matter did much to pave the way for better relationships between the two world powers, and enhanced Kennedy's prestige both here and abroad.

While few presidential decisions have such potential consequences (as Kennedy put it, there is a great difference in a bill's being defeated and the country's being wiped out), many involve difficulties not present in the Cuban missile crisis. The facts of a case are often more difficult to come by than the placement of the offensive missiles, for political, social, and economic matters are more subject to differing interpretations than the physical presence (or absence) of a weapon system. Moreover, the alternatives (including taking no action) available to a President in a given situation may be more restricted or infinitely more complex. The President also generally finds it very difficult to rally support from as many groups as sided with Kennedy about Cuba: domestic issues breed more political rivalries than an incident that threatens the very survival of the nation and all its people.

PRESIDENTIAL METHODS AND TECHNIQUES
OF DECISION-MAKING

As decisions vary, so do the means by which Presidents seek to reach them. President Eisenhower, for example, employed methods he had learned in the army. His administration was characterized by an extensive delegation of authority to subordinates, together with a chain-of-command principle whereby many decisions were made by lower-level interagency committees. Even those decisions he ultimately made were facilitated by members of his staff who condensed the facts and alternatives in brief memoranda that the President could examine in a short period of time.

In sharp contrast were the methods of Franklin Roosevelt. Rather than make a clear delegation of authority to specific individuals for particular programs, FDR deliberately created overlapping responsibilities between different administrative units. Termed the "competitive" theory of administration, his policy was deliberately designed to create rivalries between individuals, a practice Roosevelt justified on the basis that each, therefore, tried to do a better job than his counterpart. (This technique also provided FDR with more information than he would have gained from one individual alone, and so enabled him to stay on top of situations.) Roosevelt also frequently bypassed the chain of administrative command by dealing directly with assistant secretaries and bureau chiefs without informing cabinet officials (their superiors) of such actions.

Presidents also differ on how they utilize the institutions of the executive branch. As might be expected, Eisenhower's commitment to the concept of an executive "team" led him to have frequent cabinet meetings, complete with an established agenda; on the other hand, FDR and Kennedy seldom convened the body, and when they did they made no real effort to transact important business. Each preferred to deal directly with individual cabinet secretaries or their subordinates. Kennedy, like Roosevelt, frequently called startled underlings on the telephone to get their advice on a matter or to prod them to greater efforts on an assignment.

Whatever administrative techniques particular Presidents employ, they seek a common goal: to get others to help them make vital decisions. This effort requires a delicate balance that is difficult to maintain. Roosevelt and Kennedy were both criticized for involving themselves personally with so many matters and obtaining advice from so many sources that they got bogged down in minor concerns and had trouble making up their minds in the face of contradictory suggestions. On the other hand, Eisenhower was accused of abdicating his responsibility for major matters by permitting his advisors to make decisions that rightfully belonged to him.

All Presidents share the problem of getting advice from individuals who can look at matters from the Chief Executive's perspective rather than just from their own. Presidents cannot depend on their cabinets to provide such advice, since department heads tend to view concerns from the vantage point of their own particular group and its clientele.* For this reason Presidents have at times sought counsel from private individuals outside the government who have no particular axe to grind. Woodrow Wilson, for example, depended on Colonel Edward M. House for suggestions on both domestic and foreign affairs, and a series of recent Presidents of both political parties solicited recommendations from the late financier Bernard Baruch on a variety of matters. Since the creation of the White House Office, Chief Executives have been able to place persons they trust on the staff, as John Kennedy did with Theodore Sorensen and Lyndon Johnson, with William Moyers.

Ultimately, however, when all the advice is in, it is the President alone who must make the final decision whether to press hard for a particular piece of legislation, issue an executive order, hire or fire a major executive official, campaign extensively in a midterm election, or go on television to address the American people on a delicate problem in domestic or foreign affairs. As former President Harry Truman expressed the situation in a terse sign on his desk in the White House: "The Buck Stops Here."

---

*Some individual cabinet members, however, do have broader interests and perspectives and are expected to do more than merely administer their departments. The late Robert Kennedy and John Mitchell advised Presidents Kennedy and Nixon respectively on many matters not related to their duties as Attorney General.

ASSESSMENT

The Presidency as it has evolved over the course of our history is almost precisely the opposite of what the Founding Fathers had in mind for the office. Rather than representing minority property interests and checking the actions of the popular body, the House of Representatives, many Presidents in recent years have initiated proposals benefiting social, political, and economic underdogs in American society. Woodrow Wilson's "New Freedom," Franklin Roosevelt's "New Deal," Harry Truman's "Square Deal," John Kennedy's "New Frontier," and Lyndon Johnson's "Great Society," all were liberal legislative programs advocated by Democratic Chief Executives. And, while Republican Presidents like Theodore Roosevelt, Dwight Eisenhower, and Richard Nixon have not proposed such sweeping changes in the *status quo* as their Democratic counterparts, nevertheless they have been more liberal in their orientation than most of their Republican congressional colleagues, particularly those serving in the House of Representatives. Thus the first Roosevelt took the leadership in regulating business trusts; social security and unemployment compensation benefits were expanded to cover more pepole during the Eisenhower administration; and Nixon proposed sweeping changes in the welfare program to bring larger payments to more persons.*

A major factor in this development in the Presidency is the change that has occurred in the method of selecting our Chief Executives. As previously indicated, the electoral college designed to allow elites in various states to choose the President has been converted into a nationwide popularity contest favoring large, politically competitive states in which blacks, Mexican-Americans, Puerto Ricans, and other ethnic groups are heavily concentrated. In these circumstances it is not surprising to find Presidents (particularly Democratic ones, but liberal Republican ones as well) receptive to the interests of such disadvantaged groups.

The President is also in a better position than other public officials to initiate proposals for change. He has important communication linkages to his political party and to the American public in general; he also has a variety of tools he can utilize to persuade legislative and executive officials to follow his political lead. In a pluralistic society where power is widely distributed among a wide variety of private groups and many public officials, the Presidency is a focal point for developing positive public policies and rallying majorities within and without government to their support.

Yet there are many limitations on what an ambitious Chief Executive can do. He has limited influence over his party in Congress and finds it difficult to control the activities of the three million employees of the executive

---

*The social security, unemployment compensation, and welfare programs will all be discussed in Chapter 16.

branch. Particularly powerful are the triangular alliances that exist among private groups, executive units, and congressional committees and subcommittees that often foster and protect the interests of economically advantaged minorities at the expense of an over-all program of presidential priorities. Nor are Presidents uniformly successful in rallying Congress, the general public, or attentive publics to their support. It is significant to note that almost none of Truman's "Fair Deal" and Kennedy's "New Frontier" legislative proposals were enacted into law.

Over the years students of the Presidency have advocated a number of improvements designed to strengthen the office: an item veto to permit him to nullify parts of a bill without having to turn down the whole measure; the right of cabinet members to go on the floor of Congress; increased staff assistance for the Chief Executive; and simultaneous elections for the Presidency, House, and Senate to facilitate party majorities. Yet there is little indication that any of these would make much difference in the conduct of the office or that Presidents even need them to be politically effective. More helpful in this latter regard is Neustadt's suggestion that we choose political professionals for the office who are experienced in wielding power and who can persuade other officials to do what the President wants them to do, not just for his sake, but for their own as well.

It would be a mistake, however, to accept wholeheartedly the idea of the "strong" President as always a good thing for democracy or the country. Former White House aide George Reedy has charged in his recent book, *The Twilight of the Presidency*, that an incumbent of the office is sheltered from the harsh realities of life by a protective staff that courts favor from him rather than telling him when and why he is wrong. Other liberals who have typically supported the Franklin Roosevelt model of the Presidency have become alarmed at the power the Chief Executive wields in foreign policy, as well the unwillingness or inability of recent incumbents of the office to properly handle many of the major domestic problems of our society. We will withhold judgment on this latter sentiment until we examine in the last part of the book the President's role in three major areas of public policy—race, poverty, and foreign affairs.

Selected Readings

The problems the President faces as party leader are analyzed by James Burns in the *Deadlock of Democracy: Four-Party Politics in America* (Englewood Cliffs, N.J.: Prentice-Hall, 1963). Lester Seligman treats the President's personal party in "The Presidential Office and the President as Party Leader," *Law and Contemporary Problems* (Autumn 1956), 724–735.

For an excellent analysis of the President's role as leader of public opinion, see Elmer Cornwell, *Presidential Leadership of Public Opinion* (Bloomington, Ind.:

Indiana University Press, 1965). The Chief Executive's relationships with the press are treated by Douglass Cater, "The President and the Press," *The Annals of the American Academy of Political and Social Science* (September, 1956), 55–66.

Wilfred Binkley's revised edition, *The President and Congress* (New York: Vintage Books, 1962), chronicles the relationships that have prevailed between the two over the course of our history. Lawrence Chamberlain's analysis of the respective parts that the President and Congress have played in the formulation of major legislation is dealt with in *The President, Congress, and Legislation* (New York: Columbia University Press, 1946).

A recent general analysis of the national executive is James Davis, Jr., *The National Executive Branch* (New York: Free Press, 1970). An excellent study of the cabinet is Richard Fenno, *The President's Cabinet* (Cambridge: Harvard University Press, 1959). For an historical analysis of Senate action on presidential nominations, see Joseph Harris, *The Advice and Consent of the Senate* (Berkeley: University of California Press, 1953). Excellent studies of close presidential advisers are Louis Koenig, *The Invisible Presidency* (New York: Holt, Rinehart and Winston, 1960), and Patrick Anderson, *The President's Men* (Garden City: Anchor, 1969). Studies of high-level civil servants and political executives include John Carson and R. Shael Paul, *Men Near the Top* (Baltimore: Johns Hopkins University Press, 1966), Dean Mann, *The Assistant Secretaries* (Washington: The Brookings Institution, 1965), and Marver Bernstein, *The Job of the Federal Executive* (Washington: The Brookings Institution, 1958). For a study of reorganization efforts of the late 1930s, see Barry Karl, *Executive Reorganization and Reform in the New Deal* (Cambridge: Harvard University Press, 1963). A political analysis of budget-making is Aaron Wildavsky, *The Politics of the Budgetary Process* (Boston: Little, Brown, 1964).

A penetrating analysis of the problems of presidential decision-making is Richard Neustadt, *Presidential Power*, rev. ed. (New York: John Wiley, 1968). For a brief treatment of the same subject by a former White House aide of President Kennedy, see Theodore Sorensen, *Decision-Making in the White House* (New York: Columbia University Press, 1963).

A very good over-all analysis of the Presidency which favors a "strong" Chief Executive is James Burns, *Presidential Government* (Boston: Houghton Mifflin, 1965). George Reedy, *The Twilight of the Presidency* (New York: World, 1970), expresses a fairly pessimistic view of the ability of the Presidency to cope with the current problems of our society.

CHAPTER 13

Law and Justice

Clarence Earl Gideon reading a law book. It was in the prison library that he learned of his right to counsel, a discovery that led to a landmark Supreme Court decision. (Flip Schulke/Black Star)

I N JANUARY 1962 the Clerk of the United States Supreme Court received a petition from Clarence Earl Gideon, a prisoner serving a five-year term in the Florida State Prison for breaking and entering a pool hall and stealing coins from a cigarette machine inside the building. In the petition Gideon asked that the Court get him out of jail because during his trial in the county court in Panama City, Florida, his request for a lawyer (he was too poor to hire one himself) had been refused initially by that court and later by the Supreme Court of the State of Florida. Gideon contended that the failure to provide him with an attorney when he was being tried for a felony crime* violated the provisions of the Fourteenth Amendment of the national Constitution guaranteeing that "no state shall deprive any person of life, liberty or property without due process of law."

Gideon, a poorly educated man who had been in and out of jails most of his life, could hardly have been expected to understand the subtleties of the law bearing on his case. Although the Supreme Court had previously ruled in a 1938 case, *Johnson* v. *Zerbst*, that defendants who could not afford an attorney in criminal trials in federal courts were entitled to have one appointed for them, it had refused to apply the same ruling to state criminal proceedings. Instead, in a 1942 case, *Betts* v. *Brady*, the Court had formulated the rule that a defendant had the right to counsel in a noncapital state criminal case (one not involving the death penalty) only if it could be demonstrated that "special circumstances" prevailed, such as the defendant's illiteracy, ignorance, youth, or mental incapacity; that the charge was complex; that there was community hostility; or that the conduct of the prosecutor or judge at the trial was improper. Yet Gideon's petition contained no indication that any of these circumstances were present in his trial before the county court in Florida. If the Supreme Court were to follow its former ruling, it would refuse to hear Gideon's case, and he would remain in the Florida jail.

Fortunately for Gideon the *Betts* v. *Brady* ruling was unpopular with many persons, including three justices of the Supreme Court who had refused to go along with the majority. Moreover, the courts had experienced difficulties in deciding cases under the "special circumstances" rule. In a number of decisions prior to 1962 (including all those in the past twelve years), the Supreme Court had reversed state criminal convictions on the grounds that "special circumstances" unacknowledged by state officials war-

*A felony is a serious crime; a minor one is a misdemeanor. A felony ordinarily has a potential penalty of imprisonment for at least a year and a day.

ranted the appointment of counsel. Several new justices had also joined the Court in the twenty years since the *Betts* decision. All these factors contributed to the Court's decision in June 1962 to hear the Gideon case for the purpose of reconsidering the *Betts* v. *Brady* decision.

The Supreme Court appointed an eminent lawyer, Abe Fortas, to represent Gideon in the case. Fortas (later to become a Supreme Court Justice himself) was widely respected as one of the finest legal minds in the nation; at fifty-one a senior partner in a prominent Washington law firm, he was an experienced advocate who had successfully argued major cases before the Supreme Court. To assure a thorough preparation of the *Gideon* case, he assigned young men in his firm to research the problem. In addition, *amicus curiae* briefs were filed on Gideon's behalf by the attorneys general of twenty-three states and by the American Civil Liberties Union.*

In contrast, the task of persuading the Supreme Court to retain the *Betts* v. *Brady* ruling fell to Bruce Jacob, a twenty-six-year-old inexperienced lawyer from Florida who had never even seen the Supreme Court, let alone tried a case before it. Originally assigned to the case in the spring of 1962 while he was a member of the state attorney general's office, by the following fall when the brief for the State of Florida was due to be filed with the Supreme Court, Jacob had entered private practice. He prepared the case entirely on his own, working on it over weekends, when he drove 250 miles to use the facilities of the Florida State Supreme Court library. Although Jacob wrote to the attorneys general of all fifty states to solicit *amicus curiae* briefs on behalf of Florida's side of the case, only two, in Alabama and North Carolina, responded to his request. (Ironically, it was Jacob's letter that stimulated the *amicus curiae* briefs favoring Gideon's side of the case to be filed by the attorneys general from twenty-three states.)

The following January, a year after Gideon originally filed his case before the Supreme Court, oral arguments were heard. Jacob and an assistant attorney general of Alabama argued that the *Betts* v. *Brady* ruling should be followed by the Supreme Court because it was consistent with the principle of federalism that states should be free to experiment with the use of counsel in criminal proceedings so long as defendants' interests were not harmed by "special circumstances." They also cautioned that if the *Betts* case were overruled, prisoners in Florida and other states who were convicted in proceedings in which they were not represented by counsel would suddenly be released *en masse* on society. Fortas's major contentions were that the *Betts* v. *Brady* ruling was unworkable and that it did a disservice to the principle of federalism by requiring the Supreme Court to intervene in state criminal

*A brief is a written statement setting forth the facts of the case and the arguments for a particular finding which a party to litigation files with a court to persuade it to rule in his favor. An *amicus curiae* (literally, "friend of the court") brief is one filed by some individual or group that is not a direct party to the suit but has an interest in its outcome.

proceedings to determine whether or not "special circumstances" were present in each individual case. A representative of the American Civil Liberties Union who joined Fortas in the oral argument made another basic point: a man cannot get a fair trial when he represents himself.

Two months later in mid-March, 1963, the Court handed down a decision in favor of Gideon which specifically overruled the *Betts* v. *Brady* case. Delivering the decision for the Court was Justice Black; joining in with him in the unanimous ruling were the other eight members of the Court. (Three, however, Douglas, Clark, and Harlan, filed separate opinions in which they concurred with Black's result but set forth different reasons for reaching it.) A few weeks later, Black, who had been in the minority twenty years before, confided to a friend: "When *Betts* v. *Brady* was decided, I never thought I'd live to see it overruled."

Subsequently, Gideon was tried again before the same county judge who had been involved in the first proceeding against him. A stubborn man, Gideon initially contended that he could not get a fair trial ("It's the same court, the same judge, everything,") and refused the assistance of counsel provided by the Florida Civil Liberties Union. (Ironically, this time Gideon wanted to plead his own case.) The judge subsequently appointed a local attorney to represent him and in the subsequent trial, the jury found Gideon not guilty. Later a newspaper reporter asked Gideon if he thought he had accomplished anything. "Well I did," he replied.

Relatively few of the millions of cases tried in the courts at all levels of our political system are as dramatic and far-reaching in their impact as the Gideon one. Yet the law, and the various courts in which the law is enforced, play a major part in regulating the activities of individuals and groups in American society. We first examine the basic elements of our legal system; the next chapter concentrates on the federal courts, including the one in which Gideon's case was ultimately decided—the Supreme Court of the United States.

THE NATURE AND PURPOSES
OF THE LAW

The law is a term that is used in various ways. It refers to personal authority, as in the phrase "so-and-so's word is law," meaning that what he says goes as far as his associates are concerned. In some societies, the father of a family makes the major decisions, which the remainder follow with little or no question. The word also describes certain basic immutable principles governing human behavior—that is the sense of "natural laws" or the "laws of nature," which are held to be rational and applicable to all individuals and societies. The problem is to discover what natural laws are and how to utilize them in governing human affairs.

Here I will use "laws" to mean the rules and regulations that a government imposes on individuals or groups. (In the United States, laws can emanate from national, state, or local governments.) As we saw in Chapter 1, these rules differ from those made by other individuals or other social institutions: only the government can enforce its regulations through its monopoly on legitimate force. Thus a father's command is not "law" in the sense in which I am using the term, because it does not apply generally. Indeed, the government places limits on the sanctions a father is permitted to impose on his children: he cannot legitimately imprison them or take their lives for disobeying his commands. Nor is natural law the law we are talking about: it refers to general principles that *should* regulate human affairs, not necessarily those that *actually do*. Only if enacted into governmental rules and regulations would such principles constitute laws in the sense meant here.

Every organized society has to resort to law to govern the behavior of its members, primarily to avoid or resolve *conflicts* over a variety of matters: sexual rivalry, distribution of material goods, what use should be made of the resources of the society, and so on. Some means have to be developed to settle such conflicts. One possibility is force: the stronger claimant prevails. But that approach leads to chaos and destruction.

Another possibility is for antagonists to turn to a third party to settle the conflict. In a dispute between two individuals over, say, a piece of land, a disinterested party could hear the facts of the case and the reasons why each party feels he is entitled to the land. *A* may say he is entitled to the property in question because the former owner made an oral promise to give it to him; *B* may, in turn, produce a piece of paper signed by the owner which describes the land and details the terms of sale to *B*. The person deciding the dispute might rule that *B* has a better claim to the land because he has specific written evidence of the former owner's intentions. The arbitrator has thereby developed a rationale for his decision, and such a rationale constitutes a principle of law. Assuming that *A* accepts the principle, the law will serve its major purpose: *to settle disputes peacefully*.

Principles of law also provide individuals with *advance notice of their rights* by letting them know ahead of time what they must do to accomplish a certain result. A person wanting to lay claim to a piece of land might deduce from the dispute between *A* and *B* that he had better get a written statement of transfer from the former owner. Thus the law introduces an element of certainty and predictability in human affairs and thereby serves *to prevent future disputes*: someone without written evidence of his right to a piece of land might not think it worthwhile to contest the claim of another person who has such evidence.

Another function of the law is to *render justice in society*. It is admittedly difficult to define "justice" precisely, but generally it refers to the idea of giving every man "his due," what he is entitled to in life. Basically, then, justice is fairness in deciding disputes between individuals, and fairness means that the results of a dispute ought not to depend on who the parties to it are: the same principles of law should be applied to all individuals regardless of their background or station in life. The belief that this is so does much to insure that decisions in disputes will be accepted by the losing party and by other persons as well. Thus the contribution of the law to just decisions not only serves the interests of the immediate parties concerned but also fosters a peaceful society.

SOURCES OF AMERICAN LAW

American principles of law evolved from certain developments in England in the eleventh and twelfth centuries, when its monarchs gradually developed a central system of courts to administer justice. The rules of law developed to decide disputes came to be known as the "common customs of the realm," or more simply "common law." What was "common" to the law was that it was applied throughout the country so that the same general legal principles governed disputes in the various local units.

Common law was "judge-made" law, developed on a case-by-case basis by representatives of the king hearing disputes. In determining what principles to apply, the judges sometimes drew upon customs that had been followed in the community and sometimes they derived their own notions of sound, commonplace principles of fairness that would help prevent similar disputes in the future.

To avoid deciding each individual case anew, and also to give some certainty to the law, judges followed the general principle of *"stare decisis,"* which means literally "to adhere to the decision." That is, they looked at what judges in the past had done in similar situations and applied the earlier results and rationale to the immediate case before them. Out of this practice there developed a body of common law principles that were utilized to settle disputes throughout England.

THE DEVELOPMENT OF "EQUITY"

Although the common law thus provided continuity and certainty in the handling of legal matters, it also became exceedingly rigid. Unless an individual could fit his particular grievance and the relief he sought within the special categories of common law actions which the courts recognized, he could receive no redress for his difficulty. In time aggrieved persons began to petition the King to hear their cases "in the interests of justice and charity." He, in turn, referred such matters to his Chancellor, the most important figure in his Executive Council. Separate courts of chancellery were developed to hear such cases; in time they came to be known as courts of "equity," because they were based on general principles of fairness and conscience.

Equity thus developed as a distinct type of law. Although still "judge-made," it was based less on the principle of *stare decisis* and more on the merits of each particular case. In time, however, precedents developed for deciding these matters also. Nonetheless, equity did retain two special characteristics that differentiated it from regular common law. One was the type of relief it granted: courts of equity were not restricted to compensating a grieved party for past damages; they could also issue decrees preventing future wrongs. (Thus an individual who was concerned about his neighbor's plans to build a dam on adjoining property that would flood his land could ask a court of equity to grant an injunction forbidding its construction rather than wait for the flooding to occur and then seek compensation.) The second distinction was that courts of equity did not use juries (bodies of lay persons) to find the facts in the case as common law courts often did; the judge performed this function, along with developing and applying rules of law as in common law courts.

The principles of common law and equity law, together with dual courts to administer them, were brought to the New World by the English colonists in the seventeenth and eighteenth centuries. After the American Revolution the states adopted them as the foundation for their own law and court systems. Later, in the nineteenth century, states began to abolish separate courts of common law and equity (there never have been separate courts at the federal level), and today in virtually all states, the same judges administer both types of law, with their distinctive remedies and procedures.

The development of the English common law and equity law had certain far-reaching consequences for American society. For one thing, as in England, it produced a special group trained in developing and applying the complexities of law on a case-by-case basis: the legal profession,* including both judges and attorneys. (Judges were selected from the ranks of practicing attorneys rather than constituting a group set apart by special training as in some countries.) Both the judges and the attorneys tended to be conservative in their social and economic views. Often drawn from upper-class families, they were also exposed to the common law's solicitude for the property rights of individuals, as well as its concern for precedent in deciding present cases on the same basis as those of the past.

STATUTORY LAW

Although Americans tend to think of legislatures rather than courts as the primary source of law, in fact legislative statutes did not take on much significance in the United States until the second quarter of the nineteenth century. The change was linked with the spread of the franchise and the Jacksonian Revolution, which resulted in the election of legislators with dif-

---

*Traditionally lawyers received their training in the law office of a practicing attorney, but since the end of World War I attendance at a law school (typically associated with a university) has replaced the apprenticeship method.

ferent views from those of the judiciary. In time legislative bodies began to pass laws that modified those previously developed by the courts. For example, although common-law rulings provided that an employee who was injured because of the carelessness of a fellow employee could not receive damages from his employer if the latter were not at fault, eventually legislation made the employer liable as a means of protecting workers against the dangers of industrial employment.

Today statutes enacted by legislative bodies are a major source of laws at all levels of government. Americans are governed by acts of Congress and state legislatures, as well as regulations of local bodies such as city councils. These statutes spell out in detail the rules governing a great variety of human relationships in our increasingly complex and interdependent society.

ADMINISTRATIVE LAW

The increasing complexity of American society has resulted in still another major source of law: rules and regulations of administrators in the executive branch of government. As explained in Chapter 10, Congress no longer has the time, expertise, or political inclination to deal with all the varied problems in society, so it delegates authority to executive agencies to fix regulations within broad guidelines. To refer to an earlier example, Congress has entrusted the Federal Highway Safety Bureau with developing automobile safety standards that are "appropriate" and "practicable," "meet the need for motor vehicle safety," and are "stated in objective terms." State legislatures make similar authorizations to agencies in the states' executive branches.

CONSTITUTIONAL LAW

One final source of American law is the national Constitution and the constitutions of the fifty states. Constitutions differ from other sources of law in that they are adopted through extraordinary processes. The national Constitution was originally written by the delegates to the Constitutional Convention and then ratified by action of conventions called in the various states. State constitutions were also framed by delegates to special conventions and then ratified by the voters. Changes in constitutions also typically require extraordinary procedures: extramajority votes of legislatures, special constitutional conventions, and actions of the voters.

INTERRELATIONSHIPS AMONG LAWS
FROM DIFFERENT SOURCES

American law thus stems from a variety of sources—all three branches of the government, special conventions, and the public. Out of this mixture comes a wide variety of rules and regulations that govern the activities of individuals and groups in society.

Because of potential conflicts among the various sources of law, priorities among them are required. Statutory law takes precedence over common law and equity law; thus legislators can change judges' rules, as in establishing the liability of employers for injuries suffered by their employees. Legislatures also have the power to change regulations developed by administrative agencies; Congress could enact automobile safety regulations of its own if it were dissatisfied with those developed by the Federal Highway Safety Bureau. Finally, common law, equity, and statutory and administrative regulations, all must give way to constitutional provisions.

In actuality, of course, legal regulations from one branch of government are affected by the other branches. Although legislators can change common law rulings and overrule administrative regulations, the wording of statutes they pass is interpreted initially by executive officials and, in many instances, later by the courts. As we will see in the next chapter, the courts also have the power in the United States to determine whether statutes or executive actions violate the national or state constitutions. But the judiciary does not even have the final say, for the Congress can change judicial rulings through constitutional amendments—which, in turn, are subject to interpretation by the courts. Thus the law is a seamless web subject to actions and counteractions of various public officials as well as the people themselves.

APPLICATIONS OF LAW

Law can be analyzed in terms not only of its sources but also of its applications. One important distinction is between *private* law and *public* law. Regulations regarding contractual agreements, marriage and divorce, wills, deeds of land, and the like determine the legal rights and obligations among individuals and nongovernmental groups. Much of the law (derived in this instance primarily from common law, equity, and statutes) is of this nature. Although public officials develop, apply, and enforce legal regulations on private individuals and groups, the officials themselves are not directly affected by them.

Legal rules and regulations that apply to government officials are known as *public law*. They define the rights and obligations that exist among the officials themselves as well as those that govern relationships between them and private citizens and groups. For instance, the power of the President to veto acts of Congress is governed by public law, as is the right of a private individual to criticize actions of public officials. The primary sources of public law are constitutional provisions, administrative regulations, and statutes, but common law also plays some role. Judges too shape the public law through their power to interpret and apply constitutional, administrative, and statutory provisions.

JUDICIAL PROCEDURES
FOR ENFORCING LAW

The hallmark of a law, as compared to an informal custom or a moral principle, is that it can be enforced through sanctions that are considered legitimate by affected parties and that can involve the use of force. Thus the means by which laws are enforced and the purposes of enforcement are central to a legal system.

The two major means to enforce laws are *civil* and *criminal* procedures. The former has as its major purpose the personal interest of the individual whose rights have been violated by others. In a civil proceeding the affected party brings a legal action to compensate him for some unjustified loss he has suffered because of the activities of the individual or group he is suing. A may bring an action against B for injuring him in an automobile accident, for breaking an agreement to sell him goods, for trespassing on his property and damaging it, or the like. In such circumstances A seeks money damages to reimburse him for a wrong he has suffered at the hands of B.

Civil proceedings can also be instituted to prevent threatened actions that would harm A's interests if they did occur. Thus A might ask a court to issue an injunction (a remedy in equity) forbidding B to build a manufacturing plant next to his private home that would interfere with A's rights to clean air and a pleasant view. Or A might ask the court to order B to take some action to protect A's interests. For example, B might be permitted to build the plant, provided he uses a certain kind of "clean" fuel and builds a fence around the property.

For the most part, civil procedure is utilized to enforce the rights of private individuals and groups against other private groups and individuals, but public officials can be parties to a civil proceeding. The Commissioner of Internal Revenue, for instance, can bring a civil action against an individual who fails to pay his taxes in order to recover the monies owed to the federal government. Also, in some instances, public officials can be sued by private individuals. For example, if a public official mistakenly computes an individual's income tax with the result that he is required to pay more than he actually owes, the taxpayer can sue the official for the amount he is overcharged if the official refuses to return the money to him.*

A criminal procedure involves the rights of society in general, not merely those of the particular individual wronged. For example, in the *Gideon*

---

*Under the doctrine that the king can do no wrong, governments cannot be sued without their permission. However, legislative bodies generally grant individuals and groups the right to bring certain types of actions (such as those growing out of a breach of contract) against public officials.

case it was the state of Florida, not the owner of the pool hall into which Gideon was alleged to have broken, that brought the criminal suit. The actions of the state were based on the premise that Gideon's alleged action was of legitimate concern to others besides the pool hall owner.

One reason for employing criminal procedures is the basic idea that a person who commits a serious wrong must be punished for it: justice requires that he pay—by a fine, by imprisonment, or in extreme circumstances with his life—for the harm he has done his fellow man. Another purpose of criminal proceedings is to deter future wrongdoing by establishing the expectation of punishment. Finally, there is the motive of protecting society. If a convicted criminal is imprisoned or put to death, he has been removed as a potential threat to society, and during imprisonment he may be successfully rehabilitated so that he can be safely returned to society. (Frequently, however, rehabilitation efforts fail because few prisons have adequate programs or facilities and also because a released prisoner often finds it hard to find a job and so returns to crime to sustain himself.)

An act that gives rise to a criminal proceeding can generally give rise to a civil suit as well since they involve harm to property or persons. Thus in the *Gideon* case the owner of the pool hall could have brought a civil proceeding against Gideon to recover the money he allegedly stole from the cigarette machine. However, both the small amount of money involved and the unlikelihood that it could be collected from Gideon made the step not worthwhile.

COURTS FOR CONDUCTING JUDICIAL PROCEDURES

In the American legal system there is a variety of courts in which judicial procedures are conducted. One basic distinction is between *trial courts*, which hear cases originally, and *appellate courts*, to which cases are taken on appeal from the decisions of the trial tribunals.

It is in the trial court that the excitement and drama of the judicial process occur. Attorneys argue their cases, using witnesses to testify to various facts that are important to the case; the judge referees the spirited contest, indicating what kind of evidence can be introduced by the two sides to the case. The jury, composed of laymen, hears the evidence and decides what facts are true, guided by the judge who advises them on points of law. The final outcome of the case depends on the decisions made by the judge and the jury. The overwhelming share of cases that courts hear (most disputes are settled out of court by the parties) end in the trial court.

In some cases, however, the losing party seeks a reversal of the decision of the trial court by filing an appeal in a higher, or appellate, court. In such a tribunal the only participants are the opposing attorneys and the judges (most frequently more than one), who read the written briefs and hear the oral arguments of the attorneys. In hearing appeals the court determines whether any errors of law occurred in the trial court that operated against the interests of the losing party. If the appellate court finds that errors did occur, it either reverses the decision of the lower court outright or sends the case back to that court for a new trial.

Another important division in American courts exists between the *states* and the *national government*. As we saw in Chapter 3, one feature of the federal system is that each level of government has its own distinct political institutions, including separate systems of courts. Each state provides through its constitution and laws for its judiciary, but there is a fairly standard system that includes general trial courts at the county level and state courts of appeal.* As discussed in detail in the following chapter, there are also federal trial and appellate courts. Despite our dual court system in the United States, state and federal courts are not entirely separate. As discussed in Chapter 14, some kinds of cases can be tried originally in either state or federal courts, depending on the wishes of the parties. Moreover, as shown by the *Gideon* case, some litigation that begins in a state court is eventually appealed to a federal one.

With this basic information on the law, judicial procedures, and the courts in mind, we can turn to more specific aspects of the American legal system.

CRIMINAL PROCEDURE

It has long been a central feature of Anglo-American legal systems that the serious sanctions available in criminal procedures cannot be invoked against an accused person arbitrarily. As early as the fourteenth century, English courts provided that no man could be imprisoned or put to death except by "due process of law." English settlers in America brought with them a concern for the rights of the accused and a determination to protect those rights in criminal procedures. This solicitude for the rights of the accused in criminal cases has continued to be a hallmark of the American legal system. The late Supreme Court Justice Felix Frankfurter observed that "the history of liberty has largely been the history of the observance of procedural safeguards."

This concern derives from a number of fundamental beliefs. The right of an individual to privacy and to freedom from arbitrary governmental action are basic values in democracies in general and the American society in

*States also have special courts at the local level to hear certain kinds of cases, such as traffic violations and other misdemeanors, small civil claims, and juvenile matters. In addition, the larger states have intermediate courts of appeal, as well as a final one (usually called the State Supreme Court).

particular. Justice, or giving every man his due, is also a major purpose of the law. Finally, democracy attempts to protect the citizen from the state. Government is a powerful institution and in a criminal case the parties are seldom of equal strength. The state can marshal its vast resources against a single individual who must struggle to defend himself against charges that he has committed a wrong against society.

These considerations are reflected in the American system of criminal justice. The government is forbidden to violate the privacy of the individual through unreasonable searches and seizures of his home or person. Nor may it arrest him for arbitrary reasons. In the trial the state must prove its charge "beyond a reasonable doubt." Such prohibitions and requirements are deliberately designed to favor the accused by making it difficult for the government to succeed in its attempt to deny him his property, his freedom of movement, or his right of life itself.

SOURCES OF CRIMINAL PROCEDURE
AND RIGHTS OF THE ACCUSED

The dual legal system in the United States has resulted in separate lists of criminal offenses and trial procedures for the nation as a whole and for the fifty states. The overwhelming proportion of criminal acts violate state rather than federal laws and are tried in the state courts. Included are such major crimes as auto theft, burglary, rape, and murder. There are criminal offenses against the national government, however: for example, assassination of the President and taking a stolen automobile across state lines violate federal criminal laws and are subject to prosecution by federal officials in federal courts.*

There are several sources for rules governing criminal procedure and the rights of the accused in federal cases. The principal source is the United States Constitution, particularly the Fourth, Fifth, Sixth, and Eighth Amendments, which spell out certain prohibitions and procedural methods that must be respected. Specifically, the Fourth Amendment protects an individual against unreasonable searches and seizures of his person or his property; the next two Amendments detail how he must be charged and tried for a federal offense; while the Eighth Amendment restricts the severity of sanctions that can be imposed upon him as well as the amount of the bail that he must post in order to gain release from custody pending trial.

In addition to the specific procedural protections spelled out in these four amendments, the Fifth Amendment contains the historical English protec-

---

*Since a single act can violate both state and national criminal laws, the accused can be prosecuted by both jurisdictions. Such dual prosecutions do not violate the double jeopardy prohibition of the Fifth Amendment because under our federal system two separate levels of government are involved.

tion that an individual cannot be denied his life, liberty, or property without due process of law. The federal courts have interpreted that broad clause to mean that a person is entitled to a hearing before a fair and impartial tribunal. In the process they have held that an individual is entitled to other protections besides those specifically spelled out in the Fourth, Fifth, Sixth, and Eighth Amendments—for example, that a plea of guilty or not guilty must be made before a trial proceeds and that he must be personally present at every stage of the trial where his substantial rights may be affected.*

In addition to national constitutional provisions, acts of Congress also govern the rules of the federal criminal process. As discussed below, the omnibus Crime Control and Safe Streets Act of 1968 spells out the conditions under which confessions can be introduced in federal courts. Moreover, the federal courts themselves also issue certain rules pertaining to their handling of criminal matters.

Each of the fifty states also has its own constitution, and state legislatures and courts develop rules for criminal procedures.

Federal and state criminal processes are thus based on separate and distinct sources, but there is one provision of the national Constitution that has served to link them, the provision of the Fourteenth Amendment which declares that a state cannot "deprive any person of life, liberty, or property, without due process of law," an extension to the states of the restriction on the national government in the Fifth Amendment.

The due process clause of the Fourteenth Amendment is open to various interpretations. One is to equate it with the same clause in the Fifth Amendment. Under this interpretation the accused in a state criminal procedure, as in a federal court, is entitled to a hearing before a fair and impartial tribunal with the protection of specific safeguards (such as the right to be present at every stage of the trial). This is an interpretation of minimal procedural protection.

The interpretation of maximum procedural protection would construe the clause to include all the specific prohibitions and procedural methods spelled out in the Fourth, Fifth, Sixth, and Eighth Amendments. This is the interpretation favored by former Supreme Court Justice Black: the clause *incorporates* every safeguard mentioned in these four amendments.†
By this reasoning the accused in a state criminal case should enjoy all the

---

*Although this is the general rule, the courts have recently been faced with the problem of how to deal with defendants who deliberately try to disrupt their trial. In *Illinois* v. *Allen* (1969) the Supreme Court upheld the right of a judge to remove a defendant from the courtroom who used vile and abusive language.

†Black's incorporation theory covers not only the procedural safeguards spelled out in these four amendments but also other rights included in the first ten amendments. It would have the effect of making all such rights a person enjoys vis-à-vis the federal government also available in relation to the states.

procedural rights he has in federal proceedings (plus any other protections granted by a particular state's constitution or laws).

The Supreme Court has followed a middle ground in its interpretation of the matter by including within the coverage of the clause the general concept of a hearing before a fair and impartial tribunal along with certain of the specific procedural matters spelled out in the four earlier amendments. In choosing among such safeguards the Court has applied a general test first enunciated by Justice Benjamin Cardozo in a 1937 case, *Palko* v. *Connecticut*: is the particular procedural right at issue "of the very essence of ordered liberty?" Is it "so rooted in the traditions and conscience of our people as to be ranked as fundamental?"

For a number of years the Supreme Court was rather selective about the procedural safeguards it was willing to bring under the due process clause of the Fourteenth Amendment. For example, in the *Palko* case it refused to consider the double jeopardy prohibition of the Eighth Amendment as "fundamental" so as to prevent the state of Connecticut from appealing cases in which an accused person was acquitted in a lower court as a result of errors of law. Subsequently the Court refused to transfer other federal procedural rights to the states, including the right to a jury trial and—the issue in the *Gideon* case—the right to counsel in all criminal cases.

In so refusing, the Court took the position that Bruce Jacob argued in the *Gideon* case: under the federal system of government states ought to be free to experiment with different criminal procedures so long as they do not violate the nation's fundamental traditions or "the scheme of ordered liberty." Just because the Founding Fathers reacted to particular circumstances of their time and provided specific safeguards in federal criminal cases, the justices held, it does not follow that identical procedures need be followed by all the individual state governments 200 years later.

Gradually, however, the Supreme Court has read more and more of the specific provisions of the Fourth, Fifth, Sixth, and Eighth Amendments over into the due process clause of the Fourteenth Amendment. In *Benton* v. *Maryland* (1969) the same right at issue in the *Palko* case was extended to the states: the Eighth Amendment prohibition against double jeopardy. In the decision specifically overruling that earlier case, Justice Thurgood Marshall stated that the prohibition "represents a fundamental ideal in our constitutional heritage." Today as a result of a series of such decisions, of all the safeguards spelled out in the four amendments, only the one requiring the use of a grand jury to indict the accused in capital or "otherwise infamous" crimes remains outside the coverage of the due process clause of the Fourteenth Amendment.

What has happened is that the Supreme Court has maintained the same test first developed in the *Palko* case; however, it has come to regard more and more procedural rights as "traditional," "fundamental," or as "of the very essence of a scheme of ordered liberty." Although the test applied is still Cardozo's, the results now approach Black's preference for the wholesale application of all federal rights in criminal cases to the states.

A byproduct of this trend in the Court's attitude has been the convergence of the rights of the accused and of court procedures in federal and state criminal actions. As a result, today there is a substantial similarity in the criminal procedures of both types of jurisdiction.

GENERAL PROCEDURE IN CRIMINAL CASES

Criminal procedures in the American dual legal system are complex and detailed, but it is possible to get a general overview of them.

The initial step is the *apprehension* of the suspect—either through voluntary surrender or by swearing out a warrant empowering a police officer to arrest him. A police officer can also arrest a person without a warrant if an offense is committed in his presence or, in the case of a felony, if he has good reason to believe that the person did commit it.

Within a reasonable time after the suspect has been taken into custody, authorities must take him before a magistrate (in federal courts a commissioner) for a *preliminary hearing* to determine whether there is probable cause to believe that a crime has been committed and that the arrestee committed it. The hearing is designed to protect the accused against hasty or malicious action and the state against useless expense of subsequent proceedings if it doesn't have sufficient evidence to convict him. The magistrate examines the government's evidence, not to decide whether the accused is guilty or innocent, but to determine whether further proceedings are justified. If the evidence is insufficient the accused is released; otherwise he is held to answer the allegations against him.

Jurisdictions differ in handling the next step. Cases in federal (and many state) courts are taken before a *grand jury*, a group of citizens who hear the evidence against the accused to decide whether it is sufficient to warrant further proceedings. If they decide it is, they return a "true bill," or "indictment," against him; if they decide it is not, they return a "no bill" and charges are dropped.

Because the Supreme Court has held that indictment by a grand jury is not included within the due process clause of the Fourteenth Amendment, states can use some other method at this stage. About half the states, particularly those west of the Mississippi, permit the prosecutor to file an *information* consisting of charges supported by sworn statements of evidence against the accused.

The accused is next brought before the court for *arraignment* and *pleading*. The former is an official reading of the terms of the indictment or information by the court, after which the accused is given the opportunity to plead guilty or not guilty. In most criminal cases the parties engage in a process known as "plea bargaining" whereby the prosecutor agrees to reduce the charges against the accused in return for his pleading guilty to the lesser charges. If a guilty plea is entered, the judge decides on the *sentence*. (Usually he will accept the prosecutor's recommendations.) If the accused pleads not guilty, then the case must go to trial.

A person accused of violating a serious federal or state crime is entitled to have his case heard by a *jury* of citizens.* Federal court rules provide for a jury of twelve, but some states use smaller juries; in *Williams* v. *Florida* (1970) the Supreme Court upheld Florida's use of six-man juries.

Choosing a jury can be a long and tedious process. Both the government and defense attorneys interrogate prospective jurors (called *veniremen*) to determine whether they have prejudices that may interfere with their ability to hear the case objectively. Both sides are entitled to challenge veniremen for "cause," that is, to ask the judge to dismiss them for certain reasons, such as personal acquaintance with persons involved in the case or the fact they have already formed a judgment about the case. Both sides also have a certain number of "peremptory" challenges for which they need give no reasons.

When the composition of the jury is set, the *trial* itself begins. Both sides make opening statements setting forth the general nature of their case and the evidence they plan to introduce to support it. Witnesses testify about the events in question, and each side has the right to cross examine the other's witnesses. The judge acts as the referee of the contest, ruling on what kinds of evidence are admissible and the propriety of the questions put to the witnesses. At the end of the trial he also gives the jury instructions on questions they have to consider and what matters they may legitimately take into account in answering the questions.

The jury then retires to deliberate and reach a verdict. In federal and many state courts the verdict must be unanimous, which frequently means that the jury is "out" for a considerable period of time. If the jury is "hung"—that is, unable to reach agreement—it is necessary to choose a new one and begin the trial all over again.

Proceedings that follow the jury verdict include the *sentencing* of guilty defendants, the *appeal* of some cases to higher courts, and the final *execution* of the sentence.

CURRENT TRENDS AND CONTROVERSIES
IN CRIMINAL PROCEDURE

The Supreme Court has been very much concerned in recent years with the protection of the accused in criminal cases. Not only has it extended more and more procedural rights from federal courts to state tribunals, but

*In *Baldwin* v. *New York* (1970) the Supreme Court ruled that a defendant is entitled to a jury trial if the offense carries a potential sentence of six months or more in prison.

it has also liberalized its interpretation of a number of basic rights so as to benefit accused persons. The Court's aim has been to extend the concept of equal justice under the law to the poor and uneducated, who so often get into difficulty with legal authorities.

One area in which this is particularly apparent is *the right to counsel.* The *Gideon* case described at the beginning of this chapter established a basic principle: every person accused of a serious crime (felony) is entitled to have the assistance of an attorney. If he cannot afford to have one himself, then the government is obliged to provide one.

Gideon was a landmark case in that it opened the door to a series of specific questions involving the right to counsel. One concerns the kind of criminal cases to which it applies. Some legal experts have advocated that the right should apply to misdemeanors (minor crimes) as well as felonies. It remains to be seen whether the Supreme Court will extend the principle that far.

Another question involves the particular stages of the criminal process to which the right to counsel applies. The Supreme Court has extended the right to proceedings before and after the actual trial. It thus ruled in an important 1964 case, *Escobedo* v. *Illinois,* that the accused is entitled to the assistance of an attorney when an investigation is no longer a general inquiry into an unsolved crime but has begun to focus on a particular suspect, taken into custody, whose statements under interrogation will be used at his trial. And the Supreme Court held in a 1963 case, *Douglas* v. *United States,* that defendants are entitled to have an attorney at the appellate stages of the criminal process.

Since the *Gideon* case the federal government and the states have wrestled with the problems of who should act as attorneys for the accused and how they should be compensated for their services. In 1966 the national government passed legislation providing funds for attorneys appointed by federal courts to assist defendants in criminal proceedings. States have handled the matter in different ways. Some have provided *public defenders,* attorneys paid by public funds who concentrate on providing a legal defense in criminal cases for all persons who cannot afford an attorney of their own. Others have provided funds to compensate attorneys appointed in individual cases. Still others have refused to face up to the problem at all, with the result that lawyers have had to provide their services free of charge.

The Supreme Court has also been concerned about *confessions.* It has utilized its powers to supervise the administration of justice in federal cases by imposing strict limitations on the interrogation of suspects by federal agents. For example, in a 1957 case, *Mallory* v. *United States,* the Court ruled that a confession obtained during a ten-hour questioning of the accused between arrest and arraignment was inadmissible at the defendant's trial because the delay gave the opportunity for the extraction of the confession.

The Supreme Court has also become increasingly vigilant about the use of confessions in state proceedings. Not only has it invalidated those involving physical force or the threat of such force; it has also shown increased concern about the use of psychological pressures. In this connection the Court has looked at the "totality of the circumstances" surrounding a confession to determine whether it was voluntary or involuntary. Under that test the Court has balanced the pressures exerted against the ability of defendant to resist them, taking into account such factors as the kind and duration of the interrogation, and the age, intelligence, and literacy of the accused.

The Supreme Court has also changed its rationale for excluding involuntary confessions. Formerly they were excluded because they were likely to be unreliable. In a 1961 decision, *Rogers* v. *Richmond*, the Court suggested another reason: that because ours is an *accusatory* not an *inquisitorial* system, the state should be required to prove the guilt of the defendant by evidence other than that which it obtains by coercion out of his own mouth. Since the Supreme Court subsequently held in a 1964 decision, *Mallory* v. *Hogan*, that the Fifth Amendment privilege against self-incrimination expressly applies to state proceedings, confessions extracted by state officials can be invalidated on that basis, rather than merely on the grounds that they may be unreliable.

Thus the Supreme Court has increasingly expanded the right to counsel and prohibitions against incriminating confessions so as to protect accused persons. Moreover, it has linked the two in a way that provides even further safeguards. The classic instance, with respect to state proceedings, was a 1966 case, *Miranda* v. *State of Arizona*, the crux of which was that after a two-hour questioning by police officers the accused had confessed to kidnapping and rape. In overturning his conviction the Court ruled that once he had been taken into custody or deprived of his freedom of action in any significant way, law enforcement officials should have informed him that he had the right to remain silent and that anything he said could later be used against him. They had the additional obligation to tell him that he had the right to an attorney at the questioning and that if he lacked funds to hire one, he would be provided one by the state. Since officials had not complied with these procedural requirements, the Court ruled that the defendant's confession was illegally introduced into evidence and his conviction was invalid.

Few Supreme Court cases have evoked the storm of protest that followed the announcement of the *Miranda* decision. Law enforcement officials complained that it would handcuff their efforts to deal with criminals, that in its zeal to protect the rights of the accused the Court had forgotten that the real victim was the person against whom the offense was directed, not the one who committed it. Some critics even went so far as to link the nation's mounting crime rate with the permissive attitude of the Supreme Court.

Eventually this sentiment was found in many members of Congress, and when that body passed the Omnibus Crime Control and Safe Streets Act of 1968, it included a provision that sought to prevent the application of the *Miranda* ruling in federal criminal proceedings. The Act stated that if a judge, after looking at all the circumstances surrounding a particular confession, found it to have been given voluntarily, then it would be admissible in evidence even though each procedural requirement established in the *Miranda* decision had not been met. In addition, the law sought to alter the effect of the *Mallory* decision by providing that delay in bringing a person before a federal commissioner would not invalidate a confession if it were found to be voluntary and were given within six hours after the arrest of the accused.

The Supreme Court has not yet, at the writing of this book, ruled on the constitutionality of these provisions of the Omnibus Crime Control and Safe Streets Act affecting federal criminal procedures. Meanwhile, debate rages on the extent to which the *Miranda* decision has actually affected law enforcement at the state level. Law enforcement officials have generally claimed that the ruling has made it much more difficult to get convictions of criminals, while many civil libertarians have argued that criminals continue to confess in great numbers despite the *Miranda* decision and that many convictions are based on other evidence than confessions.*

Another controversial area of criminal procedure is the question of what should be done with an accused person who must wait for a long time (often a year or more) until his trial can be held. The traditional practice at both national and state level has been to permit someone charged with a noncapital offense to post *bail*, a sum of money insuring his appearance at trial. (Bail is usually handled through a professional surety who, for a fee, posts a bond that is forfeited if the defendant does not show up at the trial.) This procedure clearly discriminates against the poor defendant who cannot afford to post bond: he sits in jail, unable to prepare his defense adequately or to support his family, while the more affluent, including those involved in organized crime, have no trouble in posting bond and securing release from custody.

Recent attempts to develop alternatives to bail include the practice in some states of releasing persons simply on their personal promise to appear at the trial. In 1966 Congress authorized judicial officers in the District of Columbia to use this approach in both noncapital and capital federal offenses unless the judicial officer had reason to believe the accused would flee or pose a danger to others.

---

*In *Harris* v. *New York* (1971) the Court qualified the *Miranda* ruling by holding that if a defendant takes the witness stand in his trial and makes statements that differ from those made to officers while in custody, the earlier statements can be introduced in the trial for the purpose of discrediting his testimony (though not as evidence in the prosecution's case).

There has been much criticism of this approach, however, particularly in the District of Columbia where the crime rate has been high. What has especially troubled many citizens, including President Nixon and his Attorney General John Mitchell, is that a number of crimes have been committed by persons awaiting trial who had been released from custody. At the urging of the administration, Congress, in a 1970 act governing criminal procedure in the District of Columbia, provided for "preventive detention" for sixty days of those charged with dangerous (but noncapital) crimes whose release might endanger the community, individuals accused of crimes of violence, drug addicts, anyone who allegedly committed an offense after being released in connection with a previous offense, and persons accused of threatening a prospective juror or witness.

As might be expected, the concept of preventive detention has been attacked as violating the cardinal principles of Anglo-American justice that a man is considered innocent until proven guilty and that he is entitled to the basic elements of due process. Students of the problem also charge that neither psychiatrists, judges, nor lawyers can predict with any accuracy who will commit crimes if they are released; therefore, they claim, the concept of preventive detention is built on a false assumption. They suggest that the solution to the problem lies not in long imprisonment but in improving the administration of justice so that the accused are tried soon after their arrest.

The rights of persons accused of crimes versus those of society in protecting its members against dangerous individuals remains a major issue in a democracy. Drawing the line between these competing values is a difficult and perennial test in a free but orderly society.

CIVIL JUSTICE AND THE POOR

Along with the increased concern for "equal justice under the law" in criminal matters has come a realization that the poor also need assistance in their civil law problems. As the late Attorney General Robert Kennedy put the case some years ago:

> We have secured the acquittal of an indigent but only to abandon him to eviction notices, wage attachments, repossession of goods and termination of welfare benefits. To the poor man, "legal" has become a synonym simply for technicalities and obstructions, not for that which is to be respected. The poor man looks upon the law as an enemy, not as a friend. For him the law is always taking something away.

Kennedy's statement points up the kinds of legal problems poor people encounter in their everyday lives and their experience that the law is what other people use to take away their meager possessions. A classic case of this sort occurred some years ago in Washington, D.C., where an appliance store sold a mother of seven children who was on relief $1800 worth of merchandise on an installment contract, whereby she paid for them over a long period of time. Five years later, when she had only $170 more to pay, the same firm sold her a $515 stereo set. When she was unable to pay for that set, the firm repossessed not only it but all the other merchandise that she had been paying for over the years. The company's justification was an obscure provision in fine print in the sales contract that unpaid balances on any item could be distributed among all prior purchases so as to make her liable for all of them.

The poor have become prey for unscrupulous companies that have not hesitated to extend them credit for goods despite their inability to pay for them. Not only have they become the victims of repossession (frequently without notice), but they also find their wages garnished—that is, attached through legal orders served on their employer, a practice which not only denies them the fruits of their labor but also frequently gets them discharged by employers who dislike the inconvenience. The poor are at the mercy of landlords who force them to sign thirty-day leases (typically for dilapidated, crowded quarters) and then evict them without notice for any default in rent.

The poor also suffer at the hands of government agencies, particularly those concerned with welfare and public housing. Traditionally, they have found their benefits cut off without any hearing being held or even any reasons being given for the action. Even when they do receive governmental services, they do so at the price of an invasion of their privacy on such matters as where they live and with whom, what they spend their money for and at which stores, and where they go when they are sick.

Because the poor have so few possessions, it is important they be able to keep the little they have. Yet their usual lack of education and knowledge of their rights makes them vulnerable to persons who take unfair advantage of them. Thus poor people desperately need the assistance of the one individual in society who can make them aware of their rights and how to protect them: the lawyer.

PROVIDING LEGAL SERVICES FOR THE POOR

Although the *Gideon* decision and others that followed have extended the right to counsel in criminal cases, the courts have not been disposed to extend the right to civil matters. Even if it did, such a ruling probably could not be implemented. Estimates of the number of poor people needing subsidized legal services has been set as high as forty million. This fact of life has led some urban law experts to suggest that if all the lawyers in the United States did nothing but help poor people with their legal problems, they still would be unable to meet the need. Nonetheless, there has been a marked improvement in the situation since the midsixties.

Traditionally, servicing the legal problems of the poor in the United States has been the responsibility of the *Legal Aid Societies* that first came into

A legal services office brings legal assistance to a poor neighborhood. (Skarn)

existence at the turn of this century. These societies have been supported through local charitable organizations, such as the United Fund or Community Chest; in some instances, local bar associations also provided free legal service to needy persons. Even so, the aid extended through voluntary programs has always been sparse: in 1949 there were only thirty-seven legal aid offices and twenty local bar associations in the United States where the indigent could obtain legal assistance. The case loads of these agencies have always been heavy. They have also been accused of not being aggressive enough in fighting for the rights of the poor for fear of antagonizing private contributors, as well as leaders of the bar.

The most significant development in the provision of legal services for the poor was the establishment in 1965 of the Legal Services Division of the Office of Economic Opportunity, a part of the Executive Office of the President. Its approach has been the funding of law offices in ghetto neighborhoods and of traveling attorneys in rural areas. The emphasis has been on taking legal services to the indigent in their own locales rather than expecting them to travel to the usual locations of law offices—central-city business districts, suburban areas, and small towns. The Legal Services Programs have also dispensed justice in untraditional surroundings such as storefronts.

The Legal Services Program has grown over the years since its establishment in the mid-1960s. By the end of the decade it had a full-time staff of more than 1800 lawyers and operated through 850 neighborhood offices in 265 communities located in 49 states, the District of Columbia, and Puerto Rico. It has also handled a large volume of work with good success: in 1968 its lawyers processed 800,000 cases, winning 70 percent of its court trials and 60 percent of its appellate cases.

While the Legal Services Program has placed its primary emphasis on the neighborhood law office, it has also experimented with other methods of providing legal services for the poor. One known as *Judicare*, patterned after legal aid in Britain, permits the indigent individual to choose his own lawyer, whose services are subsidized by the government. Tried in rural counties in Wisconsin and in New Haven, Connecticut, it has been found to be more expensive than dispensing legal aid through neighborhood law of-fices but more acceptable to the organized bar. Some students of the prob-lem have also concluded that the quality of legal services dispensed through these law offices tends to be better than that provided by Judicare because the storefront lawyers specialize in the problems of the poor while the indi-vidual practitioners must handle them as part of their general practice.

In recent years private groups and individuals have also contributed in-creased legal assistance to the poor. Law schools have made it possible for their students to work with indigent clients and to receive academic credit for the experience, and private foundations have provided fellowships for young lawyers who want to specialize in the legal problems of the poor. Large law firms have also opened branch offices in ghetto areas where they have handled legal matters at fees far below their standard charges; they have also permitted their members to devote a certain portion of their time (for which the firm pays them) to assisting the poor. (This practice has helped such firms to recruit bright, idealistic young lawyers.) Moreover, many older attorneys have donated their services to the indigent.

Thus, providing legal services for the poor has undergone a revolution in recent years as a number of groups have contributed toward the goal of equal justice under the law. The entire movement has been strengthened by the substantial endorsement and support of the organized bar in the United States. Yet as the following section shows, there have been controversies over its objectives, particularly as these have been reflected in the activities of the Legal Services Program of the Office of Economic Opportunity.

OBJECTIVES AND CONTROVERSIES
IN THE LEGAL SERVICES PROGRAM

One of the major controversies in the Legal Services Program has been the question of its major goal. Some observers have taken the position that those assisting the indigent should concentrate on servicing their needs as they exist within the present structure of law. In other words, poor people should be informed what their legal rights are in dealing with merchants, landlords, spouses, welfare agencies, and public housing authorities, and what they need to do to protect such rights. This concept of helping the poor with their legal problems (often referred to as "Band-Aid" law) has traditionally been pursued by legal aid societies.

In contrast, some experts, including many who have occupied high positions in the Legal Services Program, have argued that much of the present common, statutory, and administrative law discriminates against the poor and in favor of merchants, landlords, and the government itself. Helping the poor, therefore, means more than just protecting their present rights; it also involves helping to establish new rights for them through a reform of the law. And reform involves encouraging clients to challenge present legal rules through test cases taken to the apellate courts with the purpose of getting them to overturn past decisions. It also means helping the poor to organize themselves politically so that they can get Congress and state legislatures, as well as administrative agencies at both levels, to enact laws and regulations favoring the indigent.

As might be expected, that aproach has not been popular with a number of groups. Some elements of the bar, representing merchants and real estate interests, credit companies, and other commercial concerns, have sought to maintain the *status quo* in their relationships with consumers, tenants, debtors, and the like. Many public officials have not taken kindly to suits brought against the government itself that seek to establish new rights for welfare recipients or those who live in public housing. What they have particularly resented is that public funds have been channeled through the Legal Services Program to lawyers who have proceeded to challenge many aspects of government programs affecting the poor. Some public officials have also charged that Program funds have been used to provide assistance to militant groups who resort to violence to achieve their goals.

Attempts have been made to curb the legal-reform activities of the Legal Services Program. In 1967 its officials and the American Bar Association successfully resisted legislation introduced by former Senator George Murphy of California to prohibit lawyers in the Program from suing federal, state, or local agencies. Two years later Murphy introduced another amendment to the Program that would have granted governors a final veto over all Legal Services projects within their state. (Governors presently can veto projects, but the national Director of the Legal Services Program has the power to override their vetoes.) It too failed of passage. In 1970, however, two top officials of the Program were dismissed by Donald Rumsfeld, the Director of its parent organization, the Office of Economic Opportunity; he also granted regional directors of the OEO greater control over Legal Services Programs in their areas. Thus the Program continues to evoke controversy among lawyers and public officials at all levels of government.

Meanwhile, the reform efforts have begun to bear fruit in a number of areas affecting the legal rights of the poor. Courts have declared that grossly exorbitant interest rates and unfair repossession clauses make contracts "unreasonable" and hence unenforceable; they have also recognized tenants' rights against landlords who fail to keep their properties in proper repair or who try to evict them for reporting housing code violations to public officials. Test cases have also established rights for the poor against the government: state residency requirements for welfare benefits have been invalidated; hearings must now be provided before a person's welfare rights can be terminated or he can be evicted from public housing; welfare inspectors cannot invade recipients' privacy at any time; benefits cannot be cut off just because a mother is living with or seeing another man than her husband; and urban renewal projects cannot proceed until adequate provision is made for relocating residents of the area affected. These and other matters have continued to engage the efforts of those interested in providing equal justice under the law in civil, as well as criminal, cases.

ASSESSMENT

American law as it has evolved over the years consists of a vast body of legal rules and regulations that has served two major purposes: peacefully settling disputes and giving people advance notice of their rights. However, it has been less successful in another goal of the law: rendering justice, giving every man his due. The development of the legal profession composed of persons from socially advantaged backgrounds, a preoccupation with property values, and the use of *stare decisis*, have all combined to make the law generally a conservative force in society, primarily committed to protecting the *status quo* and hence the interests of the "haves."

Recent developments, however, have led to better protection of the rights of "have-nots" in American society. Supreme Court decisions have created greater procedural safeguards for those accused of crime and have also granted them the right to an attorney to assist in the protection of their rights. Governmental and private efforts have also led to better representation for the poor in civil cases and to the reform of civil law in the direction of better protection for the interests of debtors, tenants, wage-earners, and welfare-recipients. Although the poor still do not receive as high-quality legal services as the affluent and although they are more likely to be detained pending trial and to receive longer sentences than the socially advantaged for similar offenses, our legal system has made substantial progress toward the goal of "equal justice under the law."

Yet all is far from well with American justice. Our courts are clogged with cases: in some urban areas it takes as long as five years to get a judgment in automobile damage suits. As a result injured persons frequently have to settle for less compensation than is properly due them in order to get money needed immediately to pay medical bills and other losses.

The deficiencies in criminal justice are even more serious. Poor people who cannot afford bail have to stay in jail for as long as a year awaiting trial. Delays also make it difficult for the prosecution to locate important witnesses. Judges are so overwhelmed with cases that they cannot hear them with proper care. The result is that all parties to the proceedings are encouraged to enter into plea bargaining to avoid the consequences of going to trial. Innocent men sometimes plead guilty to avoid a long wait for trial or the possibility that they will mistakenly be found guilty and sentenced to a long term in prison; on the other hand, men guilty of committing serious crimes are let off with minor penalties because the prosecution and judge do not have the time to properly prepare and try their cases.

What is needed is a two-pronged attack on the overcrowding of the courts. One approach is to eliminate some of the cases that now go to trial. Thus the automobile damage suits that clog our civil courts can be avoided by "no-fault" insurance that reimburses the policy-holder for injuries no matter which party to the accident is to blame. (Some states like Massachusetts have enacted such legislation with impressive results in handling damage claims.) Similarly, problems of drug-addiction, alcoholism, and homosexuality can be handled outside the regular criminal process. The other approach is to make a major investment in more and better-paid judges, and in the criminal courts, prosecutors, and public defenders as well. As Supreme Court Justice Frankfurter commented years ago: "No single aspect of our society is more precious and distinctive than that we seek to administer criminal justice according to morally fastidious standards."

Selected Readings

The information on the Gideon case is taken from the highly readable account of it by Anthony Lewis, *Gideon's Trumpet* (New York: Random House, 1964).

An excellent over-all analysis of the law and the judicial process written for students of political science (rather than law students) is Henry J. Abraham, *The Judicial Process* (New York: Oxford University Press, 1968). Another brief general treatment of the American legal system prepared by members of the Harvard Law School faculty for broadcasts to foreign audiences is Harold J. Berman (ed.), *Talks on American Law* (New York: Vintage, 1961). Both these books contain basic information on the development of law, the various types of laws and judicial procedures, and the kinds of courts that exist for enforcement of the law.

Both the above books treat of various aspects of the criminal process. A general analysis of the subject is contained in David Fellman, *The Defendant's Rights* (New York: Holt, Rinehart and Winston, 1958). A critical account of the criminal process is Arnold S. Trebach, *The Rationing of Justice* (New Brunswick: Rutgers University Press, 1964). Chapters 19 and 20 of James S. Campbell, Joseph R. Sahid, and David P. Stang, *Law and Order Reconsidered* (New York: Bantam, 1970), analyzes current developments and problems in criminal procedure. (The latter is a Report of the Task Force on Law and Law Enforcement to the National Commission on the Causes and Prevention of Violence.) An interesting attack on the *Miranda* decision is Fred Graham, *The Self-Inflicted Wound* (New York: Macmillan, 1970). Chapter 3 of the Report of the Task Force analyzes recent developments and problems in providing civil justice for the poor.

CHAPTER 14
The Federal Judiciary

(Above) **Judge G. Harrold Carswell with supporters on the Senate Judiciary Committee: Senators James Eastland of Mississippi, Roman Hruska of Nebraska, and Hiram Fong of Hawaii. (Below) Senator Birch Bayh of Indiana testifies before the committee against confirmation. (Wide World Photos)**

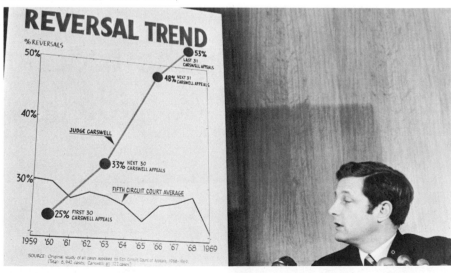

O~N~ June 13, 1968, the Chief Justice of the Supreme Court, Earl Warren, informed President Lyndon Johnson of his intention to retire as soon as a successor was chosen. Two weeks later President Johnson nominated Associate Justice Abe Fortas, a longtime friend whom Johnson named to the Court in 1965, to fill the Chief Justiceship. A freshman Republican Senator from Michigan, Robert Griffin, immediately began a fight against the nomination on several grounds: it was based on "cronyism"; no vacancy existed since the incumbent Chief Justice had not yet retired; and the new Chief Justice should be chosen not by a lame duck President but by the one to be elected the following November.

During the course of the Senate's consideration of the nomination, other objections to Fortas's appointment developed. He was found to have participated at President Johnson's request in White House conferences regarding the Vietnam war and urban riots, and to have accepted a fee (raised by a former law partner) for a seminar at American University. Decisions involving obscenity and criminal procedure in which Justice Fortas participated were also subjected to criticism. When the nomination came to the Senate floor for action in early October, Republicans and Southern Democrats joined in successfully defeating a cloture motion to terminate a filibuster on the issue. The following day Justice Fortas wrote to the President requesting that his nomination be withdrawn to avoid further attacks on the Court.

Justice Fortas's troubles did not end with that incident. A *Life* magazine article claimed that while on the Court he had accepted a fee from the family foundation of a man later imprisoned for illegal stock manipulation. Congressmen called for Fortas to resign, and some of his former supporters conceded that his actions were indiscreet. Attorney General John Mitchell, reportedly on orders from President Richard Nixon, met with Chief Justice Warren to press for Fortas's resignation. Ultimately, on May 14, 1969, claiming no wrongdoing, Justice Fortas submitted his resignation in the interest of protecting the work and position of the Court. In doing so, he became the first Supreme Court justice to resign under threat of impeachment.

President Nixon had no difficulties with his initial appointment to the Court. When Chief Justice Warren retired that same month, the President nominated as his successor Warren Burger, a judge on a United States court of appeals (the function of such courts will be discussed below); Burger, originally from Minnesota, was confirmed by the Senate on June 9, less than three weeks after his nomination. When the President moved to replace

Fortas, however, his nominee, Clement Haynsworth, a court of appeals judge from South Carolina, met major oposition. Civil rights groups accused him of foot-dragging on school desegregation, and a labor union charged that at the time Judge Haynsworth voted against it in a legal dispute with management, he was part owner of a firm doing business with the company he favored in the labor-dispute case. Judge Haynsworth was also found to have purchased stock in a company after a case involving it was decided by his court, but before the decision was announced. Demands that Nixon withdraw the nomination were refused, and a coalition of Northern Democrats and liberal Republicans combined to defeat the nomination on November 21, 1969. Particularly embarrassing for the President was the fact that seventeen Republicans, including Minority Leader Hugh Scott of Pennsylvania, Minority Whip Robert Griffin of Michigan, and the Chairman of the Republican Conference, Margaret Chase Smith of Maine, voted against his nominee.

Two months later President Nixon submitted another nominee to the Senate, G. Harrold Carswell, another court of appeals judge, this time from Florida. Opposition was slow to rise to the nomination, largely because the Senate was hesitant to enter into another battle with the President over a Supreme Court judgeship. However, civil rights groups charged that Carswell's record showed that he was a segregationist. Moreover, a newspaper discovered that in an unsuccessful race for the Georgia legislature in 1948, Carswell declared his belief in white supremacy; he was also involved in the transfer of a municipal golf course to private ownership to avoid desegregating the course. A number of law school deans and faculty members also testified that Judge Carswell did not have the professional competence to sit on the Supreme Court. Ultimately a combination of Northern Democrats and liberal Republicans similar to that which opposed Judge Haynsworth defeated the nomination on April 8, 1970.

President Nixon reacted bitterly to Judge Carswell's defeat, stating that it was obvious to him that the present Senate would not confirm a conservative nominee from the South. Some Southern senators who opposed the President's nominees responded that he had not sent the names of the best Southern judges to the Senate for consideration. A week after Carswell's defeat, the President nominated Harry Blackmun, a Minnesota court of appeals judge and longtime friend of Chief Justice Burger. He was confirmed unanimously within a month's time.

Thus ended a chain of events that resulted in the first defeat of the nomination of a Chief Justice of the Supreme Court since 1795 (President Grant withdrew two nominations in the 1870s before the Senate could consider them) and a Court vacancy (Fortas's) of over a year's duration for the first time since the Civil War. Before turning to a general analysis of the selection of federal judges, however, we need to examine the federal court system to determine what kind of tribunals it includes, the types of cases these courts hear, and the way they conduct their business.

THE JURISDICTION
OF FEDERAL COURTS

The general jurisdiction of the federal courts is set forth succinctly in Article III, Section 2 of the Constitution. Two words used there, "cases" and "controversies," have been construed by the federal courts to mean that the litigation they hear must involve an actual dispute. Two parties cannot trump up a law suit just to have the Court interpret a federal statute or determine its constitutionality. Nor will federal judges render *advisory opinions* about how or whether a particular law should be enforced. Only a party that has actually been adversely affected by the provisions of a law can obtain an interpretation or test its constitutionality.

Assuming an actual case brought by a legitimate plaintiff, it can still be heard by federal courts only if it falls within one of two broad categories. One concerns the *subject matter* of the suit, which is limited to litigation involving the federal Constitution, a federal law, or a treaty, along with admiralty and maritime matters.

The other category relates to the *particular parties* to the suit. If the United States is suing or being sued, the federal courts can hear the case. They have jurisdiction over cases affecting ambassadors and other agents of foreign governments, disputes between a state or one of its citizens and a foreign government or one of its citizens. Interstate conflicts can also come to the federal courts. These include litigation between states, between citizens of different states, between citizens of the same state who claim lands under grants of different states, and between a state and a citizen of another state (but only if the state is bringing suit).

The jurisdiction of federal courts is established by the Constitution, but the way they exercise it is for the most part determined by Congress. The only constitutional provision that restricts its discretion is the stipulation in Article III, Section 2 that in cases involving ambassadors, other public ministers, and consuls, and those in which a state is a party, the Supreme Court has original jurisdiction (the power to hear the case for the first time).

With this exception Congress can make what rules it wishes. For example, it may forbid the federal courts to handle a particular kind of case. Indeed, a suit between citizens of different states must involve $10,000 or more before a federal court will hear it; Congress has turned over to the state courts controversies involving lesser amounts of money. Or Congress may allow both federal and state courts to hear a particular type of case, in other words, to exercise *concurrent* jurisdiction. Suits between citizens of different states involving more than $10,000 are in that category: if both parties desire, they can litigate the matter in a state court. Finally, Congress has the power to retain *exclusive* federal jurisdiction; for instance, cases involving alleged violations of a federal criminal statute must be heard in a federal court, not a state one.

In addition to its power to allocate cases between federal and state courts, Congress can also decide at which level in the federal judiciary a matter will be heard. The only judicial tribunal specifically mentioned in the Constitution is the Supreme Court; Article II, Section 1 empowers Congress to create "inferior" (that is, lower) courts to assist with the processing of federal litigation. The following section of that same Article also empowers Congress to regulate the appellate jurisdiction of the Supreme Court, determining what matters it will review that have initially been tried in the lower federal courts. The federal judicial system today, as developed through statutes passed by Congress over the years since the initial Judiciary Act of 1789, includes, in addition to the United States Supreme Court, the United States district courts and the United States courts of appeals.*

MAJOR FEDERAL COURTS

THE DISTRICT COURTS

The United States district courts are primarily courts of original jurisdiction. Although they get some cases from state courts and review some actions of federal administrative agencies, for the most part the district courts are the trial tribunals of the federal judiciary. It is here that spirited battles occur, involving opposing attorneys, witnesses, a jury (though often, particularly in civil cases, the parties waive a jury trial), and a single presiding judge (however, when an injunction is sought to declare federal or state statutes or the order of a state administrative agency unconstitutional, three judges sitting as a group hear the case). The overwhelming proportion of federal cases—some ninety percent—start and end in the district courts.

District courts concern themselves with a wide variety of matters. The most prevalent is bankruptcy, which cannot be heard in a state court. It is there, too, that the federal government brings antitrust suits and prosecutes persons who steal automobiles and take them across a state line. Cases involving citizens of different states are like those that fill the dockets of state courts: automobile accidents, breaches of contract, and labor cases. Over 300,000 cases, about two-thirds of them bankruptcy proceedings, are filed

---

*In addition to the federal courts of general jurisdiction authorized by Article III, there are special federal courts that handle disputes arising from particular functions of Congress under powers granted by Article I. Included are United States Customs Courts, the United States Court of Custom and Patent Appeals, the United States Court of Military Appeals, Territorial Courts, and the United States Court of Claims, which hears claims brought against the national government.

annually in federal district courts; of these some 15,000 actually go to trial.

This flood of cases is processed through eighty-eight district courts located in the fifty states, plus several more in the District of Columbia and the territories. In size they range from one judge to twenty-four judges (in the New York City area). They are national courts, but they are oriented to a considerable degree to states and localities. Each state has at least one federal district court, and no court jurisdiction crosses state lines. And although district court judges occasionally are assigned to hear cases in other districts (for example, a visiting North Dakota district court judge issued the famous injunction in 1957 prohibiting Governor Faubus and other Arkansas officials from interfering with the integration of the Little Rock schools), for the most part they preside over disputes arising in their own area.

THE UNITED STATES COURTS OF APPEALS

The United States Courts of Appeals serve as the major appellate tribunals in the federal court system. They review principally the civil and criminal decisions in cases initially heard in federal district courts and the orders and decisions of federal administrative units, particularly the independent regulatory agencies. Over ninety percent of the 10,000 cases heard annually by the courts of appeals end right there; only a small proportion go to the United States Supreme Court for final disposition.

There are ten regional courts of appeals located in various parts of the United States, plus one in Washington, D.C. The size of the courts varies from three judges in the First Circuit in the New England area to fifteen in the Fifth Circuit in the South.* In some instances judges sit in different cities located within a court's jurisdiction.

To expedite their considerable case load, courts of appeals are divided into panels of three judges. The Chief Justice of each court determines the composition of the various panels, which are changed from time to time so that a judge does not always have the same colleagues. On application of the parties or the judges themselves, a case can be heard *en banc*, that is, by the entire court. The procedure is fairly rare, being restricted to legal questions of exceptional importance or cases in which the court feels that a full tribunal is necessary to secure uniformity in its decisions, or compliance with a controversial one.

Courts of appeals judges tend to be less closely tied to particular states and localities than their counterparts in district courts. Thus Fifth Circuit judges have been more likely to vote in favor of blacks in civil rights cases than have their brethren in the federal Southern trial courts, and they have

*The courts of appeals were formerly called circuit courts because initially they were staffed by Supreme Court justices who would make the "circuit," that is, come to various regions of the country to hear cases.

overruled a number of lower court decisions that originally favored white litigants.

THE UNITED STATES SUPREME COURT

Attorneys frequently assure clients who have lost cases in state or lower federal courts that they will take the matter to the United States Supreme Court where it will be settled in their favor. Designed as a tactic to console individuals who have suffered a courtroom defeat and to convince them that their attorney will stand by them, the promise is seldom realized. For one thing, most people lack the financial resources needed to carry legal battles to the highest tribunal. Costs naturally vary with the nature of the suit and the court level at which it is first tried, but at a minimum, tens of thousands of dollars will be involved in court and attorneys' fees and in many instances the figure will be in the hundreds of thousands.* For another, even if a person has the money to fight his case to that level, he may not be willing to take his chances on the decision.

Besides, there is a great difference between taking a case to the United States Supreme Court and getting the justices to hear it. In recent years over 3000 cases have been filed annually, but the Court generally takes on only a few hundred. Over ninety percent of those who seek the assistance of the Court have come away disappointed.

In fact, the Supreme Court has almost complete discretion over the cases it will hear. Litigation that comes within the original jurisdiction of the Court (cases involving foreign ambassadors, ministers, and consuls, and those in which a state is a party) may come to it for initial consideration. But even here there is some leeway since Congress has granted to district courts *concurrent* jurisdiction over controversies pertaining to foreign diplomatic personnel and some involving a state. As a result, most cases heard for the first time before the Supreme Court involve two states. In any event, cases of original jurisdiction constitute a very minor part of the case load of the Supreme Court. For example, in 1969 only one case was original, the previous year only two. For all practical purposes, then, the Supreme Court is an appellate body.

Congress, which regulates the appellate jurisdiction of the Supreme Court, has established two major sources of cases: the United States courts of appeals and the highest courts of the various states.† Yet the Court is granted discretion over which cases it will actually review. Typically it chooses only

---

*It has been estimated that the litigation that eventually resulted in the 1954 school desegregation decision, *Brown* v. *Board of Education*, cost the National Association for the Advancement of Colored People over $200,000.

†Certain cases, such as those involving challenges to state or federal statutes, come directly to the Supreme Court from the federal district courts, as do some from special federal courts like the United States Court of Claims or territorial courts.

those that involve a "substantial federal question" or that, for "special and important reasons," the Court feels it should deal with. The Court chose to hear Gideon's controversy, for instance, because it felt that the right to counsel in state criminal cases was an important constitutional issue and that the previous ruling in the 1942 *Betts* v. *Brady* decision had not dealt with the matter satisfactorily.* In other instances, the Court may choose a case because it involves the interpretation of an important federal statute or because it raises a legal issue on which various district courts or courts of appeals have ruled differently. It is not enough that members of the Supreme Court believe that the wrong party won in the lower court or that a legal injustice has been done. Before they accept a case (four justices must agree to do so), they must also feel that it raises important issues transcending the particular parties and case involved, with important consequences for the American political system or society in general.

The most important factor affecting decision-making by the Supreme Court is that it is a *collegial* body. Unlike the courts of appeals, it does not divide itself into separate panels to hear different cases. Members have taken the position that the Constitution refers to one Supreme Court, not several, and therefore all judges should normally participate in each case. (The fact that the Court has almost complete discretion over the cases it will hear enables it to concentrate its attention on relatively few; otherwise, the Court could never employ collective decision-making.)

The annual session of the Supreme Court is spread over a thirty-six-week period from October to June. During that time the Court sets aside about four days a week during two weeks of each month to hear oral arguments of opposing counsel on cases the Court has chosen for a full hearing. Typically the time is divided between the two sides, with each attorney having half-an-hour to an hour to present and defend his case. The justices feel free to interrupt them for questions at any point: interrogation by former Justice Frankfurter was a harrowing experience, not unlike a searching oral examination of a graduate student. Contributing to the tension for many, if not most, attorneys is the fact that this may be their first and last appearance before the Court. Only the Solicitor General, who presents cases in which the United States is a party (about half of all those argued before the Court), gets extensive experience in the nation's highest Court.

The overwhelming proportion of the work of the Supreme Court, however, takes place behind the scenes, or behind the "purple curtain" (which forms the backdrop for the public appearances of the Court). The justices spend most of the time individually reading and studying cases and discussing them with their law clerks (recently graduated students of the nation's

---

*Gideon's case was considered by the Supreme Court under special rules that permit it to review appeals filed by indigents (designated as "paupers") even though they do not satisfy requirements such as the filing of forty copies of a typewritten petition in proper form and the paying of court costs.

top law schools) as well as some of their colleagues. Members do come together as a single group for conferences, held on Friday and continued on Saturday if necessary, to make joint decisions on certain matters.

One major matter settled in conference is the choice of cases that the Court will hear that term. Another is the way cases already heard by the Court should be decided. In both matters the Chief Justice gives his views first, then the associate justice with the longest service on the Court speaks, and so on to the most junior man, who speaks last. The voting on both issues proceeds in reverse order with the Chief Justice voting last.

After the case is decided, it must be determined who will write the opinion setting forth the decision of the Court and the reasons behind that decision. If the Chief Justice votes with the majority, he decides who should write the opinion. If the case is a major one, he will probably assume the responsibility himself, as Chief Justice Warren did in the *Brown* v. *Board of Education* decision in 1954. Most opinions, however, are assigned so as to spread the work load of the Court among its nine members. If the Chief Justice is not on the prevailing side, the most senior justice who is, writes the opinion himself or assigns it to one of his colleagues.

The assignment of an opinion is a delicate decision. An opinion is often assigned to the justice whose views are closest to those of the minority, the idea being that he may be able to win them over to the majority's side. This tactic is often pursued when a premium is placed on getting a unanimous or nearly unanimous opinion by the Court, a particularly desirable goal in controversial decisions when the justices want maximum public acceptance. For the same reason an opinion may be assigned to a justice with personal or background characteristics that help to make the result more palatable: the decision in a 1944 case, *Smith* v. *Allwright*, invalidating white primaries in the South was once taken from Justice Felix Frankfurter, a Northern Jew not particularly sympathetic with the Democratic party in the past, and assigned to Justice Stanley Reed, a Protestant from an old-line Kentucky Democratic family.

The assignment of an opinion to a justice, however, does not necessarily end the collegial process. Negotiation may continue as he strives to write the opinion so that a maximum number of the justices join with him in it. He may even adopt suggestions and reasoning of other justices in order to dissuade them from writing opinions of their own. (Separate opinions may be either *concurring* ones, in which the writer agrees with the result reached by the majority opinion but not the reasons for it, or *dissents*, those reaching the opposite result.) It is often not possible to settle differences: because most cases heard by the Supreme Court are controversial and because the justices are typically men with strongly held views, a great number of divided opinions result.

Getting nine men with strong, diverse views to work together well as a group is not an easy feat. One close student of the subject, political scientist

David Danelski, has pointed out that it calls for both "task" leadership, or expediting the work of the Court, and "social" leadership, or helping establish good interpersonal relationships among the justices. The key part that the Chief Justice plays in conference discussions and in the assignment of opinions provides him with the opportunity to provide both types of leadership. How well a given Chief Justice does, however, depends on his personality and skills in interpersonal relationships. Danelski feels that former Chief Justice Hughes was successful in providing the Court with both "task" and "social" leadership, whereas Chief Justice Stone failed on both counts. Chief Justice Taft performed the social role effectively, but let his good friend, Justice Van Devanter, become the task leader during his tenure.

The final stage in the decision-making process of the Supreme Court is the announcement of its decisions and the reasons for them in open session on "opinion day," typically held on two or three Mondays each month while the Court is in session.* The justices present their opinions orally: some read them verbatim, others merely summarize their major points. These sessions are frequently enlivened by caustic comments and even verbal exchanges between judges who differ strongly on cases under discussion.

The operation of the federal courts, of course, depends not only on their jurisdiction and their customs but also on the individual judges. The following section explains how judges are chosen and describes the kinds of individuals who become judges at all three levels of the federal judiciary.

THE SELECTION AND BACKGROUNDS OF FEDERAL JUDGES

Unlike most state judges, who are elected by the people, federal jurists are appointed. The Constitution specifically states that the President shall nominate and, by and with the advice and consent of the Senate, appoint Supreme Court judges. Congress provides for the same process to be used for staffing the lower federal courts, so the President and the Senate are partners in the appointment process for all federal judges.

THE POLITICS OF SELECTION

Both the President and the Senate have sought the assistance of other officials to help them carry out their responsibilities of appointment. The Attorney General's office recommends judicial candidates to the President. And the Senate judiciary Committee considers the nominees, and votes as a

*By delivering all its opinions on Monday, the Court creates problems for the mass media, which frequently must report and comment on a variety of cases at one time. Former Chief Justice Warren initiated a practice of releasing some opinions on other days, but most are still delivered on Monday.

group recommending confirmation or rejection. Although neither the President nor the entire Senate is obligated to accept the advice of the Attorney General's office or the Senate Judiciary Committee, they are both generally inclined to do so.

The selection of federal judges involves many other individuals and groups, both inside and outside the government. Their interests are different and their influence is felt at different stages of the selection process.

The earliest and perhaps the most important part of the process is *recruitment* of candidates. Senators (of the President's party) from states in which district courts and courts of appeals appointees are to serve are a major source of suggestions. State and even local party officials are sometimes drawn into the process, especially if the state has no senators of the President's political party. The President himself, as well as his representatives in the Attorney General's office, also recruits judicial candidates, especially for the Supreme Court and the United States courts of appeals.

Other individuals and groups involved in the process do not belong to either the party in the government or the party organization. A prime example is a lawyer who is a self-starter, that is, one who promotes his own candidacy for the federal bench and lines up influential support. Sitting federal judges may also become involved, although most of them are inclined to wait for others to seek their advice on prospective nominees rather than to advance candidates of their own. Although they are important on occasions, neither judicial self-starters nor sitting judges are as significant in the recruitment process as are public and party officials.

The second stage is the *screening* of candidates. It is here that the President and the senators scrutinize one another's nominees. The analysis of the various candidates by the Attorney General's office includes a check into their backgrounds and activities by the Federal Bureau of Investigation.

Interest groups also enter the process at this juncture. In particular, the Committee on the Federal Judiciary of the American Bar Association evaluates persons being considered for nomination to the federal bench. They have customarily used the ratings "exceptionally well-qualified," "well-qualified," "qualified," and "not qualified." Although Presidents are not required to refer prospective nominees to the Committee for consideration, they have all done so since 1946. Other interest groups (including state and local bar associations, labor unions, and business groups) may also play some part in evaluating nominees, but their role in the process is not as institutionalized or considered as legitimate as that of the Committee of the American Bar Association.

After the President makes his nomination for a federal judgeship, the Senate must act to *confirm* or *reject* it. The Senate Judiciary Committee, operating through subcommittees of three, conducts hearings and invites testimony. Interest groups, including nonlegal ones, often become involved at this point. Those that have been unable to prevent the President from nominating a person they do not favor may carry the fight against him to the Committee. The Senate Committee gets the view of the American Bar Association and gives any senator of the President's party from the state concerned a chance to register opposition by returning a "blue slip" (a standard blue form used for this purpose) or by invoking the informal rule of "senatorial courtesy," declaring that the nominee is "personally noxious" to him. This merely means that the senator opposes him for political reasons or has a candidate of his own whom he prefers over the President's man; when this occurs—rarely of late—the Senate may refuse to confirm the nomination as a matter of political custom. Unless the nomination is withdrawn by the President, the Judiciary Committee makes a recommendation on the nomination, but the final decision is up to the entire Senate.

PATTERNS AND TRENDS
IN THE SELECTION OF FEDERAL JUDGES

The variety of individuals and groups that participate in the selection of federal judges makes the process a complex one. Those who are especially influential in the choice of one judge may not be nearly so important in the selection of another. The eventual outcome depends on a number of factors: the level of federal court involved, the attitudes and political skills of the President and particular senators involved, the characteristics of the candidate, and the general political tenor of the times. Nonetheless, it is possible to discern certain basic patterns and trends in the selection of federal judges.

Although the Constitution clearly provides that the President is to nominate and, by and with the advice and consent of the Senate, to appoint all federal judges, the process for the district courts typically works in reverse. The initiative comes from the Senate, or more precisely the senator or senators of the President's party from the state concerned. The President has a veto power over those who are offensive to him politically or who fail to meet the minimum qualification standards of the organized bar, but the rule of senatorial courtesy, which has been in effect since the Washington administration, is a powerful weapon for use against the President. Moreover, few Chief Executives are willing to risk the loss of Senate political support over a district court judgeship since the work of those tribunals is seldom crucial to his own political goals or programs.

The President is generally more influential in the selection of judges to the United States courts of appeals. He takes more of a personal interest in them than in district court appointments for two reasons. First, the courts of appeals handle matters of more importance to him. For example, their review of actions of the independent regulatory commissions can affect his over-all economic program. Second, courts of appeals judgeships are less numerous and more prestigious, inviting the interest of his major political supporters. Furthermore, with the courts of appeals appointments senators are in weaker bargaining positions. Since these courts encompass several states, no senator (or pair of senators) from any one state can lay a special claim to name an appointee that is recognized by the entire Senate. By political custom these judgeships are apportioned among the various states involved, but the President and his advisors determine how and in what sequence to do so.

The President clearly dominates the selection process for the Supreme Court. He is, of course, vitally interested in the decisions reached by that tribunal since they affect the operation of the entire political system and the functioning of American society in general. Since a Supreme Court judgeship is so prestigious, few, if any, lawyers would be inclined to turn down the post. And with the entire nation as the Court's geographical jurisdiction, no senator, or even group of senators, has a special say over the allocation of judgeships. Only the entire Senate can thwart the President's wishes.

The historical record of Supreme Court appointments is that about one in five presidential nominations has either been rejected outright or not acted on by the Senate, a far higher proportion of failure to confirm than for any other federal office. There has been considerable variation in the fate of nominees at different times. Bitter political battles led to a number of failures to confirm in the period from 1829 when Andrew Jackson took office until Grant left the Presidency in 1877. At the other extreme, from 1894 (when two of President Cleveland's nominees were rejected) until 1968 when the Senate failed to act on Lyndon Johnson's nomination of Associate Justice Abe Fortas to the Chief Justiceship, only one nominee, a Southern court of appeals judge, John J. Parker, failed to be confirmed. The Fortas matter, of course, was soon followed by the outright rejections of two of President Nixon's nominees, Clement Haynsworth and G. Harrold Carswell, within a few months' time in late 1969 and early 1970.

An analysis of the circumstances surrounding the four incidents in this century reveals the factors that contribute to the Senate's failure to confirm presidential nominees. Perhaps the most basic is the presence of major political differences between key senators and the President. Democrats joined with progressive Republicans of the day (Borah, Norris, and Johnson) in defeating the nomination of Judge Parker by Republican President Herbert Hoover. The same type of coalition formed to defeat Haynsworth and Carswell. On the other hand, prominent Senate Republicans allied themselves with conservative Democrats from the South to filibuster successfully against Justice Fortas.

These four failures to confirm also reflected broader political divisions in the nation. All three of the rejected Republican nominees, Parker, Haynsworth, and Carswell, were Southerners who were bitterly opposed by Negro and liberal interest groups for their rulings on civil rights cases. The former two were also considered antilabor. Fortas, in turn, had incurred the enmity of a number of conservative groups through his liberal decisions in obscenity cases and suits involving the rights of the accused in criminal proceedings.

Other issues have played a role in the three most recent incidents. Several senators who had originally supported Fortas's elevation subsequently joined with others in urging that he resign from the Court when his acceptance of a fee from a family foundation became known. Some senators were also opposed to Fortas's continuing to advise President Johnson on political matters while he was serving on the Court. Judge Haynsworth was criticized for ruling on cases involving companies in which he had a financial interest, while Judge Carswell's role in helping incorporate a segregated social club in his hometown in Florida contributed to the defeat of his nomination. While the political infighting in these three nomination battles was particularly vicious, and although these issues represented outward manifestations of deeper partisan and philosophical differences between the contending parties, it is very possible that the financial affairs of Supreme Court nominees, as well as their off-the-bench activities in general, may in the future come under closer scrutiny.

The opposition to Justice Carswell's nomination by members of the bar, particularly law professors who claimed his opinions were mediocre, may indicate that the legal qualifications of Supreme Court nominees will also be analyzed more carefully in the future. This development would suggest an increased role for the American Bar Association's Committee on the Federal Judiciary in future appointments.* The fact that the Committee found Carswell to be qualified for the position may lead it to analyze candidates more thoroughly in the future and to check their legal credentials with both the academic segment of the bar and practicing attorneys.

CHARACTERISTICS OF FEDERAL JUDGES

The characteristics of federal judges reflect a number of the considerations that bear on their appointment. The most basic qualification is membership in the *legal profession*. Although this is not a legal requirement, it is an informal custom: no nonlawyer has ever been appointed to a federal judgeship. Moreover, in keeping with contemporary preparation of lawyers, virtually every judge appointed to the federal bench since the end of World War II has been a graduate of a law school.

Another common attribute of federal judges is *public experience*. All except one of the ninety-eight judges who have served on the Supreme Court previously engaged in public service at some level of government or participated in political activities. Lower federal court judges also have political backgrounds; in fact, they are frequently described as "lawyers who knew a United States senator," particularly those on district benches. Attorneys

*Republican Presidents have been more inclined than Democratic ones to pay heed to the Committee's ratings; it has also played a more important role in the selection of lower federal judges than of Supreme Court justices.

who refrain from participation in public affairs (and there are relatively few of them) are not likely to be as visible to senators or to Presidents or their advisors as are lawyers who are active in public life.

As might be expected, the most prevalent kind of previous public office is one connected with the *courts*. Judges have often been city, county, or state prosecutors, or district attorneys. Some have also served as United States attorneys or their associates, while a few have been Solicitor General or Attorney General of the United States.

Previous *judicial experience* is also common among federal judges, although not as common as might be supposed. About one-third of the present district judges have previously been state judges; two in five judges on courts of appeals have been on the bench previously, most of them as federal district judges. The Supreme Court draws its appointees from both pools: of the ninety-eight justices in the nation's history, twenty-one came from an inferior federal court, and the same number from a state bench.*

Whatever the particular public experience of potential judicial appointees has been, they tend to be affiliated with the *same political party* as the President who appoints them. Few Chief Executives fall below the ninety percent mark in making partisan appointments to the lower federal courts. The ratio for the Supreme Court is somewhat lower, but even there the tendency has been to stay within party ranks: only twelve of the ninety-eight justices have been named by a President of another party.

When a President does cross party lines, it is likely to be because he has a high personal regard for the person concerned and a realization that the nominee, while affiliated with the opposition, shares the President's *general political philosophy* and views on public policy issues. A vivid statement of this consideration is contained in a letter Republican President Theodore Roosevelt once sent to his good friend, Senator Henry Cabot Lodge of Massachusetts, explaining a nomination:

> . . . the *nominal* politics of the man [Horace H. Lurton, a Democrat] has nothing to do with his actions on the bench. His real politics are all important. . . . He is right on the Negro question; he is right on the Insular business; he is right about corporations; and he is right about labor. On every question that would come before the bench, he has so far shown himself to be in much closer touch with the policies in which you and I believe.†

*Extensive judicial experience among Supreme Court justices is not common: of the ninety-eight justices, only twenty-three had ten or more years experience on some court. Although the lack of such experience has been criticized, some of the most eminent jurists, including John Marshall, Roger Taney, Louis Brandeis, Felix Frankfurter, and Earl Warren, had no prior judicial experience at all.

†Lodge replied that a Republican with similar views could be obtained and persuaded Roosevelt to nominate William Moody, the Attorney General of Massachusetts. Lurton was subsequently appointed by Roosevelt's successor, another Republican, President William Howard Taft.

Former Chief Justice Earl Warren. (United Press International)

Although Presidents attempt to choose men for the Supreme Court who share their general political views, they are not always successful in doing so. Justices often behave in ways not anticipated by their benefactors. Immediately after he was appointed to the Court by Theodore Roosevelt, Oliver Wendell Holmes, Jr. voted on the side of private enterprise and against the administration in a famous antitrust case, *Northern Securities* v. *United States* (1904). And President Eisenhower had little reason to suspect that his nominee for Chief Justice, Earl Warren, would become one of the most liberal, "activist" jurists in the history of the Supreme Court. Yet once the Chief Executive has placed a man on the Court, there is little he can do about his appointee's decisions since for all practical purposes, he is there for life.*

A Supreme Court appointment is so important because many social, economic, and political issues of the day become involved in litigation that comes to the Court for a decision. Most of these decisions require the Court to interpret major congressional statutes. Some, however, involve the judges of the Supreme Court in an even more demanding and controversial task: interpreting the Constitution itself.

JUDICIAL REVIEW

Although the term "judicial review" might conceivably be applied to a Court's reexamination of any matter already handled by a lower tribunal, it has a much more precise meaning. It refers to the power of a court to review the actions of all public officials—legislative, executive, and judicial—to see whether they are inconsistent with the governing constitution and, if the court finds that they are, to declare them unconstitutional and hence unenforceable.

In exercising judicial review, a court thus regards a constitution as being superior to ordinary laws or executive and judicial decrees; in determining that an official action is unconstitutional and therefore invalid, the court must find that a legislator, an executive, or a judicial official has done something that he has no authority to do under the constitution, or that he has taken some action that is forbidden by the constitution.

Judicial review exists at various levels of our political system. For example, state courts have the power to determine whether actions of state legislators, executives, or judicial officials violate the state constitution and to render invalid those that do. On such matters the decision of the highest state court is final. State courts also have the power to interpret the national Constitution as it applies to state actions. It can also decide whether a federal law or treaty is in violation of the national Constitution. But the rulings of state courts are not final on these issues; they may be appealed to the federal courts for final disposition.

The federal judiciary has the final say on whether actions of state or national officials violate the national Constitution. In the *Gideon* case the Supreme Court ruled that state judicial officials in Florida violated the due process clause of the Fourteenth Amendment when they tried and convicted Gideon for a state felony offense without providing legal counsel for him. In an earlier case, *Johnson* v. *Zerbst* (1938), the Court had decided that the Sixth Amendment granted indigent persons accused of violating federal crimes the right to counsel and that therefore the defendant's trial by a

---

*All federal judges hold office during "good behavior" or until they die or choose to retire voluntarily. They can also be impeached, but only four have been removed in that manner, and none of them was a Supreme Court justice.

lower federal court without the assistance of an attorney was unconstitutional.

Some aspects of judicial review are more controversial than others. The right of a court to set aside actions of political officials—that is, legislators and executives—has been of more concern to students of the democratic process than their power to invalidate what other judges have done. The power of the federal courts to review the actions of national officials has been more seriously questioned than their authority to render unenforceable the activities of state officials. And it is the combination of these two most-criticized aspects of judicial review, the power of federal courts to invalidate actions of legislative and executive officials of the national government, that has provoked the greatest controversy.

Very few nations grant courts the power of judicial review as it is exercised in the United States. Typically, in countries with a federal form of government the power is granted to judicial tribunals, as in Australia, Canada, India, and West Germany. Even in these nations, however, the role of the courts in invalidating actions of political officials has never taken on the significance it has in the United States. It would, therefore, be instructive to examine how the courts acquired the power of judicial review and the ways in which they have used it over the years.

THE ESTABLISHMENT OF JUDICIAL REVIEW
IN THE UNITED STATES

Ironically, judicial review is not specifically provided for in the Constitution. Nowhere does it expressly grant federal courts the right to nullify actions of public officials. The power has been derived by implication from certain wording in the Constitution and from interpretation of the intentions of the Founding Fathers. Article V, Section 2, which provides that the *national* Constitution, law, or treaties shall be "supreme" over state constitutions or laws, has been used to justify the power of federal courts to invalidate state actions. The clause itself, however, does not state that national courts should pass on such conflicts; in fact, it specifically mentions state judges and provides that they shall be bound by the supremacy clause, which might be construed to mean that state, rather than federal, judges should have the power of judicial review. The argument for federal courts' invalidating actions of the other two branches of the national government is even less supported by the wording of the Constitution.

Nonetheless, most historians agree that the Founding Fathers favored judicial review and expected the federal courts to exercise it over both state and national actions. Why, then, did they not provide for it specifically in the Constitution? One theory is that everyone took the power for granted anyway, since most of the state courts of the time were exercising judicial review over the actions of state officials. Another is that the delegates were aware that because of the secrecy of the Convention and constitutional provisions for a Senate and a President that the people did not elect, many citizens would view the new government as too elitist. Specifically granting to appointed judges with life tenure the power to overrule actions of popularly elected officials would make matters even worse and almost ensure that the Constitution would not be ratified. Therefore, for reasons of political expediency the delegates may have deliberately omitted any reference to judicial review.

Hamilton, however, was not so cautious or discrete. In *Federalist* 78 he specifically stated that the federal courts possess the power of judicial review and gave justifications for it. Some of his justifications are legalistic. He held that a constitution is a type of law and that, since it is the province of the courts to interpret laws, they necessarily interpret the Constitution. He also pointed out that the Constitution is a fundamental law, which means that if judges find ordinary legislation in conflict with it, the Constitution prevails and the legislation is invalid.

Hamilton also drew on his views of human nature to justify judicial review. Legislators cannot be trusted always to respect the limitations placed on them by the Constitution; when they do not, the courts must intervene to protect the rights of the people. Nor are the people themselves to be entirely trusted; they too will suffer "the effects of ill humor" on some occasions and threaten the minor party or the rights of particular classes of citizens. Again it is the judges, trained in settling controversies growing out of "the folly and wickedness of mankind," who can be counted on to protect the rights of minorities.

Although Hamilton's views were thus set forth in a frank and bold fashion, they were simply that, his own, and not binding on anyone else. The issue could only be settled ultimately by public officials. It remained for the Supreme Court itself to establish its power of judicial review through actual exercise of that prerogative. This it did in the famous case of *Marbury* v. *Madison*, decided by Chief Justice Marshall in 1803.

Whereas Hamilton had based his case for judicial review on legalistic arguments, the circumstances of the *Marbury* decision could hardly have been more political. After the Federalists were defeated in the election of 1800, they labored in the interval until the Republicans assumed control of the Presidency and the Congress to retain a foothold in the one remaining branch still open to them: the judiciary. The lame-duck Congress passed legislation creating a number of new circuit judgeships, along with justiceships of the peace in the District of Columbia. In the waning days of his administration, departing President Adams appointed Federalists to these new judicial posts (they became known as "midnight" appointments because they were accomplished shortly before that time on March 3, 1801). In the last-minute rush, however, John Marshall, who was then Secretary of State (as well as Chief Justice of the Supreme Court) did not get all the necessary commissions of office signed; included among them was one making William Marbury a justice of the peace in the District of Columbia. The new Republican Secretary of State, James Madison, who, along with the new President, Thomas Jefferson, resented the Federalists' attempt to pack the bench, refused to deliver the commissions to Marbury or otherwise honor his appointment.

Frustrated in his attempts to obtain his commission, Marbury turned for help to the Supreme Court over which John Marshall presided as a result of his appointment by President Adams. Marbury asked that the Court issue a *writ of mandamus* (an order requiring a public official to perform an official duty over which he has no discretion) compelling Madison to deliver the commission. As his authority for the suit, he invoked a provision in the Judiciary Act of 1789 granting the Court the power to issue such writs.

Marbury's case placed Chief Justice Marshall (who should have disqualified himself from hearing it, since he was the one who failed to deliver the commission while he was still Secretary of State) on the horns of a dilemma. If he (and the rest of the Federalist judges on the Court) ruled that Marbury was entitled to the commission, his political enemy, President Jefferson, could simply order Madison not to deliver it, which would serve to demonstrate that the judiciary could not enforce its mandates. On the other hand, to rule that Marbury had no right to the commission would seem to justify Jefferson's and Madison's claim that the midnight appointments were improper in the first place.

But the Chief Justice was up to the challenge. He slipped off the horns of the dilemma by ruling that, while Marbury had the right to the commission and a *writ of mandamus* was the proper remedy to obtain it, the Supreme Court was not the tribunal to issue it. In reaching this result, he reasoned that the original jurisdiction of the Supreme Court is provided for in the Constitution and Congress cannot add to that jurisdiction. Therefore, the section of the Judiciary Act of 1789 granting the Supreme Court the power to issue *writs of mandamus* in cases it hears for the first time is unconstitutional and, hence, unenforceable.

The ruling extricated Marshall from an immediate difficulty; it had other effects as well. It created the possibility that the Federalists could use this new-found power to check actions of the Republican Congress and President. And most crucial of all from a long-term standpoint, it established the power of the courts to declare acts of public officials invalid.

Crucial as the *Marbury* v. *Madison* ruling was, it did not settle all the aspects of judicial review. For one thing, it applied only to the actions of the national government. Not until seven years later, in the case of *Fletcher* v. *Peck* (1810), did the Court invalidate a state law on the grounds that it violated the national Constitution. Moreover, the *Marbury* case did not define the scope of judicial review. As some persons, like Jefferson, reasoned, the ruling merely meant that the Court could strike down laws that affected the judiciary itself (as the Judiciary Act of 1789 did), but that it had no power over matters pertaining to the other two branches of government because each was the judge of the constitutionality of matters within its own province. Indeed, not until the *Dred Scott* case (1857), in which the Court invalidated Congress's attempt to abolish slavery in the territories, did the Court lay that theory to rest by striking down a law that had nothing to do with the courts.

THE SUPREME COURT'S USE OF JUDICIAL REVIEW

Although judicial review puts a powerful weapon in the hands of the Supreme Court, for the most part the power has been used with considerable restraint, particularly with respect to federal laws. In the 170 years since *Marbury*, the Court has invalidated some 100 provisions of national laws, an average of only one every two years. In the same period of time, it has declared close to 800 state laws unconstitutional, or about four per year.

The Court's use of judicial review has not been uniform over the years, however. After all, fifty-four years transpired between the *Marbury* v. *Madison* decision at the beginning of the nineteenth century and the *Dred Scott* case decided on the eve of the Civil War. In contrast, the Court declared unconstitutional no less than thirteen New Deal laws during the period from 1934 to 1936.

The types of issues of concern to the Supreme Court have changed over the years. Subject matter has naturally varied from case to case, but different basic themes have dominated the Courts attention in different eras of our constitutional history. The issues have reflected both the major problems of American society at the time and the justices' own conceptions of the values they should protect through the power of judicial review.

The major issue facing the Court from 1789 until the Civil War was nation-state relationships. As we saw in Chapter 3, Chief Justice Marshall took the leadership in providing support for a strong national government. The constitutional basis for its expansion came in the form of a broad interpretation of both the interstate commerce power and the "necessary and proper" clause. At the same time, state activities that affected the powers of the national government were invalidated. Toward the end of the era, when Marshall died and was replaced by Roger Taney, the Court moderated its stand on nation-state relationships. For example, it ruled that states could regulate interstate commerce, provided that the regulation concerned local matters and did not affect a subject requiring uniform treatment throughout the United States. As a whole, however, the era was clearly a time of general support for the nation over the states in constitutional conflicts.

The pre-Civil War period was also characterized by judicial protection of private property. In fact, there was a connection between the nation-state and property-rights issues: for the most part, the federal government was promoting business and commercial interests, while the states were more involved in trying to regulate them. Thus judicial support for a strong national government dominant over the states favored commercial interests. Furthermore, Chief Justice Taney's decision in the *Dred Scott* case invalidating Congress's attempt to abolish slavery in the territories showed his solicitude for another type of property-holder: the large landowner in the South.

The Civil War settled the nation-state problem, and the courts became preoccupied with one overriding issue in the period that followed: business-government relations. Unlike the earlier era, however, now both the national government and the states were involved in regulating burgeoning industrial empires, along with smaller commercial enterprises. Therefore, favoring one level of government over the other would not accomplish the goal of many justices of the day: protecting business against what they conceived to be improper governmental interference.

The Court thus embarked upon a two-pronged judicial attack on governmental regulation of business by the two political levels. It frustrated the national government's control of industry by limiting the scope of the interstate commerce power so as to cover only businesses that were actually involved in interstate commerce (such as railroads, shipping companies, and the like) and those that directly affected that commerce; this approach freed concerns involved in agriculture, mining, and production from control by the federal government. Similarly, the taxing power of the national government was contracted through judicial rulings inquiring into congressional motives behind the use of that power: for instance, a special tax on businesses using child labor was invalidated on the grounds that the purpose of the tax was not to raise money but to discourage the use of child labor. State regulation of business was also thwarted through a novel interpretation of the due process clause of the Fourteenth Amendment. Although, as previously indicated, historically that clause had always referred to procedures of public officials, the Supreme Court now gave it a substantive meaning by holding that what the justices considered to be unreasonable regulations of private interests denied persons of their property without due process of law.*

This dual approach served to protect business against regulation by government, either national or state. It dominated the Court's thinking in the early part of this century, continuing into the 1930s when it was utilized to

---

*Another tactic the Court used to protect business was to interpret the word "person," which appears in the Fourteenth Amendment, to include corporations. Thus the Court utilized an amendment that was designed to safeguard the civil liberties of individuals to protect the property rights of business interests.

strike down many New Deal laws. President Roosevelt, following his re-election in 1936, sought to curb the Court's power over his programs by introducing legislation permitting him to appoint additional justices equal to the number sitting on the Court who had reached the age of seventy and had not retired. This proposal provoked a storm of protest from critics who charged that FDR was trying to pack the Court, and it ended in a congressional defeat for the President on the issue. Although FDR lost the battle in the Congress, he won the war in the courtroom: Justice Owen J. Roberts, who had, to that point, generally been aligned with the four justices on the Court invalidating social and economic legislation, began in 1937 to vote with the four on the other side. With this change (a satirical description was "a switch in time saves nine"), the era of the Court's preoccupation with property rights came to an end.

Since 1937 the Supreme Court has focused almost all its attention on protecting the personal liberties of individuals against infringement by either the national government or the states. Some twenty provisions of congressional laws have been struck down since 1943, including violations of First Amendment freedoms, along with procedural rights of the accused spelled out in the Fourth, Fifth, Sixth, and Eighth Amendments. In addition, the due process clause of the Fifth Amendment has been utilized to invalidate criminal statutes for the vagueness of their language and to outlaw the segregation of the schools in the District of Columbia. The Court has been even more vigilant against infringements of personal liberties at the state level, relying on the due process and equal protection clauses of the Fourteenth Amendment to protect individuals against actions violating freedom of expression and religion, denials of procedural safeguards in criminal cases, and racial discrimination.

This brief review of the uses to which the Court has put judicial review over the years raises the issue of how individual judges conceive of the power of judicial review. What is the nature of the process? That is, what specifically does a judge do when he goes about deciding whether a law or executive order is unconstitutional? What role does he think judicial review should play in the political process?

CONCEPTS OF JUDICIAL REVIEW

Former Supreme Court Justice Owen Roberts is most closely associated with the legalistic concept of judicial review. He once described the process as a rather simple one: all a judge does is to lay the constitutional provision involved beside the statute being challenged and decide whether the latter squares with the former. According to Justice Roberts, judges don't "make" law; they "find" it.

Another former Associate Justice of the Supreme Court, Felix Frankfurter, had a much different concept of judicial review. According to him many of the key words and phrases that appear in the Constitution, such as "due process of law" and "equal protection of the law," are so vague and undefined that they compel a judge to read his own views into them. Those views, in turn, depend on the judge's own personal philosophy and scheme of values, which he acquires from his particular background and experiences in life. Since matters of discretion are involved, judges, in Frankfurter's view, do "make" law rather than just "find" it.

Few students of the judicial process, including judges themselves, would agree with Judge Robert's simplistic concept of judicial review. If deciding whether a law is constitutional or not is as simple as he claims, why is there so much disagreement among justices hearing the same case? Or why does the Court overrule its former decisions, as it has done on many occasions over the years? Frankfurter's concept of the process of judicial review is much more realistic.

But even if a judge concedes that values do play a part in his thinking, he still has the problem of deciding the extent to which he will allow his values to affect his rulings on constitutional issues. Perhaps because Frankfurter was so sensitive to how an individual's background and experiences shape his personal values, he is generally identified as a "nonactivist" judge, one who was hesitant to substitute his constitutional values for those of legislators and executives. For example, in a 1940 decision, *Minersville School District* v. *Gobitis*, Frankfurter, upholding the right of a school board to expel students who refused to salute the flag as required by Pennsylvania state law, took the position that the courts have no competence to tell political authorities that they are wrong to use this method of instilling patriotism in children.

The "activist" attitude on the role that judges feel they should play in constitutional issues is exemplified by Justice Robert Jackson's opinion in *West Virginia State Board of Education* v. *Barnette*, decided three years later, which specifically overruled the *Gobitis* case. In declaring a similar West Virginia flag-salute law unconstitutional, Jackson reasoned that such an action interfered with a child's freedom of speech because he had the right to be silent and not be compelled to utter what was not in his mind. The Justice went on to assert that the right of legislative discretion to which Frankfurter referred should be more restricted when it affects civil liberties than when property rights are involved.

This last comment of Justice Jackson points up another important aspect of the concept of judicial review: how activist or nonactivist a judge is, may well depend on the particular value that is at stake in a given case. Thus Justice Jackson was less willing to defer to the judgment of political authorities on civil liberties than he was on those affecting property rights. Other judges like Frankfurter may be unwilling to permit freedom of speech or racial tolerance to occupy a higher place in their scheme of values than property interests.

Analysis of Supreme Court decisions over the years reveals the attitudes of individual judges that underlie the positions they take in a series of cases reaching the Supreme Court. Some judges, for example, consistently vote on the side of the individual on civil liberties cases; others tend to favor economic have-nots in litigation against affluent interests; still others generally prefer one side in litigation between individuals; and federalism is also an issue that some justices respond to in a fairly consistent manner.

Of course, discerning the factors that dispose a judge to vote the way he does is a difficult task, particularly since he is frequently faced with deciding between competing values. For example, had Justice Frankfurter still been on the Court at the time of the *Gideon* case, he would have faced such a problem. As indicated previously, he considered procedural safeguards basic to liberty, so he would have been disposed to favor furnishing the accused the assistance of counsel so that he could take full advantage of such safeguards. On the other hand, the former Justice was a strong advocate of federalism and the right of the states to experiment with their own legal and political processes; also, as a nonactivist he was hesitant to have a Supreme Court Justice substitute his judgment for that of other public officials. Those attitudes would have inclined him toward allowing Florida to decide how it should handle its own criminal proceedings. He thus would have had to do what he conceived the major function of a judge to be: balance the interests and values involved in each case and decide which should prevail.*

Personal values are not always controlling in a case. A judge sometimes puts other considerations ahead of them. He may, for example, respect the views of an influential colleague on a case or decide to go along with his fellow judges in order to present a unanimous decision to the public. He may also respect the principle of *stare decisis* and so refuse to overrule a former precedent; nonactivist judges also hesitate to invalidate actions of other public officials.

There is little question, however, that in exercising the right of judicial review, Supreme Court justices have considerable discretion in deciding cases on the basis of their own value systems. (As Max Lerner commented some years ago, "Judicial decisions are not babies brought by constitutional storks.") Unlike many cases at the lower levels of our judicial system, those that reach the Supreme Court do not typically involve technical legal issues but rather broad philosophical questions for which there are no easy or automatic answers. In passing on such matters, justices of the Supreme Court, then, like legislative and executive officials, make public policy.

Judicial review is certainly an important feature of American democracy, but its role in public policy-making must be kept in perspective. For one

---

*Justice Frankfurter is reported to have told Justice Black that if he had still been on the Court at the time, he would have voted to grant counsel to Gideon.

thing, most of the work of the Supreme Court consists of the interpretation of statutes passed by Congress, not in determining whether they are constitutional or not. Moreover, as the following section indicates, even when the Supreme Court does decide a constitutional issue, the controversy is not necessarily ended.

THE SUPREME COURT
IN THE POLITICAL PROCESS

Even though the life tenure of Supreme Court justices protects them from the kinds of pressures that elected officials face, they are not totally insulated from the political process. In particular, the two coordinate branches of the national government are in a position to check the Court's actions in a number of significant ways. Included are direct checks involving specific judicial decisions and indirect methods designed to affect general activities of the Supreme Court.

THE COURT AND CONGRESS

Congress has the power to affect Supreme Court decisions by passing laws that reverse or modify what the Court has previously done on an issue. Examples of this technique, already referred to in Chapter 3, are the enactment of legislation deeding tideland oil properties to the states after the Court had ruled that the national government, not the states, owned such lands and the passage of legislation permitting states to regulate insurance companies following a Court decision holding that they fell under the control of the national government through its interstate commerce power. Another instance previously cited was the enactment of the Omnibus Crime Control and Safe Streets Act of 1968, which limited the effect of the *Mallory* case by allowing up to six hours for prearraignment questioning of suspects in federal criminal proceedings.

Some reversals of Supreme Court decisions cannot be accomplished through ordinary legislation, and Congress must initiate constitutional amendments to achieve its purposes. When the Court ruled in *Chisholm* v. *Georgia* (1793) that a state could be sued in a federal court by a citizen of another state, the Eleventh Amendment was enacted to deny jurisdiction in such cases. The *Pollock* v. *Farmers' Loan and Trust Company* decision (1895) that invalidated a national income tax was ultimately reversed through the passage of the Sixteenth Amendment granting Congress the power to enact such a tax without apportioning it among the various states. More recently, when the Supreme Court ruled in 1970 that Congress could not grant eighteen-year-olds the right to vote in state and local elections, the Twenty-Sixth Amendment was enacted in 1971 to achieve that result.

In addition to reversing specific judicial decisions, the national legislature can affect the Court's consideration of particular kinds of issues through its power to determine the appellate jurisdiction of the Supreme Court. A famous example of the use of this power was the passage in the immediate post-Civil War period of legislation that had the effect of denying the Court appellate jurisdiction over certain cases in which the constitutionality of the Reconstruction Acts was at issue. The tactic was particularly effective in that instance because the Court bowed to Congress's will by dismissing a case on which it had already heard arguments but had not yet ruled.

Taking away the Court's jurisdiction over a case it has already heard is rare; trying to prevent the justices from deciding certain issues in future litigation is much more common. This was the approach used by Senator William Jenner of Indiana in the late 1950s when he introduced legislation that would have denied the Court appellate jurisdiction over a number of issues on which he felt the Court had unduly favored the rights of individuals at the expense of internal security. Included in the statute's coverage were the rights of witnesses before congressional committees, the removal of federal employees for reasons of national security, state antisubversion laws and regulations regarding the activities of school teachers, and state statutes pertaining to admission to the bar. Although the Jenner bill failed to pass, it constituted one of the major threats to the independence of the Court in recent years.

Control over Court personnel is still another power whereby Congress can affect the actions of the tribunal. Thus the number of justices is determined by legislation, and this number has varied from five to ten over the years since 1789. An example of the use of this power for political purposes was the enlargement of the Court by the Radical Republicans in 1869 after President Johnson left office so that President Grant (whom they controlled) could appoint an additional justice. Franklin Roosevelt tried a similar technique in 1937 with his Court-packing bill. The number of justices has remained at nine since 1869, however, which may mean that manipulating the size of the Court is now considered improper and will, as in Roosevelt's case, be unsuccessful.

The concern of Congress with Court personnel can also be directed at particular individuals. As previously indicated, the Senate can interject constitutional issues into its consideration of nominees to the Court. In recent years nominees have frequently been questioned by the Senate Judiciary Committee about their judicial philosophy and "activist" or "nonactivist" views; at the time of his nomination for the Chief Justiceship, Associate Justice Fortas was criticized by Senators Eastland and McClellan for his rulings in obscenity cases. Nor do attacks on judges necessarily cease once they are confirmed. Justice William Douglas, who went on the Court in 1939, has on two occasions—the first in 1953 and the second in 1970—been the object of impeachment resolutions in the House of Representatives. Neither attempt was successful.

Thus the Congress does have a number of weapons it can use to affect the

activities of the Supreme Court. For the most part it has used the less drastic of these measures, such as reversals or revisions of Supreme Court decisions and the failure to confirm nominees, rather than more severe anti-
Court actions, such as altering the appellate jurisdiction of the Court,
tampering with its size, or impeaching sitting judges.*

THE COURT AND THE PRESIDENCY

Like the Congress, the President has several powers at his disposal which
can have major effects on the actions of the Supreme Court. One such power
has already been discussed: the appointment of justices. As Robert Dahl
has pointed out, over the years one new justice has been appointed on the
average of every two years; a President, then, can expect to appoint two
judges for each term he has in office. Thus a Chief Executive can, through
judicious choice of persons with policy views similar to his own, influence
the general direction of the Court's thinking, as Franklin Roosevelt did
through his nine appointments. If the Court is a divided one, even a smaller
number of appointments can be crucial: immediately after President Nixon
chose Chief Justice Burger and Associate Justice Blackmun,† the Court began to modify the general tenor of its previous rulings, particularly with
respect to procedural rights of the accused in criminal proceedings.

The President also shares with Congress the power to enact legislation
affecting the Court. In fact, the initiative for such legislation may come
from the Chief Executive, as it did in the court-packing plan of 1937. Even
when this is not the case, however, the President's veto power means that
legislation affecting the Court will probably not be successful unless it meets
with his approval.

Finally, the President does have the ability to affect Supreme Court decisions that require his action for implementation. Recall one of Chief Justice Marshall's problems in the *Marbury* v. *Madison* decision: if he ruled
that the former had a right to his justice-of-the-peace commission, President
Jefferson might tell Madison not to deliver it to him. Just such an eventuality later occurred when Marshall ruled in two separate decisions, *Cherokee Indian* v. *Georgia* (1831) and *Worcester* v. *Georgia* (1832), that the
state had no legal authority over land occupied by the Cherokee Indian

---

*There are other potential weapons Congress could use against the Court, but past ex-
perience demonstrates that they have little chance of passage. Included are requirements
that decisions invalidating national laws be either unanimous or by extra-majorities, that
Congress be empowered to overrule Supreme Court decisions by extra-majority votes,
and that the electorate be given the power to overturn such decisions. Attempts to require that Supreme Court justices have previous judicial experience have also failed to
gather sufficient congressional support to pass.

†During the October 1970 term Justices Burger and Blackmun disagreed in only four of
some 120 decisions, which led Court observers to label them the "Minnesota Twins."

tribe, and President Jackson refused to take steps to implement either ruling. On the other hand, the positive effect a Chief Executive can have on a Supreme Court ruling is demonstrated by President Truman's order to Secretary of Commerce Charles Sawyer to return the steel mills to their private owners after the Court's decision in *Youngstown Sheet and Tube Company* v. *Sawyer* (1952) that the Chief Executive had no authority to seize them. Further evidence of the key role the President plays in implementing Court rulings is provided by the actions of Presidents Eisenhower and Kennedy in sending federal troops and marshals to enforce school desegregation decisions.

The combination of powers of the Congress and the President with respect to the Supreme Court means that they can have a major effect on its actions. Robert Dahl, who has analyzed the ultimate outcome of Court decisions declaring acts of Congress unconstitutional, concludes that legislation reversing and revising such decisions and new presidential appointees to the Court who vote to overrule them, eventually mean that if the two political branches are agreed on a matter of public policy, they will eventually get their way. The most the Court can do is delay the application of a policy for a number of years, as occurred, for example, between the 1895

The justices of the Supreme Court in mid-1971: (front row) John M. Harlan, Hugo L. Black, Chief Justice Warren E. Burger, William O. Douglas, and William J. Brennan; (back row) Thurgood Marshall, Potter Stewart, Bryon R. White, and Harry A. Blackmun. (Paul Conklin/Pix)

ruling in the Pollock case and the passage of the Sixteenth Amendment in 1913.

While congressmen and the President have positive powers that they can use to check the Supreme Court, other public officials are frequently able to have a negative effect on its actions through delaying, or even avoiding, the execution of its orders. For just as some Supreme Court decisions require the President to enforce them, others depend for their ultimate effectiveness on what individuals in various political positions do about implementing them.

LOWER COURTS AND SUPREME COURT DECISIONS

Typically a Supreme Court decision does not end a legal controversy; rather, it remands the case to a lower court which is entrusted with proceeding further on the matter in light of the Court's opinion. One might assume that inferior tribunals would promptly carry out the orders of the highest Court; as a matter of practice lower courts frequently delay or modify the upper Court's wishes in significant ways.

The possibilities of lower courts' altering the intentions of the Supreme Court are particularly promising when the highest Court's order itself is uncertain and vague. The classic instance was the Supreme Court's directive following the 1954 desegregation decision to the federal district courts to supervise the integration of the public schools in their areas so that it occurred with "all deliberate speed." The exceedingly slow pace of integration in parts of the South led some critics to charge that many judges emphasized the "deliberativeness" of the process to the exclusion of its "speed."

But even when the Court does not grant the lower federal tribunals such broad discretion in implementing its decisions, judges are frequently able to avoid the Court's rulings by distinguishing them in subsequent cases, that is, drawing distinctions between the facts of the cases in which these rulings were made and those present in the litigation before them. This occurred in the aftermath of the *Mallory* decision, which provided that defendants in federal criminal cases must be arraigned a short time after they are arrested. Studies of subsequent proceedings in both federal district courts and courts of appeals indicate that judges avoided the *Mallory* doctrine by distinguishing it from cases before them.

State tribunals, like lower federal courts, can also obstruct Supreme Court decisions. After the Court ruled in 1958 that Alabama could not require the National Association for the Advancement of Colored People to furnish copies of its membership lists as a condition for operating in the state, a prolonged legal battle was carried on at the state level. Through a combination of delays and avoidances with respect to the upper Court's rulings, Alabama was able to keep the NAACP from operating in the state for over six years after the 1958 decision was handed down.

STATE AND LOCAL OFFICIALS
AND SUPREME COURT RULINGS

The dramatic events following the 1954 school desegregation decision attest to the role that state officials can also play in obstructing rulings of the Supreme Court. It will be recalled that Governor Orval Faubus intervened after a federal district court approved the decision of the school board in Little Rock, Arkansas, to integrate the schools of that area in the fall of 1957, and that it became necessary for President Eisenhower to send federal troops to enforce the district court's order. Similarly, the legislature of Virginia tried to avoid the integration of the public schools by repealing compulsory school attendance laws and permitting students to attend private schools subsidized by the state. (As with the Faubus incident, however, the Supreme Court's will eventually prevailed as it invalidated Virginia's attempt to circumvent its rulings in this way.)

In many instances the effectiveness of Supreme Court rulings depends on local officials. Studies have indicated, for example, that despite decisions outlawing Bible-reading and prayers in the public schools, boards of education still permit such practices in some communities, particularly in rural areas. Similarly, the effect of cases like *Miranda* and *Mallory* turn on the actual interrogation practices of local law enforcement officials, while book and magazine dealers determine the consequences of the host of obscenity cases with which the Court has dealt in recent years.

Even though the Supreme Court must depend on others to effect compliance with its rulings, for the most part compliance does occur. Attempts to delay and avoid its edicts are reserved to more controversial areas of public policy in which the Court's opinions run counter to traditional practices and beliefs. Even then, however, the Court's will eventually prevails in most cases. Despite the unpopularity of school desegregation decisions in the South, the general opposition to the outlawing of prayers and Bible-reading in the schools, and the natural reluctance of legislatures to reapportion themselves along the lines required by the Court, the fact of the matter is that schools are becoming integrated, religious exercises are disappearing from the schools, and state legislatures all over the nation have redistricted themselves, as well as the House of Representatives. Such sharp departures from former practices in controversial areas of public policy testify to the major influence the Court continues to exercise on American life.

ASSESSMENT

It is difficult to reconcile judicial review with some of the major principles and assumptions of democracy. Granting to nine men (or more precisely, five, since that constitutes a majority of the Court), who are appointed and who serve for life, the power to overturn the actions of elected legislative and executive officials violates the idea of majority rule. It also is at variance with the democratic assumption that there are no elites who are intelligent enough or unselfish enough to make decisions that vitally affect the interests of the remaining members of society.

As indicated in Chapter 1, however, democracy does not always trust the majority; it also seeks to protect certain fundamental rights of minorities. In passing on constitutional questions, the Supreme Court is in a position to safeguard fundamental rights with which democracy has traditionally been concerned: freedom of speech, the press, and religion; social equality; procedural due process in criminal proceedings; and private property. Thus Supreme Court justices can and have acted under the power of judicial review to protect both rights "in" the government and rights "from" government.

But assuming that such minority rights should be safeguarded, there still remains the question of why Supreme Court justices should be granted that power: what is special about their training and/or position in the political system that qualifies them, rather than legislative or executive officials, to protect the rights of minorities?

If the major issues that come to the Supreme Court for decision were narrow legal ones, it could be argued that the training of the justices gives them a special expertise to pass judgment on such matters. But as previously suggested, this is not so: the issues that are resolved there are mostly broad philosophical ones involving basic values such as racial equality, the separation of church and state, and freedom of speech and the press. There is nothing in his law school education that specifically prepares a judge to deal with such matters; indeed, students of sociology, religion, and communication are probably better qualified than jurists to deal with these three issues. (One area where Supreme Court judges do have special training, and sometimes experience as well, is in dealing with the procedural rights of accused persons, but even then they are not necessarily familiar with the practical consequences their rulings have on the work of policemen, prosecutors, defense counsels, and trial judges.)

A more valid argument for the Court's prerogative in protecting the rights of minorities is the rather unique political situation justices enjoy compared to elected legislative and executive officials. It is unrealistic to expect the latter to fully protect the rights of minorities when they are elected by majorities, particularly in times of emergency and stress when the general public is likely to show little concern for the rights of unpopular minorities. A classic example is the contemporary "law and order" issue, which has led many congressmen and executive officials to advocate stricter policies towards persons accused of crime. Only officials who enjoy life tenure could afford to take the position that some Supreme Court judges have with respect to the procedural rights of the accused.

Whether judicial review is consistent with democracy or not, it will in all probability continue to be a part of our governing process. It has some 170 years of tradition behind it. Moreover, persons of all different political persuasions support judicial review when it favors values they cherish. Thus conservatives in the 1930s applauded the Court's role in seeking to protect property interests from the incursions of Franklin Roosevelt's New Deal; in the last three decades, liberals have praised Supreme Court judges for their role in the desegregation of public schools, the reapportionment of state legislatures, and the provision of additional procedural safeguards for persons accused of crime.

Judicial review will also survive because it is not an absolute power. Judges are sensitive to public attitudes, as was indicated by Justice Robert's switch in voting on New Deal issues after the 1936 presidential election that Franklin Roosevelt won by a landslide. Furthermore, the Congress and the President have important powers by which to affect decision-making by the Supreme Court. That body is very much a part of the democratic process.

Selected Readings

Henry J. Abraham, *The Judicial Process* (New York: Oxford University Press, 1968), contains basic information on all the subjects treated in this chapter.

A recent analysis of the lower federal courts written from a political, rather than a legal, standpoint is Richard J. Richardson and Kenneth N. Vines, *The Politics of Federal Courts* (Boston: Little, Brown, 1970). A similar approach to all the federal courts, including the Supreme Court, as well as to the judicial process in general, is Herbert Jacob, *Justice in America* (Boston: Little, Brown, 1965). Two good general treatments of the Supreme Court are John R. Schmidhauser, *The Supreme Court* (New York: Holt, Rinehart and Winston, 1960), and Glendon A. Schubert, *Constitutional Politics* (New York: Holt, Rinehart and Winston, 1964). David Danelski analyzes the role of the Chief Justice in "The Influence of the Chief Justice in the Decision Process," which appears in Walter F. Murphy and C. Herman Pritchett (eds.), *Courts, Judges, and Politics* (New York: Random House, 1961).

Chapter 4 of the Richardson and Vines book analyzes judicial selection and the backgrounds of judges of the lower federal courts. An historical account of the Senate's role in the selection of federal judges (as well as executive officials) is Joseph P. Harris, *The Advice and Consent of the Senate* (Berkeley: University of California Press, 1953). For an excellent analysis of the role that the Federal Judiciary Committee of the American Bar Association plays in the selection of federal judges, see Joel B. Grossman, *Lawyers and Judges: The ABA and the Politics of Judicial Selection* (New York: John Wiley, 1965). Chapters 2 and 3 of Schmidhauser's book discuss the selection and backgrounds of Supreme Court judges.

A general treatment of judicial review is Robert K. Carr, *The Supreme Court and Judicial Review* (New York: Farrar and Rinehart, 1942). An historical analysis of the subject is Robert G. McCloskey, *The American Supreme Court* (Chicago: University of Chicago Press, 1960). For an analysis of judicial review from the standpoint of democratic theory, see Howard E. Dean, *Judicial Review and Democracy* (New York: Random House, 1967).

For a book favoring judicial activism, see Charles L. Black, Jr., *The People and the Court: Judicial Review in a Democracy* (New York: Macmillan, 1960). Another, counseling judicial restraint, is Alexander M. Bickel, *The Least Dangerous Branch: The Supreme Court at the Bar of Politics* (Indianapolis: Bobbs-Merrill, 1962). Two early studies of attitudes of Supreme Court justices are C. Herman Pritchett, *The Roosevelt Court* (New York: Macmillan, 1948), and his subsequent *Civil Liberties and the Vinson Court* (Chicago: University of Chicago Press, 1954). A more recent and more sophisticated analysis of the same subject is Glendon A. Schubert, *The Judicial Mind* (Evanston: Northwestern University Press, 1965).

An early study urging that the courts be viewed within a political framework is Jack Peltason, *The Federal Courts in the Political Process* (New York: Doubleday, 1953). Two recent books analyzing the consequences of Supreme Court decisions are Theodore Becker (ed.), *The Impact of Supreme Court Decisions* (New York: Oxford University Press, 1969), and Stephen Wasby, *The Impact of the United States Supreme Court: Some Perspectives* (Homewood, Ill.: Dorsey, 1970). Two good studies of conflicts between the Supreme Court and the Congress are Walter F. Murphy, *Congress and the Court* (Chicago: University of Chicago Press, 1962), and C. Herman Pritchett, *Congress Versus the Supreme Court* (Minneapolis: University of Minnesota Press, 1961). Jack Peltason, *Fifty-Eight Lonely Men* (New York: Harcourt, Brace, 1961) treats of the pressures that federal judges in the South face in the enforcement of Supreme Court decisions on school desegregation. Chapter 6 of Robert Dahl, *Pluralist Democracy in the United States* (Chicago: Rand McNally, 1967), analyzes the extent to which the Court has been able to check actions of the Congress and the President over the years.

PART IV

ISSUES
AND PUBLIC POLICY

U*P TO THIS POINT* we have been examining the general operation *of the American political system, the process by which a broad range of decisions is made that bind all our citizens. In this last section of the book we look in more detail at specific decisions our government has made to deal with particular issues in American society. Three general areas are singled out for analysis—race relations, poverty and welfare, and foreign and military affairs.*

Public policy—or more precisely, "policies"—encompasses those decisions or rules that officials in the three branches of government make to deal with various social problems that they believe demand governmental action. In each of the three chapters that follow, we will examine the process by which the officials concerned arrived at the decisions they did with respect to race relations, poverty and welfare, and foreign and military affairs. It should be noted that the way policies were developed in these three areas vary greatly. Governmental decisions on the race issue involved all three branches of government and were influenced greatly by blacks themselves, particularly the actions and demands of their leaders and interest groups. In contrast, the poverty program was developed, not by poor people, but by middle-class social reformers largely outside the government who persuaded executive officials what should be done to help the economically disadvantaged; these officials, in turn, pushed the program through Congress with little initial resistance from that body. Finally, the policies pertaining to foreign and military affairs were developed almost exclusively within the executive branch of the government itself; citizens, interest groups, political parties, the courts, and even Congress had little to do with the decisions our government made in international matters in the post-World-War-II period.

Chapters 15, 16, and 17 also examine the substance of governmental decisions relating to race, poverty and welfare, and foreign and military affairs. Particular attention is focused on how the approaches to these problems have changed over time as governmental officials and affected individuals and groups have reacted to the results of past policies. Also included in the analysis are assessments of how successful the decisions made in these areas have been in bringing about greater social and economic equality in our society and in protecting and advancing our nation's interests in the world.

CHAPTER 15

The Race
Revolution

In December 1956, after a year-long boycott, victorious Negroes, vindicated by the Supreme Court, ride on desegregated buses in Montgomery, Alabama. Among the riders are Ralph D. Abernathy and Martin Luther King. (Wide World Photos)

I N DECEMBER 1955 a Negro seamstress named Rosa Parks boarded a bus in Montgomery, Alabama and sat in the front section reserved for whites. When the driver asker her to get up and give her seat to a white man, she refused and was arrested. The black community quickly organized a bus boycott to protest the incident and chose a young Baptist minister, Dr. Martin Luther King, to direct the effort. An improvement association composed of Montgomery Negroes called for the end of segregated seating in the city's buses. After some violence and the jailing of King and other protest leaders, the association prevailed: a federal district court—and ultimately the Supreme Court—ruled against segregated seating on municipal buses.

This incident set off a chain of events that had a major impact on race relations in the United States. Blacks in other Southern cities followed the Montgomery example in using boycotts to protest segregated facilities. More important still, the incident brought into national prominence the Reverend Dr. King who led the fight for racial integration through the principle of nonviolence. From that time until he was shot in April 1968 King was the most important figure in the civil rights struggle in the United States.

About two years before King's death, however, another incident occurred that also had a major effect on that struggle. James Meredith (whose enrollment at the University of Mississippi in 1962 had touched off a riot that led to the intervention of federal troops) began a Freedom March through that state in the summer of 1966 to interest Negroes in registering to vote. The march had barely begun when Meredith was shot and wounded. King rushed to the scene to resume the march, cautioning the participants to remain nonviolent. In contrast, however, a young Howard University graduate, Stokely Carmichael, chairman of the Student Nonviolent Coordinating Committee, urged Mississippi blacks to follow a new approach in the civil rights battle: "Black Power."

Although Carmichael never defined what he meant by the term (we will explore its possible meanings below), his general message was that blacks must stop being ashamed of their race and take their destiny into their own hands. The importance of the slogan lay in evoking an emotional response from the crowd—which chanted in unison, "Black Power! Black Power! Black Power!"—and in ushering in a new era in the civil rights struggle.

Both incidents are part of what students of race relations in the United States call a "revolution" or a "revolt." Generally the words refer, not to a violent overthrow of the present system (though some militant groups today advocate such action), but rather to a sharp break from the past in the nature of the civil rights movement, particularly in the tactics used and the kinds of persons involved in the struggle. To understand the present race revolution we must, therefore, know something of the situation that preceded it; the chapter thus begins with a brief resumé of major developments that ultimately led to the bus incident in Montgomery. In particular, this resumé focuses on the events, leaders, and governmental actions that shaped race relations in the ninety-year period from the end of the Civil War until the mid-1950s.

RACE RELATIONS IN AMERICA, 1865–1955

During the Reconstruction Period following the Civil War, Northern churches and the federal government embarked upon a program of bringing liberated slaves into the mainstream of American life. Public schools were created for them, and a number of major Negro universities, including Howard, Atlanta, and Fisk, along with Hampton Institute for Industrial Education, were founded. Congress passed legislation granting Negroes the right to sue, to give evidence in court, and to buy, sell, and inherit property; Congress also outlawed segregation in transportation, schools, and public accommodations. Southern state constitutions were redrawn to extend suffrage to all adult male citizens, and the Fifteenth Amendment specifically prohibited states to deny the right to vote on the basis of race, color, or previous condition of servitude. Benefiting from their new-found political rights, blacks were elected to the United States Senate, to the House of Representatives, and to state and local offices as well. But the halcyon days of Southern Negroes ended when a political deal was struck between Northern Republicans and Southern Democrats in the disputed presidential election of 1876:* the latter acquiesced in the choice of the GOP standard-bearer, Rutherford B. Hayes, over the Democratic candidate, Samuel J. Tilden, in return for Hayes's agreement to withdraw Northern troops from the South when he came to office. When President Hayes fulfilled that promise in 1877, the decade of Reconstruction came to a close.

There then followed the systematic exclusion of Negroes from various facets of Southern life. Initially based on custom, in time state laws were passed providing for segregation in public schools, transportation, and accommodations. When, as we saw in Chapter 7, the Populist alliance of blacks and poor whites in the early 1890s threatened the interests of the Bourbon Democrats, the latter split the alliance, and then proceeded to disenfranchise Negroes through a series of techniques, including poll taxes,

*The dispute arose over competing groups of electors in certain states. An electoral commission chosen to resolve the issue settled it in the Republicans' favor.

literacy tests, and the exclusion of blacks from participation in the primaries of the dominant Democratic party. A Virginia Democratic leader, Carter Glass, described the goal frankly as ". . . the elimination of every Negro voter that can be gotten rid of, legally, without materially impairing the numerical strength of the white electorate." Nor did all Southerners stick to legal means to subordinate the Negro: during the 1880s and 1890s there were on the average one hundred lynchings a year. By the early years of the twentieth century, the process of segregation, disenfranchisement, and intimidation was complete.

About this same time the locus of race problems began to shift away from the rural South, where the overwhelming proportion of Negroes lived, to the urban North and West, to which they migrated in increasing numbers after the turn of the century. Just before World War I, damage to Southern agriculture by the boll weevil and floods combined with a rising demand for labor (occasioned by the decline in European immigration due to the war) to swell the Negro migration: Chicago's black population more than doubled from 1910 to 1920, while Cleveland's quadrupled. The depression of the 1930s slowed the migration somewhat, but since that time industry's demands for labor beginning in World War II and the increased mechanization of agriculture since the War have sent increasing numbers of Negroes to Northern and Western cities. By 1960 three-fourths of blacks in the United States lived in urban areas, almost half of them outside the South.

While many Negroes bettered themselves economically by moving to the North, they found it far from the promised land they sought. Typically they settled in the low-rent areas of the city, forming black ghettoes in the process: even before World War II New York had its Harlem and Chicago its State Street district. Although some blacks preferred to remain in such areas to be near to their own people and institutions—particularly Negro churches—those who could afford it and who wanted to move to white neighborhoods found themselves thwarted by residential segregation ordinances, restrictive covenants in deeds forbidding the sale of property to non-Caucasians, and, in many cases, violence in the form of personal beatings and the stoning and bombing of their homes. Residential segregation, in turn, resulted in separation of blacks from whites in the neighborhood school system. Blacks seeking employment found their way barred by their limited education and skills, white workers who feared the loss of their own jobs, and labor unions that discriminated against them. Thus while blacks found life in the Northern ghetto better than that on the Southern plantation, discrimination and segregation were part of their everyday lives.

THE NEGRO RESPONSE

Negroes reacted in a variety of ways to the conditions they faced in both the rural South and the urban North. The leader most associated with accommodation to the situation, particularly in the South, was Booker T. Washington. Born a slave and educated at Hampton Institute, he urged Negroes to prepare themselves for jobs that whites would permit them to hold: those involving manual skills. The program he developed at Tuskegee Institute stressed farming and handicrafts. Washington also urged Negroes to develop their own businesses as a means of advancing their race economically. Thus Washington felt that economic self-help and a striving after middle-class virtues and responsibility should be the goals of his race.

At the same time Washington urged Negroes to accept segregation and political disenfranchisement. In a famous speech in 1895 which brought him world fame, he stated: "In all things that are purely social, we can be as separate as the fingers, yet one as the hand in all matters essential to natural progress." Washington criticized Negro political activity and approved literacy and property qualifications for voting on the grounds that they would stimulate Negroes to obtain education and wealth.

As might be expected, Washington's philosophy was well-received by whites, particularly philanthropists who wanted to do "good work" but who opposed racial equality. Contributions poured into Negro private schools from Carnegie, Rockefeller, and other donors on Washington's say-so. However, his hopes for a major economic uplift of Negroes proved illusory: urbanization and technological change made farming skills and manual labor obsolete, and most black capitalists failed because of a lack of managerial experience, low-income clients, and rivalry from white merchants. (Some black businesses, particularly banks and insurance and realty companies, did flourish and support a small black-capitalist class.)

Although Washington was the major Negro political figure at the turn of the twentieth century, he came under increasing criticism from a small group of Northern intellectuals—editors, lawyers, ministers, and teachers. The most prominent of these critics was W.E.B. Du Bois, a Harvard-educated Negro social scientist who taught at Atlanta University. He agreed with Washington's support for black businessmen but was opposed to his emphasis on vocational education. Du Bois felt that the race could best be improved by providing a liberal education to its "talented tenth," who would eventually lift their less-gifted brethren. He was opposed to segregation as well as the political disenfranchisement of the Negro and placed the responsibility for the race problem on whites.

Du Bois originally tried to develop a program to fight for Negroes' rights through the Niagara Movement, but it failed, and he subsequently joined with a group of white liberals to found the *National Association for the Advancement of Colored People* in 1909. Given visibility through the efforts of well-known white leaders—including the philosopher and educator, John Dewey; the founder of Hull House, Jane Addams; and the eminent lawyer, Clarence Darrow—its best-known spokesman was Du Bois, who served as the publicity director and editor of its organ, *Crisis*. The Association, which soon became the major group fighting for Negro rights, later led the way in the court battles to end segregation and disenfranchisement described below.

The migration of Negroes to the cities led to the establishment in 1914 of another important organization, *The National Urban League*. Founded by conservative Negroes, white philanthropists, and social workers, it concentrated its efforts on finding employment opportunities for Negroes and helping them adjust to urban life. It adopted a conciliatory approach in persuading employers that Negroes were good workers. Like the NAACP, the organization was strongly middle-class in its orientation.

The interests of lower-class Negroes were articulated by a variety of leaders and organizations. A Jamaican citizen, Marcus Garvey, founded the Universal Negro Improvement Association in 1914, which sought to liberate American Negroes from their oppression through their wholesale migration to Africa. A. Philip Randolph, the editor of *Messenger,* advanced a Marxist approach to the problems of poor blacks by urging them to join with white workers to fight the capitalist system that enslaved them both. Still another outlet for blacks trapped in the ghetto was provided by the religious sects led by charismatic preachers like Father Divine and Daddy Grace, who enriched themselves by offering urban Negroes salvation, healing, and miracles. All three approaches—nationalism, Marxism, and religion—had one thing in common: they were escapist and offered little in concrete results for lower-class Negroes.

Negro efforts to improve their situation, however, did lead to some results, as public officials eventually responded to their demands. But as indicated below, this response was both slow in coming and limited in its scope.

THE GOVERNMENTAL RESPONSE

The major governmental arena for asserting Negro rights in the period from Reconstruction to the Negro Revolution was the courtroom. Yet in the early years judges were not responsive to the interests of blacks. In the Civil Rights Cases of 1883 the Supreme Court ruled that legislation enacted by Congress in 1875 providing for equality in public accommodations could not be used to forbid discrimination by private persons, since the Fourteenth Amendment applied only to the states. In another landmark decision, *Plessy* v. *Ferguson* (1896), upholding the segregation of the races on railroads, the Court announced its "separate but equal" doctrine: separate facilities for blacks and whites met the requirements of the equal protection of the laws clause of the Fourteenth Amendment so long as the facilities were equal. (Justice John Marshall Harlan, however, wrote a famous dissenting opinion proclaiming the Constitution to be "color-blind" and warning that "the thin disguise of equal accommodations will not mislead anyone nor atone for the wrong done this day.")

The NAACP, however, soon after its founding embarked upon a series of successful test cases on several civil rights fronts. Its initial victory came in *Guinn* v. *United States* (1915), in which the Supreme Court invalidated the "grandfather clause" of the Oklahoma constitution exempting persons from a literacy test if their ancestors were entitled to vote in 1866; the Court viewed this provision as a deliberate (and not too subtle) attempt to evade the Fifteenth Amendment. The Association subsequently waged a number of battles against the white primary, culminating in *Smith* v. *Allwright* (1944), in which the Court held such an election to be a *public* function (rather than the business of a *private* organization, the Democratic party) and hence forbidden by that same Amendment.

The NAACP also fought segregation successfully in the courts. In 1917 the Supreme Court outlawed municipal ordinances providing for residential segregation; the organization then focused its attention on restrictive covenants in deeds, which were used to prevent Negro incursions into white neighborhoods. In 1926 the Court ruled that since these were agreements between private parties they did not violate the Fourteenth Amendment; however, in *Shelley* v. *Kraemer* (1948) the Court held that judicial enforcement of such covenants involved the power of the state, and so contravened the equal protection clause of that amendment. Over the years the Court also struck down segregation on railroads and buses as constituting interference with interstate commerce. (In 1955 the Interstate Commerce Commission issued regulations outlawing segregation on interstate trains and buses, as well as in waiting rooms, restaurants, and other facilities at stations.)

Most significant, however, was the long battle the NAACP waged against segregation in the public schools. Its initial victory came in *Missouri ex rel Gaines* v. *Canada* (1938), in which the Supreme Court ruled that a state did not meet its constitutional responsibilities by refusing to admit a Negro to its law school and then offering to pay his expenses to a school in a neighboring state that admitted Negroes: the "separate but equal" doctrine meant separate but equal within the state. Subsequently the Court began to examine whether facilities and practices in higher education were actually equal, ruling that a special Texas law school established for Negroes did not have the faculty, library, and reputation of its regular law school, and that Oklahoma could not force a Negro graduate student to sit in separate sections of classrooms, libraries, and dining facilities.

All these cases were a prelude to the famous *Brown* v. *Board of Education of Topeka* (1954) case in which the Court, in a unanimous opinion written by Chief Justice Earl Warren, specifically voided the use of the separate but equal doctrine in public educational facilities at any level. In ruling that separate educational facilities are inherently unequal the Chief Justice held that segregation creates a feeling of inferiority in Negro children that may affect their hearts and minds in a way unlikely ever to be undone. The following year the Court entrusted the federal district courts with requiring local school boards to make "a prompt and reasonable start toward full compliance" with the 1954 ruling and with seeing to it that desegregation proceed "with all deliberate speed."

In contrast to the judiciary, the other two branches of government did little for the rights of Negroes. Despite the lobbying efforts of the NAACP, the Senate even refused to enact antilynching legislation, as Southern senators used the filibuster successfully against it. Nor were many "liberal" Presidents of this century committed to civil rights: Theodore Roosevelt arbitrarily discharged three black companies of soldiers on unproven charges of rioting in Brownsville, Texas; Virginian Woodrow Wilson did not permit Negroes in the Marines in World War I; and Franklin Roosevelt introduced no major civil rights legislation and only issued an executive order establishing a Committee on Fair Employment practices in 1941 after A. Philip Randolph threatened to lead a march on Washington to secure job opportunities for Negroes. It remained for a border state politician, Missourian Harry Truman, to take the first significant steps for racial equality by outlawing segregation in the armed services and civilian jobs in the national government, ordering firms doing business with the federal government not to discriminate in hiring, proposing a broad civil rights program to the Congress, and appointing a committee to study race relations in the United States. Subsequently Republican President Dwight Eisenhower continued the process of desegregating the armed forces that Truman had begun and took the leadership in ending segregation in the District of Columbia as well.

Thus by the mid-1950s the judicial and executive branches of the national government had begun to respond to Negro demands. As the next sections indicate, however, these demands stepped up in the period that followed.

GENERAL NATURE AND CAUSES
OF THE RACE REVOLUTION

As indicated earlier, what we term the Race "Revolution" or "Revolt" is the sharp break from the past that occurred in the civil rights movement in the postwar period as epitomized by the Montgomery bus boycott. A central feature of the shift in the movement was the increased determination of Negroes no longer to accept the *status quo* in race relations as most of them had done over the years. For the first time a large segment of the black community refused to accommodate itself to its inferior position in American society and decided to take action to change that position. What had heretofore been a battle in which a relatively few well-educated, middle-class Negroes participated, became a movement that involved a large number of working- and lower-middle-class blacks as well.

The Revolt was not only against the system of race relations that Negroes had tolerated over the years but also against Negro leadership. A new breed of black leaders expressed dissatisfaction with the approaches of the NAACP and the National Urban League to the race problem, namely, pursuing the battle for Negro rights in courtrooms and legislative chambers or behind the scenes in conciliatory conversations with white governmental leaders and private employers. What was needed, according to the new leaders like King, was to have masses of blacks take direct action in the form of boycotts, sit-ins, marches, and the like to win rights for themselves.* There was also a new sense of urgency in the civil rights movement. Negroes were not willing to wait until legal cases eventually won rights for their children; they wanted these rights for themselves now.

Of course, this new direction and sense of urgency in the civil rights movement did not occur overnight; it developed over a period of time and involved a number of events and factors. World War II contributed to the eventual Revolt in a number of ways. Many black men had a novel experience in their lives—being treated well by whites. Those who served overseas received respect and social acceptance from citizens in France, Great Britain, and elsewhere that they had never enjoyed in the United States. When they returned home, the reversion to an inferior position was naturally resented by many former Negro GI's who determined to do something about it. Moreover, the irony of the nation's fighting a war against Nazi Germany with its racist philosophy and at the same time practicing a brand of racism of our own (not only were our troops generally segregated, but we also kept separate supplies of blood from blacks and whites) was not lost on Negro soldiers.

Events in the post-World-War-II era contributed to the development of the Negro Revolution. The end of colonialism in Africa and the emergence of new free nations there under the leadership of blacks gave American Negroes a new sense of pride in their race and a desire to enjoy the same freedom as their brethren. Also helping the Negroes' cause with political leaders was the fact that our rivals in the Cold War, the communists, held up American pretentions of equality to the uncommitted nations of the world.

For the attitudes and actions of whites in the United States on the race issue also affected how Negroes themselves viewed the situation. Many began to perceive that whites were growing more sympathetic towards their cause. Particularly influential were the Supreme Court cases and exec-

---

*As indicated later in this chapter, these tactics were used prior to King's arrival on the civil rights scene; however, he gave them wider notoriety and in the eyes of most Americans came to symbolize their use.

utive actions invalidating voting restrictions and segregation in education, transportation, and the armed services. Thus as blacks gained additional rights, they came to want ever more, as a natural rise in expectations set in.

New black leaders and greater publicity for the Negro cause helped channel these new perspectives and expectations into effective action. The rapid growth in the Negro middle class and the availability of a large pool of persons with the experience and skills needed for political activities gave the Negro Revolution the dynamic leadership it had lacked in the past. Adding to the increasing militancy of some blacks was the gap between educational and economic levels—more people became aware of the advantages of American society in which they did not fully share.

All these factors helped pave the way for the Race Revolution analyzed in the following section.

DIRECTIONS AND TRENDS IN THE RACE REVOLUTION

Although the Race Revolution represented a break from the past in the continuing civil rights struggle in the United States, a uniform movement did not result, for its participants differed in their approaches to the race problem. As indicated below, the movement also went through different phases over the years after 1955.

EARLY DIRECTIONS

The initial phase of the Race Revolution was dominated by the Reverend Martin Luther King, who worked to achieve full integration of Negroes in all aspects of American life. His approach was that of nonviolence, or passive resistance, a technique which he borrowed from Mahatma Gandhi, who had used it successfully against the British in India. In 1957 King founded the *Southern Christian Leadership Conference* (SCLC), a loose organization of Southern clergymen who joined together to fight against segregation and for Negroes' voting rights, particularly in the South. King's dominant role in the civil rights struggle, however, stemmed not from his position with that organization but from the symbolic leadership he provided for blacks generally, many of whom were affiliated with other organizations.

One such group that came to prominence in the early 1960s was the *Student Nonviolent Coordinating Committee* (SNCC). Composed of Negro college students who initially protested against segregation at Southern lunch counters early in 1960, it was officially founded in April of that year at a meeting attended by King and other civil rights leaders. SCLC provided SNCC with financial and other assistance, as did other Negro organizations such as the NAACP. In time Northern college students also helped with the group's primary activities: sponsoring sit-ins and freedom rides to protest segregation in public accommodations and transportation, and registering Southern Negroes to vote. As its name implied, SNCC under the leadership of John Lewis was also committed to the principle of non-violence.

A third group, which also assisted SNCC and joined the civil rights effort in the South, was the *Congress of Racial Equality* (CORE). Established in Chicago in 1942, the organization (which developed out of the activities of a pacifist, religious group, the Fellowship of Reconciliation) carried out a successful sit-in the following year to protest segregation in restaurants in that city. The group attracted little attention during the remainder of that decade or in the one that followed; but in the spring of 1961, shortly after James Farmer became its national director, the organization launched freedom rides through the South to test whether nondiscrimination policies were actually being observed in interstate transportation.

These three organizations formed the nucleus of the movement to achieve integration and secure Negro political rights through direct-action techniques designed to bring quick results. The NAACP's legislative approach to the same goals came under increased attack, and the organization responded to the criticism by supplementing its traditional activities with involvement in direct action. The organization paid the fines of persons who were jailed for protest activities, and many NAACP members joined the protesters and went to jail themselves. The National Urban League under the directorship of Whitney Young also began to exert more concerted pressure on employers to hire blacks, using the threat of direct action by other groups to serve their own behind-the-scenes negotiations.

Thus a variety of organizations pushed for integration and Negroes' rights through different approaches. The division of labor in the civil rights struggle proved to be fruitful as the groups supplemented one another's efforts. Sympathetic whites from the North contributed financially to the movement, and many of them, particularly college students, went to the South to assist with the integration of public facilities and the registering of Negroes to vote. The coalition of blacks and white liberals reached a high point in August 1963 when some 200,000 persons responded to the call of A. Philip Randolph and the pacifist Socialist Bayard Rustin (who had first experimented with personal sit-ins in the 1940s when he was Youth Secretary of the Fellowship of Reconciliation) to join a march on Washington as a means of persuading Congress to enact civil rights legislation. It was at this gathering (remarkable for its orderliness given the numbers of people that participated) that the Reverend Dr. King delivered his famous "I have a dream" speech ("I have a dream that my four little children will one day live in a nation where they will not be judged by the color of their skin but by the content of their character").

Just as the civil rights movement seemed to reach new heights, however, it began to develop frustrations. Direct-action techniques failed to bring results in desegregating facilities in Mississippi and Alabama; the Negro Mississippi political party, the Freedom Democratic party, that came to the Democratic presidential convention in the summer of 1964 to challenge the seating of the regular Democratic delegation on the grounds of Negro disenfranchisement was granted only token representation: two at-large seats. In the North direct action proved ineffective both against *de facto* segregation of the schools occasioned by residential segregation of the races and against job discrimination by employers and labor unions alike. Violence broke out in some of the nation's major cities: Harlem experienced difficulties in the summer of 1964, and the nation was shocked the following summer when the Watts section of Los Angeles exploded in the worst riot in the nation's history.

In the period from 1964 to 1966 more and more blacks became dissatisfied with nonviolent, direct action as a means of achieving their goals. Contrariwise, many white liberals became alarmed at the incidents of violence and began to withdraw their support (particularly financial) from the civil rights movement. Martin Luther King experienced increased difficulty in bridging the gap between Negro factions and between the two races. The stage was thus set for a new phase in the Race Revolution represented by Stokely Carmichael's call for Black Power.

THE SHIFT TO BLACK POWER

The shift in approach to the race problem occurred first in two of the interest groups that had played a prominent part in the initial phase of the Race Revolution: SNCC and CORE. At about the same time in 1966, both organizations changed their leadership. SNCC replaced its nonviolent leader, John Lewis, with Stokely Carmichael; CORE elected Floyd McKissick (who refused to denounce the violence in Watts the previous year) to its top position. With these changes the two organizations moved to a more militant approach to the race issue, as represented by Carmichael's urging Mississippi Negroes to use Black Power to better their situation in life.

As previously mentioned, Carmichael never defined what he meant by the term Black Power. It has remained vague, partly because it represents a general mood or call for action rather than a specific program with concrete goals, and partly because it means different things to different people. Nonetheless, it is possible to spell out certain ideas that have come to be identified with Black Power.*

*One recent survey of interpretations given the term by black citizens in Detroit indicated that many of them associated it with a traditional goal of the civil rights movement: "a fair share," that is, equal rights for Negroes. However, most Negro leaders appear to regard Black Power as involving new approaches to race relations, as discussed below.

One idea is the conviction that blacks should control their own organizations rather than depend on the leadership of whites, who traditionally played a major role in the activities of the NAACP and CORE. As a matter of fact, however, the replacement of whites by blacks in such organizations had already occurred by 1965: that year only two whites were on the staff of the NAACP and less than one-fourth of its national board was white. CORE went through a similar process of drawing upon blacks for leadership positions. Negroes also came to provide the major support, financial and otherwise, for these groups as both organizations added large numbers of blacks (including working-class people) to their memberships.

Black Power has also become associated with economic power for the Negro race. Ironically, this represents a revival of the idea of black capitalism that the conservative Booker T. Washington had advocated two-thirds of a century before. The notion of economic power for blacks includes a number of other things now, however: the formation of Negro cooperatives; increasing the number of blacks employed by white companies; getting the latter (especially those in the ghetto) to do business with Negro banks, contractors, and insurance firms.

Black Power also means political power for the Negro; the concentration of blacks in Northern ghettoes and Southern rural counties creates the potential for electing members of their race to political offices, especially at the city and county level. Black Power advocates differ, however, on the kind of organization that offers the best chance for maximizing black political strength. SNCC has called for the formation of independent political parties such as the Black Panther Party in Lowndes County, Alabama, while CORE has preferred working within the regular Democratic party. The two thus differ on whether blacks can work effectively with whites to advance their own political interests. SNCC's concentration in the South naturally made its leaders less sanguine on this point.

Behind these various facets of Black Power lies a feeling that Negroes cannot depend on the good will of whites to secure additional rights; such dependence might end as it did in 1876 when Northern political leaders valued reconciliation with the South more than they did the rights of Negroes. The best way to insure that such rights will be advanced, according to Black Power advocates, is for blacks to operate from a position of strength that will force a change in race relations whether whites want such a change or not.

Perhaps the vaguest aspect of Black Power is the question of whether it includes the use of violence, and, if so, under what circumstances. The leaders of CORE sanction it only in self-defense, while the *Black Panthers*, described below, advocate the use of guerrilla warfare to achieve advances in Negro rights. Individual leaders like Carmichael himself have also vacillated on the issue. In many instances, it is difficult to determine whether spokesmen actually intend that blacks resort to violence or whether they

Two advocates of Black Power: (left) Stokely Carmichael, seen with Black Panther Party posters in Lowndes County, Alabama; (right) the late Malcolm X addressing a Black Muslim meeting. (Left: John Ford/Pix; right: Eve Arnold/Magnum)

are only engaging in emotional rhetoric designed to win support from the black community.

Another feature associated with Black Power is the idea of black consciousness, a feeling of pride in the race. This was an important part of the initial message of Carmichael: blacks should cease feeling inferior to whites and identify with their own race. It is this aspect of Black Power that has led to the establishment of Black Studies programs in schools to acquaint members of the race with their cultural heritage. Related to this source of racial pride is the desire for unity and solidarity among blacks.

For a small core of blacks, racial pride and unity can best be achieved through a separation of blacks from whites. This sentiment is reflected in their effort to control schools in their communities, substituting black teachers for whites and tailoring the curriculum to fit the special needs of their children. The same is true of efforts by blacks to determine the content and personnel of Black Studies programs at the university level and to live in special dormitories. Thus, ironically, militant Black Power has become associated with the same general goal espoused by the conservative Booker T. Washington—segregation of the races—only in this instance it is the blacks who want to separate themselves from the whites.

Two black interest groups in particular have carried the policy of segregation to the extreme by advocating that separate geographical territories be set aside for blacks. The *Black Muslims* (originally founded in 1930 and now under the leadership of Elijah Muhammad) want to establish an exclusive black state in the United States where no whites are to be allowed. Believing that blacks originally lived in a high state of civilization in Mecca but were conquered by whites and made to worship a white Jesus, the Muslims believe in the superiority of the black race and hence the desirability of separation. One of the former leaders of the organization, Malcolm X (who was slain in 1965 by another Muslim), likened blacks in the United States to a colonized people such as those in Africa who must win their freedom from their white oppressors.

The second separatist group with beliefs similar to those of Malcolm X is the *Black Panthers*, who want the central cities to be controlled by blacks. Marxist in orientation, Black Panthers leaders like Eldridge Cleaver seek ties with the ex-colonial Third World, as well as with white revolutionaries in the United States, to overthrow the capitalistic system which they feel enslaves both blacks and whites. Founded in Oakland, California in 1966 to protect blacks there against alleged police brutality, the Black Panthers continue to be involved in periodic shoot-outs with police (admittedly, however, some of these have not been entirely of the Panthers' making) whom they consider to be agents of the white society that holds them in colonial bondage. While the Panthers advocate guerrilla revolutionary tactics to accomplish their goals of liberating blacks, they have also inaugurated a free breakfast program for hungry ghetto children and have instilled in them a sense of racial pride.

THE RACE REVOLUTION TODAY

The development of Black Power and its many interpretations has divided the forces working for racial progress into several distinct factions. On the right of the civil rights movement are the NAACP, the National Urban League, and the SCLC, all of which still work for integration of the races through peaceful means involving political coalitions with whites. Further to the left is CORE, which preaches Black Power but which does not openly advocate the use of violence or call for total physical separation of the races. On the far left are the separatists, the nationalist Black Muslims and the even more extremist Marxists, the Black Panthers, who are willing to use violence and engage in it with police in urban areas.*

Unlike the situation in the initial phase of the Race Revolution when the participants supplemented one another's efforts, many of today's broad spectrum of black interest groups work at cross purposes. Spokesmen for the NAACP have termed Black Power a brand of racism, while those from militant organizations like the Muslims and Panthers call representa-

*SNCC, for all practical purposes, has disappeared from the scene in recent years.

tives of the NAACP "ugly Americans" who have sold out their black breth-ren to the white power structure. Thus the ends of integration versus separa-tion and the means of peaceful persuasion versus violence are basically incompatible.

The result of these developments has been a lack of cohesion and over-all leadership in the black community. No individual comparable to Martin Luther King exists today in whom the overwhelming proportion of blacks have faith. Black leadership tends to be fragmented and localized, with new aspirants acquiring (and often then losing) influence with certain kinds of blacks in particular communities.

Recent studies of attitudes of blacks towards various leaders indicate, however, that the more conservative spokesmen still draw the greatest support of the Negro community. A *Time*-Louis Harris poll in 1970 re-vealed that sixty-two percent of the Negroes questioned thought a great deal of the Reverend Ralph Abernathy, president of the SCLC, and fifty-five percent had the same attitude towards Roy Wilkins, Executive Director of the NAACP; in contrast Stokely Carmichael and Elijah Muhammed drew support from only twenty-six and twenty-three percent of the re-spondents, respectively.

At the same time there is evidence that more blacks are beginning to believe that violence may be necessary to achieve their rights. A 1966 Harris poll showed that twenty-one percent of Negroes thought they might have to resort to violence to win rights; by 1970 thirty percent of those questioned expressed that sentiment. Moreover, among teenage blacks the figure rose to forty percent.

To get some appreciation of why Negroes feel as they do, we need to look at the governmental response to the Race Revolution and the actual results that have been achieved in bettering conditions for blacks in the United States.

GOVERNMENTAL RESPONSE
TO THE RACE REVOLUTION

Unlike the governmental response in the earlier period, that associated with the Race Revolution covered many aspects of the race problem and in-volved all three branches of the national government. Congress, which had passed its last major civil rights legislation in 1875, enacted no less than six statutes in the period from 1957 through 1970, along with a constitu-tional amendment. As indicated below, the Presidents who served in this period also had varying degrees of commitment to civil rights.

THE BREAKTHROUGH

Because President Eisenhower wanted to retain the political support of Southern Democrats (which Truman lost after he presented his civil rights program to Congress), and also because Ike felt that laws had little effect in changing racial attitudes (such changes could occur only in the "hearts of men"), he asked for no civil rights legislation during his first three years in office. In the late fall of 1955, however, Clarence Mitchell of the NAACP initiated a meeting of congressmen from both parties sympathetic to civil rights to push for the enactment of such legislation. It was decided that the right to vote should have priority in the legislative program. Meanwhile, Attorney General Herbert Brownell and other liberal Republicans who disagreed philosophically with the President on the race issue and who also wanted their party to strengthen itself in the upcoming presidential election in the Northern states with large Negro populations, persuaded the cabinet, and subsequently the President, to agree to the presentation of a civil rights proposal in early 1956. Brownell framed a bill with four sections: one creating a Civil Rights Commission, a second upgrading the status of the Civil Rights Division in the Department of Justice, a third (known for a decade as "Title III") granting the Attorney General the power to seek injunctive relief against the violation of any civil right, and a fourth authorizing that same official (or an aggrieved individual himself) to seek relief in voting rights' matters only. Despite the President's reservations about the last two sections of the bill, the Attorney General's wishes eventually prevailed, and the bill passed the House in 1956 and again in 1957.

The real battleground was the Senate, where Southerners who opposed the bill had the advantage of the right of filibuster. Liberal Democrats and Republicans wanted to change the cloture rule to permit less than two-thirds of the membership to cut off debate, but Democratic Majority Leader Lyndon Johnson contended that civil rights legislation could be enacted without changing the cloture rule. Johnson proved true to his word, but the price was the watering down of the bill to eliminate Title III and also to provide that persons cited for contempt for violating voting rights would have the right to a jury trial. (Southern juries might be expected to be more sympathetic than federal judges.) The Leadership Conference on Civil Rights representing some twenty organizations decided to support the weakened bill as a breakthrough to be built upon in future years. Thus the 1957 legislation, a moderate law with limited protection for voting rights and the organizational provisions of sections one and two, was enacted into law.

Although the Civil Rights Act of 1957 constituted a beginning in the long quest to counteract discrimination, it did not begin to meet the nation's racial problems. Two weeks after the President signed the bill, he was forced to send federal troops into Little Rock, Arkansas to enforce court orders to desegregate the schools there. Branches of the Ku Klux Klan as well as White Citizens' Councils spread throughout the South. Shootings, stabbings, and bombings of Negro homes and churches increased as the tempo of violence rose. Moreover, a report of the Civil Rights Commission issued in 1959 indicated that intimidation and obstruction by Southern officials were successfully preventing Negroes from voting.

These events were soon reflected in a series of bills introduced in Congress by Lyndon Johnson, by Democratic Senator Paul Douglas of Illinois, and by the Eisenhower administration. These proposals called for various attacks on racial problems, including criminal penalties for bombings, community-relations services in racially torn areas, technical and financial assistance for desegregation, the preservation of voting records, the use of federal officials to assist Negroes in registering and voting, and resurrection of Title III of the original 1957 bill. The legislative struggle again ended in victory for the South, however, when the Act of 1959 was passed, only strengthening somewhat the enforcement of voting rights and providing limited criminal penalties for bombings and the obstruction of federal court orders (dealing primarily with school desegregation). Thus the governmental response in the 1950s to the Race Revolution was a moderate one.

THE PERIOD OF ACCELERATION

In the first year of the new decade it was apparent that the political system was beginning to respond more vigorously to the Race Revolution. Both political parties at their national conventions that summer rejected the moderate congressional approach of the 1950s by adopting strong civil rights planks in their platforms, including support for civil rights demonstrations and the use of legal means to hasten school desegregation. During his campaign John Kennedy pledged to introduce a broad civil rights bill in early 1961, to provide moral leadership on the race issue, and to eliminate discrimination in federally assisted housing by a "stroke of the presidential pen."

When Kennedy actually took office, however, he became much more cautious on the race issue. His general approach called for advancing civil rights through executive action. He thus spoke out against the moral evil of discrimination, appointed Negroes to high public office, dispatched troops to Mississippi and Alabama to protect Negroes entering state universities, and eventually in 1962 signed the executive order forbidding discrimination in federally assisted housing. But the President's desire to retain the support of the Southern bloc for other proposals (for example, on reciprocal trade), plus his assessment that significant civil rights legislation could not get past that bloc in the Senate, caused him to delay sending any civil rights message at all to Congress until early 1963.* Even that one was de-

*President Kennedy did, however, support a constitutional amendment to ban the use of poll taxes in federal elections. The measure cleared Congress in 1962 and was ratified as the Twenty-fourth Amendment in 1964. Only five states—Alabama, Arkansas, Mississippi, Texas, and Virginia—still used this tax as a requisite for voting at the time the Amendment was ratified.

voted primarily to reports of his executive accomplishments and recommendations for minor legislation to be introduced later that year.

The events of that spring ended Kennedy's cautious approach to civil rights legislation. When Martin Luther King led a major effort to desegregate facilities in Birmingham, Alabama, officials there responded by jailing thousands of Negroes and resorting to police brutality, including the use of vicious dogs on helpless demonstrators. All this was dramatically brought to life for millions of Americans who watched the tragic display on television. Equally important was the political response of the nation's churches, which for the first time entered the civil rights arena in force.

The Conference on Civil Rights, with a new Washington headquarters and now representing fifty organizations, put pressure on the President for comprehensive legislation, including equality of access to public accommodations, fair employment, provisions for cutting off federal funds to state and local programs practicing discrimination, and Title III of the original 1957 bill. The administration resisted some of these provisions as being too ambitious but agreed that the civil rights forces were free to try to convince Congress to include them. This they accomplished in a liberal bipartisan bill which the House Judiciary Committee reported to the Rules Committee just as the President departed for Dallas.

The new President, Lyndon Johnson, who had favored moderation when he was Senate Majority Leader, threw his support behind the strong bill and used all his political skills to get it enacted into law. The Democratic Whip, Hubert Humphrey—working with his Republican counterpart, Thomas Kuchel of California, the administration, and the Leadership Conference, and aided by outside pressures from churches, organized labor, and other liberal groups—steered the bill through the Senate, even managing to invoke cloture for the first time ever on a civil rights bill. Also involved in the effort was Republican Minority Leader Everett Dirksen, who quoted Victor Hugo: "Stronger than all the armies is an idea whose time has come." In the summer of 1964 the most comprehensive civil rights bill in history was enacted into law.

Not satisfied with this accomplishment, the first Southerner to serve in the White House since Wilson, pushed forward on the civil rights front. President Johnson appointed Thurgood Marshall to the Supreme Court and Robert Weaver to his cabinet, the first Negroes to serve in these bodies. Moreover, in 1965 he supported new legislation to eliminate barriers to voting. This time voting rights demonstrations led by the Reverend Dr. King in Selma, Alabama performed the same function that Birmingham had two years before: the mass media reported as police bombarded praying Negroes with tear gas and waded into their ranks with clubs, whips, and ropes. Addressing Congress before a nationwide television audience in March, the President linked Selma with Lexington, Concord, and Appomattox as places that shaped a "turning point in man's unending search for freedom," and he ended his address with a refrain from the civil rights hymn, "We Shall Overcome." Five months later Congress passed the Civil Rights Act of 1965, thereby suspending literacy tests and authorizing the appointment of federal examiners to supervise electoral procedures in areas using such tests where less than one-half the voting·population was registered or voted in November 1964.

THE SLOWDOWN

One major area of concern to civil rights activists remained outside the legislative accomplishments of the 1950s and 1960s: housing. As early as 1959 the Civil Rights Commission reported the high incidence of discrimination in housing and noted its effects on disease, juvenile delinquency, and crime. President Kennedy's executive order of 1962 excluded existing homes and its restriction to housing insured or guaranteed by federal agencies left about eighty percent of new housing unaffected. A President's Committee on Equal Opportunity in Housing chaired by Governor David Lawrence of Pennsylvania requested after the 1964 election that the order be broadened; some observers feared that some of the committee's Negro members would resign if President Johnson rejected the group's recommendations. The President decided not to use the executive-order approach of his predecessor but rather to go to Congress with the issue. In early 1966 he asked that body to enact broad housing legislation and to provide protection from physical harm for Negroes and civil rights workers.

This time, however, the political situation differed greatly from that of the early 1960s, for this particular legislation aimed not just at discrimination in the South but also at all-white suburbs in the North. The National Real Estate Association rallied its 80,000 members against the housing bill, while the churches that were so active in 1963 did not come to its support. Rather than the peaceful demonstrations and singing of "We Shall Overcome" of Birmingham and Selma, there were riots in Chicago and Cleveland and cries of "Black Power." Congressional mail ran heavily against the housing bill, and Senate Minority Leader Dirksen, who had helped deliver Republican votes for cloture in the past, voted against it. The housing bill failed to come to a vote in the upper chamber in 1966 and 1967.

In early 1968 the prospects for the bill looked no brighter. However, Clarence Mitchell, chief lobbyist for the Leadership Conference (now composed of over 100 church, labor, civil rights, and civic groups), continued to prod the Johnson administration and Senate liberals on its behalf. Republican Senator Edward Brooke of Massachusetts and Democratic Senator Walter Mondale of Minnesota sponsored legislation covering most of the nation's homes and apartments. Senator Dirksen again changed his mind and agreed to support cloture, which was successfully invoked on the fourth try in early March. Mitchell and others worked hard to get the

House to approve the Senate bill. On April 4 Martin Luther King was assassinated; six days later the House agreed to the upper chamber's proposal (which also included protection for civil rights participants), and a major civil rights housing bill was enacted into law.

In the 1968 campaign Richard Nixon pursued what was dubbed a Southern strategy and received a very small share of the Negro vote. When he came to office he appointed no Negro to the Supreme Court or to his cabinet and generally took a "go-slow" approach to school desegregation, including outright opposition to busing to achieve greater racial balance in the schools. He asked for no new civil rights legislation and proposed that the 1965 Voting Act that was due to expire in 1970 be made nationwide in its application. Liberal congressmen and most civil rights leaders (including Clarence Mitchell) opposed Nixon's suggestion on the grounds that such a law could not be administered as effectively as one that concentrated on the areas where interference with voting rights was most serious. This latter view prevailed as the 1970 Act adopted the approach of the earlier one (it extended the date of determination of registration or voting from November 1964 to November 1968) and abolished all literacy tests until 1975.*

Thus the long civil rights battle in the Congress and the executive branches reflected a variety of pressures and events occurring both inside and outside the political process. At the same time, progress was also being made on another governmental front: the judiciary.

THE COURTS

The Supreme Court under Chief Justices Earl Warren and Warren Burger, continued the process begun earlier of outlawing discrimination in many areas of American life. It invalidated Southern efforts to delay school desegregation and to circumvent it through laws repealing compulsory school attendance and granting tuition subsidies to students attending private schools; in 1971 the Court also upheld the busing of children to achieve greater racial balance in the schools. It declared segregation to be illegal in public parks, swimming pools, transportation facilities, and the like, and also forbade discrimination in private organizations that used public property. The Court also construed an 1866 statute as barring racial discrimination in the sale or rental of all property and struck down the use of poll taxes in statewide and local elections.

---

*President Nixon's approach to improving the racial situation was essentially economic: he proposed the "Philadelphia Plan" whereby contractors on construction projects financed by federal funds set quotas for the employment of blacks; he also established an Office of Minority Business Enterprise in the Department of Commerce.

Thus the national government has provided a wide variety of legal weapons in recent years to better the situation of the Negro race. The following section analyzes the extent to which these weapons have helped to bring results in improving life for blacks in America.

RESULTS OF THE RACE REVOLUTION

The Race Revolution has involved a broad array of leaders and interest groups that have been successful in getting the national government to respond to their demands for an improvement in race relations. Yet the results achieved have varied considerably in different areas of the battle against discrimination.

POLITICAL POWER:
VOTING AND OFFICEHOLDING

Blacks have made their greatest gains in the political arena. The progress has been particularly marked since the passage of the 1965 Voting Rights Act. Statistics compiled by the Voter Education Project of the Southern Regional Council, a biracial, nonpartisan organization, show that in the eleven Southern states (Alabama, Arkansas, Florida, Georgia, Louisiana, Mississippi, North Carolina, South Carolina, Tennessee, Texas, and Virginia), registration of Negroes rose from 2,194,200 in November 1964 to 3,324,000 in spring-summer 1970. In the process the proportion of Negroes of voting age registered to vote rose from forty-three to sixty-six percent. This increase in registration was particularly impressive in Mississippi, where it increased from about seven to sixty-seven percent of the voting-age blacks in less than six years.

Despite this increase, however, fewer Southern blacks than Southern whites were registered in spring-summer 1970: the figures were sixty-six and eighty-three percent of the voting-age citizens, respectively. The disparity was particularly great in Alabama, where ninety-six percent of whites compared to sixty-four percent of Negroes were registered. In Texas, however, proportionately more blacks (eighty-five percent) were registered than whites (seventy-four percent).

Negroes have also been successful in winning political office. Statistics compiled by the Metropolitan Applied Research Center and the Joint Center for Political Studies show that the number of Negroes in public office increased more than sixty percent between the fall elections of 1968 and those of 1970. By the latter date 1769 blacks held a political office at some level of the political system.

The most famous Negro officeholder at the national level remained Senator Edward W. Brooke of Massachusetts, a Republican first elected in 1966. In the Ninety-first Congress there were thirteen blacks in the

One practical result of the Race Revolution: rural Southern Negroes line up to vote in large numbers for the first time in history. (United Press International)

House of Representatives, including Shirley Chisholm of New York, the first woman of the race ever elected to Congress. The eleven Southern states account for more than one-third of the nation's black officials, including 105 from Alabama alone. Outside the South, Negro officials tend to come from Northern industrial states, notably Michigan and New York, along with California. Most black mayors are in the South, but the early 1970s saw some serving in Northern cities such as Cleveland, Ohio; Gary, Indiana; and Newark, New Jersey. (Negroes also lost close mayoralty races in Detroit and Los Angeles in 1969.)

Despite the increase in officeholders, Negroes are still not as well-represented in public office as their numbers would warrant. Although they constitute about one-tenth of the voting population, Negroes occupy only about three-tenths of one percent of the more than 500,000 elected political positions in the United States.* In 1970, eight states with small black populations (Idaho, Maine, Montana, New Hampshire, North Dakota, South Dakota, Utah, and Vermont) had no Negro elected officials at all. None of the nation's fifty governors was black, and only two other statewide executive positions, California's Superintendent of Public Instruction and Michigan's Secretary of. State, were occupied by Negroes.

*One factor that may contribute to this underrepresentation is the small numbers of blacks who live in suburban and rural areas of the North, which have more public offices to be filled in proportion to population than do large cities.

EDUCATION

The combination of court actions and guidelines established by the Department of Health, Education and Welfare has brought considerable progress in integrating the public schools. Statistics issued by that Department in January, 1971 revealed that, nationwide, about one in three Negroes attended a majority white school in the fall of 1970; in the fall of 1968 the comparable figure had been less than one in four. Moreover, the percentage of Negroes going to all-black schools declined from forty percent to sixteen during that two-year interval.

The progress in desegregation varied by geographical region. It was especially marked in the Southern states, where one in three Negro students attended a majority white school in the fall of 1970 compared to one in five in 1968. The proportion of Southern blacks attending all-Negro schools meanwhile fell drastically from sixty-eight percent to just over eighteen percent. In Northern and Western states, however, almost no progress was made in the comparable period of time: the proportion of Negroes attending majority white schools remained at about one in four, while those in all-black ones stayed at one in eight. The same situation prevailed in Border jurisdictions (Delaware, the District of Columbia, Kentucky, Maryland, Missouri, Oklahoma, and West Virginia): those in majority white schools rose only from twenty-eight to twenty-nine percent while the all-black school attendance fell slightly from twenty-five to twenty-two percent.

Thus the school problem shifted from the battle against *de jure* segregation in the rural areas and small towns in the South to *de facto* segregation in large cities in both the North and South, a condition brought about by residential segregation. Only extensive busing of children to schools outside their neighborhoods or a breakdown in the living pattern of the two races in the nation's urban areas is likely to bring significant change in school desegregation in the future.

Aside from the integration issue, blacks do not achieve as high a level of education as do whites. A report issued by the Bureau of the Census showed that in 1969 forty-two percent of Negroes aged twenty and twenty-one had not graduated from high school; only eighteen percent of whites of the same age were not high school graduates. The figures were reversed for college attendance: twenty-one percent of blacks had attended college for one year or more compared to forty percent of whites.

HOUSING

A report issued by the United States Commission on Civil Rights* in October 1970 indicated that sanctions against discrimination in housing

*The first federal Civil Rights Commission authorized by Congress to investigate discrimination and to recommend corrective measures was established in 1957. Its authority has been continued over the years since that time.

have seldom been applied. The government has not been willing to cut off aid for its own housing programs or to use its mortgage insurance or loan guarantees to insure that housing is made available to Negroes. Moreover, according to the Commission, neither the Department of Justice nor the Department of Housing and Urban Development has the personnel to effectively enforce the Civil Rights Act of 1968.

Blacks living in urban areas have been concentrated in the central cities where housing conditions are very bad. By the end of the 1960s, however, about 220,000 Negroes moved each year to the suburbs, compared to about 19,000 annually in the first half of the decade. Most of those moving were better-educated and affluent Negroes, but some less-advantaged ones have contributed to the growth of suburban ghettoes immediately adjacent to central cities. Negro housing in rural areas is also inferior to that of whites. The Bureau of the Census reported in 1968 that while blacks constituted about eleven percent of the population, they occupied thirty-two percent of substandard housing units.

ECONOMIC POWER:
EMPLOYMENT AND INCOME

Census Bureau reports indicate that the most significant economic gains among blacks have been among those in professional and managerial positions. The number of Negroes in such positions doubled between 1960 and 1969. Even so, most blacks continue to hold unskilled and semi-skilled jobs; in fact, the proportion of Negroes in such occupations actually rose from thirty-eight to forty-two percent between 1960 and 1969.

The federal government has become a major employer of Negroes. Civil Service Commission reports show that in November 1969 fifteen percent of federal employees were black (at that time Negroes constituted about eleven percent of the nation's population), but they were concentrated in the lower positions: over twenty percent of employees earning between $6548 and $11,647 were Negroes, compared to two percent of those with salaries above $14,192.

Recent indications are that black capitalism has failed to develop to any appreciable extent. Only two percent of the five million private businesses in the nation are owned by Negroes, and many of these are small service operations such as barbershops, funeral homes, or neighborhood stores for which profit margins are small. The same problems plague black businessmen today as in Booker T. Washington's time: small capital, poor clientele, and lack of managerial experience.

In terms of unemployment and income, Negroes also compare unfavorably with whites. Statistics compiled by the Bureau of Labor Statistics for the first nine months of 1970 showed that in twenty of our largest central cities, 7.4 percent of Negroes were unemployed while 4.6 percent of whites

were out of work. The disparity in unemployment was even greater between teenagers of the two races: thirty-one percent compared to twelve
percent. The Census Bureau also reported in 1969 that, while the income
of blacks had increased faster since 1965 than that of whites, the median
family income of Negro families ($5999) that year was still only sixty-one
percent of that of white families ($9794).

Thus the improvement in various aspects of the Negro's life in America has
depended on a number of factors: the seriousness of the particular situation sought to be remedied; how well it lent itself to correction; the efforts
put forth by those seeking change (including the attitudes of public officials entrusted with protecting civil rights); and the amount of resistance
that change has met from those favoring the *status quo* in race relations.
The concluding section assesses the race situation in terms of the principles
of democracy.

ASSESSMENT

No situation has been more of an anomaly in our democracy than the status
of the American Negro. In a classic study of the race problem, *An American
Dilemma,* published in 1944, the Swedish scholar Gunnar Myrdal noted
the conflict that existed between the principles of what he termed the
American Creed—the essential dignity of the individual, the basic equality
of all men, and certain inalienable rights to freedom, justice, and fair
opportunity—and the treatment accorded to Negroes in our society. According to Myrdal, it is this conflict between the ideals on the one hand and, on
the other, fears and jealousies, considerations of prestige and conformity,
and prejudices against particular types of people that constitutes the dilemma
in America—not for Negroes, but for whites.

Race relations have changed considerably in the United States in the
three decades that have passed since Myrdal observed them. Progress has
been notable in some areas, especially in the enfranchisement of Negroes
and in the passage of laws outlawing discrimination in various areas of
American life. Thus we have made significant strides toward the achievement of political equality and equality under the law for blacks. Even
today, however, fewer Negroes than whites are registered to vote, and many
laws and executive decrees against discrimination have not been effectively enforced.

The Race Revolution to date has benefited primarily middle-class Negroes who no longer face discrimination in public accommodations and
who now have more jobs and educational opportunities made available to
them by legal regulations, as well as by a growing desire of many whites
to demonstrate their racial tolerance. The Revolution has had virtually no
impact at all on lower-class blacks, however. Without income or education,

it means little to the ghetto or rural black to know that members of his race are entitled to dine at the finest restaurant or be eligible for the executive training program of a major corporation.

The reason that so little has been done for lower-class blacks is that their problem is essentially one of poverty—the lack of educational, social, and occupational skills needed in our society today. As indicated in the following chapter, attacking that problem involves a commitment of resources that our society has been unwilling to make to date. Until it does, the situation of the poor black (as well as poor white) in America will continue to be dismal.

It would be unrealistic, however, to assume that even massive economic programs for the poor black will solve the race problem and bring social equality in America. For tension between the races is based on factors that transcend economic considerations. Many low-income whites in particular, but others as well, feel a genuine sense of social and psychological insecurity and threat from Negroes. These feelings may, in fact, intensify as poor blacks begin to experience more gains. At the same time, many Negroes today find it difficult to trust whites, who have so often failed them in the past, and to maintain a sense of racial pride without, at the same time, feeling contempt for whites. Moreover, as Negroes win more rights, it is not surprising that whites expect them to be satisfied with their improved situation while blacks become increasingly restive to achieve still further gains. Clearly, tolerance and patience will be needed by both races in the days ahead as the nation continues to wrestle with its most difficult social problem.

Selected Readings

The classic historical study of the Negro problem in America is John Hope Franklin, *From Slavery to Freedom* (New York: Knopf, 3rd edition, 1967). An excellent short treatment covering the entire historical period is August Meier and Elliot Rudwick, *From Plantation to Ghetto* (New York: Hill and Wang, rev. ed., 1970). A very good study of the Reconstruction period and its aftermath is C. Vann Woodward, *The Strange Career of Jim Crow* (New York: Oxford University Press, 3rd ed., 1966). Booker T. Washington expresses his attitudes on race relations in his autobiography, *Up From Slavery* (originally published in *The Outlook*; Garden City, N.Y.: Doubleday, 1946). Those of W.E.B. Du Bois appear in a volume of essays, *The Souls of Black Folk* (Greenwich, Conn.: Fawcett, 1961). Two studies of the ghetto are Robert C. Weaver, *The Negro Ghetto* (New York: Harcourt, Brace, 1940), and Kenneth Clark, *Dark Ghetto* (New York: Harper & Row, 1965).

A study of the Race Revolution is contained in Louis Lomax, *The Negro Re-*

volt (New York: New American Library, 1962). Included among studies of various Negro interest groups are Howard Zinn, *SNCC: The New Abolitionists* (Boston: Beacon, 1964), Inge Bell, *CORE and the Strategy of Non-Violence* (New York: Random House, 1968), and C. Eric Lincoln, *The Black Muslim in America* (Boston: Beacon, 1961). Martin Luther King expresses his views in *Why We Can't Wait* (New York: Harper & Row, 1964), as do James Farmer in *Freedom—When?* (New York: Random House, 1965), and Whitney Young, Jr. in *To Be Equal* (New York: McGraw-Hill, 1964)

The concept of Black Power is analyzed in Stokely Carmichael and Charles V. Hamilton, *Black Power* (New York: Random House, 1967). For two excellent analyses of black militancy, see Chapter IV, Jerome H. Skolnick, *The Politics of Protest* (New York: Simon & Schuster, 1969), and Chapter 5, James S. Campbell, *et al, Law and Order Reconsidered* (New York: Bantam, 1970). For interpretations of the term by a sample of Detroit residents see Joel Aberbach and Jack Walker, "The Meaning of Black Power: A Comparison of White and Black Interpretations of a Political Slogan," *The American Political Science Review* LXIV (1970), 367–389.

James Sundquist has an excellent account of the forces that produced the succession of civil rights acts in Chapter 6 of his *Politics and Policy: The Eisenhower, Kennedy and Johnson Years* (Washington: Brookings, 1968). Another good source of information on these developments is *Revolution in Civil Rights* (Washington: Congressional Quarterly Service, 4th ed., 1968). An assessment of the effectiveness of such actions is *Civil Rights Progress Report* (Washington: Congressional Quarterly, 1970).

Gunnar Myrdal's classic sociological study, *An American Dilemma* (New York: Harper & Row, 1944), is condensed in Arnold Rose, *The Negro in America* (New York: Harper & Row, 1948). Another sociological study is E. Franklin Frazier, *The Negro in the United States* (New York: Macmillan, rev. ed., 1957).

CHAPTER 16

Poverty and Welfare

The family of an unemployed farm worker in the Ozarks prepares for a dinner of potatoes and biscuits. (Wide World Photos)

I N HIS FIRST STATE OF THE UNION MESSAGE, in January 1964, Lyndon Johnson told Congress that "this Administration here and now declares an unconditional war on poverty." He asked the director of the Peace Corps, Sargent Shriver, to serve as his special assistant in developing means to fight that war. In six weeks' time, drawing on ideas of people within and without the government, Shriver and his associates developed a comprehensive bill that included, among other proposals, "Community Action Programs" to fight poverty involving "maximum feasible participation" of the poor themselves. By August Congress had enacted the Economic Opportunity Act of 1964, making relatively few changes in the administration bill and none at all in the Community Action Programs. When the President appointed Shriver to head the new Office of Economic Opportunity (located in the Executive Office of the President), the stage was set for an attack on the exceedingly ambitious goal set forth in the 1964 Act—"to eliminate the paradox of poverty in the midst of plenty in this nation."

In time, however, the crusade against poverty ran into difficulties. The first major targets were the Community Action Programs; local government officials did not want federal officials and representatives of the poor deciding how money should be spent in their communities. The Legal Services Program experienced the problems previously discussed in Chapter 13. The entire war against poverty increasingly became an economic casualty of the demands of another war: the one in Vietnam. By the time Richard Nixon was ready to assume office in 1969, a sign in the elevator of the OEO headquarters announced: "This building will self-destruct on January 20."

It did not, however. Although the new President recommended some changes in the antipoverty program, he did not eliminate it. In fact, he persuaded Donald Rumsfeld, a young Republican Congressman, to give up a safe seat to head the OEO. Nixon also supported another program for the poor begun by his predecessor in calling for increased federal spending for food for the needy.

Most surprising, however, was President Nixon's own contribution to the battle against poverty: a new Family Assistance Plan, which he announced in a nationwide television broadcast in August 1969. This proposal called for a radical overhauling of the existing welfare system to guarantee a minimum yearly income. Besides protecting the unemployed, it also covered the "working poor" whose income fell below acceptable standards. Although the proposal ran into opposition from the Democratic Congress (as well as some members of his own party), the President continued to back it until August 1971, when he asked Congress to postpone action on it as part of his general program to fight inflation.

Thus the problems of the poor have been a principal concern of government since the mid-sixties, under Presidents representing both major political parties. But, as we shall see below, for most of our history poverty was not recognized as something with which the federal government should concern itself. Before examining changes in American attitudes and practices towards this issue, however, we need to analyze the general nature of poverty and examine the different interpretations given to it.

THE GENERAL NATURE
OF POVERTY

The word "poverty" has no absolute meaning that everyone accepts. Most commonly it refers to a lack of income needed to purchase a minimum amount of basic goods and services—food, clothing, shelter. Even if one accepts that general definition, however, how does one decide what quantity of what particular kinds of goods and services are needed for a minimum standard of living? Moreover, expectations change over time: forty years ago electricity and inside plumbing would have been thought luxuries; today they are considered necessities.

Despite these complications, in order to establish a program for distributing benefits there has to be some way of dividing the poor from the nonpoor. An approach used by most government agencies is to use an economy food plan (one for temporary or emergency use when funds are low) to determine the cost of food needed to provide adequate nutrition. On the assumption that food costs constitute a certain percentage of total family expenditures (the percentage varies by family size), the official poverty line in 1970 for a nonfarm family of four was set at $3968; for those living on farms (who presumably can grow some of their own food), the line was eighty-five percent as much, or $3373. Although these figures fail to take into account such factors as regional differences in living costs and the frequent inability of the poor to spend their money wisely, the general approach is reasonable and simple and does a relatively good job of distinguishing the poor from the nonpoor in terms of a minimum living standard.

Some observers feel, however, that poverty is a *relative* matter and that it should be determined, not by amount of income, but rather by its distribution. Even if incomes rise, those with substantially less than the bulk of the population (frequently the figure is set at one-half the national median income) feel they are poor, and everyone else regards them as such as well. Thus in this view poverty is a *subjective* rather than an *objective* condition.

Certain experts carry this notion further: Oscar Lewis, for one, wrote of a "culture of poverty," that is, a distinctive set of feelings and behavior patterns associated with poverty. Impoverished persons have a sense of fatalism, helplessness, and powerlessness that makes it impossible for them to control their lives. They live only for the present and refuse to defer current pleasures for future rewards; thus they spend whatever money they have impetuously and save nothing for tomorrow.

One other concept of poverty focuses on *communities* rather than individuals. John Kenneth Galbraith refers to "insular" poverty, which applies to "islands" or "pockets" with a low economic potential, a high incidence of unemployment, poor public services, and related deficiencies. These regions include Appalachia, parts of the Southern coastal plain, the cutover lands of the Great Lakes states, and the Ozarks. While some residents of these areas are not poor, most are. In a sense these are economically "sick" communities.

These different conceptions of poverty affect how people view poverty and what, if anything, they think can be done about it. The following section explores some of the traditional attitudes of Americans toward the problems of the poor.

TRADITIONAL ATTITUDES
AND PRACTICES
REGARDING THE POOR

Early American attitudes towards the poor (derived largely from British practices) placed the major responsibility for caring for them on their immediate families, their relatives, and private charities. If help from these sources was not available, public assistance then became the duty of local governmental units (typically the township or county), which financed aid through a poor tax. Needy people who could work were sent to workhouses; those who could not were placed in poorhouses. (Frequently both were located in separate sections of the same building.) In some instances payments in cash, food, or clothing were made in lieu of institutionalization. In any event, the provisions for the poor were woefully inadequate: the poorhouses were dilapidated, and they frequently harbored petty criminals and mental defectives along with the indigent; the cash payments, designed only for emergencies, were kept below the income received by the lowest-paid worker. This inhumane treatment pricked few consciences because poverty was regarded as a reflection of moral deficiencies: to be poor was sinful.

In fact, some contended that public assistance for the poor interfered with the operation of natural economic laws. One prominent spokesman for this point of view was a nineteenth-century English economist, Thomas Malthus, who developed the theory that population rises at a faster rate than food supply, resulting in a shortage of the latter; feeding the poor thus only keeps them alive and worsens the situation. A similar view was espoused by Herbert Spencer, an English sociologist prominent in the latter half of the century, who contended that laws of natural selection allow only the fittest to survive; providing help for the poor enables the unfit to continue to exist, thus weakening the human race.

Although Malthus and Spencer had some impact on attitudes in the United States (the "robber barons" naturally seized on the Englishmen's philosophies to justify their own exploitation of the poor), as the nineteenth century progressed the idea gradually became accepted that certain people simply could not care for themselves and that, therefore, the general public had an obligation to assist them. More of the responsibility for aid began to be assumed by states (rather than counties), which developed specialized institutions for the blind, the deaf, the delinquent, and the insane. Cash payments to the handicapped also were increasingly provided by the states: by 1930 twenty had programs for the blind, forty-five gave aid to mothers with dependent children, and twelve provided assistance to the aged.

Another institution of the late nineteenth and early twentieth centuries also assumed some responsibility for the poor: the urban political machine. The precinct captain was ready to dispense aid in the form of food, clothing, and the like to the needy who, in turn, were expected to vote for the machine's political candidates. It was particularly appealing to the poor that the assistance provided by the political boss was dispensed without the long forms and embarrassing questions that typically accompanied public assistance programs.

The national government was not considered responsible for the needy, with the exception of certain special groups such as Indians, merchant seamen, and veterans. The Depression, however, suddenly changed that. By 1932, when about one in four workers was unemployed, poverty had changed from the condition of a relatively few "unworthy" Americans to the plight of millions, most of whom had previously been employed as "worthy" citizens. Moreover, the existing system for handling the problems of the poor collapsed as local governments and states ran into financial difficulties. Only the national government remained as a potential provider for the poor, but President Hoover clung to the traditional belief that relief should be handled by local governments. He eventually approved a limited federal relief program, but it remained for the new President, Franklin D. Roosevelt, to persuade the nation to assume a new attitude toward the role of the national government in providing for the needy.

SOCIAL SECURITY
WELFARE MEASURES

In the early stages of Roosevelt's New Deal efforts were directed toward the recovery of the economy. Included among the measures passed to meet that problem were the Federal Emergency Relief Act and work programs such as the Civilian Conservation Corps (CCC) and the Works Progress Administration (WPA). These programs were temporary in nature, designed to get money quickly into the hands of vast numbers of people who had been thrown out of work by the Depression.

Subsequently the Roosevelt administration turned its attention to providing permanent assistance for particular groups of persons who needed special help. The President appointed a special Committee on Economic Security to look into the matter and then endorsed its recommendations in a congressional message. Congress responded with the passage of the Social Security Act of 1935, the most important welfare measure ever enacted.

The Social Security Act provided for a number of programs built around two distinct approaches to providing income to persons with special needs. The first type was based on the *insurance* principle: contributions were made to a trust fund from which benefits were drawn. The most prominent of these programs was old age insurance, under which both the employer and the employee made monthly payments based on the latter's salary. When he reached the age of sixty-five, he was entitled to benefits based on the amount of his earnings prior to retirement.

Another program that operated on this same principle provided unemployment benefits for anyone thrown out of work through no fault of his own. However, unlike the old age insurance program, which was administered entirely by the federal government, unemployment insurance was handled by the states, and the amount and duration of benefits granted to the unemployed were left up to them. The federal government's role in these programs was indirect: under the terms of the Social Security Act each employer was required to pay a three percent federal payroll tax but he got nearly all of it back in the form of a federal tax credit if his state had an unemployment insurance program in which the employer participated. By 1939 the Act had achieved its purpose: programs were in effect in all states.

These two programs were and still are essentially self-financing in that the money for the benefits comes primarily from contributions made by employees and employers themselves. Only if the trust funds become exhausted can general governmental revenues be used. They have little of a charity aspect to them since persons receive benefits prescribed by law and are not required to show need to receive them. (The unemployment compensation programs are generally financed through contributions from employers alone; only a few states require employees to make payments from their salaries.)

The second major approach under the Social Security Act produced *public assistance* programs. Initially these covered three major groups—the aged, the blind, and dependent children deprived of normal parental support by the death, incapacity, or absence of a parent—all of whom are special cases of need in the sense that they cannot be expected to earn a living for themselves. (The aged in question either are not eligible for old age insurance benefits or have requirements beyond those benefits.)

These three public assistance programs are self-financing but essentially charitable: recipients do not contribute to them and funds are paid from general revenues. All three are administered through grants-in-aid as described in Chapter 3: the federal government provides part of the funds for them and the individual states pay the remainder. The amount and scope of benefits thus vary by state. The administration of these programs is also handled by state governments, subject to certain national standards relating to the use of merit systems in hiring personnel, provision for hearings for applicants denied benefits, and other procedures. Unlike the insurance plans, in which benefits are paid without regard to need, under the public assistance programs welfare workers investigate the financial situation of recipients.

The Social Security Act of 1935 was essentially an achievement of the Democrats. In time, however, the Republicans came to accept this basic welfare program. It is significant that social security benefits were increased during the Eisenhower administration, which was also responsible for the establishment of the Department of Health, Education and Welfare.

Changes have been made over the years in the insurance programs. Old age insurance has been broadened to cover not only urban workers, for which it was originally designed, but also most of the work force, including self-employed persons, farm and domestic workers, state and local governmental employees, and those employed by nonprofit organizations. Benefits have been increased and the retirement age reduced; if an employee dies before he retires, benefits are paid to his surviving wife and children. Moreover, insurance benefits are now available to disabled persons. Originally an Old Age Insurance program, it is now known as Old Age, Survivors and Disabled Insurance (OASDI).

A parallel development has occurred in the public assistance programs. Benefits have increased, and the federal government has assumed a greater share of the costs of such benefits. The Aid to Dependent Children program has been liberalized to provide for benefits to parents as well as to needy children; it is also now possible for these payments to be made even if a healthy father is living at home, provided he is looking for work and cannot find it. In addition, it is possible for indigent, aged persons to receive assistance for medical expenses. Finally, an entirely new assistance program for the permanently and totally disabled has been added.

Although changes have been made in the Social Security Act over the years, it is significant to note that there were no radical departures in either the insurance or public assistance programs during the 1930s, '40s, and '50s. Democratic recommendations that medical care be financed through increased Social Security contributions and Republican proposals that the government guarantee private insurance companies against potential heavy medical losses in extending coverage to persons not under existing programs were both defeated in Congress during the Truman and Eisenhower years. Nor did either administration propose any new approaches to the problem of poverty. This was the situation when John Kennedy came to office in January 1961.

NEW APPROACHES TO POVERTY

During the New Deal and postwar period, the problems of the poor were viewed almost exclusively from the standpoint of the first definition of poverty discussed at the beginning of this chapter: providing needy persons with enough income to cover the bare essentials of life. Little or no attention was given to the other ideas relating to poverty, such as "the culture of poverty" or "pockets" of poverty. A growing concern with these two concepts brought major changes in the approaches to the problems of the poor in the late 1950s and early 1960s.

A major attempt to deal with these broader concepts of poverty occurred in the Lower East Side of New York City, where a group of private citizens joined with public officials to fight juvenile delinquency. They operated on the theory that young people resort to antisocial behavior because they cannot achieve traditional goals through conventional means (denied jobs, they cannot earn money to buy things they want, so they steal them); their general approach was to provide "opportunities" for youth in the form of employment, programs of remedial education, skills training, and the like. To accomplish that goal they organized a nonprofit corporation called Mobilization for Youth (MFY) and proposed that a target area with a population of some 100,000 people be used as the site of a demonstration project to test the effects of using this broad approach to fight juvenile delinquency. Drawing on the expertise of various government agencies as well as the School of Social Work of Columbia University, MFY eventually obtained financial support from a variety of sources: private foundations, the City of New York, President Kennedy's Committee on Juvenile Delinquency and Youth Crime, the Labor Department, and the National Institute of Mental Health.

Paralleling the effort of the MFY in New York City was a national Public Affairs program of the Ford Foundation that sought to rehabilitate deteriorating areas of central cities through coordinated community efforts involving public and private agencies. One of the better-known of its ventures was located in New Haven, Connecticut, where a progressive mayor sought to minister to the needs of the city's poor, particularly those displaced by urban renewal projects. Assisted by a Ford Foundation grant, along with federal and local money, a nonpartisan body called Community Progress, Incorporated, composed of representatives of the redevelopment agency, the

Board of Education, social agencies, Yale University, and a supporting citizens' group, embarked on a coordinated approach to provide the poor with a wide variety of services—education, skills training, health care, welfare, home management, and the like.

The MFY and Ford Foundation programs thus differed from previous approaches to poverty in several ways. Rather than merely ameliorate conditions by providing needy persons with income, they sought to rehabilitate individuals by helping them overcome the handicaps—lack of education, few job skills, poor health—that held them in poverty. They also stressed a coordinated attack on poverty rather than piecemeal programs. Finally, they viewed poverty as a community phenomenon that could be effectively dealt with only through the efforts of a broad variety of public and private agencies.

Some of the initial programs of the Kennedy administration reflected elements of this new approach to the problems of the poor. The Area Redevelopment Act of 1961 aimed at "insular" poverty by providing financial assistance to industrial and rural areas of high unemployment and low income. The Manpower Redevelopment Act of 1962 sought to retrain workers whose skills were no longer needed (such as coal miners) for work in which they were needed; the following year Congress amended the bill to provide remedial education for the illiterate and to give training to young workers seventeen years and older. The Juvenile Delinquency and Youth Offenses Control Act of 1961 adapted the MFY approach of providing demonstration and training projects to determine the most effective ways of using a community's total resources to combat juvenile delinquency locally. The full adaptation of the new approach to poverty did not occur, however, until the launching of what has been called the "War on Poverty."

LAUNCHING
THE WAR ON POVERTY

Although the War on Poverty is generally associated with Lyndon Johnson, it was actually begun by his predecessor, John Kennedy. In December 1962 the President told the chairman of his Council of Economic Advisers, Walter Heller, that he wanted to go beyond the programs that had already been undertaken to help the disadvantaged; he asked to be given facts and figures on the things that still had to be done. He specifically asked Heller to look into the poverty problem in the United States.

There has been a great deal of speculation about the factors that prompted Kennedy to focus on poverty. As James Sundquist, a participant in the War on Poverty, points out, the term "poverty" (unlike "race") was not a word that appeared in presidential speeches or congressional debates at that time. There were no polls showing that the public was concerned about poverty (again this differed from the nation's preoccupation with the race issue), nor were there interest groups representing the poor like those that spoke for blacks. Heller remembers that Kennedy asked him for a copy of Michael Harrington's study of poverty, *The Other America*, and Arthur Schlesinger, Jr. suggests in his book on Kennedy, *A Thousand Days*, that the President was also influenced by John Kenneth Galbraith's *The Affluent Society*. Both Schlesinger and Sundquist stress that the President was searching for a broad, unifying theme that would pull together existing programs for the needy and at the same time allow him to go forward with new ideas and programs for the poor. The term "poverty" provided a promising focus for a "new frontier" in the President's agenda of public problems.

Heller put one of his staff members to work gathering data on poverty in the United States. The evidence showed that, although there had been a decline in the number of poor people, the trend had slowed down. Heller forwarded the information to the President. Concerned that the Republicans were planning their own antipoverty program, the chairman of the CEA also sent the President some proposals for his own program. By October 1963 the President was working on a comprehensive attack on poverty; he asked Heller to assemble a list of specific proposals for inclusion in his 1964 legislative program.

THE WAR ON POVERTY
UNDER PRESIDENT JOHNSON

The Council of Economic Advisers, the Bureau of the Budget, and the White House staff were in the midst of reviewing departmental antipoverty proposals for Kennedy's 1964 legislative program when the news of the assassination came from Dallas. In his first meeting with Heller on November 23, President Johnson said that the attack on poverty was "his kind of program," and that Heller should move ahead on it at full speed. The Bureau eventually winnowed the proposals down to thirty-five, many of which were already pending in some form in Congress. What was still missing, however, was something new, a unifying theme that would tie the legislative program together.

The focus that emerged toward the end of December was a community-wide attack on the problems of the poor patterned after the juvenile-delinquency and urban programs previously discussed. Originally suggested by men who had served on the President's Committee on Juvenile Delinquency and Youth Crime and the Ford Foundation's Public Affairs Program, the new program was adopted by the Budget Bureau, whose officials liked the idea of coordinated efforts against poverty initiated by local groups (both public and private) that the federal government would help finance in a limited number of demonstration projects.

Changes were made in the proposed program after Sargent Shriver was appointed its special administrator. Provisions for increased employment through job training and for business loans were added to the community-action features of the bill. The idea of confining the undertaking to a few demonstration areas was abandoned as not being consistent with an all-out War on Poverty. It was also decided that these community programs could not await the development of comprehensive, coordinated plans; permitting individual projects to be funded would bring faster political results.

Given the breadth of the program and the innovative nature of the community-action approach, the bill developed by Shriver and his group encountered relatively little difficulty in Congress. It benefited from the fact that President Johnson was still in the honeymoon stage of his relationship with the legislature. Should the Republicans have opposed the measure, they would have been placed in the position of appearing to be against the alleviation of poverty. The legislative strategy called for winning the support of Southern Democrats. To this end, Representative Phil Landrum of Georgia was chosen as the bill's sponsor. In addition, concessions were made to Southern legislators: an amendment was added to the bill permitting governors to veto most projects; and it was agreed that Adam Yarmolinsky (who had ruffled some congressional feathers) would not serve as deputy director of the antipoverty program as had been originally contemplated. In August President Johnson signed the Economic Opportunity Act of 1964.

MAJOR FEATURES OF THE PROGRAM

The Economic Opportunity Act of 1964 provided for a variety of anti poverty programs. Several focused on *education* and *training*. One, the Job Corps, which was designed to help youths from greatly disadvantaged backgrounds escape the culture of poverty, called for taking them out of their home environment and placing them in residential settings where they would receive remedial education in reading and arithmetic, vocational training in mechanical and clerical work, as well as health care, personal guidance, and counseling. A somewhat less ambitious project, The Neighborhood Youth Corps, involved work-training programs for unemployed teenagers in their home communities. In addition to these measures for the young, the Act established an adult literacy program, as well as work experience for the hard-core unemployed, especially those receiving benefits under the Aid to Families with Dependent Children program.

Other features of the Economic Opportunity Act of 1964 included loans for rural areas and small businesses; assistance for migrant workers; and a domestic version of the Peace Corps, the Volunteers in Service to America (VISTA), whose members would work in slums, migrant camps, Indian reservations, and other depressed areas.

Finally, the most distinctive feature of the Act was the Community Action Program providing for a comprehensive attack on poverty on a local basis. The Act itself provided almost no guidelines except to require that projects were to be administered through public or private nonprofit organizations (or combinations thereof) and were to involve the "maximum feasible participation" of residents and groups of the area.

Thus the Economic Opportunity Act of 1964 included a variety of anti-poverty programs. Unlike the welfare approach of the 1930s, however, the new tack was primarily rehabilitative rather than ameliorative.* Some of the new projects attacked poverty at the community level rather than merely focusing on the individual. At this point the War on Poverty represented a victory for middle-class reformers concerned with the plight of the poor who sold the program first to the President and other executive officials and then steered it through Congress.

DIFFICULTIES
IN THE WAR ON POVERTY

If conflicting political forces were remarkably absent from the launching of the War on Poverty, they soon had an impact on the administration of the program. They were felt in local communities, in Congress, and within the executive branch itself. The Community Action Program in particular became the target of bitter political controversies.

COMMUNITY ACTION CONTROVERSIES

The particular sources of difficulties in the Community Action Program were its two unique features: administration at the local level through public or private nonprofit organizations and the "maximum feasible participation" of the residents and groups of the area. These provisions of the Act of 1964 were so vague that they invited a variety of interpretations. For example, did "maximum feasible participation" mean that the residents were merely to help carry out these programs or that they were also to be involved in planning them and deciding how funds should be spent? The representation of the residents on Community Action boards also raised some thorny questions: how were they to be chosen, and what ratio of residents to outsiders was appropriate?

Daniel Moynihan, an early participant and close subsequent observer of the War on Poverty, claims that the provisions for the participation of the poor were placed in the Act as a means of insuring that Southern blacks would receive benefits from the program, and that it was assumed the

*Two programs passed in 1965 were in the second category: amendments to the Social Security Act that year provided medical insurance for persons over 65 (Medicare) and assistance to the medically indigent (Medicaid).

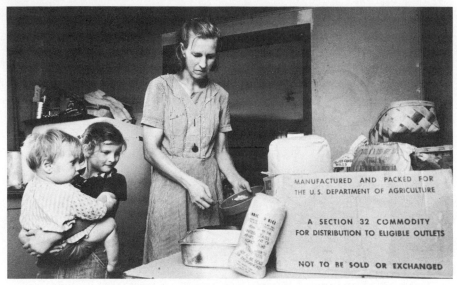

Antipoverty programs: (above) A family benefitting from the distribution of food surpluses; (below) a Community Action Program in North Carolina. (Ken Heyman)

Antipoverty programs: (above) A Job Corps class in New Jersey; (below) an adult education class for Navahos in Arizona. (Ken Heyman)

programs would be planned and dominated by regular local public officials. However, the OEO itself issued a Community Action program guide in February 1965 suggesting that residents of the area were to be involved in "planning, policy-making and operation" of the program. The guide also recommended that, wherever it was feasible, elections of the poor to local Community Action boards be held. And while the guide made no specific provisions for a definite fraction of the poor on the boards, the OEO was using a rule-of-thumb standard of one-third.

Whatever the merits of these respective positions may be, mayors in cities with Community Action Programs preferred the former interpretation. Mayor Daley of Chicago was quite willing to allow the poor there to receive benefits, but he wanted his organization to decide how the money should be spent. What the mayor did not want was the development of a rival political group building up support for itself among the city's poor blacks and whites who owed their allegiance to the Daley organization. The nation's mayors formed a committee, with Daley as its chairman, to urge that OEO recognize local agencies endorsed by city hall as the proper channels for Community Action projects. Daley and his committee lost little time in taking that message to the Vice President, Hubert Humphrey.

Besides this built-in political conflict, the Community Action Program developed other problems. The group in Newark was accused of encouraging the 1967 riots, the one in Syracuse of issuing remedial reading manuals suggesting that poor blacks could reach their goals only through the use of force. Rivalries broke out in some areas between blacks and Puerto Ricans for control of the local program. High salaries for local OEO officials and careless administration of funds brought allegations that some persons were getting rich off poverty at the expense of the poor who received little in the way of benefits.

As might be expected in a political system where congressmen are dependent on local political organizations for support, these grievances were soon felt in the legislative arena. The Act of 1964 was amended to give local political officials greater control over Community Action boards.* Limitations were placed on the size of salaries paid to OEO officials, and participants in disorders were denied funds. Congress also began to earmark more and more of the Community Action funds for specific matters, such as the popular Head Start Program (discussed below).

The executive branch also began to reflect dissatisfaction with the program. The Bureau of the Budget took a position directly opposite to the OEO's guideline on "maximum feasible participation," contending that this phrase referred to carrying out Community Action Programs, not de-

---

*It should be noted that another new government program launched in 1966, "Model Cities," provided that federal assistance to communities for coordinated neighborhood projects be channeled through a single agency designated by the local governing body.

signing them. And most important of all, President Lyndon Johnson cooled on Community Action; in time he was confiding to friends in Congress that it was not exactly his favorite program.

Thus what had started out as the most innovative antipoverty program to date soon became a political disaster. Two aspects of the Community Action Program, however, did achieve success. These were the Legal Services Program described in Chapter 13 and the Head Start Program of special instruction for preschool poor children that was designed to compensate for disadvantages in their home life. Inaugurated in the summer of 1965 after being developed by national officials of the Community Action Program, Head Start was acclaimed throughout the country and soon became a congressional favorite.

OTHER OEO PROGRAMS

The experiences with other OEO programs were mixed. The Job Corps turned out to have almost as many headaches as Community Action Programs: many youths dropped out of it after a short time; the costs of maintaining them in residential camps proved to be expensive (about $7500 per person a year); and people in rural areas where some of the camps were located were shocked by the behavior of some of the more incorrigible youths in the program. In contrast, the Neighborhood Youth Corps that provided work training for young people in their own communities was popular because it was less expensive to administer, helped keep young people off the streets and in school, and brought money into local communities. It also tended to attract less difficult youths than the Job Corps; furthermore, the trainees were not thrown into new environments as were the Job Corpsmen. The remaining programs in OEO—training for adults, loans to rural communities and businesses, and VISTA received limited funding and never became significant features of the War on Poverty.

In the waning years of the Johnson administration, the war in Vietnam was costing so much (about $20 billion a year) and preempting so much of the President's time that the War on Poverty that he had launched with such hope and enthusiasm clearly began to wind down. This was the general situation when the new President came into office.

SHIFTING EMPHASIS
IN THE WAR ON POVERTY

During the presidential campaign of 1968 Richard Nixon stressed the importance of a private enterprise approach to solving the problems of the poor. This emphasis, plus the political difficulties the War on Poverty experienced in the latter years of the Johnson administration, led many observers to predict the termination of the program, as epitomized by the "self-destruct" sign in the elevator at the Office of Economic Opportunity.

Rather than eliminate the antipoverty program, however, the new President shifted its emphasis. On his recommendation, certain OEO programs were transferred from that agency to appropriate regular departments. For example, Head Start was shifted to the Department of Health, Education and Welfare, and the Job Corps to the Department of Labor. In 1971 he proposed that the Legal Services Program be assigned to a government corporation to be known as the National Legal Services Corporation.

These proposals were consistent with the President's thinking that the OEO should focus its attention on innovation and research. That is, it should develop new ways of fighting poverty and also evaluate how well existing programs were operating. Once programs had proven to be successful, they should be transferred to appropriate permanent agencies to administer. Thus the OEO should serve as an "incubator" for antipoverty programs.

In keeping with this philosophy, the OEO under Donald Rumsfeld carried out experimental programs. One already begun during the Johnson administration involved testing the effect of giving a guaranteed income to families headed by a working male who earned a low income; it showed that the incentive to work did not decline as a result of such payments. Another involved experimenting with contracts to private companies to teach reading and mathematics to disadvantaged children in selected urban and rural areas.

These shifts brought the Nixon administration into conflict with Democratic senators like Gaylord Nelson of Wisconsin (Chairman of the Labor and Public Welfare Committee's Subcommittee on Employment, Manpower, and Poverty), who charged that OEO was "retreating from the War on Poverty" and becoming an "antiseptic laboratory doing pure research on assorted small pilot projects." Struggles also developed between the agency and the Democratic Congress over earmarking funds for specific purposes (such as Head Start or Legal Services), which Rumsfeld opposed as creating inflexibility in the agency's operations. Some Capitol Hill Democrats were also critical of the agency's experiment in allowing the Oklahoma state government to process all antipoverty projects there. Thus the traditional Republican preference for administering national programs through the states rather than allowing direct federal-local relationships to develop was reflected in the new approach to OEO operations.

These changes in the OEO program, however, did not represent the real focus of President Nixon's concern with poverty. Welfare reform became his major approach to the problems of the poor.

WELFARE REFORM

During the 1968 presidential campaign Richard Nixon stressed the importance of getting people off the welfare rolls and onto payrolls. According to former presidential adviser Daniel Moynihan, the new President had decided by April 1969 to push for a total reconstruction of the welfare system, but heated discussions of the issue within his cabinet continued until late July. On August 8 the President went before a nationwide television audience to propose a series of governmental reforms, including radical changes in the welfare system in the direction of what the Chief Executive called "workfare." Three days later, in a special message to Congress, he spelled out the deficiencies of the present system, together with his proposals for change.

President Nixon's particular target of criticism was the Aid to Families with Dependent Children program (AFDC). He pointed to the disparity in benefits the program provided in various states: a family of four in the most generous state received $263 a month; in the most parsimonious, $39. Particularly distressing to the President was the fact that in most states a family with an unemployed male was not entitled to benefits; thus the system encouraged a poor father to desert his wife and children in order to assure that they would receive benefits. He also stressed the unfairness of a system that made no provision for the "working poor," that is, a family in which the head was employed but not earning enough to provide the family a minimum standard of living. The President also cited the rising number of persons on welfare and the consequent costs: since 1960 the welfare rolls had risen by one-third while the expenditures had doubled. Thus, according to the Chief Executive, more and more Americans were being caught up in a life of dependence which the states in particular were finding increasingly difficult to finance.

The President recommended that the AFDC program be eliminated and a Family Assistance system be adopted in its place. Under the new program dependent families headed by a female or unemployed male would be eligible to receive a minimum welfare payment: for a family of four it would amount to $1600 a year. The "working poor" would, however, also be brought under the system if their income fell below a certain figure: a family of four, for example, would receive some payment until their income reached $3920. The system had a built-in work incentive: the first $720 of earned income would not count in reducing the $1600 guarantee; fifty percent of income above that level would be deducted. Thus a family of four with a $2000 income would receive a $960 supplement to that earned income.

The President proposed other means to stimulate present welfare recipients to seek employment. Unemployed males capable of working, and mothers with school-age children, would have to accept job training or employment, or have their benefits cut off. Women with preschool-age children would not be required to work, but child-care centers would be established to facilitate their doing so. The program also provided for expanded training and job development programs, together with a $30-a-month bonus as an incentive for persons to go into job training.

The President acknowledged that the Family Assistance Plan would be more expensive than the existing system by an estimated $4 billion the first year. (Two million of the "working" poor would for the first time receive benefits.) He proposed, however, that the federal government assume the increase. No state would be required to spend more than ninety percent of its present welfare costs. Thus even states that made higher payments than the minimum ones proposed by the President, would have the excess (plus ten percent more of their existing benefits) absorbed by the national government.

Heralded as the most significant social welfare proposal in four decades, the President's message met with general approval from a variety of groups: social workers, academicians, political figures (especially state governors), and many of the poor themselves. The administration bill that was introduced in October 1969 passed the House the following April, but stalled in the Senate Finance Committee where it was attacked by liberals because the payments were set too low and by conservatives because it was too costly. The Committee included welfare reform in a package with social security and foreign trade legislation that was ultimately filibustered in the waning days of December 1970.

The President resubmitted the Family Assistance program as one of six major goals in his 1971 State of the Union Message, and told Republican governors in April that it would have number-one priority with the administration until it was enacted. The following June the House passed a comprehensive welfare reform bill patterned after that originally proposed by the President. The floor for a needy family of four was raised to $2400; "working poor" families of the same size with incomes as high as $4140 were to be paid partial benefits based on a deduction of two-thirds of their incomes above $720. Also included in the bill were a five percent increase in social security payments and improvements in assistance for the aged, blind, and disabled, together with liberalization of the Medicare and Medicaid benefits, all of which had the strong support of the Nixon administration. The Senate was considering the measure when in August 1971 President Nixon, as a part of his anti-inflation program, asked that welfare reform be postponed for a year.

Thus the Nixon administration turned away from a concern with the "culture of poverty" or poverty as a community-wide phenomenon and returned to the traditional view that it is the absence of sufficient income to purchase a minimum amount of goods and services. The following section analyzes the extent and nature of that kind of poverty in the United States today.

POVERTY
IN THE UNITED STATES TODAY

In 1959 the Census Bureau first began to gather data on poverty in the United States. Since that time it has published information on the subject periodically, revising its poverty threshold upward to reflect increases in living costs. It is, therefore, possible to determine what changes have occurred in the poverty situation over time. Because the Bureau also analyzes its data by sex, age, race, and the like, we can see which particular groups are most likely to be poor.

The period from 1959 through 1969 showed a significant decline in poverty in the nation. In 1959 over 39 million persons, constituting some 22.4 percent of the population, had incomes below the poverty line; in 1969 the comparable figures were 24.3 million, and 12.2 percent, respectively. While the decline was fairly constant over the entire period, it was greatest from 1963 through 1969 when more than 11 million persons crossed the poverty threshold.

Between 1969 and 1970, however, the situation changed. For the first time since 1959 the number of poor people increased: from 24.3 million and 12.2 percent of the population in 1969, to 25.5 million and 12.6 percent in 1970. Although differences in the antipoverty programs of the Johnson and Nixon administrations may have played some role in the increase, more likely it is associated with the general state of the economy. Bureau of Labor statistics show that from 1963 to 1968 the unemployment rate fell from 5.7 percent to 3.6 percent of the work force; from 1969 to 1970 it rose from 3.5 percent to 4.9 percent. Thus a downturn in the economy that throws people out of work forces some of them across the poverty threshold.

It should not be assumed, however, that only persons who are unemployed are poor. For example, Census Bureau statistics show that in 1969, 61 percent of male heads and 43 percent of female heads of poor families worked at some time during the year. Moreover, about one-third of the poor male and one-eighth of the poor female family heads worked 50 to 52 weeks of the year. Thus part-time and low-paying full-time jobs also contribute to poverty in the United States.

Poverty tends to be concentrated in certain categorical groups. Families headed by *women* tend to be poor. Although only 14 percent of the total populace lived in such a household in 1970, 44 percent of the poor did. *Blacks* also have a disproportionate number of poor people: in 1970 about one-third of them fell below the poverty line compared to one in ten whites. *Family status* and *age* are also associated with poverty. In 1970 one-third of persons over 14 not living with families and almost one-half of those over 65 living alone were poor. *Family size* also affects poverty: 23 percent of all poor families in 1970 consisted of seven or more persons.

Poverty also varies by *residence*—it is twice as prevalent among farm families as among urban ones—and by *region*—Southern families are twice as likely to be poor than are those who live in the Northeast. Outside the South poverty is concentrated in metropolitan areas: in 1969, 63 percent of the poor in the North and West lived in or near large cities; only 36 percent of poor Southerners did.

The *degree* of poverty also varies among groups. In 1970 the median income deficit (the difference between the poverty line and the income actually received) was about $1000 for poor white families compared to $1300 for poor Negro families. This difference was mostly attributable, however, to the smaller family size of the whites: the deficit per family member was about the same for both races.

Some idea of the magnitude of the poverty problem in the United States can be gained from an estimate of how much money would be required to raise the income of all poor persons (those living in families as well as those alone) above the poverty line. In 1970 the Census Bureau set that figure at $11.4 billion.

ASSESSMENT

Americans have long stressed the democratic value of equality of opportunity, but for most of our history that term has been interpreted to mean formal opportunity in the sense that positions are open to anyone on the basis of his capacities. Beginning in the 1930s, however, and increasingly in the 1960s, the concept has been construed more literally. The national government has accepted the responsibility of equalizing conditions in our society by providing the disadvantaged with a minimum level of goods and services. It is significant that a Republican President, Richard Nixon, has proposed that a floor be placed under the incomes of all Americans. Should his Family Assistance Plan (or some variation of it) be adopted, as seems likely, we will have moved a long way towards the goal of providing all individuals with the necessities—food, education, job training, and the like—that are required for individual self-development.

The question remains, however, whether merely placing money in the hands of the poor will solve the poverty problem and permit individuals to develop themselves to the fullest extent of their capacities. If many poor people do possess feelings of fatalism, helplessness, and powerlessness, and are unable to postpone present pleasures for future rewards, then there is no assurance that they will be able to take full advantage of the material resources provided them. They may simply squander them. If this is the case, we may want to consider trying to rehabilitate them through broad programs designed to deal with these handicaps.

It should be recognized, however, that the rehabilitation process is an exceedingly difficult one. We know relatively little about how to go about rescuing poor people from a "culture of poverty" or about whether it can even be accomplished for many of them.* Rushing to the task with the

*Some observers even question the right of middle-class reformers to impose their values and life style on lower-class individuals. The primary justification for doing so is to protect the interests of the latter's dependents who may well suffer from their irresponsible attitudes and behavior.

best of intentions but with little information on the techniques necessary to accomplish it, will only bring frustrations to all parties concerned.

There has also been a great amount of romanticism about the part the poor can be expected to play in the political process. If our information on political socialization and political participation tells us anything, it is that the acquisition of political interests and values takes place over a long period of time and that persons with low levels of income and education do not exercise their political rights to the same extent or as effectively as others do. We should, therefore, anticipate that there will be limits to what the poor can accomplish in the political arena until they have gone through a period of acculturation in the values and acceptable political techniques of the democratic process and have acquired the kinds of resources needed for political effectiveness. Certainly it does them no good to pit them against established political institutions and experienced politicians as was done in the Community Action Program.

Selected Readings

Two books that did much to stimulate interest in poverty as a public issue are John Kenneth Galbraith, *The Affluent Society* (Boston: Houghton Mifflin, 1958), and Michael Harrington, *The Other America: Poverty in the United States* (New York: Macmillan, 1962). Chapter 1 of Louis Ferman, Joyce Kornbluh, and Alan Haber (eds.), *Poverty in America* (Ann Arbor, Michigan: University of Michigan Press, rev. ed., 1968), discusses the general nature of poverty and various definitions of it.

An excellent historical treatment of welfare in the United States is contained in Chapter 9 of Jack Peltason and James M. Burns, *Functions and Policies in the United States* (Englewood Cliffs, N.J.: Prentice-Hall, 2nd ed., 1962). Good analyses of welfare programs enacted in the postwar period in the United States are Chapter 8 of *Congress and the Nation, 1945–1964* (Washington: Congressional Quarterly Service, 1964), and Chapter 14 of the supplementary volume, *Congress and the Nation, 1965–1968.*

Two very good analyses of the intellectual roots of the Kennedy and Johnson antipoverty programs are Daniel Moynihan, *Maximum Feasible Misunderstanding* (New York: Free Press, 1970), and Chapter 4 of James Sundquist, *Politics and Policy: The Eisenhower, Kennedy, and Johnson Years* (Washington: Brookings, 1968). Both books also contain excellent accounts of the factors that led to the enactment of the Economic Opportunity Act of 1964. Moynihan's study also analyzes the reasons that contributed to the difficulties of the Community Action Program, as does John C. Donovan, *The Politics of Poverty* (New York: Pegasus, 1967).

Evaluations of the War on Poverty include Moynihan and Joseph A. Kershaw, *Government against Poverty* (Chicago: Markham, 1970). Chapters 3 and 10 of

Edward Banfield, *The Unheavenly City* (Boston: Little, Brown, 1970), contain a provocative analysis of the psychological attitudes and behavior of the lower class in the United States and the problems of rehabilitating its members. Chapter 6 of Thomas Weaver and Alvin Magid, *Poverty: New Interdisciplinary Perspectives* (San Francisco: Chandler, 1969), includes a perceptive analysis by political scientist Harry Scoble of inherent limits in the ability of the poor to exercise political power.

CHAPTER 17

Foreign and Military Policy

During a visit to South Vietnam in July 1965, Secretary of Defense Robert McNamara inspects a map of Vietcong-controlled territory. The shaded areas on the map mark the sites of search-and-destroy missions. (Wide World Photos)

I N MID-1967, discouraged by the course of events in Vietnam, Secretary of Defense Robert McNamara ordered a study be made of the record of America's involvement in that war. An analysis of documents in the files of the Department of Defense by thirty-six civilian and military officials led to a classified forty-seven-volume study entitled, "The History of the United States Decision-Making Process on Vietnam Policy," or what came to be known simply as "the Pentagon papers." By the time McNamara left the administration the following year, he was so disheartened with the war that he sent the study largely unread to the National Archives. Convinced that Richard Nixon was repeating the mistakes in Vietnam of the previous administration, Daniel Ellsberg, one of the study's participants, unsuccessfully urged Nixon's Assistant for National Security, Henry Kissinger, to read the papers. When Ellsberg got no better results from other officials, he decided to leak the classified documents to Democratic Senator George McGovern of South Dakota (who turned them down), then to Republican Representative Paul McCloskey (who accepted some without classified markings and locked them in his safe), and ultimately to the press.

Beginning in mid-June 1971, the *New York Times* and the *Washington Post* ran stories based on their interpretations of the Pentagon papers. The *Times* accounts suggested that the Johnson administration during 1964 launched clandestine attacks against North Vietnam and planned to obtain a congressional resolution to legitimize open warfare against the North (all prior to the events leading up to the Gulf of Tonkin Resolution), that the administration decided to bomb the North before the 1964 presidential election, and that in April 1965 it determined to commit American ground troops, but ordered the decision kept secret.* The *Post* reported that the Eisenhower administration fought unsuccessfully to prevent the Geneva Conference of 1954 from calling for elections throughout North and South Vietnam for fear the communist leader Ho Chi Minh would win, and that President Kennedy knew of and approved plans for the military coup d'état that overthrew President Ngo Dinh Diem in 1963. Subsequent accounts also indicated that United States officials early subscribed to the "domino theory" (if Vietnam goes Communist, all Southeast Asia will fall to the Reds) and rarely reexamined this assumption afterwards; it was further revealed that administration planners continued to place faith in American ability to cow North

---

*This version of events, particularly the decision to bomb the North prior to the 1964 election, is disputed, even by some persons who participated in the Pentagon Study.

Vietnam through progressive applications of force, despite the lack of evidence that this course of action was working.

Concerned that the disclosure of the papers would jeopardize the government's ability to conduct foreign policy in a confidential way, the Nixon administration asked officials of the *Times* and *Post* to stop publication. When they refused, the government filed lawsuits in the federal district courts in New York and Washington, D.C. to restrain further disclosures. After proceedings were taken to the appropriate United States courts of appeals, both cases ended up in a consolidated suit (*New York Times Co.* v. *United States*) in the United States Supreme Court, which ruled in a six-to-three decision on June 30, 1971 in favor of the newspapers. Speaking for the majority, the late Justice Black argued that "in revealing the workings of government that led to the Vietnam war, the newspapers nobly did precisely that which the Founders hoped and trusted they would do"; in dissent, Chief Justice Burger countered that it was a duty of a citizen to report to responsible public officers "the discovery or possession of stolen property or secret government documents . . . this duty rests on taxi drivers, Justices, and the *New York Times*."

Eventually, copies of the study were provided to Congress. Daniel Ellsberg was indicted by a Los Angeles federal grand jury on two counts: for unauthorized possession of . . . documents and writings related to the national defense" and for putting copies of classified, top-secret documents to "his own use." Facing the fact that conviction on either count could bring a sentence of ten years, Ellsberg declared, "Ten years in prison is very cheap if that would contribute to ending this war."

The Pentagon papers raise some of the most fundamental issues of American foreign policy. What is the process by which we make foreign policy decisions? What general goals has the United States pursued in the international arena since the end of World War II? Upon what assumptions have these goals been based? Before examining such issues, however, we will explore an even more basic matter, the general nature of foreign policy.

THE GENERAL NATURE
OF FOREIGN POLICY

Foreign policy is frequently defined as the official acts of government taken in relation to other countries. Although such official *acts* constitute the essence of foreign policy, *anything* that affects relationships with other nations bears on foreign policy. *Statements* as well as actions by governmental officials often influence how other countries view their intentions. The United States has often seemed to judge Communist China more by Mao Tse-tung's boasts of worldwide domination than by his nation's relatively cautious policies—for example, the failure to invade the offshore islands of Quemoy and Matsu still occupied by the Nationalists.

Although domestic and foreign policy are interrelated (consider the effect of the Vietnam war on the War on Poverty), the two take place within essentially different settings. For the government responds in the one case to demands of groups that are active in internal politics and in the other to initiatives taken by other nations. At the same time, of course, the United States originates actions of its own in the international arena. The essential problem of governance in both foreign and domestic policy is the same: working out accommodations among competing interests. Virtually absent from the international arena, however, is the ultimate means available in domestic politics for controlling conflict: laws that can be enforced through the government's monopoly on the use of legitimate force. Although international law does exist, it is only binding on nations to the extent that they are willing to subject themselves to it. And history demonstrates that when a nation's vital interests are at stake, it is seldom willing to do so. Political scientist Stanley Hoffmann has stressed the fact that while procedures for cooperation exist in both domestic and world politics, the "permanent possibility of free and legitimate recourse to violence remains the mark of international relations." As evidence of the relative importance violence plays in international affairs, consider that we typically refer to military and foreign policy but not to police and domestic policy.

Like domestic policy, however, American foreign policy today is broad in scope. The time has long past when our foreign affairs were the concern of a relatively small number of professional diplomats who concentrated their efforts on major European powers and countries in this hemisphere; currently a wide range of individuals in many departments of the government, together with persons from private life, play a role in our relationships with over 130 nations around the globe.

Our foreign policy is pursued through a variety of means. *Political* channels include membership in international organizations like the United Nations, as well as the exchange of diplomatic representatives and the signing of bilateral agreements with individual nations. *Economic* aspects of foreign policy involve reciprocal trade agreements and financial assistance to other nations. The *military* component is reflected in forming mutual defense alliances, sending arms to friendly nations, negotiating agreements such as the one banning the testing of nuclear weapons, and actually resorting to force, as in Korea and Vietnam. Also of increasing importance is the *cultural* side of foreign policy, as represented by broadcasts to foreign countries, overseas libraries, student exchange programs, and goodwill tours of popular entertainers like the late Louis Armstrong. Together these activities shape foreign policy, or what Arthur Schlesinger, Jr. calls the "face a nation wears to the world."

This range of activities involves various individuals and groups both inside and outside the government. The following section discusses the major participants in foreign and military policy and their comparative importance.

THE POLICY-MAKING PROCESS
THE PRESIDENT

Harry Truman once told a group of Jewish War Veterans that he "made" American foreign policy. Although this statement is a bit exaggerated, it is fair to say that the Chief Executive dominates foreign policy in a way that he does not dominate the making of domestic policy. As political scientist Aaron Wildavsky puts it, we have one President but "two Presidencies," one for domestic affairs and the other for foreign and military defense policy.

The great influence of the Chief Executive in foreign affairs stems in part from certain broad legal powers. He has a number of constitutional prerogatives that enable him to play the role of the nation's *chief diplomat.* He can, for example, negotiate agreements with foreign countries, either by a formal treaty, for which he must receive Senate approval by a two-thirds vote (and usually does),* or by an executive agreement. Of the latter, some he negotiates under legislative authority (for instance, reciprocal trade agreements adjusting tariffs within limits set by Congress) and some he can exercise entirely on his own (for a notable example, the Yalta agreements Franklin Roosevelt entered into in 1945 with the Soviet Union affecting postwar developments in Central Europe and the Far East).

Aside from his agreement-making authority, the President determines formal diplomatic relationships with other nations. He has the prerogative to recognize foreign countries diplomatically. When rival groups purport to represent a nation, as with China for over twenty years, the President's decision regarding the diplomats he receives determines which government we regard as the legitimate one. The Chief Executive can also break off diplomatic relationships with a nation by asking that their representatives be withdrawn as President Wilson did a few weeks before the declaration of war against Germany in 1917.

The President also chooses, and can dismiss as well, the major officials involved in the making of foreign policy. Although he must seek Senate approval for his nominees for cabinet positions, such as the Secretary of State, and for diplomatic representatives abroad, he is seldom turned down. Moreover, the Chief Executive can avoid this possibility altogether by appointing personal envoys to conduct diplomatic activities. Thus Franklin Roosevelt used Harry Hopkins to handle delicate matters with our allies in

---

*The Senate has turned down or refused to act on only about ten percent of the treaties negotiated over the years. It can, however, indirectly defeat a treaty through attaching reservations to it which are unacceptable to the Chief Executive or foreign country involved. President Wilson's opponents used this technique to defeat the Treaty of Versailles.

World War II, although the latter held no official diplomatic post in FDR's administration.

Finally, the President can employ "personal" diplomacy. Woodrow Wilson, for example, attended the Paris Peace Conference as the head of the United States delegation. Richard Nixon's dramatic plan to go to Communist China is another example of personal diplomacy, a technique employed by virtually every President since World War I.

If anything, the powers the President exercises over military matters are even more awesome than those he wields over diplomacy. He claims the authority (some persons argue that he has usurped it) to send American forces anywhere in the world, including into actual combat if he so desires. Recent major commitments of American troops into battle were made by executive action alone: President Truman's decision to order American forces into Korea in 1950, along with presidential actions with respect to the use of Americans in Vietnam. These current examples have many precedents. In the century after 1815, historian Arthur Schlesinger, Jr. counted no less than forty-eight separate occasions of the use of armed forces abroad without formal declaration of war by Congress.

As Commander in Chief of the armed forces, the Chief Executive possesses other major powers that enable him to dominate military policy. He chooses, with Senate approval, the major functionaries, both civilian and military, such as the Secretary of Defense, the Joint Chiefs of Staff, and other high-ranking officials. He can also remove them. Thus Abraham Lincoln went through a series of commanders of the Northern forces in the Civil War until he found a man to his liking, Ulysses S. Grant; President Truman eventually decided to relieve General Douglas MacArthur from his command in Korea when the General persisted in advocating policies (such as bombing Red China) that Truman did not favor.

That event points up another prerogative of the President as Commander in Chief: determining major strategic decisions governing the conduct of hostilities. Truman decided to fight a "limited" war in Korea because he was concerned about drawing the Soviet Union into the war on the side of Red China (the two at that time were partners in a defense pact) and because he did not want to involve the United States in an all-out war in Asia at a time when it had major military commitments in Europe. Franklin Roosevelt also made a number of strategic decisions that affected how World War II was fought, including giving the war in Europe initial priority over the one in Asia.

Basic decisions involving weapons are also up to the President. Thus Truman proceeded with Roosevelt's initial commitment to the development of the atomic bomb and then made the awesome decision to use it against the Japanese in the closing days of World War II. He also decided later to go ahead with the manufacture of the hydrogen bomb, even though some of his advisors opposed this course of action. On the other hand, President Kennedy terminated the development of the Skybolt missile (to be launched from high-speed bombers) in favor of the Minuteman and Polaris weapons that could be fired from underground silos and submarines.

As Commander in Chief the President even has the authority to make tactical military decisions. Although they generally leave such matters to professional officers, Chief Executives have been known to enter into the details of military operations. At the time of the Cuban missile crisis in 1962 President Kennedy insisted on planning the positioning of American ships off Cuba. Lyndon Johnson not only decided to bomb North Vietnam in 1965 but also chose the targets.

Thus the President has a wide range of powers affecting foreign affairs that he can exercise in the manner contemplated by Hamilton in the *Federalist Papers*—with "decision, activity, secrecy and despatch." For his pre-eminence in this area of public policy stems both from the breadth of his prerogatives and from his ability to take decisive initiatives that others find it difficult to counter or reverse. Although the Congress has the power to refuse to appropriate funds for military ventures such as those in Korea and Vietnam, it is reluctant to exercise its authority when the lives of Americans fighting there depend on supplies and equipment. Another advantage the President enjoys over the Congress (and over other participants in foreign policy-making) is the superior information about international developments that executive-branch members located here and abroad provide him.

MAJOR EXECUTIVE-BRANCH PERSONNEL

The wealth of resources available to the President in foreign affairs is reflected in the size of the two major departments involved: Defense and State. As of January 30, 1970, the former had some one and one-quarter million *civilian* employees (military personnel numbered over three million), the latter, over 40,000. In addition, other departments, such as Commerce, Labor, and Agriculture, have people assigned to international affairs.

The three top presidential advisors in foreign affairs are the Secretary of State, the Secretary of Defense, and a member of the White House Staff, currently designated as the Assistant to the President for National Security Affairs. The first official is expected to bring a political perspective to foreign policy, the second offers a military view, and the third presumably takes both these interests into account in counseling the Chief Executive. Of course, the division between the Secretaries of State and Defense is by no means complete: each is expected to appreciate the perspective of the other. At times, individuals holding these positions have appeared to reverse roles. Former Secretary of State Dean Rusk was considered by many observers to have adopted an essentially military stance towards the problems of the Vietnam war, while Secretary of Defense Robert McNamara (particularly towards the end of his term) and his successor, Clark Clifford, were supposedly convinced that the conflict there was essentially political and could not be won on the military battlefield.*

The relative influence that each of these three officials exercises in foreign-policy-making depends on the relationship he enjoys with the President. Dwight Eisenhower had great admiration for and confidence in John Foster Dulles and gave him broad discretion in handling a variety of matters: conducting high level negotiations with foreign leaders, representing the American position on issues before the United Nations, and the like.

The importance of Dulles in the Eisenhower administration is to be contrasted with the part assigned to the Secretary of State in the Administrations of Kennedy and Richard Nixon. Kennedy chose Dean Rusk, a low-key figure from a private foundation with no political support of consequence, and so limited Rusk's role in foreign affairs that the Chief Executive, in effect, became his own Secretary of State. Richard Nixon followed a similar course of action by appointing William Rogers, a close personal friend with very limited experience in foreign affairs. Secretary Rogers seems not to have been briefed ahead of time on the Cambodian invasion and to have played no role in helping to work out the arrangements for the most dramatic diplomatic event of recent years: President Nixon's announcement of his contemplated trip to Communist China to confer with leaders there.

The man who did play a major part in both of these latter decisions was Henry Kissinger, Assistant to President Nixon for National Security Affairs. The fact that McGeorge Bundy, who held that same post under Kennedy (as well as under Johnson for a period) was also an important figure suggests that Presidents (especially those who want to take a major leadership role themselves) want the advice of strong figures who are knowledgeable about foreign affairs. At the same time Chief Executives prefer having such advisors on the White House staff where they can be controlled and where they are also free from questioning by congressional committees and members of the press that might lead to disclosures of vital information.

The role of the Secretary of Defense in foreign policy also varies with the incumbent and his relationship with the President. Robert McNamara, a highly competent, forceful figure who advised both Kennedy and Johnson, had a major impact on policies during his six years in office. In contrast, of the three Secretaries who served in that post in the eight years of the Eisenhower administration (Charles Wilson, Neil McElroy, and Thomas Gates), only the first appears to have had much say in major foreign policy decisions.

*This assessment is by no means unanimous: some analysts believe it was Rusk, rather than Clifford, who convinced Lyndon Johnson to stop the bombing of the North in the spring of 1968.

Presidential Assistant for Security Affairs Henry A. Kissinger in Peking with Premier Chou En-lai of the People's Republic of China; in July 1971 they made preliminary arrangements for a visit to China by President Nixon. (Wide World Photos)

Although the Secretaries of Defense and State and the President's Assistant for National Security Affairs are generally the key figures in foreign-policy making, the Chief Executive depends on other top-ranking officials for advice and recommendations. He may, for example, look to other members of the White House staff for assistance in special areas of concern as Kennedy did to Arthur Schlesinger, Jr. on Latin American affairs, or the President may seek the counsel of second- or third-level officials in executive departments. Thus Franklin Roosevelt completely bypassed his Secretary of State, Cordell Hull, and dealt with Under Secretary of State Sumner Welles on a range of foreign policy issues. Assistant Secretaries of State with expertise in a certain region (Europe, Africa, East Asia and the Pacific, and so on) and the Director assigned to a specific country are also important sources that Chief Executives can tap for information and advice.

As a result of experiences in World War II a number of official organizations have been created through statute (primarily by the National Security Act of 1947) to assist the President in foreign and military affairs. One is the National Security Council (composed of the President, the Vice President, the Secretaries of State and Defense, and the Director of the Office of Emergency Preparedness), which operates as a kind of miniature cabinet to advise the President on the integration of domestic, foreign, and military policies relating to national security. But like the larger cabinet, it operates at the sufferance of the President. Truman and Eisenhower convened it regularly, whereas Kennedy preferred to utilize *ad hoc* groups such as the one he assembled at the time of the Cuban missile crisis. Even if a President presents a problem to the NSC, he need not accept its recommendations: Eisenhower declined to do so when that body recommended intervention in Indo-China in 1954 on the side of the French against the Vietnamese forces.

Reporting to the NSC is another body of considerable significance in foreign and military policy: the *Central Intelligence Agency*. Developed from the Office of Strategic Services (OSS) during World War II, in 1947 this agency was entrusted with coordinating the intelligence work (gathering and interpreting information about other nations) carried on by units operating under the Army, Navy, Air Force, and State Departments. The CIA was also given a monopoly on espionage and other covert activities undertaken in foreign countries. Over the years since that time, the agency has reportedly undertaken a wide variety of activities, including successful ventures, such as helping rebels to overthrow the leftist Arbenz government in Guatemala in 1954, and fiascos, such as training Cuban exiles to invade their island in 1961 at the Bay of Pigs where they were slaughtered by Castro's forces. Despite the imposing nature of the CIA (its exact budget is secret but it has been estimated at about $2 billion a year) and the scope of its operations (it has sometimes had closer diplomatic relations with foreign governments than the State Department), like all agencies in the executive branch its influence ultimately depends on the President. After the CIA mistakenly assured Kennedy that if we helped the Cuban exiles invade the island there would be internal uprisings against Castro, the President had all overseas operations placed under the ambassadors concerned. He also ordered the entire range of intelligence activities to be reexamined by a special board reporting to him and asked the Director of the CIA, Allen Dulles, to resign.

The President's major professional military advisers are the *Joint Chiefs of Staff*. Created by Franklin Roosevelt in World War II and placed on a permanent statutory basis by the National Security Act of 1947, the Joint Chiefs presently include a chairman and the military chiefs of the three services (Army, Navy, and Air Force). Their expertise puts them in a position to exercise a major influence on military policy. Like other executive agencies, however, they are under the President's control. Almost as soon as he took office, Dwight Eisenhower inaugurated a "New Look" in military policy, which emphasized nuclear "massive retaliation" as provided by the Air Force over conventional warfare as favored by the Army. The President, who placed great stress on obtaining unanimous recommendations from the Joint Chiefs, maneuvered the then Army Chief of Staff, Matthew Ridgeway (who naturally opposed the new policy), into appearing publicly to endorse it. President Kennedy also used his power effectively over the Joint Chiefs. Angered by the bad advice he got from them on the Bay of Pigs operation, the Chief Executive replaced the chairman, General

Lyman Lemnitzer, with a military man more to his liking—General Maxwell Taylor.

These, then, are the major agencies of the executive branch that are involved in foreign and military policy.* Of course, as previously mentioned, others such as the Departments of Commerce, Agriculture, and Labor, which are primarily concerned with domestic matters, engage in some activities relating to foreign affairs. Moreover, those agencies concerned with the financial and budgetary control of government operations (such as the Treasury and the Office of Management and Budget) play a role in establishing limits on, as well as the direction of, the activities undertaken in international affairs. Both these agencies, for example, had an important part in developing and implementing the "New Look" military policy of the Eisenhower administration, which was designed to produce "more bang for the buck" than conventional weaponry.

OTHER BRANCHES OF GOVERNMENT

Congress has much less influence in foreign and military affairs than it has in domestic matters. As previously suggested, concern for the attributes of "decision, activity, secrecy and despatch" prompted the Founding Fathers to grant the President, rather than the Congress, the more important constitutional powers in the field of national security. For example, he can officially recognize a foreign government diplomatically; Congress can only pass resolutions in favor or opposition. Even where the national legislators do have prerogatives, they are often placed in a position of having to react to presidential initiatives. He negotiates the treaties and makes the diplomatic and military appointments that senators must then consider. And although Congress alone has the formal power to declare war, the President can render that power virtually meaningless by committing troops to battle on his own, as was done in both Korea and Vietnam.

Congress, moreover, has been less disposed since World War II to use its traditional powers when it is dealing with matters of national security. While it exercises its power-of-the-purse prerogative vigorously in cutting domestic programs proposed by the President, for much of the post-World-War-II period it gave the Chief Executive all he requested in the way of military funds—usually more, in fact. Major conflicts between Congress and the President in the 1950s and for most of the 1960s occurred because the legislators wanted to spend more money and maintain higher levels of military force than the President did. While this situation began to change, especially in the Senate, in the late 1960s, the House (which traditionally

---

*Other units that play a part in the day-to-day operation of our foreign policy include the Foreign Service, the Agency for International Development, and the United States Information Agency.

is more tight-fisted with money than the upper chamber) has been more reluctant to use its power of the purse to reduce military expenditures or to even alter the conduct of the war in Vietnam.

Nor has the congressional power of investigation been as potent in foreign and military affairs as it has been in domestic policy. Such investigations suffer because they often occur considerably after major executive actions have taken place: the inquiry into the events at Pearl Harbor in 1941 took place five years later, after the war was over. Even when investigations are held at a time when they could have influence on the administration's course of action, they often seem not to have much effect: the series of hearings that the Senate Foreign Relations Committee held on Vietnam in 1966 appeared to have limited consequences (if any) on the conduct of the war there.

There are some areas of foreign affairs in which Congress does have considerable influence on policy. These include foreign trade, foreign aid, and immigration. It should be noted that these involve long-range economic matters of considerable concern to domestic groups rather than military or diplomatic crises.

There are, however, some instances when national legislators do become involved in military matters. Thus several congressmen (including the Senate Majority Leader, Lyndon Johnson) were consulted by President Eisenhower on the issue of intervening in Indo-China in 1954; their advice not to become involved unless our allies (such as Great Britain) agreed to participate (which they did not) is credited with influencing Eisenhower's decision not to commit American forces at that time. Political scientist Samuel Huntington also points to the influence the Joint Committee on Atomic Energy exercised in executive decisions to develop the hydrogen bomb and nuclear-powered aircraft. Both these instances, however, involved individual congressmen and congressional committees rather than the entire body.

Recent studies point up the inferior part the legislative branch plays in foreign and military affairs compared to the executive. Aaron Wildavsky's analysis of congressional voting on executive proposals from 1948 through 1964 indicates that, including refugees and immigration bills, Presidents prevail about seventy percent of the time on defense and foreign policy, compared with forty percent in the domestic sphere. Similarly, James Robinson's study of foreign and military policy issues from the late 1930s to the early 1960s shows that the executive rather than the Congress had most to do with virtually all the major decisions reached during that period. In the final analysis, Congress must be considered a very junior partner to the executive in the making of foreign and military policy.*

*If Congress is a junior partner to the executive in foreign and military policy, the Supreme Court is for all practical purposes not a member of the firm at all. Throughout

Thus the making of foreign and military policy is primarily an executive matter, with Congress playing a limited role in the process and the Supreme Court virtually none at all. The following section analyzes the part that individuals and groups outside the government structure play in influencing foreign and military affairs.

POPULAR CONTROL

Generally speaking, Americans are not as well informed about foreign policy issues as they are about domestic concerns. For one thing, such issues usually have less *immediacy* for them. If the President orders a temporary freeze on prices and wages, the average citizen can appreciate the impact that the policy has on his own life. It is much less clear how he is affected by a change in the government of Chile. As indicated by the Pentagon papers incident, moreover, a great deal of *secrecy* necessarily surrounds our relationships with other countries, and thus the public is not privy to information that would enable it to make informal judgments about international developments. Furthermore, foreign and military affairs are often so *complex* and *technical* that the average citizen would have trouble comprehending them even if he had the necessary information.

To compound the problem for the average citizen, the ordinary reference groups that help to guide his opinions on domestic concerns are not as meaningful for foreign policy issues. An individual who is not conversant with the advantages and disadvantages of the Family Assistance Plan, for example, may get some clues from how business or labor leaders feel about it. His party affiliation, too, may help him make up his mind on the matter if one candidate favors the Plan and another opposes it. However, because different social and economic groups, as well as political parties and candidates, have been less likely in recent years to be lined up on one side or the other of foreign and military concerns, helpful clues are missing.

The result is that mass opinion on foreign and military issues tends to be superficial, lacking depth and understanding. Gabriel Almond, who pioneered the study of the subject in the late 1940s, refers to general public opinion on foreign policy as constituting a "mood." By this he meant that mass attitudes on foreign policy matters are highly generalized and emotional rather than specific and rational. He also suggested that, like "moods," their opinions are subject to sudden change. Because this is so, Almond expressed concern in 1950 that the American public might not provide stable support for our international commitments. He suggested, for example, that if for tactical reasons Russia temporarily eased its pressures

---

American history the Court has deliberately declined to intervene in such matters. Although the Court, in a 1952 decision, *Youngstown Sheet and Tube Co.* v. *Sawyer*, did invalidate President Truman's seizure of the steel industry (where a strike was, in the President's judgment, imperiling our situation in Korea), that action occurred after a cease-fire had been declared.

on neighboring countries, the American public might be encouraged to demand that our troops be demobilized.

While Almond's "mood" theory is helpful in understanding the nature of public opinion as it relates to foreign policy, his prediction of instability has not turned out to be true for public support of international commitments. Public opinion polls taken in the post-World-War-II period indicate a consistently high level of support for a continuing active role in world affairs. Moreover, this support held solid even in the face of considerable changes in the public's attitudes toward the likelihood of war or in the extent of its concern with international problems.

Most Americans adopt a rather permissive attitude toward the actions the government takes in international affairs. When Presidents have involved the nation in the world's problems (as all of them have since World War II), the public has been willing to support their efforts. In time of crisis, Americans rally around their leader, as evidenced by the increased ratings President Kennedy received in public opinion polls even at the time of the Bay of Pigs fiasco. The same reaction occurred when President Truman first sent American troops into Korea in 1950 and President Johnson extended commitments in Vietnam in 1965.

At the same time, however, public support for particular military ventures (as contrasted to a general policy of involvement in world affairs) erodes when they run into difficulties. After the Chinese entered the Korean war in late 1950 and our casualties began to mount, opposition to the war increased. The same thing occurred in Vietnam when American troops began to experience heavy losses there. Moreover, public disenchantment with this latter war continued even after casualties declined: in May 1971 a Gallup poll showed that sixty-one percent of the public thought we had made a mistake in sending our troops there.

It is difficult to determine what effect public opinion actually has on even such a basic matter as the conduct of a major war. Presidents Truman and Johnson persisted in waging unpopular ones: Johnson was quoted as saying he would continue his course of action in Vietnam even if his public opinion ratings fell to one percent. On the other hand, neither Truman nor Johnson ran for reelection, and in both cases the minority party's candidate (Eisenhower and Nixon) won the subsequent election. Although one cannot say that the Korean and Vietnamese wars were necessarily the determining factors in the 1952 and 1968 presidential contests (Eisenhower had great personal popularity, and race relations and law and order were also prominent issues in the 1968 contest), it is at least arguable that both incumbent Presidents *thought* that their war policies would lead to political defeat. In this sense, candidates' perceptions of adverse public reactions may affect their decisions not to seek reelection.*

*Voting a new President into office does not necessarily mean a change in policy, however. Eisenhower followed the Truman administration's approach of negotiating an end to the Korean War; he succeeded in that effort when Stalin died in March 1953 and a more conciliatory group of men came into power in the Soviet Union.

Although the general public's interest in foreign affairs is sporadic, responding mostly to dramatic events (such as military encounters), there is an "attentive public" that follows a range of international developments with some regularity. These are the persons who pride themselves on having a cosmopolitan outlook on the world. They keep informed on what happens in world politics by reading books, articles, and editorials on the subject, attending lectures and debates dealing with such matters, and discussing current events with one another. Composed primarily of professionals such as academics, lawyers, bankers, newspaper editors, and school teachers, this group of individuals also constitutes an important source of information on foreign developments for members of the general public who may look to them for advice and clues.

Joining this group from time to time are those who develop a particular interest in a specific issue. Thus individuals with a Jewish background are likely to be concerned about events in the Middle East that affect Israel. Economic considerations also play a part in stimulating interest in certain issues: businessmen who are threatened by competition from Japanese imports respond to actions the government takes affecting foreign trade.

In many instances, these attentive publics organize themselves into interest groups to try to influence foreign policy. These groups may take the form of a general-purpose organization (such as the Foreign Policy Association) or they may adopt a particular approach or point of view (like the Committee for a Sane Nuclear Policy). They may reflect ethnic (Zionist Organization of America) or economic (American Tariff League) concerns. Also active in trying to influence American foreign policy are other governments, such as that of Taiwan trying to prevent our recognition of Communist China.

Another general type of lobby that has been given great attention in recent years is the so-called "military-industrial" complex. This is the general name given to the combination of professional military men, defense contractors, and their congressional allies (who want military installations and defense industries in their districts), who are said to exert tremendous pressures to keep military spending at a high level and to further a "hard-line" policy with communist nations. Although there is no over-all formal organization that speaks for all these groups, they do coordinate their efforts through such interest groups as the American Security Council, which actively supported the ABM.

It is difficult to determine just how much influence attentive publics and organized interest groups actually have on foreign and military policy because of the secrecy and complexity of the decisions involved. Those decisions that are made in a short period of time, that affect all the members of American society fairly equally, and about which private groups have no presumed expertise (for example, the decision in the Cuban missile crisis) are unlikely to be much influenced by interest groups. On the other hand, long-term policies that have a particular impact on certain segments of the population and that concern matters about which such groups are considered to possess special knowledge (such as businessmen are thought to have about foreign trade) presumably reflect a higher degree of group influence. In any event, most students of interest groups attribute less influence to them on foreign affairs than in domestic policy.

The same generalization applies to *political parties*. The necessity of presenting a united front to the world and the desire to achieve continuity in our policies toward other nations means that party leaders and candidates are less likely to take opposite stands on foreign than on domestic affairs. Even when they do (as when the Republican party in the 1952 presidential campaign called for the "liberation" of Eastern European countries behind the Iron Curtain), the policies that the new administration actually follows when it comes to political office tend to parallel those of the former party in power. Thus partisan factors that characterize so much of domestic policy-making are much less important in foreign and military affairs.

One final group that plays a role in foreign affairs is made up of the representatives of the *mass media*. Reporters and commentators of the press, radio, and television act as potential *intelligence-gathering* and *communication links* for the various participants in the policy process. Thus executive officials and congressmen learn of each other's attitudes on international developments from the media. The media also furnish the electorate with information on the activities of public officials and at the same time provide the officials with feedback on how their actions are (or are likely to be) received by the American public and the publics of other nations as well. Finally, representatives of foreign governments look to the media for clues on the attitudes and intentions of American officials.

But the media do more than transmit information on the actions and attitudes of other individuals and groups that are involved in policy-making in foreign affairs. The media themselves become active *participants* in the process. They are in a position to *interpret* international developments for the public, and frequently their version of developments differs markedly from the impressions that public officials are trying to create. Thus the Johnson administration tried to picture the Tet offensive in Vietnam in early 1968 as a last-ditch military effort of the communists which failed; large elements of the media construed it, rather, as evidence that major cities in the South were still vulnerable to enemy attacks. At times the media, especially commentators and editorial writers, even become *advocates* of certain courses of action that may run counter to the policies being pursued by public officials: Walter Lippmann, for one, has been a long-time critic of our involvement in land wars in Asia.

The Pentagon papers incident points up the natural conflict that exists in a democratic society between the media representatives and officials involved in foreign and military affairs. The former believe in maximum disclosure of official actions, in the people's "right to know" what their public servants are doing in any area of public concern (including that of national security), and in the soundness of their own analyses of international developments. On the other hand, public officials are concerned lest such disclosures interfere with the delicate operations involved in protecting the nation's security, and they are highly suspicious that the media are more interested in producing their own versions of official actions and intentions in order to create conflict so they can better sell their services.

Thus the process by which American foreign and military policy is made is highly complex and involves basic issues of decision-making in a democratic society. The following section takes up an equally difficult problem: what goals and approaches does a democratic society like the United States pursue in international affairs?

GENERAL GOALS
AND APPROACHES

The United States, like other nations, naturally pursues a variety of goals in foreign affairs. Like individuals, the nation has been motivated in international relations by two general purposes: *ideals* and *self-interest*. The former has led us to seek moral goals that transcend national boundaries. The latter source of action has caused us to pursue our own selfish concerns or what is generally referred to in foreign affairs as the "national interest."

The ideals involved in the conduct of foreign policy are the same kinds of values that any democratic nation seeks in domestic politics: liberty, equality, justice, good will, peace, and the like. The important consideration is that as a nation we have not been satisfied with merely implementing these ideals in the United States; we have rather sought to have them extended to other nations as well. The individual most associated with this doctrine in foreign affairs is Woodrow Wilson: in his speech to Congress on April 2, 1917, asking for a declaration of war on Germany, he explained that the nation was fighting ". . . for the rights of nations great and small, and the privilege of men everywhere to choose their way of life and of obedience. The world must be made safe for democracy." At the same time the Chief Executive assured the legislators: "We have no selfish ends to serve. We desire no conquest, no dominion. We seek no indemnities for ourselves, no material compensation for the sacrifices we shall freely make."

It is somewhat more difficult to define precisely what is included in the national interest. At the minimum it means self-preservation for a nation. Survival involves maintaining territorial integrity, basic governmental institutions, and political independence. Closely akin to the latter is a nation's political self-sufficiency, that is, the ability to conduct its affairs without depending on other countries. One aspect of that self-sufficiency is reflected in the United States' general withdrawal from international involvement when it pursued a policy of isolationism during the nineteenth and early part of the twentieth century.

The national interest can be construed, however, to cover additional concerns, such as the protection of citizens and property beyond the country's territorial boundaries or the right of access of businessmen to foreign markets. Some persons would also include the nation's honor and prestige, along with its "way of life," as worthy of protection as part of the national interest. At times, the nation has also been willing to embark on imperialistic ventures (as in Texas, Cuba, and the Philippines) in order to *increase* national honor or prestige.

A varied array of persons have advocated the national interest approach to international affairs. The late theologian Reinhold Niebuhr, journalist Walter Lippmann, professional diplomat George Kennan, and political scientist Hans Morgenthau have all advocated that the United States stop trying to pursue universal idealistic goals (such as bringing liberty and justice or democratic institutions to other countries) and concentrate on protecting and advancing our own national interest. Generally such spokesmen are referred to as "realists," as against "idealists," in the field of foreign affairs.

Although the "idealism–self-interest" dichotomy is helpful in assessing what a nation's goals are (or should be) in international affairs, it is deficient in some other respects. For one thing, nations do not pursue one approach exclusively to the detriment of the other. Few persons advocate pursuing idealistic goals if they threaten national survival: there has been little disposition to bring democracy to nations behind the Iron Curtain at the risk of a major war with the Soviet Union. On the other hand, there are moral limits to what realists propose to further the national interests: none of those mentioned above, for example, has advocated a preventive war to protect the national interest. Thus a democratic nation's foreign policy involves reconciling both ideals and self-interest.

It is even difficult in some instances to separate the two types of goals, especially when the national interest is defined broadly. Thus Walt Rostow, an economic historian who served in major foreign policy posts in the 1960s, conceives of the American national interest as including our basic societal values and what he terms our "still developing way of life." To protect these interests Rostow suggests that we *maintain a world environment* in which the societies of the area he terms Eurasia (Europe, Asia, the Middle East, and Africa) develop along lines consistent with our own values and way of life. These include societies with a solicitude for the "dignity of the individual as against the claims of the state," and societies that may not necessarily be democratic at the present time but that "accept as a goal a version of the democratic value judgments consonant with their culture and their history." Thus Woodrow Wilson's idealistic goal of making the world safe for democracy and Rostow's conception that the American national interest requires a world environment composed of nations with democratic values and aspirations turn out to be quite similar.

Conflicts over the goals of American policy often turn, not on the "idealist–self-interest" dichotomy, but rather on what is to be included within the definition of national interest and, perhaps even more importantly, *the kind of world environment* deemed necessary to protect such interests. Rostow's statement that ". . . under modern conditions, it is difficult to envisage the survival of a democratic society as an island in a totalitarian sea" reveals his assessment that the internal political order of a country will determine its relationships with other nations. As he views the situation, totalitarian societies are inherently dangerous to democratic ones. Not everyone, however, believes this to be the case. Realists generally believe that what counts is the specific relationships that exist between nations: Yugoslavia, for instance, is a totalitarian society but is not hostile to the United States. This reasoning suggests that our national interest is not necessarily jeopardized by the presence of totalitarian societies in the world.

Another consideration that plays a part in determining the goals and approaches a nation pursues in foreign policy is an assessment of the *power* it is able to wield in the international arena. Realists have been critical of many commitments the United States has made in recent years on the grounds that they exceed our resources. In their view we have failed to maintain a balance between our goals and the means we possess for accomplishing those goals. Specifically the realists charge that the nation has pursued a general policy of *globalism*, of trying to affect international relations on all kinds of matters in all parts of the world, rather than practicing a doctrine of *limitation*, of restricting our activities to those concerns in particular areas where we have the actual power to make our policies effective.

Thus views concerning the policies the government should follow in international affairs turn on different conceptions of goals, the kind of world environment needed to protect and foster such goals, and the means we have to make those goals effective. The following section utilizes these frames of reference to analyze the major policies the nation has followed in the post-World-War-II period.

AMERICAN FOREIGN POLICY SINCE WORLD WAR II

World conditions at the end of the war in 1945 were radically different from those that prevailed at the beginning of hostilities in 1939. When the second war began there were seven great powers in the world—Germany, Italy, Japan, Great Britain, France, Russia, and the United States. The fighting resulted in the defeat of the first three and the exhaustion of the next two, leaving only Russia and America as significant powers in international affairs. Of these two, the United States was by far the more powerful: unlike Russia we had not been invaded; we also possessed the atomic bomb while the Soviets did not. Thus the United States stood at the pinnacle of world power and influence at the end of the war. Moreover, unlike the situation after World War I, we were determined not to retreat to a policy of isolationism but rather to involve ourselves actively in international affairs.

American foreign policy in the quarter-century after the end of the war was indeed characterized by active involvement on a global basis. The following analysis focuses on three geographical areas in which the United States has made major economic and military commitments that greatly affect international relations and our role in them.

EUROPE: 1945–1950

Even while the United States and the Soviet Union were allies during World War II, difficulties arose that eventually led to conflicts between the two major powers in the postwar period. Stalin never forgot that American troops, along with British and Japanese forces, tried unsuccessfully to put down the Bolshevik Revolution following World War I. He also resented the Allies' decision to wait until 1944 to launch a second front against Germany, meanwhile leaving the Soviet Union with the major burden of fighting Hitler's armies. To these suspicions and resentments was added a major conflict on the future of Eastern Europe. The Soviets (who regarded this area, across which armies had marched in successive invasions of Russia, as vital to their security interests) wanted control over the countries of Eastern Europe when the war was over. While Churchill acceded to Stalin's wishes in this regard (Russia, in turn, was to give Britain a free hand in Greece), the policy was not acceptable to the United States. Scholars differ about the reasons: Arthur Schlesinger, Jr. attributes our attitude to the acceptance of a general "universalist" view that national security could only be assured by international organization (as compared to a balance of power in Europe) and to a refusal of liberals to accept the spread of police states in the area. William A. Williams suggests that the United States position was consistent with our historic policy of seeking open access to economic markets. In any event, allowing Bulgaria, Hungary, Poland, and Rumania to be controlled by the Soviets, it was felt, would constitute a recognition of political and economic spheres of influence of which we disapproved.

The postwar future of Germany also created conflicts with the Soviets. During the war the United States considered the possibility of weakening Germany economically by making it a "pastoral" nation, but subsequently it became our purpose (after destroying its war-making capabilities) to restore Germany economically and politically so it could serve as a counter-weight to Soviet influence in Central Europe. These policies intensified Soviet fears of the reemergence of a powerful Germany, an eventuality they hoped to prevent by keeping the conquered nation economically weak and politically divided. Moreover, Russia's desire to exact reparations (for damages suffered during the war) by stripping German industries was also at odds with our policy of keeping the plants intact.

The war had barely ended before both sides began to engage each other in verbal battle. In late October 1945 President Truman announced that the United States would "refuse to recognize any government imposed upon any nation by the force of any foreign power." Within a week, Soviet Foreign Minister Molotov responded that peace could not be reconciled with an armaments race "preached abroad by certain especially zealous partisans of the imperialist policy. . . . In this connection we should mention the discovery of atomic energy and the atomic bomb." In February 1946 Stalin predicted that the capitalist world would once again split into hostile camps leading to war, and he suggested that the Soviet Union prepare itself for that development by increasing its industrial capacity at the expense of producing consumer goods. One month later Churchill gave his famous speech at Westminster College in Fulton, Missouri, charging that "From Stettin in the Baltic to Trieste in the Adriatic, an iron curtain has descended across the continent, allowing police governments to rule Eastern Europe."

Meanwhile, along with words, actions taken by the American and Russian governments began to contribute to what soon became known as the "Cold War." When the Soviet Union applied for a loan from the United States in the fall of 1946, our government claimed to have "lost" it until the following March when it suddenly turned up, to the great suspicion of the Soviets. In May 1947 we forbade the Soviets from taking any more reparations from the parts of Germany we occupied. In turn, the Soviets refused to evacuate troops from Iran and demanded that they be granted oil concessions there. Russia also put pressure on Turkey to allow it to share control over the Dardenelles between the Black Sea and the Mediterranean. (American demands for the withdrawal of the troops in Iran and the movement of a carrier into the Mediterranean eventually caused Stalin to back down on both fronts.) The two nations also failed to agree on the control of atomic energy: the Soviets turned down an American proposal for international control because they were unwilling to allow inspection of the natural resources and interior of their country and also because they felt that the proposed plan served to guarantee an American monopoly on the bomb.

Most important of all the factors in heightening the tensions of the Cold War was the Soviet Union's treatment of the countries of Eastern Europe. In the Yalta agreements signed in February 1945, it was agreed that "free elections" would be held in those nations at "the earliest possible time."

British Prime Minister Clement Attlee, American President Harry S. Truman, and Soviet Premier Joseph Stalin during the Potsdam Conference on postwar problems (summer 1945) in a brief moment of amity before the onset of the Cold War. (Wide World Photos)

Initially, some contests were held (for example, in November 1945 the non-communists won the elections in Hungary), but in late 1946 and early 1947 police actions removed opposition candidates in Rumania and Poland, and the Soviets also began to subvert the government of Hungary. Thus American hopes for self-determination and democracy for these countries, together with economic markets for American products, came to a bitter end.

In this atmosphere, in February 1947, the British Ambassador informed the U.S. State Department that despite his nations traditional commitments, it could not provide the economic and military aid needed by Turkey and Greece. The following month Truman asked Congress to provide $400 million of American-controlled military and economic aid to stop communist-supported rebellions in those two countries. The late Dean Acheson, then an Under Secretary of State, told leading congressmen that the aid was needed to control the expansion of Russia in the Middle East and other areas, an expansion that was part of a communist plan to "encircle and capture the ultimate objective of Germany." Two months later Congress met the President's request, which came to be known as the Truman Doctrine.

Soon that Doctrine evolved into an even more ambitious venture: the Marshall Plan. In June 1947, at a commencement address at Harvard University, Secretary of State George C. Marshall explained the Plan's aims: to restore the nations of Europe economically by providing credits to buy American goods to help them rebuild their industries. Although Marshall invited the Soviet bloc countries to participate in the Plan, Stalin refused to let them do so because of the requirement that the economic records of each country be opened for scrutiny and also because he wanted each country to be able to draw up its own plans for assistance rather than have to participate in a general European proposal. (The Soviets then responded with a plan of their own to integrate the economies of Eastern European countries with that of Russia.) President Truman sold Congress on both the economic advantages of the Marshall Plan for American business and its value as a means of preventing the spread of communism in Western European countries weakened economically by the war (the Communist coup overthrowing the democratic government of Czechoslovakia in February 1948 provided evidence of recent subversion); the President saw the Plan become a reality in June 1948, when he signed a bill creating more than $5 billion of aid.

One more major program remained to make Western Europe safe from feared Russian expansion and subversion: the formation in 1949 of the North Atlantic Treaty Organization in which the United States joined with other nations in pledging joint action in the event that any of them was attacked. That same year the Soviet blockade of access to West Berlin (located within the Soviet Zone of Germany) came to an end after the United States successfully used an airlift to supply food and other essentials to the city for over eleven months. Although the latter days of the decade thus looked generally favorable to America and our Western European allies, the explosion of an atomic bomb by the Soviets in September 1949 meant that the days of our nuclear monopoly were at an end.

Thus American foreign policy in Europe in the immediate postwar period reflected major conflicts with the Soviet Union. Its over-all assumptions and objectives were best articulated in an article, written by George Kennan under the pseudonym "Mr. X.," which appeared in *Foreign Affairs* magazine in July 1947. In it Kennan attributed Soviet conduct to what he termed a "traditional and instinctive Russian sense of insecurity"; a communist ideology that advocates revolution to defeat capitalist forces in the outside world; and Stalin's determination to use the threat of "capitalist encirclement" to regiment his people and consolidate his own political power. Kennan suggested that Soviet aggression be "contained by the adroit and vigilant application of counterforce at a series of constantly shifting geographical and political points," a policy he predicted would eventually lead to "either the break up or gradual mellowing of Soviet power." As indicated below, "containment" became the basis of our policy not only in Europe but in Asia as well.

KOREA

Another area of controversy between the United States and the Soviet Union in the postwar period was Korea, a country that had been occupied by Japan since 1910. As early as 1943 President Roosevelt expressed his preference for the eventual independence of the country. He felt, however, that an apprenticeship period would be necessary to prepare the Koreans to rule themselves and that during that interval (Roosevelt had in mind twenty years or longer) the country should be placed under the trusteeship of the United States, Russia, and one or two other countries. Stalin informally agreed to this proposal but nothing definite concerning Korea's future was planned either at Yalta in February 1945 or at Potsdam the following July. The Potsdam meeting did, however, provide for the entry of the Soviet Union into the war in the Far East. When it did so, after the United States dropped two atomic bombs on Japan in early August 1945, the two major powers made a hasty decision to divide Korea at the thirty-eighth parallel so that the Japanese could surrender to Russian troops north of that line and to American forces below it.

During the months following the end of the war, two separate Korean regimes emerged to lead their countrymen. In the North a communist-dominated government set up a People's Republic that had Russian support. In the South right-wing groups under the leadership of Syngman Rhee emerged victorious in elections held under the auspices of the American military government.

The development of the two rival regimes backed by the two major powers contributed to the difficulties that followed. A five-year trusteeship approved by the United States and the Soviets in late 1945 met violent opposition from Koreans, especially Rhee who wanted immediate independence. Proposals for free elections to be held throughout the country made first by the United States and later by the United Nations were not acceptable to the People's Republic or to the Soviets, who feared the North would lose the elections since twice as many Koreans lived south of the thirty-eighth parallel. As a result the two zones continued their separate governments. In 1948 the Soviets withdrew their troops and we followed suit the next year. However, while Russia provided the North with extensive equipment and training for their troops, American military assistance for the South was extremely limited.

Nor did the United States give any indication that it would send troops of its own to help defend South Korea if it were attacked. In March 1949

General Douglas MacArthur, Supreme Commander of the occupation forces in Japan, told a British journalist that America's line of defense ran through a chain of islands from the Philippines to the Aleutians through the Ryukyus (this line lay west of Korea); he was also quoted as saying that "anyone who commits the American army on the mainland of Asia ought to have his head examined." In January 1950 Secretary of State Acheson defined essentially the same defense perimeter in a speech before the National Press Club, saying that if South Korea were attacked, it would be the responsibility of the United Nations to come to its assistance.

When the North Koreans attacked across the thirty-eighth parallel on June 25, 1950, however, President Truman responded by committing air and naval forces and, when that aid did not stem the tide, American ground troops as well. The United Nations also asked its members to come to the aid of the Republic of Korea. Ultimately, sixteen nations did contribute to the United Nations' forces fighting in Korea, but the United States provided the overwhelming share of the air and naval power and, with South Korea, most of the ground forces also.

It is not entirely clear why North Korea decided to attack, but it appears that the Soviet Union was concerned about our unilateral action in negotiating a peace treaty with Japan without Russian participation and hoped to bring all of Korea under communist control in order to counteract the threat posed by a strongly anticommunist Japan. It is also possible that Stalin wanted to divert Western pressure from Europe to the Far East or to test American will to resist an armed attack. In any event, the Soviet Union apparently took the United States at its word about its defense perimeter, and assumed that the South could be taken militarily without risking direct confrontation with us.

Why the United States decided to resist the aggression after previously stating that Korea lay outside its defense perimeter is also not completely certain. However, President Truman reveals in his *Memoirs* that he viewed the invasion as the same kind of aggression that Japan, Italy, and Germany engaged in during the 1930s and concluded that this time the aggressors must be taught that force would meet with resistance. The President also explained to MacArthur that "we are fighting in Korea . . . to carry out our commitment of honor to the South Koreans and to demonstrate to the world that the friendship of the United States is of inestimable value in time of adversity." Dean Acheson, now Secretary of State, told a congressional committee that the aggression was "a challenge to the whole system of collective security, not only in the East, but everywhere in the world." Korea was also considered important to the security of Japan.

Whatever the reasons, the commitment of American forces soon began to turn the war around. In mid-September United Nations troops under MacArthur conducted a landing behind the enemy lines at Inchon and within two weeks linked up with forces from the South to cut off large numbers of North Korean troops. Although President Truman had announced in June that our objective was to restore the division of the country at the thirty-eighth parallel, in September he declared that Koreans had a right to be "free, independent and united." Late that month he ordered MacArthur north of the parallel, and on October 7 the United Nations General Assembly endorsed the President's order as the first troops moved into the North.

The war, however, soon took another dramatic turn. Communist leader Chou En-lai told the Indian ambassador to mainland China that if the UN troops crossed the thirty-eighth parallel and included within their forces South Koreans, China would send in troops to help the North Koreans. This message was relayed through the Indian government (the main link to China since Washington had no direct diplomatic contacts with Peking), but the American government discounted the threat as communist propaganda passed on by the ambassador, who was considered to be friendly to Communist China. In mid-October MacArthur assured President Truman that the Chinese had no air force and that if their troops tried to move into Korea without air cover, they would be slaughtered. In late October, however, the first Chinese prisoner was captured, and on November 25 Chinese "volunteers" crossed the Yalu River in force, trapping and destroying large numbers of UN troops. Within three weeks the UN forces were pushed back across the thirty-eighth parallel, and it looked for a time as if they might be driven from the peninsula altogether.

Reinforcements, however, enabled MacArthur once again to turn the tide, and in January 1951 UN troops moved back towards the parallel. Here the fighting stabilized, while a conflict arose within the United States government over how the war should now be waged. MacArthur urged instituting a naval blockade of China, bombing its military and industrial installations, and utilizing Chinese Nationalist troops, perhaps on the Chinese mainland itself. Truman, however, concerned lest Russian troops come to the aid of the Chinese and apprehensive about the possibility of tying the United States down in a major war in Asia at a time when Europe was still threatened by the Soviets, chose instead to fight a limited war and to seek negotiations with Peking. When MacArthur refused to follow orders and his actions threatened to hamper the negotiations, the President relieved him of his command in April 1951.

Truman's policy soon brought results. In late June 1951 the Russians suggested an armistice and a withdrawal of both forces from a neutral zone across the thirty-eighth parallel. The following month negotiations began, but not until July 1953 after Eisenhower had come into office and a group of new leaders had replaced Stalin was an armistice signed. Some twenty years later no final peace settlement had yet been agreed to and the nation was still partitioned. The United States has a mutual defense treaty with South Korea, and some 45,000 American troops remain stationed there.

Thus the containment policy originally intended for Europe was applied in Asia as well, under the assumption that China and the Soviet Union were allies and that together they constituted a major communist threat to America and the free world. As indicated below, the developments in Korea also had a major influence on still another area of increasing American concern: Vietnam.

VIETNAM

As with Korea, President Roosevelt's initial preference for Vietnam in the postwar period (the Japanese occupied it in 1940 after a period of French rule) was a multi-nation trusteeship, with eventual independence to be granted in twenty years or more. However, concern about the communist background of Ho Chi Minh, the strongest local figure, and the desire to favor a wartime ally led to a decision at the end of the war to permit France to reoccupy Vietnam for a period prior to the granting of independence. In early 1946 Ho's forces (called the Vietminh) occupied the northern part of the country and the French the south. Tentative plans called for an eventual referendum in the South to see if its people wished to have the authority of the Vietminh extended there, and for the inclusion of Vietnam in the French Union. Tensions increased between the French and the Vietminh, however, and in December 1946 hostilities broke out between the two.

In the early stages of the fighting the United States did not make a firm commitment to either side. We were torn between our fears of Ho's communist connections and a distaste for supporting French colonialism. Gradually, however, the former took precedence over the latter. After the Chinese Communists defeated the Nationalists in 1949, we became concerned that Vietnam would come under Chinese control; that fear intensified after the Chinese entered the Korean War, a development we viewed as a prelude to expansion throughout East Asia. At the same time, the United States became increasingly concerned with obtaining French support for containing the Soviet Union in Europe. One means for accomplishing this objective was to relieve France of the burden it was carrying in waging the war in Vietnam.

American policy in Vietnam from 1950 to 1954 was to assist the French economically to fight that war. After the termination of the hostilities in Korea, we stepped up this assistance as we absorbed more and more of the costs of the Vietnamese war. Despite these efforts, however, the Vietminh became increasingly successful in the fighting. By early 1954 it became obvious that economic assistance alone would not defeat Ho Chi Minh's forces; outside military assistance would have to be provided. We tried to interest the British to join with us in sending troops to Vietnam. They felt, however, that the Communist movement there was indigenous rather than

Chinese- (or Russian-) inspired, and that the settlement should reflect the realities of the power situation there. When President Eisenhower determined not to commit American troops alone, France pursued the course of action advocated by the British.

The settlement of the war came as a result of a conference held in Geneva, Switzerland, from May to July, 1954. Participants in the conference included Britain and the Soviet Union (as joint chairmen), France, the United States, Communist China, Cambodia, Laos, the French-sponsored state of (South) Vietnam, and the Democratic Republic of (North) Vietnam. One document signed by France and North Vietnam provided for the temporary division of Vietnam at the seventeenth parallel into two zones pending reunification; the withdrawal of French and Vietminh troops to their respective zones; the movement of Vietnamese to the North or South as they chose during a 300-day period; a ban on receiving military material or personnel in either zone; and the appointment of an International Control Commission to supervise the carrying out of the terms of the agreement. A second document, a Final Declaration, expressing approval of the first agreement and fixing July 1956 for the holding of general elections throughout the country for the purposes of reunification, was signed by no one, but was verbally supported by all the conference participants except South Vietnam and the United States. We stated that we were not "prepared to join" in the declaration, but would "refrain from the threat or use of force to disturb" the agreements reached, and we warned that we viewed with grave concern "any renewal of aggression in violation" of them.

The reason why the Geneva settlement was not acceptable to the United States was that we did not want to be associated with any agreement that consigned territory to communist rule. (Secretary of State John Foster Dulles considered any such action "appeasement.") The South Vietnamese opposed the Geneva agreement because they felt that they would lose to the Communists in the elections for two reasons: more people lived in the North than the South, and there was no noncommunist leader with the popular appeal of Ho Chi Minh.

Our subsequent actions and those of the South Vietnamese reflected these attitudes. In September 1954 the United States entered into a treaty with Britain, France, Australia, New Zealand, the Philippines, Thailand, and Pakistan to create the South East Asia Treaty Organization (SEATO) to provide security against aggression in the area. South Vietnam was specifically included in the territory covered by the treaty. At the same time we backed a native leader Ngo Dinh Diem against the French puppet, Bao Dai, for the leadership of South Vietnam. Bao Dai was deposed and Diem came to power pledged to give Vietnam genuine national independence. We supported Diem's regime economically and backed his decision to call elections for South Vietnam alone, and to refuse to consult with the North

Vietnamese about the national elections to be held in 1956. As justification for this course of action, Diem argued that honest elections could not be held in the North and that South Vietnam had refused to endorse the Geneva agreements and hence was not bound by them.

In the years that followed, Diem tried with American assistance to consolidate his regime in the South. His political base, however, was narrow: he was a Catholic and enjoyed his greatest strength among the educated class living in the cities; he had virtually no support from the largest religious sect, the Buddhists, or from the lower classes, especially the peasants who lived in villages outside the major population centers. Diem also alienated many South Vietnamese by jailing his political opponents. When the Communists in the South (called the Viet Cong) saw their hopes for a unified Vietnam under Communist control dashed by the failure to hold the 1956 elections, they began a program to detach the rural population from the Diem administration. To accomplish that end, they began a terrorist campaign against government officials and also interfered with the collection of taxes by the central government. The Viet Cong won the support of large sections of the village population through political appeals calling for land distribution and the end of unfair taxation. This village population became an important source of recruits, food, and information on the movement of enemy forces in the guerrilla warfare the Viet Cong launched against the South Vietnamese government. By the end of the 1950s, large sections of rural Vietnam were under the control of the Communists.

In the early 1960s the war entered a new phase. The military operations of the Viet Cong stepped up as they penetrated more and more areas of the South and began to mount larger-scale attacks on the South Vietnamese army. Along with these developments, those fighting to overthrow Diem began to receive more assistance from the North in the form of equipment, military advisers, and even some troops. The Viet Cong also established a political arm, the National Liberation Front, which included non-Communists, such as Social Democrats. The religious intolerance of Diem's family alienated more and more South Vietnamese, including the Buddhists, who mounted demonstrations against his regime.

The United States responded to these challenges with changes in its policies. Soon after President Kennedy took office in 1961, he decided to increase aid to Diem and to send American military men to serve as advisers to the South Vietnamese troops. The American government also inaugurated programs designed to break the hold of the Viet Cong on the villages and put pressure on Diem to initiate social and economic reforms. None of these efforts met with much success: the military situation worsened; we made little headway with the pacification of the villages; and the corruption and nepotism of the South Vietnamese government persisted. In November 1963 the Diem regime was overthrown by a military coup which American officials were apparently aware of and did nothing to prevent.

The problems of South Vietnam did not end, however, with the demise of Diem. A succession of governments headed by generals-of-fortune followed, resulting in increasing instability in the South. As the military situation grew worse, the United States increased its commitment of American troops; by 1964 they numbered 25,000. In August 1964, following torpedo attacks on American warships in the Gulf of Tonkin, President Johnson sent retaliatory strikes against North Vietnamese torpedo boat facilities. He also used the incident to obtain a congressional resolution authorizing the Chief Executive "to take all necessary measures to repel any armed attack against the forces of the United States and to prevent further aggression."

In 1965 the moment of truth arrived. The United States would have to take over the war or see South Vietnam fall to the Communists. President Johnson chose the former course of action. In February the United States began the systematic bombing of the North; that same spring American forces abandoned the role of "advisers" and were openly committed to combat in the South. That June, Air Vice Marshall Ky became premier. With our prodding, elections were held the next year to choose delegates to write a constitution and in balloting held in 1967 a government was chosen with Nguyen Van Thieu as President and Nguyen Cao Ky as Vice President. Meanwhile the commitment of American troops accelerated: by early 1967 some 400,000 Americans were stationed there.

The massive commitment of American troops halted the Communist tide and in the words of one observer, made the war "unlosable." At the same time the North Vietnamese stepped up their infiltration of supplies and troops to the South. A stalemate in the fighting occurred as President Johnson came under competing advice: the military wanted him to commit still more troops to the fray, while Secretary of Defense Robert McNamara proposed an end to the escalation and the consideration of a political solution to the war.

In 1968 President Johnson decided upon the latter course of action. Following the Tet offensive in late January, in which the Communists demonstrated their ability to attack urban areas in force, the military asked for an additional 206,000 men (at that time the United States had over half a million men in Vietnam), a request that would have necessitated calling up the reserves. The President refused, and in a dramatic announcement to a nationwide television audience on March 30, 1968, ordered a halt to the bombing of the North, called for a convening of peace talks to end the war, and took himself out of contention for the presidential contest in November. As that election was being held, peace talks convened in Paris involving representatives of North Vietnam, the National Liberation Front, South Vietnam, and the United States.

When Richard Nixon took office in January 1969, he embarked on a program of what he called "Vietnamization," which involved turning over more and more of the fighting to the South Vietnamese and the systematic withdrawal of American troops. The Paris peace talks appeared to make no progress. (In 1971 the President announced his intention to visit Communist China in late February 1972, possibly with the hope of persuading its leaders to help bring the war to a close.) Meanwhile, in elections held in October 1971, President Thieu ran unopposed after two announced opponents (former premiers Ky and Minh) withdrew from the race, charging that the contest was "rigged" by Thieu.

Thus the war in Vietnam constitutes the major military commitment of the United States after World War II, a commitment that had cost some 45,000 American lives by the end of 1971. Over the years our leaders have justified their actions there on a number of grounds. In some instances they have emphasized "idealistic" goals, such as permitting the Vietnamese to choose their own form of government and fulfilling promises made to them. At other times the reasons given for our fighting there have related to America's own interests: the loss of valuable raw materials (tin, rubber, and rice) that would occur if the area fell to the Communists, or the damage to American prestige, honor, and credibility that would accompany a defeat or a failure to keep our commitments. Our involvement there has also reflected a view of the conditions in the world environment that threaten our freedom and that of other nations. We have thus subscribed to the "domino" theory (if Vietnam is lost to the Communists, then one by one other nations in Asia would fall), and to the even more inclusive assumption that if the Communists win a war of "national liberation" in Vietnam, then Communists in underdeveloped countries all over the world —particularly South America and Africa will be encouraged to launch similar wars. These goals and assumptions of our foreign policy, together with the process by which that policy is made, are assessed in the following section.

ASSESSMENT

The checks and balances that exist among the three branches of government and the influence of public opinion, political parties, and interest groups that characterize the making of domestic policy are virtually absent from the process by which decisions in foreign and military affairs are made. About the only political weapon citizens have at their disposal to affect decisions in those two areas is the ballot: they can vote against an incumbent President whose policies they disapprove of. Even that possibility has its limitations, however: anyone unhappy with the major commitment of American troops in Vietnam beginning in 1965 had to wait three years to express his electoral disapproval, and then President Johnson chose not to run again.

There are, of course, valid reasons why certain decisions pertaining to national security cannot be made by normal procedures for making domestic policy. Considerations of secrecy, dispatch, and expertise preclude the involvement of a wide range of individuals and groups both inside and outside the government. It is to be expected that such decisions be made primarily by the President and his advisors in the executive branch.

Given these facts of life, it is particularly important that vital checks and balances be built into the system by which the Chief Executive reaches the awesome decisions regarding foreign and military policy. As this process operates, the presidential advisers structure the situation and shape the options from which he chooses; the prize in the political struggle thus becomes not the public's mind, but that of the President. Each participant has the goal of convincing the Chief Executive that his concept of political reality (the intentions of other nations, our own capacities, the significance of a particular event) is the *true* one. If the process is to operate as it should, then, the President must be exposed to as wide a range of views and proposals as possible so that he can choose intelligently among them.

One possibility for effecting a better policy-making process is a suggestion of former presidential advisor Adam Yarmolinsky, namely, to apply an *adversary* system to decision-making in foreign and military policy similar to the one we employ in courts of law. Thus one team of executives would be assigned the responsibility of proving a certain proposition while another would be required to try to disprove it. In addition, knowledgeable persons outside government could be brought in to examine particular situations. Such procedures might well broaden (as well as refine) the advice and options a President receives on foreign- and military-policy matters.

Thought also needs to be given to how we can make better separation of those matters in foreign affairs that require secrecy from those that do not. Events such as the release of the Pentagon papers indicate that officials frequently invoke claims for the necessity of secrecy when what is really involved is a desire to avoid embarrassment over serious mistakes of judgment. Insofar as possible, actions of our public officials should be made known to Congress and attentive publics; such a procedure would make it more likely that we would learn from (or perhaps even avoid) such mistakes. It would also help avoid the damage that is done to the credibility of public officials when the American public ultimately learns about what they have done.

The record of our government in protecting and furthering our national interest in the international arena in the postwar period is a mixed one. Although some "revisionist" historians have suggested in recent years that the United States overestimated the Soviet threat of expansion in Europe after the war and underestimated its concern with its own security, their evidence for such allegations is not convincing, particularly from the standpoint of what was known about possible Soviet intentions *at that time*, not from the vantage point of hindsight. We can never know for sure what Stalin might have done had the United States not inaugurated the Truman Doctrine, the Marshall Plan, and NATO to protect the countries of Europe. Given our cultural ties with Western Europe, its industrial potential, and the importance of preserving these historic Western democracies, the policies instituted to prevent their possible fall to the Soviets were clearly in the American national interest. Certainly few persons would quarrel with the results achieved: the economic and political reemergence of these countries within a short period of time. At the same time we avoided a direct confrontation with Russia in Eastern Europe, the area of primary concern to her.

The justifications for American policies in Korea are less certain. If the United States intended to provide South Korea with protection in the postwar period, the government clearly erred in indicating that it was not within our defense perimeter. On the other hand, there were good reasons for our going to the aid of that country when it was attacked. It was the South Koreans who asked for free elections which the North refused; moreover, a United Nations Commission confirmed that the North was the aggressor. The geographical location of Korea *did* affect the security of Japan, in which we had a vital interest. In addition, the attack on June 25, 1950 came soon after the coup in Czechoslovakia, the blockade of Berlin, the first Soviet explosion of an atomic device, and the coming to power of the Peking government in China (which soon developed close relationships with Russia); all these events gave the appearance of an increasing Communist offensive against the Free World. Once the commitment was made, the most serious mistake in Korea was to change the goal of the intervention from restoring the division of the country at the thirty-eighth parallel to trying to occupy the North, a decision that brought about Chinese intervention.

With the exception of the decision not to intervene in Vietnam on the side of the French in 1954, our policy with respect to that country suffered from questionable goals and dubious assumptions. We badly underestimated the ability and popular appeal of Ho Chi Minh as the outstanding nationalist leader of Vietnam; on the other hand, we overestimated the amount of support Diem enjoyed, as well as his commitment to establishing a democratic regime. We interpreted the enemy as international communism, with close connections among the Russians, Chinese, North Vietnamese, and Viet Cong; in actuality the Soviets and Chinese have been at odds with each other since the late 1950s, and North Vietnam has tried to avoid domination by China, a nation that has occupied Vietnam in the past. We were also overly optimistic about our ability to crack the will of the Viet Cong and the North Vietnamese and about our own capacity to fight a guerrilla war in the jungles of Vietnam with weapons better suited for conventional warfare involving major engagements across definite lines (as occurred in Korea, for example). Most of all, we failed to understand that the conflict in Vietnam is primarily a political, not a military, struggle, for the allegiance of the South Vietnamese people.

There is little doubt that, as in Vietnam, we have frequently overmilitarized our foreign policy to the detriment of political and diplomatic considerations. It is tempting to attribute this development to the role of the military or the "military-industrial complex" in the making of policy. The fact of the matter is, however, that the major decisions in the postwar period that have expanded our military commitments have been made by Presidents on the advice of top-level *civilian* officials in the State and Defense Departments, as well as special presidential assistants.

It is difficult to determine what particular factors have shaped the attitudes of these civilian officials. One possibility is that the appeasement of dictators in the 1930s (which led to further aggression and eventually to World War II) conditioned our leaders (who lived through those perilous days) to perceive similar aggression in the postwar period and to resist it this time. In the complex, baffling world of international relations where the intentions of other nations are difficult to determine and the course of future events virtually impossible to predict (who, after all, can prove or disprove the domino theory?), it is natural to use historical analogies to try to understand the present and deal with it. Yet a lot of mistakes have been made in American foreign policy on the basis that the war in Korea in 1950 was like the one in Poland in 1939 and that the Vietnam conflict involved essentially the same considerations as one or both of those wars.

There is a similar danger that the United States will try to read too much from the bitter experience in Vietnam and withdraw too precipitously and too extensively from world affairs. Given the limited ability of the United Nations to keep peace in the world, it will be important for the United States, as the world's most powerful nation, to help bring peace and stability to the world. At the same time, Americans must learn to make better discriminations among our commitments than we have in the past, taking into account how vital a particular area is to our national interest, the actual danger posed to that interest, the degree of determination the nations concerned evince in defending themselves and establishing viable governments, and the limits of our own political and military power. We should also recognize that formerly weak nations (such as those of Western Europe and Japan after the war) are now capable of joining with us in helping to keep peace in our turbulent world.

Selected Readings

Daedelus, the journal of the American Academy of Arts and Sciences, devoted its Fall 1962 issue to a broad analysis of American foreign policy. Two selections in that issue that are particularly helpful in conveying the essentials of foreign policy are Ernest May, "The Nature of Foreign Policy: The Calculated Versus the Axiomatic," and Stanley Hoffmann, "Restraints and Choices in American Foreign Policy." Another good discussion of the unique nature of foreign policy is Martin Hickman, "The Distinctive Environment of Foreign Policy," which appears in a book edited by him, *Problems in American Foreign Policy* (New York: Glencoe, 1968).

Two valuable books that treat the general process by which foreign and military policy are made are Roger Hilsman, *The Politics of Policy-Making in Defense and Foreign Affairs* (New York: Harper & Row, 1971), and Kenneth Waltz, *Foreign Policy and Democratic Politics* (Boston: Little, Brown, 1967). The President's role in foreign affairs is treated by Sidney Warren, *The President as World Leader* (Philadelphia: Lippincott, 1964), and in military affairs by Ernest May (ed.), *The Ultimate Decision: The President as Commander-in-Chief* (New York: Braziller, 1960). Aaron Wildavsky compares the President's role in foreign and domestic affairs in "The Two Presidencies," *Transaction* (December 1966), pp. 7–14. The best treatment of defense policy is Samuel Huntington, *The Common Defense* (New York: Columbia University Press, 1961). For an analysis of the way that the American administrative structure shapes foreign policy, see Henry Kissinger, "Domestic Structure and Foreign Policy," in his book, *American Foreign Policy: Three Essays* (New York: Norton, 1969).

For a treatment of the role of Congress, see James Robinson, *Congress and Foreign Policy Making* (Homewood, Ill.: Dorsey, 1962). For a discussion of the role that the Supreme Court has played in foreign policy, see Chapters V and VI of Edward Corwin, *The President: Office and Powers* (New York: New York University Press, 3rd ed., 1948).

The best discussion of the role of public opinion in foreign policy is Gabriel Almond, *The American People and Foreign Policy* (New York: Harcourt, Brace, 1950). An historical analysis of the subject is Frank Klingberg, "The Historical Alteration of Moods in Foreign Policy," *World Politics* (January 1952), 239–273. Three studies of the attitudes of the American people on foreign policy and recent wars are William Caspary, "The Mood Theory: A Study of Public Opinion and Foreign Policy," *The American Political Science Review* (June 1970), 536–547; Sidney Verba *et al.*, "Public Opinion and the War in Vietnam," *The American Political Science Review* (June 1967), 317–334; and John Mueller, "Trends in Public Support for the Wars in Korea and Vietnam," *The American Political Science Review* (June 1971), 358–375.

The role interest groups play in the making of foreign policy are analyzed in Bernard Cohen, *The Role of Non-Governmental Groups in Foreign Policy-Making* (Boston: World Peace Foundation, 1959); Raymond Bauer et al., *American Business and Public Policy* (New York: Atherton, 1963); and Lester Milbrath, "Interest Groups and Foreign Policy," in James Rosenau (ed.), *Domestic Sources of Foreign Policy* (New York: Free Press, 1967). Two selections in that same volume that deal with the part that elections play in foreign policy are Warren Miller, "Voting and Foreign Policy," and Kenneth Waltz, "Electoral Punishment and Foreign Crises." Bernard Cohen, *The Press and Foreign Policy* (Princeton: Princeton University Press, 1963), is the best treatment of that subject.

For an analysis of the goals of American foreign policy, see Robert Osgood,

Ideals and Self-Interest in America's Foreign Relations (Chicago: University of Chicago Press, 1953). Walt Rostow gives his definition of the national interest in Appendix A of his book, *The United States in the World Arena* (New York: Harper & Row, 1960). For an excellent analysis of a related concept, see Arnold Wolfers, " 'National Security' as an Ambiguous Symbol," *Political Science Quarterly* (December 1952), 481–503. Two excellent statements of the "realist" point of view on the goals and approaches of foreign policy are George Kennan, *American Diplomacy, 1900–1950* (Chicago: University of Chicago Press, 1951), and Hans Morgenthau, *Scientific Man versus Power Politics* (Chicago: University of Chicago Press, 1946).

The best treatment of American foreign policy in the postwar period is William Carleton, *The Revolution in American Foreign Policy*, (New York: Random House, 2nd ed., 1967). A traditional view of the Cold War is Arthur Schlesinger, Jr., "Origins of the Cold War," *Foreign Affairs* (October 1967), 22–53. Two of the better "revisionist" treatments of the subject are William A. Williams, *The Tragedy of American Diplomacy* (New York: Dell, rev. ed., 1962), and Walter LaFeber, *America, Russia, and The Cold War, 1945–1971* (New York: Wiley, 2nd ed., 1972). The best account of the events leading up to the Korean War is Soon Sung Cho, *Korea in World Politics, 1940–1950* (Berkeley: University of California Press, 1967). An excellent study of the situation in Vietnam is Beranard Fall, *Vietnam Witness* (New York: Praeger, 1966).

A very good analysis of American foreign policy in the postwar years is Robert Osgood *et al.*, *America and the World from the Truman Doctrine to Vietnam* (Baltimore: John Hopkins Press, 1970). An excellent analysis of the Vietnam experience is James C. Thomson, Jr., "How Could Vietnam Happen?" *The Atlantic* (April 1968), 47–54. A broad variety of specialists give their views on that subject in Richard Pfeffer (ed.), *No More Vietnams?* (New York: Harper & Row, 1968). Two books that are highly critical of American foreign policy are William Fulbright, *The Arrogance of Power* (New York: Vintage, 1966) and Gabriel Kolko, *The Roots of American Foreign Policy* (Boston: Beacon, 1969).

The Constitution of the United States of America

We the People of the United States, in Order to form a more perfect Union, establish Justice, insure domestic Tranquility, provide for the common defence, promote the general Welfare, and secure the Blessings of Liberty to ourselves and our Posterity, do ordain and establish this Constitution for the United States of America.

Article I

Section 1. All legislative Powers herein granted shall be vested in a Congress of the United States, which shall consist of a Senate and House of Representatives.

Section 2. The House of Representatives shall be composed of Members chosen every second Year by the People of the several States, and the Electors in each State shall have the Qualifications requisite for Electors of the most numerous Branch of the State Legislature.

No Person shall be a Representative who shall not have attained to the age of twenty five Years, and been seven Years a Citizen of the United States, and who shall not, when elected, be an Inhabitant of that State in which he shall be chosen.

Representatives and direct Taxes shall be apportioned among the several States which may be included within this Union, according to their respective Numbers, which shall be determined by adding to the whole Number of free Persons, including those bound to Service for a Term of Years, and excluding Indians not taxed, *three fifths of all other persons.** The

* Italics indicate passages altered by subsequent amendments. This was revised by the Sixteenth (apportionment of taxes) and Fourteenth (determination of persons) Amendments.

actual Enumeration shall be made within three Years after the first Meeting of the Congress of the United States, and within every subsequent Term of ten Years, in such Manner as they shall by Law direct. The Number of Representatives shall not exceed one for every thirty Thousand, but each State shall have at Least one Representative; and until such enumeration shall be made, the State of New Hampshire shall be entitled to chuse three, Massachusetts eight, Rhode-Island and Providence Plantations one, Connecticut five, New-York six, New Jersey four, Pennsylvania eight, Delaware one, Maryland six, Virginia ten, North Carolina five, South Carolina five, and Georgia three.

When vacancies happen in the Representation from any State, the Executive Authority thereof shall issue Writs of Election to fill such Vacancies.

The House of Representatives shall chuse their Speaker and other Officers; and shall have the sole Power of Impeachment.

Section 3. The Senate of the United States shall be composed of two Senators from each State, *chosen by the Legislature thereof,*† for six Years; and each Senator shall have one Vote.

†Revised by Seventeenth Amendment.

594

Immediately after they shall be assembled in Consequence of the first Election, they shall be divided as equally as may be into three Classes. The Seats of the Senators of the first Class shall be vacated at the Expiration of the second Year, of the second Class at the Expiration of the fourth Year, and of the third Class at the Expiration of the sixth Year, so that one third may be chosen every second Year; *and if Vacancies happen by Resignation, or otherwise, during the Recess of the Legislature of any State, the Executive thereof may make temporary Appointments until the next Meeting of the Legislature, which shall then fill such Vacancies.*°

No Person shall be a Senator who shall not have attained to the Age of thirty Years, and been nine Years a Citizen of the United States, and who shall not, when elected, be an Inhabitant of the State for which he shall be chosen.

The Vice President of the United States shall be President of the Senate, but shall have no Vote, unless they be equally divided.

The Senate shall chuse their other Officers, and also a President pro tempore, in the Absence of the Vice President, or when he shall exercise the Office of President of the United States.

The Senate shall have the sole Power to try all Impeachments. When sitting for that Purpose, they shall be on Oath or Affirmation. When the President of the United States is tried, the Chief Justice shall preside: And no Person shall be convicted without the Concurrence of two thirds of the Members present.

Judgment in Cases of Impeachment shall not extend further than to removal from Office, and disqualification to hold and enjoy any Office of honor, Trust or Profit under the United States: but the Party convicted shall nevertheless be liable and subject to Indictment, Trial, Judgment and Punishment, according to Law.

Section 4. The Times, Places and Manner of holding Elections for Senators and Representatives, shall be prescribed in each State by the Legislature thereof; but the Congress may at any time by Law make or alter such Regulations, except as to the Places of chusing Senators.

The Congress shall assemble at least once in every Year, and such Meeting shall be *on the first Monday in December,*† unless they shall by Law appoint a different Day.

Section 5. Each House shall be the Judge of the Elections, Returns and Qualifications of its own Members, and a Majority of each shall constitute a Quorum to do Business; but a smaller Number may adjourn from day to day, and may be authorized to compel the Attendance of absent Members, in such Manner, and under such Penalties as each House may provide.

Each House may determine the Rules of its Proceedings, punish its Members for disorderly Behavior, and, with the Concurrence of two thirds, expel a Member.

Each House shall keep a Journal of its Proceedings, and from time to time publish the same, excepting such Parts as may in their Judgment require Secrecy; and the Yeas and Nays of the Members of either House on any question shall, at the Desire of one fifth of those Present, be entered on the Journal.

Neither House, during the Session of Congress, shall, without the Consent of the other, adjourn for more than three days, nor to any other Place than that in which the two Houses shall be sitting.

Section 6. The Senators and Representatives shall receive a Compensation for their Services, to be ascertained by Law, and paid out of the Treasury of the United States. They shall in all Cases, except Treason, Felony and Breach of the Peace, be privileged from Arrest during their Attendance at the Session of their respective Houses, and in going to and returning from the same; and for any Speech or Debate in either House, they shall not be questioned in any other Place.

No Senator or Representative shall, during the Time for which he was elected, be appointed to any civil Office under the Authority of the United States, which

---

°Revised by Seventeenth Amendment.   †Revised by Twentieth Amendment.

shall have been created, or the Emoluments whereof shall have been encreased during such time; and no Person holding any Office under the United States, shall be a Member of either House during his Continuance in Office.

Section 7. All Bills for raising Revenue shall originate in the house of Representatives; but the Senate may propose or concur with Amendments as on other Bills.

Every Bill which shall have passed the House of Representatives and the Senate, shall, before it become a Law, be presented to the President of the United States; if he approve he shall sign it, but if not he shall return it, with his Objections to that House in which it shall have originated, who shall enter the Objections at large on their Journal, and proceed to reconsider it. If after such Reconsideration two thirds of that House shall agree to pass the Bill, it shall be sent, together with the Objections, to the other House, by which it shall likewise be reconsidered, and if approved by two thirds of that House, it shall become a Law. But in all such Cases the Votes of both Houses shall be determined by Yeas and Nays, and the Names of the Persons voting for and against the Bill shall be entered on the Journal of each House respectively. If any Bill shall not be returned by the President within ten Days (Sundays excepted) after it shall have been presented to him, the Same shall be a Law, in like Manner as if he had signed it, unless the Congress by their Adjournment prevent its Return, in which Case it shall not be a Law.

Every Order, Resolution, or Vote to which the Concurrence of the Senate and House of Representatives may be necessary (except on a question of Adjournment) shall be presented to the President of the United States; and before the Same shall take Effect, shall be approved by him, or being disapproved by him, shall be repassed by two thirds of the Senate and House of Representatives, according to the Rules and Limitations prescribed in the Case of a Bill.

Section 8. The Congress shall have Power To lay and collect Taxes, Duties, Imposts and Excises, to pay the Debts and provide for the common Defence and general Welfare of the United States; but all Duties, Imposts and Excises shall be uniform throughout the United States;

To borrow Money on the credit of the United States;

To regulate Commerce with foreign Nations, and among the several States, and with the Indian Tribes;

To establish an uniform Rule of Naturalization, and uniform Laws on the subject of Bankruptcies throughout the United States;

To coin Money, regulate the Value thereof, and of foreign Coin, and fix the Standard of Weights and Measures;

To provide for the Punishment of counterfeiting the Securities and current Coin of the United States;

To establish Post Offices and post Roads;

To promote the Progress of Science and useful Arts, by securing for limited Times to Authors and Inventors the exclusive Right to their respective Writings and Discoveries;

To constitute Tribunals inferior to the Supreme Court;

To define and punish Piracies and Felonies committed on the high Seas, and Offences against the Law of Nations;

To declare War, grant Letters of Marque and Reprisal, and make Rules concerning Captures on Land and Water;

To raise and support Armies, but no Appropriation of Money to that Use shall be for a longer Term than two Years;

To provide and maintain a Navy;

To make Rules for the Government and Regulation of the land and naval Forces;

To provide for calling forth the Militia to execute the Laws of the Union, suppress Insurrections and repel Invasions;

To provide for organizing, arming, and disciplining, the Militia, and for governing such Part of them as may be employed in the Service of the United States, reserving to the States respectively, the Appointment of the Officers, and the Authority of training the Militia according to the discipline prescribed by Congress;

To exercise exclusive Legislation in all Cases whatsoever, over such District (not exceeding ten Miles square) as may, by

Cession of particular States, and the Acceptance of Congress, become the Seat of the Government of the United States, and to exercise like Authority over all Places purchased by the Consent of the Legislature of the State in which the Same shall be, for the Erection of Forts, Magazines, Arsenals, dock-Yards, and other needful Buildings;—And

To make all Laws which shall be necessary and proper for carrying into Execution the foregoing Powers, and all other Powers vested by this Constitution in the Government of the United States, or in any Department or Officer thereof.

Section 9. The Migration or Importation of such Persons as any of the States now existing shall think proper to admit, shall not be prohibited by the Congress prior to the Year one thousand eight hundred and eight, but a Tax or duty may be imposed on such Importation, not exceeding ten dollars for each Person.

The Privilege of the Writ of Habeas Corpus shall not be suspended, unless when in Cases of Rebellion or Invasion the public Safety may require it.

No Bill of Attainder or ex post facto Law shall be passed.

*No Capitation, or other direct, Tax shall be laid, unless in Proportion to the Census or Enumeration herein before directed to be taken.**

No Tax or Duty shall be laid on Articles exported from any State.

No Preference shall be given by any Regulation of Commerce or Revenue to the Ports of one State over those of another: nor shall Vessels bound to, or from, one State, be obliged to enter, clear, or pay Duties in another.

No Money shall be drawn from the Treasury, but in Consequence of Appropriations made by Law; and a regular Statement and Account of the Receipts and Expenditures of all public Money shall be published from time to time,

No title of Nobility shall be granted by the United States: And no Person holding any Office of Profit or Trust under them, shall, without the Consent of the Congress, accept of any present, Emolument, Office, or Title, of any kind whatever, from any King, Prince, or foreign State.

Section 10. No State shall enter into any Treaty, Alliance, or Confederation; grant Letters of Marque and Reprisal; coin Money; emit Bills of Credit; make any Thing but gold and silver Coin a Tender in Payment of Debts; pass any Bill of Attainder, ex post facto Law, or Law impairing the Obligation of Contracts, or Grant any Title of Nobility.

No State shall, without the Consent of the Congress, lay any Imposts or Duties on Imports or Exports, except what may be absolutely necessary for executing its inspection Laws: and the net Produce of all Duties and Imposts, laid by any State on Imports or Exports, shall be for the Use of the Treasury of the United States; and all such Laws shall be subject to the Revision and Controul of the Congress.

No State shall, without the Consent of Congress, lay any Duty of Tonnage, keep Troops, or Ships of War in time of Peace, enter into any Agreement or Compact with another State, or with a foreign Power, or engage in War, unless actually invaded, or in such imminent Danger as will not admit of delay.

Article II

Section 1. The executive Power shall be vested in a President of the United States of America. *He shall hold his Office during the Term of four Years,†* and, together with the Vice President, chosen for the same Term be elected as follows:

Each State shall appoint, in such Manner as the Legislature thereof may direct, a Number of Electors, equal to the whole Number of Senators and Representatives to which the State may be entitled in the Congress but no Senator or Representative, or Person holding an Office of Trust or Profit under the United States, shall be appointed an Elector.

The Electors shall meet in their respective States, and vote by Ballot for two Persons, of whom one at least shall not be an Inhabitant of the same State with

---

*Revised by Sixteenth Amendment.　　　　†See Twenty-second Amendment.

themselves. And they shall make a List of all the Persons voted for, and of the Number of Votes for each; which List they shall sign and certify, and transmit sealed to the Seat of the Government of the United States, directed to the President of the Senate. The President of the Senate shall, in the Presence of the Senate and House of Representatives, open all the Certificates, and the Votes shall then be counted. The Person having the greatest Number of Votes shall be the President, if such Number be a Majority of the whole Number of Electors appointed; and if there be more than one who have such Majority, and have an equal Number of Votes, then the House of Representatives shall immediately chuse by Ballot one of them for President; and if no Person have a Majority, then from the five highest on the List the said House shall in like Manner chuse the President. But in chusing the President, the Votes shall be taken by States, the Representation from each State having one Vote; A quorum for this purpose shall consist of a Member or Members from two thirds of the States, and a Majority of all the States shall be necessary to a Choice. In every Case, after the Choice of the President, the Person having the greatest Number of Votes of the Electors shall be the Vice President. But if there should remain two or more who have equal Votes, the Senate shall chuse from them by Ballot the Vice President.*

The Congress may determine the Time of chusing the Electors, and the Day on which they shall give their Votes; which Day shall be the same throughout the United States.

No Person except a natural born Citizen, or a Citizen of the United States, at the time of the Adoption of this Constitution, shall be eligible to the Office of President; neither shall any Person be eligible to that Office who shall not have attained to the Age of thirty five Years, and been fourteen Years a Resident within the United States.

In case of the Removal of the President from Office, or of his Death, Resignation, or Inability to discharge the Powers and Duties of the said Office, the Same shall devolve on the Vice President, and the Congress may by Law provide for the Case of Removal, Death, Resignation or Inability, both of the President and Vice President, declaring what Officer shall then act as President, and such Officer shall act accordingly, until the Disability be removed, or a President shall be elected.†

The President shall, at stated Times, receive for his Services, a Compensation which shall neither be encreased nor diminished during the Period for which he shall have been elected, and he shall not receive within that Period any other Emolument from the United States, or any of them.

Before he enter on the Execution of his Office, he shall take the following Oath or Affirmation:—"I do solemnly swear (or affirm) that I will faithfully execute the Office of President of the United States, and will to the best of my Ability, preserve, protect and defend the Constitution of the United States."

Section 2. The President shall be Commander in Chief of the Army and Navy of the United States, and of the Militia of the several States, when called into the actual service of the United States; he may require the Opinion, in writing, of the principal Officer in each of the executive Departments, upon any Subject relating to the Duties of their respective Offices, and he shall have Power to grant Reprieves and Pardons for Offences against the United States, except in Cases of Impeachment.

He shall have Power, by and with the Advice and Consent of the Senate, to make Treaties, provided two thirds of the Senators present concur; and he shall nominate, and by and with the Advice and Consent of the Senate, shall appoint Ambassadors, and other public Ministers and Consuls, Judges of the supreme Court, and all other Officers of the United States, whose Appointments are not herein otherwise provided for, and which shall be established by Law: but the Congress may by Law vest the Appointment of such in-

---

*Superseded by Twelfth Amendment.

†Revised by Twenty-fifth Amendment.

ferior Officers, as they think proper, in the President alone, in the Courts of Law, or in the Heads of Departments.

The President shall have Power to fill up all Vacancies that may happen during the Recess of the Senate, by granting Commissions which shall expire at the End of their next Session.

Section 3. He shall from time to time give to the Congress Information of the State of the Union, and recommend to their Consideration such Measures as he shall judge necessary and expedient; he may, on extraordinary Occasions, convene both Houses, or either of them, and in Case of Disagreement between them, with Respect to the Time of Adjournment, he may adjourn them to such Time as he shall think proper; he shall receive Ambassadors and other public Ministers, he shall take Care that the Laws be faithfully executed, and shall Commission all the Officers of the United States.

Section 4. The President, Vice President, and all civil Officers of the United States, shall be removed from Office on Impeachment for, and Conviction of Treason, Bribery, or other high Crimes and Misdemeanors.

Article III

Section 1. The judicial Power of the United States, shall be vested in one supreme Court and in such inferior Courts as the Congress may from time to time ordain and establish. The Judges, both of the supreme and inferior Courts, shall hold their Offices during good Behavior, and shall, at stated Times, receive for their Services, a Compensation, which shall not be diminished during their Continuance in Office.

Section 2. The judicial Power shall extend to all Cases, in Law and Equity, arising under this Constitution, the Laws of the United States, and Treaties made, or which shall be made, under their Authority;—to all Cases affecting Ambassadors, other public Ministers and Consuls;—to all Cases of admiralty and maritime Jurisdiction;—to Controversies to which the United States shall be a Party;—to Controversies between two or more

States;—*between a State and Citizens of another State**;—between Citizens of different States;—between Citizens of the same State claiming Lands under Grants of different States, *and between a State or the Citizens thereof, and foreign States, Citizens, or Subjects.**

In all cases affecting Ambassadors, other public Ministers and Consuls, and those in which a State shall be Party, the supreme Court shall have original Jurisdiction. In all the other Cases before mentioned, the supreme Court shall have appellate Jurisdiction, both as to Law and Fact, with such Exceptions, and under such Regulations as the Congress shall make.

The Trial of all Crimes, except in Cases of Impeachment, shall be by Jury; and such Trial shall be held in the State where the said Crimes shall have been committed; but when not committed within any State, the Trial shall be at such Place or Places as the Congress may by Law have directed.

Section 3. Treason against the United States, shall consist only in levying War against them, or in adhering to their Enemies, giving them Aid and Comfort. No Person shall be convicted of Treason unless on the Testimony of two Witnesses to the same overt Act, or on Confession in open Court.

The Congress shall have Power to declare the Punishment of Treason, but no Attainder of Treason shall work Corruption of Blood, or Forfeiture except during the Life of the Person attainted.

Article IV

Section 1. Full Faith and Credit shall be given in each State to the public Acts, Records, and judicial Proceedings of every other State. And the Congress may by general Laws prescribe the Manner in which such Acts, Records, and Proceedings shall be proved, and the Effect thereof.

Section 2. The Citizens of each State shall be entitled to all Privileges and Immunities of Citizens in the several States.

A Person charged in any State with

*Revised by Eleventh Amendment.

Treason, Felony, or other Crime, who shall flee from Justice, and be found in another State, shall on Demand of the executive Authority of the State from which he fled, be delivered up, to be removed to the State having Jurisdiction of the Crime.

*No person held to Service or Labour in one State, under the Laws thereof, escaping into another, shall, in Consequence of any Law or Regulation therein, be discharged from such Service or Labour, but shall be delivered up on Claim of the Party to whom such Service or Labour may be due.**

Section 3. New States may be admitted by the Congress into this Union; but no new State shall be formed or erected within the Jurisdiction of any other State; nor any State be formed by the Junction of two or more States, or Parts of States, without the Consent of the Legislatures of the States concerned as well as of the Congress.

The Congress shall have Power to dispose of and make all needful Rules and Regulations respecting the Territory or other Property belonging to the United States; and nothing in this Constitution shall be so construed as to Prejudice any claims of the United States, or of any particular State.

Section 4. The United States shall guarantee to every State in this Union a Republican Form of Government, and shall protect each of them against Invasion; and on Application of the Legislature, or of the Executive (when the Legislature cannot be convened) against domestic Violence.

Article V

The Congress, whenever two thirds of both Houses shall deem it necessary, shall propose Amendments to this Constitution, or, on the Application of the Legislatures of two thirds of the several States, shall call a Convention for proposing Amendments, which, in either Case, shall be valid to all Intents and Purposes, as Part of this Constitution, when ratified by the Legislatures of three fourths of the several States, or by Conventions in three fourths

thereof, as the one or the other Mode of Ratification may be proposed by the Congress; Provided that no Amendment which may be made prior to the Year One thousand eight hundred and eight shall in any Manner affect the first and fourth Clauses in the Ninth Section of the first Article; and that no State, without its Consent, shall be deprived of its equal Suffrage in the Senate.

Article VI

All Debts contracted and Engagements entered into, before the Adoption of this Constitution, shall be as valid against the United States under this Constitution, as under the Confederation.†

This Constitution, and the Laws of the United States which shall be made in Pursuance thereof; and all Treaties made, or which shall be made, under the Authority of the United States, shall be the supreme Law of the Land; and the Judges in every State shall be bound thereby, any Thing in the Constitution or Laws of any State to the Contrary notwithstanding.

The Senators and Representatives before mentioned, and the Members of the several State Legislatures, and all executive and judicial Officers, both of the United States and of the several States, shall be bound by Oath or Affirmation, to support this Constitution; but no religious Test shall ever be required as a Qualification to any Office or public Trust under the United States.

Article VII

The Ratification of the Conventions of nine States, shall be sufficient for the Establishment of this Constitution between the States so ratifying the Same.

Done in Convention by the Unanimous Consent of the States present the Seventeenth Day of September in the Year of our Lord one thousand seven hundred and eighty seven and of the Independence of the United States of America the twelfth. In witness whereof We have hereunto subscribed our Names.

. . .

*Superseded by Thirteenth Amendment.   †See Fourteenth Amendment, Section 4.

ARTICLES IN ADDITION TO, AND AMEND-
MENT OF, THE CONSTITUTION OF THE
UNITED STATES OF AMERICA, PROPOSED BY
CONGRESS, AND RATIFIED BY THE SEVERAL
STATES, PURSUANT TO THE FIFTH ARTICLE
OF THE ORIGINAL CONSTITUTION.
(Ratification of the first ten amendments
was completed December 15, 1791.)

Amendment I

Congress shall make no law respecting an establishment of religion, or prohibiting the free exercise thereof; or abridging the freedom of speech, or of the press; or the right of the people peaceably to assemble, and to petition the Government for a redress of grievances.

Amendment II

A well regulated Militia, being necessary to the security of a free State, the right of the people to keep and bear Arms, shall not be infringed.

Amendment III

No Soldier shall, in time of peace be quartered in any house, without the consent of the Owner, nor in time of war, but in a manner to be prescribed by law.

Amendment IV

The right of the people to be secure in their persons, houses, papers, and effects, against unreasonable searches and seizures, shall not be violated, and no Warrants shall issue, but upon probable cause, supported by Oath or affirmation, and particularly describing the place to be searched, and the persons or things to be seized.

Amendment V

No person shall be held to answer for a capital, or other infamous crime, unless on a presentment or indictment of a Grand Jury, except in cases arising in the land or naval forces, or in the Militia, when in actual service in time of War or public danger; nor shall any person be subject for the same offence to be twice put in jeopardy of life or limb; nor shall be compelled in any criminal case to be a witness against himself, nor be deprived of life, liberty, or property, without due process of law; nor shall private property be taken for public use, without just compensation.

Amendment VI

In all criminal prosecutions, the accused shall enjoy the right to a speedy and public trial, by an impartial jury of the State and district wherein the crime shall have been committed, which district shall have been previously ascertained by law, and to be informed of the nature and cause of the accusation; to be confronted with the witnesses against him; to have compulsory process for obtaining witnesses in his favor, and to have the Assistance of Counsel for his defence.

Amendment VII

In Suits at common law, where the value in controversy shall exceed twenty dollars, the right of trial by jury shall be preserved, and no fact tried by a jury, shall be otherwise reexamined in any Court of the United States, than according to the rules of the common law.

Amendment VIII

Excessive bail shall not be required, nor excessive fines imposed, nor cruel and unusual punishments inflicted.

Amendment IX

The enumeration in the Constitution, of certain rights, shall not be construed to deny or disparage others retained by the people.

Amendment X

The powers not delegated to the United States by the Constitution, nor prohibited by it to the States, are reserved to the States respectively, or to the people.

Amendment XI (January 8, 1798)

The Judicial power of the United States shall not be construed to extend to any suit in law or equity, commenced or prosecuted against one of the United States by Citizens of another State, or by Citizens or Subjects of any Foreign State.

Amendment XII (September 25, 1804)

The Electors shall meet in their respective states and vote by ballot for President and Vice President, one of whom, at least,

602   The Constitution of the United States of America

shall not be an inhabitant of the same state with themselves; they shall name in their ballots the person voted for as President, and in distinct ballots the person voted for as Vice President, and they shall make distinct lists of all persons voted for as President and of all persons voted for as Vice President, and of the number of votes for each, which lists they shall sign and certify, and transmit sealed to the seat of the government of the United States, directed to the President of the Senate; —The President of the Senate shall, in the presence of Senate and House of Representatives, open all the certificates and the votes shall then be counted;—The person having the greatest number of votes for President, shall be the President, if such number be a majority of the whole number of Electors appointed; and if no person have such majority, then from the persons having the highest numbers not exceeding three on the list of those voted for as President, the House of Representatives shall choose immediately, by ballot, the President. But in choosing the President, the votes shall be taken by states, the representation from each state having one vote; a quorum for this purpose shall consist of a member or members from two-thirds of the states, and a majority of all the states shall be necessary to a choice. And if the House of Representatives shall not choose a President whenever the right of choice shall devolve upon them, *before the fourth day of March next following,** then the Vice President shall act as President, as in the case of the death or other constitutional disability of the President.— The person having the greatest number of votes as Vice President shall be the Vice President, if such number be a majority of the whole number of Electors appointed, and if no person have a majority, then from the two highest numbers on the list, the Senate shall choose the Vice President; a quorum for the purpose shall consist of two-thirds of the whole number of Senators, and a majority of the whole number shall be necessary to a choice. But no person constitutionally ineligible to the office of President shall be eligible to that of Vice President of the United States.

*Revised by the Twentieth Amendment.

Amendment XIII (December 18, 1865)

Section 1. Neither slavery nor involuntary servitude, except as a punishment for crime whereof the party shall have been duly convicted, shall exist within the United States, or any place subject to their jurisdiction.

Section 2. Congress shall have the power to enforce this article by appropriate legislation.

Amendment XIV (July 28, 1869)

Section 1. All persons born or naturalized in the United States, and subject to the jurisdiction thereof, are citizens of the United States and of the State wherein they reside. No State shall make or enforce any law which shall abridge the privileges or immunities of citizens of the United States; nor shall any State deprive any person of life, liberty, or property, without due process of law; nor deny to any person within its jurisdiction the equal protection of the laws.

Section 2. Representatives shall be apportioned among the several States according to their respective numbers, counting the whole number of persons in each State, excluding Indians not taxed. But when the right to vote at any election for the choice of electors for President and Vice President of the United States, Representatives in Congress, the Executive and Judicial officers of a State, or the members of the Legislature thereof, is denied to any of the male inhabitants of such State, being twenty-one years of age, and citizens of the United States, or in any way abridged, except for participation in rebellion, or other crime, the basis of representation therein shall be reduced in the proportion which the number of such male citizens shall bear to the whole number of male citizens twenty-one years of age in such State.

Section 3. No person shall be a Senator or Representative in Congress, or elector of President and Vice President, or hold any office, civil or military, under the United States, or under any State, who, having previously taken an oath, as a member of Congress, or as an officer of the United States, or as a member of any State legislature, or as an executive or judicial officer of any State, to support the Constitution of the United States, shall have engaged in insurrection or rebellion against the same, or given aid or comfort to the enemies thereof. But Congress may by a vote of two thirds of each House, remove such disability.

Section 4. The validity of the public debt of the United States, authorized by law, including debts incurred for payment of pensions and bounties for services in suppressing insurrection or rebellion, shall not be questioned. But neither the United States nor any State shall assume or pay any debt or obligation incurred in aid of insurrection or rebellion against the United States, or any claim for the loss or emancipation of any slave; but all such debts, obligations, and claims shall be held illegal and void.

Section 5. The Congress shall have power to enforce, by appropriate legislation, the provisions of this article.

Amendment XV (March 30, 1870)

Section 1. The right of citizens of the United States to vote shall not be denied or abridged by the United States or by any State on account of race, color, or previous conditions of servitude.

Section 2. The Congress shall have power to enforce this article by appropriate legislation.

Amendment XVI (February 25, 1913)

The Congress shall have power to lay and collect taxes on incomes, from whatever source derived, without apportionment among the several States, and without regard to any census or enumeration.

Amendment XVII (May 31, 1913)

The Senate of the United States shall be composed of two Senators from each State, elected by the people thereof, for six years; and each Senator shall have one vote. The electors in each State shall have the qualifications requisite for electors of the most numerous branch of the State legislatures.

When vacancies happen in the repre-

sentation of any State in the Senate, the executive authority of such State shall issue writs of election to fill such vacancies: *Provided,* That the legislature of any State may empower the executive thereof to make temporary appointments until the people fill the vacancies by election as the legislature may direct.

This amendment shall not be so construed as to affect the election or term of any Senator chosen before it becomes valid as part of the Constitution.

Amendment XVIII (January 29, 1919)

Section 1. After one year from the ratification of this article the manufacture, sale, or transportation of intoxicating liquors within, the importation thereof into, or the exportation thereof from the United States and all territory subject to the jurisdiction thereof for beverage purposes is hereby prohibited.

Section 2. The Congress and the several States shall have concurrent power to enforce this article by appropriate legislation.

Section 3. This article shall be inoperative unless it shall have been ratified as an amendment to the Constitution by the legislatures of the several States, as provided in the Constitution within seven years from the date of the submission hereof to the States by the Congress.

Amendment XIX (August 26, 1920)

The right of citizens of the United States to vote shall not be denied or abridged by the United States or by any State on account of sex.

Congress shall have power to enforce this article by appropriate legislation.

Amendment XX (February 6, 1933)

Section 1. The terms of the President and Vice President shall end at noon on the 20th day of January, and the terms of Senators and Representatives at noon on the 3rd day of January, of the years in which such terms would have ended if this article had not been ratified; and the terms of their successors shall then begin.

Section 2. The Congress shall assemble at least once in every year, and such

*Repealed by the Twenty-first Amendment.

meeting shall begin at noon on the 3rd day of January, unless they shall by law appoint a different day.

Section 3. If, at the time fixed for the beginning of the term of the President, the President elect shall have died, the Vice President elect shall become President. If a President shall not have been chosen before the time fixed for the beginning of his term, or if the President elect shall have failed to qualify, then the Vice President elect shall act as President until a President shall have qualified; and the Congress may by law provide for the case wherein neither a President elect nor a Vice President elect shall have qualified, declaring who shall then act as President, or the manner in which one who is to act shall be selected, and such person shall act accordingly until a President or Vice President shall have qualified.

Section 4. The Congress may by law provide for the case of the death of any of the persons from whom the House of Representatives may choose a President whenever the right of choice shall have devolved upon them, and for the case of the death of any of the persons from whom the Senate may choose a Vice President whenever the right of choice shall have devolved upon them.

Section 5. Sections 1 and 2 shall take effect on the 15th day of October following the ratification of this article.

Section 6. This article shall be inoperative unless it shall have been ratified as an amendment to the Constitution by the legislatures of three-fourths of the several States within seven years from the date of its submission.

Amendment XXI (December 5, 1933)

Section 1. The eighteenth article of amendment to the Constitution of the United States is hereby repealed.

Section 2. The transportation or importation into any State, Territory, or possession of the United States for delivery or use therein of intoxicating liquors, in violation of the laws thereof, is hereby prohibited.

Section 3. This article shall be inopera-

tive unless it shall have been ratified as an amendment to the Constitution by conventions in the several States, as provided in the Constitution, within seven years from the date of the submission hereof to the States by the Congress.

Amendment XXII (February 26, 1951)

Section 1. No person shall be elected to the office of the President more than twice, and no person who has held the office of President, or acted as President, for more than two years of a term to which some other person was elected President shall be elected to the office of President more than once. But this Article shall not apply to any person holding the office of President when this Article was proposed by the Congress, and shall not prevent any person who may be holding the office of President, or acting as President, during the term within which this Article becomes operative from holding the office of President or acting as President during the remainder of such term.

Section 2. This article shall be inoperative unless it shall have been ratified as an amendment to the Constitution by the legislatures of three-fourths of the several States within seven years from the date of its submission to the States by the Congress.

Amendment XXIII (March 29, 1961)

Section 1. The District constituting the seat of Government of the United States shall appoint in such manner as the Congress may direct:

A number of electors of President and Vice President equal to the whole number of Senators and Representatives in Congress to which the District would be entitled if it were a State, but in no event more than the least populous State; they shall be in addition to those appointed by the States, but they shall be considered, for the purposes of the election of President and Vice President, to be electors appointed by a State; and they shall meet in the District and perform such duties as provided by the twelfth article of amendment.

Section 2. The Congress shall have power to enforce this article by appropriate legislation.

Amendment XXIV (January 23, 1964)

Section 1. The right of citizens of the United States to vote in any primary or other election for President or Vice President, for electors for President or Vice President, or for Senator or Representative in Congress, shall not be denied or abridged by the United States or any state by reason of failure to pay any poll tax or other tax.

Section 2. The Congress shall have the power to enforce this article by appropriate legislation.

Amendment XXV (February 10, 1967)

Section 1. In case of the removal of the President from office or of his death or resignation, the Vice President shall become President.

Section 2. Whenever there is a vacancy in the office of the Vice President, the President shall nominate a Vice President who shall take office upon confirmation by a majority vote of both Houses of Congress.

Section 3. Whenever the President transmits to the President pro tempore of the Senate and the Speaker of the House of Representatives his written declaration that he is unable to discharge the powers and duties of his office, and until he transmits to them a written declaration to the contrary, such powers and duties shall be discharged by the Vice President as Acting President.

Section 4. Whenever the Vice President and a majority of either the principal officers of the executive departments or of such other body as Congress may by law provide, transmit to the President pro tempore of the Senate and the Speaker of the House of Representatives their written declaration that the President is unable to discharge the powers and duties of his office, the Vice President shall immediately assume the powers and duties of the office as Acting President.

Thereafter, when the President transmits to the President pro tempore of the Senate and the Speaker of the House of Representatives his written declaration that no inability exists, he shall resume the powers and duties of his office unless the Vice President and a majority of either the principal officers of the executive departments or of such other body as Congress may by law provide, transmit within four days to the President pro tempore of the Senate and the Speaker of the House of Representatives their written declaration that the President is unable to discharge the powers and duties of his office. Thereupon Congress shall decide the issue, assembling within forty-eight hours for that purpose if not in session. If the Congress, within twenty-one days after receipt of the latter written declaration or, if Congress is not in session, within twenty-one days after Congress is required to assemble, determines by two-thirds vote of both Houses that the President is unable to discharge the powers and duties of his office, the Vice President shall continue to discharge the same as Acting President; otherwise, the President shall resume the powers and duties of his office.

Amendment XXVI (June 30, 1971)

Section 1. The right of citizens of the United States, who are eighteen years of age or older, to vote shall not be denied or abridged by the United States or any state on account of age.

Section 2. The Congress shall have the power to enforce this article by appropriate legislation.

Index